Strategic Marketing in Fragile Economic Conditions

Irene Samanta
Graduate Technological Education Institute of Piraeus, Greece

A volume in the Advances in Marketing, Customer Relationship Management, and E-Services (AMCRMES) Book Series

BUSINESS SCIENCE Reference
An Imprint of IGI Global

Managing Director: Lindsay Johnston
Production Editor: Jennifer Yoder
Development Editor: Allison McGinniss
Acquisitions Editor: Kayla Wolfe
Typesetter: James Knapp
Cover Design: Jason Mull

Published in the United States of America by
Business Science Reference (an imprint of IGI Global)
701 E. Chocolate Avenue
Hershey PA, USA 17033
Tel: 717-533-8845
Fax: 717-533-8661
E-mail: cust@igi-global.com
Web site: http://www.igi-global.com

Library of Congress Cataloging-in-Publication Data

Strategic marketing in fragile economic conditions / Irene Samanta, editor.
pages cm
Includes bibliographical references and index. ISBN 978-1-4666-6232-2 (hardcover : alk. paper) -- ISBN 978-1-4666-6233-9 (ebook) -- ISBN 978-1-4666-6235-3 (print & perpetual access) 1. Marketing--Management. 2. Consumer confidence. 3. Financial crises. I. Samanta, Irene,1956- editor of compilation.
HF5415.13.S87767 2014
658.8'02--dc23
2014013819

This book is published in the IGI Global book series Advances in Marketing, Customer Relationship Management, and E-Services (AMCRMES) (ISSN: 2327-5502; eISSN: 2327-5529)

British Cataloguing in Publication Data
A Cataloguing in Publication record for this book is available from the British Library.

All work contributed to this book is new, previously-unpublished material. The views expressed in this book are those of the authors, but not necessarily of the publisher.

For electronic access to this publication, please contact: eresources@igi-global.com.

Advances in Marketing, Customer Relationship Management, and E-Services (AMCRMES) Book Series

Eldon Y. Li
National Chengchi University, Taiwan & California Polytechnic State University, USA

ISSN: 2327-5502
EISSN: 2327-5529

Mission

Business processes, services, and communications are important factors in the management of good customer relationship, which is the foundation of any well organized business. Technology continues to play a vital role in the organization and automation of business processes for marketing, sales, and customer service. These features aid in the attraction of new clients and maintaining existing relationships.

The Advances in Marketing, Customer Relationship Management, and E-Services (AMCRMES) Book Series addresses success factors for customer relationship management, marketing, and electronic services and its performance outcomes. This collection of reference source covers aspects of consumer behavior and marketing business strategies aiming towards researchers, scholars, and practitioners in the fields of marketing management.

Coverage

- Database Marketing
- Online Community Management and Behavior
- Mobile CRM
- B2B Marketing
- Telemarketing
- Data Mining and Marketing
- Mobile services
- Social Networking and Marketing
- Cases on Electronic Services
- Customer Retention

IGI Global is currently accepting manuscripts for publication within this series. To submit a proposal for a volume in this series, please contact our Acquisition Editors at Acquisitions@igi-global.com or visit: http://www.igi-global.com/publish/.

The Advances in Marketing, Customer Relationship Management, and E-Services (AMCRMES) Book Series (ISSN 2327-5502) is published by IGI Global, 701 E. Chocolate Avenue, Hershey, PA 17033-1240, USA, www.igi-global.com. This series is composed of titles available for purchase individually; each title is edited to be contextually exclusive from any other title within the series. For pricing and ordering information please visit http://www.igi-global.com/book-series/advances-marketing-customer-relationship-management/37150. Postmaster: Send all address changes to above address.

Titles in this Series

For a list of additional titles in this series, please visit: www.igi-global.com

Handbook of Research on Effective Marketing in Contemporary Globalism
Bryan Christiansen (PryMarke, LLC, USA) Salih Yıldız (Gümüşhane University, Turkey) and Emel Yıldız (Gümüşhane University, Turkey)
Business Science Reference • copyright 2014 • 463pp • H/C (ISBN: 9781466662209) • US $325.00 (our price)

Brand Management in Emerging Markets Theories and Practices
Cheng Lu Wang (University of New Haven, USA) and Jiaxun He (East China Normal University, China)
Business Science Reference • copyright 2014 • 337pp • H/C (ISBN: 9781466662421) • US $200.00 (our price)

Handbook of Research on Retailer-Consumer Relationship Development
Fabio Musso (University of Urbino, Department of Economics, Society and Politics (DESP), Italy) and Elena Druica (University of Bucharest, Department of Economic and Administrative Sciences, Romania)
Business Science Reference • copyright 2014 • 589pp • H/C (ISBN: 9781466660748) • US $380.00 (our price)

Strategies in Sports Marketing Technologies and Emerging Trends
Manuel Alonso Dos Santos (Universidad Católica de la Santísima Concepción, Chile)
Business Science Reference • copyright 2014 • 363pp • H/C (ISBN: 9781466659940) • US $235.00 (our price)

Handbook of Research on Consumerism in Business and Marketing Concepts and Practices
Hans-Ruediger Kaufmann (University of Nicosia, Cyprus & International Business School at Vilnius University, Lithuania) and Mohammad Fateh Ali Khan Panni (City University, Bangladesh)
Business Science Reference • copyright 2014 • 668pp • H/C (ISBN: 9781466658806) • US $365.00 (our price)

Handbook of Research on Management of Cultural Products E-Relationship Marketing and Accessibility Perspectives
Lucia Aiello (Unviersitas Mercatorum, Italy)
Business Science Reference • copyright 2014 • 486pp • H/C (ISBN: 9781466650077) • US $345.00 (our price)

Marketing in the Cyber Era Strategies and Emerging Trends
Ali Ghorbani (Payame Noor University, Iran)
Business Science Reference • copyright 2014 • 357pp • H/C (ISBN: 9781466648647) • US $185.00 (our price)

Transcultural Marketing for Incremental and Radical Innovation
Bryan Christiansen (PryMarke, LLC, USA) Salih Yıldız (Gümüşhane University, Turkey) and Emel Yıldız (Gümüşhane University, Turkey)
Business Science Reference • copyright 2014 • 588pp • H/C (ISBN: 9781466647497) • US $185.00 (our price)

IGI GLOBAL
DISSEMINATOR OF KNOWLEDGE
www.igi-global.com

701 E. Chocolate Ave., Hershey, PA 17033
Order online at www.igi-global.com or call 717-533-8845 x100
To place a standing order for titles released in this series, contact: cust@igi-global.com
Mon-Fri 8:00 am - 5:00 pm (est) or fax 24 hours a day 717-533-8661

Table of Contents

Detailed Table of Contents

Foreword

We live in a phenomenal and unprecedented period of world history. No one could ever predict the duration and depth of the crisis created by the transition from the 2nd to the 3rd industrial revolution. The comparison made with data of the 1970s, with the successive oil crises, is unsuccessful. In the '70s we had a shock to the global economy, but afterwards, investments were made to rebuild from the ruins of the crisis. Companies at the time were small. Today, companies have grown too much, proving to be much easier to change course to a boat rather than the Titanic. At the time, there was tremendous flexibility. Current sizes make a company's adjustment to the new normal difficult and very painful. It is said that we should go back ten years and adapt business accordingly. This, however, is an exercise that cannot be accomplished. A company is a dynamic organization and expands into new areas within changing market conditions and regulatory requirements, particularly in a globalized economy whose main feature is the "sharing economy." Companies have to operate at low cost and generate a high turnover with very small margins. At the beginning of the first decade of 2000, companies had low turnover but high profit margins. Today, within the context of the economic crisis experienced by Europe, companies are trying to reduce employee compensation to the levels of the past decade, but this will not increase their competitiveness, and as a matter of fact, this by itself is extremely dangerous. As long as there is demand for qualified executives and when the company decides to shoot itself in its foot, it is highly probable that it will lose its best executives, who are its intangible capital, and capital should not be laid off. Pay cuts are a slippery and dangerous road.

Today there is only one option. A company must find a way to continue to grow even in a declining market. This is key. Companies do not shrink to profitability. Even this can be achieved temporarily, perhaps for one year, but it is not sustainable. When a company follows the path of a downward trend, it will surely lead to bankruptcy. Therefore, it must find ways to grow by adapting its strategy. These issues lead scholars to deal with issues related to fragile economies.

This book consists of affairs dealing with the tourist industry, social media, Web marketing, customer loyalty and retention, corporate social responsibility and return to communities part of their profits, and sustainable competitive; these are some of the challenges facing today's businesses, and scholars have an obligation to analyze them comprehensively.

This book is of particular interest and will be discussed both within academic circles and by senior management to preempt the problems they will face in the near future.

Panagiotis Kyriazopoulos
Graduate Technological Education Institute of Piraeus, Greece

Panagiotis Kyriazopoulos *received his Bachelor degree in Business Administration from University of Piraeus, MSc in Marketing from Liverpool John Moores University, UK, MA in Economics and PhD degree in TQM from the Aristotelian University of Thessaloniki, Greece. After several years in industry as a marketing manager, he joined as Professor of Marketing and Operation Management at the Graduate Technological Education Institute of Piraeus, where he has worked for the last 35 years. His research interests include marketing and entrepreneurship and social media marketing. He is the founder and director of the MSc in International Business Management, a course running in Department of Business Administration of TEI of Piraeus. He was a local course leader for nine years for the PgD/MSc in International Marketing course running in collaboration with the University of the West of Scotland, UK, and TEI of Piraeus. He is a founder of the research laboratory of Marketing Research and editor of Working Paper Series, a monthly edition published by TEI of Piraeus from 2004 to 2013 and editor of Selection of Research Papers, an annual edition journal published by TEI of Piraeus from 2007 to 2013. He is Editor in Chief of the Journal of Marketing and Operation Management Research published by Nova Publishers (USA) and President of Marketing and Operation Management Society.*

Preface

In the last few years, the business environment has been characterized by strong economic crisis. The Euro zone countries are in an economic "nervousness." Countries such as Greece, Ireland, Spain, Portugal, Cyprus, and Italy are in a recession, while northern European countries such as Germany, The Netherlands, Austria, etc. and the USA are situated in strong economic "nervousness."

The global financial crisis continues to be a severe shock to most enterprises and has affected organizations significantly. The initial economic downturn, the worst since the Great Depression, has affected almost all sectors of the economy.

The viability of businesses may depend on their ability to identify and respond to trends and opportunities presented and threatened by their external environment; yet, smaller firms have little ability to shape their macro-environment. Successful firms may be those that recognize potential threats and through adjustment convert them into opportunities.

In this fragile economic environment marketing called upon to play a dominant financial and social role. Moreover, in times of crisis there may be a lack of marketing strategy to cope with a turbulent environment where crises lurk around every corner. Different levels in information and knowledge society and, in particular, the network economy have acknowledged the significance of the role of Strategic Marketing. Therefore, it is important to understand how Strategic Marketing is manifested and how it can be enhanced at various levels in organizations in Fragile Economic Conditions. Every organization private or public that has felt the pain would do well to ask:

- What can one reasonably expect in such a climate of crisis?
- What role can marketing strategy play in shaping responses?
- Do organizations with well-established marketing strategy processes fare better than those that are primarily opportunistic?

New marketing tools such as e-marketing, mobile marketing, social media, etc. have developed in the third industrial revolution. Therefore, researchers, academics, and practitioners have to develop new ideas about how they can use all these tools in order to bring a new economic equilibrium between firms and consumers in the global environment.

Many firms lack expertise and management skills. Many businesses do not have the resources to implement marketing strategy, and in particular, require flexibility, self-sufficiency, and trust with their partners. However, strategy is often more implicit than explicit, so that leadership and management skills become extra important. Barringer and Greening (1999) identified that successful firms engaged in marketing strategy and those that failed did not, and that it is an important factor in business performance. Effective firms were those that were flexible, participative, and adaptive.

Organization with the most commitment to marketing strategy made critical decisions and were better able to pursue growth opportunity during the crisis, as they were more confident about their prospects. An organization's trust and confidence in marketing strategy as a decision making discipline is a strong indicator of potential success, allowing businesses to take advantage of growth opportunities as they appear in times of economic disruption. Moreover, linking strategy directly to resources and performance measures and having more direct leadership involvement in the process are well-accepted ways to encourage an organization's embrace of strategic marketing.

THE CHALLENGES

In order to be able to lead organizations through crises, executives need to have knowledge about the structures and processes they introduce with the goal of maintaining the organization's capacity for action. However, many organizations are not aware of this fact. These concepts also include a lot of well-founded knowledge about what customers need in the time of crisis. Executives can also use this knowledge during crises or during change processes.

One of the most important topics does not get addressed openly within most organizations: the joint leadership performance. Leadership is not an individual process, but rather a form of cooperation with mutual interdependencies. All executives can jointly ensure that the information gets to the right places, that decisions are made within the allotted time frame, and that performance can be achieved within the organization as best as possible. The more pronounced this taboo is, the more difficult it will be to correct decisions quickly and to adapt to rapidly changing circumstances.

Because the current crisis is an event that requires extra resources, organizations often rely on social relational networks made up of many interconnected relationships in order to acquire resources for their survival (Lin, 2002).

Lee et al. (2009) state that sudden change can offer benefits to companies that have invested in and developed flexible capabilities and resources.

In the last two decades, the study of "trust in business and industrial marketing has experienced phenomenal growth," recognizing trust as central to business marketing. Trust is important and useful in a range of organizational and inter-organizational activities (Elangovan, et al., 2007). The study of trust in external buyer-seller relationships has also received much more attention and firmly anchors the belief that trust is an essential part of long-term and value-adding marketing relationships. In this context, and in the context of the resource-based view of the company, good internal trust organizational relationships (with employees) and trust external organizational relationships (with customers, suppliers, etc.) may be seen as a key company resource and source of competitive capabilities. That high-loyal relationships between employers, employees, customers, and suppliers lead to long-term commitment and long-term contracting, and may be seen as a way out of critical situations and crises. Thus, some companies may even view a crisis as an opportunity to change and build a competitive advantage (Lee, et al., 2009). The motives for building and engaging trust and loyalty in new inter- and intra-company relationships, while redesigning existing ones, may be the result of external challenges and/or internal needs (Ballantyne, 2003).

When linking internal contexts (HRM, internal marketing, and innovations) and external contexts (market orientation and customer expectations) that are characterized by a turbulent economic environment, various organizational processes face different pressures to change and adapt to new circumstances. In this context, with their focus on creating value-adding, trusting, and long-term relationships with all types of "customers," marketing strategy processes are under even greater pressure because they are focused on both satisfying "internal customers" (employees) and external customers (e.g. buyers, suppliers).

SEARCHING FOR A SOLUTION

During the economic downturn, many people are looking for value (saving money, products that last long), rather than luxury. Expect growing demand for retail outlets that offer well-made, basic things at low cost.

Marketing strategy will struggle to meet the challenge of online communities. Most consumers trust the opinion of friends and strangers more than official advertising. That is why online communities become so powerful. You can type in the name of a hotel into Google, but if the comments by people who stayed recently are awful, you are not likely to believe the claims on the hotel's own Website, so future marketing strategies will look for ways to encourage positive news and word-of-mouth in order to spread the brand online.

The rapid growth of technology has brought about the adoption of electronic processes in the firm's production, e-marketing, and mobile marketing, where advertising is triggered by where you are or by what you are doing. It could be a special offer arriving in your mobile phone, for example, just as you are walking by a restaurant, or advertising while you are surfing the Web, which is linked to lifestyle choices you have made in the past (Mavondo, et al., 2005).

In a crisis, people return to brands they know, and that will be a key theme as well as value for money. Budgets for marketing will be reduced and companies will look for more cost-effective ways to reach their target audiences. In a turbulent economic environment with increased organizational uncertainty, innovation relies on the acquisition and exploitation of new knowledge in which external ties as sources of diverse information may be vital to any innovative activity (Jiminez, et al., 2008). On the other hand, quality perceived by the customer that can be defined as a customer's judgment of a product's excellence as well as customers' perceptions of price are often considered the most crucial determinants of their behavior and final product choice. Jiminez et al. (2008) found that quality generates customer loyalty and that the impact of market orientation on performance is mediated by innovation through the Web. In sum, we suspect that there is also a positive relationship between e-marketing strategy and performance in a crisis because companies with information technology capabilities will be able to respond to environmental change and challenge faster and in a better way than their counterparts. E-marketing strategy is thus becoming important as a means of survival.

One simple truth is the key to all marketing strategy in fragile economic conditions:

- Building trust is the big value, the key to selling in an economic crisis
    - **Satisfy Customers:** Value (perceived quality/perceived cost)
    - **Strengthen Community through Social Marketing:** Your neighborhood, city, nation
    - **Strengthen the Web Presence:** Through e-marketing and social media
    - **Sustain The World:** Life on earth, environment, your own world

This book identifies the effect that suspected drivers of success in marketing strategy during the economic crisis would have on key outcomes. The drivers examined through this chapter include:

- **Structure:** Does your organization have a structured marketing strategy with great leadership involvement?
- **Embrace:** Does your organization use marketing strategy to truly shape the future and to allocate resources?
- **Reliance:** Has the marketing strategy been highly effective and important in your organization during the economic crisis?

Areas of improvement based on organizational experience are identified in the book:

- **Enhancing of strategic thinking:** Place more emphasis social marketing, and build customer loyalty and trust.
- **Make a stronger conjunction to resource allotment:** Ensure that marketing strategy allocates capabilities and resources to manage complexity.
- **Increasing leadership participation:** More visibility and direct involvement in the organizational trust and knowledge by senior leaders.
- **Improve strategic action:** Enhance operational execution through better change and performance management through e-marketing as well as overall communications through word of mouth

This book will aim to provide relevant theoretical frameworks and the latest empirical research findings in the area. It will be written for professionals who want to improve their understanding of the strategic role of trust at different levels of the information and knowledge society, that is, trust at the level of the global economy, of networks and organizations, of teams and work groups, of information systems, and finally, trust at the level of individuals as actors in the networked environments.

The target audience of this book will be composed of professionals and researchers working in the field of information and knowledge management in various disciplines (e.g. library, information and communication sciences, administrative sciences and management, education, adult education, sociology, computer science, and information technology). Moreover, the book will provide insights and support executives concerned with the management of expertise, knowledge, information, and organizational development in different types of work communities and environments.

ORGANIZATION OF THE BOOK

The book is organized into 15 chapters. A brief description of each of the chapters follows:

Chapter 1 examines customer loyalty across the supply chain during the economic crisis in Greece. The importance of this study lies in the fact that no sufficient literature exists relating to the impact of the current financial crisis on customer loyalty across the supply chain.

Chapter 2 researches corporate ownership in Japan and focuses on corporate networks: horizontal and vertical *keiretsu*. The research examines the Japanese organisational structure and presents a review of the main stages of the change that has affected vertical *keiretsu*, together with the factors that have contributed to this change. Finally, the chapter analyses the evolution of trust within *keiretsu*.

Chapter 3 examines how public trust can be transformed into customer retention initiatives, and thereby, public sectors can regain their market position. Relying on the best practices and data from Edelman Trust Barometers and World Bank, the chapter addresses the trust deficit concerns. The research identifies the sources for creation of trust deficit in public sectors across the world.

Chapter 4 examines the main criteria that influence customer satisfaction and its effects on a case bank. The study identifies the actions that banks take into account and analyse and the elements that can be improved in order to keep their customers satisfied and loyal during the economic recession.

Chapter 5 argues that in unstable business environments the integration of internal and external perspectives of strategy formulation is necessary for a firm to sustain advantages. The proposed model presents four stages of corporate strategy development: Scouting, Maintenance, Dominance, and Appraisal. The chapter describes their applicability by using two cases of companies that adopted similar long-run strategies.

Chapter 6 examines the challenge that businesses and consumers confront today in protecting and preserving the earth's resources and the environment. Manufacturers and retailers are observing this trend and are trying to gain an edge in the competitive market by exploiting the potential in the green market industry. The aim of this chapter is to identify and analyze how eco-label can influence consumer buying behavior and awareness towards the various eco-labels in the Mumbai market.

Chapter 7 examines how marketing can partner with organisational leadership for a mutually beneficial exchange of skills and capabilities in order to be able to reinvent organisations rapidly enough to cope with shifts in the external business environment and create a sustainable future for the business.

Chapter 8 refers to small family businesses in Greece and examines the impact of their marketing strategy during an economic crisis period. The chapter shows how small family businesses indicate marketing strategy using Carson's model.

Chapter 9 introduces the role of brand management in emerging markets, thus explaining the concepts of brand management system, corporate branding, brand performance, brand equity, brand awareness, perceived brand quality, brand association, and brand loyalty; the importance of brand strategy in emerging markets; and brand relationships toward effective brand management.

Chapter 10 aims to undertake empirical research investigating the nature and magnitude of the determinants of word-of-mouth behaviour from the point of view of service performance and post-purchase perceptions. A theoretical model linking service quality issues and word-of-mouth behaviour was developed and tested using structural equation modelling of 280 surveyed participants at various day spa locations.

Chapter 11 examines the internal market orientation in the food retail industry. One reason for this may be the difficulty of measuring its benefits in such a context. The service industry and business-to-business companies have remained at the forefront of studies into internal marketing due to the close contact between employees and customers in such companies.

Chapter 12 identifies the Internet growth in India, as it is increasing at an alarming rate, which is indicating a fast growth future for the many e-marketing companies in India. The young population of the country prefers the new technology. Young buyers of India prefer to buy online due to easy mode of transaction, preferred mode of payment, safe delivery, and effective after-sales service, in terms of return and refund policy.

Chapter 13 seeks to study the application of information technology status of tourism promotion, particularly through Internet with a future plan to develop this type of promotion. In the context of tourism management, this chapter penetrates different usage of Web technology to disseminate maximum level of information for tourism promotion.

Chapter 14 examines whether the changes that take place in the global business environment have modulated the way firms do business or whether it is simply transient details that have caused such excitement. Should firms be wary of any proclamations of "new" ways of doing business?

Chapter 15 presents the textile industry, which has completely changed over the last few years. New innovation products have been launched in the market. Electrotextiles is one of them: a new category of textile products that has conducting properties contrary of the traditional textile products but keeps the "textile" properties like softness, lightness, and "washableness."

Irene Samanta
Graduate Technological Education Institute of Piraeus, Greece

REFERENCES

Ballantyne, D. (2003). A relationship mediated theory of internal marketing. *European Journal of Marketing*, *37*(9), 1242–1260. doi:10.1108/03090560310486979

Barringer, B. R., & Greening, D. W. (1998). Small business growth through geographic expansion: A comparative case study. *Journal of Business Venturing*, *13*(5), 467–492. doi:10.1016/S0883-9026(97)00038-4

Jimenez, G., Ongena, Peydro, & Saurina. (2008). *Hazardous times for monetary policy: What do twenty-three million bank loans say about the effects of monetary policy on credit risk-taking?*. Banco de España documento de Trabajo 0833.

Lee, T., Chung, W., & Taylor, R. (2011). A strategic response to the financial crisis: An empirical analysis of financial services advertising before and during the financial crisis. *Journal of Services Marketing*, *25*(3), 150–164. doi:10.1108/08876041111129146

Lin, H.-F. (2007d). Knowledge sharing and firm innovation capability: An empirical study. *International Journal of Manpower*, *28*(3/4), 315–332. doi:10.1108/01437720710755272

Mavondo, F. T., Chimhanzi, J., & Stewart, J. (2005). Learning orientation and market orientation: Relationship with innovation, human resource practices and performance. *European Journal of Marketing*, *39*(11-12), 1235–1263. doi:10.1108/03090560510623244

Praest Knudsen, M. (2007). The relative importance of inter firm relationships and knowledge transfer for new product development success. *Journal of Product Innovation Management*, *24*(2), 117–138. doi:10.1111/j.1540-5885.2007.00238.x

Acknowledgment

I would like to thank the advisory board; this chapter book could not have been completed without their help.

Special thanks to the authors of the chapters who have made special contributions.

I also want to thank Professor Michael Danson, specialist in Economics and Management at Herriot Watt University, for his invaluable advice and support.

Finally, I would like to thank Professor Bill Donaldson at the Robert Gordon University, responsible for research in Marketing within the Aberdeen Business School, for his advice on the research field.

Irene Samanta
Graduate Technological Education Institute of Piraeus, Greece

Section 1
Relationship Marketing

Chapter 1
Loyalty in Crisis: Evidence from Greece

Ilias P. Vlachos
Northumbria University, UK

Dimitra Skoumpopoulou
Northumbria University, UK

ABSTRACT

This chapter examines customer loyalty across the supply chain during the economic crisis in Greece. The authors posit the following research questions: How does customer's loyalty change in light of the financial crisis and to what extent does customer loyalty contribute to a firm's performance during an economic crisis? The factors discussed are satisfaction, exchange of information, trust, competition, and finally, customer loyalty in fragile economic conditions. In order to examine customer loyalty in a period of crisis, the authors drew their sample from Greek manufacturing companies in 2012. They received 131 usable questionnaires. The total response rate was 13.1%. The results indicate that there is a quite high level of loyalty, which drives them to continue their partnership in the future, but also to recommend their partner to other firms.

1. INTRODUCTION

This chapter examines customer loyalty across the supply chain during the economic crisis in Greece. Financial crisis started in Greece in 2008 and has resulted in severe recession. In 2011 Greece's total economic output was 16% below the pre-crisis peak. Government deficit and government debt in 2010 reached −10.6 and 144.9% of Gross Domestic Product, respectively (Eurostat, 2013).

The current economic climate in Greece and elsewhere in Europe means that firms have to deal with high uncertainty and difficulties into remaining within competition. Hence, it is vital for firms to keep their customers since economic crisis means that it is not easy to invest into the acquisition of new customers.

The construct of loyalty has gained a lot of interest in marketing research since the '70s while the customer loyalty within business gained attention in early '90s due to changes in the business environment, such as the intensified competition and a shift to satisfy customers across different cultures globally (Jacoby & Chestnut, 1978). Gorbatenko

DOI: 10.4018/978-1-4666-6232-2.ch001

(2011) argued that although the phenomenon of customer loyalty has been studied for decades, the question of the best method for measuring loyalty still has no definitive answer.

Soulaki (2010) claimed that a major impact of the economic crisis is the fear and uncertainty of the future with more consumers seeking to better manage their expenses. Mansoor (2011) concluded that the economic recession forced consumers' behaviour to include aspects such as "the need for simplicity," "temperance," "smart consumption," "green consumerism" and "ethical consumerism." Voinea and Filip (2011) suggested that consumers will continue to purchase goods in order to satisfy their basic needs however the way they do this will change as they have new preferences and the desire to be more active and responsible of their lives is intensified.

The importance of this study lies to the fact that no sufficient literature exists relating to the impact of the current financial crisis on customer loyalty across the supply chain. This gap of knowledge in the existing literature should be addressed as companies and academics would be interested in the results of our research since it could enlighten them regarding the marketplace and the customer needs, while it can help them to better manage, formulate and implement a customer driven marketing strategy.

Thus, the aim of our study is to analyze the customer loyalty across the supply chain during the economic crisis in Greece. We posit the following research questions:

1. How does customer's loyalty change in the light of the financial crisis and
2. To what extend customer's loyalty contributes to a firm's performance during an economic crisis?

The structure of the chapters is as follows: the next section discusses the background of this research by exploring in greater detail aspects of the current literature such as customer loyalty in supply chain management and factors that have an impact on customer loyalty. Section 3 presents the methods employed when undertaking this research while section 4 discusses the solutions and recommendations derived from our findings. Finally section 5 provides our concluding remarks and suggests areas for future research.

2. BACKGROUND

There is consensus that true loyalty is demonstrated when individuals choose to remain customers of a company even when they are not offered the best quality of products and services (Ahluwalia et al., 2000). The type of loyalty that is characterized by commitment is called premium quality (Gounaris & Stathakopoulos, 2004). Loyal customers are characterized by repetitive purchasing of products and services, recommending the company to others, defending it against bad comments by strongly supporting their choices (Akhter et al., 2011).

Loyalty can be measured with both attitudinal and behavioral items (Jacoby & Kyner, 1973; Dick and Basu, 1994; Fathollahzadeh et al., 2011; Akhter et al., 2011). Attitudinal measurements, due to the fact that they reflect the psychological and emotional attachment to loyalty, are used in order to understand the cognitive elements that underlie purchasing motives and future actions (Bowen & Chen, 2001; Fathollahzadeh et al., 2011). They are viewed to add some degree of value to the product or service (Wu, 2011). Behavioural measurements, on the other hand, focus on the customer's purchasing history (Vesel & Zabkar, 2009; Fathollahzadeh et al., 2011) and have been measured by the repetitive purchasing behaviour that a customer shows towards a product or service (Wu, 2011).

Due to the economic crisis consumers are seeking to better manage their expenses out of fear and uncertainty of the future. Consumers are becoming more rational in terms of purchasing decisions which means that they are spending more time searching for specific information and are focusing on buying cheaper products in smaller quantities (Leinwand, Moeller & Shriram, 2008). Limited literature exists relating to the impact of the financial crisis on customer loyalty thus this section presents relevant literature and existing research in order to shed light to the economic factors that affect customer loyalty in the supply chain.

2.1 Customer Loyalty in Supply Chain Management

2.1.1 Types of Loyalty

Customer loyalty is well connected with the loyal behaviour of a consumer towards a company. Dick and Basu (1994) claimed that there is not a certain model of customer loyalty; instead there are different levels and interpretations of customer loyalty depending on the nature of the industry, the industry norms and how the firm perceives what is loyalty and what is not. Dick and Basu (1994) provided four different modes of customer loyalty:

1. The "no loyalty" mode where there is low relative attitude and low repeat patronage,
2. 'The "spurious loyalty" which is when there is a low relative attitude and high repeat patronage,
3. the "latent loyalty" with high relative attitude and low repeat patronage and finally
4. The "loyalty" which corresponds in a favourable behaviour between the firm and its customer which leads into a relative positive attitude and repeated patronage.

In order to reach a status where a firm would have created loyal customer, it would first need to understand how a customer can fit into the loyal category but also to understand his needs and how the firm can correspond on those needs. According to Cahill (2007) customer loyalty has been subject to changes due to the economic recession. Having examined the case of the recession which affected Britain in the late 1990s, Chaill (2007) claims that customer preferences are subject to changes during an economic crisis since their income is affected while the nature of competition changes. A study made in 2009 on a sample of 2400 people in France, U.S. and UK, by Euro RSCG C and O, in partnership with Harris Interactive, was aimed at understanding the factors that influence preferences and consumer choices after the crisis (Salzman & O'Reilly, 2010). The study showed that most consumers surveyed changed their consumption behaviour by adopting a logical standby or a replacement, distinguishing their purchases or dropping different brands. Thus, before being interested in the price of products, consumers are asking questions about their usefulness (64% of respondents wonder whether they really needed the product, 60% if they could not find a lower price elsewhere and 59% if they can afford to acquire it). In the context of crisis, perhaps contrary to many expectations, quality is what comes first for the new consumer before the lower price. Consumers surveyed defined quality by: looking for healthy products (42%), looking for strong and sustainable products (47%) and for responsible products (http://www.eurorscgco.com). Thus, consumers have become more vigilant and more aware of their ability to influence the world with their consumer choices (Salzman & O'Reilly, 2010).

Although consumers will continue to purchase goods in order to satisfy their basic needs however the way they do this will change as they have new preferences and the desire to be more active and responsible of their lives (Voinea and Filip, 2011). Therefore companies need to build strong foundations of trust and the ability to solve problems along the supply chain in order to maintain a competitive advantage over other industry players (Arli et al., 2013). The next section discusses how companies can achieve loyalty across their supply chain.

2.1.2 Loyalty in Supply Chains

Several studies have stressed the importance of various operational factors in determining customer retention and loyalty and ultimately the success of firms (Collier & Bienstock, 2006; Hsiao, 2009). Some of these studies have focused on the relationship between company performance and logistics performance. Logistics performance has been either studied as a single factor or as a part of a set of operational factors (Karpinski, 1999). While the role of logistics on firm performance has been well researched in a traditional context (Wisner, 2003; Green et al., 2008; Yang et al., 2009), this topic has received relatively less attention in a manufacturing context. Traditionally, logistics services are built to facilitate efficient flow of goods, information, and cash. Logistics plays a very important role in ensuring customer loyalty. The factors related to logistics are experienced by customers after making payments, and are often grouped as one of the post-purchase factors. Studies have found that customers generally considered physical delivery as a very important factor (Esper et al., 2003; Agatz et al., 2008) and that logistics capability is positively associated with firm performance in the computer and consumer electronics retailing industry (Cho et al., 2008) and container shipping services (Yang et al., 2009). Logistics performance mainly deals with delivery speed and reliability but several studies have also included responsiveness, communication, order-handling and distribution (Cho et al., 2008) in the scope of logistics. While the impact of these factors on customer loyalty/firm performance has been extensively studied in the traditional context (Yang et al., 2009), there seems to be limited research on how customer loyalty has been affected due to the economic crisis and in a supply chain context.

Companies often are focusing on customer satisfaction to cultivate loyalty within their customer base (Levesque & McDougall, 1996; Reichheld, 2003). As the benefits of increased loyalty are becoming better understood, customer satisfaction is increasingly becoming a more important corporate goal (Bitner, 1990; Das et al., 2010; Reichheld, 2009). The degree to which customer satisfaction can be enhanced depends on how well the trading partners are integrated (Johnston et al., 2004). Mutual knowledge created through information shared along the supply chain increases the probability of a common understanding among the parties (Cramton, 2001). Hence a customer's expectations are kept consistent with the supply chain's ability to meet the customer's needs. For example, through collaboration with customers and suppliers firms can learn to tailor service offerings to more closely match specific customer requirements (Stank et al., 2001). Integration with customers and suppliers is related to customer satisfaction and given the relationship between customer satisfaction and loyalty, and then there are a larger number of transactions with the same customers when the firm is integrated with its trading partners. Greater numbers of transactions means that companies achieve improved service levels, reduced costs, greater responsiveness, and improved decision making (Wong et al., 2011). Information about customer requirements, expectations, and preferences can be used in order to create better service and product offerings. When suppliers can exchange information through supply chain integration this can lead to reduced product development times, more reliable products, and products with which customers are more satisfied (Carr and Pearson, 2002; Eltantawy et al., 2009; Lau et al., 2010; Sharland et al., 2003; Shin et al., 2000; Tracey & Tan, 2001; Vonderembse & Tracey, 1999; Wong et al., 2011). Customer integration entails gathering information from customers and combining it with existing information for the purpose of product and service innovation and improvement (Edvardsson et al., 2012). It is possible that the information gathered from collaboration partners could be embodied in the products and services offered thus leading to a superior product/service through which competitive advantage is attained. This principle is supported in the operations management literature as previous studies have shown that the particular way in which customers are integrated has a major impact on the quality of information gained, and therefore on product and service development and customer satisfaction (Magnusson et al., 2003). Heikkila (2002) suggested that understanding the customer's needs together with the right product offering contributes to improving the demand chain, which further leads to superior supply chain efficiency and high customer satisfaction.

2.2 Effects of Customer Loyalty to the Firms

Customer loyalty, a key variable, is concerned with the likelihood of a customer returning, making business referrals, providing strong word-of-mouth, as well as providing references and publicity (Bowen & Shoemaker, 1998). There are a number of issues related with loyalty and its effects on firms, such as increase on revenues, stronger customer base, and impact on internal environment as well as decrease on costs.

Reicheld et al (2000) argued that there are three key advantages from prioritizing customer loyalty. The first one is an increase in the revenues and in the market share as customers feel satisfied and loyal to the brand hence they tend to increase their repurchases but also to make referrals which increase the customer base. The second impact is that a strong and loyal customer base means that the firm would have to decrease the costs given for acquiring new customers but also for declining the old ones and those who have left the brand. Furthermore, the decrease on promotion costs can allow a space for better prices or to provide resources in some other functions of the firm, such as its R&D. A third point is that customer loyalty has an impact on the internal environment. This is because the employees feel proud of been part of this firm and this affects job satisfaction and job climate, which in the end leads into better quality services and customer retention. The latter argument indicates also that there is a circle of functions, related with service quality. For example, a satisfied customer will affect the job climate and a high satisfied and committed employee will also affect his customers. Hence, we have a circle where customer satisfaction and employee satisfaction are interrelated and they are highly associated with customer loyalty (Reicheld et al, 2000). The most important aspect which was mentioned from Reicheld et al., (2000) is that customer loyalty helps a firm to decrease the costs given to acquire new customers. The same argument has been mentioned from Knemeyer et al. (2003) and Neal (1999). Indeed, it seems that when there is a high volume of loyal customers, then it is expected to spend less resources, especially from the marketing and sales department for acquiring new customers and to focus on resources related with customer retention. Furthermore, customer retention due to their loyalty to the brand is expected to have a financial value as mentioned from Gupta et al., (2004).

However, besides the benefits there is a knowledge gap which is the lack of a related literature which will link customer loyalty with success. Cahill (2007) reported that most of the studies are focusing on revenues and often they rely on empirical data that derives from small-scale studies. Yet studies such as Reichdeld and Sasser (1990) give evidence that there is a link between customer loyalty and firm success but they rely mostly on case studies rather than large survey samples. Kalwani and Narayandas (1995) studied a large sample of firms in order to show that there is a relation between high customer loyalty and high revenues and a higher return on investments. Their key assumption is the highest level of customer loyalty the highest are expected to be the revenues and the profitability of the firm. This assumption relies on the fact that the key source of revenues for a firm is its consumers. Therefore, when the customers are satisfied, it is expected to have also a rise in the revenues of the firm, while a loyal customer will bring more customers and will spread a positive word of mouth. At the same time, the firm is able to reduce the amount of money spent for acquiring new customers and therefore to increase its profit margins. On the other hand, there is a view, expressed from Reinartz et al., (2005), that the efforts made to increase customer loyalty may mean also high costs due to the efforts made to keep the customers close to the brand, though this increase can be short-term and on the long term the firm can enjoy the benefits of the customer loyalty. However, Reinartz et al., (2005) raised the alarm since some efforts to retain customers, such as product improvements, can lead into an increase on the costs which will bring an increase in the profitability of the firm. Hence, customer loyalty is expected to bring profitability for a firm, but there is a need to look into the factors that can enable companies to achieve all the benefits associated with customer loyalty.

2.3 Customer Loyalty Factors

The financial sector relies on the maintenance of a long-term relationship with its customers, due to the nature of the products and services it provides, thus losing a customer is a matter that raises concern (Sweeney & Swait, 2008). The importance of customer satisfaction in financial services has been studied extensively in the existing literature (Arbore & Busacca, 2009) and the marketing activity of many companies has focused on achieving customer loyalty (Vesel & Zabkar, 2009). The studies that recognise the significance of customer loss and the impact that this has on a company's profitability are abundant (Sweeney & Swait, 2008; Chi & Gursoy, 2009; Fathollahzadeh et al., 2011; Akhter et al., 2011; Keisidou et al., 2013).

Cahill (2007) proposed three key categories of factors affecting customer loyalty. Those are the customer related factors, the relationship related factors and the company related factors. In the case of the customer related factors, those are factors such as the customer's personality and characteristics, his culture, his habits and his stereotypes. In the aspect of the relationship related factors, we have to find factors which determine the relationship of the consumer with the firm. Those can be variables such as the quality of the products or services, the experience that the customer has from the relationship with the firm, his trust towards the firm and emotional detachment with the firm. The company-related factors are related with issues such as the corporate reputation, the loyalty scheme programmes, and so on.

Schweizer (2008) suggested that we shall not try to classify the factors affecting customer loyalty into internal and external as made from Cahill (2007), since they are too many, but instead to rate them according to their importance. Schweizer (2008) has identified a number of variables such as the pricing policy, the reputation of the firm and the brand image, consumer trust and commitment, customer involvement, product importance, switching barriers and other variables. According to Schweizer (2008) the customer's loyalty depends on the combination of various factors and it also depends on the situation. However, it is important that customer loyalty to be part of the overall business strategy that a firm has adopted, in order to bring benefits (Duffy, 2003). In the next sections we will discuss a number of customer loyalty factors and their impact on an organization's performance. The factors discussed are satisfaction, exchange of information, trust, competition and finally customer loyalty in fragile economic conditions.

2.3.1 Satisfaction

It has been stated that customer satisfaction is the most influential factor on customer loyalty (Kanning & Bergmann, 2009; Hoq & Amin, 2010). Oliver (1980) defined customer satisfaction as the difference between an individual's expectations before the consumption of a product or service and the actual experience that results after the consumption. The term satisfaction describes the sense of fulfilment (Vesel & Zabkar, 2009), that a customer feels after having interacted with a company (Wu, 2011). Additionally, it can be defined as the evaluation that occurs after the consumption of a product or service and at what degree it has met or exceeded the customers' expectations (Yu & Dean, 2001; Akhtar et al., 2011). Ladhari et al., (2011) defined customer satisfaction as the total evaluation of the overall level of services provided. It is thought that satisfaction is likely to increase customer loyalty (Vesel & Zabkar, 2009; Akhter et al., 2011) and it is suggested that satisfied customers result in better financial performance (Bernhardt et al., 2000; Chi & Gursoy, 2009; Fathollahzadeh et al., 2011; Keisidou et al., 2013).

Customer satisfaction means success when we have to deal with services (Lovelock, 2007). For Rocco and Andrew (2011) customer satisfaction is the essence of service marketing and it can guarantee customer loyalty. Customer satisfaction is the positive state of mind that a customer has over his partner (Wallenburg, 2004). Often researchers state that customer satisfaction is something vague and this has led into a variety of conceptualizations over what is customer satisfaction. Homburg et al (2003) suggest that it is about having structures and processes which will also keep the customer satisfied. They have also used the exchange theory in order to report that in such a relation both the customer and the firm are expecting from each other something. The customer expects from the supplier to receive top quality services and to have signs that the supplier has understood the customer's needs, while the supplier expects a long-term relationship with the appropriate benefits (Homburg et al., 2003).

Various researchers, such as Brady et al., (2002) and Spreng et al., (1996) indicated that there is a direct link between customer satisfaction and customer loyalty. This assumption relies on the hypothesis that a satisfied customer tends to be also a loyal customer. However, there are also cases of customers who are satisfied but not loyal and vice versa (Rowley, 2005). Someone may be satisfied from a brand but he/she may not buy it for economic reasons or because at that time the brand is not found. On the other hand, someone may not be fully satisfied but he/she can proceed with frequent repurchases of the product.

2.3.2 Exchange of Information

A key characteristic of industrial marketing is inertia and the relationship between the partners (Kotler & Keller, 2009). In order to have a sustainable relationship, the partners must be fair and frank to each other. A vital point of customer loyalty is the perception that the customer has concerning the ability of his partner to provide him with adequate and accurate information (Wallenburg, 2004). Cahill (2007) argues that loyalty is determined based on the perception that the customer has on whether his partner provides him with anything that would help his business. Providing the customer with accurate information is granted from the firm as a key contribution to its success and hence, it constitutes a construct of customer loyalty in business to business relations.

2.3.3 Trust

Trust is an inter-organizational element which leads into sustainable and long-term relationships with benefits for all parties (Arrow, 1975). Cahill (2007) suggested that trust is extremely important when firms are operating in highly competitive markets. Companies can gain a lot of advantages through establishing collaborative relationships between their suppliers. Crutchfield (2001) mentioned that in today's environment firms have to face a business climate which is particular uncertain. This means that firms need to rely in a partner who will not let them down and they will believe in him; hence to have someone to trust. Creating relationship under the umbrella of trust helps firms to reduce uncertainty and the feeling that their projects may end up in failure. However, it is important to stress that trust can overcome the psychological handicap but this surely cannot guarantee the success of the partnership. Nonetheless, customers who trust their supplier feel safe and comfortable in this relationship and they are willing to cooperate with some that has gained their trust. Hence they are willing to take some risks together with their partner (Morgan & Hunt, 1994). According to Wellenburg (2004), trust in industrial relationships can occur between organizations or between the customer and some members of the organization. This is something that shall not worry the organizations. In this kind of relationships it is very common an organization to communicate only one member or even a small team of their supplier and vice versa. In the long run the trust will develop between those persons.

Trust has been defined as the willingness to rely on an exchange partner in whom one has confidence or confidence in an exchange partner's reliability and integrity (Morgan & Hunt, 2004). Trust causes dedication because it reduces the costs of negotiating agreements and lessens customers' fear of opportunistic behaviour by the service provider (Bendapudi & Berry, 1997). In social psychology trust is considered to consist of two elements: trust in the partner's honesty, and trust in the partner's benevolence. Honesty is the belief that a partner stands by his/her word, while benevolence is the belief that the partner is interested in the customer's welfare, and will not take actions with negative impact on the customer (Afsar 2010).

2.3.4 Competition

Under a climate of a free market economy, a firm can pick up its partner between a number of competitors. The buyer will compare the offers made from the potential suppliers and he will select the ideal offer. However, unlike commercial marketing, in industrial marketing the buyer will hardly switch supplier. One of the reasons is customer loyalty. However, loyalty depends a lot on the number of competitors that exist and on the quality of their offers (Cahill, 2007). It is important to mention that this is an area where not many researches have taken place and surely this research will provide some more information about this variable. An example of such research is Wallendurg (2004) who stated that the quality and availability of alternatives seems to affect customer loyalty.

2.3.5 Customer Loyalty in Fragile Economic Conditions

The recent financial turmoil has not had too large effects on the overall customer satisfaction in the European manufacturing sector. However, the crisis has affected final consumers differently, and the satisfaction has gone down more in some countries (like Denmark, Baltic States, and Russia) than in others (Skowron & Kristensen, 2012). Additionally, Skowron and Kristensen (2012) report that the perception among the customers of a business now varies much more than before which means that the spread between satisfied and dissatisfied customers is higher now than during previous years. For example in the banking sector, expectations as well as availability and comfort of using banking products and services became less important for potential customers when compared to the bank's image, real quality of a given bank's offer and the level of customer service. Summing up, during financial crises companies should concentrate on building the image of stable and well-prepared businesses. The proper communication strategy with actual and potential clients becomes one of the most important elements of success. Clients demand from companies' detailed and understandable information about different products and services offered by the various organisations. It is extremely important for enterprises to be able to give all the necessary information in an easy and convenient way to meet all the customers' demands and suggestions (Skowron & Kristensen, 2012).

3. METHODS: RESEARCH DESIGN

In order to examine customer loyalty in a period of crisis, we drew our sample from Greek manufacturing companies in 2012. The questionnaire was pretested on randomly selected firms with in-depth interviews of key decision makers. The respondents were mainly or supply chain managers or, in some instances, the managing directors of the firms.

We selected a random stratified sample of 1.000 manufacturing companies in Greece, which accounts for about 20% of the Greek population. We included in the sample companies that have used at least once international 3PL services during the last 12 months. We got 131 usable questionnaires. The total response rate was 13.1%.

Table 1 provides information about demographics of the sample companies (Size in Number of full time employees, Sales (Euros) Imports Exports Trading Sector) and the Greek food manufacturing population. Size, Sales, and Trading Sector were recoded and transformed into control variables. To ensure that the respondents were comparable to non-respondents, analyses of variances were conducted between these groups. The non-response bias was assessed by comparing early respondents with late respondents (Armstrong & Overton, 1977). We also found no significant differences between supply chain managers and managing directors.

Respondents were asked to indicate their firm's loyalty to a specific international 3PL service provider in the above four items. For perceived items, a 5-point scale ranging from bad (1) to very good (5) was used.

Table 1. Sample demographics and structure of Greek manufacturing sector in 2010 (N=20.235)

Characteristic	Population	Sample
Number of full time employees		
1-5	20.5%	26%
6-10	18.0%	26%
11-50	45.9%	33%
51-250	12.9%	12%
251-500	1.4%	4%
>500	1.2%	0%
Sales		
0-500.000 €	9.9%	24.5
501.000-1.000.000 €	20.4%	16.7
1.000.001-10.000.001 €	58.5%	36.0
>10.000.000 €	11.3%	22.8
Imports		
West Europe	56%	45%
East Europe	11%	9%
North America	6%	13%
South America	4%	2%
Australia	3%	2%
Africa	9%	2%
East Asia	7%	21%
West Asia	4%	6%
Exports		
West Europe	40%	33%
East Europe	33%	42%
North America	6%	5%
South America	1%	1%
Australia	5%	4%
Africa	9%	3%
East Asia	3%	7%
West Asia	3%	5%
Trading Sector		
Food products	30%	11%
Furniture	1%	1%
I.T. Electronics	10%	11%
Medical supplies	3%	16%
Medicine and Cosmetics	3%	9%
Professional / Household commodities	3%	11%
Other*	47%	42%

Sources: Compilation of various sources: ICAP (www.icap.gr), PSE (www.pse.gr), Eurostat/Comext (www.eurostat.gr), Statistics.gr, mfa.gr

4. SOLUTIONS AND RECOMMENDATIONS

We calculated the degree of acceptance of Loyalty factors among respondents (Table 2). We also analyzed the loyalty factors across three demographic variables: size (Table 3), revenues (Table 4) and Trading Region (Table 5). We report the results by each loyalty factor in turn. To construct the cross-tables, we added the strongly agree and agree into one category 'agree' and respectively the strongly disagree and disagree into one category 'disagree'.

4.1 Satisfaction

Overall respondents reported that they are satisfied from the services delivered from their partners (62%) mostly from the ability of the partner to correspond immediately on their demands (62%), while they claim that they are satisfied generally from their partnership but also from the fact that their partner's services cover all of their needs (61%). Only 3% of the respondents reported that they were strongly dissatisfied by their partners, thus there is still room for improving business partnerships, given that about 35% of respondents gave a neutral position about satisfaction (Table 2). Cross-tabulation and Chi-Square Tests of Loyalty Factors vs Company Size measured by number of employees showed that there is a difference of perception based on the size of the companies (Table 3). Specifically, small-size companies are more satisfied overall from a partnership (30.7%) with only 7% of the large companies reported to be satisfied from their partnership. The same difference is also found in the question about quality services and response time. Companies with

Table 2. Results: loyalty factors

Loyalty Factors	Strongly Disagree	Disagree	Neutral	Agree	Strongly Agree
Satisfaction: We are fully satisfied from our partnership	0%	3%	35%	49%	13%
Satisfaction: The partner's services cover all of our firm needs	0%	4%	35%	46%	16%
Satisfaction: The partner offers top quality services and immediate responses	0%	7%	32%	41%	20%
Exchange of Information: Effective	5%	9%	31%	44%	11%
Exchange of Information: Immediate	4%	6%	35%	37%	17%
Exchange of Information: Reliable	4%	9%	22%	44%	21%
Price: Reflects the provided service quality	2%	4%	32%	42%	21%
Price: Partners's prices are better than market average price	0%	7%	48%	30%	15%
Price: The discounts given from the partners is in our firm's advantage	4%	13%	30%	39%	14%
Trust: The partner keeps his promises	2%	4%	29%	40%	25%
Competition: A better price offer from our partner's competitor would not affect our partnership	6%	22%	31%	31%	10%
Competition: We do not care of other alternatives and their prices	10%	18%	33%	29%	11%
Loyalty Under Crisis: We will continue working together in the future	3%	4%	29%	42%	21%
Loyalty Under Crisis: I would recommend my partner to other firms	5%	9%	27%	37%	21%

Table 3. Results of cross-tabulation and chi-square tests of loyalty factors vs. company size (no employees)

Loyalty Factors	Small Size		Large Size		Chi-Square Tests			
	Agree	Disagree	Agree	Disagree	Value	Asymptotic Significance	Likelihood Ratio	Fisher's Exact Test
Satisfaction: We are fully satisfied from our partnership	30.7%	52.6%	7.0%	9.6%	.187	.666	.667	.796
Satisfaction: The partner's services cover all of our firm needs	1.8%	81.6%	0	16.7%	.407	.523	736	1.000
Satisfaction: The partner offers top quality services and immediate responses	30.7%	52.6%	7.0%	9.6%	.187	.666	.667	.796
Exchange of Information: Effective	35.1%	48.2%	9.6%	7.0%	1.597	.206	.208	.219
Exchange of Information: Immediate	35.1%	48.2%	10.5%	6.1%	2.829	*.093*	.092	.130
Exchange of Information: Reliable	28.1%	55.3%	6.1%	10.5%	.070	.791	.792	.796
Price: Reflects the provided service quality	29.8%	53.5%	7.0%	9.6%	.271	.602	.605	.611
Price: Partners's prices are better than market average price	39.5%	43.9%	14.9%	1.8%	11.315	*.001*	.000	.001
Price: The discounts given from the partners is in our firm's advantage	35.1%	48.2%	11.4%	5.3%	4.408	.036	.035	.045
Trust: The partner keeps his promises	1.8%	81.6%		16.7%	.407	.523	.391	1.000
Competition: A better price offer from our partner's competitor would not affect our partnership	3.5%	79.8%	0.9%	15.8%	.042	.838	.842	1.000
Competition: We do not care of other alternatives and their prices	28.9%	54.4%	6.1%	10.5%	.031	.861	.861	1.000
Loyalty Under Crisis: We will continue working together in the future	45.6%	37.7%	14.0%	2.6%	5.715	*.017*	.012	.021
Loyalty Under Crisis: I would recommend my partner on other firms	34.2%	49.1%	7.0%	9.6%	.007	.932	.932	1.000

smaller revenues appear to be less satisfied from their partners than larger ones, i.e. only 16.7% agree that are fully satisfied from their partnership compared to 25.4% of equivalent large-size companies. However, the chi-square tests indicate that there was not statistical difference between small- and large-size companies (Table 4). Results of cross-tabulation and chi-square tests of loyalty factors vs trading region did not produce significant difference between the EU and the rest of the world regions (Table 5).

4.2 Exchange of Information

There is a high satisfaction rate (65%) regarding the ability to provide reliable exchange of information between the reporting companies and their partners (Table 2). On the other hand, the ability to provide immediate exchange of information seems to lag behind for some firms which have claimed that they are only enough satisfied from their partner (54%). Overall, 55% of respondents reported an effective exchange of information.

Table 4. Results of cross-tabulation and chi-square tests of loyalty factors vs. revenues

Loyalty Factors	Small Size Companies		Large Size Companies		Chi-Square Tests			
	Agree	Disagree	Agree	Disagree	Value	Asymptotic Significance	Likelihood Ratio	Fisher's Exact Test
Satisfaction: We are fully satisfied from our partnership	16.7%	21.1%	25.4%	36.8%	.123	.726	.726	.845
Satisfaction: The partner's services cover all of our firm needs	0.9%	41.2%	0.9%	57.0%	.052	.820	.821	1.000
Satisfaction: The partner offers top quality services and immediate responses	15.8%	26.3%	21.9%	36.0%	.002	.967	.967	1.000
Exchange of Information: Effective	21.1%	21.1%	23.7%	34.2%	.929	.335	.335	.348
Exchange of Information: Immediate	17.5%	24.6%	28.1%	29.8%	.521	.471	.470	.568
Exchange of Information: Reliable	15.8%	26.3%	18.4%	39.5%	.399	.528	.528	.554
Price: Reflects the provided service quality	14.9%	27.2%	21.9%	36.0%	.072	.788	.788	.846
Price: Partners's prices are better than market average price	19.3%	22.8%	35.1%	22.8%	2.445	.118	.118	.132
Price: The discounts given from the partners is in our firm's advantage	18.4%	23.7%	28.1%	29.8%	.250	.617	.617	.705
Trust: The partner keeps his promises	1.8%	40.4%		57.9%	2.799	**.094**	.061	.175
Competition: A better price offer from our partner's competitor would not affect our partnership	1.8%	40.4%	2.6%	55.3%	.010	.922	.922	.923
Competition: We do not care of other alternatives and their prices	16.7%	25.4%	18.4%	39.5%	.736	.391	.392	.431
Loyalty Under Crisis: We will continue working together in the future	28.1%	14.0%	31.6%	26.3%	1.696	.193	.191	.247
Loyalty Under Crisis: I would recommend my partner on other firms	16.7%	25.4%	24.6%	33.3%	.093	.761	.761	.848

There are a significant number of firms (11%) which reported that they are hardly or not satisfied at all from the exchanged information (Table 2). The cross-tabulation and chi-square tests versus company size revealed a statistical significant difference in the immediate exchange of information (chi-square value = 2.829, asymptotic significance=.093). Small-size companies agreed 35.1% and disagreed to 48.2% while larger companies 10.5% and 6.1% respectively. Reliable exchange of information also had significant differences, specifically, Small-size companies agreed 28.1% and disagreed to 55.3% while larger companies 6.1% and 10.5% respectively. Regarding revenues as the cross-tabulation variable, there were not significant differences, i.e. regarding effective Exchange of Information, Small-size companies agreed 21.1% and disagreed to 21.1% while larger companies 23.7% and 34.2% respectively. The same figures were also reported for the trading region as cross-tabulation variable.

4.3 Price

Overall, not all firms are satisfied from the pricing policy of their partners (Table 2). For example there is evidence of low satisfaction levels from the discounts (14%), since it appears to have a

Table 5. Results of cross-tabulation and chi-square tests of loyalty factors vs. trading region

Loyalty Factors	EU		Rest of World		Chi-Square Tests			
	Agree	Disagree	Agree	Disagree	Value	Asymptotic Significance	Likelihood Ratio	Fisher's Exact Test
Satisfaction – We are fully satisfied from our partnership	16.7%	25.4%	21.1%	36.8%	.123	.726	.726	.845
Satisfaction -The partner's services cover all of our firm needs	0.9%	41.2%	0.9%	57.0%	.052	.820	.821	1.000
Satisfaction -The partner offers top quality services and immediate responses	15.8%	26.3%	21.9%	36.0%	.002	.967	.967	1.000
Exchange of Information - Effective	21.1%	21.1%	23.7%	34.2%	.929	.335	.335	.348
Exchange of Information - Immediate	17.5%	24.6%	28.1%	29.8%	.521	.471	.470	.568
Exchange of Information - Reliable	15.8%	26.3%	18.4%	39.5%	.399	.528	.528	.554
Price - reflects the provided service quality	14.9%	27.2%	21.9%	36.0%	.072	.788	.788	.846
Price - Partners's prices are better than market average price	19.3%	22.8%	35.1%	22.8%	2.445	**.118**	.118	.132
Price - The discounts given from the partners is in our firm's advantage	18.4%	23.7%	28.1%	29.8%	.250	.617	.617	.705
Trust - The partner keeps his promises	1.8%	40.4%		57.9%	2.799	**.061**	.094	.175
Competition - A better price offer from our partner's competitor would not affect our partnership	1.8%	40.4%	2.6%	55.3%	.010	.922	.922	.922
Competition - We do not care of other alternatives and their prices	16.7%	25.4%	18.4%	39.5%	.736	.391	.392	.431
Loyalty Under Crisis - We will continue working together in the future	28.1%	14.0%	31.6%	26.3%	1.696	**.193**	.191	.247
Loyalty Under Crisis - I would recommend my partner on other firms	16.7%	25.4%	24.6%	33.3%	.093	.761	.761	.848

significant portion of firms which claim enough satisfied and very little satisfied but also it seems that they do not perceive that their partners' prices are better than the market average. A positive claim is that the firms reported in a great extent that the prices given from their partners reflect the quality of services that they receive (21%) (Table 3). Small Size Companies seem less satisfied from partner price than large companies and 22.8% of them disagree that Partners' prices are better than market average price when only 19.3% agree. On the other hand, large companies gave almost equal responses and 28.1% of them disagree that Partners' prices are better than market average price when only 29.8% agree (Table 4).

4.4 Trust

It seems that the respondents are quite satisfied (Agree 40% Strongly Agree 25%) from their partners who are regarded as trustworthy (Table 2). This is a positive outcome and it indicates that trustworthiness is an important factor for having customer loyalty. However, small companies seem to be disappointed from their partners trust (81.6% based on number of employees) and 40.4% based on revenues (Table 3). Regarding the results of cross-tabulation and chi-square tests of loyalty factors vs revenues the asymptotic significance of chi-square tests was .094 and the chi-square value 2.799, likelihood Ratio .061, and Fisher's exact test .175 (Table 4).

4.5 Competition

A significant evidence of the loyalty of a firm towards its partner is given from the level of willingness to shift partner (Table 2). Not all respondents share the same opinion regarding possible alternative offers. Most respondents seem skeptical and open in the possibility that a more attractive offer could change their existent partnerships. For example, 31% agree and 10% strongly agree with the question '*A better price offer from our partner's competitor would not affect our partnership*'. However, the percentage of skeptical companies are high i.e. 33% did not give a clear answer to the question '*We do not care of other alternatives and their prices*'. This may be justified because in an era of economic recession, sometimes even quality can be sacrificed in the pursuit of a better financial deal. The Cross-tabulation and Chi-Square Tests of Loyalty Factors vs Company Size (no employees) sheds more light to this relation. It is the large companies that are more skeptical since 28.9% of small companies agree with the question '*We do not care of other alternatives and their prices*' and 54.4% disagree while the corresponding percentages for large companies are 6.1% and 10.5% respectively, therefore the 83.4% of large companies are skeptical about competition (Table 3). Responses are different when referring to revenues, and 18.4% of large companies agree and 39.5% disagree with the previous question '*We do not care of other alternatives and their prices*' (Table 4). The same picture is found when comparing companies depending on the region they trade i.e. 16.7% of companies trading within EU agree and 25.4% disagree with the above statement, while the percentages for the 'rest of the world' companies are 18.4% and 39.5% respectively.

4.6 Customer Loyalty during Crisis

The most important goal of a company which makes efforts to acquire and retain loyal customers is to ensure as much as possible a future collaboration with its current customers as well as to obtain the most efficient type of advertisement, which is the one emanating from its own customers.

The results indicate that there is a quite high level of loyalty which drives them to continue their partnership in the future, but also to recommend their partner to other firms (Table 2). 42% of respondents agree and 21% strongly agree that will continue working together in the future with their partners, thus remaining loyal to them. Further, they reported that they wound recommend their partner to other firms (37% agree and 21% strongly agree). The figures are statistically the same for different sizes of the company (Table 3) and revenues generation (Table 4). There is a statistically significant difference to the question '*We will continue working together in the future*' depending on the trading region (Chi-Square value 1.696, significance: .193), which can be attributed to the large number of skeptical companies (neither agree or disagree).

5. CONCLUSION

The first set of questions referred on the geographical regions that the firms choose for their transactions and how the economic crisis has affected the firms and the nature of their operations. The key clue which derived from this set of questions was that they tend to export and import mostly with countries which are nearby. In addition, the economic crisis has affected significantly their economic performance.

The next part of the survey was about the selection factors that companies would use in order to choose their partner. There is a strong indication that there is not a single motive for choosing a partner. Instead there is a clear set of motives which would persuade a firm to work with someone else (Rocco & Andrew, 2011). Indeed, from the answers given we realized that there is not a single motive but a combination of motives. Service-related factors such as having friendly staff and providing quality driven services (Homburg et al., 2003) are among the most important. However, there is also strong evidence that the possibility of providing financial credits, such as having a longer time of payments and debts towards each other, has become a key factor. This has not been identified previously in the literature. As a matter of fact, it seems that the lack of cash in the Greek market has brought forward the need to ensure that each partner will show an understanding of the current situation and he will provide any possible convenience in order to help the customer.

In the case of satisfaction, it seems that there is a good level of satisfaction, though the participants claim that they are just satisfied from their partnership but also from the fact that their partner covers all of their needs. Authors such as Lovelock (2007) and Wallenburg (2004) have stressed the fact that customer satisfaction is strongly linked with customer loyalty. However Homburg et al (2003) have written that most of the research in this field had taken place with firms that address to consumers and not in B2B. Of course customer satisfaction is not the only determinant of loyalty, as mentioned by Rowley (2005), who indicates that when we have a business partnership, satisfaction is not the only variable that will determine customer loyalty.

Regarding the exchange of information factor the questionnaire focused mainly on the ability of the partner to provide accurate and important information as a sign of being fair to his customer. From the results it appears that they are in balance with their partners. According to Neuert et al., (2005) this affects in a great extend customer loyalty; the essence that the customer feels when his partner provides him with all the necessary information without a hesitation. The factor of trust was used as a unique question. The respondents deemed that trust is an important factor when they choose their partners. Cahill (2007) argues that trust is even more important when firms are operating in highly competitive markets and it brings advantages through collaborative relationships between the service provider / supplier and the buyer. The fact that the Greek market is not only highly competitive but it is under a crisis makes the existence of trust between the involved parties even more important. As a matter of fact, the willingness of a customer to share his risks with his partner is a sign of loyalty. Wallenbrg (2004) and Cahill (2007) have indicated that trust is highly associated with customer loyalty. A customer who trusts his partner surely is a loyal customer.

The factor of price was not previously included in the literature but under the current situation, it is necessary to include it because price is a major factor that influences customer loyalty in a time of economic crisis. It seems that there is still space for improvements, such as having better discounts and try to make better price offers. The positive clue was that the prices are reflecting the quality of services delivered to the customer. Finally, we examined the alternatives that the firms have on their disposal. Wallendurg (2004) stated that the quality and availability of alternatives seems to affect customer loyalty. In this case the firms have a plethora of alternatives to choose from. Cahill (2007) suggests that the tendency to avoid searching for new choices, despite of the wide offers that they exist, is due to customer loyalty and to the uncertainty from changing the partner. However, the sample of our survey does not seem to be so absolute about this factor. This could be explained again by the current crisis in Greece and the possible existence of more attractive offers.

REFERENCES

Afsar, B., Rehman, Z. U., Qureshi, J. A., & Shahjehan, A. (2010). Determinants of customer loyalty in the banking sector: The case of Pakistan. *African Journal of Business Management*, *4*(6), 1040–1047.

Agatz, N. A. H., Fleischmann, M., & van Nunen, J. A. E. E. (2008). E-fulfillment and multi-channel distribution – A review. *European Journal of Operational Research*, *187*(2), 339–356. doi:10.1016/j.ejor.2007.04.024

Ahluwalia, R., Burnkrant, R. E., & Unnava, H. R. (2000). Consumer response to negative publicity: The moderating role of commitment. *JMR, Journal of Marketing Research*, *37*(2), 203–214. doi:10.1509/jmkr.37.2.203.18734

Akhtar, M. N., Hunjra, A. I., Akbar, S. W., Rehman, K. U., & Niazi, C. S. K. (2011). Relationship between customer satisfaction and service quality of Islamic banks. *World Applied Sciences Journal*, *13*(3), 453–459.

Arbore, A., & Busacca, B. (2009). Customer satisfaction and dissatisfaction in retail banking: Exploring the asymmetric impact of attribute performances. *Journal of Retailing and Consumer Services*, *16*(4), 271–280. doi:10.1016/j.jretconser.2009.02.002

Arli, V., Dylke, S., Burgess, R., & Soldo, E. (2013). Woolworths Australia and Walmart US: Best practices in supply chain collaboration. *Journal of Economics, Business, and Accountancy Ventura*, *16*(1), 27–46.

Armstrong, J. S., & Overton, T. S. (1977). Estimating nonresponse bias in mail surveys. *JMR, Journal of Marketing Research*, *14*(3), 396–402. doi:10.2307/3150783

Arrow, K. J. (1975). Gifts and Exchanges. In *Altruism, Morality, and Economic Theory* (pp. 13–28). New York: Academic Press.

Bendapudi, N., & Berry, L. L. (1997). Customers' motivations for maintaining relationships with service providers. *Journal of Retailing*, *73*(1), 15–37. doi:10.1016/S0022-4359(97)90013-0

Bernhardt, K. L., Donthu, N., & Kennett, P. A. (2000). A longitudinal analysis of satisfaction and profitability. *Journal of Business Research*, *47*(2), 161–171. doi:10.1016/S0148-2963(98)00042-3

Bitner, M. J. (1990). Evaluating service encounters: The effects of physical surroundings and employee responses. *Journal of Marketing*, *54*(2), 69–82. doi:10.2307/1251871

Bowen, J. T., & Shoemaker, S. (1998). Loyalty: A strategic commitment. *The Cornell Hotel and Restaurant Administration Quarterly*, *39*(1), 12–25. doi:10.1177/001088049803900104

Bowen, T. J., & Chen, S. (2001). The relationship between customer loyalty and customer satisfaction. *International Journal of Contemporary Hospitality Management*, *13*(5), 213–217. doi:10.1108/09596110110395893

Brady, M. K., Cronin, J. J. Jr, & Brand, R. R. (2002). Performance-only measurement of service quality: A replication and extension. *Journal of Business Research*, *55*(1), 17–31. doi:10.1016/S0148-2963(00)00171-5

Cahill, D. (2007). *Customer loyalty in third party logistics relationships: Findings from studies in Germany and the USA*. New York: Springer.

Carr, A. S., & Pearson, J. N. (2002). The impact of purchasing and supplier involvement on strategic purchasing and its impact on firm's performance. *International Journal of Operations & Production Management*, *22*(9/10), 1032–1055. doi:10.1108/01443570210440528

Chi, C. G., & Gursoy, D. (2009). Employee satisfaction, customer satisfaction and financial performance: An empirical examination. *International Journal of Hospitality Management*, *28*(2), 245–253. doi:10.1016/j.ijhm.2008.08.003

Cho, J. J.-K., Ozment, J., & Sink, H. (2008). Logistics capability, logistics outsourcing and firm performance in an e-commerce market. *International Journal of Physical Distribution & Logistics Management*, *38*(5), 336–359. doi:10.1108/09600030810882825

Collier, J.E., & Bienstock, C.C. (2006, Fall). How do customers judge quality in an e-tailor?. *MIT Sloan Management Review*, 35–40.

Cramton, C. D. (2001). The mutual knowledge problem and its consequences for dispersed collaboration. *Organization Science*, *12*(3), 346–371. doi:10.1287/orsc.12.3.346.10098

Crutchfield, T. N. (2001). The Effect of Trust and Commitment on Retention of High-Risk Professional Service Customers. *Services Marketing Quarterly*, *22*(2), 17–27. doi:10.1300/J396v22n02_02

Das, A., Kumar, V., & Saha, G. C. (2010). Retail service quality in the context of transition economies. *International Journal of Quality & Reliability Management*, *27*(6), 658–683. doi:10.1108/02656711011054542

Dick, A., & Basu, K. (1994). Customer loyalty: Toward an integrated conceptual framework. *Journal of Marine Science*, *22*(2), 99–113.

Duffy, D. (2003). Internal and external factors which affect customer loyalty. *Journal of Consumer Marketing*, *20*(5), 480–485. doi:10.1108/07363760310489715

Edvardsson, B., Kristensson, P., Magnusson, P., & Sundström, E. (2012). Customer integration within service development. *Technovation*, *32*(7-8), 419–429. doi:10.1016/j.technovation.2011.04.006

Eltantawy, R. A., Giunipero, L., & Fox, G. L. (2009). A strategic skill based model of supplier integration and its effect on supply management performance. *Industrial Marketing Management*, *38*(8), 925–936. doi:10.1016/j.indmarman.2008.12.022

Esper, T. L., Jensen, T. D., Turnipseed, F. L., & Burton, S. (2003). The last mile: An examination of effects of online retail delivery strategies on consumers. *Journal of Business Logistics*, *24*(2), 177–203. doi:10.1002/j.2158-1592.2003.tb00051.x

Eurostat. (2013). *Government statistics*. Retrieved September the 1st from http://epp.eurostat.ec.europa.eu/portal/page/portal/government_finance_statistics/data/database

Fathollahzadeh, M., Hashemi, A., & Kahreh, M. S. (2011). Designing a new model for determining customer value satisfaction and loyalty towards banking sector of Iran. *European Journal of Economics. Finance and Administrative Sciences*, *28*(1), 126–138.

Gorbatenko, A. (2011). *Customer loyalty as the factor of a company's competitiveness in the time of depression*. Retrieved September the 15th from http://www.changing-europe.org/download/CESS2011/gorbatenko.pdf

Gounaris, S., & Stathakopoulos, V. (2004). Antecedents and consequences of brand loyalty: An empirical study. *Journal of Brand Management*, *11*(4), 283–306. doi:10.1057/palgrave.bm.2540174

Green, K. W. Jr, Whitten, D., & Inman, R. A. (2008). The impact of logistics performance on organizational performance in a supply chain context. *Supply Chain Management: An International Journal*, *13*(4), 317–327. doi:10.1108/13598540810882206

Gupta, S., Lehmann, D. R., & Stuart, J. A. (2004). Valuing Customers. *JMR, Journal of Marketing Research*, *41*(1), 7–18. doi:10.1509/jmkr.41.1.7.25084

Heikkila, J. (2002). From supply to demand chain management: Efficiency and customer satisfaction. *Journal of Operations Management*, *20*(6), 747–767. doi:10.1016/S0272-6963(02)00038-4

Homburg, C., Giering, A., & Menon, A. (2003). Relationship Characteristics as Moderators of the Satisfaction-Loyalty Link: Findings in a Business-to-Business Context. *Journal of Business-To-Business Marketing*, *10*(3), 35–62. doi:10.1300/J033v10n03_02

Hoq, H. Z., & Amin, M. (2010). The role of customer satisfaction to enhance customer loyalty. *African Journal of Business Management*, *4*(12), 2385–2392.

Hsiao, M.-H. (2009). Shopping mode choice: Physical store shopping versus e-shopping. *Logistics and Transportation Review*, *45*(1), 86–95. doi:10.1016/j.tre.2008.06.002

Jacoby, J., & Chestnut, R. W. (1978). *Brand Loyalty: Measurement and Management*. New York: Wiley.

Jacoby, J., & Kyner, D. B. (1973). Brand loyalty vs repeat purchasing behaviour. *JMR, Journal of Marketing Research*, *10*(1), 1–9. doi:10.2307/3149402

Johnston, D. A., McCutcheon, D. M., Stuart, F. I., & Kerwood, H. (2004). Effects of supplier trust on performance of cooperative supplier relationships. *Journal of Operations Management*, *22*(1), 23–38. doi:10.1016/j.jom.2003.12.001

Kalwani, M. U., & Narayandas, N. (1995). Long-term manufacturer supplier relationships: Do they pay off for supplier firms? *Journal of Marketing*, *59*(1), 1–16. doi:10.2307/1252010

Kanning, U. P., & Bergmann, N. (2009). Predictors of customer satisfaction: Testing the classical paradigms. *Managing Service Quality*, *19*(4), 377–390. doi:10.1108/09604520910971511

Karpinski. (1999). The logistics of e-business—Web commerce demands new approach to inventory, shipping. *Internet Week, 767*, 1096.

Keisidou, E., Sarigiannidis, L., Maditinos, D. I., & Thalassinos, E. I. (2013). Customer satisfaction, loyalty and financial performance: A holistic approach of the Greek banking sector. *International Journal of Bank Marketing*, *31*(4), 259–288. doi:10.1108/IJBM-11-2012-0114

Knemeyer, A. M., Corsi, T. M., & Murphy, P. R. (2003). Logistics Outsourcing Relationships: Customer Perspectives. *Journal of Business Logistics*, *24*(1), 77–109. doi:10.1002/j.2158-1592.2003.tb00033.x

Kotler, P., & Keller, K. (2009). *Marketing Management* (13th ed.). Pearson.

Ladhari, R., Ladhari, I., & Morales, M. (2011). Bank service quality: Comparing Canadian and Tunisian customer perceptions. *International Journal of Bank Marketing*, *29*(3), 224–246. doi:10.1108/02652321111117502

Lau, A. K. W., Yam, R. C. M., & Tang, E. P. Y. (2010). Supply chain integration and product modularity: An empirical study of product performance for selected Hong Kong manufacturing industries. *International Journal of Operations & Production Management*, *30*(1), 20–56. doi:10.1108/01443571011012361

Leinwand, P., Moeller, L. H., & Shriram, K. (2008). *Consumer Spending in the Economic Downturn: The wide ranging Impact on consumer behaviour*. Booz & Company. Retrieved from www.interbrand.com/.../33_IP_Consumer_Spending_in_a_Recession.pdf

Levesque, T., & McDougall, G. H. C. (1996). Determinants of customer satisfaction in retail banking. *International Journal of Bank Marketing*, *14*(7), 12–20. doi:10.1108/02652329610151340

Lovelock, C. (2007). *Services Marketing*. Prentice Hall.

Magnusson, P. R., Matthing, J., & Kristensson, P. (2003). Managing user involvement in service innovation. *Journal of Service Research*, *6*(2), 111–124. doi:10.1177/1094670503257028

Mansoor, D. (2011). The Global Business Crisis and Consumer Behavior: Kingdom of Bahrain as a Case Study. *International Journal of Business and Management*, *6*(1), 104–115.

Morgan, R. M., & Hunt, S. D. (1994). The Commitment-Trust Theory of Relationship Marketing. *Journal of Marketing*, *58*(3), 20–38. doi:10.2307/1252308

Neal, W. D. (1999). Satisfaction is Nice, But Value Drives Loyalty. *Marketing Research*, *11*(1), 20–23.

Oliver, R. L. (1980). A cognitive model of the antecedents and consequences of satisfaction decisions. *JMR, Journal of Marketing Research*, *17*(4), 460–469. doi:10.2307/3150499

Ramanathan, R. (2010). The moderating roles of risk and efficiency on the relationship between logistics performance and customer loyalty in e-commerce. *Transportation Research Part E, Logistics and Transportation Review*, *46*(6), 950–962. doi:10.1016/j.tre.2010.02.002

Reichheld, F. (2003). The one number you need to grow. *Harvard Business Review*, *81*(12), 46–54. PMID:14712543

Reichheld, F. (2009). Closing the customer feedback loop. *Harvard Business Review*, *87*(12), 43–47.

Reichheld, F. F., Markey, R. G. J., & Hopton, C. (2000). The loyalty effect - The relationship between loyalty and profits. *European Business Journal*, *12*(3), 134–139.

Reichheld, F. F., & Sasser, W. C. J. (1990). Zero defections: Quality comes to services. *Harvard Business Review*, *68*(5), 105–111. PMID:10107082

Reinartz, W., & Kumar, V. (2002, July). The mismanagement of customer loyalty. *Harvard Business Review*, 86–94. PMID:12140857

Rocco, M. A., & Andrew, N. V. (2011). *Hospitality Today: An Introduction* (7th ed.). Educational Institute of the American Hotel Motel Association.

Rowley, J. (2005). The four Cs of customer loyalty. *Marketing Intelligence & Planning*, *23*(6), 574–581. doi:10.1108/02634500510624138

Salzman, M., & O'Reilly, A. (2010). *10 trends in mindful consumption*. Retrieved 25/09/2013 from http://www.thenewconsumer.com/2010/10/29/10-trends-in-mindful-consumption/

Schweizer, B. (2008). *An Examination of Factors Leading to Abating Customer Loyalty Towards Magazine Subscriptions*. Berlin: GRIN Verlag.

Sharland, A., Eltantawy, R. A., & Giunipero, L. C. (2003). The impact of cycle time on supplier selection and subsequent performance outcomes. *Journal of Supply Chain Management*, *39*(3), 4–12. doi:10.1111/j.1745-493X.2003.tb00155.x

Shin, H., Collier, D. A., & Wilson, D. D. (2000). Supply management orientation and supplier/buyer performance. *Journal of Operations Management*, *18*(3), 317–333. doi:10.1016/S0272-6963(99)00031-5

Skowron, L., & Kristensen, K. (2012). The impact of the recent banking crisis on customer loyalty in the banking sector: Developing versus developed countries. *The TQM Journal*, *24*(6), 480–497. doi:10.1108/17542731211270052

Soulaki, A. (2010). *Can a financial crisis shaken Greek consumers' brand loyalty?* Retrieved September the 20th from http://www.ihu.edu.gr/gateway/files/document/dissertations/Soulaki_Antonia.pdf

Spreng, R. A., MacKenzie, S. B., & Olshavsky, R. W. (1996). A Reexamination of the Determinants of Consumer Satisfaction. *Journal of Marketing*, *60*(3), 15–32. doi:10.2307/1251839

Stank, T. P., Goldsby, T. J., & Vickery, S. K. (1999). Effect of service supplier performance on satisfaction and loyalty of store managers in the fast food industry. *Journal of Operations Management*, *17*(4), 429–447. doi:10.1016/S0272-6963(98)00052-7

Sweeney, J., & Swait, J. (2008). The effects of brand credibility on customer loyalty. *Journal of Retailing and Consumer Services*, *15*(3), 179–193. doi:10.1016/j.jretconser.2007.04.001

Tracey, M., & Tan, C. L. (2001). Empirical analysis of supplier selection and involvement, customer satisfaction, and firm performance. *Supply Chain Management: An International Journal*, *6*(4), 174–188. doi:10.1108/EUM0000000005709

Vesel, P., & Zabkar, V. (2009). Managing customer loyalty through the mediating role of satisfaction in the DIY retail loyalty program. *Journal of Retailing and Consumer Services*, *16*(5), 396–406. doi:10.1016/j.jretconser.2009.05.002

Voinea, L., & Filip, A. (2011). Analyzing the Main Changes in New Consumer Buying Behavior during Economic Crisis. *International Journal of Economic Practices and Theories*, *1*(1), 14–19.

Vonderembse, M. A., & Tracey, M. (1999). The impact of supplier selection criteria and supplier involvement on manufacturing performance. *Journal of Supply Chain Management*, *35*(3), 33–39. doi:10.1111/j.1745-493X.1999.tb00060.x

Wallenburg, C. M. (2004). *Kundenbindung in der Logistik: Eine empirische Untersuchung zu ihren Einflussfaktoren*. Bern: Academic Press.

Wisner, J. D. (2003). A structural equation model of supply chain management strategies and firm performance. *Journal of Business Logistics*, *24*(1), 1–26. doi:10.1002/j.2158-1592.2003.tb00030.x

Wong, C. Y., Boonitt, S., & Wong, C. W. Y. (2011). The contingency effects of environmental uncertainty on the relationship between supply chain integration and operational performance. *Journal of Operations Management, 29*(6), 604–615. doi:10.1016/j.jom.2011.01.003

Wu, L. W. (2011). Beyond satisfaction: The relative importance of locational convenience, interpersonal relationships, and commitment across service types. *Managing Service Quality, 21*(3), 240–263. doi:10.1108/09604521111127956

Yang, C.-C., Marlow, P. B., & Lu, C.-S. (2009). Assessing resources, logistics service capabilities, innovation capabilities and the performance of container shipping services in Taiwan. *International Journal of Production Economics, 122*(1), 4–20. doi:10.1016/j.ijpe.2009.03.016

Yu, Y., & Dean, A. (2001). The contribution of emotional satisfaction to consumer loyalty. *International Journal of Service Industry Management, 12*(3), 234–250. doi:10.1108/09564230110393239

KEY TERMS AND DEFINITIONS

Competition: The activity or condition of striving to gain or win something by establishing superiority over other companies.

Crisis: A time of intense difficulty or danger that threatens the survival of the firm.

Exchange of Information: Exchange of information between partners.

Loyalty: Demonstrated when individuals choose to remain customers of a company even when they are not offered the best quality of products and services.

Satisfaction: Fulfillment of one's wishes, expectations, or needs, or the pleasure derived from this.

Trust: Firm belief and reliance in the reliability, truth, or ability of a business partner.

Chapter 2
The Evolution of Trust in Japan:
The Case of Vertical Keiretsu Groups

Nabyla Daidj
Institut Mines-Télécom, France

ABSTRACT

Research on corporate ownership in Japan focus mainly on corporate networks: horizontal and vertical keiretsu. Horizontal keiretsu are networks of firms whose small individual equity stakes in each other collectively sum to control blocks structured around a main bank. Vertical (manufacturing) keiretsu are similar structures that encompass the suppliers and customers of a single large firm. Vertical networks, representative of long-lasting and stable relationships (especially in the Japanese car industry), are undergoing drastic changes. Many authors insist there have been significant changes observed within keiretsu since the end of the 1990s. To have a better understanding of the evolution of trust within keiretsu, it is necessary to analyse its industrial organisation evolution. The authors first situate the Japanese organisational structure and then present a review of the main stages of the change that has affected vertical keiretsu, together with the factors that have contributed to this change. Finally, they analyse the evolution of trust within keiretsu. The authors illustrate the evolution of keiretsu via a case study: the Nissan keiretsu closely related to the Renault-Nissan alliance.

INTRODUCTION

The Japan spectacular growth originated partly in *keiretsu*. *Keiretsu* and more specifically 'vertical *keiretsu*' have been widely recognized as an important source of strength in Japanese industries. They contributed largely to boost the Japanese post Second World War growth. They were a key feature of Japan's economy, affecting directly or indirectly economic transactions within and across industries. They also structured the Japanese industrial system. They can be analyzed as both an organizational phenomenon and a means which has enabled Japanese firms to expand their production capacities, their competitiveness and their exports growth (Aoki, 1988) until the 1990s.

The corporate governance structure is dynamic, developing in response to country-specific factors

DOI: 10.4018/978-1-4666-6232-2.ch002

and new market conditions (Kester, 1990). Until the 1990s, the consortium of *keiretsu* members led to an exclusion of foreign competitors from the Japanese market. But, the automotive industry has undergone major changes over the past years in Japan. More recently in the automobile industry, one of the most exposed to the competitive global market, three major firms had been taken over by foreign concern: Mazda by Ford in 1996, Nissan by Renault in 1999, and Mitsubishi by Daimler-Chrysler in 2000. These operations have had a great impact on *keiretsu* and more specifically on supplier relationships (Daidj et al., 2008) and corporate governance leading to a reorganization/dissolution of keiretsu.

This study whose aim is to propose a framework to discuss the evolution of trust practices within an international strategic alliance follows previous analysis on *keiretsu* issue (Daidj, 2009, 2011, 2013a). Several coordination and corporate mechanisms exist: some are formal (contract, authority), others are informal (trust, reputation, reciprocity). *Keiretsu* values are mainly 'trust and dependence'. We'll analyze the Nissan case to illustrate the implications of changes in subcontracting and purchasing system and consequently in trust. How trust has evolved within the former Nissan keiretsu?

This paper is organized as follows; the first section briefly reviews the relevant literature to clarify the concept of trust as this notion has become an important topic of research in a variety of disciplines, including management, ethics, sociology, psychology, and economics. Trust is a multidimensional and multifaceted concept. We focus our attention on ties between trust, alliances and organizational networks such as *keiretsu*. The second section investigates the evolution of vertical *keiretsu* using the case of Nissan and examines the impact of these changes on trust within the Renault-Nissan alliance. The final section concludes.

1. TRUST, ALLIANCES, AND INTER-ORGANIZATIONAL NETWORKS

Scholars in various disciplines (institutional economics, sociology, strategic management, organization studies) have referred to trust in different ways. But, "trust remains an under-theorized, under-researched, and, therefore, poorly understood phenomenon" (Child, 2001, p. 274). In this part, we propose a general formulation of trust to facilitate the study the evolution of trust within inter-firms groups such as Japanese *keiretsu* in part 2.

1.1 The Determinants of Trust

1.1.1 Trust: A Polysemantic Concept

Bigley and Pearce (1998) consider that concepts of trust depend on the research problem. The notion of trust is very broad, it encompasses many meanings. In fact, it is a polysemantic concept presenting an ambiguous theoretical status (Ingham & Mothe, 2003).

The general definitions emphasize the key role of trust: it an "important lubricant of social systems" (Arrow, 1974, p. 23). Trust is closely related to transactions: "there is an element of trust in every transaction" (Arrow, 1973, p. 24) and trust results from belief formulations in repeated transactions (Breton & Wintrobe, 1984).

Common thoughts stand out from definitions relationships between trust and several concepts: cooperation, confidence, control, risk, vulnerability and predictability. The interrelationships of these factors lead to a confusion in the definition of trust (Table 1). For example, as it explained by Mayer et al., (1995), the association is ambiguous regarding trust and predictability. Following Deutsch (1958), they consider the fact that "to be meaningful, trust must go beyond predictability (1995, p. 714). Another illustration

Table 1. The different meanings of trust and related concepts

Authors	Definitions
Bromiley and Harris	Trust is defined as "one's *non-calculative* belief in another's honesty in negotiations, good-faith efforts to keep commitments, and forbearance from opportunism." (2006, p. 125).
Cook and Wall	Trust is "the extent to which one is willing to ascribe good intentions to and have confidence in the words and actions of other people." (1980, p. 39)
Farris, Senner, and Butterfield	Trust is "a personality trait of people interacting with peripheral environment of an organization." (1973, p. 145)
Fukuyama	"Trust constitutes the expectations which are formed inside of a community governed by a consistent behavior, honest and cooperative, usually based on standards shared by the other members of this community." (1995, p. 26)
Gambetta	"Scholars tend to mention (trust) in passing, to allude to it as a fundamental ingredient or lubricant, an unavoidable dimension of social interaction, only to move on to deal with less intractable matters." Trusting someone means "the probability that he will perform an action that is beneficial or at least not detrimental to us is high enough for us to consider engaging in some form of cooperation with him." (1988, p. 217)
Johnson-George and Swap	"Willingness to take risks may be one of the few characteristics common to all trust situations." (1982, p. 1306)
Luhmann	"If you do not consider alternatives (every morning you leave the house without a weapon!), you are in a situation of confidence. If you choose one action in preference to others in spite of the possibility of being disappointed by the action of others, you define the situation as one of trust." (1988, p. 102)
Mayer, Davis and Schoorman	"(Trust) is the willingness of a party to be vulnerable to the actions of another party based on the expectation that the other will perform a particular action important to the trustor, irrespective of the ability to monitor or control that other party." (1995, p. 712)
McEvily et al.	"Trust is the willingness to accept vulnerability based on positive expectations about another's intentions or behaviors." (2003, p. 92)
Piricz and Mandják	"Trust is calculable, risk decreasing, relationship based, soft resource embedded in a permanent changing environment." (2012, p. 5)
Rotter	Interpersonal trust is defined "as an expectancy held by an individual or a group that the word, promise, verbal or written statement of another individual or group can be relied upon." (1967, p. 651)
Sabel	"Trust is the mutual confidence that no party to an exchange will exploit another's vulnerabilities." (1993, p. 1133)
Zucker	Trust is "a logical set of expectations shared by all involved in an economic exchange" (1986, p. 50)

Source: Developed by the author, based on analysis of the articles cited.

of this lack of clarity is related to the confusion between 'trust' and 'trustworthiness."

Several scholars consider that trust involves two principle concepts: reliance (Giffin, 1967; Rotter, 1980) and risk (Gambetta, 1988; Mayer et al., 1995). Currall and Inkpen (2002, p. 484) define reliance as "action through which one party permits its fate to be determined by another. Risk is the potential that the trusting party will experience negative outcomes, i.e. "injury or loss" if the other party proves untrustworthy (March & Shapira, 1987; Sitkin & Pablo, 1992)."

In addition, trust is also determined by contextual factors and the level of trust evolves as the parties interact (see section 2). In particular, the cultural context is an important issue for researchers studying trust. People with different developmental experiences, personality types, and cultural backgrounds vary in their propensity to trust (e.g., Hofstede, 1991). Culture, time, tacit knowledge and trust, value identification, language and preferential sharing are contextual factors.

Informal trust mechanisms can also occur at a more collective level and a trust culture might develop within villages, ethnic groups, countries. This is "a system of rules – norms and values – regulating granting trust and meeting, returning, and reciprocating trust; in short, rules about trust and trustworthiness" (Sztompka, 1999, p. 99).

The Japanese context has been explored by several authors who try to determine "how and to what extent trust is embedded in Japanese business culture" (Evans, 2012, p. 59). Culture represents the values and beliefs that individuals of a same organization share. It defines how individuals are involved in the company and what is relevant for learning (Schein, 1992). Personal relationships among key individuals have played a crucial role in producing trust between organizations in Japanese industrial groups (Lincoln et al., 1996). Evans has explained that the aim of relationships within firms in Japan is finally to create 'trust': "(…) If transaction negotiating and business activity is treated as a very human activity, we observe another characteristic of the entire process that somehow all component parts i.e. cultural values, meld into one another and naturally so. Relations, Japanese social values, information exchange, product and the self, private life and company life, trust, all connect and blend into a singularity. Thus, a Japanese championing the virtues of a "personal relationship" or a reference to my "uchi" (home) could mean my "company," a mention of "giri" presumes the existence of an "on" and so on and so forth. A "kimochi," either good or not, night be substituted by a product evaluation, favorable or otherwise. And there are more; a job viewed as "well-done" equates with a 'trustworthy' collaborator, a worker's personal life in conjunction with his professionalism can be assessed as exemplary and therefore that person may be suited to be given a challenging task" (2012, p. 157).

1.1.2 The Multi-Level Approach of Trust

According to Currall and Inkpen (2002), the concept of trust can be applied to persons, groups and firms: "(…) all three are capable of trust decisions and the measurable actions that follow. Organizational researchers often study decision making by individuals (e.g., Bazerman, 2001), groups (e.g., Bar-Tal, 1990), or organizations (e.g., Huber, 1990). Therefore, our definition of IJV (international joint venture) trust may be said to "travel" (Osigweh, 1989) across levels because viewing trust as a decision to take action rather than an expectation also allows the researcher to extend the level of measurement to the group or firm" (2002, p. 484). Informal arrangements have to be built on trust (Tullock, 1965, p. 37).

At the personal level, the study of inter-personal trust is closely linked with the discipline of psychology (Deutsch, 1958; Rotter, 1967). Zaheer et al., (1998) analyzed distinctions at an empirical level between inter-organizational and interpersonal trust. Within firms, members are very often linked by relations of interpersonal trust. Ties among members can take multiple forms and in some cases they are informal. At the firm level, trust could increase competitive advantage (Barney & Hansen, 1994; Jarillo, 1988; Mohr & Spekman, 1994). Trust is the basis for mutual confidence between firms (Johnston *et al.*, 2004).

Trust has been analyzed in a context of cooperation: dyadic alliances and networks. There is a distinction between dyadic and network forms. When two firms are involved in an alliance, trust becomes a 'strategic asset' and contributes to the success of the operation. The notions of 'commitment' and of 'mutual trust' in the case of horizontal strategic alliances have been analysed by several authors (Lane et *al.*, 2001; Parkhe, 1998; Cullen et *al.*, 1995, 2000). Trust has to be analyzed carefully in particular in the case of non-equity alliances and strategic alliances.

- Non-equity alliances include a host of inter-firm co-operative agreements such as R&D collaboration, technology sharing, co-production contract, marketing agreements, R&D and production consortia, supply arrangements, long-term sourcing agreements. The non-equity alliance is often a preliminary step to create a joint-venture. It is therefore the most flexible and potentially the least committed form of alliance;
- Strategic alliances are agreements between rival companies (with the aim of developing a sustainable competitive advantage) from other forms of co-operation which are more traditionally regarded as 'tactical' (Porter & Fuller, 1986), in other words, responding to a specific and isolated problem. This classification is important because of the different implications it has on the management of the alliance. Alliances with competing firms impose the protection of the company from losing its distinctive resources and core competencies (such as knowledge). Though this is true for all alliances involving rival firms, it is more important for complementary alliances like that of Renault and Nissan (analyzed in part 2). Within an alliance, the interests between the partners could be conflicting and: "actors use their knowledge of the network as well as their relationships with other actors in order to increase their control" (Haakansson & Johanson, 1992, p. 30). Commitment and trust are difficult to achieve in business relationships involving competitors.

In addition, strategic alliances do not only have an impact outside the coalition, but also within it on the partners themselves, because the partners, while developing close collaborations in certain fields, find themselves in competition in others. Cooperation is not simple (Doz and Hamel, 1998). It merely prolongs competition in a different form. This form is what is known as coopetition. Trust is very often associated with coopetition. As Morris et al. explain it: "Coopetition is a relationship which is characterized by trust, engagement and mutual benefits (...). "Coopetition produces a unique context for trust, in that a firm must trust its partner in two quite different arenas (…). A coopetive partner develops trust regarding how the other firm will share resources, communicate, meet deadlines, use information, and other aspects of the cooperative dimension of the relationship" (2007, p. 10).

Regarding business networks (such as business ecosystems, clusters, Japanese *keiretsu*, and Korean *chaebols*), they are determined by various interdependences between partners (Daidj, 2013b) and generated by personal and trust-based relationships (Aliouat, 2004). "Networks are viewed as structured and articulated contract-governed entities comprising at least two partners engaged in more or less long term exchange relationships. They are created as the result of specific organisational and regulatory action, based on somewhat formalised and elaborated control modes, as well as on trust." (Daidj et al., 2008, p. 100).These trustworthy relationships within these networks lower risks by reducing the amount of information unknown to each party. Within networks, one of the most important issues is the management of purchase-supply relations. The relationship could be trust-based or contracting.

1.2 Review of Literature

This section gives a theoretical perspective and overview of the literature on the linkages between transaction costs, resources and competencies and trust. An increasing number of theoretical and empirical studies, both in economics and strategic management, have focused on trust. These studies are based on a variety of theories including the theory of the firm (mainly the transaction costs economics (TCE) and the agency theory), the resource-based view (RBV), the Knowledge-based view (KBV) and game theory. We propose here to present briefly three conceptual approaches: game theory, the TCE and the RBV.

1.2.1 Game Theory: Trust and/or Cooperation?

Games can be *non-cooperative* or *cooperative*. In non-cooperative games, players move according to individualistic behaviour, without taking into account the general interest, i.e. they exclusively pursue their own interests. Cooperative games describe specific situations in which players jointly seek a collectively satisfying solution. In this type of situation, communication among players is possible. In this field, games are often based on the "cake-sharing" problem, i.e. the allocation of the aggregated outcome that results from a common cooperative action, i.e. a "core" notion or Nash bargaining solution. It is about determining an allocation that gives each player (or initial coalition of players) at least the payoff that he might individually obtain through an independent action. Nevertheless, as shown by the classical *prisoner's dilemma*, players' individualistic strategies make it difficult to implement the cooperative solution. In game-theoretic models, each firm's action depends on what it believes its rivals will do: co-operative and non co-operative players' behaviour.

Trust between trading parties can be seen as a cooperative solution of a prisoners' dilemma. However, cooperation may occur in a situation where no trust has been identified (Axelrod, 1984). As explained by Schelling (1956, p. 301): "What makes many agreements enforceable is only the recognition of future opportunities for agreement that will be eliminated if mutual trust is not created and maintained, and whose value outweighs the momentary gain from cheating in the present instance."

1.2.2 Resource-Based View (RBV). Trust: An Intangible Distinctive Resource or a Core Competence?

Introduced by Wernerfelt (1984, 1989), the resource-based view (RBV) has become an influential framework for analyzing corporate strategy (Barney, 1991; Peteraf, 1993; Hoopes et al., 2003). This approach considers the firm as a "collection" of resources which are tied to the firm's management: firms are heterogeneous with respect to their resources and capabilities.

The resources are of various kinds: physical (machines, manufacturing facilities), human (qualifications, degree of adaptability of employees), and financial (the various sources of liquid assets). They may also be intangible and may be based on goodwill (existence of intangible assets such as a patent, brand or knowhow). "By a resource is meant anything which could be thought of as strength or weakness of a given firm. More formally, a firm's resources at a given time could be defined as those (tangible and intangible) assets which are tied semi-permanently to the firm." (Wernerfelt, 1984, p. 172). Amit and Schoemaker have defined resources as "stocks of available factors that are owned or controlled by the firm. Resources are converted into final products or services by using a wide range of other firm assets and bonding mechanisms such as technology, management information systems, incentive systems, trust between labor, and more" (1993, p. 35).

The analysis of the strategic capacity of a company depends on several factors. The concept of resources is thus often associated with the concept of organisational competencies, i.e. the routines, know-how and processes that are specific to the company and to its collective learning process. They must be difficult to imitate in order to create a sustainable advantage. They form part of the "core competencies that are the collective learning in the organization, especially how to coordinate diverse production skills and integrate multiple streams of technologies" (Prahalad & Hamel, 1990, p. 82).

Trust could be considered finally as a distinctive intangible resource (Barney, 2001; Barney & Clark, 2007; Barney & Hansen, 1994) as mentioned by Kraaijenbrink et al., (2009, p. 18), "since attributes such as trust, cost leadership, economies of scale, and learning curve economies might also be considered resources."

1.2.3 Transaction Cost Economics (TCE)

1.2.3.1 Trust vs. Opportunism? An Old Debate

Coase (1937) considered first that transaction costs lead the firm to prefer outright ownership of complementary assets, rather than bearing the costs of contracting in the open market. The TCE is very useful to understand corporate strategies (Williamson, 1981). Williamson (1975, 1985) presented a conceptual framework that contrasted the market and the hierarchical firm as the two main transaction modes. Two assumptions are important in this theoretical framework: bounded rationality, asset specificity and opportunism. Opportunism manifestations, according to Williamson, include "calculated efforts to mislead, distort, disguise, obfuscate or otherwise confuse" (1985, p. 47). Several authors explain that within *keiretsu* transaction costs are reduced (Hill, 1995; Aoki, 1988) and that *keiretsu* is organized to prevent suppliers' information opportunism (Aoki & Lennerfors, 2013; Tabeta, 1998).

Transaction costs represent all of the costs associated with conducting exchanges between firms (Williamson, 1985). They are divided into ex ante transaction costs (search and contracting costs), and ex post contracting costs (monitoring and enforcement costs). Williamson (1975) suggested that organizations must act as if individuals cannot be trusted and has added that the concept of "credible commitments' provides an effective response to the substantive challenge of effective contracting, and eliminates the need for references to trust" (Williamson, 1993, p. 100).

As it is summarized by Bromiley and Harris (2006, pp. 128-129): "led by Williamson's writings, TCE scholars have offered three justifications for ignoring trust. First, they argue that individuals and organizations cannot discern the trustworthiness of other actors *ex ante* and so must act as if others cannot be trusted. Second, they argue that trust *per se* does not manifest itself in economic exchanges; rather, economic actors are always calculative whereas trust is reserved for very special social relations. Third, they assert that trust does not add any explanatory power to organizational research. We consider each of these justifications in turn, arguing that they are not only inconsistent and incorrect, but also inadequate reasons to ignore the intra- and interorganizational implications of trust."

1.2.3.2 Trust Within Keiretsu?

TCE is also useful to understand transaction modes between hierarchy and market even if Williamson didn't focus his attention on transaction modes that fell in between these two poles: make or make make. There is a continuum of operations from arm's-length market transactions to integrated activities (in-houses), including short and long-term contracts, partnerships, and strategic alliances.

According to Imai and Itami (1984), following the transaction cost approach in the continuity of Williamson (1985), *keiretsu* can be considered as intermediate (or hybrid) forms between two extreme types of economic organization, markets on the one hand and firms on the other. The two authors underlined the fact that the allocation of the resources is based on principles which are a mixture of mechanisms of market (M) and organizational mechanisms (O). Based on Imai and Itami analysis, we can now classify the various organizational configurations (table 2). We con-

Table 2. Cooperation and mechanisms of allowance of the resources

Decision Principle	Membership Principle		
	M2 (Free entry and exit)	**M2 + O2**	**O2 (Fixed and sustainable relations between participants)**
M1 (Maximization of the individual interest)	Subcontracting Licenses		
M1 + O1		Joint-venture Consortia Mutual organization *Vertical Keiretsu* Strategic alliances	
O1 (Common interest maximization)			Wholly-owned subsidiary

Source: adapted from Imai and Itami (1984: 289) and Daidj (2011)

sider that the concept of *Keiretsu* (vertical *keiretsu)* combines principles of market and hierarchy.

In the case of (M2+O2), a rule O2 prevails but there is also a fear of M2, where entry and exit of participants are possible (table 2). "This is exemplified by the case of the auto maker who has organized a network of parts subcontractors but reserves the right to freely drop any arbitrarily and does sometimes exercise this right" (Imai & Itami, 1984, p. 288). This situation corresponds to relationships within vertical *keiretsu* as it was the case of Nissan before its alliance with Renault. Indeed, the "cooperative" evolution of vertical keiretsu is recent (Daidj et *al*, 2008). 'Traditional' *keiretsu* of (1950-1970) were characterized by a hierarchical organization: vertical groups of companies that are more or less independent from one another (subcontracting small firms, suppliers and equipment manufacturers) but under the umbrella of a prime manufacturer. Trust was then a key factor between members of *keiretsu*. "The traditional keiretsu consisted of obligational relationships based on trust and goodwill." (Aoki & Taro Lennerfors, 2013a, p. 110).

The other case of (M2+O2) is based on the idea that participants could freely enter or exit but it is not possible for them as they are involved in fixed and durable relations. This situation describes the links between the main Japanese banks and the companies belonging to the same horizontal *keiretsu.*

Since the end of the 1990s, there are significant changes observed within *keiretsu* and two main evolutions: several *keiretsu* tend to disappear (Nissan, Mitsubishi). Others such as Toyota have changed and can be considered as vertical *keiretsu* II. They have introduced new types of relations between their suppliers. The "classic" subcontracting model led by a prime manufacturer, has progressively shifted toward closer relationships between the prime manufacturer and, in particular, its 1st level equipment suppliers. This cooperation mode established between the different players tends to impose itself and has been reinforced. In addition, Toyota has continued to strengthen its *Keiretsu* by increasing its financial participations in the capital of its main suppliers.

1.3 *Keiretsu* and Trust Practices: The Conceptual Framework

Whether called *zaibatsu* or more recently *keiretsu,* corporate groupings have been a distinctive part of Japanese industry for decades.

1.3.1. Horizontal vs. Vertical *Keiretsu*

The *keiretsu* has its origins in the Meiji era. At the end of the 19th century, the Meiji government accelerated the industrialisation of Japan by creating family-controlled large industrial and financial enterprises (banking, insurance, mining, shipbuilding, manufacturing of cement, paper) known as the *zaibatsu*. These giant conglomerates, controlled by ten families (or clans), became the drivers of the pre–World War II Japanese industry and economy. They were very powerful groups (among them Mitsubishi, Mitsui, Sumitomo and Yasuda) and were involved in industries such as steel, shipbuilding, international trading and banking. During World War II, *zaibatsu* produced a large part of the country's weaponry. In addition, they were seen to be monopolies by the Americans after the war. Consequently, between 1946 and 1948, following the American occupation forces, the zaibatsu dissolution program was imposed by different laws. But in the end of the 1940s, the allied forces changed policy. This resulting change in occupation policy is often called the "reverse course" focusing on the economic recovery and political rehabilitation of Japan. Consequently, to prevent the weakening of its economy, the Japanese government concerned with concentrating on scarce industries crucial to Japan's long-term economic security encouraged a re-formation of the old zaibatsu, to be known as keiretsu. Several *keiretsu* emerged from the *zaibatsu,* whereas others were new groupings of companies.

Most large Japanese firms have links with affiliated companies with which they form a system called *keiretsu*. A keiretsu is a "cluster" of firms in different industries (or within a sector), bound by interlocking shareholdings. There are mainly two types of *keiretsu* (Miyashita & Russel, 1994), which may be horizontal (conglomerate) or vertical (many suppliers – subcontractors under the "umbrella" of a large industrial firm):

- Horizontal (financial) keiretsu include a large number of major companies belonging to a wide range of unrelated industries with common ties to a main and powerful bank (*shuryoku ginkô*). The main bank provides debt financing to member firms with favourable conditions (low interest rates, long term loans) and owns large amounts of their common stock.
- Vertical ("production" or non financial) keiretsu are quite different. They represent a pyramidal structure of intercorporate equity holdings. They are generally industry-based (mainly in manufacturing such as automobile, steel and electronics industries but also in trading activities and financial services) with a large manufacturing company having equity (controlling in some cases affiliated suppliers) and other links to firms up and down the "production chain" and along the value chain.

1.3.2 The Organisational Structure of Vertical *Keiretsu*

1.3.2.1 A "Pyramidal" Structure Based On Long Term Agreements and a Nexus of Relationships

Vertical *keiretsu* represents a group of independent firms developing complementary resources (human, technological) and competencies, organized around a prime manufacturing company, the main company (*motouke*). The cohesion of the *keiretsu* is based on a long term commitment between the main manufacturer and other firms and on regular (formal and informal) relationships (supply chain, production, financial, commercial) between members.

The economic logic is based on mutual trust and self-enforcing commitments. The contracts are generally determined for several years and are adjusted every six months depending on economic evolution and the respect of quality and cost conditions by subcontractors. They help to ensure consistent and reliable quality, dependable delivery etc. The supply structure, following the *keiretsu* model with 1st, 2nd and 3rd tier suppliers, has been widely imitated by a large number of manufacturers worldwide.

1.3.2.2 Culture and Trust within Networks

The influence of culture in organizations and relationships has been analysed by different authors such as Hofstede (1991). "The cultural predisposition of the Japanese to recognize the importance of fulfilling reciprocal in-group obligations contributes to an atmosphere of trust that lays the foundations upon which the keiretsu system is organized (Dore, 1983; Hill, 1995). Compared with other societies, which do not share similar value systems promoting in-group loyalty, ''the value system of Japanese society makes this economically efficient organizational arrangement [keiretsu] relatively easy to formulate and implement'' (Hill, 1995, p. 128)." Peng et al., (2001, p. 261).

Managers of these firms possess strong social interaction ties, develop trusting relationships, and share common values and norms. Long term relationships involve trust and simplify communication (Milgrom & Roberts, 1992).

Other scholars have advanced the importance of tacit knowledge shared within networks of individuals and firms in Japan and based on trust. There are two distinctly different types of knowledge (explicit and tacit) than can be shared within an organisation. "When the Japanese want to express their thoughts, they constantly make reference to the context in order to interpret the non-explicit dimensions of the messages (communication with implicit message and strong context). Consequently, they are used to guessing what the other wants to say, and to a rather sophisticated thinking process whereby they always must guess the meaning rather than find it in an explicit sentence. Indeed, the Japanese are usually very alert to the signals, whereas westerners are primarily concerned about the clarity of what they communicate (communication with explicit message and weak context)" (Blanchot & Kalika, 2002).

1.3.2.3 Corporate Governance and Stable Shareholding (Kabushiki Antei Hoyuu)

Cross-shareholding is at the centre of business-to-business relationships (keiretsu), of business-to-bank relationships (main bank relationships) and business-to-employee relationships (Okabe, 2001), representing a system of mutual support and of "institutional complementarity" (Aoki, 1995; Aoki & Okuno-Fujiwara, 1996). Each *keiretsu* member holds some of the shares issued by the others and agrees not to trade them (around 70% of a firms equity is never traded). These stable shareholders (e.g. banks, financial institutions, industrial firms) explain partly why there is no market for corporate control (Nakamura, 2003; Jackson & Moerke, 2005). Sheard (1994) emphasized the importance of reciprocal shareholdings and other transactional ties to the stability of the Japanese system. Sheard (1994) and Berglof and Perotti (1994) considered that this cross-shareholding structure fosters long-term relationships among members and substitutes for external monitoring by the market for corporate control.

Keiretsu networks can be finally defined as ''institutionalized relationships among firms based on localized networks of dense transactions, a stable framework of exchange, and patterns of periodic collective action'' (Gerlach, 1992, p. 3). Fujiki (2002, p. 45) explains 'The *keiretsu* concept is difficult to define. Very often it indicates that firms engaged in commercial transactions are bound in a financial relationship. Other terms such as subsidiaries, relationship companies (*kankei gaisha*) and related companies (*kanren gaisha*) are often used. A subsidiary, prior to the 1998 definition, was one where the parent company held a controlling interest of over 50%. Relationship companies and related companies are cases where the parent company held more than 20% of controlling interest. They are part of a *keiretsu* and when one wants to stress the parent-subsidiary aspect of the relationship; we refer to them as horizontal *keiretsu.*'

2. THE EVOLUTION OF TRUST WITHIN VERTICAL *KEIRETSU*: THE RENAULT-NISSAN CASE STUDY

The spectacular growth of Japan originated partly from *keiretsu. Keiretsu* and more specifically 'vertical *keiretsu*' have been widely recognized as an important source of strength for Japanese industries. They contributed largely to boost post Second World War Japanese growth. They were a key feature of Japan's economy, affecting directly or indirectly economic transactions within and across industries. They also structured the Japanese industrial system. They can be analyzed as both an organizational phenomenon and a means which has enabled Japanese firms to expand their production capacities, their competitiveness and their exports growth (Aoki, 1988) until the 1990s. In this part, we analyse the evolution of *keiretsu* and try to identify factors that have influenced trust.

2.1 Methodology

The Renault-Nissan case is analyzed below with the aim of illustrating our proposed framework. This case cannot test whether our framework applies to other (or all) settings that would require large scale empirical research (Box 1). However, the literature suggests that our finding is not an exception, but may be indicative of a range of inter-organizational networks and to a lesser extent to strategic alliances. The case illustrates our contribution to the debate about trust within network (such as *keiretsu)* and strategic alliance: do coordination mechanisms (Assens, 2003) and/or governance mechanisms rely mainly on trust?

The nature of this qualitative research is exploratory and descriptive, using the case study method (Yin, 1994). Yin (1989) defined the case study as "an empirical study that investigates a contemporary phenomenon within its real life context, when the boundaries between phenomenon and context are not clearly evident and in which multiple sources of evidence are used" (p. 23). Case studies can be exploratory, explanatory or descriptive. Yin also differentiates between single, holistic case studies and multiple-case studies. Case studies can be used to provide description, test theory or generate theory (Eisenhardt, 1989). The case study method allows for analytical generalizations based on the research findings. The analysis of the Renault-Nissan Alliance provides the analytical basis for generalizing some findings of this research and its transferability to other companies to a certain extent.

Our tools for collecting data include archival records, surveys, documentation review and interviews. To analyze the competitive landscape of the automotive industry, secondary data have also been collected. As Stewart and Kamins have underlined, we need to "question information collected and reported by others" (1993, p. 18) and we have tried to assess the trustworthiness of these qualitative data. Therefore, information on markets, competitors, and technologies is derived from a large variety of sources such as company press releases and presentations, materials from conferences, company annual reports and press releases. Triangulation (information and data) was used during this research.

Other research reports on industry and company developments reviewed and downloaded include:

XERFI: World carmakers - Market analysis – Corporate strategies 2011-2016 (October 2011, 239 pages); DATAMONITOR: Company profiles: Renault (28 September 2012, 34 pages); Nissan (6 June 2012, 31 pages).

We conducted in-depth interviews with Renault KM managers in December 2012 and February 2013. Most of these interviews were open-ended based on facts, events and opinion. In addition, we have had the opportunity to attend workshops and meetings chaired by several managers of Renault in France.

2.2 From Nissan *Keiretsu* to the Renault-Nissan Alliance: A Historical Retrospect and Strategic Analysis

The history of the automotive industry in Japan and the main automotive manufacturers (Toyota, Honda, and Nissan) during the last half century has been shaped by the existence *of keiretsu* defining the boundaries for the players' behaviours. Nissan Motor, created in 1933 is a vertical *keiretsu* affiliated with the horizontal *keiretsu* Fuyo but largely independent. At its origin, Nissan was a small automaker producing components before becoming in the 1980s one of the world leaders in automobiles.

2.2.1 Structural Changes

The dramatic changes in the Japanese economy in the last decade linked with the economic recession, the bursting of the financial bubble, the deregulation of domestic capital markets and finally the slow recovery since the early 1990s have had a great impact on firm competitiveness. Japanese groups have to compete more and more, in sectors where they were very competitive for many years such as automobiles, chemicals, and consumer electronics. Both horizontal and vertical *Keiretsu* are directly concerned. In particular, stable shareholders (around a main bank) and closer supplier relationships have finally inhibited fair competition among firms in Japan and have led to market share reductions on a worldwide scale.

The 1990s saw significant growth in international strategic alliances (Mowery, 1988; Mytelka, 1991; Hagedoorn, 1996), paralleling the increase in cross-border mergers and acquisitions (M and As). The "hypercompetition" context (D'Aveni and MacMillan, 1994) has created a significant incentive for organizations to collaborate particularly in the automotive industry. In this sector at a general level, car manufacturers look for alliances to achieve global economies of scale in production (and then to reduce costs), to attain a critical mass, and also to secure sufficient financial resources to develop leading-edge technologies for the next generation of "eco-friendly" cars (Kang & Sakai, 2000).

Until the 1990s, the consortium of *keiretsu* members led to an exclusion of foreign competitors from the Japanese market. But more recently in the automobile industry, which is one of the most exposed to the competitive global market, three major firms had been taken over by foreign concerns: Mazda by Ford in 1996, Nissan by Renault in 1999, and Mitsubishi by Daimler-Chrysler in 2000 (even if the break-up between DaimlerChrysler and Mitsubishi in 2004 put a halt to this trend as Tokyo-Mitsubishi bank intervened once more to save the group from bankruptcy). These operations have had a great impact on *keiretsu.*

2.2.2 The Objective of the Renault-Nissan Alliance

In the 1990s, Nissan lost money and market share. Finally in 1999, Nissan was nearly bankrupt in spite of the implementation of the *Global Business Reform Plan.* The 1998 Nissan annual report emphasises the implementation of a *Global Business Reform Plan* to achieve a sustainable competitive advantage, to favour profitability and to continue overseas development, especially in the US. But this plan was adopted too late. Debt was huge. In this context, an agreement was signed in Tokyo on March 27th 1999 between Nissan and the French automobile manufacturer Renault, giving birth to the Renault-Nissan alliance. The first meetings were initiated as early as June 1998 whereas Louis Schweitzer, Renault's CEO, had been looking for an Asian partner since 1997. According to Louis Schweitzer, Nissan was a "weak keiretsu."

The objective of the alliance is to combine the strengths of both companies and developing synergies through common organisations, cross company teams, shared platforms and components. The main complementarities can be analysed in terms of market breakdown, technology and costs reduction: Renault is strong in Europe and is mainly a European manufacturer, Nissan has a presence in Asia and the U.S., design is Renault's strong advantage (offers conceptually innovative car models, such as: Espace, Twingo, Kangoo, Vel Satis), while Nissan's production and engine technology could benefit Renault. Combining platforms and purchasing will cut costs.

The Renault-Nissan set up joint project structure covering most of both companies' activities. In July 1999, a Charter signed sets out the principles of "a shared ambition, mutual trust, respect of each partners of the Renault-Nissan Alliance, completed by operating and confidentiality rules." It promotes the common values of the new Group and common work rules for everyday. The agreement calls for an equity investment of Renault in Nissan. Renault holds a 44.3% stake in Nissan, while Nissan owns 15% of Renault shares (each company has a direct interest in the results of its partners). Renault-Nissan bv (RNBV), was founded on March 28, 2002 to oversee the strategy of the alliance and all activities undertaken by the two firms. Renault-Nissan bv is jointly and equally owned by Renault and Nissan and hosts the Alliance Board, which met for the first time on May 29, 2002.

2.2.3 The Evolution of Nissan *Keiretsu* in the Context of Renault-Nissan Strategic Alliance

2.2.3.1 Towards a Greater Rationalization of Nissan Purchasing System

Although their brands are still fully autonomous from an operational point of view, two major cooperation areas have led to the creation of two joint-ventures between Renault and Nissan. RNPO (Renault-Nissan Purchasing Organization) was founded in April 2001 to optimize purchasing performance across the Alliance. To achieve its goal, RNPO defines worldwide purchasing strategy by product family and selects the best suppliers' project by project (table 3). The Renault and Nissan Alliance Board agreed in July 2002, to establish Renault-Nissan Information Services (RNIS), the second joint venture between Alliance partners following the establishment of Renault Nissan Purchasing Organisation. RNIS was established to deliver global information services to Renault's and Nissan's information systems departments, thereby combining their knowledge.

According to Aoki and Taro Lennerfors (2013b), before the alliance with Renault, Nissan had organized its own suppliers' association emphasizing the importance of close and strong links within its *keiretsu*. There was a form of "trust" among vertical trading partners. Several suppliers' associations were created and renamed: *Takarakai* (1954), *Nishokai* (1991) and then the "merger" between *Takarakai* and *Shohokai*.

The creation of RNPO and to a lesser extent of RNIS has led to structural changes in Nissan purchasing system: "this inevitably expanded Nissan's potential suppliers to include globally competitive suppliers ordinarily selected by Renault, thus reducing the sales volume of old keiretsu suppliers" (Aoki & Taro Lennerfors, 2013b, p. 78). When Carlos Ghosn became Nissan's COO on July 1st 1999, he underlined the lack of flexibility of the keiretsu system that was leading to a large chain

Table 3. Factors of change affecting manufacturing keiretsu

	Keiretsu		
	1952- late 1980s	**1990-2000**	**since 2000**
	Emergence and development of *keiretsu*	Shift toward closer cooperation amongst partners	Shift toward more complex and global network system
General context	Dismantling of the *zaibatsu* after 1945 driven by the United States: anti-monopoly law, ban on holdings	Stronger competition within a global context (increase in number of relocations, also in number of alliance agreements)	Acceleration in technological changes and increase in shares bought by foreign companies
Internal structure • resources • competences • dependence Economic transactional analysis	Creation of *keiretsu*, vertical groups: - pyramidal structure with companies highly specialised in resources, connected to a lead company (*Motuke*). Internalisation of production. Frequent and long-term sub-contracting relations permitting just-in-time production and total quality. - Prime manufacturer take shares in SMEs	Evolution toward a real partnership between the prime manufacturer and certain 1st tier subcontractors who possess specific competences based on strategic resources (exclusive technological know-how, design-defining of specific sub-systems, etc.). Certain subcontractors become real partners.	Weakening of the pyramid structure and creation of a network structure within which the relations between the partners are no longer exclusive (possibility of supplying to other *keiretsu*) Relations based on competitiveness criteria: cost and innovation effects (in production processes, manufacturing capacity etc). Trust is less relevant to explain the relationships between main members within *keiretsu*. However, trust is still a key success factor of the Renault-Nissan strategic alliance. Use of social networking, Web and KM 2.0 tools to collaborate within the alliance structure.

Source: adapted from Daidj et al., (2008, p. 114).

of suppliers demanding high disadvantageous prices. Consequently, as mentioned by Lim (2012, p.28), "Ghosn revealed that maintaining keiretsu was not among the company's objectives. Instead, the system would be founded on the basis of a cost/benefit analysis." Finally, the restructuring of Nissan occurred under the watchful supervision of Renault, and involved a drastic downsizing in the number of its suppliers. Relying increasingly on the best-price system, orders are given to companies offering interesting prices in the short term, even though they are not members of the *keiretsu*.

2.2.3.2 Coordination and Governance Mechanisms and Perspectives: Trust Oriented?

Keiretsu are dynamic systems and the role of trust has also evolved. In the case of the Renault-Nissan alliance, the concept of trust has to be analyzed at different levels: on the one hand, within Nissan *keiretsu* (i.e. between firms of Nissan keiretsu) and between Nissan and Renault in the context of the alliance process on the other hand.

If trust is viewed as a structural factor explaining the duration and success of vertical *keiretsu*, there is a need for research on the evolution of trust since the development of links between the traditional "Nissan *keiretsu*" and foreign investors such as Renault.

In fact, trust has not disappeared within Nissan *keiretsu* as Aoki and Taro Lennefors explain it in a recent paper. "Having moved toward Western-style supplier relationships under Carlos Ghosn, Nissan shifted its stance again in 2004, announcing a new purchasing policy that represented a reevaluation of keiretsu. It has increased its investment in one large supplier and continues to rely on goodwill and trust in its dealings with many vendors. One example of its recent keiretsu-like practices is a program in which its engineers and those of its suppliers take up process-improvement projects in the suppliers' factories" (2013b, p. 112).

Several years after the launch of the strategic alliance, the long lasting relationship between Nissan and Renault is characterized by:

- A high degree of cooperation between the two car manufacturers. Co-operative arrangements have been actively implemented leading to common platforms several years after the signature of the alliance;
- Repeated transactions based on trust and a continuous flow of information and knowledge. Knowledge transfers have been also important between the two firms even if they are difficult to evaluate (Fujimoto & Arturo Heller, 2001; Freyssenet, 2003). Within *Keiretsu,* culture is one of the key factors explaining knowledge sharing and transfer issues. "Many observers have praised Japanese firms' ability to share knowledge within and among themselves. However, there are, arguably, differences in the learning that occurs within a Japanese firm (or related ones), and the learning that takes place in Silicon Valley. Ideas seem to circulate in Japan through more structured channels, such as those organized around membership in a firm, university, or high school alumni associations. Keiretsu, or keiretsu-type relationships, as well as the tradition of the "network state" inserting itself as a mediator among competing firms, may constrain cross-firm knowledge-sharing" (Rowen & Toyoda, 2002, p. 20). Tacit knowledge-sharing is explained by the presence of trust.

In addition, since 2004, KM 2.0 and Web 2.0 tools have been developed (Daidj, 2011, 2013a). The adoption of these tools by Renault has led to increased collaboration between the two manufacturers. This should probably develop in the future not only coordination, which was the initial goal of Renault-Nissan Alliance, but also cohesion teams. This will give rise to a number of new opportunities by building common purposes with the active contribution of employees of both companies.

CONCLUSION

Several scholars have identified the main features of vertical *keiretsu* in terms of cooperation, commitment, close and long term relationships and trust. Trust is considered as an important factor embedded in Japanese culture (Fukuyama, 1995) and often presented as an explanation to the specificity of the Japanese subcontracting system (Sako, 1992) has become less relevant. Created and maintained by long term exchanges and by the relational dimension, this subcontracting has been shaken by the weakening of this latter.

Nissan, in the wake of a strategic alliance with a foreign group has restructured its *keiretsu* based on the rationalisation of relationships between their different subcontractors. However, trust is still a factor explaining how parts' manufacturers, subcontractors and automobile assemblers interact to achieve their products in order to improve competitiveness. Aoki and Taro Lennerfors (2013a, p. 113) underline "the keys to keiretsu-like-partnerships: support, cooperation, trust."

Two main research orientations should be conducted in the future: an in-depth analysis of trust on the entire performance of the Renault-Nissan alliance. The second axis concerns the comparative analysis with other car manufacturers involved in international strategic alliances.

REFERENCES

Aliouat, B. (2004). Un regard nouveau et global sur l'organisation en réseau: Compétences relationnelles et métamorphoses des organisations. *Revue Management International*, *8*(2), 51–56.

Amit, R., & Zott, C. (2001). Value creation in e-business. *Strategic Management Journal*, *22*(6/7), 493–520. doi:10.1002/smj.187

Aoki, K., & Lennerfors, T. (2013a). The new improved Keiretsu. *Harvard Business Review*, (9), 109–113.

Aoki, K., & Lennerfors, T. (2013b). Whither Japanese keiretsu? The transformation of vertical keiretsu in Toyota, Nissan and Honda 1991-2011. *Asia Pacific Business Review*, *19*(1), 70–84. doi:10.1080/13602381.2011.652832

Aoki, M. (1988). *Information, incentives, and bargaining in the Japanese economy*. Cambridge, UK: Cambridge University Press. doi:10.1017/CBO9780511571701

Aoki, M. (1995). Towards a Comparative Institutional Analysis. *The Japanese Economic Review*, *47*(1), 1–19. doi:10.1111/j.1468-5876.1996.tb00031.x

Aoki, M., & Okuno-Fujiwara, M. (Eds.). (1996). *Comparative Institutional Analysis: A New Approach to Economic Systems*. Tokyo: University of Tokyo Press.

Arrow, K.J. (1973). *Information and economic behavior*. Stockholm: Federation of Swedish Industries.

Arrow, K. J. (1974). *The limits of organization. New-York*. W. W. Norton & Company.

Asanuma, B. (1989). Manufacturer-Supplier Relationships in Japan and the Concept of Relation-Specific Skill. *Journal of the Japanese and International Economies*, *3*(1), 1–30. doi:10.1016/0889-1583(89)90029-4

Assens, C. (2003). Le réseau d'entreprises: Vers une synthèse des connaissances. *Management international, 24*(1), 120-136.

Axelrod, R. (1984). *The Evolution of Cooperation*. New York: Basic Books.

Barney, J. B. (1991). Firm resources and sustained competitive advantage. *Journal of Management*, *17*(1), 99–120. doi:10.1177/014920639101700108

Barney, J. B., & Clark, D. N. (2007). *Resource-Based Theory: Creating and Sustaining Competitive Advantage*. New York: Oxford University Press.

Barney, J. B., & Hansen, M. H. (1994). Trustworthiness as a source of competitive advantage. *Strategic Management Journal*, *15*(S1), 175–190. doi:10.1002/smj.4250150912

Berglof, E., & Perotti, E. (1994). The Governance Structure of the Japanese Financial Keiretsu. *Journal of Financial Economics*, *36*(2), 259–284. doi:10.1016/0304-405X(94)90026-4

Bigley, G. A., & Pearce. (1998). Straining for Shared Meaning in Organization Science: Problems of Trust and Distrust. *Academy of Management Review*, *23*, 405–421.

Blanchot, F., & Kalika, M. (2002). The Renault-Nissan Alliance, Case study. (Y. Meyer, Trans.). Paris: Centrale de Cas et de Médias Pédagogiques (CCMP).

Breton, A., & Wintrobe, R. (1982). *The logic of bureaucratic conduct: An economic analysis of competition, exchange and efficiency in private and public organizations*. Cambridge, UK: Cambridge University Press. doi:10.1017/CBO9780511896033

Bromiley, P., & Harris, J. (2006). Trust, transaction cost economics, and mechanisms. In R. Bachmann, & A. Zaheer (Eds.), *Handbook of Trust Research* (pp. 124–143). Northampton, MA: Edward Elgar. doi:10.4337/9781847202819.00014

Coase, R. (1937). The Nature of the Firm. *Economica*, *4*(16), 386–405. doi:10.1111/j.1468-0335.1937.tb00002.x

Cook, J., & Wall, T. (1980). New work attitude measures of trust, organizational commitment, and personal need nonfulfillment. *Journal of Occupational Psychology*, *53*(1), 39–52. doi:10.1111/j.2044-8325.1980.tb00005.x

Cullen, J. B., Johnson, J. L., & Sakano, T. (1995). Japanese and local partner commitment to IJVs: Psychological consequences of outcomes and investments in the IJV relationship. *Journal of International Business Studies*, *26*(1), 91–115. doi:10.1057/palgrave.jibs.8490167

Cullen, J. B., Johnson, J. L., & Sakano, T. (2000). Success through commitment and trust: The soft side of strategic alliance management. *Journal of World Business*, *35*(3), 223–240. doi:10.1016/S1090-9516(00)00036-5

Currall, S. C., & Inkpen, A. (2002). A Multilevel Approach to Trust in Joint Ventures. *Journal of International Business Studies*, *33*(3), 479–495. doi:10.1057/palgrave.jibs.8491027

Currall, S. C., & Inkpen, A. C. (2006). On the Complexity of Organizational Trust: A Multi-level Co-Evolutionary Perspective and Guidelines for Future Research. In R. Bachmann, & A. Zaheer (Eds.), *Handbook of Trust Research* (pp. 235–246). Edward Elgar. doi:10.4337/9781847202819.00021

D'Aveni, R., & MacMillan, I. C. (1994). *Hypercompetition*. New York: Free Press.

Daidj, N. (2009). The evolution of corporate governance in Japan: The case of vertical keiretsu groups. In G. Aras & D. Crowther D. (Eds.), Global perspectives on Corporate Governance and Corporate Social Responsibility (pp. 73-106). Aldershot, UK: Gower Publishing Limited.

Daidj, N. (2011). The evolution of KM practices: The case of the Renault-Nissan International strategic alliance. In *Knowledge Management 2.0: Organizational Models and Enterprise Strategies*. IGI Global. doi:10.4018/978-1-61350-195-5.ch010

Daidj, N. (2013a). Different perspectives on KM 2.0 new practices and Web 2.0 tools at Renault-Nissan alliance since 2000. *International Journal of Strategic Information Technology and Applications*, *4*(2), 1–20. doi:10.4018/jsita.2013040101

Daidj, N. (2013b). The evolution of new entrants' strategies in the media sector in a context of convergence: The case of Apple, Google and Microsoft. In S. Ben Letaifa, A. Gratacap, & T. Isckia (Eds.), *Understanding business ecosystems: How firms succeed in the new world of convergence* (pp. 165–192). De Boeck.

Daidj, N., Gardet, E., & Mothe, C. (2008). The manufacturing keiretsu: A changing inter-company network? The case of the car industry. In S. Dzever, J. Jaussaud, & B. O'Callaghan (Eds.), *Evolving corporate structures and cultures in Asia* (pp. 97–117). London: ISTE/Wiley Ltd.

Deutsch, M. (1958). Trust and suspicion. *The Journal of Conflict Resolution*, *2*(4), 265–279. doi:10.1177/002200275800200401

Doz, Y., & Hamel, G. (1998). *Alliance Advantage*. Boston: Harvard Business School Press.

Eisenhardt, K. (1989). Building theories from case study research. *Academy of Management Review*, *14*, 532–550.

Evans, W. (2012). *Trust in Japanese Culture and Management*. (Unpublished doctoral dissertation). Telecom Ecole de Management, Evry, France.

Farris, G., Senner, E., & Butterfield, D. (1973). Trust, culture, and organizational behavior. *Industrial Relations*, *12*(2), 144–157. doi:10.1111/j.1468-232X.1973.tb00544.x

Freyssenet, M. (2003). Renault: Globalization, But For What Purpose? In M. Freyssenet, K. Shimizu, & G. Volpato (Eds.), *Globalization or Regionalization of European Car Industry?* (pp. 103–131). London: Palgrave Macmillan. doi:10.1057/9780230554818

Fujiki, K. (2002). Keiretsu Kaitai – Kawaru Jiodousha Buhin Torihiki. In *The Breakdown of Keiretsu – The Changing Automobile Parts Transactions*. Tokyo: Ekonomisto Sha.

Fujimoto, T., & Arturo Heller, D. (2001). *Recent Trends in Alliance-Enabled Capability Building: Implications for Firm Performance in the Global Auto Industry: A Dynamic View of the Ford-Mazda, Renault-Nissan & DaimlerChryslerMitsubishi*. Paper presented at the Ninth GERPISA International Colloquium: Reconfiguring the Auto Industry: Merger & Acquisition, Alliances and Exit. Paris, France.

Fukuyama, F. (1995). *Trust: The Social Virtues and the Creation of Prosperity*. The Free Press.

Gambetta, D. G. (1988). Can we trust trust? In D. G. Gambetta (Ed.), *Trust* (pp. 213–237). New York: Basil Blackwell.

Gerlach, M. (1992). *Alliance Capitalism: The Social Organization of Japanese Business*. Berkeley, CA: University of California Press.

Giffin, K. (1967). The contribution of studies of source credibility to a theory of interpersonal trust in the communication process. *Psychological Bulletin, 68*(2), 104–120. doi:10.1037/h0024833 PMID:6065581

Haakansson, H., & Johanson, J. (1992). A model of industrial networks. In *Industrial networks: A new view of reality* (pp. 28–34). London, UK: Routledge.

Haakansson, H., & Johanson, J. (1993). The Network as a Governance Structure: Interfirm Cooperation Beyond Markets and Hierarchies. In G. Grabher (Ed.), *The Embedded Firm On the Socioeconomics of Industrial Networks* (pp. 35–51). London: Routledge.

Hagedoorn, J. (1996). Trends and Patterns in Strategic Technology Partnering since the Early Seventies. *Review of Industrial Organization, 11*(5), 601–616. doi:10.1007/BF00214825

Hill, C. (1995). National institutional structures, transaction cost economizing, and competitive advantage: The case of Japan. *Organization Science, 6*(1), 119–131. doi:10.1287/orsc.6.1.119

Hofstede, G. (1991). *Cultures and Organizations: Software of the Mind*. London: McGraw-Hill Book Company.

Hoopes, D. G., Madsen, T. L., & Walker, G. (2003). Guest Editors' Introduction to the Special Issue: Why is There a Resource-Based View? Toward a Theory of Competitive Heterogeneity. *Strategic Management Journal, 24*(10), 889–902. doi:10.1002/smj.356

Imai, K., & Itami, H. (1984). Interpenetration of Organization and Market. *International Journal of Industrial Organization, 2*(4), 285–310. doi:10.1016/0167-7187(84)90001-8

Ingham, M., & Mothe, C. (2003). Apprentissages et confiance au sein d'une alliance technologique. *Revue Française de Gestion, 29*, 111–128. doi:10.3166/rfg.143.111-128

Jackson, G., & Moerke, A. (2005). Continuity and Change in Corporate Governance: Comparing Germany and Japan. *Corporate Governance: An International Review, 13*(3), 351–361. doi:10.1111/j.1467-8683.2005.00429.x

Jarillo, J. C. (1988). On strategic networks. *Strategic Management Journal, 9*(1), 31–41. doi:10.1002/smj.4250090104

Johnson-George, C., & Swap, W. (1982). Measurement of specific interpersonal trust: Construction and validation of a scale to assess trust in a specific other. *Journal of Personality and Social Psychology, 43*(6), 1306–1317. doi:10.1037/0022-3514.43.6.1306

Johnston, D. A., McCutcheon, D. M., Stuart, F. I., & Kerwood, H. (2004). Effects of Supplier Trust on Performance of Cooperative Supplier Relationships. *Journal of Operations Management, 22*(1), 23–38. doi:10.1016/j.jom.2003.12.001

Kang, N.-H., & Sakai, K. (2000). International Strategic Alliances: Their Role in Industrial Globalisation. *STI Working Paper, 5.*

Kester, C. (1990). *Japanese Takeovers: The Global Contest for Corporate Control*. Cambridge, MA: Harvard Business School Press.

Kraaijenbrink, J., Spender, J.C., & Groen. (2009). The resource-based view: A review and assessment of its critiques. *MPRA Paper No. 21442*. Retrieved from http://mpra.ub.uni-muenchen.de/21442/

Lane, P. J., Salk, J. E., & Lyles, M. A. (2001). Absorptive capacity, learning, and performance in international joint ventures. *Strategic Management Journal, 22*(12), 1139–1161. doi:10.1002/smj.206

Lim, W. M. (2012). The Voyage of the Renault-Nissan Alliance: A Successful Venture. *Advances in Management, 5*(9), 25–29.

Lincoln, J. R., Gerlach, M. L., & Ahmadjian, C. L. (1996). Keiretsu Networks and Corporate Performance in Japan. *American Sociological Review, 61*(1), 67–88. doi:10.2307/2096407

Luhmann, N. (1988). Familiarity, confidence, trust: Problems and alternatives. In D. G. Gambetta (Ed.), *Trust* (pp. 94–107). New York: Basil Blackwell.

Mayer, R. C., Davis, J. H., & Schoorman, F. D. (1995). An integrative model of organizational trust. *Academy of Management Review, 20*, 709–734.

McEvily, B., Perrone, V., & Zaheer, A. (2003). Trust as an Organizing Principle. *Organization Science, 14*(1), 91–103. doi:10.1287/orsc.14.1.91.12814

Milgrom, P., & Roberts, J. (1992). *Economics, Organization and Management*. Englewood Cliffs, NJ: Prentice Hall.

Miyashita, K., & Russel, D. W. (1994). *Keiretsu: Inside the hidden Japanese conglomerates*. New York: McGraw Hill.

Mohr, J., & Spekman, R. (1994). Characteristics of partnership success: Partnership attributes, communication behavior, and conflict resolution techniques. *Strategic Management Journal, 15*(2), 135–152. doi:10.1002/smj.4250150205

Morris, M., & Koçak, A., & Özer. (2007). Coopetition as a Small Business Strategy: Implications for Performance. *Journal of Small Business Strategy, 18*(1), 35–55.

Mowery, D. C. (Ed.). (1988). *International Collaborative Ventures in U.S. Manufacturing*. Cambridge, MA: Ballinger.

Mytelka, L. K. (1991). *Strategic Partnerships and the World Economy*. London.

Nakamura, M. (2003). *Corporate Governance and Management Practices in Japan: Current issues*. Paper presented at the EAMSA 20th Annual Conference. Stockholm, Sweden.

Okabe, M. (2001). Are cross-holdings of Japanese corporations dissolving? Evolution and implications. *Nissan Occasional Paper Series, 33.*

Parkhe, A. (1998). Understanding Trust in International Alliances. *Journal of World Business, 33*(3), 219–240. doi:10.1016/S1090-9516(99)80072-8

Penga, M. W., & Leea, S.-H. (2001). The keiretsu in Asia: Implications for multilevel theories of competitive advantage. *Journal of International Management, 7*(4), 253–276. doi:10.1016/S1075-4253(01)00047-3

Peteraf, M. A. (1993). The Cornerstones of Competitive Advantage: A Resource-Based View. *Strategic Management Journal, 14*(3), 179–191. doi:10.1002/smj.4250140303

Piricz, N., & Mandják, T. (2012). *The relationship among trust conflicts and perceived satisfaction in B2B context*. Paper presented at the 28th Annual IMP Conference. Rome, Italy.

Porter, M., & Fuller, M. B. (1986). Coalitions and Global Strategy. In M. Porter (Ed.), *Competition in Global Industries* (pp. 315–343). Boston, MA: Harvard Business.

Prahalad, C. K., & Hamel, G. (1990). The core competence of the corporation. *Harvard Business Review*, *68*(3), 79–91.

Rotter, J. (1980). Interpersonal trust, trustworthiness and gullibility. *The American Psychologist*, *35*(1), 1–7. doi:10.1037/0003-066X.35.1.1

Rotter, J. B. (1967). A new scale for the measurement of interpersonal trust. *Journal of Personality*, *35*(4), 651–665. doi:10.1111/j.1467-6494.1967.tb01454.x PMID:4865583

Rowen, H. S., & Toyoda, A. M. (2002). *From Keiretsu to Startups: Japan's Push for High Tech Entrepreneurship* (Working Paper). Asia/Pacific Research Center, Stanford University. Retrieved from http://iis-db.stanford.edu/pubs/20027/rowen_toyoda.pdf

Sabel, C. F. (1993). Studied trust: Building new forms of cooperation in a volatile economy. *Human Relations*, *46*(9), 1133–1170. doi:10.1177/001872679304600907

Sako, M. (1992). *Price, Quality and Trust*. Cambridge, UK: Cambridge University Press. doi:10.1017/CBO9780511520723

Schein, E. H. (1992). *Organizational Culture and Leadership*. San Francisco: Jossey-Bass Publishers.

Schelling, T. C. (1956). An essay on bargaining. *The American Economic Review*, *46*, 281–306.

Sheard, P. (1994). The Main Bank System and Corporate Monitoring and Control in Japan. *Journal of Economic Behavior & Organization*, *11*(3), 399–422. doi:10.1016/0167-2681(89)90037-1

Stewart, D., & Kamins, M. (1993). *Secondary Research: Information, Sources, and Methods*. Thousand Oaks, CA: Sage Publications.

Sztompka, P. (1999). *Trust: A sociological theory*. Cambridge, UK: Cambridge University Press.

Tabeta, N. (1998). The Kigyo keiretsu organization and opportunism in thc Japanese automobile manufacturing industry. *Asia Pacific Journal of Management*, *15*(1), 1–18. doi:10.1023/A:1015428707475

Tullock, G. (1965). *The Politics of Bureaucracy*. Washington, DC: Public Affairs Press.

Wernerfelt, B. (1984). A Resource-Based View of the Firm. *Strategic Management Journal*, *5*(2), 171–180. doi:10.1002/smj.4250050207

Williamson, O. E. (1975). *Markets and Hierarchies*. New York: Free Press.

Williamson, O. E. (1981). The Economics of Organization: The Transaction Cost Approach. *American Journal of Sociology*, *87*(3), 548–577. doi:10.1086/227496

Williamson, O. E. (1985). *The Economic Institutions of Capitalism*. New York: Free Press.

Williamson, O. E. (1993). Opportunism and its critics. *Managerial and Decision Economics*, *14*(2), 97–107. doi:10.1002/mde.4090140203

Yin, R. (1989). *Case study research: Design and methods*. Newbury Park, CA: Sage Publishing.

Yin, R. (1994). *Case study research: Design and methods* (2nd ed.). Thousand Oaks, CA: Sage Publishing.

Zaheer, A., McEvily, B., & Perrone, V. (1998). Does trust matter? Exploring the effects of interorganizational and interpersonal trust on performance. *Organization Science*, *9*(2), 141–159. doi:10.1287/orsc.9.2.141

Zucker, L. G. (1986). Production of Trust: Institutional Sources of Economic Structure. *Research in Organizational Behavior*, *8*, 53–111.

KEY TERMS AND DEFINITIONS

Culture: The values and beliefs that individuals of a same organization share.

Purchase-Supply Relations: Can be defined as supply arrangements and/or long-term sourcing agreements. They are considered as non-equity forms of partnerships between clients and suppliers, subcontractors and manufacturers.

Strategic Alliance: Cooperative agreement between rivals that involves exchange, sharing, and/or co-development. Strategic alliances do not only have an impact outside the coalition, but also within it on the partners themselves, because the partners, while developing close collaborations in certain fields, find themselves in competition in others.

Trust: The notion of trust is very broad and it encompasses many meanings. Trust is closely related to transactions and results from belief formulations in repeated transactions.

Vertical Keiretsu: Vertical groups of companies that are more or less independent from one another (small subcontracting firms, suppliers and equipment manufacturers) but are under the umbrella of a prime manufacturer.

Chapter 3
Trust Deficit in Public Sector:
Causes, Consequences, and Strategies to Mitigate

Vedantam Leela
National Law University, India

ABSTRACT

Deficit trust is considered a cause for further deterioration of the public sector delivery systems. It has raised concerns in the modern political scenario. The author identifies the sources for creation of deficit trust in public sectors across the world. Considering that individual trust perceptions are susceptible to fluctuation, the author argues that there is a possibility to shift distrust to trust. Thereby, relying on the best practices and data from Edelman Trust Barometers and World Bank, this chapter addresses the trust deficit concerns. Some countries have maintained trust requirements, but others are struggling to mitigate. Mentioning the best practices of established, credible, and sound mechanisms to improve the trust relationships, the author highlights the modern intervention techniques used by various organisations to instil the public trust. Throughout this chapter, the author suggests how public trust can be transformed into customer retention initiatives and thereby public sectors can regain their market position.

INTRODUCTION

In this chapter, the author examined the theoretical base on the nature and significance of the organisational trust model. This chapter attempts to explore the possibilities to identify the reasons for creation of deficit trust in public sectors across the world. By specifically mentioning the best practices of established, credible and sound mechanisms to improve the trust relationships, it is intended to highlight the modern intervention techniques used by various organisations to instil the public trust and attainment of customer retention. As the term 'trust' may be contested, therefore, it is referred as to 'trust enhancing approaches' as a strategic tool, for the better public sector's performance outcomes. Trust can be described as an enriching relationship based on business or individual, personal or professional (Lorenz, 1988; Lewicki & Bunker 1996; Mayer *et al.*, 1995; Gilson, 2003). Can, for example, the stated concepts of trust and deficit trust improve the functioning of public sector or an outcome?

DOI: 10.4018/978-1-4666-6232-2.ch003

Over the past two decades, trust continued as a subject of study of sociologists (Coleman, 1990), economists (Fukuyama, 1995) and organizational scientists (Gambetta, 1988; Kramer & Taylor, 1996). A few questions may arise and they could be (1) What constitutes trust among various stakeholders in the Public sector and government? (2) Whether the public sector organisations adopts mechanisms to build trust linkages and how this trust strategy can be formulated? (3) Are there any environmental factors (internal and external) or contingencies for generating a need for public sector institutions to adopt trust building measures? (4) Is it possible to isolate and figure out the various models of trust building processes by reputed organisations? Most importantly (5) for public sector and their stakeholders, who are looking ways to gain a comparable and competitive advantage, the impact of these trust related interventions, will it matter at all?

This chapter also examines the possible options of implementing various counter-strategies to deficit trust and measure the gap and existing deviations in the existing process in various public sectors across the world. The author then considered some common initiatives associated with trust, including international and comparative trust interventions. In the current chapter, a number of question, of which some are quite inherent and essential to the understanding of how trust works, and how public sectors have evolved mechanisms to satisfy the demands of their customers. The author also has addressed through various examples as to how large public sector corporates have decided to impact the public trust and regain their market position. There is a common thread i.e. the theme of 'trust creation' and which runs in the chapter, much of the interventions are quite fundamental to plug out the deficit trust and constraints therein, that further the cause of reputation building and maintaining a balanced approach among various stakeholders.

Trust remained under-theorized, under-researched and, therefore, poorly understood 'phenomenon' (Child, 2001) and the casualty was organizational trust which remained unaddressed (McEvily et al., 2003). On the other hand, distrust is the confident expectation that another individual's motives, intentions, and behaviours are sinister and harmful to one's own interests. In interdependent relationships, this often entails a sense of fear and anticipation of discomfort or danger. On account of raising distrust levels it naturally initiates the Government and the agencies to take such measures to vulnerabilities, in an attempt to protect customers' interests. Accordingly, presence of distrust among others is likely to induce an unfair competitiveness which encourage and aggravate disputes.

The concept of trust is essential for any interpersonal (Frederique, & Sorge, 2008), interactive and interdependent relationships to exist in any organisation. Building trust is often seen as a proactive measure to nurture commitment, involvement and gain organisational citizenship behaviour (Wicks, Berman. & Jones, 1999). Researchers argue that the constant engagement of the internal and external stakeholders in trust based relationship (Julia, 2006), leads to two situations, namely (1) professional trust and (2) personal trust. The issue of concern for research is why there is growing deficit trust in public sector. Many researchers have concentrated their works on building trust and nurturing trust among leaders and followers (Galford & Drapeau, 2003). But there is scanty literature in the areas of deficit trust. In this backdrop, it is true that the public sectors which are primary governed by the principles of social welfare, utilitarian, justice, service without capitalistic approach but they are predominantly governed by deficit budgets. Public sectors may be projected as poor performers, ironically, the leaders and employees of public sector may be growing richer. With the growing concerns on

Figure 1. Trust in the government in Washington (1958 – 2001)
Source: (Chanley, 2002)

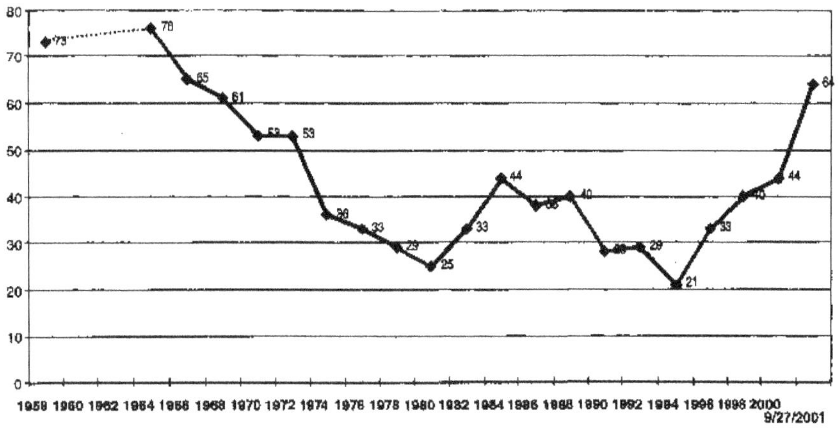

the not so impressive performance and sharply declining quality of services of public sector, it attracts critical evaluation and also tends to get scrutinised by social audits, non-governmental organisations and media.

Due to its destructive character, the emergence of resolution of distrust and enhancing trust relationships management in public sector has gained attention. Researchers have been probing into dimensions of the distrust and provide suggestions on how it can be managed more effectively. The objectives for this chapter are as follows:

CHAPTER OBJECTIVES

1. Explain the meaning and develop conceptual framework of trust.
2. Describe the factors that cause deficit trust.
3. Examine the challenges of building and maintaining trust, and measures for instilling trust.
4. Highlight the vulnerabilities of public sector leading to distrust.
5. Outline the international and comparative strategies to rebuild trust.

DISTRUST IN THE PUBLIC SECTOR: CAUSES FOR DECLINE

There could be divergent views about how to isolate the causes for public distrust. The information is by and large based on hearsay, observation and reported cases of grievances. The growing tendency among the recipients of public sector services is that they have a strong dissentient and dislike for the poor services provided by the public sector organisations. On account of over-bureaucratisation, public sectors may be regarded as rule based, procedure centric and dominated by centralised authority. Many governmental bodies and public sectors have not adopted transparent and efficient delivery systems on account of lack of political will. To illustrate an example of varied fluctuations in Public Distrust, the author presents the decline of trust in US citizens Figure 1 (Chanley, 2002).

In United States, since 1960, there has been a growing public disillusionment after US' involvement in Vietnam conflict which led to increase in public cynicism in government. 1970's saw the decline in government trust after the Watergate scandal, followed by President Nixon's resignation. The growing public dissatisfaction was also present during the period of presidency of Mr. Carter. During the first term of President Reagan, there was substantial increase of trust in US government. On the contrary, during the Reagan's second term, due to the Iran-contra scandal, however, trust again began to decline. The early years of the Clinton's presidency, i.e., 1992, witnessed the House bank policy. Later, unimpressive health care policies and reforms added to the public distrust of US government. After 1994, the trust level against US government hit a record low. The situation is much the same now as majority in US says that the Federal Government threatens their personal rights. The latest national survey by the Pew Research Center for the People and the Press, conducted Jan. 9-13 among 1,502 adults, finds that 53% think that the federal government threatens their own personal rights and freedoms while 43% disagree. (www.people-press.org, 2013)

The other causes are as follows:

1. **The Service Delivery System of Public Sectors:** The employees of public sector may have negative attitudes like low faith, commitment and sense of belongingness towards their employer. The motto of every public sector is to serve large number of people with deficit finance. Taking this consideration, the performance of employees also may be low, which incidentally reflects in services delivered by them.
2. **No Performance Evaluation of Public Sectors:** The functioning of governmental institutions and public sectors often get scrutinised by citizens and those who approach the concerned under right to information. But, these organisations should develop their internal mechanism to evaluate and improve their performance standards. For example, after the Bernard L. Madoff investment scandal, the Securities and Exchange Commissions' (SEC) inspector general conducted an internal investigation into the agency's failures to uncover the scheme despite a series of red flags and tips. In September 2009, the SEC released a report on how the SEC missed these red flags and identified repeated opportunities for SEC examiners to find the fraud and how ineffective their efforts were. There should be a internal control mechanism to control the deviations.
3. **Scandals in Public offices:** United Stated had witnessed higher degree of corruption in government, where people holding administrative positions were held responsible for their corrupt or dishonest practice. Of the prominent ones, (1) Iran-Contra Scandal, 1996 where it did damage the Reagan's presidency, (2) House banking scandal where the House of Representatives Bank found that 450 members had overdrawn their checking accounts, but not been penalized Such scandals can also be interpreted as irregularities and increased crimes in public offices where public share their growing concerns (Chanley et al., 2000). Six were convicted of charges, most only tangentially related to the House Bank itself. Twenty two more of the most prolific over-drafters were singled out by the House Ethics Committee. (1992), (3) Environmental protection Agency (EPA) Scandal like, a scandal in which funds from the EPA were selectively used for projects which would aid politicians friendly to the Reagan administration. On account of these scandals, skepticism continued to grow and it leads to negative attitude formation(Chanley et al., 2000, 2001).

ENHANCING TRUST: WHAT IS IT?

In management context, 'Trust' is associated with a cognitive element based on reasonable and influential value oriented decisions, supported by strong interaction for long term planning - to affectively dominate the relationship and form bondage through constant interaction, compassion and cooperation with others (Deutschn & Coleman, 2008; Osgood, 1959). This endeavour of trust process is undertaken by top level management, to maintain favourable relations with stakeholders like employees, customers and suppliers and ensure attainment of the organisation's performance goals. The short term trust measures could be perceived as transactions costs rather than ensure long term association as investment on reciprocal and mutual gain basis for creation of enduring value (Parkhe, 1993). It takes time to form and build trust in an "incremental and accumulating manner" (Rotter, 1980). Employees who are the internal customers assess trust, by their experience and dependency processes and they would address their personal gains rather than fulfilment of institutional vision. On a similar note, the agents, partners and distributers of supply value chain aim at small rewards and incentives resulting into instant transaction cost on the basis of zero-sum-game, instead of long term and mutually exclusive relationships. According to Jake Freivald, Vice President of corporate marketing at Information Builders Inc. (IBI), "Corporations definitely understand the relative importance of trust. Consumers buy more products from companies that they trust. Therefore, corporations have to face the challenge to find new ways to measure trust and enforce putting mechanisms in place to increase it."

The Definitions of Trust

Trust as willingness for discovering owns vulnerability towards other person whose behaviour cannot be controlled, in the situation in which potential benefits are much smaller in relation to the potential losses if other person takes advantage of that vulnerability (Zand, 1997).

Trust among the individuals and groups in an organization are very important and significant for a long-term stability of organization and well-being of its members (Cook & Wall, 1980).

Trust is an essential fluid for all social activities, allowing people to work and live together, without creating unnecessary stresses and conflicts during negotiations (Cohen & Prusak, 2001).

These definitions help in determining how much the top level management would invest in scrutiny of organizational trust. Such an attempt leads to investigations of organizational functioning and existence of working relations. The top level management must assure of high level trust by evaluating the job content factors like working conditions, accomplishments, achievements, empowerment, rewards and recognitions, training and developmental initiatives. The presumption of institutional leaders is that high trust between employer and employees leads to higher productivity, efficiency and improved commitment. High level of trust includes behaviour like stimulation of innovations; movement towards high emotional stability; facilitation of acceptance and openness for free expression and encouragement for risk acceptance (De Furia, 1997). Similarly, job context factors like organisational policy, culture, relations with the supervisor, work environment reflect upon impact of trust relationships (Daley & Vasu, 1998). Organizational trust is not a simple concept for understanding. "Examination of trust" requires the consideration of numerous factors. According to Mishra's model (1996) of organizational trust, few important dimensions of 'Organizational Trust' are (i) willingness to risk, (ii) benevolence, (iii) competence, (iv) openness and (v) reliability. Latest studies discovered another factor i.e., measurement of the level of individual relations of employees towards common objectives, norms, values and beliefs, joint with organizational culture which is also known as identification (Shockley - Zalabak, Ellis & Winograd, 2000). Savage (1982) presents a few important elements characteristic for the organizations where the trust level is low, or there isn't any: the atmosphere is often quiet with the low level of energy and engagement; there are no conflicts, anyone who impairs the system or expresses dissatisfaction is punished or fired; each change is observed with doubt and alarm, managing is from top to bottom, status is important, decisions are verified through the chain of commanding, people feel as if they are incarcerated within their work.

On the other hand, there is a range of behaviour typical for organizations of high performances. According to Phillips (1997), organizations with high performance contain five common elements: leaders who understand the value of accepting work tasks in current operating; leaders are visionary, and clearly articulate their visions leader believes in sharing the wealth with employees and they realize; when understand the values of intellectual capital and invest in it and importantly; they understand the values of loyalty and look for the way to support and develop the same.

Organizational climate of trust allows the employees to express their ideas, feelings and mutual learning. Organization without trust can make a negative position with people, which will prevent them in learning. Development of trust occurs in the situations where the individuals have freedom to express themselves in their daily tasks, without unnecessary control, monitoring and supervision (Fairholm, 1994). Supporting those freedoms will also develop the environment of high trust between the employees and management. According to Sonnenburg (1994), high confidence level within an organization implies: reducing discord and conflicts between the employees; mutual obligation of people; productivity increase; stimulation of development; improving the morale of employees; reducing the abstinence of employees; creating the environment where the innovations can be developed and advanced.

During recent years, organizational form was often discussed. Such organizations that focus on trust, cooperation, and teamwork and reject typical individual approaches are very often referred to as organizations of high performance since they tend to take what is best from individuals and create extraordinary abilities for transferring the valuable results to all the employees in organization (Dalton, 2000). Such organizations create goods and services with a lot greater quality in relation to traditional hierarchical organizations (Jordan, 1999). With such identity, organizations of high performances, apparently take over the position from traditional hierarchical organizations.

Faced with severe competitive demands for lower costs, high performance and greater outreach to larger cross-sections in the society, the public sector organisations are increasingly turning to employee trust to enhance the involvement, commitment and productivity levels of their employees. This chapter presents the importance of trust building interventions aimed to arrive at better interpersonal relationship and improvise the functioning of governance in public sector. The increased trust based relationship between the organisational leaders and the stakeholders can lead to more responsive decisions, continuous improvement in performance outcomes and leads to a higher level of employee job satisfaction, motivation and organisational citizenship. Figure 1 depicts the changing levels of trust and distrust in government in US.

Although trust is a broad term, it encompasses the conduct of inter-personal (Frederique, & Sorge, 2008), interactive and interdependent relationships in any organisation. Building trust is a proactive measure to nurture commitment, involvement and organisational citizenship behaviour (Wicks, Berman & Jones, 1999) in public sector organisations. Organisations like Infosys Technologies Ltd, Southwest Airlines, Johnson and Johnson adopted ethical and transparent practices to build trust among the stakeholders. For e.g. since 1980's the Malaysian public sector has adopted number of direct Employee Participative programs like the Look East Policy, Clean, Efficient and Trustworthy Policy, Total Quality Management, ISO, 5s' and in-house union in order to encourage employees direct involvement. Although the participative programs introduced are less in number, yet the Malaysian Government attempted to address the problems, efficiency, productivity and attitudinal development of the public sector including in the Malaysian Public Universities (Parasuraman & Rathakrishnan, 2011). Figure 2 exhibits the responses of majority of countries which reflect the distrust in their governments. (www.Edelman.com). According to this figure, in a survey conducted by Edelman, countries like Russia, Poland, China, Poland, Italy, Netherlands, South Korea, France Argentina, Indonesia, Spain, Japan and Brazil have reflected drop in the trust level in 2012.

According to the survey conducted by Edelman Trust Barometer 2012, trust in government officials and CEO's, experienced its biggest decline in Barometer history in 2009. Only 29 percent of those surveyed view them as credible. The drop in trust in the credibility of CEOs in mature markets such as the US, UK, France and South Korea fell more than or as dramatically as it did when the recession hit in 2008-2009. Overall, CEO credibility dropped 12 points to 38 percent, biggest drop in Barometer history (trust.edelman.com/trusts/path-forward/credibility-of-goverment-officials-and-ceos-plummets). The exhibit 1 on

Figure 2. Drop in trust level in various countries
Source:the Edelman Trust Barometer -2012 report

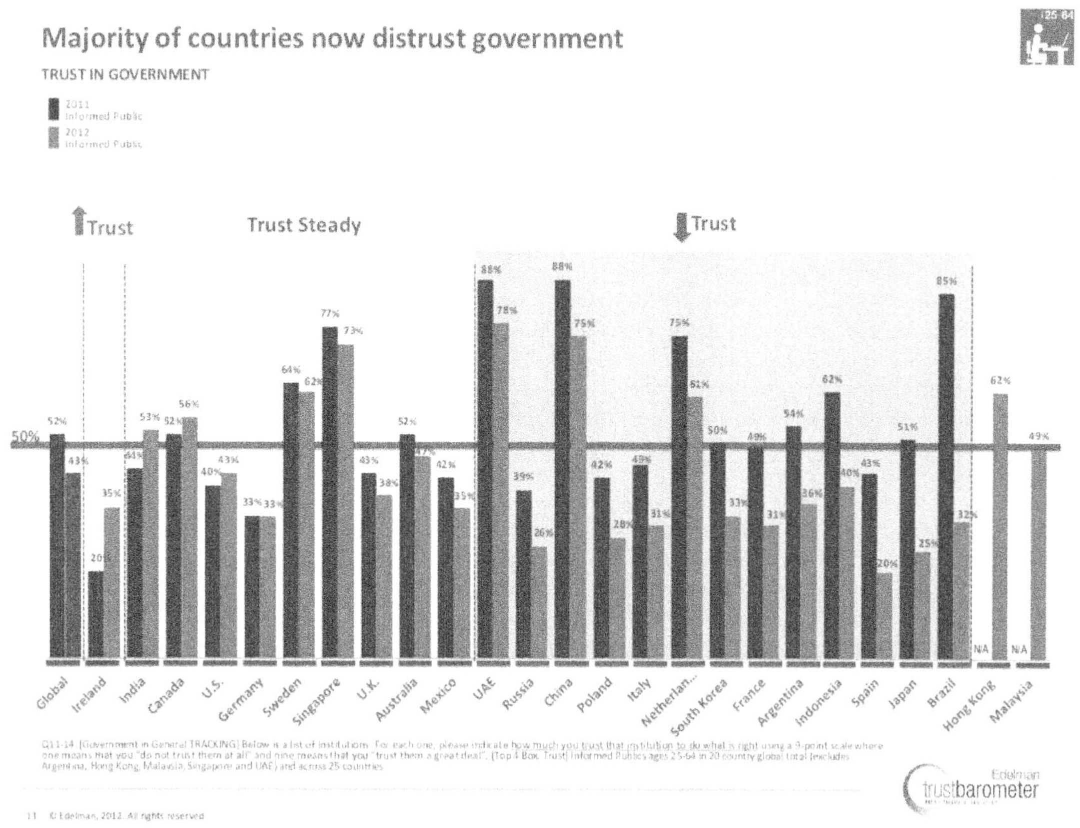

Exhibit 1. IRS, US: Transforming services delivery through accenture

The Internal Revenue Service (IRS), a bureau of the United States Department of the Treasury, is one of the world's most efficient tax administrators. The IRS functions under the immediate direction of the Commissioner of Internal Revenue and is responsible for collecting taxes and the interpretation and enforcement of the Internal Revenue Code of the United States. One and a half century old, what makes the IRS the head turner is its present standing. With a workforce of about 106,000, a budget of $12 Billion and collections crossing $2.4 Trillion even calling IRS a success would be an understatement. The juggernaut named IRS was not always so and has actually skyrocketed in past one and a half decade. IRS was earlier often thought to be an ineffective agency due to its notorious delay in tax refunds and poor administration. To deal with the situation, IRS had attempted to implement various managerial reforms. The IRS Restructuring and Reform Act of 1998 provided the gateway for formulation of the most comprehensive reorganization and modernization of IRS. IRS provides enhanced online capabilities services to improve the cost effectiveness and improves just in time delivery of service. Accenture had a pivotal role in making the system more comprehensive by providing appropriate solutions that encompassed technology, web design, infrastructure, help desks and change management. Accenture transformed the IRS outlook taxpayers toward attainment of self-service, thereby enabling the IRS to focus on its core business and reduce its cost-to-serve. With the constant assistance of Accenture, IRS was able to handle analysis of existing IRS governance on websites, implement sound systems of hardware and software and managed volumes of transactions in peak time i.e., tax seasons. IRS -Accenture collaborative deal provided the following integrated systemic services:

1. *Support of structured and accessible documents*
2. *User-friendly interactive development*
3. *Easily manageable formats and conversions*
4. *Conversions of text formats to XML*
5. *Outbound services like emails, fax, text messages.*
6. *Multichannel capability*
7. *E-forms download*
8. *Customer friendly and helps user feel empowered*
9. *Manageable Templates*
10. *User Controlled environment*

IRS services attempts to reach to such world class that it aims to provide an environment where the customers feels he has got over delivered that the assurances he claims. This endeavour of total enablement and customer execution friendly strategy ultimately lead to attainment of three important decisions. First of all these endeavours create industry specific standard integration that are synchronised and they enable rapid and flexible incorporation within the company's existing infrastructure, and provide for seamless policy administration system. Secondly, IRS as it is common with similar organisations around the world faces increasing demand from its customers for multi-channel and personalised engagements. With the arrival of the eFiling system, IRS has also continuously improved its customer satisfaction continuously according to the American Customer Satisfaction Index (ACSI). The eFiling system has provided the public with a faster, more effective, more accurate, and safer tax filing services.

Today, with more than 24 million page views at peak volume, irs.gov is now considered as one of the largest online offerings worldwide. The site has had 100 percent uptime since its launch—even during the heavy tax season and despite 30 percent annual increases in usage. Accenture created a multi-channel helpdesk for additional support service to ensure access to taxpayers. The multi-channel support allows for the creation of a single customer view and the development of richer, more relevant customer communications it also offered robust functionality that will enable us to improve the overall context and relevancy of each individual communication.

The supporting help desk guarantees that 80 percent of taxpayer calls are answered within 40 seconds. As a result, the site has dramatically enhanced the IRS's ability to connect with its taxpayers through a highly cost-effective channel while creating a more reliable and more dependable web experience for US taxpayers. In fact, IRS.gov has top response time among dozens of government Internet sites and has won several awards, including "Best of the Web" from Forbes magazine and a "Pioneer Award" for its innovative approach to e-Government in initiatives.

Source: M. Jae Moon, Can IT Help Government to Restore Public Trust?: Declining Public Trust and Potential Prospects of IT in the Public Sector, < http://citeseerx.ist.psu.edu/viewdoc/download?doi=10.1.1.4.2836&rep=rep1&type=pdf > (last visited on 13th September, 2013)

NIS Latvia reflects the corruption in public and private sectors.

Another emerging dimension of Public Sector distrust is due to 'subcontracting'. Although the constant engagement of the internal and external stakeholders in trust based relationship (Julia, 2006) leads to the emergence of two situations (1) professional trust and (2) personal trust; the issue of concern for research is why there is growing deficit trust in public sector. Under the garb of sub-contracting, a complex network of relationships developed between principal employer, agents and sub agents to accomplish the goals of various institutions under Public Sector. Due to the involvement of various actors and active players on account of contractual agreements and public-private partnerships, there was an increasing phenomenon of deficit trust, violation of trust (Charley, 1997) and non accountability. Consequently, institutions for example railways, aviation, transport, food supplies, hospitals, manufacturing units and industrial establishments, were subjected to the evil side of political, administrative and bureaucratic leadership (Galford, & Drapeau, 2003). It was difficult to trace out amongst these actors, who were actually responsible for creation of deficit trust. Trust was said to be declining, and this decline was generally seen as detrimental to public service delivery. Yet, on account of the strong under-currents in 'power' plays among the government, public servants, and third party agents, the presence of collusion is inevitable, leading to corruption, nepotism, sidestepping formal rules and regulations. Concerns with declining public trust in government have become a new phenomenon in contemporary political debates. This concern also extended to levels of individuals' trust in the public administration and public services. Individuals' trust in the public sector although found to fluctuate; reports did not reflect consistently declining levels of trust. The Edelman Barometer found that the lack of trust is driven by the perception of unethical behaviour, and, unfortunately, scandals continue to emerge. In 2012, investigators in Europe, the U.S., Canada and Asia found that bankers knowingly submitted false data for the calculation of the London Interbank Offered Rate, an interest rate benchmark that influenced the value of hundreds of trillions of dollars in financial contracts around the world, including floating-rate mortgages, corporate loans and interest rate swaps. The ruses were committed to hide their institutions' financial problems or to boost their traders' profits. The Edelman survey found that more than one in two people, globally (56 percent) were aware of the financial services scandals (78 percent in the United Kingdom, where Barclays paid a $450 million fine), with 59 percent saying the cause of those scandals was behaviour, specifically corruption, poor corporate culture, or poor leadership. In this scenario, instilling trust or measurements to track trust was an increasingly important phenomenon among the Business Leadership across the world. "In countries where the middle class is emerging, trust seems to be on the rise," said Ben Boyd, chair of corporate practice and lead trust spokesperson of Edelman which conducted survey in 26 countries. He also mentioned that "in industrialised countries, trust is on the decline." In this context, Figure 3 exhibits the distrust that is growing with very few countries in the neutral zone.

Figure 3 indicates leader's willingness to facilitate expectation and opportunity on one hand and risk and ensure compliance on the other. Trust is not merely taking risk per se; rather, it is a willingness to take risk (Granovetter, 1985). Leaders are respected when they possess knowledge and gain cooperation. Stakeholders also believe those leaders who are worthy of their trust (Julia, 2006). On account of globalisation, liberalisation and privatisation, the institutions of public sectors have become vulnerable to the corrupt approaches and succumb to competitive forces like MNCs and TNCs. To contain the growing opportunism of among the people, customers, and stakeholders, the public sector has to carve out an edge for itself and mark its achievements by building trust

Figure 3. Growing distrust and shift away from trust in various countries
Source: The Edelman Trust Barometer, 2012.

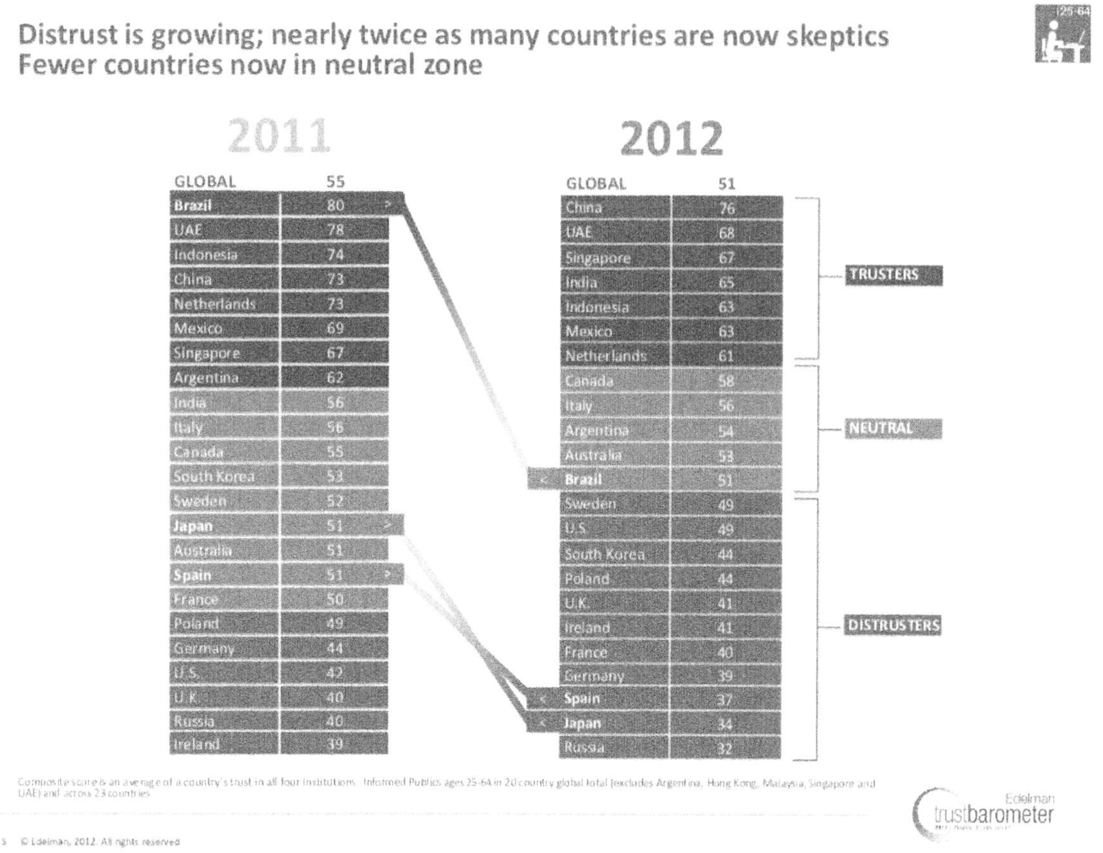

linkages, by making the system more transparent (Julia, 2006), ethical and provide services for value for money spent.

Trust Model

Figure 4 depicts the most popular trust model that was provided by Mayer, Davis, and Schoolman. Mayer et al., (1995) argued that there were three major factors that determine organizational trust: (1) characteristics of the trustor, (2) characteristics of the trustee, and (3) the perceived risk. They suggested that the perceived risk tends to moderate the relationship between trust and risk taking in our model. Trust is the "willingness to take risk," and the level of trust is an indication of the amount of risk that one is willing to take. The propensity of the trustor and the elements of trustworthiness that the trustee possesses influence the current level of trust. Researchers like McEvily et al., (2003); Sitkin and George, (2005); highlighted the dominance of relationship between trust and control systems in dealing with risk.

The characteristic traits of the trustor were considered as factors to determine the propensity of the trustor to trust. In other words, some individuals are more trusting than others. The characteristics of the trustee are presented as trustworthiness. According to Mayer et al., there were three elements of trustworthiness namely (1) ability the competence the trustee possesses in the specific domain; (2) benevolence the willing-

Figure 4. Trust model
Source: Mayer, Davis, and Schoorman, 1995

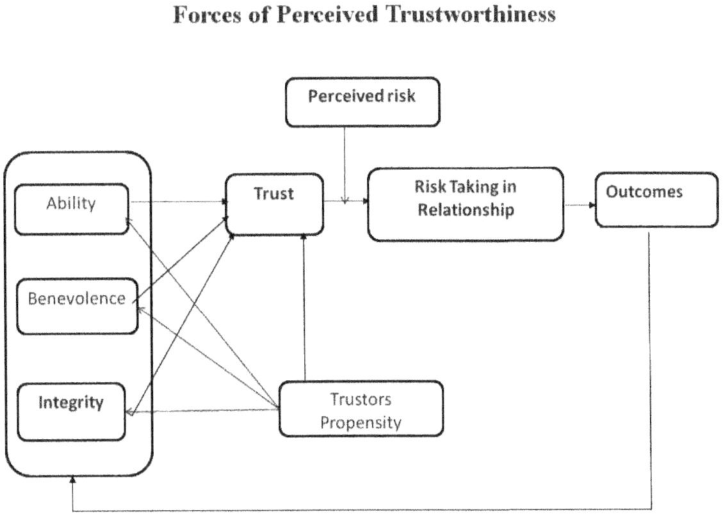

ness of the trustee to do good for the trustor; and (3) integrity whether the trustee has a core set of values to guide behavior.

Further, Mayer et al., in their model presented that the current situation of trust will have a specific amount of perceived risk that reaffirms the existence of trust. Most common of all, higher the trust level and lower the perceived risk in the current context, more likely it is that risk taking will occur in the trust relationship. The outcomes of the risk taking could vary from extremely positive to extremely negative in a continuum. The probable outcomes provided scope for evaluation to the trustee and level of trustworthiness may increase or decrease.

Given the importance of trust to key organizational outcomes, our trustworthiness results would provide a guide for increasing trust in organizations. Ability, benevolence, and integrity provide three distinct avenues for fostering trust, as all three are highly correlated with trust and all three had significant, unique relationships with it. Researchers stated that the ability results reinforce the importance of recruitment and selection strategies geared towards maximizing general abilities and training strategies targeted at building task-specific expertise (Arthur, Bennett, Edens, & Bell, 2003). Colquitt et al., (2007) in their meta-analysis of above mentioned integrated model found strong correlations between trust propensity, trustworthiness, and trust. They also found a good statistical fit to support the integrated model proposed by Mayer et al., 2007.

DEVELOPMENT OF TRUST AND CO-EVOLUTION OF TRUST ACROSS LEVELS

The dynamics of trust relationship occur in three dimensional levels (1) at the interpersonal level, (2) at intergroup level and at inter-organizational level. Currall and Epstein (2003) proposed trust's evolutionary phases as shown in Figure 5. To begin with, as shown in the figure, the trust starts at an initial level of zero. At this point there is no firm expression of either trust or distrust. Between two individuals or groups or in two organisational contexts, trust emerges once there is exchange of information and the possible outcomes thereupon.

Based on the degree of mutual and reciprocal exchange of series of critical information exchanges and confidence that gets generated, trust develops. Although Currall and Esptein (2003) acknowledged that the development of trust is often slow and incremental because parties tend to be reticent about trusting. This is perhaps true because the information that is known is little and there are self doubts about others' behaviour leading to speculation of the improbability. Trust building is essentially a very slow process as it is based on 'walking firmly while constantly testing the waters'. As individuals make small beginnings, they remain conscious about the possible violations. As individuals perceive trust being upheld, they continue to gain faith and proceed. Individuals build trust with lot of caution and alertness in trusting others and continue to take one step at a time.

With over a series of positive experiences of trust-building approaches, the level of trust grows until it attains an optimum level of 'maintaining trust' phase. At this level, both parties share a stable relationship of trust although one of them may tend to trigger the violations of trust. If either of the parties constantly violates the trust, the degree of violations, will however, determine the fissures to occur in the relationships. Trust then gets instantly destroyed. It is true that it takes time, efforts and patience to build trust, but the process of trust maintenance is tedious and must be nurtured carefully. Currall and Esptein (2003) argued that trust at one level may impact trust at another level during the 'developing trust' phase. It is important to note that the level of distrust is where the trust suddenly encounters a fall and the revival is equally challenging to handle. When the organizational context for trust falls at

Figure 5. Evolutionary phases of trust
Source: Currall and Epstein (2003).

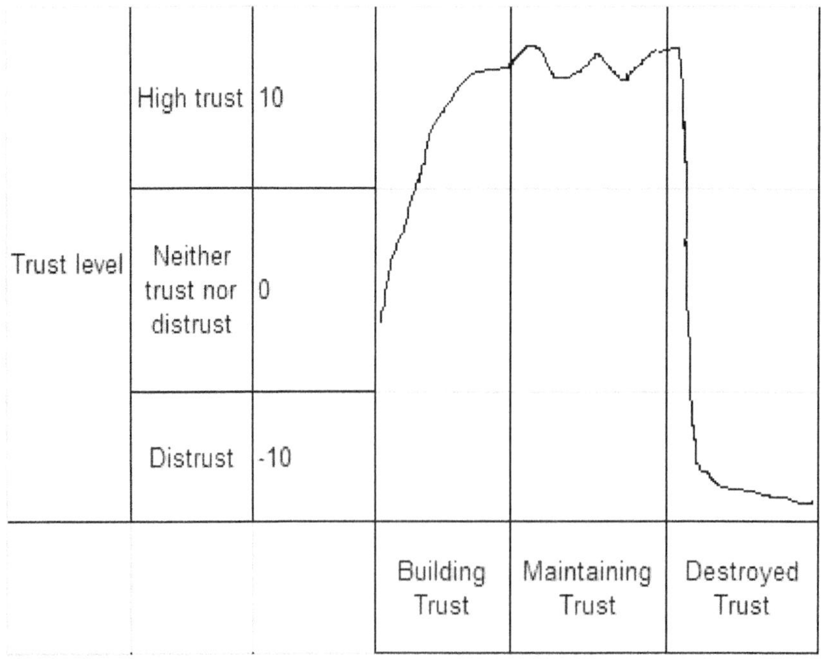

another lower level, this demands a kick start of the evolution process of trust at different levels to gain the momentum.

Distinction between Trust and Distrust

Although trust and distrust can be understood as two ends of same continuum (Worchel, 101), yet the origin of trust and distrust are different. The terms 'Trust' and 'Distrust' may appear as if they are opposite to each other, but in reality there is considerable difference between the two. The main differences between the two are as follows:

1. Trust exists when two individuals are willing to depend upon each (Fox, 1974) and other even though they are conscious of the potential problems in their relationships. Distrust exists when one individual suspects the motives and intentions of the others (Sitkin & Roth, 1993) which might lead to some dire consequences.
2. In trust relationships, there is a strong presence of positive emotion (Deutsch, 1958) like an element of security, in spite of lack of control over the party, and even though there are possibilities of negative consequences. In situations where distrust exists, it is governed by negative emotions like anger, suspicion and fear of what will happen (Luhmann, 1988; Deutsch, 1958).
3. The sustenance of trust is not dependent on situation; it is based on the overall strength of the interpersonal relations (Gabarro, 1978) between the two individuals. In case of distrust, it is inherently governed by difference or doubt that makes one try to find other means. Distrust occurs on account of sudden breakdown in a given situation.
4. Presence of trust develops positive expectations (Lewicki et al., 1998) in a relationship, while presence of distrust develops antagonist relationship, where use of power, dominance (Bies, 1996) and control increases the feeling of vulnerability.
5. The potential outcomes in trust relationship is dependency (Luhmann, 1988), faith, loyalty and respect for each other. The potential outcomes of distrust relationships are lack of cooperation, increased disagreements, refusal to accept power, lack of confidence, vengeance and retaliation (Webb, 1996; Lewicki et al., 1998).

Types of Trust Relationships

There are three types of trust identified in professional relationships which are linked and sequential. By understanding how trust changes, grows and declines, we learn about change, growth and decline in relationships.

Deterrence Based Trust: Deterrence-based trust based on consistent fear and threat of punishment. It is primarily governed by apprehension of what will happen if people don't follow what they ought to. It is a fragile form of relationship, susceptible to breakdown. This form of trust based relationship is based on fear of reprisal, if the trust is violated (Lewicki & Bunker, 1996). For example when two individuals trust each other, deterrence can be an effective threat, as both of them are concerned of the potential loss of a relationship which may outweigh the gain created by defecting from it. There must be common rules which tend to monitor, exchange information and ensure proper reporting between the parties. It is the fear of losing a relationship that makes a person to confirm to do right things. Little knowing about their obligations, individuals may do what they are asked to, for fear of consequences of not following the orders.

Calculus-Based Trust: It is similar to deterrence based trust but this form of trust is grounded not only in the fear of punishment for violating trust, but also in the rewards for preserving it. Individuals indulging in calculus based trust often compare the costs and benefits of creating and sustaining

Figure 6. Types of trust in organisations
Source: Graham Dietz, Deanne N. Den Hartog, (2006)

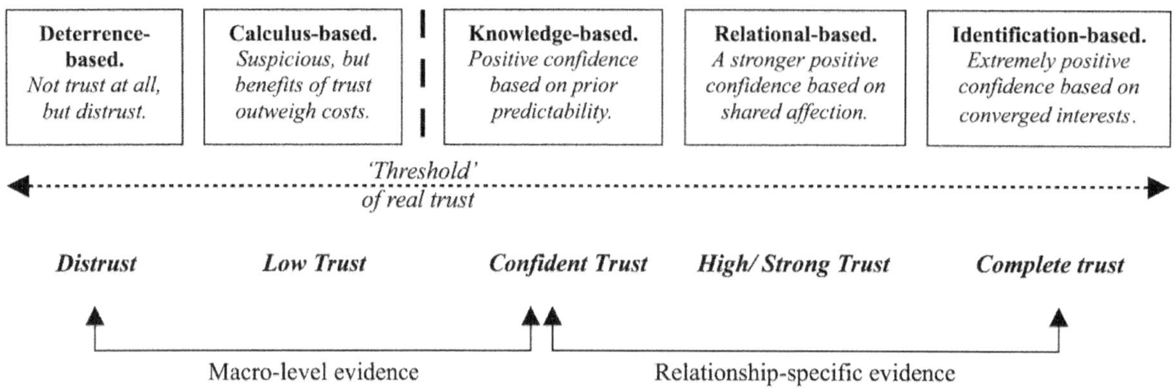

a relationship versus the costs and benefits of severing it (Lewicki & Bunker, 1996). However, delayed reciprocity may actually reduce a party's ability to extricate itself from relationships that have ceased to generate value or have become less valuable than other opportunities. For example, a purchasing manager may feel compelled to continue dealing with a particular supplier, even when better alternatives exist, because of outstanding obligations to that supplier representative (McEvily et al., 2003).

Knowledge-Based Trust: Knowledge based Trust occurs when an individual has enough information and understanding about another person to predict that person's behaviour. Having adequate knowledge about a person, thing or situation helps in making accurate prediction. Making predictions about possible behavioural outcomes depends on overall understanding about the person like identification of traits, personality, strengths and weakness develops from repeated interactions, communication, and building a relationship. Unlike calculus-based trust, knowledge-based trust (KBT) is founded not on control, but information. For example, customers cultivate knowledge of various products and services by gathering data, seeing each other in different contexts, and experiencing each other's range. Knowledge based trust encourages knowledge sharing by increasing the disclosure of knowledge to others and by proving access the knowledge in one's possession (Dirks 2000; Ferrin 2001).

Relational Trust: The relational trust in its essence is interpersonal. Such trust is based on reliance on and/or confidence in some event, process or person. It reflects an expectation of positive outcomes. Trust arises from institutional or organisational situations. In both, personal and interpersonal trust two or more people or groups trust each other in a specific situation. Interpersonal trust is situational or relationship specific, where as personal trust is based on one person trusts another person, persons or thing(s) in a specific situation. The trusting entity is one person and trust is directed to another party of persons. In both personal and interpersonal trust, the basis for trust is dependent on the attributes the trusted person or group possess in a given situation or relationship. Interpersonal and personal trust develops when there is a trusting belief system between both parties. The development of a trusting belief system is dependent on the extent to which individuals in a relationship consistently display behaviours associated with trustworthiness. The beliefs and perceptions of trustworthiness, the trust or holds of the trustee, significantly influences the level of trust between both parties. In interpersonal and personal relationships, the most common factors or attributes associated with the nurturing, development and maintenance of trust based on a belief system are:

Identification-Based Trust: Identification based trust happens when parties understand and endorse one another, and can act for each other in interpersonal transactions. Based on the degree of familiarity and repeated interactions among individuals, identification based trust requires parties to fully internalize and harmonize with each others' desires and intentions. Certain activities enhance trust based on identification. Identification -based trust has a strong emotional component and so it is sensitive to a number of non-logical factors. Predictability is defined as reliability and consistent behaviour. Predictability means that one's actions are consistent enough that another can forecast what one will do in a given situation. It assumes objectivity, good judgement and impartiality in handling situations. Having predictability means that one's willingness and ability to serve another's interest does not vary or change over time. This makes managing identification-based strust difficult (Lewicki & Wiethoff, 2000). For example, employees working in same profession or problem solving teams or organizations can assume a common identity. For example, players of IPL cricket team often develop deep trust relationships with one another based on long term association. Cricket players come to know about their teammates, draw their expectations, share core values and develop consensus based decisions to respond to different game plans and ensure situations are predictable and evolve acceptable norms.

Other Forms of Trusts are Based on Contingent Situations

System, Impersonal or Structural Trust: Founded upon social or institutional structures in the situation, and not on the person or personal attributes of the trusted parties. System trust exists to the extent that a company's practices, rules, regulations and processes make employees feel secure and assured. In most of the public sectors across the world, bureaucracy is recognised as the backbone of the administrative functions.

Dispositional Trust: Trust connotes a generalized expectancy that one can rely on the word, the promise, the verbal or written statement of another person or institution and it arises from the personality attributes of the trusting party. Unlike interpersonal and structural trust, dispositional trust is not situation or relationship specific. Dispositional trust exists to the extent that a person displays a sense of basic trust – a consistent tendency to trust across a broad spectrum of situations and persons. It is directed towards people. Public sector services across the world are meant to provide reasonable services with a service orientation. Such services provided could be at parent institution level or through the agency. In the process of transactions between the institution and customers, the public sector has to prove five basic elements to generate the trust namely (1) integrity, (2) competence, (3) consistency, (4)loyalty, and (5) openness (Butler & Cantrell, 1984). Of these all, willingness to take risks is common to all trust situations (Mishra & Mishra, 1994).

Integrity Based Trust: It refers to honesty and truthfulness where the stakeholders expect the management to uphold its promises and commitments and not to act immorally or unfairly (Whitener, Brodt et al., 1998; Hoy & Tschannen - Moran, 1999; Pavlou, 2002; Mishra & Spreitzer, 1998). The term honesty can be defined by integrity and truthfulness. Honesty means one makes bona fide agreements, tells the truth and fulfils any promises made. With honesty, one proves one's willingness to be trustworthy by making and fulfilling agreements to do so. It emphasizes that stakeholders need to see a 'track-record' of ethical and honest behaviour. For example, customer trust might increase when a firm voluntarily issues a recall of products suspected to be defective; forced recalls may lead trust to diminish.

Competence Based Trust: Competence is defined as the technical and interpersonal knowledge and skills, required to do one's job. The essence of competence is self efficacy which relects the capacity or ability to produce a desired result. It means one party has the ability to do what the other party or person needs to have done. It also refers to individual's technical and interpersonal knowledge and skills. Ideally, stakeholders rely on the organization's *ability* to perform in the manner that is expected or promised where in return customers expect high performance and expect quality services. Investor trust might also be predicated on attributions of organizational competence. For example, investors might question whether the top management team is capable of competing and thriving in the market (Ellis & Shockley-Zalabak, 1999; Jarvenpaa & Tractinsky, 1999; McKnight & Chervany, 2002).

Benevolence Based Trust: It refers to individual's reliability, predictability and good judgements in handling skills that the organizations care about the particular stakeholder and will thus act in ways that are in the stakeholder's best interest. The term benevolence means one cares about the welfare of the other and is therefore motivated to act in the other person's interest. Loyalty, the willingness to protect and "save face for another," is associated with benevolent motives. The essence of benevolence is the willingness to serve another's interest. Organizational stakeholders perceive benevolence when concern, care and interest are expressed by the organization (Edmondson, 1999). For example, an employee might trust the organization because management has consistently provided merit raises, even when the organization has not been doing well financially. South west airlines example

Reliability-Based Trust: Stems from a stakeholder's experience that the organization has behaved consistently and predictably in ways that meet expectations. Importantly, in the context of trust, these expectations are positive—we do not think of trust in relation to a serial killer, even if he behaves predictably (Baier, 2001). Reliability may be important to stakeholders that have little information regarding the motives or integrity of the organization, but who still rely on consistent and dependable behaviour. Suppliers who expect to be paid on time and customers who expect timely delivery of their goods seem to meet these criteria.

Transparency-Based Trust: Transparency based trust refers to the individual's ability to reveal complete information and state the full truth (Butler and Cantrell, 1984); (Mishra & Mishra, 1994). It is relevant to stakeholders who are interested in evaluating the routines, processes, and decisions of the organization. For example, investors may want to have access to information that reveals how management is making the decisions that are necessary to secure the long-term viability of the organization; employees who want to ensure that their jobs and pensions are secure might want similar information. Transparency has come to be seen as a key element of organizational trust, especially in the wake of recent corporate scandals such as those involving Enron (Turnbull, 2002).

In the inter-organizational context, identification and similarity "can generate homogenous expectations and common assumptions regarding a partner and partnership" and thus lead to trust and cooperation (Parkhe, 1998; Pavlou, 2002). As this discussion suggests, all six of these antecedents—or bases—of trust are potentially relevant to different stakeholders. Hence, when it is considered all stakeholders together (i.e., if we do not distinguish between stakeholder types), one should find that organizational trust is positively influenced by attributions regarding each of these antecedents.

The ability to build and maintain trust in a public sector, is dependent on the relationship between any two individuals, be it an agent and a customer or between two institutions. An organization which intends to nurture trust based relationships must encourage upfront communication and keep up the promises. It must be fostered through the rest of the company. Public sectors must set the example and the standard for all employees to follow. Integrity is crucial to building an environment of trust in any relationship, including those between an organization and its employees on every level. Excellent and open communication is also very crucial in the development of trust; employees must know the company's vision and its plan to achieve the vision. This type of communication includes sharing information (including negative information), which should not be minimized. Employees should be considered and treated as equals in the company to foster a sense of community, and all ideas should also be considered equally. Employers should also be able to empathize with their employees, as it is hard to trust someone who cannot put themselves in someone else's shoes. Employees also very much appreciate when a company leader can own up to a mistake they have made. Employers that take the time and care to develop trust in their organization will reap the rewards.

WHY INSTITUTIONS OF PUBLIC SECTOR SUFFER FROM TRUST DEFICIT?

Most of the public sectors are facing the deficit trust. It is more than ever that organisational leadership is put to question and asked to find relevant answers as to why deficit trust is created? Events in the recent past have definitely contributed for formulation of low trust or deficit trust. In the wake of Enron, WorldCom, AIG and Satyam scandals, organizations took cognisance of falling trust levels relationships. Lack of trust can be identified when there is non-acceptance of values, decisions of supervisors are questioned to justify the motives and intentions, inefficient communication; reduced possibility of recognizing and accepting good ideas; increasing efforts for obtaining relevant information; increase in rejection, defensiveness and hostility; delayed implementation of activities and projects; win-win mentality is replaced by win-lose (De Furia, 1997). Expecting and mobilising trust from the others often leads to the zone of cold behaviour, because people mostly believe in other people on the basis of moral characteristics. This type of behaviour can lead to the environment of no confidence, rather than mutual confidence.

Global Transparency International conducts several research based studies n bribes across various countries. Accordingly, Bribe Payers Index scores reflects that 28 of the world's largest economies, from these countries pay bribes abroad. The countries and territories ranked in the Index cover all regions of the world and represent almost 80 per cent of the total world outflow of goods, services and investments. The 2011 report examines different types of bribery across sectors – including, for the first time, bribery among companies ('private-to-private' bribery). Foreign bribery has significant adverse effects on public well-being around the world. It distorts the fair awarding of contracts, reduces the quality of basic public services, limits opportunities to develop a competitive private sector and undermines trust in public institutions. Engaging in bribery also creates instability for companies themselves and presents ever-growing reputational and financial risks. This is particularly relevant in light of recent anti-bribery reforms in a number of key countries around the world, such as China and the United Kingdom. Companies from Russia and China, which invested US $120 billion overseas in 2010 and, are increasingly active in global business, are seen as most likely to pay bribes abroad. Companies from the Netherlands and Switzerland are seen as least likely to pay bribe.

Most prevalent and often critiqued for poor performance is public sector services, often for spending huge amounts of taxpayers' money on public services. Figure 5. depicts the perception of general population in 25 countries across the globe (www.edelmantrust barometer, 2012). The responses got were for a question asked how important each of the following in building trust in

Figure 7. Government not meeting public expectations
Source The Edelman Trust Barometer, 2012

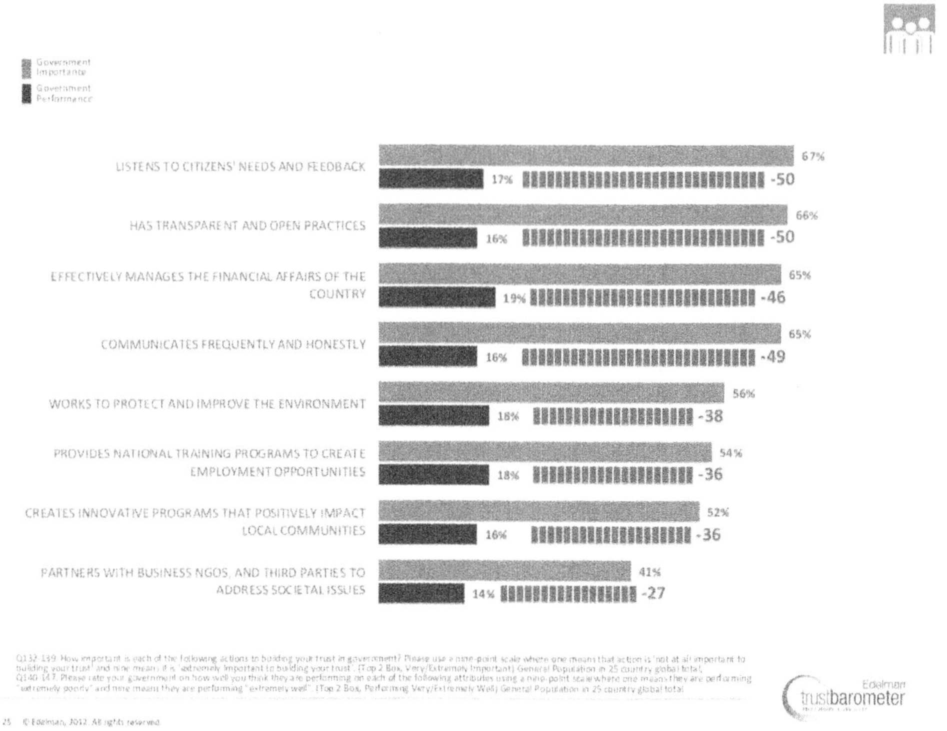

government is. The figure shows that the public expectations from government services are much more and there is always unmet demand which leads to distrust.

The measures of public policy are mostly evaluated in terms of financial performance and quality of production, services and attainment of objectives. Because of systemic flaw i.e., bureaucratic relationship, the performance of public sector tends to deteriorate on account of corruption, red tape or wastage; the size of any shadow economy (i.e. untaxed income); the strength of the rule of law; the health and life expectancy of its population; the educational achievement of its population and the quality of its communications and transport infrastructure. Such 'macro' indicators help to chart the effectiveness of public sector reforms in different countries.

In addition, there are several global frameworks like OECD, Transparency International, World Bank, International Monetary Fund, which specifically assess countries' public sectors on various measures such as service delivery, strength of financial systems, accountability and quality of regulatory environment. The performance of the public sector is an important driver for economic growth in that country, as it is the public sector which provides a fit and well-educated workforce; a regulatory and investment environment conducive to business and the infrastructure (physical and virtual) to enable the movement of goods and information. Again, different countries face different challenges. Many Countries adopting market led public sector reform are shrinking their public sectors, or blurring the boundaries between public and private sectors by outsourcing services to the private sector; or inviting private sector or third sector providers to provide services.

There are several mechanisms to increase private sector participation in the delivery of public goods like Public-Private Partnerships (PPP). Public-private partnerships are collaborations between local or central government and private companies have been a more successful global trend. Since the mid 1990s developing countries experienced a seven-fold increase in PPP activity, similar to Europe. The trend was even higher in the US. Most of these PPP related to transport and highways. The advantages to the public authority were transfer to risk to (1) the private partner; and, or (2) reallocation of capital expenditures into operating expenditures. Taking UK as an example, various governments encouraged or required outsourcing of finance and other processes, payroll and recruitment, procurement and medical and social care. The resultant outcome showed that public to private outsourcing constitutes a 40% of the outsourcing industry in the UK, which was as much as to UK's GDP of financial services. (Rowe & Calnan, 2006)

Factors Which Influence Trust Based Relationships

The following are some of the factors which influence trust based relationships.

1. **Vulnerabilities:** The critical role of trust is often exposed in partnership or collaborative relationships, joint ventures, and mergers and acquisitions. Sources of distrust originate on account of contributing partners, intentions of private sector during joint partnership with public sector (Muraskin, 2002). Trust is considered essential in stakeholder relationship development (Wilson, Bunn, & Savage, 2010). Researchers argue that breach of trust between partners occurs on account of little information sharing process, fewer strategic opportunities, and scarcity of resources basis of partners' potential skills and abilities, as opposed to their prior social relationships (Edelenbos & Klijn, 2007). For example, in the 1990, the Child Vaccine Initiative (CVI), was founded by as an alliance of United Nations, World Health Organization, United Nations Development Program, United Nations Children's Fund, World Bank and non-governmental organizations like Rockefeller Foundation, following the 1990 for upliftment and improvement of child health across the globe. It was disbanded in 1998 due to high level of distrust between the private and public sectors, conflicts over the distribution of different aspects of the project like authority, formulation of committees, decision making led to friction between the contributing partners. The contribution of private sector was perceived to be innovative as it geared up profit maximisation but, the public sector was considered to be overly bureaucratic and inefficient. This difference in opinions and objectives rendered the CVI unsuccessful in the achievement of its goals (Musaskin, 2002; Ezezika et al., 2013).
2. **Non Attainment of Public Sector Reforms, Performance Standards and Outcomes:** Public sector is mostly service oriented and caters to services based on utilitarian functions i.e., where larger good for larger cross-sections of the society is associated. Public sector should prioritise building performance measures, straighten pilferages, and identify measures for attainment of performance. Arriving at an agreement on a reasonable performance target is a challenge, more so, when the costs associated with getting it are wrong. In view of this, is there a strong need for public sector governance. A question to ponder over will be as to why in such cases the developing countries oppose to public sector reforms?

The government's aim to demonstrate political commitment so as to bring public sector reforms is grounded in wider sustainable goals. In Germany, the increased efforts by the government during the crisis, has increased the public trust levels. Exhibit 2 reflects the increased perception of public trust levels in German government.

Consistent political commitment is emphasized by Sarker (2006) in the case of Singapore. The Government of Singapore initiated a New Public Management model where systematic reforms were enunciated in 1989. The aim was to attain dual goals. The leaders in Singapore perceived attainment of broad outreach with excellence in meeting the public needs and be a driving force to ensure the economic growth and development. This type of motivation is required in developing and maintaining sustainable public sector reforms in several other authoritarian countries in Asia. On a similar note, the World Bank also has taken several measures to instil the culture of performance standards and outcomes in the public sectors (Bunse & Fritz, 2012).

Figure 8 reflects the Measureable Performance Improvements in Public Management Systems. It exhibits the efforts put in by the World Bank to provide financial aid and thereby assist governments in their efforts to improve transparency, accountability and service delivery, which has remarkably shown improvement. The World Bank through aid dependency has addressed the concerns of public sector governance and public sector management. It lays emphasis on strengthening the public sector management systems in two areas namely (1) public sector management systems and (2) public sector governance. World Bank aid develops dependency among the beneficiaries, such as parliaments and offices of the ombudsman and the support to these institutions has raised the level of public accountability, and ensured tracking improvements by the measures of the rule of law, state legitimacy and trust in government institutions. Such efforts ensured reduction of corruption in assisted organisations, and equip firms and households with better services, such as health and education. A better public sector

Exhibit 2. GfK Verein: In Germany, people trust the government

The GfK Verein was established in 1934 as a non-profit organization. The purpose of the Verein is to develop innovative research methods in close cooperation with academic institutions, to promote the training and further education of market researchers, to observe the structures and developments in society, the economy and politics that play a key role in private consumption, and to research their effects on consumers. It has an impressive membership of companies, individuals and academic institutions.

GfK Global Trust Report 2013 conducted a survey and interviewed around 28,000 respondents in a total of 25 countries worldwide between September and November 2012 on trust among 12 institutions, 11 business areas and in other individuals. The scale identified was on "trust completely", "mostly trust", "don't really trust" and "don't trust at all". It was observed that in Germany, the police are the most trusted institution clearly top of the rankings with 81 percent. In comparison with the previous year, however, trust dropped by four percentage points. Second in the rankings by a clear margin is the judiciary, which recorded a trust value of 65 percent.

The German government is the only institution that saw an improvement in its trust value. Although it is in the lower third of the rankings, with 34 percent, this is 5 percentage points higher than in the previous year. Professor Dr. Raimund Wildner, Managing Director of the GfK Verein, comments: "This development could be attributable to the positive perception, as reported in the media, of how the German Chancellor is managing the current crisis."

In Germany, the political parties have again remained bottom in the rankings, with only one in six Germans trusting them. However, faith in German political parties is relatively average in an international comparison.

With only a few exceptions, trust values have remained relatively stable in Germany in comparison with the 2012. The only improvement has been registered for trust in the government. The automotive industry maintained its high level, while energy and water providers saw a slight decrease. When looking at trust in institutions across all 25 countries, the highest value is registered for the military and the army, at 79 percent. This is followed by the church and religious communities, which are trusted by 66 percent on average.

Source: (www.gfk-verein.org) Nuremberg, 7 February 2013)

Figure 8. Measureable performance improvements in public management systems: FY 2010-2012
Source: www.worldbank.org/poverty reduction and economic management

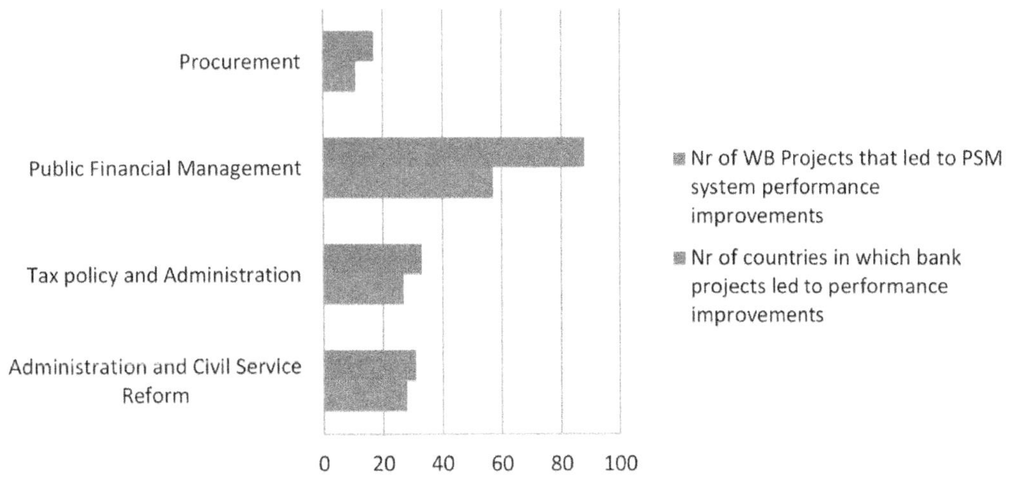

means better regulation of social and economic behavior, such as food or road transport safety. (Source:www.worldbank.org/SGO4LFRS S0).

3. **No Transformational Leadership:** Transformational leaders trigger changes in the organisation and make proactive decisions to suit to the institutional growth. Literature on transformational leaders highlights the presence of greater scepticism and pessimism regarding leader's ability to reflect transformational style in public sector, other than private sector (Wright & Pandey, 2010). The reasons attributed to the negative approach are on account of public sector inherited culture i.e., bureaucracy coupled with centralised decision control systems (Shamir and Howell 1999). Public sector as a system restrains the development of transformational leaders.
4. **Presence of Relational Bureaucracy:** According to Gittell and Douglass, (2012), relational bureaucracy is a hybrid of the relational and bureaucratic forms in which the reciprocal interrelatedness enables the participants to respond to each other in knowledgeable and caring ways, while formal structures embed reciprocal interrelatedness in the roles, thus enabling the scalability and sustainability typically associated with the bureaucratic form. It comprises of leader-follower relationship in worker-supervisor, a working and coordinated relationship between any two co-workers and a relationship between the employee and the customers. First of all, in such relational bureaucracies, decisions emerge after a series of interactions among the key agents/groups and levels of decision processes and analysis shifts from the two member to the system or network of relationships. Secondly, there are chances of knowledge overlap or excessive gap between the members. Thirdly, leader's behavior is seen from the context of emerging situation and not from the leader's perspective.
5. **No Professional Approach:** Professionals in the public sector are constantly exposed to indifference and interpersonal conflicts. Application of distinctive competence undergrids professionalism (Schon, 1983) and these interpersonal conflicts originate on account of attitudinal approaches which

stem out of inactive responses, politicking, nepotism and favouritism. When the environment is drastically changing, the non-responsive and unwillingness to adapt to market situations raises suspicion for the very services that the public sector delivers. Preferring to concentrate on stability strategy and consciously ignoring differentiation or focus strategy may prove to be detrimental in the long run. Due to the competitive forces and indulgence of private players, public sector loses its reputation and market share. However, innovation pushes professionals into unexplored territories which are beyond their comfort zones. Static ethical prescriptions, such as those found in deontology, are ill-fitted for professionals under such conditions. Professionals in public sector need to have space for innovative practices, and prefer tried-and-true approaches (Gerald, 2010).

Consequences of Violation of Trust

1. **Low Demand for Goods and Services:** Due to cut-throat competition, Indian companies have constantly engaged customers to switch between the competitors wherein the focus gets shifted to a company rather than the quality of goods and services. Most of the car manufacturing companies like Hyundai; other insurance companies like Max New York Life Insurance etc. have kept their focus on switch-and-save strategy that has commoditized the entire industry. Though the decisions to switch over are customers centric, customers face the challenge of self created vicious cycle of low trust. This process of continuous exchange of untrustworthy and disgruntled customers among few competitors will never help for a sustainable organisational growth or market share.

Accordingly to a survey conducted by Thunderhead (www.thunderhead.com), a customer communication management software vendor, 66 percent of insurance customers currently do not feel their communications needs are being met by their insurer; 50 percent of respondents agreed that insurers communicate without regard to customer preference. Leaders engaged in Customer Experience in any industry, share certain common traits when it comes to execution (Mitchell, 2011). Thunderhead focused on importance of comprehensive training to all associates of a large companies, and emphasised on developing mutually beneficial delivering system with quality services across every touch point. By doing so, Thunderhead was able to create high differentiation especially in building trust, loyalty and ultimately growth as customers and their relatives (www.thunderhead.com). Firms with the highest customer advocacy ratings like Forrester research, reports that customer retention is very important aspect in today's business scenario. But many companies are not undertaking the requisite steps to engage employees and keep them engaged in the long run. Customer loyalty and retention reflect upon the shareholder value and provide consistent returns than those engaged in switching and swapping between two or more entities. Forrester research report describes the specific steps that can be pursued by the organizations to ensure that the customers experience a central role and feel motivated, equipped, and empowered during the engagement process (www.Forrester.com).

2. **Public Procurement Deals**: Public procurement is a process by which large amounts of public funds are utilized by public entities to purchase goods and services from the private sector. Vast amounts of money are therefore expended through the public procurement system. A procurement system that has loose or opaque rules, are poorly enforced, and provides opportunities for misuse of the

contract award process through corruption or other patronage arrangements. Those in the private sector and their collaborators in the public institutions who benefit from such flawed systems have a very deep vested interest in the maintenance of the status quo. Vested interests in such systems can also manifest themselves in various other ways. They could, for example, include local business cartels that may have an interest in maintaining a legal framework that prohibits competition from foreign suppliers. In many developing countries, access to public contracts also serves as a means to reward political supporters and of financing political parties.

3. **Corruption:** Most of the corporate and public sector organisations are entrapped in corruption across the world. For example, BNP Paribas - France's biggest bank, caused hiking in their own interbank rates with other banks on everyday lending to each other, concerned at the possibility of more bad debts being carved out from interbank lending rates. This led to credit - crunch. Having witnessed two events of recessions and consumers have been hit by a series of bank scandals, the economy was further exposed to the breakdown of culture and mismanagement in the UK industry. To quote the chief executive, Peter Vicary-Smith, "Five years on from the beginning of the financial crisis, public confidence in the banking industry is at an all-time low, with a series of scandals exposing mismanagement and corruption at the very heart of the banking system that have costed UK consumers dearly" (www.theguardian.com, 2012). In 2007, heightened inter-bank lending rates, along with the closure of the mortgage securities market, placed the finances of Northern Rock under intolerable pressure. The way the group financed itself, "a reckless business model excessively reliant on wholesale funding," according to MPs, had been caught short by the credit crunch. Panicking customers queued to grab back their savings and the UK's first bank run in 140 years was under way. Both the Royal Bank of Scotland and Halifax Bank of Scotland (HBOS) have been forced to raise billions of pounds in extra capital from their shareholders to shore up the finances. Since the crunch, house prices have fallen, consumer confidence has plummeted and, prices and unemployment have risen. The Rock – the fast-growing banking success story of the previous decade – was on the road to nationalization, a £27bn taxpayer bailout and huge political embarrassment for the government. The public is more disillusioned with the banking sector than ever. (www.theguardian.com, 2012).

4. **Loss of Integrity**: Although the kind of service delivery systems across the supply chain of public sector may differ from country to country, it becomes imperative to ensure that the services are valued and public service ethos be reinforced. Demonstration of disrespect to civilians, dishonesty, partiality, inequity, unaccountability and ineffectiveness in the delivery of services, destroys the integrity between the public sector and recipients of services (Bouder, Bertok & Beschel, 2001). Although there is no perfect definition of integrity (Cox, La Case and Levine (2008), governments which propose to undertake a reformist approach may have to adopt transparency and uphold service towards attainment of such services, which will cater to the public interest. Such an endeavour could reflect the role of public sector and the government to serve the general public and uphold their integrity. Integrity, therefore, would mean a moral character. Integrity is often referred to doing the right thing even when there is no regulatory authority. or even though others do not confirm to the same.

5. **Lack of Transparency**: As recipients of public funds and executors of the public trust, public sector organizations should have high standards of scrutiny and disclosure. Their operations and decisions may be reviewed by bodies such as, the BC Auditor General, the Ombudsman's Office or Select Standing Committees of the Legislature. Disclosure is at the heart of best practice in corporate governance. The duty to disclose information on governance applies with special force on public sector organizations, where there are high expectations of public service and accountability. For these organizations, the duty to make governance-practice accessible to public review accompanies other disclosure requirements established by a provincial legislation or policy. While some public sector organizations in British Columbia publicize their governance practices, full public disclosure is not yet in commonplace.
6. **Disclosure and Transparency**: As recipients of public funds and executors of public trust, public sector organizations are open to high standards of scrutiny and disclosure. Their operations and decisions may be reviewed by bodies such as the BC Auditor General, the Ombudsman's Office or Select Standing Committees of the Legislature. Various "shareholders," including members of the public, often bring diverse viewpoints for their examination of the decisions or the decision-making processes used by public sector organizations. They sometimes rely on the Freedom of Information and Protection of Privacy Act while making their inquiries. The scrutiny of public sector organizations may also extend to the board members. Therefore, individuals joining public sector organization boards should be aware that their actions are potentially subject to the same level of interest and inquiry as other members of the public sector, such as public servants and politicians.

For these and some other reasons, public sector organizations should have good systems in place to ensure that their operations and decision-making processes are consistent with the public sector standards; and these systems should ensure that organizations report appropriately to all the interested parties through accessible avenues of disclosure.

Functional and Dysfunctional Aspects of Distrust

Functional Distrust: Distrust in general context is considered detrimental for a continued relationship. Although subconsciously present, but rarely spoken upfront. Presence of distrust provides potential ground for constructive criticism and change for many individuals. When people have malicious intentions, ulterior motives or they wilfully intend to get favourable gains, they try to exploit others. Therefore, distrust can be a valuable mechanism that send caution signals and makes us alert. The element of distrust makes us more aware of information, environment and prevents us from falling prey to a naive view of other

A certain level of distrust provides scope for introspection and audit to self queries and suggestion improvements. This will automatically avoid compliances and excessive group cohesive behaviour. In addition, a certain amount of distrust quality decision making and arrests, group think and wrongful group stances affects the quality of decision making, and permits functional interaction. Appropriate boundaries should be set for maintaining reasonable relationships and performance outcomes. Having vigilance and building checks and balances by periodic monitoring of their behaviour helps in constructive outcomes and compliance as well. In short, it is possible (and even advisable) to have a blind trust on others as the saying goes "appearances are deceptive." Distrust is particularly encouraged when you do not know them well.

Dysfunctional Distrust: A slight dose of distrust can lead to unwarranted outcomes. Presence of distrust in an element, is associated with a lack of sense of belongingness, wilful cooperation, lower satisfaction and commitment, and leads to possibly vindictive approaches, vengeance and hostile behaviour. Distrust can also lead to over suspicious behaviour and too much of emphasis may be laid on information disclosure. Public sectors and governments take up activities which are sensitive and confidential. Distrust leads the parties to reduce their willingness to share information and engage in problem solving in conflict situations, and hence to distributive bargaining approaches with the other party, an approach that usually overlooks integrative, value-creating opportunities. Distrust can also cause conflicts to escalate to the point of intractability, as positions harden and the parties become increasingly reluctant to yield concessions. Adams and Freedman (1976) recognized individuals who perceive inequity would display anger and may desire for a systemic change. Such change may bring in an upliftment in self image whereby individuals may resist to indulge in personal or intentional attack on institutions. (Adams, & Freedman, 1976; Tepper, 1995). The negative emotions that emerge with distrust, fear, suspicion and anger, cause the trust to vilify and demonize the other party, and can even produce paranoid cognitions. Hence, even though there could be competitive opportunities to create comprehensive agreements or sort out the relationship, on account of distrust, talented individuals are ignored or discounted.

PRACTICAL IMPLICATIONS FOR MANAGING LEVELS OF DISTRUST: WHAT INDIVIDUALS CAN DO

It is important to note that the first element of distrust begins at the individual level. When individuals encounter sudden and provocative distrust, it is perhaps the most disturbing and emotionally challenging. It might cause sudden psychological stress and generate panic. For individuals who have faced distrust might take some time to heal with the experience they had and overcome the fear of occurrence of the same. Some individuals may feel frustrated and even go withdrawn. One of the ways through which individuals can counter distrust against the public sector systems is to expose the systems failure to deliver quality services. More the number of individuals raise their voices and try to highlight the inherent reasons which cause trust deficit, this strategy can help alleviate the apprehension and marginalise the threat of the feeling of vulnerability. When more aggrieved individuals join hands, the public sector organisations will be compelled to address their concerns.

Individuals can also develop derivative plans to implement better services. In order to rectify the negative attitudes against the public sector services, individuals may develop a series of initiatives to present a correct perspective to eliminate the distorted perceptions. Constant public engagement will marginalise the heightened anxiety, and create an atmosphere of mutual trust. Mutual and exclusive reciprocal relationships strengthen the negotiating power. The relationships between Public sector organisations and the third party intermediaries can ensure improved effectiveness and efficiency.

Essentially, when the change is a volunteered by public sectors, the indications will be strong enough to ensure willingness so as to prevent trust deficit. There will be calls for the initiating party to make a general statement indicating a desire to reconstruct the trust levels. When public sector takes steps to provide clear-cut measures which contain direction, clarity, specific, supported by strong political will, it will serve as a benchmark and there will be a new level of verifiable quotient, to depend upon. Trust cycle starts when things changes without much of attention, glare and demand. Conscious efforts with credible performance will ensure that the level of distrust is made non-existential. Consistency in performance delivery will be seen as an essential driving force for triggering the required change. Moreover, public sectors should develop their schemes of actionable plans to be implemented with due diligence, sincerity and reliability.

Impact of Building Trust in National and International Scenario

On account of various interventions developed by the Organisation for Economic Co- operation and Development, Securities and Exchange Commission, anti corruption laws, integrity packs guidelines, anti corruption and bribery conventions, and ratifications, countries across the world are opening up their information and intend to comply with the transparency regime. Interventions to develop trust basis in public sector are as follows:

1. **Transparent Service Delivery Systems:** In such cases, the leadership of the government and the public response to comply with the leadership direction showcases the political will to enhance the trust levels. This further, depends upon the organisational response to the building leaders who nurture a trust based relationship. One has to identify a new imperative for governments: move beyond with a focus on the quality of the service transaction to develop a new kind of relationship with the citizens. This relationship should foster deeper trust; improve the relevance and transparency of government decision making, service design and delivery; and transform the relationship between public services and customers/ citizens from one of dependency to that of shared responsibility. One of the ways, the leaders in customer service are facilitating this relationship is by implementing citizen services portals. Public sector reforms have been achieved with the aid and support of the World Bank. In Vietnam, the Financial Management Information System now operates nationwide and is used for budget execution, accounting and fiscal reporting for the central and all 63 provinces and 700 districts. In Armenia, an Electronic Document Management System (EDMS) has been rolled-out to the entire civil service system, allowing real time communication between central and regional governments and the automation of work planning and performance management process in civil service. In Yemen, the government budget is now published on the Web at the time of its submission to the parliament to obtain citizen's feedback. This has led to a 15-point increase (5th largest in the world) in the Open Budget Index (OBI) between 2008 and 2010.
2. **Integrity Framework Reviews:** The OECD helps countries to review and modernize their integrity framework by mapping out good practices and developing principles, guidelines and tools. Our approach focuses on mapping "at risk" areas vulnerable to misconduct, fraud and corruption. The OECD has developed Principles for Managing Ethics in the Public Service. The Principles were approved as a recommendation by the highest body of the OECD, the Council, in April 1998. The OECD supports and measures progress in the implementation of the Principles by developing frameworks for countries to review and modernize their integrity systems, conducting Integrity Framework Reviews, assembling comparative cross-country benchmarks and indicators. Countries are shifting their efforts from policy design and implementation to assessment of these efforts. The Integrity Framework is a systemic and comprehensive approach to view integrity management within government. It includes firstly, the integrity management systems: the instruments, processes and actors within public sector organisations to stimulate and enforce integrity and prevent corruption and secondly, the integrity context (or supporting

environment) that can have an impact upon the integrity of the members in public sector organisations. With these portals, agencies are able to provide premier services to citizens by making user friendly support service systems.

Exhibit 3 reflects the initiative taken by the US government to develop an comprehensive framework to deal with integrity revenue systems.

3. **Promote Anti Corruption Regime:** The Bribe Payers Index is a unique tool capturing the supply side of international bribery, specifically focussing on bribes paid by the private sector. The 2011 Bribe Payers Index is the fifth edition of the index, ranking 28 of the world's largest economies according to the likelihood of firms from these countries to bribe when doing business abroad. It is based on the results of Transparency International's 2011 Bribe Payers Survey. This asked 3,016 senior business executives in 30 countries around the world for their perceptions of the likelihood of companies, from countries they have business dealings with, to engage in bribery when doing business in the executive's country. A total of 19 sectors were scored and ranked in 2011 using the same methodology as the 2008 index. The 2011 Bribe Payers Survey, on which the index is based, asked business executives how common bribery was in the sectors with which they have business relations. The survey asked how often three different types of bribery were perceived to occur in each sector: firstly, bribery of low-ranking public officials; secondly, improper contributions to high-ranking politicians to achieve influence; and thirdly, bribery between private companies.
4. **RatificationsofInternationalConventions:** OCED has developed a comprehensive anti-bribery Convention which has legally binding standards to criminalize bribery of foreign public officials in international business transactions. It also provides for various measures that make conventions enforceable and ensure that the implementation is effective. It is the first and only international anti-corruption instrument focused on the 'supply side' of the bribery transaction. The 34 OECD member countries and six non-member countries - Argentina, Brazil, Bulgaria, Colombia, Russia, and South Africa - have adopted this Convention. (www.oecd.org/corruption/oecdantibriberyconvention.htm).
5. **Due Diligence on Procurement Deals:** Public Sectors are mostly prone to ill effects

Exhibit 3. Loss of integrity: Transparency international, national integrity system assessment latvia

usiness, Public Sector and the Ombudsman are the most vulnerable pillars of NIS in Latvia. Business operations suffer from extreme and unnecessary administrative burden as state institutions are adamantly controlling on business activities. Their consultations further prove to be a hindrance in overall outcome. The dominant presence of grey economy is incompatible with overall transparent and accountable business sector. The current legal framework limits disclosure of beneficial owners by giving only the controlling authorities access to such information. The apathetic response of the business organisations towards anti-corruption activities further worsens the position.

Situation is nonetheless the same, if not worse, in public sector. Ample number of public officials occupying corruption-sensitive positions are susceptible to particularly daring corruption risks by virtue of radical cut-offs in salaries in wake of economic crisis. At the zenith of public administrative services, it is manifested or ostensible political approval and not actual qualification, which determines selection. Nevertheless, the darkest blot is administration's failure to provide for public education and cooperate with CSOs and other private parties in tackling the corruption issues. It is thus, the prime need of government to fine-tune its anti-corruption policies in order to trigger public agencies to perform within the ambit of their roles, risks and possibilities.

of procurement deals. Asian Development Bank (2003) and the World Bank have provided adequate guidelines to ensure that the parties confirm to the lawful ways of handling transactions. Fundamental reforms to a system in which some or all of those vested interests exist calls for the dismantling of entrenched practices and institutions (both formal and informal) with a view to injecting greater transparency and competition in the system and increasing the level of accountability of the public officials. However, those wishing to maintain the *status quo* resist the change quite strongly because such reforms will normally involve the loss of direct economic and/or political benefits. Furthermore, the political leadership often lacks the will to expend the necessary political capital to overcome the resistance of the often powerful economic forces.

Increased litigation costs due to the procurement deals: Like the private sector, government organizations are beginning to realize substantial reductions in purchasing costs and greater efficiency in administrative operations by transforming procurement from a tactical, transaction-oriented function into a strategic one. A leading-edge approach to strategic sourcing and vendor relations helps governments capture and apply fact-based information about vendor selection and performance. Such an approach creates a shared environment for agencies and their suppliers to communicate coordinate and conduct commerce. By transferring the procurement process from traditional channels—such as paper, mail and telephone—to secure, easy-to-access Web-based applications, governments are transforming purchasing operations and bringing them into line with industry's best practices. These strategic solutions integrate and streamline the entire procurement process, from buyer to supplier and back again. And they're allowing agencies to use buying power to realize a number of valuable and tangible benefits, including: reducing the budget needed for goods and services; capitalizing on declining prices on term contract items; reducing the overall cost of materials management operations; accelerating payments to take advantage of vendor discounts; legal and risk mitigation and increasing productivity.

6. **Self Governance:** Transparency International and Non-governmental body, based in Berlin, aims to fight corruption. It has got 90 chapters and it takes initiatives to create awareness of detrimental effects of corruption. It also provides the consequences and damaging effects when corruption is prevalent among. It also suggests implement effective measures to tackle it (www.transparency.org). The surveys and assessments used to compile the index include questions relating to the bribery of public officials, kickbacks in public procurement, embezzlement of public funds, and questions that probe the strength and effectiveness of public-sector anti-corruption efforts. Public outcry at corruption, impunity and economic instability had sent shockwaves around the world in 2011. Protests in many countries have escalated quickly from small scale action to mass demonstration, uniting people from all parts of society. Their backgrounds may be diverse, but the message is the same: more transparency and accountability from our leaders is needed. The 2011 Corruption Perceptions Index shows that public frustration is well founded. According to the survey reports New Zealand, Denmark and Finland top the list, while North Korea and Somalia are at the bottom. "This year we have seen corruption on protestors' banners be they rich or poor. Whether in a Europe hit by debt crisis or an Arab world starting a new political era, leaders must heed the demands for better government," said Huguette Labelle, Chair of Transparency International. Public-

sector governance that puts the interests of its citizens first is a responsibility that is not restricted to any border. Governments must act accordingly. For their part, citizens need to continue demanding better performance from their leaders.

FUTURE RESEARCH AND EMERGING TRENDS

Declining trust in the public sector is almost an emerging global trend today. Last two decades have seen most of the serious cases like where the trust levels hit a record low across the world. People's trust in the public sector has continuously declined since the 1980s, entered a period of slight recovery in 2000, and then began to fall again in 2010 (www.edelmantrust.com). Generating the public trust can become a reality only by citizenship engagement. Although it is long drawn process by adopting a democratic mechanism citizenship engagement is instrumental in determining acceleration for public trust. Since liberalisation and globalisation, there has been a growing challenge has been the increase in the public's expectations and demands against the government. The limitation has been the public sector institutions constantly weren't able to meet the customers' expectations. The growing gap between government capacity to meet the customers' demands and needs, led to public mistrust toward government and has widened the gap leading to a deficit trust. Across the world in the public sectors and government, policies and enforcement challenges occasionally encounter failures as the public officials' indulge in malpractice and corruption. Lack of distributive and procedural fairness in implementation of public policies often leads to distrust in government. These are some of the significant factors that lead to mistrust in the government. Foreign Investors and people's trust in the government is one of the key factors that determine the government's competitiveness to be at par across the world. A high level of trust leads to better cooperation from the public in implementation of public policies, and this in-turn improves effective policymaking and implementation. For example, more number of people pay their taxes, when their trust in tax-related administrative agencies is high (Mayer *et al.*, 1995). Since 1960, the world has witnessed significant deterioration in political trust. Trust can be build only when consumers' are provided with tangible benefits from the public organizations. The services provided by the government should attempt to minimise the conflict of interests. (Neustadt, 1990). Absence of trust in the government and public sectors occurs when people perceive that their sacrifices do not lead to better future for everyone. (Hetherington, 2005). A high level of public distrust threatens the legitimacy of the government (Miller, 1974) For example, the emergence of internal conflict and disruption within society that occurred in Middle East, Egypt, and Africa reflects the level of public distrust.

CONCLUSION

The author began this chapter by providing a broad view about how trust and distrust are interrelated. The dynamics of interpersonal and intergroup relations among the organisations leads to varied levels of trust and distrust. When the transactions between any two individual donors provide the required degree of trust related outcomes, the dynamics of trust changes over various phases of time. Therefore, the author argues that deficit trust in public sector can play a constructive role in adopting reciprocal and multilayered, and bilateral relations (public-private) promoting government reforms and developing a more responsive administration (Barber, 1983). Too much of corruption leads to continuous decline of public trust in the government. It, not only often creates burden on building capabilities and competitiveness, but also the country may face poor reputation, and may not attract global attention and Foreign Investments which in turn accelerates the economic development. With the high degree of deficit trust in public sector and governmental agencies, the systems enter into a chain reaction causing a vicious cycle. The only remedy available is a strong intervention from the state having a political will. People in democratic systems may perceive that participative forums may provide respite but it will only create an environment of venting out emotional outcry but will not help in policy making. The public sector must develop a robust transparent model to boost the trust levels.

REFERENCES

Adams, J. S., & Freedman, S. (1976). Equity theory revisited: Comments and an annotated bibliography. In L. Berkowitz, & E. Walster (Eds.), *Equity theory: Toward a general theory of social interaction* (pp. 43–90). New York: Academic Press. doi:10.1016/S0065-2601(08)60058-1

Baier, A. (1986). Trust and Antitrust. *Ethics*, *96*(2), 231–260. doi:10.1086/292745

Barber, B. (1983). *The Logic and Limits of Trust*. New Brunswick, NJ: Rutgers University Press.

Barney, J. B., & Hansen, M. H. (1994). Trustworthiness as a Source of Competitive Advantage. *Strategic Management Journal*, *15*(S1), 175–190. doi:10.1002/smj.4250150912

Bies, R. J., & Tripp, T. M. (1996). Beyond Distrust: Getting Even and the Need for Revenge. In *Trust in Organizations: Frontiers of Theory and Research* (pp. 246–260). Thousand Oaks, CA: Sage. doi:10.4135/9781452243610.n12

Bouder, F., Bertok, F., & Beschel, R. (2001). Fostering Public Ethics and Preventing Corruption. In Schiavo-Campo & Sundaram (Eds.), To Serve and Preserve: Improving Public Administration in a Competitive World. Manila: Asian Development Bank.

Bunse, S., & Fritz, V. (2012). *Making Public Sector Reforms Work Political and Economic Contexts, Incentives and Strategies* (working paper 6174). The World Bank.

Butler, J. K. Jr, & Cantrell, R. S. (1984). A behavioral decision theory approach to modeling dyadic trust in superiors and subordinates. *Psychological Reports*, *55*(1), 19–28. doi:10.2466/pr0.1984.55.1.19

Chanley, V. A. (2002). Trust in Government in the Aftermath of 9/11: Determinants and Consequences. *Political Psychology*, *23*(3), 469–483. doi:10.1111/0162-895X.00294

Chanley, V. A., Rudolph, T. J., & Rahn, W. M. (2000). The origins and consequences of public trust in government: A time series analysis. *Public Opinion Quarterly*, *64*(3), 239–256. doi:10.1086/317987 PMID:11114267

Chanley, V. A., Rudolph, T. J., & Rahn, W. M. (2001). Public trust in government in the Reagan years and beyond. In J. R. Hibbing, & E. Theiss-Morse (Eds.), *What is it about government that Americans dislike?* (pp. 59–78). Cambridge, UK: Cambridge University Press.

Charley, B. (1997). Organisational Infidelity: How Violations of Trust Affect the Employee-Employer Relationship. *The Academy of Management Executive*, *11*(4), 94–99.

Child, J. (2001). Trust–the fundamental bond in global collaboration. *Organizational Dynamics*, *29*(4), 274–288. doi:10.1016/S0090-2616(01)00033-X

Cohen, D., & Prusak, L. (2001). *In Good Company: How Social Capital Makes Organizations Work*. Boston, MA: Harvard Business School Press.

Coleman, J. S. (1988). Social capital in the creation of human capital. *American Journal of Sociology*, *94*(s1Supplement), S95–S120. doi:10.1086/228943

Colquitt, J. A., Scott, B. A., & LePine, J. A. (2007). Trust, Trustworthiness, and Trust Propensity: A Meta-Analytic Test of Their Unique Relationships With Risk Taking and Job Performance. *The Journal of Applied Psychology*, *92*(4), 909–927. doi:10.1037/0021-9010.92.4.909 PMID:17638454

Cook, J., & Wall, T. (1980). New Work Attitude Measures of Trust, organizational commitment and personal need no fulfilment. *Journal of Occupational Psychology*, *53*(1), 39–52. doi:10.1111/j.2044-8325.1980.tb00005.x

Cox, D., La Caze, M., & Levine, M. P. (1999). Should We Strive for Integrity? *The Journal of Value Inquiry*, *33*(4), 519–530. doi:10.1023/A:1004614232579

Currall, S. C., & Inkpen, A. C. (2006). On the complexity of organizational trust: A multi-level co-evolutionary perspective and guidelines for future research. In *Handbook of Trust Research*. Edward Elgar Publishing Limited. doi:10.4337/9781847202819.00021

Daley, D. M., & Vasu, M. L. (1998). Fosternig Organizational Trust in North Carolina, The Pivotal Role Of Administrators And Political Leaders. *Administration & Society*, *30*(1), 62–84. doi:10.1177/009539979803000105

Dalton, D. (2000). Understanding High Performance Organizations. *Security*, *37*, 69.

De Furia, G. L. (1997). *Facilitators Guide to the Interpersonal Trust Surveys*. Pfeiffer & Co.

Deutsch, M. (1958). Trust and Suspicion. *The Journal of Conflict Resolution*, *2*(4), 265–279. doi:10.1177/002200275800200401

Deutsch, M. (1973). *The Resolution of Conflict: Constructive and Destructive Processes*. New Haven, CT: Yale University Press.

Dietz, & Hartog. (2006). Measuring trust inside organisations. *Personnel Review*, *35*(5), 557–588.

Dirks, K. T. (2000). Trust in leadership and team performance: Evidence from NCAA basketball. *The Journal of Applied Psychology*, *85*(6), 1004–1012. doi:10.1037/0021-9010.85.6.1004 PMID:11125648

Doyle, B. (2008). Customer Advocacy: How US Consumers Rate Their Banks, Brokerages, And Insurers. *Forrester Research Inc*. Retrieved September 2, 2013, from http://www.forrester.com/rb/Research/customer_advocacy_2008_how_us_consumers _rate/q/id/46083/t/2

Edelenbos, J., & Klijn, E. (2007). Trust in complex decision-making networks: A theoretical and empirical exploration. *Administration & Society*, *39*(1), 25–50. doi:10.1177/0095399706294460

Ellis, K. & Shockley-Zalabak. (1999). *Communicating with management: Relating trust to job satisfaction and organizational effectiveness*. Paper presented at the National Communication Association Convention. Chicago, IL.

Ezezika, O. C., Deadman, J., Murray, J., Mabeya, J., & Daar, A. S. (2013). To trust or not to trust: A model for effectively governing public-private partnerships. *AgBioForum*, *16*(1), 27–36.

Fairholm, G. W. (1994). *Leadership and the Culture of Trust*. Westport, CT: Praeger.

Ferrin, D. L. (2001). The role of trust in organizational settings. *Organization Science*, *12*(4), 450–467. doi:10.1287/orsc.12.4.450.10640

Fomburn, C. J. (1996). *Reputation*. Boston: Harvard Business School Press.

Fox, A. (1974). *Beyond Contract: Work, Power and Trust Relations*. Faber.

Frederique, S., & Sorge, A. (2008). Creating a High-Trust Organisation: An Exploration into Organisational Policies that Stimulate Interpersonal Trust Building. *Journal of Management Studies*, *45*(5), 857–884. doi:10.1111/j.1467-6486.2007.00763.x

Fukuyama, F. (1995). *Trust: Social Virtues and the Creation of Prosperity*. New York: Free Press.

Fukuyama, F. (2001). Social capital, civil society, and development. *Third World Quarterly*, *22*(1), 7–20. doi:10.1080/713701144

Gabarro, J. J. (1978). The Development of Trust, Influence, and Expectations. In *Interpersonal Behavior: Communication and Understanding in Relationships* (pp. 290–303). Englewood Cliffs, NJ: Prentice-Hall.

Galford, R., & Drapeau, A. S. (2002). *The Trusted Leader: Bringing Out the Best in Your People and Your Company*. The Free Press.

Galford, R., & Drapeau, A. S. (2003). Enemies of Trust. *Harvard Business Review*, *81*(2), 1–8. PMID:12577656

Galford, R., & Drapeau, A. S. (2003). Trusted Leadership. *Executive Excellence*, *20*(1), 12.

Gambetta, D. (1988). *Trust: Making and Breaking Cooperative Relations*. Oxford, UK: Blackwell.

Gerald, A. E. (2010). Ethics of Innovation for Public Service Professionals. *The Innovation Journal: The Public Sector Innovation Journal, Volume, 15*(3), Article 2.2.

GfK Global Trust. (n.d.). Germans place more trust in government again. *GfK Global Trust Report 2013*. Retrieved August 26, 2013, from http://www.gfk-verein.org/index.php?article_id=301&clang=1

Gittell, J. H., & Douglass, A. (2012). Relational Bureaucratic Form: Embedding Reciprocal Relationships into Roles. *Academy of Management Review*, *37*(4), 709–733. doi:10.5465/amr.2010.0438

Governance and Public Sector Management. (n.d.). Retrieved September 5, 2013, from http://siteresources.worldbank.org/PUBLICSECTORANDGOVERNANCE/Resources/285741-1348676611027/PSGDataSheet.pdf

Granovetter, M. (1985). Economic Action and Social Structure: The Problem of Embeddedness. *American Journal of Sociology*, *91*(3), 481–510. doi:10.1086/228311

Hetherington, J. M. (2005). *Why Trust Matters: Declining political Trust and the demise of American Liberalism*. Princeton, NJ: Princeton University Press.

Hoy, W. K., & Tschannen-Moran, M. (1999). Five faces of Trust: An Empirical Confirmation in Urban Elementary Schools. *Journal of School Leadership*, *9*(3), 184–208.

Jacobs. (2013). What can HR do to change the banking culture and rebuild trust? *JD Power and Associates*. Retrieved August 24, 2013, from http://www.jdpower.com/autos/ratings/auto-insurance-provider-ratings/

Jarvenpaa, S. L., Tractinsky, N., & Vitale, M. (1998). *Consumer trust in an internet store* (Working Paper). Department of MSIS, University of Texas, Austin, TX.

Jordan, S. A. (1999). Innovative Cultures + Empowered Employees = High Perfomanse Organizations. *Public Productivity and management. RE:view*, *23*, 109–115. doi: doi:10.2307/3380798

Julia, J. (2006). Organisation-Stakeholder-relationships: Exploring Trust and Transparency. *Journal of Management Development*, *25*(10), 942–945. doi:10.1108/02621710610708577

Lewicki, R. J., & Bunker, B. B. (1996). Developing and Maintaining trust in work relationships. In *Trust in Organisations* (pp. 119–124). Thousand Oaks, CA: Sage Publications. doi:10.4135/9781452243610.n7

Lewicki, R. J., McAllister, D. J., & Bies, R. J. (1998). Trust and distrust: New relationships and realities. *Academy of Management Review*, *23*, 438–458.

Lewicki, R. J., & Wiethoff, C. (2000). Trust, Trust development and Trust Repair. In *The Handbook of Conflict Resolution*. San Francisco: Jossey-Bass.

Lewicki & Wiethoff. (2000). Trust, Trust Development, and Trust Repair. In *The Handbook of Conflict Resolution: Theory and Practice* (pp. 86–107). San Francisco: Jossey-Bass Publishers.

Lewiski, R., Tomlinson, E., & Gillespie, N. (2006). Models of interpersonal trust development: Theoretical approaches, empirical evidence and future directions. *Journal of Management*, *32*(6), 991–1022. doi:10.1177/0149206306294405

Luhmann, N. (n.d.). Familiarity, Confidence, Trust: Problems and Alternatives. In *Trust: Making and Breaking Cooperative Relations* (pp. 94–107). New York: Blackwell.

Mayer, R. C., Davis, & Schoormann. (1995). An Integrative Model of Organisational Trust. *Academy of Management Review*, *20*(3), 709–734.

McCauley, D. P., & Kuhnert, K. W. (1992). A Theoretical Review and Empirical Investigation of Employee Trust in Management. *Public Administration Quarterly*, *16*, 265–285.

McEvily, B., Perrone, V., & Zaheer, A. (2003). Trust as an organizing principle. *Organization Science*, *14*(1), 91–103. doi:10.1287/orsc.14.1.91.12814

McKnight, D. H., & Chervany, N. L. (n.d.). While trust is cool and collected, distrust is fiery and frenzied: A model of distrust concepts. In D. Strong, D. Straub, & J.I. DeGross (Eds.), *Proceedings of the Seventh Americas Conference on Information Systems* (pp. 883–888). Boston: Omnipress.

Mishra, A. K. (1996). Organizational responses to crisis: The centrality of trust. In R. M. Kramer, & T. R. Tyler (Eds.), *Trust in Organizations: Frontiers of Theory and Research* (pp. 261–287). Thousand Oaks, CA: Sage. doi:10.4135/9781452243610.n13

Mishra, A. K., & Mishra, K. E. (1994). The role of mutual trust in effective downsizing strategies. *Human Resource Management*, *33*(2), 261–279. doi:10.1002/hrm.3930330207

Mishra, A. K., & Spreitzer, G. M. (1998). Explaining How Survivors Respond to Downsizing: The Roles of Trust, Empowerment, Justice, and Work Redesign. *Academy of Management Review*, *23*(3), 567–588.

Mitchell, C. (2011). *Achieving Customer-led Growth in Insurance-Three steps to improve retention and return to growth* (IBM Global Business Services, White Paper). IBM Corporation.

Moon. (2003). Can IT Help Government to Restore Public Trust? Declining Public Trust and Potential Prospects of IT in the Public Sector. In *Proceedings of the 36th Hawaii International Conference on System Sciences*. Retrieved September 9, 2013, from http://citeseerx.ist.psu.edu/viewdoc/download?doi=10.1.1.4.2836&rep=rep1&type=pdf

Muraskin, W. (2002). The last years of the CVI and the birth of GAVI. In M. R. Reich (Ed.), *Public-private partnerships for public health* (pp. 115–168). Cambridge, MA: Harvard University Press.

Neustadt, R. (1990). *Presidential Power and the Modern Presidents: The Politics of Leadership from Roosevelt to Reagan*. New York: Free Press.

Osborn, C. (Ed.). (2000). *Public-private partnerships: Theory and practice in international perspective*. London: Routledge.

Parasuraman, B., & Radhakrishnan, B. (2011). Employee participation in the Public sector in Malayasia: A General Overview. *Journal of Arts. Science and Commerce*, *2*(1), 55–69.

Parkhe, A. (1993). Strategic Allaince Structure, A Game theoretic and transaction cost examination of inter-firm cooperation. *Academy of Management Journal*, *24*(4), 794–829. doi:10.2307/256759

Pew Research Center. (2013). Majority Says the Federal Government Threatens Their Personal Rights. *Pew Research Center for the People and & the Press*. Retrieved September 4, 2013, from http://www.people-press.org/2013/01/31/majority-says-the-federal-government-threatens-their-personal-rights/2/

Pfeffer, J. (1998). *The Human Equation*. Boston, MA: Harvard Business School Press.

Phillips, C. J. (1997). Do you Trust me? *Executive Excellence*, *14*, 7–10.

Press Association. (n.d.). Financial crisis, five years on: trust in banking hits new low. *Press Association*. Retrieved September 15, 2013, from http://www.theguardian.com/business/2012/aug/09/financial-crisis-anniversary-trust-in-banks

Public Sector Integrity Reviews. (n.d.). Fighting corruption in the public sector - Why integrity matters for governments? *Public Sector Integrity Reviews*. Retrieved August 24, 2013, from http://www.oecd.org/governance/ethics/publicsectorintegrityreviews.htm

Rotter, J. B. (1980). Interpersonal Trust, Trustworthiness, and Gullibility. *The American Psychologist*, *35*(1), 1–7. doi:10.1037/0003-066X.35.1.1

Rousseau, D. M., Sitkin, S. B., Burt, R. S., & Camerer, C. (1998). Not so Different After All: A Cross-Discipline View of Trust. *Academy of Management Review*, *23*(3), 393–404. doi:10.5465/AMR.1998.926617

Rowe, & Calnan. (2006). Trust relations in health care: Developing a theoretical framework for the new NHS. *Journal of Health Organization and Management, 20* (5), 376 – 396.

Sarker, A. E. (2006). New Public Management in Developing Countries – An analysis of success and failure with particular reference to Singapore and Bangladesh. *International Journal of Public Sector Management*, *19*(2), 180–203. doi:10.1108/09513550610650437

Savage, D. (1982). Trust as a Productivity Management Tool. *Training and Development Journal*, *36*, 54–57.

Schon, D. (1983). *The Reflective Practitioner*. New York, NY: Basic Books.

Shockley-Zalabak, P., Ellis, K., & Winograd, G. (2000). Organizational Trust: What it Mean and Why it Matters. *Organization Development Journal*, *18*, 35–48.

Sitkin, S. B., & Roth, N. L. (1993). Explaining the Limited Effectiveness of Legalistic Remedies for Trust / Distrust. *Organization Science*, *4*(3), 367–392. doi:10.1287/orsc.4.3.367

Stern, S., Manning, H., & Connor, C. O. (2013). *Sharpen Customer Experience Focus With Employee Engagement*. Retrieved September 3, 2013, from http://www.forrester.com/Sharpen+Customer+Experience+Focus+With+Employee+Engagement /fulltext/-/E-res101141

Temkin. (n.d.). Customer Experience Boosts Revenue. *Forrester Research, Inc*. Retrieved September 5, 2013, from http://www.forrester.com/rb/Research/customer_experience_boosts_revenue/q/id/54750/t/2

Tepper, B. J. (1995). Upward maintenance tactics in supervisory mentoring and nonmentoring relation-ships. *Academy of Management Journal*, *38*(4), 1191–1205. doi:10.2307/256626

Tepper, B. J. (2000). Consequences of abusive supervision. *Academy of Management Journal*, *43*(2), 178–190. doi:10.2307/1556375

Tucker, T. (1998). A Critical Analysis of the Procurement Procedures of the World Bank. In S. Arrowsmith, & A. Davies (Eds.), *Public Procurement: Global Revolution* (pp. 139–157). London: Kluwer Law International.

Turnbull, S. (1997). Corporate governance: Its scope, concerns & theories, *Corporate Governance. International Review (Steubenville, Ohio)*, *5*(4), 180–205.

Webb, E. J. (1996). Trust and Crisis. In *Trust in Organizations: Frontiers of Theory and Research* (pp. 288–301). Thousand Oaks, CA: Sage.

Whitener, E. M., Brodt, Korsgaard, & Werner. (1998). Managers as Initiators of Trust: An Exchange Relationship Framework for Understanding Managerial Trustworthy Behavior. *Academy of Management Review*, *23*(3), 513–530.

Wicks, A. C., Berman, S. L., & Jones, T. M. (1999). The Structure of Optimal Trust: Moral and strategic Implications. *Academy of Management Review*, *24*(1), 99–116.

Wilson, E. J., Bunn, M. D., & Savage, G. T. (2010). Anatomy of a social partnership: A stakeholder perspective. *Industrial Marketing Management*, *39*(1), 76–90. doi:10.1016/j.indmarman.2008.06.005

Worchel, P. (1979). Trust and Distrust. In *The Social Psychology of Intergroup Relations* (pp. 174–187). Wadsworth.

World Bank. (2009). *Governance and Anticorruption in Lending Operations: A Benchmarking and Learning Review*. Retrieved from http://siteresources.worldbank.org/EXTLAWJUSTINST/Resources/GAC_review_2009.pdf

Wright, B. E., & Pandey, S. K. (2010). Transformational Leadership in the Public Sector: Does Structure Matter? *Journal of Public Administration: Research and Theory*, *20*(1), 75–89. doi:10.1093/jopart/mup003

You, J. (2005). *A Study of Social Trust in South Korea, with Comparative Perspectives*. Paper presented at the Annual Conference of the American Sociological Association. Philadelphia, PA.

Zalabak, P. S., & Winograd, G. (2000). Organizational Trust: What It Means, Why It Matters. *Organization Development Journal*, *18*(4), 35–49.

Zand, D. E. (1972). Trust and Managerial Problem Solving. *Administrative Science Quarterly*, *17*(2), 229–239. doi:10.2307/2393957

Zand, D. E. (1997). *The Leadership Triad – Knowledge, Trust and Power*. Oxford University Press.

KEY TERMS AND DEFINITIONS

Trust (1): As willingness for discovering owns vulnerability towards other person whose behaviour cannot be controlled, in the situation in which potential benefits are much smaller in relation to the potential losses if other person takes advantage of that vulnerability" (Zand, 1997).

Trust (2): Among the individuals and groups in an organization are very important and significant for a long-term stability of organization and well-being of its members" (Cook and Wall, 1980).

Chapter 4
Customers' Satisfaction and Loyalty in the Economic Recession:
The Case of a Greek Bank

Irene Samanta
Graduate Technological Education Institute of Piraeus, Greece

ABSTRACT

This chapter examines the main criteria that influence customer satisfaction and its effects on a case bank. The study identifies the actions that banks take into account and analyses the elements that can be improved in order to keep their customers satisfied and loyal during the economic recession. The research clarifies the satisfaction criteria, including ease of access, service provided, products and personnel, that are perceived as important in the evaluation of customer satisfaction. Quantitative research was conducted with 419 customers of a Greek bank. The results unexpectedly showed that respondents were satisfied with the bank. Competitive advantages were based mainly on quality service and personnel. Customers continue to use the bank for their transactions and to recommend new customers. The results also confirm the hypotheses that "total customer satisfaction" is related to "loyalty," "recommendation," and "complaints handling." However, in general their interrelationships did not fit the linear regressions cases.

INTRODUCTION

Financial services have experienced several changes over the last decade with a growing attention to customer needs. The National Bureau of Economic Research (NBER) defines recession as "a period of falling economic activity spread across the economy, lasting more than a few months, normally visible in real GDP, real income, employment, industrial production, and wholesale-retail sales." Financial institutions (banks) realised the strategic importance of customer value and seem to be continuously seeking innovative ways to enhance customer relationships. The bank sector the recent years is becoming ever more competitive,

DOI: 10.4018/978-1-4666-6232-2.ch004

as price competition intensifies and the shifting of loyalty becomes an acceptable practice.

Banks have realised the importance of loyalty, customer satisfaction, customer retention and profitability in order to understand customer preferences and to diagnose the switching behaviours of their customers or elements that should improve. Little is known between about the bond between customer and bank with the results that the payoffs of such marketing activities are uncertain. Although the studies on the effects of economic recession and customer loyalty are rather scarce, some empirical evidence is available. Williams and Naumann (2011:20) investigated the problem of customer loyalty and its changes during the times of economic crises and recessions. Past researchers have only conducted secondary analysis of data and came to a conclusion that the recession of 2009 stimulated a decrease in customer loyalty to the large organisations. This can be explained by the worsened performance of the companies, shattered corporate governance and decreased trust of consumers in the companies. The decrease in trust can be interpreted as a result of future expectations of even worse performance that may put the customers and stakeholders of the companies at risk. So, according to Williams and Naumann (2011:20) one of the most important factors of customer loyalty during periods of economic recession is the financial performance of organisations and their solvency

Newman and Cowling (1996) stated that excellent service quality is a one-way road for modern banks. Quality differentiates one bank from another and this is perceived as important in business profitability and survival. The impact of service quality and corporate profitability seems to be dependent on high levels of customer satisfaction, on targeting "good" clients and, above all, on the retention of these customers. Jones and Sasser (1995) stated that the goal is "complete customer satisfaction." This is the key for customer loyalty and long-term financial success. Zeithaml et al., (1990) stated that management's failure to identify customer desires is one kind of quality gap. From many studies, it has been derived that the most important criteria assessed by customers for choosing a bank are related to service quality and the delivery system. Zeithaml et al., (1996) indicated that examining the link between customer satisfaction and behavioural responses helps towards understanding the link between customer satisfaction and the financial outcomes of an organisation. The traditional product-oriented bank has transformed to a customer-oriented organisation working in a very competitive environment. The internationalisation of markets, telecommunications and the technology boom as well as the liberalisation of unified geographical areas has all helped this direction.

It is obvious that modern banks have gained market share constantly because modern banks do something better. This advantage is supposed to be reflected in perceived customer satisfaction. The main subject of this survey is to measure the impact of customer satisfaction on business growth. It is supposed that the elements of perceived customer satisfaction include Ease of Access, Service provided, Products and Personnel. These elements are perceived as equally weighted antecedents of customer satisfaction and almost all of them share attributes of service quality. There were many differences in bank determinants prior to the 1990s because of the lack of technology (ATM, Internet banking and phone banking), which meant that the location and size of branches were very important. Gupta and Torkzadeh (1988) in Winnipeg (Canada) and Laroche et al., (1986) in Montreal (Canada) showed that the friendliness and politeness of bank personnel, the management of accounts, the rate of interest paid and the procedures of transactions are the most important factors for choosing a bank. Price competitiveness was proven to be of minimum importance, which was something that was derived from Zineldin's (1992) research that stated that the banking industry is unique and differs from most other service industries.

Banking is considered to be a relationship where the customer is willing to pay slightly more in order to have speedy and high-quality service. This survey aims to confirm the hypothesis that customer satisfaction has a direct relationship with complaints handling, future use, usage continuity, repurchase intention and recommendation intention and that these relationships fit a two-variable or a multivariable linear regression case.

The basic objectives are to identify satisfaction criteria that are perceived as important in the valuation of customer satisfaction. Furthermost, the present research defines the notions of customer satisfaction, service quality and customer loyalty and correlate the interrelationships between these variables and explain their impact on perceived customer satisfaction.

THEORETICAL APPROACH

Customer Satisfaction

Surveys conducted by the University of Michigan Business School (2001) found that customers feel disrespected and mistreated by banks in general. Related surveys showed that there is a decline in the level of respect given to clients and despite the fact that business is growing quality is shrinking. This reality has a direct impact not only on customer satisfaction, but also on the profitability and performance of banks.

According to Reis et al., (2003), there has been a fundamental shift in how companies treat their customers. With the help of technology, organisations can measure what are the expectations of their customers and then deliver quality products and services at a profit. Anderson et al., (1994) proved that increasing customer satisfaction leads to higher and more stable profitability, increased consumer willingness to pay price premiums, recommendations of new potential customers, more usage of the product, higher repurchase intentions (Reitchheld 1996) and higher levels of customer retention and loyalty (Fornell 1992).

Drucker (1954) underpinned that the principal purpose of a business is to create satisfied customers. According to Bloemer et al., (1998), customer satisfaction is generally described as the full meeting of one's expectations. Fornell (1992) defined customer satisfaction as an overall evaluation of the total purchase experience compared with pre-purchase expectations over time. Oliver (1999) regarded satisfaction as a fulfilment judgment, focused on a product or service, which is evaluated for one time or repeated consumption. Oliver (1997) claimed that satisfaction is derived from the Latin *satis* (enough) and *facere* (to do or make).

Bloemer et al., (1998) argued that there is confusion about the relationship between customer satisfaction and service quality. They found that service quality can be taken as a determinant of customer satisfaction. Bank customers have certain expectations prior to their contact with the bank. They develop perceptions during their service from the bank and compare these perceptions with their expectations. While customer satisfaction and service quality have similar characteristics, they have some basic differences. In the first place, it is argued that in order to form a satisfaction perception, usage of the service is a prerequisite, whereas service quality does not necessarily need experience of the service provided.

According to Levesque and McDougal (1996), the major gains in customer satisfaction derive from changes in service quality, service characteristics and successful customer complaint handling . Peter and Olson (1996) argued that pre-purchase expectations are beliefs about the expected quality and functionality of the product, while disconfirmation deals with the differences between pre-purchase expectations and post-purchase opinion. This means that when the perceived opinion, after the purchase of the product/service, is higher than the pre-purchase expecta-

Figure 1. Hypothesized bank customer satisfaction model

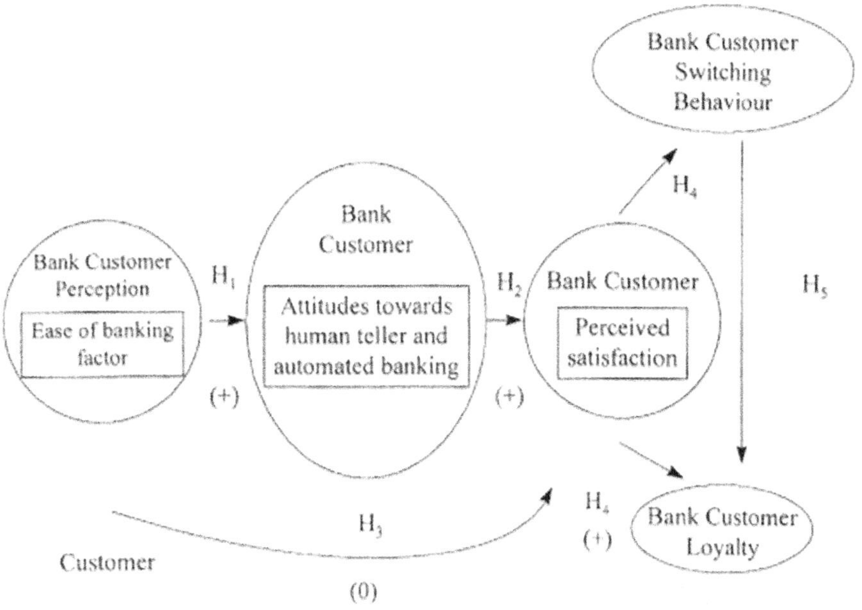

tion customers are satisfied. When the opposite happens, then customers are dissatisfied and the company deals with "negative disconfirmation."

Hallowel (1996) assumed that there is a positive relationship between customer satisfaction, service quality and loyalty, which this survey acknowledges and will try to confirm. The basic case of this survey is adapted from the research of Moutinho and Smith (2000) (Figure 1). Moutinho and Smith (2000) argued that a number of researchers have found that service-related factors such as speed, efficiency, access and services are ways of attracting, satisfying and retaining customers. Perceived customer satisfaction is confirmed and this is reflected in switching behaviour and customer loyalty.

Hypothesis 3 (H3 – perceived satisfaction) is the addition of "Ease of banking" (H1) and "Attitudes" (H2). H3 is directly linked with "Switching costs" and "Customer loyalty." Moreover, the created switching costs end up in customer loyalty. This means that H1 and H2 are indirectly connected (via customer satisfaction) with customer loyalty.

Customers' attitudes have been developed in order to measure perceptions about service delivery and how they affect customer behaviour. Moreover, the ease of banking factor includes all service channels of modern banks as well as the time needed for delivering services. Manrai and Manrai (1993) stated that there is no direct impact of ease of banking and customer attitudes on loyalty and switching costs. Their connection comes through customer satisfaction and this is confirmed by the results of the present survey (Peppers & Rogers, 2004).

Service Quality

As mentioned, research into customer satisfaction is often associated with service quality dimensions. Bitner and Hubbert (1994) defined service quality as the customer's overall impression about the perceived superiority of a company and its products/services, while satisfaction is defined as the feeling of a customer after the usage and purchase of a product or service.

Many authors have discussed the relationship between customer satisfaction and service quality. Taylor and Baker (1994) considered them as different elements that should be treated as equivalents in cases of customer decision-making. Levesque and McDougal (1996) stated that there are two overriding dimensions of service quality. The first concerns the core aspects of the service (e.g. reliability) and the second concerns the process aspects of the service (e.g. responsiveness, assurance). The outcome of the analysis of this survey confirms that these two dimensions are antecedents of customer satisfaction.

Banking services are intangible and thus it is very difficult for customers to assess service quality. This is why Bitner (1990) stated that customers make conclusions about service quality based on tangible items such as premises and the physical layouts that surround the service environment. Smith (2000) examined the dimensionality of the service quality construct and distinguished three dimensions: access/convenience, human elements and tangibles.

Access and Convenience are considered to be very important for making it easy for customers. In a service provider such as a bank, Human Resources are the main assets of the organisation. The skills and attitudes of the personnel offer competitive advantages and differentiate one bank from another. Finally, tangibles such as the architectural design or functionality of the procedures reinforce the perceived holistic image of the organisation.

For the purpose of the present survey, convenience and accessibility are treated as parts of the tangible dimension of service quality, which is perceived as an important antecedent of customer satisfaction. All the important elements of customer satisfaction and service quality will be grouped into categories and will be included in the questionnaire.

Loyalty

Reicheld and Sasser (1990) argued that the retention of customers has a strong impact on a company's results. Fornell and Wernerfelt (1987) added that less defection of customers affects market share. Reitchheld and Sasser (1993) state that building effective relationships with clients can contribute significantly to loyalty, customer satisfaction and financial results. These two authors confirmed that when a company increases by 5% its loyal customers, profits rise by 25-125%. As a result that it is better for a company to spend resources in order to keep existing customers than it is to attract new ones. Attracting new customers means expenditure on advertising and promotions and at the beginning of the relationship a compromise with profitability. Customer loyalty to banks was studied by Ehigie (2006:494) and Baumann et al., (2011: 247). Ehigie (2006: 494) evaluated the influence of customer satisfaction, expectations and perceived service quality on customer loyalty to banks. He found that customer satisfaction was the strongest factor among the rest. Baumann et al (2011: 247), in contrast found that the seeking of variety and resistance to changes were the most significant factors of customer loyalty to banks. Lee et al., (2011: 150) also revealed that the number of ads published by banks was reduced during the economic recession

Nikolopoulou (2006) wrote that the notions of customer service and customer satisfaction are connected with effective complaints handling. It must be clarified first to shareholders and then to the personnel that complaints are not "problems" or "threats" but must be perceived as "gifts." When this "gift" is used properly, it can add value to the company and improve the general image of the organisation. Politeness, promptness and smiling are necessary characteristics of the employees who serve customers or who deal with customer complaints. Despite the fact that these characteristics do not cost anything to the company, they increase customer satisfaction considerably and consequently customer loyalty and profitability.

Karatepe and Ekiz (2004) argued that unresolved problems may lead to the permanent loss of customers and negative word-of-mouth. Empirical research conducted by authors such as Bodgett and Anderson (2000) and Maxham and Netemeyer (2002) has proven that satisfied complainants tend to repurchase and to recommend new customers and feel, in general, satisfied with the entire organisation.

Bloemer et al., (1998) supported the notion that repeat purchasing or visiting sequence, as a method of measuring loyalty, must not be the only factor for assessing loyalty. For instance, a low degree of repurchasing could mean that customers do not need any other products (i.e. mortgage loan) or that the variety of products cannot satisfy their needs. Of course, this factor is very important but it is not the only one needed to be analysed.

According to East (1997), when customers are satisfied with a particular product or service, they are likely to engage in repeat purchases or cross-purchases. Taylor and Baker (1994) stated that customer satisfaction has a direct impact on the formation of future purchase intentions. File and Prince (1992) identified a strong impact of customer satisfaction on the recommendation of potential customers. They stated that satisfied customers are likely to communicate to others their good experiences and through this communication they contribute to word-of-mouth advertising. Ewing (2000) underpinned that the higher the customer's intention to purchase a brand, the higher will be his or her willingness to make a referral of a potential customer to that brand.

Banking Sector and the Case Bank

Zineldin (1996) predicted that banks would move into a competitive financial environment providing a variety of products/services. No bank can offer the best products every time in any different category. Moreover, no bank can satisfy all customers. Banks usually differentiate their products in order to reach more efficiently different market segments. Personalised service and a customer-oriented approach will lead to customer loyalty and customer retention. The banking industry was characterised by a stable environment for decades; however, modern banks operate in a very competitive, international environment that was created mainly by the growth of technology and telecommunications as well as by the deregulation of markets and economic crises.

The case bank showed tremendous growth and decisiveness because it managed to double retail branches in under than three years. From its first day in business, it created a Complaints Handling Department and it conducts customer satisfaction surveys at least twice per year. The case bank is a customer-oriented organisation that manages to grow over its competitors at an amazing pace. This is the first reason for choosing this firm as the case for this survey. The second, but no less important, reason is because the case bank is a "pure" modern firm. This means that it is not an outcome of acquisitions and mergers but strategically follows "greenfield" expansion. The third reason and at the same time one of the hypotheses, is that having achieved an amazing performance in a very short time period, it means that its customers must feel more than satisfied.

METHODOLOGICAL FRAME

After dealing with the conceptual background, an empirical study is carried out in order to test the basic hypotheses that concern Greek retail banking and customer satisfaction in a modern bank. For the data analysis, the SPSS program was used. The questionnaire was adapted from other questionnaires (Athanasopoulos & Gounaris 2001; Mihelis et al., 1998; Ewing 2000). The questions that were perceived as important were developed and added to the questionnaire.

The first section was developed in order to identify the most important factors that make customers collaborate with the case bank using a closed ranking question. The following five sections used five-item Likert scales ("Very satisfied" to "Very dissatisfied") to deal with perceived customer satisfaction and included "Access," "Service," "Products," "Personnel" and "Overall Satisfaction." "Loyalty" in the seventh section includes "Complaints handling," "Continuous Usage," "Future usage" and "Recommendation." Loyalty was measured indirectly because it was perceived as very difficult to obtain a clear answer about purchase repetition. In order to do this, a five-item Likert scale was used to measure intention to switch banks and willingness to recommend the bank to potential customers.

The presented customer satisfaction survey took place from December 2011 to February 2012 in seven branches located in Athens. This choice was made because of the focused expansion of the case bank and because a large percentage of the Greek population lives in Athens.

According to Saunders et al., (2003), in order to have a margin of error of up to 5%, for a population of 1,000,000 the suggested sample should be 384 questionnaires. The clientele of the case bank did not exceed 400,000 and so the final dataset of 419 questionnaires was considered to be acceptable. After a short test period, the questionnaires were asked of customers visiting branches to carry out transactions or to ask information about products. The response rate was more than 98%. Respondents were shared equally between the two genders. The target group of the case bank is customers from 25 to 45 years that are educated with an income from average to high. This target group is reflected here as the 68.2% of respondents are aged from 25 to 45 years old and as the education level of 47.1% was university and postgraduate education.

STATISTICAL ANALYSIS

Reasons for This Collaboration

The main purpose of the first question was to identify the most important factors that make a customer keep his or her relationship with the case bank. The task was to calculate the percentage of customers that ranked each variable between the first four positions and compare this percentage with the percentage of customers that ranked the same variable between the last four positions. Fol-

Table 1. Reasons of collaboration

	Important	*Non-Important*
Q1.1. Modern and innovative	44.80%	55.10%
Q1.2. Image and prestige	33.40%	66.50%
Q1.3. Overall quality of products and	42.70%	57.20%
Q1.4. Nearby branch	58.20%	41.90%
Q1.5. Service from personnel	87.50%	12.50%
Q1.6. Accessibility to alternative	50.80%	48.30%
Q1.7. Clarity of information provided	44.50%	55.50%
Q1.8. Speed and efficiency	63.40%	36.60%

lowing this tactic, a table was derived with two columns. The first column includes the first cumulative percentage and it is named "important," and the second column is named "non-important" and includes the second cumulative percentages (Table 1).

The least important factors for having a relationship are image and prestige (Q1.2). This is not very strange because everyone that has a relationship with a financial institution or a bank takes for granted that this organisation is trustful and prestigious (Ball 2004).

A similar conclusion can be drawn from the low rate of Q1.7 (Clarity of information provided), where it is obvious that this is not an important factor for satisfaction or trust, or for the retention of a banking relationship.

The intense competition that characterises the banking industry led to the homogeneity of products, services and charges. No competitive advantage gained from innovative products lasts more than several weeks. Of course, innovative products offer first-mover advantages but after a while all products are copied and become similar. The low rate of variable Q1.3 (Overall Quality of Products and Services) reflects this reality (H5). Products, although necessary for satisfaction, are not the most important factor or even the only factor for keeping a fruitful banking relationship.

Q1.6 (Accessibility to Alternative Channels) reflects that customers take the presence of alternative channels for granted. Today, all retail banks in Greece provide at least ATM access. This factor could be characterised as "indifferent" for keeping a relationship with modern banks but of course something that must always exist and run well. Q1.4 (Nearby Branch) is the third most important factor for retaining a good relationship. According to Thwaites and Vere (1995), access/convenience is a very important factor both for choice of bank and for customer satisfaction. Modern banks have realised this and they always try to expand more, reaching the sizes of networks that belong to old or state-owned banks.

The second most important factor is "Speed and Efficiency" (Q1.8). It is well known that queues and response time in old and very large banks are a deterrent for keeping a banking relationship. This constitutes a sustainable competitive advantage for modern banks, which helps them create satisfied and loyal customers. Finally, the most important factor analysed in this section was the quality of service provided by the personnel (Q1.5). The very high rate of this variable was a surprise. Banking is a labour-intensive industry, so it is obvious that the most important assets are its employees. This is exactly the conclusion of this analysis.

Access

Customers are very satisfied with all elements of "Access" with a slight primacy for "service systems" (Table 2).

As shown above, all the satisfaction percentages are excellent. This means that access of any kind is achieved satisfactorily. The result for the location of the branches and system availability are excellent. The lower rates of Q2.3 ("Alternative channels") and Q2.4 ("Phone banking") are easy to explain because not all customers use or want to have access to these services. Another remark here was the below 3% answers for "dissatisfied" and "very dissatisfied" customers for all questions. Concluding, one could say that with a total satisfaction rate of 89.9% "Access" is a very strong element of customer satisfaction (H4).

Service

The service provided by a bank in general is believed to be one of the most important factors of overall satisfaction. Service can differentiate one bank from another and can offer competitive advantages that are not easy to copy or transfer. As shown in Table 3, respondents are very satisfied with all the elements of "Service."

The total satisfaction level from "Service" is excellent and this has a very positive impact on

Table 2. Access

Q2.1 Location of the branches – ("Location")	90.6%
Q2.2 Availability of the computerised systems and services in the branches – ("Service systems")	85.4%
Q2.3. Availability of service systems (ATMs, Web banking, Phone Banking) – ("Alternative channels")	78%
Q2.4. Average time for response for phone banking	75.1%
Q2.5 Overall satisfaction with access	**89.9%**

Table 3. Service

Q3.1 Appearance of the branches interior – ("Image")	90.5%
Q3.2 Functionality / comfort of premises – ("Effectiveness")	77.8%
Q3.3 Queues for teller transactions – ("Queues")	88.3%
Q3.4 Waiting time for other services – ("Waiting time")	82.8%
Q3.5 Privacy while being serviced in the branches – ("Tactfulness")	77.3%
Q3.6 What is your opinion about service processes in the branches – ("Service actions")	79.7%
Q3.7 User-friendly environment for alternative channels – ("Friendly")	71.3%
Q3.8 Information received from the bank – ("Information")	81.6%
Q3.9 Overall Satisfaction with Service	**91.2%**

overall satisfaction. Although all variables show a very good performance, there are differences between them of up to 20%.

The best performance belongs to Q3.1 ("Image"), which has to do with the architectural image of branches. This is a characteristic of modern banks that have abolished non-reachable cashiers and separated desks in the branches. Two other strong performances Q3.3 ("Queues") and Q3.4 ("Waiting time") have a strong impact on the formulation of the total satisfaction rate because of "speed of service." Q3.8 ("Information") presents a very high performance that confirms the conclusion from variable Q1.7 (Clarity of information provided). This means that although "Information" of all kinds is not a basic factor for retaining a relationship, it must be provided correctly otherwise it will have a negative impact on satisfaction.

The poorest performance concerns Q3.7 ("Friendly") but as explained before this is because not all people use alternative channels because of in sufficient experience. Finally, once again the percentage rates of "dissatisfied" and "very dissatisfied" customers are below 3.1%.

Products

This section presented the lower performance not only in total but also in every different element (Table 4). With the exception of the "variety of products," "terms and conditions" and "meeting of financial needs" all the elements were performed less that 80%. The general conclusion is that this

Table 4. Products

	Ccumulative %
Q4.1 Variety of products and services – ("Variety")	79.70%
Q4.2 Meet your financiall needs? – ("Financiall needs")	73.30%
Q4.3 Deposit interest rates and investment products – ("Interest rates")	57.20%
Q4.4 Mortgage loans interest rrates – ("Mortgage loans")	59.60%
Q4.5 Cconsumer loans and Credit cards interest rates –	47.90%
Q4.6 Fees and commmissions for thee usage of products and transactions – ("Charges")	50.30%
Q4.7 How clarified is the terms of the products? – ("Terms")	69.80%
Q4.8 Bank Assurance and Car Insurance products – ("Special products")	41.50%
Q4.9 Overall Satisfaction from Products	**68%**

category of the survey is essential and must be improved (H7).

The performance of Q4.7 (Terms and conditions) means that information is hardly regulated and provided satisfactorily by all banks, which ends up being a non-competitive advantage factor. Q4.6 (Charges) gives a very poor performance. Maresca (2003) argued that a reduction in interest spreads obliges banks to impose commissions in order to recover their earnings. Although all banks set these kinds of charges, they suffer bad criticism from clients (H5). Bank assurance products Q4.8 ("Special products") show the worst performance because the vast majority of customers have never "bought" such a product.

Personnel

This section presents the best performance (Table 5). With a total satisfaction rate of 94%, the reader can easily interpret the first choice of customers (Q1.5, Service from Personnel). The basic rule that "the bank is its people" is confirmed totally. Quality service from the personnel is the bedrock of satisfaction (H5, H9). Of course, that does not mean that other factors have limited weight on the perceptions of customers. Personnel behaviour is not something that can be copied easily from rivals and at the same time create a sustainable competitive advantage (H8). Q5.1 (politeness) scored an excellent performance of 98.8%, which means that customers value this behaviour as being very important. Moreover, it seems that Q5.2 (Knowledge of personnel) is also valued as excellent 92.9%. Speed at executing requests (Q5.5) scored 89.7%. "Understanding of needs" (Q5.3) is also very good (81.3%). These observations mean that the quality of service provided by the personnel of the bank is very high and that the most important thing is that customers recognise it (H8).

A surprise was the performance of "telephone access to the branch" (Q5.4). A percentage of 77.7% is considered to be excellent. This phenomenon is rather rare, especially in very old banks or state-owned banks. An amazing performance (89%) was presented by the willingness of personnel to help and support in the emergence of problems.

Loyalty

Loyalty is measured indirectly through "usage continuity," "future usage," "recommendation" and reactions to "complaints handling." Altogether,

Table 5. Personnel

	Cumulative %
Q5.1 Politeness, Courtesy and friendliness of Personnel – ("Politeness")	98.80%
Q5.2 Employees knowledge and skills – ("Knowledge")	92.90%
Q5.3 Understand and satisfy financial needs – ("Understand")	81.30%
Q5.4 Telephone access to the branch – ("Telephone access")	77.70%
Q5.5 Speed and accuracy in execution of requests – ("Request speed")	89.70%
Q5.6 Demonstration of Alternatives Channels – ("Demonstration")	73.70%
Q5.7 Help/Support in resolution of problems – ("Help support")	89%
Q5.8 Overall Satisfaction with Personnel	**94%**

87.2% (Q8 usage continuity) of respondents agree that they will continue to collaborate with the case bank. A total of 79.7% of customers agree that when they want something in the future they will address the case bank (H1). This proves that the satisfaction of customers is profound and stable based on their holistic impression about their relationship. The correlation analysis with "future usage" (0.683), "recommendation" (0.659), "total satisfaction" (0.676) and "complaints handling" (0.642) (Table 15) showed that these variables are connected and tend to change in the same direction.

The cross-tabulation analysis with total satisfaction (Table 6) showed that 99.1% of the respondents that will address the case bank in the future are at least "satisfied." The correlation analysis with "total satisfaction" (0.67) and recommendation (0.721) (Table 15) showed that these variables are directly and strongly connected. This analysis proves once again the validity of the customer satisfaction survey. It also proves that satisfaction has a dynamism that will grow business in the future.

Recommendation is directly connected with satisfaction level (H3). A satisfied customer should feel the need to recommend his or her bank and share with other people his or her impressions. The performance of variable Q10 (Recommendation) is 80.1%. This connection with the satisfaction variable is very important for banks in order to identify future trends for business growth. The cross-tabulation analysis with total customer satisfaction (Table 7) showed that 88% of "satisfied" customers intended to make referrals.

Table 6. Cross tabulation Q9 (future usage) - Q11 (total satisfaction)

Continue use * total satisfaction Cross tabulation

		Total satisfaction				Total
		very satisfied	satisfied	indifferent	dissatisfied	
Continue use	totally agre	92	32	1		125
	agree	32	195	10		237
	indifferent	1	21	30	1	53
Total		125	248	41	1	415

Table 7. Cross tabulation Q10 (recommendation) - Q11 (total satisfaction)

recomendation * total satisfaction Crosstabulation Count						
		Total satisfaction				Total
		very satisfied	satisfied	indifferent	dissatisfied	
recommendation	Totally agree	83	40	1		124
	agree	42	165	4		211
	indifferent	1	44	35		80
	disagree			1	1	2
	Total	12 6	24 9	41	1	417

"Complaints handling" was shown to affect customer satisfaction and loyalty (H2). Only 13.7% of respondents had a problem with their relationship. A total of 87% asked for a solution from the bank and 74% of these customers were at least "satisfied" with the solution provided (Table 8). The cross-tabulation analysis between "complaints handling" and "loyalty" (Tables 9, 10) shows that every satisfied complainant is willing to repurchase, to continue bank collaboration and to recommend potential customers.

Cross Tabulation, Correlation, and Regression Analysis

The main hypothesis that "bank customers are very satisfied" by modern banks is confirmed. This result will be further tested through the analysis and testing of co-relationships with other variables that are referred to below. The researcher will try to show the connection between overall satisfaction and retention and complaints handling. The linear regression case did not fit regarding the "loyalty

Table 8. Cross tabulation Q7.3 (complaints)-Q11 (overall satisfaction)

complaints * total satisfaction Cross tabulation Count						
		total satisfaction				
		very satisfied	satisfied	indifferent	dissatisfied	Total
complaints	very satisfied	10	5			15
	satisfied	3	16	3		22
	indifferent		5	4	1	10
	dissatisfied			2		2
	very dissatisfie d			1		1
Total		13	26	10	1	50

Table 9. Cross tabulation Q7.3 (complaints handling) - Q8 (usage continuity)

complaints * continuous Cross tabulation Count					
		continuous			Total
		totally agree	agree	indifferent	
complaints	very satisfied	8	7		15
	satisfied	3	16	3	22
	indifferent		6	4	10
	dissatisfied			2	2
	very dissatisfied			1	1
Total		11	29	10	50

Table 10. Cross tabulation Q7.3 (complaints handling) - Q10 (recommendation)

complaints * recommendation Cross tabulation Count					
	recommendation				Total
	totally agree	agree	indifferent	disagree	
very satisfied	7	7	1		15
satisfied	4	13	5		22
indifferent		3	6	1	10
dissatisfied			2		2
very dissatisfied			1		1
	11	23	15	1	50

section" Q8 (usage continuity), Q9 (future usage), Q10 (recommendation) and the complaints handling Q7.3 (Tables 11–14).

However, the correlation analysis (Table 15) showed that all these variables are directly connected and have an impact on the final performance of customer satisfaction. The correlation analysis with total satisfaction, continued use, future use and recommendation (Table 15) proved that there is a strong connection between these variables with the strongest relationship with overall satisfaction (>63%). The high performance of 94.8% for Q11 (Overall satisfaction) is related to the high performance for complaints handling (68.5%). Therefore, after this analysis another hypothesis is confirmed (H2). The multiple linear regression case for Q7.3 (Offered solution to complaints), Q8 (Usage continuity), Q9 (Future usage) and Q10 (Recommendation), which was calculated only for respondents that complained to the bank, resulted in an R square = 0.674. This means that when complaints are handled efficiently and at

Table 11. Regression Q8 (usage continuity) – Q11 (total satisfaction)

Model Summary				
Model	R	R Square	Adjusted R Square	Std. Error of the Estimate
1	,676(a)	,456	,455	,467

Table 12. Regression Q9 (future usage) – Q11 (total satisfaction)

Model Summary				
Model	R	R Square	Adjusted R Square	Std. Error of the Estimate
1	,670(a)	,448	,447	,511

Table 13. Regression Q10 (recommendation) – Q11 (total satisfaction)

Model Summary				
Model	R	R Square	Adjusted R Square	Std. Error of the Estimate
1	,636(a)	,404	,403	,547

Table 14. Regression Q7.3 (complaints handling) – Q11 (total satisfaction)

Model Summary				
Model	R	R Square	Adjusted R Square	Std. Error of the Estimate
1	,685(a)	,469	,458	,681

Table 15. Connection between "total satisfaction" and variables

Correlations						
		total satisfaction	complaints	continue use	future use	recommendation
total satisfaction	Pearson Correlation	1	, 6 85(* *)	, 6 76(* *)	, 6 70(* *)	, 636(* *)
	Sig . (2 -tailed)	,	,000	,000	,000	, 000
	N	418	50	415	417	417
complaints	Pearson Correlation	, 685(* *)	1	, 6 42(* *)	, 620(* *)	, 593(* *)
	Sig . (2 -tailed)	,000	,	,000	,000	, 000
	N	50	50	50	50	50
continue use	Pearson Correlation	, 676(* *)	, 642(* *)	1	, 683(* *)	, 659(* *)
	Sig . (2 -tailed)	,000	,000	,	,000	, 000
	N	415	50	416	415	415
Future use	P e a r s o n	, 670(* *)	, 6 20(* *)	, 683(* *)	1	, 721(* *)
	Sig . (2 -tailed)	,000	,0 0 0	,000	,	, 000
	N	417	50	415	418	417
recommendation	Pearson	, 6 36(* *)	, 5 93(* *)	, 659(* *)	, 721(* *)	1
	Sig . (2 -tailed)	,000	,000	,000	,000	,
	N	417	50	415	417	418

* * Correlation insignificant 0.01 level (2 - tailed) .

the same time all other variables perform well. Thus, the connection between "total satisfaction" and these variables tend to be linear.

The principal hypotheses of this survey were confirmed. First, the improvement in market share means that customer satisfaction is better. Customers are very satisfied. High overall satisfaction is verified from the will of customers to continue using the bank to address future needs and to recommend new customers (H2). The "bank is its people" and its way of servicing customers and products are necessary (H9). If old banks with large networks continue to lose market share, modern banks will outperform in the areas of quality service and flexibility. The analysis of this survey confirms the hypotheses that "total customer satisfaction" is related to "loyalty," "recommendation" and "complaints handling" (H2). This means that the bank has to take care of pre-sales, sales and after-sales services in such a way that add value to the final performance.

CONCLUSION

Modern banks understand the importance of access to networks, which means that competitive advantages based on networks have faded away. The implementation of alternative channels has helped a lot in this direction.

Another conclusion is that no matter the satisfaction performance there are always areas that need improvement, with products being one of the first priorities. Summarising, one could say that the strong points of the case bank are: "Service systems," "Architectural image," "Queues." "Information," "Product variety," "Financial needs," "Terms," "Mortgage loans," "Deposit interest rates," "Politeness," "Knowledge," "Request speed" and "Help support." The areas that need improvement, no matter their performance rate, are "Tactfulness," "Services," "Effectiveness," "Friendliness," "Special products," "Telephone access" and "Demonstration."

According to Zairi (2000), the challenge that organisations face is the move from "introverted" profit-oriented approaches to customer-focused and market-oriented approaches. In order to increase customer loyalty, many banks create and offer innovative products and services. Worcester (1997) observed that these products are often accompanied by new charges, and so recommended that banks should focus on less tangible and more difficult to copy elements such as customer satisfaction, service quality and loyalty.

According to Jamal and Naser (2002), the importance of customer satisfaction and customer retention for a customer-focused organisation must not be underestimated. Complementary to the above statement is the opinion of Bitner and Hubbert (1994), who stated that customer satisfaction is becoming a corporate value as more and more companies try to improve the quality offered to customers in their products and services.From the above analysis, it is obvious expectantly those customers are satisfied. Moreover, it was confirmed that there is a strong relationship between customer satisfaction, complaints handling and loyalty. Elements of satisfaction such as "Access," "Products," "Personnel" and "Services" proved to be significant and equally weighted for the formulation of customers' perceptions. It is supposed that modern banks serve customers better and that this has to do with culture and services. Products are identical for all banks but the interrelationships with customers add value to the total outcome. The findings from the research reveal that consumer loyalty to the particular bank has not declined since the economic recession in the Greece.

LIMITATIONS AND FUTURE RESEARCH

Although this survey is detailed and analytical, it concerns a single bank. This means that if it was decided to cover the whole Greek banking industry the number of questionnaires and case branches should be bigger (smaller margin error) and divided into the number of banks and their market shares. Therefore, it is recommended that the same survey should be conducted for all Greek banks in order to understand better the advantages and disadvantages of Greek banks in this economic recession period and the trend for their growth in the future. At this point, it is worthwhile stating that survey outcomes present a static image. Perceived customer satisfaction is dynamic and changes over time. Thus, these kinds of surveys must be conducted periodically not only to verify the results but also to identify performance trends. Moreover, the effectiveness of marketing plans must be linked and evaluated through customer satisfaction measurement. Finally, the establishment of incentive systems for employees has proven to be directly related to customer service quality, which could be another area for future surveys. The findings contribute to the effective management of financial institutions. The recommendations aim at the management of the banks on how to improve customer loyalty amongst the banks' consumers.

REFERENCES

Anderson, E. W., Fornell, C., & Lehmann, D. R. (1994). Customer satisfaction, market share and profitability: Findings from Sweden. *Journal of Marketing*, *58*(3), 53–66. doi:10.2307/1252310

Athanasopoulos, A., & Gounaris, S. (2001). Behavioural responses to customer satisfaction: An empirical study. *European Journal of Marketing*, *35*(5/6), 687–707. doi:10.1108/03090560110388169

Ball, D., Coelho, P. S., & Machás, A. (2004). The role of communication and trust in explaining customer loyalty: An extension to the ECSI case. *European Journal of Marketing*, *38*(9–10), 1272–1293. doi:10.1108/03090560410548979

Bitner, M. J. (1990). Evaluating service encounters: The effects of physical surroundings and employee responses. *Journal of Marketing*, *54*(2), 69–82. doi:10.2307/1251871

Bitner, M. J., & Hubbert, A. R. (1994). Encounter satisfaction versus overall satisfaction versus quality. In *Service Quality: New Directions in Theory and Practice*. London: Sage.

Bloemer, J., Ruyter, K., & Peeters, P. (1998). Investigating drivers of bank loyalty: The complex relationship between image, service quality and satisfaction. *International Journal of Bank Marketing*, *16*(7), 279–286. doi:10.1108/02652329810245984

Bodgett, J. G., & Anderson, R. D. (2000). A Bayesian network case of the consumer complaint process. *Journal of Service Research*, *2*(4), 321–338. doi:10.1177/109467050024002

Drucker, P. F. (1954). *The Practice of Management*. New York: Harper and Row.

East, R. (1997). *Consumer Behaviour: Advances and Applications in Marketing*. London: Prentice Hall.

Ehigie, B. (2006). Correlates of customer loyalty to their bank: A case study in Nigeria. *International Journal of Bank Marketing*, *24*(7), 494–508. doi:10.1108/02652320610712102

Ewing, M. T. (2000). Brand and retailer loyalty: Past behaviour and future intensions. *Journal of Product and Brand Management*, *9*(2), 120–127. doi:10.1108/10610420010322161

File, K. M., & Prince, R. A. (1992). Positive word of mouth: Customer satisfaction and buyer behaviour. *International Journal of Bank Marketing*, *10*(1), 25–29. doi:10.1108/02652329210007867

Fornell, C. (1992). National satisfaction barometer: The Swedish experience. *Journal of Marketing*, *56*(1), 6–21. doi:10.2307/1252129

Fornell, C., & Wernerfelt, B. (1987). Defensive marketing strategy by customer complaint management: A theoretical analysis. *JMR, Journal of Marketing Research*, *24*(4), 337–346. doi:10.2307/3151381

Gupta, Y., & Torkzadeh, G. (1988). Redesigning bank service: Systems for effective marketing. *Long Range Planning*, *21*(6), 38–43. doi:10.1016/0024-6301(88)90157-4

Hallowel, R. (1996). The relationships of customer satisfaction, customer loyalty and profitability: An empirical study. *International Journal of Service Industry Management*, *7*(4), 27–42. doi:10.1108/09564239610129931

Jamal, A., & Naser, K. (2002). Customer satisfaction and retail banking: An assessment of some of the key antecedents of customer satisfaction in retail banking. *International Journal of Bank Marketing*, *20*(4), 146–160. doi:10.1108/02652320210432936

Jones, T. O., & Sasser, W. E. Jr. (1995, November-December). Why satisfied customers defect. *Harvard Business Review*, 88–99.

Karatepe, O. M., & Ekiz, E. H. (2004). The effects of organisational responses to complaints on satisfaction and loyalty: A study of hotel guests in Northern Cyprus. *Managing Service Quality*, *14*(6), 476–486. doi:10.1108/09604520410569810

Laroche, M., Rosenblatt, J., & Manning, T. (1986). Services used and factors considered important in selecting a bank: An investigation across diverse demographic segments. *International Journal of Bank Marketing*, *4*(1), 35–55. doi:10.1108/eb010771

Lee, T., Chung, W., & Taylor, R. (2011). A strategic response to the financial crisis: An empirical analysis of financial services advertising before and during the financial crisis. *Journal of Services Marketing*, *25*(3), 150–164. doi:10.1108/08876041111129146

Levesque, T., & McDougal, G. H. G. (1996). Determinants of customer satisfaction in retail banking. *International Journal of Bank Marketing*, *14*(7), 12–20. doi:10.1108/02652329610151340

Manrai, A. K., & Manrai, A. L. (1993). Consumer switching behaviour of banking services: A conceptual case. In *Proceedings of the Sixth Bi-Annual International Conference of the Academy of Marketing Science*, (vol. 6, pp. 100-104). Istanbul: World Marketing Congress.

Maxham, J. G. III, & Netemeyer, R. G. (2002). Caseling customer perceptions of complaint handling over time: The effects of perceived justice on satisfaction and intent. *Journal of Retailing*, *78*(4), 252–259. doi:10.1016/S0022-4359(02)00100-8

Mihelis, G., Grigoroudis, E., Siskos, Y., Politis, Y., & Malandrakis, Y. (1998). *Customer Satisfaction Measurement in the Private Bank Sector*. Decision Support Systems Laboratory, University of Chania.

Moutinho, L., & Smith, A. (2000). Caseling bank customer satisfaction through mediation of attitudes towards human and automated banking. *International Journal of Bank Marketing*, *18*(3), 124–134. doi:10.1108/02652320010339699

Newman, K., & Cowling, A. (1996). Service quality in retail banking: The experience of two British clearing banks. *International Journal of Bank Marketing*, *14*(6), 3–11. doi:10.1108/02652329610130127

Nikolopoulou, R. (2006, March 15). The importance of the right customer service in franchise networks. *Express*, p. 40.

Oliver, R. L. (1997). *Satisfaction: A Behavioural Perspective on the Consume*. New York: McGraw-Hill Companies, Inc.

Oliver, R. L. (1999). Whence consumer loyalty? *Journal of Marketing*, *63*, 33–44. doi:10.2307/1252099

Paolo. (2003). Banks Can Reduce Running Cost by 20%. *Kathimerini*, 24.

Peppers, D., & Rogers, M. (2004). *Managing customer relationships: A strategic framework*. New York: John Wiley and Sons.

Peter, P. J., & Olson, J. C. (1996). *Consumer behaviour and Marketing Strategy* (4th ed.). Irwin.

Reicheld, F., & Sasser, W. E. Jr. (1990). Zero defections: Quality comes to services. *Harvard Business Review*, *68*, 105–111. PMID:10107082

Reis, D., Pena, L., & Lopes, P. A. (2003). Customer satisfaction: The historical perspective. *Management Decision*, *41*(2), 195–198. doi:10.1108/00251740310457641

Reitchheld, F. F. (1996). *The Loyalty Effect*. Cambridge, MA: Harvard Business School Press.

Saunders, M., Lewis, P., & Thornhill, A. (2003). Research Methods for Business Studies. *Financial Times*, pp. 81–105.

Schweizer, B. (2008). *An Examination of Factors Leading to Abating Customer Loyalty Towards Magazine Subscriptions*. Berlin: GRIN Verlag.

Smith, A. M.Characteristics on the Dimensionality of the Service Quality Construct. (2000). The impact of scale characteristics on the dimensionality of the service quality construct. *Service Industries Journal*, *20*(3), 167–190. doi:10.1080/02642060000000037

Taylor, S. A., & Baker, T. L. (1994). An assessment of the relationship between service quality and customer satisfaction in the formation of consumer's purchase intentions. *Journal of Retailing*, *70*(2), 163–178. doi:10.1016/0022-4359(94)90013-2

Thwaites, D., & Vere, L. (1995). Bank selection criteria – A student perspective. *Journal of Marketing Management*, *11*(1–3), 133–149. doi:10.1080/0267257X.1995.9964334

University of Michigan Business School. (2001). *American Customer Satisfaction Index*. Retrieved from www.bus.umich.edu/research/nqrc/asci.html

Williams, P., & Naumann, E. (2011). Customer satisfaction and business performance: A firm-level analysis. *Journal of Services Marketing*, *25*(1), 20–32. doi:10.1108/08876041111107032

Worcester, R. M. (1997). Managing the image of your bank: The glue that binds. *International Journal of Bank Marketing*, *15*(5), 146–152. doi:10.1108/02652329710175244

Zairi, M. (2000). Managing customer dissatisfaction through effective complaints management systems. *The TQM Magazine*, *12*(5), 331–337. doi:10.1108/09544780010341932

Zeithaml, V., Parasuraman, A., & Berry, I. (1990). *Developing Quality Service-Balancing Customer Perceptions and expectations*. New York: The Free Press.

Zeithaml, V. A., Berry, L. L., & Parasuraman, A. (1996). The behavioural consequences of service quality. *Journal of Marketing*, *60*(2), 31–46. doi:10.2307/1251929

Zineldin, M. (1992). *Bank-Corporate Client Interactions and Relationships-A New Marketing Approach (Research Report Series, No. 4)*. Stockholm University.

Zineldin, M. (1996, March). Bank strategic positioning and some determinants of bank selection. *International Journal of Bank Marketing*, *14*(6), 12–22. doi:10.1108/02652329610130136

KEY TERMS AND DEFINITIONS

Customer Satisfaction: An overall evaluation of the total purchase experience compared with pre-purchase expectations over time.

Customer Satisfaction's Perceived Elements: Ease of Access, Service provided Products and Personnel. These elements are perceived as equally weighted antecedents of customer satisfaction and almost all of them share attributes of service quality.

Economic Recession: A period of falling economic activity spread across the economy, lasting more than a few months, normally visible in real GDP, real income, employment, industrial production, and wholesale-retail sales.

Loyalty: Customers are satisfied with a particular product or service; they are likely to engage in repeat purchases or cross-purchases.

Service Quality: The customer's overall impression about the perceived superiority of a company and its products/services.

Section 2
Marketing Strategy

Chapter 5
Sustainable Competitive Advantage in Turbulent Business Environments using Critical Organizational Capabilities and Resources to Manage Complexity

Yannis A. Pollalis
University of Piraeus, Greece

ABSTRACT

In today's turbulent economic conditions, some organizations are able to sustain their competitive positioning while others, with similar capital and technological resources, seem to struggle to survive. In addition, more and more firms seem to adopt strategies that focus primarily on their internal strengths, capabilities, and competencies, while others seem to depend more on external forces to shape their strategies, such as competition, economies of scale, and technological demands. In this chapter, the author argues that in unstable business environments the integration of internal and external perspectives of strategy formulation is necessary for a firm to sustain advantages for long. The proposed model presents four stages of corporate strategy development: Scouting, Maintenance, Dominance, and Appraisal. The chapter utilizes the concepts of Critical Success Factors (CSFs) and Critical Resources (CRs), describes its applicability by using two cases of companies that adopted similar long-run strategies, and finally offers implications for strategic management and planning practitioners.

DOI: 10.4018/978-1-4666-6232-2.ch005

INTRODUCTION

Traditional strategic management theory and research have emphasized the importance of matching a firm's internal resources and capabilities with the opportunities and risks found in the external environment (Liu, 2013; Grant, 1996; Hofer & Schendel, 1978; Glueck, 1980; David, 2005; Johnson et al., 2005). This dominant paradigm of competitive strategy has evolved from the industrial organization (IO) or industrial economics approach which argues that the external environment (i.e., the industry's structure) guides a firm's strategy for competitive advantage and that the main purpose of the firm is to identify innovative ways to defeat competition (Bain, 1956; Schumpeter, 1950). Extensions of the IO paradigm are Porter's well-known theory of competitive advantage and the PIMS marketing initiative (Buzzel & Gale, 1987; Porter, 1980; Porter, 1981 & 1985; Knott, 2003).

However, recent research in strategic management emphasizes the emergence of a new paradigm of the strategy formulation process: the *resource-based approach* (Liu, 2013; Grant, 1996; Wernerfelt, 1984; Wernerfelt, 1989; Barney, 1991; Aacker, 1989; Grant, 1991; Priem & Butler, 2001). The resource-based theory of the firm proposes that a successful competitive strategy is one that places more emphasis on the firm's internal resources and capabilities and thus develops strategic plans based on such capabilities rather than primarily focusing at the competitive environment (Barney, 1991).

Proponents of the resource-based model have questioned the effectiveness of the IO model of strategy formulation for its simplified and unrealistic assumptions regarding the homogeneity of firms within an industry and the perfect mobility of a firm's resources (Grant, 1996; Barney, 1991; Grant, 1991; Lado et al., 1992). In brief, the resource-based view argues that the best way to build the foundations of sustainable competitive advantage is *from the inside*, i.e., by exploiting the organization's resources, unique attributes and distinctive competencies. In contrast, the IO model which has emerged from the field of microeconomics suggests that the conditions, constraints, and attributes of the external environment should be the basis for a firm's strategy formulation.

The proponents of both approaches have strong arguments regarding "where the strategy analysis should start, why, and how," but it seems that a more pragmatic answer to that question comes from the integration of the two ways of thinking (Hrebiniak & Joyce, 1984). Furthermore, although the two perspectives have their own examples and "success stories" to demonstrate the validity of each approach, their differences regarding the effectiveness of each model have, for the most part, remained theoretical.

This paper argues that an integration of both the IO and the resource-based models of strategy formulation process is more likely to benefit an organization's strive for competitive advantage rather than a choice between one or the other. In other words, this paper proposes that simultaneous emphasis on both external forces and internal resources and capabilities would provide a firm with the knowledge necessary to survive and compete successfully in the long-run. In addition, this paper emphasizes the role of firm *alliances* (e.g., information-based partnerships) and *outsourcing* (e.g., renting information processing services from outside technology vendors) as another way to generate sustainable competitive advantage in today's rapidly changing business environment. Similar integrative perspectives that emphasize the combination of external and internal information-seeking activities for strategy development have appeared elsewhere in the strategic management literature (Grant & King, 1982; Hrebiniak & Snow, 1982; Hansen & Wernerfelt, 1989; Pollalis & Grant, 1994; Amit & Schoemaker, 1993; Hax & Majluf, 1991; Hofer & Schendel, 1978; Hrebiniak & Joyce, 1984; Itami, 1987).

BUILDING A NEW MODEL FOR STRATEGIC ADVANTAGE

The success stories of American companies such as 3M and Motorola, and Japanese companies such as Honda and Matsushita make it easy to identify many of the activities suggested by an integrative model: their strategic advantages are based on important organizational resources (e.g., organizational culture, motivation, capacity for innovation); their management's ability to identify opportunities and threats in their prospective markets; and their organizational structure's flexibility to absorb changes in the environment and transform them to advantages. Other authors have also identified similar resource-based processes for success in many leading organizations around the world (e.g., NEC, Canon, Casio, Philips). However, such findings remain at the descriptive level and offer limited assistance to practitioners who want to apply these approaches in new organizational contexts (Pascale, 1984; Peters & Waterman, 1982; Itami, 1987; Grant, 1991).

At the other side of this vast literature on success anecdotes, are theoretical perspectives offered by researchers and academicians who provide a plethora of normative frameworks prescribing "what should be done" to succeed. Therefore, the rich empirical evidence of unstructured innovation and creativity is met with theoretical rigidity and formal structures and processes that organizations 'must go through' to achieve their objectives. And although one has to admit that these theories and models are usually thought provoking and inspiring, they often lack realism and practicality (Pollalis & Grant, 1994).

This paper does not intend to follow either of those extremes, nor to propose a "grand theory" that will assure success and competitive advantage for all organizations. In fact, such a theory is unlikely to exist for the simple reason that there is no market where all competitors have competitive advantage (a fact attributed more to the human nature of competitiveness and individuality, rather than to social and market constraints of society). The essence of high performance is perceived uniqueness and is often achieved via innovation, so it can never be mapped on a single framework or process. The author's intention, rather, is to propose an intuitively appealing process to take advantage of important organizational resources and sustain long-term benefits. The proposed Scouting-Maintenance-Dominance-Appraisal (SMDA) approach also challenges the ends-ways-means 'rational' approach in planning and adopts a prototyping-like approach (i.e., using trial and error processes to identify internal strengths and weaknesses) of reverse-planning (Hayes, 1985).

The SMDA model focuses on both the external environment (primarily the competition and the customers) and the internal resources and capabilities, and is an extension of work previously reported in strategic management research (Hrebiniak & Joyce, 1984; Amit & Schoemaker, 1994; Pollalis & Grant, 1994). The model uses the concepts of *critical success factors* (CSFs) and *critical resources* (CRs) to build strategy and identifies a dynamic process to implement it.

The following sections include: first, a description of the IO and resource-based models, their assumptions, and their appropriateness for different situations; second, an explanation of the rationale for the integration of the two models and the SMDA strategy formulation process; finally, a conclusion with two case-examples where such an integrative approach can been demonstrated. Finally, the paper discusses implications of the SMDA model for research and practice.

DESCRIPTION OF THE I/O AND RESOURCE-BASED MODELS

Strategy from the Outside-In: The Industrial Organization Model

Industrial organization (IO) is the field of neoclassical economics that studies industry structure and process and the way they affect firm performance and profitability (Lado, 1992). The IO model focuses on the external environment (i.e., stakeholders and the competition) and it favors the outside-in approach for competitive advantage: a firm determines what the environment's pressures, constraints, and stakeholders' demands are and then builds the appropriate resources and capabilities to meet those pressures and demands. In summary, the IO model suggests that in order for a firm to develop a successful strategy for competitive advantage, it first has to establish an industry's attractiveness (i.e., the elements that define an industry's capacity for profits such as the competition, economies of scale, prices, cost structures, technological developments, etc.) and then identify what resources it should acquire to enter that industry or to defeat the competitors already in it (Bain, 1956; Porter, 1980; Porter, 1981; Porter, 1985). In general, the IO view assumes that a firm's potential for superior performance is based on its ability to generate monopolistic or oligopolistic market conditions (Conner, 1991).

The IO approach to strategy formulation dominated research and practice in strategic management from the 1950s through the 1980s and still influences strategic thinking today. Emphasizing the role of the external environment in a firm's strategy, IO proponents claimed that organizations with the ability to learn about and adopt to the competitive environment will generate substantially higher profits than those organizations without that ability. Thus, firms that are able to *match or fit* their internal resources, skills and capabilities with the opportunities and threats of the environment, will be likely to sustain competitive advantage. As an extension of the IO model, Michael Porter introduced the concept of *competitive forces* (Porter, 1980; Porter, 1985; David, 2005; Johnson, 2005) which emphasized five structural dimensions of any industry that a firm should be responding to in order to improve its competitive position: competitors, new entrants, customers, suppliers, and substitutes. Porter's model, along with his *generic strategies' toolkit* (i.e., low cost leadership, differentiation, and focus strategies) resulted in an emphasis towards the alignment between the industry's pressures and the firm's potential to build resources to meet such pressures: alignment was the prerequisite to success, misalignment was likely to guarantee failure or exit from the industry (Lado, 1992; Samanta, 2006).

Porter's competitive analysis theory along with the PIMS project initiative and studies generated a myriad of cases and examples where organizations seemed to be very successful when they managed to match the external environment's demands. Examples of such cases include: the introduction of Ford Motor Co.'s *Mustang* model after market research identified the need for a "small, inexpensive, sporty car that would be driven by the young adult..." (Hrebiniak & Joyce, 1984), the introduction of oral contraceptives (Hrebiniak & Joyce, 1984), and the introduction of information technology products and services to meet the demand generated by the new markets of EEC and Eastern Europe.

In addition, the IO model views that a firm's own resources and idiosyncratic attributes are of secondary importance and are developed or acquired only as a response to environmental opportunities and threats. Thus, the IO model represents a *reactive* type of strategy formulation process.

In summary, the IO model has adopted three major assumptions (Hitt et al., 1995; Barney, 1991; Lado, 1992): (a) the external environment determines the strategies a firm has to adopt to compete successfully in an industry, (b) the firms within an industry (or within a strategic group) are identical in terms of the resources they own and some of the strategies they adopt based on those resources, and (c) the resources owned by a firm are highly mobile and any resource differences across firms are likely to be short-lived. Figure 1 shows the basic components of the IO model.

Figure 1. The IO model. Adapted from Hitt, Ireland, and Hoskisson, 1995.

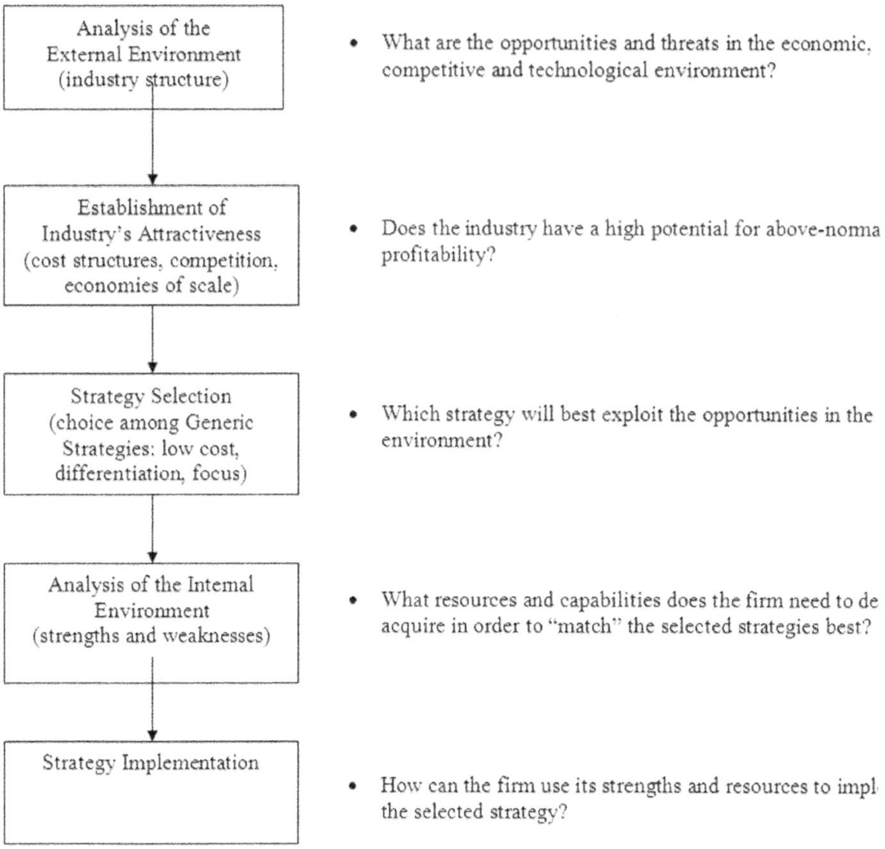

Strategy from the Inside-Out: The Resource-Based Model

The *resource-based approach* proposes that organizations should focus on their unique resources and build capabilities based on those resources to "appraise their rent-generating potential" (Grant, 1991 & 1996), as well as to sustain competitive advantage. Second, the organization should select a strategy which best exploits the firm's resources and capabilities relative to the external environment's opportunities and threats. Finally, the organization has to reinvest in those unique resources that provide competitive advantage by either augmenting or upgrading them (Barney, 1991; Grant, 1991 & 1996; Liu, 2013).

The resource-based model emphasizes that each organization has a unique set of resources, capabilities, and competencies that provide the basis for their competitive strategies. Thus, the resource-based model emphasizes a *proactive* approach to strategy formulation. Examples of firms that exemplify the resource-based model include US companies such as 3M and Motorola that used their expertise in R and D to grow in a wide range of products and markets and Japanese companies such as Honda and Matsushita (see Appendix) that used their expertise and technical excellence in one market to expand in other but related product markets (Grant, 1991; Pollalis & Grant, 1994; Hitt, 1995).

In addition, the resource-based model views firms as "seekers of costly-to-copy inputs for production and distribution" (Conner, 1991). Thus, to fulfill a firm's ultimate goal (i.e., generate above-normal returns), the strategy has to either (a) make sure that the firm's products and services are different in the eyes of the consumers or (b) if the firm is competing with firms with similar products and services, to use its unique resources to reach a low-cost position in the industry (Conner, 1991).

In summary, the major assumptions of the resource-based model are (Wernerfelt, 1984; Conner, 1991; Barney 1986a; Barney, 1986b; Barney, 1991; Lado, 1992): (i) the firms within an industry or strategic group are heterogeneous in terms of the resources they own and the capabilities they can develop based on these resources and (ii) these resources are not perfectly mobile across firms and the advantage they might generate can last long.Figure 2 describes the resource-based model and the process for sustainable competitive advantage derived from it.

THE RATIONALE FOR AN INTEGRATIVE MODEL: SYNERGY

The following arguments are in favor of an integrative approach, illustrating that neither approach is *sufficient* on its own:

1. Regardless of what resources and capabilities a firm owns, its long term success is primarily determined by the willingness of its customers to buy its products and services. Thus, firms that can "listen" to customer needs and can add value not only to their services but also to their customer's services will sustain a better position in their perspective markets. Furthermore, as others have argued (Hamel & Prahalad, 1989; Hamel & Prahalad, 1990; Ohmae, 1988; Peters & Waterman, 1982; Lado, 1992), a firm's relationships with its customers can *become* a unique resource for the firm, leading to other unique resources and competencies such as reputation, brand loyalty, and corporate image. Similar arguments can be made for the firm's relationships with its suppliers, brokers and other significant stakeholders. In other words, a firm's strategy cannot ignore the external environment by mainly focusing on its internal resources, neither can it ignore its own resources and capabilities and start searching the external environment for opportunities. The two ideologies have to be integrated and support each other's strengths toward sustainable competitive advantage.
2. Developments in information technology (IT) have spurred collaboration and partnerships among firms around the globe or within an industry resulting in synergistic benefits that do not require ownership of unique resources other than the ability to integrate each other's IT systems (e.g., EDI-based information partnerships). Thus, firms that have a strength or weakness in one area can quickly overcome it by collaborating with other firms that have a complementary set of strengths and weaknesses. Here again, a firm does not have to follow either the IO or the resource-based model to take advantage of the IT-based alliances: it can follow a combination of both approaches and exploit the market's technological developments and thus leverage its own limited resources. Similar arguments can be made for situations where a firm has to decide on whether to *outsource* or *develop-in-house* IT capabilities.
3. Finally, three other factors reinforce the use of an integrative approach: *uncertainty* about the external environment, *complexity* concerning the interrelationships across an industry's forces and *intra-organizational conflict* among those who are involved in the strategy formulation process within a firm

Figure 2. The resource-based model. Adapted from Grant, 1991 and Hitt, et al. 1995.

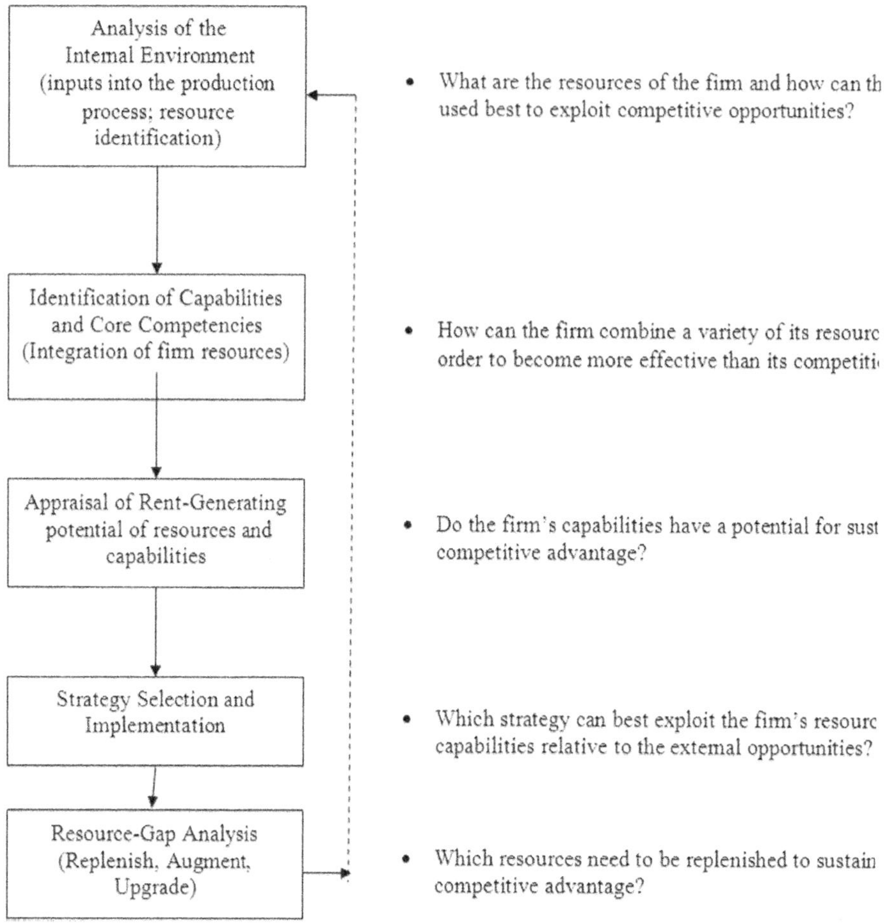

(Amit & Schoemaker, 1993; David, 2005; Johnson, 2005). Other researchers have also demonstrated empirically that the integration of both models can result in better overall performance (Hrebiniak & Snow, 1982; Hansen & Wernerfelt, 1989).

In summary, due to the environmental turbulence and change (e.g., information technology advances, global forces, customer trends, and competitive actions), as well as due to the factors of uncertainty and complexity, firms have to continue updating and changing their sets of resources and industry-based critical success factors (CSFs) in order to continue to exist and sustain their advantages. Table 1 summarizes the key characteristics, assumptions and differences between the IO, resource-based, and integrative models of strategy formulation.

The SMDA Strategy Formulation Process

Figure 3 presents the proposed SMDA model which integrates the IO and resource-based approaches for strategy formulation. The model is based on previous research (Granger, 1964; Leidecker & Bruno, 1984; Hrebiniak & Joyce,

Table 1. Comparison of the IO, resource-based, and integrative models

Model Attributes	Industrial Organization	Resource-Based	Integrative (SMDA)
Strategies for Competitive Advantage	*[Reactive]* a. Concentration on the external environment to determine the competitive forces and the industry's cost structure and potential rent-generation capability (industry attractiveness). b. Low-cost, differentiation or focus strategies can be employed to combat the competitive forces. c. Once the competitive strategies are selected, appropriate resources are acquired and/or developed to match them (strategic fit).	*[Proactive]* a. Focus on the firm's own resources, strengths and weaknesses before any attempt is made to adapt to the environment b. Development of capabilities and core competencies by integrating or innovatively combining the firm's unique resources. c. Selection of strategies that best exploit the firm's resources and capabilities (i.e., seeking costly-to-copy inputs for production and distribution functions).	*[Evolutionary]* a. Focus on both the external and internal forces by determining the critical success factors and critical resources owned by the firm. b. Determine how to match or combine CSFs and CRs in order to exploit the opportunities found in the external environment. c. Selection of most profitable strategies among the CSF-CR "fits" to establish rareness, imperfect imitability, and ltd. substitutability. d. Alliances and outsourcing capability
Major Assumptions	i. The external environment determines the strategies a firm has to adopt in order to compete successfully within an industry. ii. The firms within an industry or w/in a strategic group are identical in terms of the resources they own and their generic strategies. iii. A firm's resources are highly mobile and any resource difference between firms is short-lived.	i. The firms within an industry or strategic groups are heterogeneous in terms of the resources they own and the capabilities they can develop based on these resources. ii. The resources a firm owns are not perfectly mobile across firms and the advantage they (or the capabilities based on them) might generate can last long.	i. The resources and capabilities a firm owns are not perfectly mobile but they are substitutable with other combinations of resources, equally effective (equifinality). ii. Alliances across firms and outsourcing activities will alleviate for possible advantages of a competitor's unique resources and capabilities.
Environment Conditions for Success	• Stable environment (preferably monopolistic or oligopolistic) • Perfect information on competition • Resources are not scarce	• Turbulent Environment • Perfect information available about a firm's capabilities • Resources are scarce	• Turbulent environment • Imperfect information about external and internal environment • Resources are scarce
Related References	Schumpeter (1950); Bain (1956); Porter (1980, 1981, 1985); Hill (1988).	Lippman and Rumelt (1982); Wernerfelt (1986); Barney (1986, 1991); Lado et al. (1992); Grant (1991); Conner (1991).	Hrebiniak and Joyce (1982); Itami (1987); Hax and Majluf (1991); Amit and Schoemaker (1993) Pollalis and Grant (1994); Hitt et al. (1995).

1984; Itami, 1987; Aacker, 1989; Hax & Majluf, 1991; Amit & Schoemaker, 1993; Pollalis & Grant, 1994) and has four interrelated stages:

- **Scouting Stage:** Refers to the preliminary collection of information regarding the internal and external forces associated with an organization (i.e., by using the CSFs' methodology, benchmarking and collection of competitive intelligence information), as well as the identification of the organization's inventory of available resources.
- **Maintenance Stage:** Refers to the identification of *critical resources* (i.e., resources with unique attributes and high potential contribution), the optimal allocation of those resources to "satisfy" the demands derived from the CSFs identified in the scouting stage, as well as identification of ways to leverage critical resources (CRs) to develop organizational capabilities and competencies (e.g., by integrating CRs or mixing them with additional resources).
- **Dominance Stage:** Where the firm exploits its critical resources (e.g., techno-

Figure 3. The SMDA model. Adapted from Pollalis and Grant, 1994.

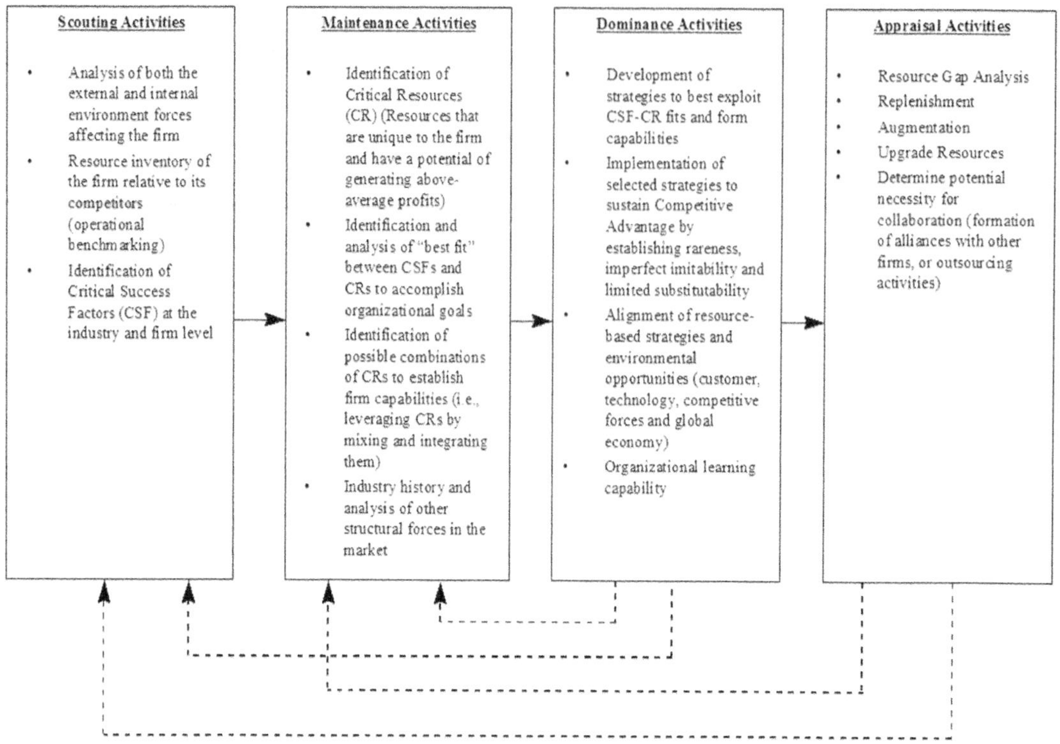

logical know-how, reputation, experience in specific processes), core competencies and capabilities by using them in complex and difficult to imitate projects and organization-wide processes, and aligning them with strategic opportunities (e.g., customer needs, technological developments, globalization pressures).

- **Appraisal Stage:** Which involves evaluation of the various strategies and implemented projects; establishment of needs to "refill" possible resource-gaps (i.e., replenish, augment, upgrade resources); divestment of resources that did not contribute to organizational performance; and finally, determine the potential or need for mixing the firm's own resources from other firms (i.e., alliances and partnerships) or renting resources and capabilities from other firms (i.e., outsourcing).

Not all firms go through these four stages during their existence. Rather, most firms complete the scouting or maintenance stage in order to catch-up with the competition and still remain profitable. It is the very few firms that manage to reach the third and fourth stages and dominate markets for extended periods, while making sure that they replenish, augment or upgrade their resources inventory frequently.

According to the SMDA model and similarly to Maslow's *hierarchy of needs* (Daft, 1983; Barney, 1991), an organization has to make sure that it can successfully complete the scouting and maintenance stages before it attains the dominance and appraisal stages (Maslow, 1943; March & Simon, 1958). However, an organization not mature enough and without adequate knowledge about its capabilities, competencies and critical resources, as well as about the external environment (especially customers, suppliers, and competitors) typically cannot understand very well the linkages between the external pressures and internal resources thus, might not be able to match successfully its resources with the industry's CSFs and its own strategy goals, let alone establish any sustainable advantage. In addition, an organization first has to establish the capability to use its resources effectively and efficiently before attempting to leverage them into resources that are rare, imperfectly imitable and with limited substitutability (Lippman & Rumelt, 1982).

Furthermore, Professor Granger proposed a *hierarchy of objectives* to facilitate decision making and planning in organizations by using a stepwise process of deriving specific objectives, analyzing alternatives and choosing strategies. According to Granger, ."..both an analysis of internal resources and an environmental analysis are called for in setting up realistic and adequately challenging criteria [to measure the success of a stated objective]. The next step requires that management define the range of possible activities which it might use to accomplish the larger objective..." (Granger, 1964).

The SMDA model described here uses the critical success factors (CSFs) methodology and the concept of critical resources (CRs). The CSFs methodology is used to identify the external and internal factors that an organization "simply cannot ignore" for establishing a business and surviving the competition (Rockart, 1979; Hofer & Schendel, 1978), while CRs could be used by a firm to develop and sustain a competitive position based on its unique resources and competencies (Aacker, 1989; Wernerfelt, 1989).

In addition, this paper defines *capability* as a three-dimensional construct that demonstrates the ability of a firm to (a) acquire, manage, and integrate the appropriate information technology and other physical resources needed for its operations (i.e., *Technological Capability*), (b) use these resources in accordance with its own needs and structural characteristics (i.e., *Organizational Capability*), and (c) align the technological and organizational capability with its strategic objectives and the broader business environment's needs (i.e., *Strategic Capability*). These three types of capabilities represent the control mechanisms for each phase of the SMDA process. The concepts of technical and organizational capability were introduced (although referred as *validity types*) by Schultz & Slevin in 1975 and were used as the two primary elements of project management success (Schultz & Slevin, 1975). Figure 4 describes each capability's characteristics, prerequisite resources, and their appropriate position and relationships within the SMDA model.

The following sections describe the stages of the SMDA process and address the various strategic activities involved to facilitate competitive advantage in turbulent environments.

Stage 1: Scouting

The scouting stage consists of two major activities: (a) the collection of external and internal environment information where the firm assesses its strengths and weaknesses (i.e., development of a *resource-inventory*) and acquires external knowledge about the opportunities and threats from its competitors, customers, and current technological developments); and (b) the identification of CSFs for the firm. As such, the scouting stage usually focuses on building and exploring the technological capability of a firm (see Figure 4).

The concept of CSFs has been discussed in the organizational and management related literature for quite some time and even going back to the ancient times, Aristotle broached the idea that leaders should create a list of simple and clear objectives for their societies (forms of organizations) and noted that those societies that did so performed better than those that did not.

The *resource inventory* includes tangible and intangible resources that a firm owns and that are potentially useful to improve the firm's competitive position. Such tangible resources can be financial, physical, human, and organizational

Figure 4. Organizational capabilities

	Technological Capability	Organizational Capability	Strategic Capability
Relevant Concerns	• What resources does the firm need to compete successfully within its industry? • What resources does the firm own to compete successfully within its industry?	• Can the firm use its resources for its operational and structural needs? • Can the firm achieve efficiency and effectiveness by integrating and mixing its various resources and capabilities?	• What projects can the firm establish to exploit its resources and capabilities and achieve its goals and objectives? • What resources does the firm need to replenish, augment or divest in order to "re-align" their contribution toward organizational goals?
Critical Resources	• Physical/Technological Resources - mostly tangible • Customer needs • Technological research and development • Competitive actions	• Integrated resources (e.g. ability to network managers, etc.) • Process improvement capability • Organizational learning • Process reengineering capability	• Imitability capability • Rareness capability • Alliances capability • Outsourcing capability • Substitutability
Appropriate position in the SMDA Model	• Scouting • Maintenance	• Maintenance • Dominance	• Dominance • Appraisal

resources (Barney, 1991; Priem & Butler, 2001), while intangible resources could include technological, innovation, and reputation resources (Grant, 1991), as well as intellectual resources such as management systems, information networks, fast organizational response systems, and corporate culture (Quinn, 1992).

Stage 2: Maintenance

The *Critical Resources (CRs)* are the resources that are unique to an organization and have a potential in either minimizing costs or maximizing profits. Critical resources could include resources that are difficult to duplicate (i.e., complex, require unique know-how, or are simply very expensive) meaning that a firm can sustain its competitive advantage depending not on the duration of it, but on the possibility of competitive duplication (Itami, 1987;Barney, 1991; Samanta, 2008). Similar to CRs are Itami's *invisible assets* (Itami, 1987), which provide a different way to recognize the vital contribution of accumulated experience and information to a firm's strategic resources.

Maintenance activities are of two kinds: (a) activities that are related to identifying CRs and (b) activities that are related to matching those CRs with the CSFs prioritized during the s-stage. For example, if one of the CSFs is *cost control* and one of the CRs is *information technology*, possible applications resulting from their integration could include the development of: a good accounting information system (fast and reliable information regarding financial performance and firm expenses); a distribution-based information system (linking customers with the firm's IS); or an order-based IS (linking suppliers with the firm's IS). Each one of these alternative information systems has a potential of decreasing the transaction costs associated with the firm. Furthermore, each alternative has a particular utility ("How much can it produce or save for the firm?") and a particular price ("How much will it cost to the firm?") which will be considered in the cost-benefit analysis of each alternative. As such, the maintenance stage usually focuses on building both the technological and organizational capability of a firm (see Figure 4).

To identify the critical resources of a firm, the following questions have to be answered: (a) *among the resources we own, which are unique?*, and (b) *does any supplier or buyer have major resources tied to us?* (Wernerfelt, 1989) The creation of CSFs-CRs combinations can provide a firm the following benefits: (1) as an extension of the CSF identification process, it can be used as a vehicle to better understand *what the firm is good at* and *what the firm is worth doing*, (2) assuming that firm resources are heterogeneous and imperfectly mobile, the combinations defined by a CSF-CR matrix could be compared with similar matrices of the leading competitors and assess the degree of heterogeneity between them (i.e., the higher the heterogeneity, the higher the probability to achieve competitive advantage), and (3) more efficient and effective processes could be identified (similarly to process reengineering attempts).

Other authors (Grant, 1991; Prahalad & Hamel, 1989; Prahalad & Hamel, 1990) use the terms *core competencies* and *strategic capabilities* respectively to describe such unique combinations of CRs. Examples include NEC's integration of computer and telecommunications expertise and Canon's integration of optical, microelectronics, and precision-mechanics expertise (Grant, 1991).

Stage 3: Dominance

This stage includes three major activities. First, the CRs identified from the most feasible cells of the CSF-CR matrix must be categorized according to their capacity (how "much" does the firm have?) (Wernerfelt, 1989). Second, those resources have to be evaluated in terms of their potential and uniqueness. Jay Barney (Barney, 1991; Priem & Butler, 2001; Johnson, 2005) suggests three attributes a resource has to have in order to contribute to sustained competitive advantage: *Rareness* (such as managerial talent), *Imperfect Imitability* (such as interpersonal relations, firm's culture, firm's reputation), and *Limited Substitutability* (such as vision). The more of those attributes a resource has, the higher the probability for obtaining advantage. For example, if a resource is rare but is imitable or substitutable, it is not considered a critical or unique resource. Although it seems intuitively easy to evaluate CRs in terms of their uniqueness, it is really a challenging perceptual task that needs to be undertaken by both top management and others knowledgeable about an industry's competitive characteristics. Brainstorming techniques can be helpful in the appropriate classification of CRs.

The following examples illustrate how firms can use different combinations of such CRs and capabilities for sustainable advantage: (a) for *rareness* effects: the ability to link the organization's information system to its customers for customized design of products (e.g., cars, homes) which in return would eliminate the need for sales representatives. The customers would have the ability to hook-up to the firm's IS and, following interactive user-friendly instructions from their screen, design their own specifications for the final product; (b) for *imperfect imitability* effect: the firm might want to use in-house prototypes of IS-applications instead of buying them from software vendors. Thus, it could create innovative applications that competitors would find very difficult to imitate; and (c) for *limited substitutability* effect: top management might be both using and providing strategic information from and to the firm's Executive Information System (EIS), to either track performance or analyze competition. Such an information system (and the management's ability to use it strategically) is difficult to substitute since it is developed on a proprietary basis to analyze internal and external information concerning the organization.

Finally, the CRs identified in the previous stages will have to be leveraged by either "mixing" them with other (existing) resources or by acquiring additional (customized) resources to complement them (Teece, 1984; Wernerfelt, 1989). Creativity, managerial talent, and analytical thinking have to be combined to assess possible benefits and costs from various resource combinations. For example, one way to accomplish this leveraging process is to hire managers with experience from an established firm (or SBU), or via a systematic study of successful firms as suggested by the scouting stage's benchmarking activities.

Stage 4: Appraisal

This final stage includes the evaluation of the implementation of the CSF-CR combinations and *resource-gap* analysis. Such evaluation involves "refilling" actions for the firm's resource base (replenishing, augmenting, and upgrading existing resources) and formulation of *alliances* and *outsourcing* types of activities with other firms. In other words, the firm has to decide how to maintain its stock of resources to sustain its position and continue its success.

Furthermore, the firm has to decide if alliances and outsourcing activities are appropriate for its strategic direction and if they should be used in addition to the resource-based activities described in the previous three stages. With the proliferation of information technologies and the increasing numbers of global competitors entering each industry, firms will have to embark on alliances and outsourcing strategies to sustain their market position and related advantages. Alliances with competitors or suppliers can exploit complementary resources, and outsourcing will allow the firm to concentrate to a few core competencies while renting resources from other firms. In that sense then, both alliances and outsourcing can be thought of as part of the *strategic capability* of a firm (see Figure 4).

CONCLUSION

The integrative approach for sustainable competitive advantage, the identification of Critical Success Factors (CSFs), the establishment of technological, organizational and strategic capability, the significance of critical resources (CRs), and the formation of alliances and outsourcing strategies have been the focus of this paper. The author has argued that by assessing the executives' perceptions on key organizational and environmental factors, and by combining them with resources that are rare, imperfectly imitable, and non-substitutable, the firm can reach the Dominance and Appraisal stages and sustain its competitive advantage. The author also assumed, that there will be iterations between the various phases of the suggested strategy development process after the basic requirements for each stage have been met (see Figure 3). The cases of Honda Corporation of Japan and Motorola Inc. of U.S. (see Appendix) illustrate the integration of the industrial organization and resource-based models of strategic management thinking, as well as demonstrate how in practice the SMDA model has been applied by two successful organizations.

Implications for Management

The end result of the proposed strategy development process should not be a long `laundry list' of critical success factors and critical resources. Rather, it should be the actions undertaken by a firm's top management (strategy conception and strategic intent) and line management (strategy implementation) after the development of winning amalgams (introduction of innovations) between CSFs and CRs, as well as the cooperation between top and line management. It is up to leadership and employees to be able to see through them and visualize new products or services, new designs, or new information systems to handle CSFs and CRs' combinations (i.e., ability to have "what-if" contingency plans). In other words it is *the ability to integrate* in a systemic and innovative way the knowledge about a firm's resources and success factors that allows the firm to gain and sustain competitive advantages in its own or other overlapping (where their boundaries meet) markets.

Implications for Strategic Planning

Perhaps the most important implication for management is the ability to facilitate strategic planning through the stages proposed by the SMDA model. It is however a benefit attributed not only to this model, but to any stage-oriented model: such models simply allow their "users" (i.e., managers, organizations) to identify "where they are now" (depending on what resources they possess and how they map on the SMDA model) and accordingly decide "how they will get where they want to move next" (again, depending on their resources' potential).

Implications for Management Control and Information Processing

The SMDA model could be used to monitor the strategy development process thus making sure that the objectives at each stage have been met before substantial resources are committed and projects are undertaken for the next stage. As appears in Figure 4, management control is more important at the initial two stages where technological and organizational capability play an important role. However, the management control facilitated by the model requires that the organization has sufficient information-processing capabilities to provide timely and accurate information regarding performance measurement. In summary, this paper has demonstrated the need for an integration of the IO and resource-based philosophies for strategy formulation. The proposed SMDA model suggests simultaneous focus on external and internal pressures to a firm's strategy formulation and complements recent theory and research on the resource-based view of the firm.

REFERENCES

Aacker, D. A. (1989). Managing assets and skills: The key to a sustainable competitive advantage. *California Management Review*.

Amit, R., & Schoemaker, P. G. H. (1993). Strategic assets and organizational rent. *Strategic Management Journal*, 14.

Bain, J. S. (1956). *Barriers to new competition*. Cambridge, MA: Harvard University Press. doi:10.4159/harvard.9780674188037

Barney, J. (1991). Firm resources and sustained competitive advantage. *Journal of Management*, *17*(1), 99–120. doi:10.1177/014920639101700108

Buzzell, R., & Gale, B. (1987). *The PIMS principles*. New York: Free Press.

Conner, K. R. (1991). A historical comparison of resource-based theory and five schools of thought within IO economics: Do we have a new theory of the firm? *Journal of Management*, *17*(1). doi:10.1177/014920639101700109

Daft, R. (1983). *Organization Theory and Design*. New York: West Publishing.

David, F. R. (2005). *Strategic Management*. New York: Prentice-Hall.

Financial Times. (1990). Mobile Communications: How Motorola Plans to Cut Off its Competitors. *Financial Times, 6*, 12.

Glueck, W. F. (1980). *Business Policy & Strategic Management*. New York: McGraw-Hill.

Granger, C. H. (1964). The Hierarchy of Objectives. *Harvard Business Review*.

Grant, J. H., & King, W. R. (1982). *The Logic of Strategic Planning*. New York: Little Brown and Co.

Grant, R. M. (1991). The resource-based theory of competitive advantage: Implications for strategy formulation. *California Management Review*, *33*(3), 114–135. doi:10.2307/41166664

Grant, R. M. (1996). Prospering in dynamically-competitive environments: Organizational capability as knowledge integration. *Organization Science*, *7*(4), 375–387. doi:10.1287/orsc.7.4.375

Hamel, G., & Prahalad, C. K. (1989). Strategic Intent. *Harvard Business Review*. PMID:10303477

Hamel, G., & Prahalad, C. K. (1990). The core competence of the corporation. *Harvard Business Review*.

Hansen, G., & Wernerfelt, B. (1989). Determinants of Firm Performance: The relative importance of economic and organizational factors. *Strategic Management Journal*, 10.

Hax, A., & Majluf, N. (1991). *The strategy concept and process: A pragmatic approach*. New York: Prentice-Hall.

Hayes, R. H. (1985). Strategic Planning--Forward in Reverse? *Harvard Business Review*.

Hitt, M. A., Ireland, R. D., & Hoskisson, R. E. (1995). *Strategic Management: Competitiveness & Globalization*. New York: West Publishing.

Hofer, C., & Schendel, D. (1978). *Strategy Formulation: Analytical Concepts*. New York: West Publishing.

Hrebiniak, L. G., & Joyce, W. (1984). *Implementing Strategy*. New York: Macmillan.

Hrebiniak, L. G., & Snow, C. (1982). Top management agreement and organizational performance. *Human Relations*, *3*(12).

Itami, H. (1987). *Mobilizing Invisible Assets*. Harvard University Press.

Johnson, G., Scholes, K., & Whittington, R. (2005). Exploring Corporate Strategy. *Financial Times*, pp. 150-157.

Knott, A. M. (2003). The organizational routines factor market paradox. *Strategic Management Journal*, 24.

Lado, A. A., Boyd, N. G., & Wright, P. (1992). A competency-based model of sustainable competitive advantage: Toward a conceptual integration. *Journal of Management*, *18*(1), 77–91. doi:10.1177/014920639201800106

Leidecker, J., & Bruno, A. (1984). Identifying and Using Critical Success Factors. *Long Range Planning*, *17*(1), 23–32. doi:10.1016/0024-6301(84)90163-8

Lippman, S., & Rumelt, R. (1982). Uncertain Imitability: An Analysis of Interfirm Differences in Efficiency under Competition. *The Bell Journal of Economics*, 13.

Liu, Y. (2013). Sustainable Competitive advantage in turbulent business environments. *International Journal of Production Research*, *51*(10), 2821–2841. doi:10.1080/00207543.2012.720392

March & Simon. (1958). *Organizations*. New York: John Wiley and Sons.

Maslow, A. H. (1943). A Theory of Human Motivation. *Psychological Review*, *50*(4), 374. doi:10.1037/h0054346

Ohmae, K. (1988). Getting Back to Strategy. *Harvard Business Review*.

Pascale, R. T. (1984). Perspectives on Strategy: The Real Story Behind Honda's Success. *California Management Review*, *26*(3), 47–72. doi:10.2307/41165080

Peters, T., & Waterman, R. (1982). *In Search of Excellence*. New York: Warner Books.

Pollalis, Y. A., & Grant, J. H. (1994). Information Resources & Corporate Strategy Development. *Information Strategy*, *11*(1), 12–28.

Porter, M. E. (1980). *Competitive Strategy*. New York: Free Press.

Porter, M. E. (1981). The contributions of industrial organization to strategic management. *Academy of Management Review*, *15*(1).

Porter, M. E. (1985). *Competitive Advantage*. New York: Free Press.

Priem, P., & Butler, J. E. (2001). Is the resource-based view a useful perspective for strategic management research? *Academy of Management Review*, *26*(1), 22–40. doi:10.5465/AMR.2001.4011928

Quinn, J. B. (1992). *The Intelligence Enterprise*. New York: Free Press.

Rockart, J. (1979). Chief Executives Define their Own Data Needs. *Harvard Business Review*, *57*(2). PMID:10297607

Samanta, I. (2006). The reinforcement of competitiveness of medium sized firms. *Applied Research Review Periodical Scientific, 11*(2).

Samanta, I. (2008). Innovation Culture Assists Knowledge Management in new era. In *Web 2.0: The business model*. Springer.

Schultz, R. L., & Slevin, D. P. (1975). *Implementing Operations Research/Management Science*. New York: Elsevier.

Schumpeter, J. A. (1950). *Capitalism, Socialism, and Democracy*. New York: Harper & Row.

Teece, D. (1984). Economic Analysis and Strategic Management. *California Management Review*, *25*(3).

Week, B. (1989, November 13). The Rival Japan Respects, Motorola's Secrets. *Business Week*, pp. 108-114.

Wernerfelt, B. (1984). A Resource-Based View of the Firm. *Strategic Management Journal*, 5.

Wernerfelt, B. (1989). From Critical Resources to Corporate Strategy. *Journal of General Management*, *14*(3).

Wiggenhorn, W. (1990). Motorola University: When Training Becomes an Education. *Harvard Business Review*.

KEY TERMS AND DEFINITIONS

Competitive Advantage: Occurs when an organization acquires or develops an attribute or combination of attributes that allows outperforming its competitors.

Critical Resources (CR): Are the resources that are unique to an organization and have a potential in either minimizing costs or maximizing profits.

Critical Success Factors (CSF): The limited number of areas in which results, if they are satisfactory, will ensure successful competitive performance for the organization.

Economic Crisis: Can be described as that period of dismal economic performance. During this time, the value of institutions, especially financial institutions, drops at unprecedented speeds and everything seems to be valueless. Production is low and often fails to meet the level of demand.

Strategic Management: Formulation and implementation of the major goals and initiatives based on consideration of resources and an assessment of the internal and external environments.

Strategic Planning: Extend to control mechanisms for guiding the implementation of the strategy. Is an organization's process of defining its strategy, or direction, and making decisions on allocating its resources to pursue this strategy.

Sustainable Advantage: When the efforts by competitors to render the competitive advantage redundant have ceased. When the imitative actions have come to an end without disrupting the firm's competitive advantage, the firm's strategy can be called sustainable.

The Industrial Organization Model of Strategy Formulation (IO): Specifies a firm's strategy based on external environment with the characteristics of general, industry and competitor environment.

The Resource-Based Model of Strategy Formulation: Specifies a firm's strategy internally to earn above-average returns based on its unique resources and capabilities.

The Scouting-Maintenance-Dominance-Appraisal Model of Strategy Evaluation (SMDA): Suggests simultaneous focus on external and internal pressures to a firm's strategy formulation and complements recent theory and research on the resource-based view of the firm.

Turbulent Economic Environment: Unpredictable and swift changes in an organization's external environment, the economy, that affect its performance.

APPENDIX

Analytical Implementation of the CR-CSF Allocation

Possible Research Problem #1: How should the firm distribute the critical resources among projects associated with the CSFs in order to maximize the firm's utility?
Objective: Max $Z = R_1(CR_1) + R_2(CR_2) + \ldots\ldots + R_n(CR_n)$ subject to the following constraints:

1. $CR_1 + CR_2 + \ldots\ldots + CR_n <= T$
2. $CR_1, CR_2, \ldots\ldots, CR_n >= 0$

where,

- $R_1, R_2, \ldots., R_n$ = Returns from various projects associated with the $CSFs_j$ (j=1..m)
- $CR_1, CR_2, \ldots, CR_n$ = Critical resources allocated to various firm projects.
- T = Total amount of resources available in the firm (determined by the economic returns of past solutions or projections of future ones).

Possible Research Problem #2: A project j associated primarily with CSF_j, can be accomplished using a variety of firm resources (CR_1, ... CR_M) each having a particular characteristic and price. assuming that we want to maximize the value (or utility, or benefits, or profits) from project j, what is the optimal solution in terms of selection of the most "profitable" (*value - costs*) combination of CSFs-CRs?
Objective: max $Z = \Sigma_i \Sigma_j R_{ij} F_{ij}$, where $(R_{ij} F_{ij})$ represents the value (total profit) generated from allocating (R_i) amount of resource -i to a project -j that has as a purpose to perform well if measured under CSF (F_j), i.e., (F_j) = operationalization of $CSF_j = (Price_j - Cost_j)$

Case 1: The "Honda Effect" Revisited

Pascale (Pascale, 1984) reports on how Honda managed to "redefine" the US and World motorcycle industry:

"The Japanese are somewhat distrustful of a single 'strategy' for in their view any idea that focuses attention does so at the expense of peripheral vision....They regard any propensity to be driven by a single-minded strategy as a weakness...." In 1975, Boston Consulting Group (BCG) identified two key factors [something like critical failure factors] for the decline of the British Motorcycle Industry, (a) market share loss and profitability declines and (b) scale economy disadvantages in technology, distribution, and manufacturing...

Table 2. Critical success factors CSF_j

	1 x 1	1 x 2	1 x n
Critical Resources CR (i) i=1 m	2 x 1	2 x 2	2 x n
	m x 1	m x 2	m x n

j=1 n

The success of the Japanese manufacturers originated with the growth of their domestic market during the 1950s...however, the Japanese have developed huge production volumes in small motorcycles in their domestic markets, and volume-related cost reductions had followed. This resulted in a highly competitive cost position which the Japanese used as a springboard for penetration of world markets with small motorcycles in the early 1960s."

In this example, Honda used its *experience* in the domestic Japanese market and then applied it to the global markets successfully. Honda has used the "knowledge about itself" (experience and superiority in specialized production systems, balancing engineering and market requirements, and cost efficiency and reliability of suppliers, and the knowledge about the external environment (markets and competitors) to develop its initial strategy process. Thus, technology and market know-how (technological capability) together with organizational learning and experience (organizational capability) in the domestic environment have been identified by Honda as Critical Resources, and matched adequately with the CSFs in the these same environments (i.e., cost sensitivity, scale, process technology, quality, etc.).

After identifying its major strengths in terms of existing or additional organizational resources (CRs) Honda continued to innovate and penetrate other markets using the same simple concepts it used in the motorcycle industry: paying attention to the "human factor," experimenting with various strategies (thus learning more about the environment's reactions), and thinking in terms of "strategic accommodation" or "adaptive persistence" (i.e., being able to move information and ideas from bottom to top and back again in continuous dialogue as Pascale observes).

Honda's competitive advantage is based on resources that have the attributes of rareness (managerial talent: "....".senior managers are humble enough not to take their initial strategic position too seriously ..." (Pascale, 1984), imperfect imitability (interpersonal relations between top management and employees allowing room for new ideas and increased productivity, firm's reputation), and limited substitutability (Honda's vision for the future). Now, Honda has moved to the stage of sustainable competitive advantage where it enjoys its "invisible assets" such as reputation for quality in motorcycles, cars or lawnmowers. Itami also mentions (Itami, 1987): "Honda used its basic technology in small engines sequentially, first in motorcycles, then in cars, and later simultaneously in the US in such varied products as generators and lawnmowers....only invisible assets can be simultaneously used in several areas." (p.13).

Honda focused on the competitive and market CSFs early on its development as a motorcycle manufacturer in Japan and thus acquired the experience and information needed to survive (Scouting Stage); it then identified its CRs and applied them towards the goals of effectiveness and efficiency, as well as managed to improve its technology-organization-strategy fit (strategic validity); that enabled Honda to maintain its position in the global market (Maintenance Stage); finally, it continued to leverage its CRs by innovating to sustain its competitive advantage both domestically and globally (Dominance Stage).

Case 2: Motorola Inc.

Motorola Inc. spends an estimated $1 million annually on competitor intelligence activities. In addition, it focuses on a few key factors to outperform its competitors: "The company embraced such Japanese tactics as driving relentlessly for market share, sharply upgrading quality, and constantly honing manufacturing processes to pare costs. And it continues to pour billions into research and development, training, and capital improvements--$1 billion, or 19% of revenues..." (Business Week, 1989).

Moreover, Motorola has emphasized the education of its employees to an extreme, spending $120 million annually in it. At "Motorola University" employees learn basic skills of reading, math and statistics, financial and risk management, as well as "relational skills" such as customer satisfaction, effective meetings, negotiations, and effective presentations (Wiggenhorn, 1990). According to the SMDA model, Motorola has successfully gone through the first stage of Scouting by focusing on a few CSFs (quality, efficiency, education, RDandD) and by learning more about its competitors (especially the Japanese) via benchmarking.

But Motorola has not been satisfied by merely managing to keep its market share in the radio communications and semiconductors industries where it initially started to establishing its reputation. Now Motorola has also entered very successfully the cellular electronics industry (mobile communications), as well as the microprocessors market. The company used its excellent technological infrastructure in radio communications and semiconductors as a base (technological capability) to develop its expertise in mobile technology. By identifying which factors were important in the young mobile market (e.g., size, weight, performance) and which unique or limited substitutable resources it possessed (e.g., expertise in communications technology, sharp focus on design, quality reputation), Motorola managed to design products that are smaller, lighter, and with more options than its rivals' (Financial Times, 1990).

"First came the MicroTac cellular phone, a Star Trekky unit that slips into a coat pocket and flips open for use. It is far sleeker and a third lighter than the next closest portable phone, from Japan's Matsushita Electric Industrial Co....with this product lineup, Motorola should grab 50% of new US cellular phone sales by 1990, says Herschel Shosteck, president of a Silver Spring (Md.) consulting firm" (Business Week, 1989) .

The combinations of certain market-driven CSFs and organization-based CRs have given Motorola an advantage and lead difficult to be followed by rivals. It is best exemplified by the adoption of Motorola's microprocessor from Canon Inc. of Japan for its best-selling EOS 35mm camera. "It's there [at the heart of the camera] says Canon, because Motorola provides superior design expertise and service, along with equal quality"(Business Week, 1989). Thus Motorola successfully managed to go through the Maintenance stage too.

However, what distinguishes Motorola from its rivals is the fact that it "builds for the future" heavily, focusing on strategic planning and strategic global alliances (e.g., has ties with Toshiba in Japan). In addition, competing with the "best-in-class" Motorola managed to take the lead in another niche market, the pager technologies. It has introduced the wristwatch pager, thus advancing at least two years ahead of the competition. By using its organizational resources such as expertise and quality focus (organizational capability), and by innovating Motorola has managed to sustain its competitive advantage in more than one domestic and global markets (strategic capability).

"That's because Motorola didn't rest on its laurels. It knew competitors would be burning the midnight oil, and Fisher [the CEO] didn't want to wind up with a me-too product because `follower positions are secondary financial positions'...Over a three-year period, with Timex Corp. as a partner, engineers shrank the numbers and size of parts until they could all be squeezed into a watch"(Business Week, 1989)

Chapter 6
Exploring the Relationship between the Eco-labels and Green Buying Behaviour with Reference to Mumbai City

Ritu Sinha
IES Management College and Research Centre, India

ABSTRACT

Today's businesses and consumers confront the challenge of protecting and preserving the earth's resources and the environment. They have become more concerned about the natural environment and are realizing that their production and consumption purchasing behavior have a direct impact on the environment. Even the consumer looks for green lifestyle and wants to make its contribution towards reducing its impact on the environment. Manufacturers and retailers are observing this trend and are trying to gain an edge in the competitive market by exploiting the potential in the green market industry. They are offering eco-friendly products that are supposed to be good for humans, nature, and companies. An eco-label is a label that certifies that a product meets overall environmental preference of a product or service based on life-cycle consideration and the important criteria to be fulfilled for achieving this label. These labels can help the companies to influence the regulatory environment, create industry standards for environmental control, and expand market share. The aim of this chapter is to identify and analyze how eco-labels can influence consumer buying behavior and awareness towards the various eco-labels in the Mumbai market.

INTRODUCTION

Over the past three decades, the environmental concerns among customers have increased and have influenced the way people consume and are willing to consume. Environmental consciousness has increased in individual consumers, and therefore has become a driving force in the business strategies that incorporates environmental aspects by most of the companies. Businesses across the world even under economic slowdown are developing strategies to sustain themselves

DOI: 10.4018/978-1-4666-6232-2.ch006

in the wake of climate change. They are working towards developing a low carbon landscape and undertaking efforts to optimize the carbon efficiency of existing products and infrastructure. As people become more conscious for their planet Earth, sustainability is becoming a part of a new value chain that respond to green enterprises offering a range of opportunities and challenges. This trend is gathering momentum and many corporate players are developing green initiatives that range from green buildings, green products, and green operations to green supply chains. Green interest group focuses on conservation, reuse, reduction of environmental footprint, enhancement of efficiencies, and a desire to preserve the environment. Although ecological products or organic products do not have a major share still there has been growing demand for these kinds of products. Consumers look for the products that are recyclable and make use of reusable packaging, nonpolluting products, and energy efficient bulbs.

BACKGROUND

In order to distinguish ecological products from conventional ordinary ones companies put special Eco-labels on them. An eco-label is a label that certifies that a product meets high environmental and performance standards and has less impact on the environment than non-labeled products. Along with this it also convey a message that the company is socially responsible. According to Williams (2004, 133), "eco-labelling is a communication label that specify the information regarding the company's commitment to "green" production principles that adhere to consumer ethic, to market demands, to industry regulation, and to the regulatory environment as determined locally or internationally." These labels include claims like recyclable, eco-friendly, low energy, and recycled content so as to catch the attention of consumers that are looking for the ways in which they could reduce adverse impacts to the environment through purchasing choices.

Ecolabels are determined on life cycle considerations; which implies that all aspects of the "life" of a product starting from design, production, operation and maintenance up to disposal are taken into consideration. This certification preferably should be done by third-party and independent from the certified company. These labels should also communicate that the awarded product has reached distinction in environmental performance in comparison to average products in the same category and this labeling is based on sound scientific evidence. These ecolabels are an answer to the growing request from consumers and committed professionals so as to provide complex information in a very straightforward way in product categories like food, appliances, housecleaning products, paper products and many more.

Eco-labelling can serve as effective forms of communication for endorsing that the product is environmentally friendly. Eco-label can address to a single dimension, two dimensions and multiple dimensions known as Type 1, Type 2 and Type 3 label. These eco-labelling can help the companies to influence the regulatory environment, create industry standards for environmental control, achieve cost savings, expand market share, as well as achieve additional indirect benefits. In the past few years, there has been a surge in corporate eco-promising i.e. practice of making claims about the environmental attributes of products. These claims have an aim of attracting consumers and convincing them to buy one product over another. But sometime these environmental claims and eco-labels create confusion among consumers and create uncertainty about which claims to trust. Also, there is lack of guiding principles or standardization with respect to these labels. Unfortunately, sometime it can backfire the company as availability of increased information content bears a risk of exceeding consumer patience and/or capacity for interpretation.

NEED OF ECO-LABELLING

The origins of eco-labelling was result of green washing phenomenon happening at commercial enterprises who recognized that environmental concerns could be translated into a market advantage for certain products. This lead to proliferation of environmental declarations and claims like "recyclable,""eco-friendly," "low energy," and "recycled content." But sometime, these claims are either not true or over exaggerated. Claims like some of bathroom cleaners were "nitrate-free" where such products had never contained nitrates! Such claims got the attention of green consumers who really want to reduce adverse environmental impacts through their purchasing choices. But over a period of time these growing numbers of claims were creating confusion in the minds of consumers. Consumers were not sure about the authenticity of these claims of environmentally preferable alternative. Hence there was a need of credible, guiding standards and investigation by an independent third party, to establish, implement and monitor these eco-labelling standards.

In an ecolabelling program, product categories and ecolabelling criteria are determined by an independent organisation with the help of complementary technical advisory group. After defining the category, life cycle review is conducted that includes raw material extraction, manufacture, distribution, use and disposal. The differentiating parameters like energy use, toxicity, etc. are then used as the basis for criteria development. The objective of setting the standards for the eco-labels helps the government in encouraging sound environmental practices by highlighting on the environmental conservation and its protection. These eco-labels serve as a market-based instrument that encourages the efficient management of renewable resources, encouraging the proper management of chemicals in products. At the same time it also foster the environmentally sound innovation and leadership.

The guiding principles of ecolabeling are voluntary participation by manufacturers, importers, service providers and other businesses. It also calls for compliance to environmental and other relevant legislation and product should able to display comparable quality and reasonable performance in relation to alternatives based on sound scientific and engineering principles. Various studies have confirmed that environmental attributes is one of many factors that is considered seriously by consumers in their purchasing decisions even under economic downturn. At the same time it is very important to have the acceptance and adoption of the ISO 14000 series of standards as it is getting accepted greatly by industry and governments around the world. Such consistency could provide legitimacy and soundness for ecolabelling programs in place and under development.

HISTORY OF ECO-LABELS

Ecolabels can serve the message for sustainable consumption and guide consumers in making informed choices about the environmental impact of the products they consume. Also, they are an element of the sustainable production which reflects that those products are certified to be environmentally superior to alternatives. Reflecting on the growing trend of environmental consciousness on the part of customers, a number of national labelling systems have been set up in different countries since 1980. The objective of putting these eco-labels on the products is to ensure that these products have been manufactured by processes and procedures with low or minimal environmental impact. Ecolabelling was first introduced in Germany in 1977 through the Blue Angel scheme and was followed by Canada's Environmental Choice Programme, introduced in 1988. Since then many countries have adopted ecolabelling and most commonly used are U.S. Environmental Protection Agency, Comprehensive Procurement Guidelines, U.S. Environmental Protection Agency, ENERGY STAR®, European Union, Eco Flower, Germany, Blue Angel, Sweden, TCO Development, Nordic Swan, Japan, Eco Mark, Japan, Green Purchasing Network and many more. Apart from this, most of these programs are also using the approach of "cradle to grave," that is, they undertake analysis which is based on the environmental consequences of their manufacture, use and disposal.

Eco-labeling makes the simple process of identifying and deciding the products or service that are less harmful to the environment in compare with the other product. There is a wide range of attributes which are taken care of these eco-labels like health issues, environmental impacts, packaging and other industrial issues to name few. In 1991, India launched its own ecolabelling system called Ecomark. Although the approach of Indian is similar to ecolabels of other countries, still it differs from rest of them in one important aspect. These ecolabels are awarded to those products that meet both environmental and quality criteria. In the India, Rugmark represents the carpets manufactured without involving child labor. Now-a- days many of packed food items having green, red dot indicating that the ingredients belong to vegetarian or non-vegetarian category. Sometime they also indicate that the packaging material with which the product is packed will be reused or recycled. These eco-labels are based on a full life cycle assessment and incorporate quality and social aspects. Still it was not accepted well by manufactures even after 15 years of existence. So far manufacturer's of around fifteen categories of various products like paper, pulp, leather and wood particle board have applied and got the Ecomark licence.

CONSUMER BEHAVIOUR

Consumer behaviour reflects on the combination of individual observation and experience, and collective communication and dissemination of information within a social market structure(Williams, 2004, 126). The role of environmental knowledge plays an important role in consumers' purchase intention, followed by environmental attitude. Green consumerism is a relatively recent phenomenon where consumers are the driving force behind environmental damage. This is causing consumer activism resulting in an increase in the concern expressed towards environmental protection leading to "green consumerism" (Eriksson, 2002). A green consumer is one who asks for green product and avoids any product which may harm damage to any living organism, cause deterioration of the environment during process of manufacturing or during process of usage, consume a large amount of non renewable energy, involves unethical testing on animals or human subjects (Elkington, 1994). Green consumers are willing to buy organic or energy consuming or recycled goods so as to demonstrate environmental responsibility. Various market research studies have confirmed that consumers are willing to pay more for eco-friendly products.

Green consumerism can affect the attitudes (i.e., the claimed behaviour) versus behaviour (i.e., the actual behaviour). People may have a motivation, desire, and thereby develop an attitude and intention to engage in environmental behavior so as to showcase themselves as role models and have a self-belief that they can help to preserve the environment. There are various factors like factors like income, age, gender, or education of customers have an important influence on their green buying behavior. Therefore eco-labels can be one of the important parameters to evaluate a product during purchasing decision. It also helps in promoting the development of products that are environmentally-sound and contribute to a sustainable consumerism. It is important to identify the groups of consumers who might be interested in buying eco-labelled products and kind of labeling they preferred. Variables like environmental attitudes, attitudes of the consumers, skepticism toward environmental product claims, consumer self-identity, and future purchase intention play an import role in buying behavior.

If consumers are able to distinguish between competing products on the basis of the products' environmental harmfulness, they will integrate this information into their decision making process. According to the multi-attribute models of the type proposed by Fishbein (1963), differences in perceived environmental harmfulness between brands should influence the choice toward the brand exhibiting the lowest harmfulness, ceteris paribus. Moreover, ethical choice models predict willingness to act on the basis of ethical judgment (Hunt & Vitell, 2006 ; Rest, 1986) and perceived moral intensity (Jones, 1991).

Consumers can contribute towards reducing the negative environmental impact of their consumption by making appropriate choices and even some percentage of customers are ready to pay higher price for the same. The objective of having eco-labels is expected to provide clear, concise and necessary information to consumers so as to differentiate between environmentally friendly products and harmful products. If consumers are aware about the products' environmental harmfulness, then they integrate this information into their buying decision process. Various studies have confirmed the fact that when consumers find a discrepancy between competing brands regarding their environmental impact, they tend to choose the most environmental friendly product. Hence there is a strong need for disseminating relevant information available and to educate consumers.

There are many factors that are instrumental in promoting green consumers to purchase green products like increased awareness of green issues and information availability on environmental sustenance; green advertising by corporations; increased concern for the environment; increase in popularity of green products by social and environmental charities as some factors. This overall increase in the environmental consciousness among different consumer profile have been identified as business opportunities by business firms to improve their marketing niche rather than just actions which need to be carried out.

STUDY OBJECTIVE

The main objective of the study is to assess the consumer awareness towards the usage of eco-labels on the products in Mumbai city of India. The study is an attempt to analyze how much customers are aware about the concept of eco-labels and does this knowledge play an important role in forming their attitudes and its influence on purchasing behavior. At the same time, it also explores the consumer's knowledge about the initiatives taken by the Indian government with respect to the eco-labels. In this study we consider "eco-label" as environmental labels, organic labels and ethical labels.

METHODOLOGY

For this study a quantitative pilot study was planned where structured questionnaire was used to collect the data from the respondents. This survey was done to find out the consumers attitudes towards the role of eco-labels on the products in their purchase behavior. The study made use of both primary and secondary data. Secondary data consists of related articles, books from both libraries and Internet resources relating to eco-labels. More than 100 questionnaires were distributed to the people of Mumbai and only 60 were found suitable for analysis, others were rejected because of incomplete information.

In order to measure the consumer attitude towards eco-labels, a structured questionnaire was used where respondents were asked to answer the statements on five-point Likert type scale ranging from 'Strongly Agree' to 'Strongly Disagree'. The demography of the respondents was also measured in terms of age, gender, education, occupation and income etc. The questions of the questionnaire aimed to know how the about the awareness, attitude of consumers when they make their decision for purchasing eco-labeled products. Some questions were asked to gain information about buying decision process such as why they buy organic products, how they gain information about the organic products and etc. Some other questions related to their demographic profile.

The questionnaire made use of several multi-item scales. These items were checked for their accuracy and applicability with the help of reliability. For this purpose, the split-half reliability of Cronbach's alpha of a scale was used. The Cronbach's alpha value can range from 0 to 1, where higher values indicating higher internal consistency. The questionnaire had a Cronbach's Alpha value of 0.695 which indicates that each item has very high internal consistency and can thus be considered reliable.

DATA ANALYSIS

Sample Profile

Majority (70%) of the respondents were male whereas female were 30% constituted the sample size of 60. Majority (35%) of the respondents was from younger age group of 26-35 years and 22% of the respondents belong to 36-45 and 46-59 years while the rest 11% of the respondents belong to more than 60+ and 10% belong to 15-25 age group. Majority of respondents have Graduation (33%) and post –graduation (16%) as their educational qualification where undergraduates were 14%, others were 13% and people belonging to vocational schools they constitute 3%. 38% of respondents belong to the income group of 2.50 to 3.50 lakhs, 28% belong to the 1.00 to 2.5 lakhs, 23% belong to more than 5.00 lakhs, 8% belong to .50-1.00 and only 1% belong to less than 0.50 lakhs. Around 23% of respondents belong to the category of working executive and housewife.

RESULTS

The data were analyzed to determine the extent to which consumer attitude and beliefs are affected by the presence of eco-labels on them. When the people were asked about the awareness regarding the environmental problems in relation to the production, use and disposal of household products, it was found out that 27% were completely aware of it whereas 37% constitute slightly aware and rest of them i.e. 36% were completely unaware of it. When these respondents were enquired about how they have received information regarding eco-labels, they attributed this information to the Friends/relatives (34%), Advertising (27%), Company publications(21%), Internet (13%) and Personal research (5%).

A cluster analysis was run on 60 cases, each responding to items on demographics (gender; qualifications, occupation, income, awareness about the environmental issues and awareness about the symbol for the eco-label), on their attitudes to buying behavior towards the green product having eco-label. A hierarchical cluster analysis was performed to arrive at the number of clusters. The coefficient of Agglomeration Schedule suggested the emergence of four clusters. (Refer to the Appendix). This was further taken by carrying out K-Means which gave rise to Final Cluster Centers, Number of Cases in each Cluster and Cluster Membership.

Cluster 1

People belonging to this cluster are neutral about the fact that Indian government supports Eco-label and uses the symbol of earthen pot for the same. They do not read the labels when they make a purchase and neutral for paying extra if the product is eco-friendly. They rarely buy eco-labelled products and prefer affordable shops even if buying eco-labelled products. They don't care whether a product carries an eco-label or not and they won't postpone their purchase if an eco-labelled product is not available. They are neutral about the fact that individual consumers can contribute to solving environmental problems but agrees to the point that humans are severely abusing the environment. They disagree that environmental problems are the responsibility of the central government but do not trust green labels. They disagree that environment-conscious consumption leads to better health but agree that it is troublesome, expensive and boring to be environment conscious

Cluster 2

People belonging to this cluster are neutral about the fact that Indian government supports Eco-label and uses the symbol of earthen pot for the same. They are neutral towards reading the labels when they make a purchase and to pay extra if the product is eco-friendly. They prefer affordable shops if they are buying a eco-labelled product. They are neutral for checking the eco-friendly product and prefer affordable shops even if buying eco-labelled products. They are neutral whether a product carries an eco-label or not and they won't postpone their purchase if an eco-labelled product is not available. They are neutral about the fact that individual consumers can contribute to solving environmental problems but agrees to the point that humans are severely abusing the environment. They are neutral about the fact that environmental problems are the responsibility of the central government and trust about green labels. They agree that environment-conscious consumption leads to better health but agree that it is expensive to be environment conscious but not troublesome and boring.

Cluster 3

People belonging to this cluster are neutral about the fact that Indian government supports Eco-label and uses the symbol of earthen pot for the same. They are neutral towards reading labels when they make a purchase and agree to pay extra if the product is eco-friendly. They prefer affordable shops if they are buying an eco-labelled product. They are neutral for checking the eco-friendly product and prefer affordable shops even if buying eco-labelled products. They don't care whether a product carries an eco-label or not and they won't postpone their purchase if an eco-labelled product is not available. They agree to the fact that individual consumers can contribute to solving environmental problems but disagrees with the fact that humans are severely abusing the environment. They disagree about the fact that environmental problems are the responsibility of the central government and trust about green labels. They agree that environment-conscious consumption leads to better health but disagree that it is expensive, troublesome and boring to be environment conscious.

Cluster 4

People belonging to this cluster are neutral about the fact that Indian government has a symbol of earthen pot for the eco-labels but are aware of the fact that Indian government supports eco-label. They are neutral towards reading labels when they make a purchase and agree to pay extra if the product is eco-friendly. They prefer affordable shops if they are buying an eco-labelled product. They are neutral for checking the eco-friendly product and prefer affordable shops even if buying eco-labelled products. They read labels when they make a purchase and willing to pay extra if the product is environment friendly. They prefer buying eco-labelled products but are not fond of affordable shops for shopping eco-label products. They also agree that humans are severely abusing the environment and being Environment-conscious consumption leads to better health. At the same time they also accepted that it is expensive to be environment conscious. These group members completely disagree with the fact that it is troublesome to be environment conscious and they do not trust green labels and also feel that Individual consumers can contribute to solving environmental problems and they often buy eco-labelled products.

From the Agglomeration Schedule Coefficient table we infer that cluster 4 represents a group who are quite aware about eco-label and have positive attitude towards the green environment. On further analysis, we profile the people who belong to cluster 4 as green consumers. On further, conducting a cross tab between the cluster 4 profile and their demographic, it has been found out that the people belonging to Cluster 4 has maximum frequency pertaining to female members belonging to an age group of 36-45 years are mostly graduates and post graduates and having an income ranging from 2.50 to 5.00 lakhs . These people are mostly executives and housewife. The items (statements) which were significant for this group were found to be that they read labels when they make a purchase and willing to pay extra if the product is environment friendly. Still they prefer affordable shops even for buying eco-labelled products. This cluster feels that if an eco-labelled product is not available, they would postpone their purchase and individual consumers can't contribute much in solving the environmental problems. They feel that humans are severely abusing the environment and environmental problems are the not the solely responsibility of the central government and they trust green labels. They believe that environment-conscious consumption leads to better health and it is troublesome to be environment conscious and expensive also. Still it is not boring to be an environment-conscious consumer. If we consider the Anova table, we find statement like I read labels when I make a purchase, I am willing to pay extra if the product is environment friendly, I prefer affordable shops even buying eco-labelled products, If an eco-labelled product is not available, I postpone my purchase, Individual consumers can contribute to solving environmental problems, Humans are severely abusing the environment, Environmental problems are the responsibility of the central government, I do not trust green labels, Environment-conscious consumption leads to better health, It is troublesome to be environment conscious, It is expensive to be environment conscious and It is boring to be an environment-conscious consumer are found to be statistically significant and these items have played an important role in forming and differentiating clusters.

FINDINGS

With the changing time, when everyday there is a news article that discusses about the aftereffects of climate change; people are becoming conscious about their planet Earth. They are more willing to purchase organic or energy-conserving or recycled goods to demonstrate their contribution towards the environmental responsibility. They are ready to shell out more money for ecological safe products that is offering an opportunity to the manufacturers to produce products that are more eco-friendly. But it has also been found out that in some of the cases the labels of green, natural, herbal or organic pertains to the content of the packaging rather than the product itself.

The pilot study conducted above also endorses the same sentiments. It suggests that there is little amount of awareness regarding the eco-labels among the Indian consumers. People are aware of green initiatives and also very positive about it. Still they are not aware of Indian government initiatives in this context. Majority of the respondent were not aware of the fact that Government of India has launched the eco-labelling scheme known as `Ecomark' in 1991 for easy identification of environment-friendly products. It uses a mark of earthern pot as a seal of approval for environmentally preferable consumer products. The logic of choosing an earthern pot as logo for the Ecomark is that this pot uses a renewable resource like earth and does the least damage to the environment and consumes little energy in its manufacturing. Also, its solid and graceful form represents strength and fragility, which is also a reflection of the eco-system. So the marketers and government should provide more information about benefits of eco-labeled products and impact of them on environment would help other groups to be familiar with eco-label and consideration of that in their purchase decisions.

But when it comes to actual buying behavior they become very much price conscious. The nature and motivations for the green products is not very high and companies need to aggressive with their eco-labels to motivate the behavioural change in them. When companies want themselves to be perceived as environmental responsibility, there is a considerable need for companies to react and create necessary strategies for creating consumer awareness of ecolabelled products. Hence it is very important for the companies to understand the underlying motives of consumer behaviour and increasing consumer awareness of eco-labelled products without which it cannot reach and benefit from a "green" way of producing, selling, and disposing of goods. The company should always find new and creative ways to reach its customers and communication regarding the ecolabels can serve as a way connects with them on environmental concern. Some customers already have a basic knowledge of eco-labels and environmental issues, but require further information and clarity delivered in a more effective and easy-to-understand way. Consumers might be ready to adapt to sustainable consumption patterns and their willingness to pay extra for eco-labelled products. Companies can encourage sustainable consumption as a trendy and fun product group for children, while highlighting healthiness for women.

LIMITATION OF THE STUDY

This primary research has certain limitations. The sample size was quite small due to time constraints. There is need of further research to be carries out at different parts of country to get the exact idea for green buying behavior in Indian context.

CONCLUSION

The main purpose of green consumption is to create a better environment. It is important to make green behaviour as a common phenomenon among people so that it can lead to the sustainability values. Under this context, attitude is an important factor that will determine a person's intention and hence, actual behaviour. A positive attitude and concern for the environment will encourage consumers to be "green-savvy." This would make them responsible for their actions and consumptions patterns and these set of customers would be more open to accept changes in their living style. Hence, there is a need to make environmental claims independently verified so as to build and retain consumer confidence. There should be transparency in what and how you communicate with your customers as it is responsible for building trust. The adoption of eco-labels has a potential for creating an increase in sales through product differentiation, increased accountability, or increased choice for consumers in a greening retail environment.But in reality, sometime too much of information, too little time, and a paucity of independent, and understandable information about environmental performance creates confusion in the mind of customers. At this junction, consumer education campaign aimed at raising the awareness of their power to influence product development and eco-labelling programs. Companies can constructively use the eco-lables as a reflection of socially responsible business practice. Various studies have confirmed the fact that eco-label has positive effect on consumer purchase intention. Therefore, it is viable choice for the companies to invest in this domain. It has a potential to be included as part of the policy mechanisms that are designed to guide consumer markets to be more environmentally friendly.

REFERENCES

Bamberg, S., & Moser, G. (2007). Twenty years after Hines, Hungerford, and Tomera: A new meta-analysis of psycho-social determinants of pro-environmental behaviour. *Journal of Environmental Psychology, 27*(1), 14–25. doi:10.1016/j.jenvp.2006.12.002

Bhattacharya, S. (2011). Consumer Attitude towards Green Marketing in India. *The IUP Journal of Marketing Management*, 62-70.

Bratt, C., Hallstedt, S., Robèrt, K.-H., Broman, G., & Oldmark, J. (2011). Assessment of eco-labelling criteria development from a strategic sustainability perspective. *Journal of Cleaner Production, 19*(14), 1631–1638. doi:10.1016/j.jclepro.2011.05.012

Brucks, M. (1985). The effects of product class knowledge on information search behavior. *The Journal of Consumer Research, 12*(1), 1–16. doi:10.1086/209031

Chan, R. Y. K. (2004). Consumer responses to environmental advertising in China. *Marketing Intelligence & Planning, 22*(4), 427–437. doi:10.1108/02634500410542789

Cherian, J., & Jacob, J. (2012). Green Marketing: A Study of Consumers' Attitude towards Environment Friendly Products. *Asian Social Science, 8*(12).

D'Souza, C., Taghian, M., & Lamb, P. (2006). An empirical study on the influence of environmental labels on consumers. *Corporate Communications: An International Journal, 11*(2), 162–173. doi:10.1108/13563280610661697

D'Souza, C., Taghian, M., Lamb, P., & Peretiatko, R. (2007). Green decisions: Demographics and consumer understanding of environmental labels. *International Journal of Consumer Studies, 31*, 371–376. doi:10.1111/j.1470-6431.2006.00567.x

Dono, J., Janine, W., & Ben, R. (2010). The relationship between environmental activism, pro-environmental behaviour and social identity. *Journal of Environmental Psychology, 30*(2), 178–186. doi:10.1016/j.jenvp.2009.11.006

Horne, R. E. (2009). Limits to labels: The role of eco-labels in the assessment of product sustainability and routes to sustainable consumption. *International Journal of Consumer Studies, 33*(2), 175–182. doi:10.1111/j.1470-6431.2009.00752.x

Kim, Y., & Choi. (2005). Antecedents of green considerations purchase behaviour: An examination of collectivism, environmental concern and PCE. *Advances in Consumer Research. Association for Consumer Research (U. S.), 32*(1), 592–599.

Rex, E., & Baumann, H. (2007). Beyond ecolabels: What green marketing can learn from conventional marketing. *Journal of Cleaner Production, 15*(6), 567–576. doi:10.1016/j.jclepro.2006.05.013

Tracy, A. P., & Oskamp, S. (1984). Relationships among ecologically responsible behaviors. *Journal of Environmental Systems, 13*(2), 115–126. doi:10.2190/6TN8-48WT-63XT-CHEN

Wulf, K. D., & Schröder, G. O. (2003). Assessing the impact of a retailer's relationship efforts on consumers' attitudes and behavior. *Journal of Retailing and Consumer Services, 10*(2), 95–108. doi:10.1016/S0969-6989(02)00013-9

KEY TERMS AND DEFINITIONS

Attitude: A person's general feeling of favorableness or unfavorableness for that concept. It is also defined as a psychological tendency that is expressed by evaluating a particular entity with some degree of favor or disfavor.

Behaviour: The result of attitude that can take different forms as people willingness and intended actions shape it. Ecological behavior: is the human behaviour regarding ecology that consciously seeks to minimize the negative impact of human actions on nature and build environment.

Eco-Label: A label that certifies that a product meets high environmental and performance standards and has less impact on the environment than non-labeled products. Along with this it also convey a message that the company is socially responsible.

Environmental Attitude: Attitude when developed towards an object such as environment is referred as environmental attitude and usually accepted as mind-set of respondents for given environment issues.

Green Consumer: One who asks for green product and avoids any product which may harm damage to any living organism, cause deterioration of the environment during process of manufacturing or during process of usage, consume a large amount of non renewable energy, involves unethical testing on animals or human subjects.

APPENDIX

Figure 1. Symbol of eco-label used by Indian government

Table 1. Are you aware of environmental problems in relation to the production, use and disposal of household products

		Frequency	Percent	Valid Percent	Cumulative Percent
Valid	1	16	26.7	26.7	26.7
	2	22	36.7	36.7	63.3
	3	22	36.7	36.7	100.0
	Total	60	100.0	100.0	

Table 2. How have you received information regarding eco-labels

		Frequency	Percent	Valid Percent	Cumulative Percent
Valid	1	3	5.0	5.0	5.0
	2	8	13.3	13.3	18.3
	3	20	33.3	33.3	51.7
	4	13	21.7	21.7	73.3
	5	16	26.7	26.7	100.0
	Total	60	100.0	100.0	

Table 3. Gender

		Frequency	Percent	Valid Percent	Cumulative Percent
Valid	1 (Female)	18	30.0	30.0	30.0
	2 (Male)	42	70.0	70.0	100.0
	Total	60	100.0	100.0	

Table 4. Age

		Frequency	Percent	Valid Percent	Cumulative Percent
Valid	1(15-25)	6	10.0	10.0	10.0
	2)26-35)	21	35.0	35.0	45.0
	3(36-45)	13	21.7	21.7	66.7
	4(46-59)	13	21.7	21.7	88.3
	5 (More than 60)	7	11.7	11.7	100.0
	Total	60	100.0	100.0	

Table 5. Marital status

		Frequency	Percent	Valid Percent	Cumulative Percent
Valid	1(Single)	11	18.3	18.3	18.3
	2 (married)	49	81.7	81.7	100.0
	Total	60	100.0	100.0	

Table 6. Education

		Frequency	Percent	Valid Percent	Cumulative Percent
Valid	1(undergraduate)	14	26.7	26.7	26.7
	2(Vocational Schools)	2	3.3	3.3	30.0
	3(Graduates)	20	33.3	33.3	63.3
	4(Post Graduates)	16	23.3	23.3	86.7
	5(Othetrs)	8	13.3	13.3	100.0
	Total	60	100.0	100.0	

Table 7. Annual income

		Frequency	Percent	Valid Percent	Cumulative Percent
Valid	1	1	1.7	1.7	1.7
	2	5	8.3	8.3	10.0
	3	17	28.3	28.3	38.3
	4	23	38.3	38.3	76.7
	5	14	23.3	23.3	100.0
	Total	60	100.0	100.0	

Table 8. Profession

		Frequency	Percent	Valid Percent	Cumulative Percent
Valid	1	5	8.3	8.3	8.3
	2	13	21.7	21.7	30.0
	3(Executive)	14	23.3	23.3	53.3
	4	13	21.7	21.7	75.0
	5(Housewife)	14	23.3	23.3	98.3
	6	1	1.7	1.7	100.0
	Total	60	100.0	100.0	

Table 9. Final cluster centers

	Cluster			
	1	2	3	4
I am aware of symbol used for Eco-label by govern	3	3	3	3
I am aware that Indian government supports Eco-label.	3	3	3	4
I read labels when I make a purchase	2	3	3	4
I am willing to pay extra if the product is environment friendly	3	3	4	4
I prefer afforable shops even buying eco-labelled products	2	4	4	3
I rarely buy eco-labelled products	4	3	3	2
I don?t care whether a product carries an eco-label or not	4	3	4	3
If an eco-labelled product is not available, I postpone my purchase	3	2	1	3
Individual consumers can contribute to solving environmental problems	3	3	4	2
Humans are severely abusing the environment.	4	4	2	4
Environmental problems are the responsibility of the central government	2	3	2	3
I do not trust green labels	3	3	2	2
Environment-conscious consumption leads to better health	1	4	4	4
It is troublesome to be environment conscious	4	3	1	2
It is expensive to be environment conscious	4	4	2	4
It is boring to be an environment-conscious consumer	4	3	2	3

Table 10. Number of cases in each cluster

Cluster	Cases
1	5.000
2	17.000
3	20.000
4	18.000
Valid	60.000
Missing	.000

Chapter 7
Towards Leadership Marketing:
An Exploratory and Empirical Study

Wilson Ozuem
Regents University, UK

Alina O'Keeffe
University of Wales, UK

ABSTRACT

In an era when collaboration is key to business prosperity, the ability to develop one truly coherent and agile brand lived by its employees and delivered to the external stakeholders has become extremely challenging. Unity between the internal brand and a company's external image, when change is the only constant, has nearly vanished. The marketing function is frequently being underemphasised at the board level. Furthermore, the existing approach to leading business devalues the importance of marketing and its role in leading organisational change. This chapter is about how marketing can partner with organisational leadership for a mutually beneficial exchange of skills and capabilities in order to be able to reinvent organisations rapidly enough to cope with shifts in the external business environment and create a sustainable future for the business. From an interpretivist perspective, the current chapter explores the novel concept of "leadership marketing," which challenges the conventional view of marketing and leadership as two separate fields and offers a holistic approach for business management and brand alignment.

INTRODUCTION

Marketing literature in the past decades has increasingly reflected the need for marketing to lead organisational change (Day 2011). Clearly most extant literature confines marketing to the functional marketing mix (Baker, 2007). There is a recognition that marketing should be looked at beyond the functionalist perspective: "To excel in a global economy, the field of marketing must take a new position, rethinking its fundamental relationship to all aspects of the organisation and

DOI: 10.4018/978-1-4666-6232-2.ch007

its external environment" (Morris, 1987). This study is aimed at establishing a new transformational concept of leadership marketing, which is based on the integration of the two academic and business terrains - leadership and marketing. Also, the study aspires to explore the role marketing plays in driving organisational change. With the speed of change the current business environment, marketing practices quickly go out of date if not attuned to market needs. Companies are required to align their internal and external perceptions of the brand with organisational competencies. Prior to determining the role that marketing plays in leading organisational change, the novel concept of leadership marketing needs to be defined. It is also necessary to discover the components and prerequisites for the successful adaptation of leadership marketing. Hence, in order to attain the above stated aims and objectives, the following research questions will be addressed: What are the determinants of the new leadership marketing paradigm? What is the role of leadership marketing in driving organisational change within the business and across its different functions?

BACKGROUND

An increasing number of companies are becoming customer-centred as a result of the long-standing recognition of the importance of marketing orientation in today's highly competitive business environment. Adoption of the marketing concept, based on customer focus and integration of departments, has been accentuated as a foundation for maintaining long-lasting business success (Kohli & Jaworski, 1990; Harris, 2002). Furthermore, the nature of business has evolved such that companies have realised the significance of internal organisational culture and strong employee relations in achieving sustainable business performance (Carrig &Wright, 2006). From the marketing perspective, employees have become internal customers due to their ability to satisfy the needs of other employees inside the organisation, which is an antecedent to external customer satisfaction. As part of a natural evolution of marketing organisation, customer satisfaction has driven many companies to establish much closer relationships with their suppliers, partners and others in the supply chain. This in turn has emphasised the importance of collaboration between all the organisations involved in delivery of the final product. As a result, lines between internal and external stakeholders have been blurred a long time ago and the distinction between the two will further lose its clarity. This implies a new way of thinking for organisations to remain successful in the face of advancing competition and new technologies. As business strategies become more complex, culture is required to grow into the level of complexity required to implement them (McGuire, et al., 2009).

The two notions mentioned above bring out opposite sides of the marketing spectrum whereby external marketing centres around customers by developing an organisation's outside image, while internal marketing focuses on employees by shaping organisational culture and identity. The link between the two lies with leadership that shapes the way employees perceive the organisation, which in turn influences the projection of the image to external audiences, including customers (Hogg & Carter, 2000). Predictably, the quality of leadership explains as much as 45 per cent of an organisation's performance (Day & Lord, 1986). The challenge for many companies is to be able to effectively represent and maintain connections between their unique and compelling identity i.e. inside brand, embodied in employee culture, and external organisational image i.e. outside brand, portrayed by the company to its customers and other external stakeholders. Quite a few companies fall short by failing to deliver the brand promise made to target customers and even more fail to effectively adapt to the changes in the business environment and reconfigure their customer value-creating processes to match the new positioning.

Amongst the first to address this were Mark and Pearson (2001) who developed a meaningful management framework that uses brand archetypes, whereby brand takes on symbolic significance and becomes an expression of meaning which leads to a consistent message being communicated to external audiences. Speak and Hanson (2008) proposed a neo-brand platform which argues that the brand needs to support employee engagement, i.e. brand inside-building, and exude creative possibilities to capture the fascination of prospective customers, i.e. brand outside-building. Both of these studies approached the problem from the brand management perspective. However, the dynamic nature of the business and ever-changing environmental conditions often demand organisational change which encompasses more than just repositioning of the company's brand. Such changes often create a need for companies to alter their direction and re-define their value proposition to meet expectations of external stakeholders. The internal organisational environment also requires readjustment to support the creation of customer value internally. As such, marketing leaders' ability to predict external trends and transform the organisation accordingly becomes imperative in achieving sustainable and superior performance. Given that organisational change and leadership are often studied within a strategic management context, but more seldom within the confines of marketing, studying leadership that is beyond the scope of the board of directors is critical to a better understanding of change management within marketing-oriented organisations. However, the two research streams – leadership and marketing – have yet to be integrated.

LEADERSHIP AND MARKETING: WHAT LIES WITHIN?

Almost no academic research has been carried out on the theme of the role of marketing in leading organisational change, despite the long history study in both leadership and marketing individually. The link between the two fields has emerged following the recognition of the importance of continuous organisational development in a constantly changing environment. Many self-published articles of opinion leaders in the field of leadership marketing form a starting point for this research, despite the lack of thorough academic backing. The emerging concepts outlined in these articles are used to lay a foundation for this study and are further enhanced by drawing on an already established pool of academic marketing and leadership knowledge. However prior to defining the concept of leadership marketing, the definition of the terms involved is provided to ensure uniformity and understanding throughout the study. This will also define the scope and the point of view on marketing and leadership for the purposes of this study. In its basic form, leadership is defined as the process of influencing others to achieve certain goals (Pass at al., 2006). As a personal quality, leadership enables a person to manage, administer, motivate and direct others, as well as earning respect of superiors (Davies at al., 2003). Drucker (1973) noted that leadership involves "the lifting of a man's vision, to higher sights, the raising of a man's performance to a higher standard, the building of a man's personality beyond its normal limits." Moving beyond personality, leadership is based on trust and courage to delegate responsibilities to others to fully exploit their potential. Leadership, as a business management discipline, is a recent phenomenon, emerged in the post-war years and took off in the 1970s (Birkinshaw, 2010). On a strategic level, successful leaders "project a clear and consistent picture of a desired organisational identity and put in place conditions that increase the likelihood of desired behaviours through enhanced employee satisfaction" (Bradshaw, 1998). The concept of "transformational leadership" suggest that leaders transform followers' personal values and self-beliefs, move them to higher levels of needs and aspirations (Jung, 2001), and raise the performance expectations of their followers (Bass, 1995). Contemporary views of strategic leadership inevitably revert to Porter's classic "five forces" competition theory, which sees strategists as practitioner economists who analyse and manage market forces, as well as practitioner psychologists who analyse and manage their own and others' thought processes (Gavetti, 2011). Drawing on the Sustainable Marketing Leadership (SML) model, it can be stated that effective leadership rests on four main components – strategic visioning, integrated planning, managing performance and marketing controllership (Shapiro, 2005). Those are enabled by compelling vision, clear organisational identity, effective culture for employee alignment and deep understanding of consumer behaviour to facilitate customer satisfaction. According to Werbach (2009), when leaders at the top instigate a strategy for sustainability and guide the organisation through the process of increasing transparency, engaging employees, and embracing network partners to accomplish important sustainability goals, they set the conditions to let everyone improve the company's strategy.

With regard to change, which perhaps is the only constant nowadays in the business environment, the true leader sees it as a challenge and the foundation for organisational growth and expansion (Billire, 2009). In choosing strategic direction, leaders are expected to estimate uncertainly and lay out a vision of future events sufficiently precise (Courtney, Kirkland & Viguerie, 1997). However there is a tendency for businesses to rely only on an explicit knowledge of numbers and data, which prevents leaders from coping with change (Nanaka & Takeuchi, 2011); this is because such knowledge is contextual and ignores people's values, goals and relationships. Hence, one of the substantial shifts in creating a sustainable future is that it must extend beyond the company – it must be about pursuing the common good and serving the higher purpose (Nanaka & Takeuchi, 2011). The main task of leadership nowadays, as argued by Martin (2007), is to create a space where employees can generate new ideas and departments can work closely together to build an organisation that is effective, agile and more prepared to respond to complex challenges. On the subject of marketing, the American Marketing Association's (AMA) provides an updated definition of marketing as "the activity, set of institutions, and processes for creating, communicating, delivering, and exchanging offerings that have value for customers, clients, partners, and society at large" (cited in Gundlach & Wilkie, 2009). Furthermore, the Chartered Institute of Marketing, the UK equivalent to the AMA, also revised its definition of marketing as "the strategic business function that creates value by stimulating, facilitating and fulfilling customer demand. It does this by building brands, nurturing innovation, developing relationships, creating good customer services and communication benefits. By operating customer-centrically, marketing brings positive return on investment, satisfied shareholders and stakeholders from business and the community, and contributes to positive behavioural change and a sustainable business future" (cited in Charles, 2007). The modern concept of marketing is based on the idea that a business should discover and then satisfy customer needs rather than focusing on sales of its existing products or services produced without any deep insight into consumers' preferences, wants and desires and do so better than its competitors. What's more, four key areas of marketing competency, as revealed by a recent Accenture survey of 400+ marketing executives, comprise operations, customer analytics, innovation and customer engagement (Smith & Nunes, 2010).

Leadership Marketing Components

This section presents a combined view on the essential parts of leadership and marketing. Firstly, the importance of marketing orientation and brand image is discussed, followed by the vital components of internal marketing, organisational culture and band identity. Lastly, major theories on culture and leadership are presented. Many theories have been developed on marketing, nevertheless many researchers agree with Deshpande and Webster's (1989) view of marketing orientation as being: "a shared set of beliefs and values that puts the consumer into the centre of the firm's thinking." While Kohli and Jaworski (1990) define marketing orientation as an activity-based characteristic of the firm, Konopa and Calabaro (1971) and Felton (1959) view it as external consumer orientation, as opposed to product development orientation, and integration of all departmental functions within the organisation. Along the same line of thought, Avlonitis and Gounaris (1999) stress satisfaction of customer needs and a business ability to adjust products and services as a response to the changes in those needs and wants so as to continue delivering customer value. Even though the main emphasis is still on customer satisfaction, Misiag (2001) defines marketing orientation as an internal driving force that influences not only customers, but also employees of the organisation. Narver and Slater (1990) present market orientation as the form of the organisationally spread culture, which in the most effective and efficient way supports necessary behaviour for the formation of higher value for customers, and by that it forms assumptions for better results of the business.

Branding is seen as one of the core elements of marketing which is used to build distinctive brand identities that will be recognised by consumers in increasingly crowded marketplaces (Low and Fullerton, 1994). Amongst many other benefits, a brand's ability to obtain a definite competitive advantage (Kim, et al., 2003) and add financial value (Murphy, 1992) has been widely acknowledged and many brand-building concepts have been developed with this in mind. Beyond a brand name that differentiates one product from others, Boulding (1956) developed the concept of brands as symbolic images. Gardner and Levy (1955) argued that a brand image, which is the external perception of the organisation in the eyes of consumers and other stakeholders, outweighs the significance of the "technical" product features. With differentiation a purpose of branding, communications refocused on building deeper emotional connection with consumers based on values (Goodyear, 1996) and feelings about the brand (Gardner and Levy, 1955). The brand positioning concept was introduced by Ries and Trout (1981) that stated that brands create unique positions in consumers' minds through distinctive brand associations. However, as consumer perceptions are continually changing, companies need to focus on building a more stable brand reputation, which represents multiple images over time (Fomburn & Van Riel, 1997). Kapferer (1997) suggested that brand identity – what the brand stands for from the firm's point of view – should take precedence over brand image or how that brand is perceived from an external perspective. This raises the significance of internal communication and employee alignment with an organisation's culture, an important component of brand identity that shapes corporate brand values and plays a unifying role to maintain the consistency of the message (Olins 1995, Mitchell, 1994). On a similar note, Mark and Pearson (2001) addressed the critical need and tremendous opportunity to create, preserve and nurture brand meaning by leveraging its deep archetypal roots. More recent developments included Andersen's (2010) view that branding occurs when the company's projected self-identity aligns positively with the consumer's projection of the company's identity. This resonates with Ind (2007) suggesting that a successful brand's essence extends from the internal vision and values into the external personality and positioning. As a result, strong brand names often are used to support new product launches where consumer perceptions of the original brands are automatically transferred to the extension (Aaker and Keller, 1990; Andersen, 2010).

Internal Marketing, Culture, and Brand Identity

Having initially emerged from service industries, internal marketing shapes organisational culture to transform the orientation of the organisation to focus upon employees, who are paramount in delivering the brand to external stakeholders. Internal marketing literature emphasized the crucial element of "communicating by deeds" organisational values and offering employees a clear vision that is worth pursuing (Berry & Parasuraman, 1992). Internal marketing has been suggested as a key instrument to implement successful internal brand building, whereby employees better accept the brand values and align their attitudes accordingly (Vallaster & de Chernatony, 2003). According to Schein's (1992) conception, organisational culture consists of collective assumptions, values and artefacts that are shared by members of the organisation. A company culture is a mix of behaviours and attitudes of those who are part of it; often unsaid, intangible but deeply ingrained and embedded in every individual within the workplace can be summarised as "the way we do things around here" (Jacobs, 2011). Organisations have frequently tried to establish cultures through written rules, policies and procedures, but in so doing misunderstood the whole concept of "culture" and such an approach has potential to adversely affect employee engagement.

Webster and Deshpande (1989) were amongst the first to address the effect of organisational culture upon marketing. Hofstede (1980) and Pfeffer (1997) linked strong culture to high business performance. As proposed by many (Narver & Slater, 1990, Grönroos, 1990), internal marketing nurtures the culture that most effectively and efficiently creates behaviours that lead to the provision of superior customer value and motivates employees toward customer-oriented performance. It ensures that staff understand the brand's promise and can deliver it thus aligning customer brand expectations with employee performance (Hatch & Schulz, 2003). From this perspective, Jacobs (2003) asserts that a brand represents the relationship an organization has with its employees just as much as it represents the relationship that it has with its customers. Therefore internal marketing and strong employee cultures represent a critical success factor in linking the external and internal view in the organisation (Dunne and Barnes, 2000). A new concept of leadership culture involves the meaning that people make of the organisation and its environment and the tools they have to create shared direction, alignment and commitment throughout the business (McGuire, et al., 2009). A hierarchy of leadership culture developed by Centre for Creative Leadership (CCL) is illustrated on Figure 1.

Closely linked with culture is the concept of an organisation's identity, which is defined as "a commonly shared understanding of the values of the firm held by employees." Organisation's image, on the other hand, is the way stakeholders view the firm from an external perspective (Hatch & Schultz, 1997). Although marketing culture is part of the broader corporate culture of an organisation, internal marketing initiative can be a catalyst to reshaping the entire culture within the firm, which leads to much greater integration between departments (Dunne & Barnes, 2000). By changing the attitudes and assumptions of the employees, so to align them with the desired organisational identity, cultural change will ensue.

Organisational Change and Leadership

Continuous change is a fact of life for organisations - significant shifts in consumer psychology resulting from recent economic turmoil and rapid technological developments are just two major changes that organisation must embrace. Those companies who capture changes in consumer mindset, and consequently transform their core practices are able to benefit from emerging opportunities and potential growth. And so, change

Figure 1. Hierarchy of leadership culture (Source: McGuire, et al., 2009)

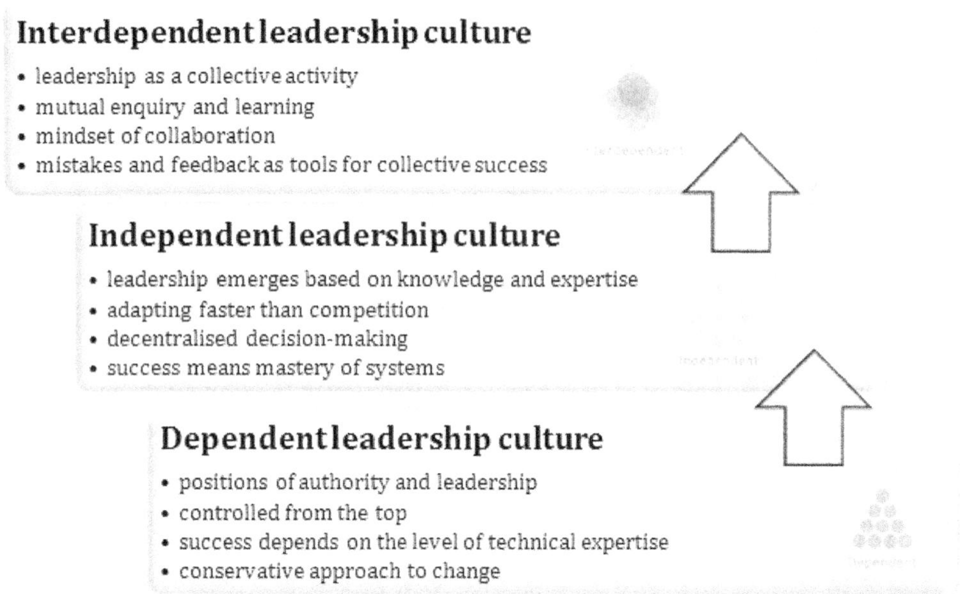

places uncertainty in the way of company's strategic development, making it extremely challenging for leaders to predict the future of their businesses accurately enough to choose a clear strategic direction (Courtney, Kirkland & Viguerie, 1997). To successfully embrace change, organisations need to adopt new leadership mindsets, not just new skills (McGuire, et al., 2009). Felton (1956) was amongst the first to recognise that marketing is a very complex management function which is also affected by change. A company's ability to respond continuously to unanticipated changes that impact its performance is referred to as "strategic flexibility" (Evans, 1991, Aaker & Keller, 1990). However, the challenge presented here is how to develop business-wide capabilities that are sustainable in the ever-changing business environment by seeing organisation as a whole and recognising interdependence of its various functions, the view which is rooted in systems theory (Felton, 1959). Collins (2001) expressed that marketing is driving organisational change that goes beyond a change programme. For the purposes of this study, organisational change is defined not as an overnight sensation with a moment of breakthrough, but a process of continuous evolvement, growth and development. This coincides with Collins' view on change, which described change not as a change programme with motivational stunts and big turnaround plans, but a rather slow progression with hardly any radical transformation (Collins, 2001). Organisations seeking to adapt during turbulent times cannot force change through purely technical approaches such as restructuring (McGuire, et al., 2009). One suggestion emerging from recent studies was to develop leadership capability, which is capacity of the company to sustain its future leaders (Ulrich & Smallwood, 2007). According to the conventional approach, the right business structures ensure efficiencies, innovation and agility for organisations to succeed and sustain (McGuire, et al., 2009). However, in reality, there is insufficient leadership capability, which is evidenced by results of the survey, conducted by the Chartered Institute of Personnel and Development (CIPD) and talent management consultancy DDI – "one-fifth of leaders and HR professionals consider their companies' leadership development programmes as ineffective" (Stevens, 2011). Moreover, Steve Newhall, managing director of DDI (2011), pointed out that while "identifying and nurturing talent is vital, most of the HR professional in the UK revealed that they lacked the ability to fill vacant leadership positions." This raises another challenge for the UK businesses.

At present, the ability to integrate systems, collaborate with partners and coordinate across the supply chain remains elusive (McGuire, et al., 2009). According to the behavioural model of charismatic leadership (Conger & Kanungo 1998; Conger, Kanungo & Menon 2000), leaders are those who possess high sensitivity to the environment and followers' needs, articulate an attractive vision for the organization and inspire subordinates to follow their attitudes and behaviours. Sisodia, Sheth and Wolfe (2007) argue that leadership from the top needs to be more inspired and catalytic rather than directive. Leadership provides direction for the whole organisation by creating a compelling vision and inspires the organisational change by motivating employees and convincing them to follow. Thus, leaders play an indispensible role in taking an organisation from where it is now to where it needs to be and instilling into employees the company's culture, values and vision and continuously communicating these through deeds (Berry, Hensel & Burke 1976; Grönroos 1990). There are emerging views on leadership as a collective activity, rather than individual competency. As evidenced by CCL's research, a view on leadership as a process that happens throughout the organisation through interdependent decision-making is becoming more dominant as considered with regards to the future (Martin, 2007). As a result of the research, CCL proposed a model, illustrated on Figure 2, for building shared direction, alignment and commitment by way of reaching the balance between inside-out leadership and outside-in management.

However Ulriuch and Smallwood (2007) went further to develop a concept of "leadership brand." It argues that successful leadership requires identity of leaders throughout an organisation that bridges customer expectations and employee and organisational behaviour. Leading by example

Figure 2. Inside-out change leadership model (Source: Martin, 2007)

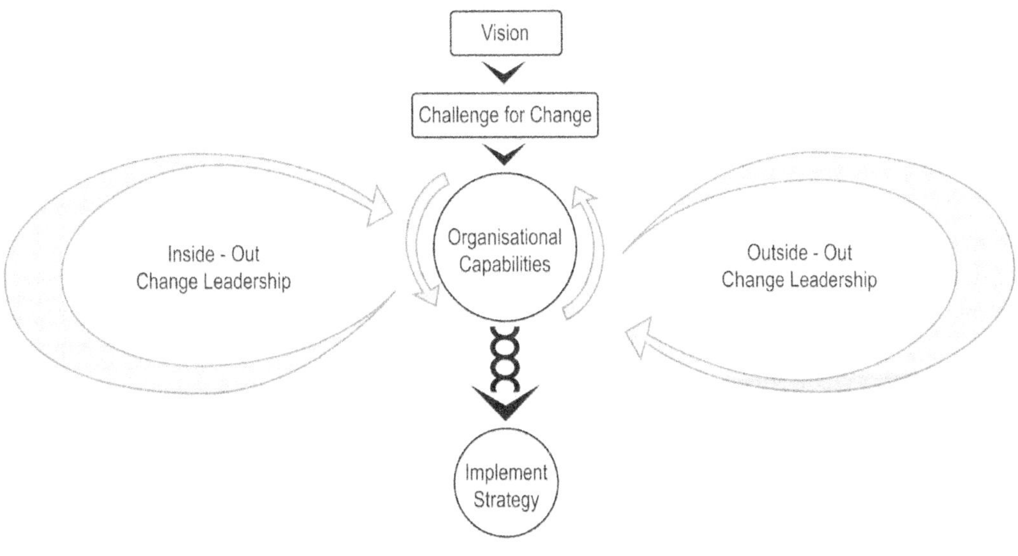

and inspirational communication are the key to persuading others to accept and support an organisation's new direction and creating a culture conductive to change (Kotter, 1995). Unsurprisingly the nature of effective leadership is changing in itself. CCL's research substantiated that flexibility, collaboration, cross boundaries and collective approaches to leadership are rising in significance as a response to challenges that are greater than individual's own capabilities (Martin, 2007). As a result, relationship-building and change management skills escalated in importance replacing such traditional skills as resourcefulness and decisiveness. Marketing leaders' concern over culture and their role in shaping it within their marketing teams - and even organisation as a whole - enables them to play a central role in driving the growth and success of the business (Brand Learning, 2011). Strategy will not succeed in a void, and leadership often makes the difference between merely reaching for great opportunities and actually realising their potential (Hsieh & Yik, 2005).

Relationship between Marketing and Leadership

With an aim to integrate the roles of marketing and leadership in organisational change an initial definition of the new concept based on the theoretical foundation suggested by the literature review is presented. Consistent with the assumption that marketing orientation initiates brand leadership in the market place and creates an internal brand culture amongst employees, the financial value of branding, inspired leadership and strong employee relations was proven in previous research (Kim, et al., 2003, Murphy, 1992; Rajagopalan & Spreitzer, 1997; Heskett, et al., 1994; Carrig and Wright, 2006; Day and Lord, 1986). While executive leadership has received significant attention in literature on organisational change (Kotter, 1995; Wu, et al., 2007; Elias, 2009), research on the role of internal marketing remains unclear focusing more on employees' perspectives on organisational commitment and job motivation (Vrontis, et al., 2010). Furthermore, absent is research that integrates marketing, leadership and change. Companies that work in a networked or cross-functional manner are delivering their brand promise in a more holistic way. Hence, leadership becomes naturally crucial in creating alignment across the different functions of the organisation. The beliefs that drive leadership behaviours within the organisation need to ally with the operational business strategy (McGuire, et al., 2009). According to Maritz research sponsored by the Chartered Institute of Marketing, many respondents felt that having a brand-literate CEO is a massive benefit in aligning the company to the brand (Brooke, 2002). As marketing's scope goes beyond a department and drives the whole business (Kotler, 2001; Brooke, 2002; Brand Learning, 2011), marketing serves as an integral link between external branding, by building organisational image in the minds of consumers, and internal culture, by shaping brand identity amongst employees. An ability to create brands through people is highly enhanced by leadership capabilities of those marketers.

Leadership shapes the way employees view their organisations, which in turn influences the projection of the brand to customers. As was proven by previous research, the quality of an organisation's leadership accounts for almost half of its performance (Day & Lord, 1986), Other research, carried out by CIPD, highlighted three drivers of leadership quality - leadership development, talent managements and management culture (Stevens, 2011). In light of its definition, marketing is undoubtedly relevant to research on organisational change and should be an integral part of organisational change. This represents a promising area that deserves further investigation. Drucker was one of the first to refer to marketing in the context of leadership. In particular he described leadership as a marketing job, which meant that "leaders must know and understand those they lead, and lead in way followers would relate to." However he did little to develop this concept (Cohen, 2010). His far-reaching idea was explicitly grounded in the following statement that "good leadership is essentially marketing." Deeply rooted in the concept of leadership marketing is the belief that marketing revolves around the customer, and insight generation and brand development play significant part, but leadership is needed to "engage the functions outside marketing that play a role in creating products, services and brand experiences that engage customers, earn their respect and retain their loyalty" (McGrath, 2009). With the emergence of the network society and collaboration, this view expands further beyond the organisation to its external network of partners - customers, suppliers and agencies, and therefore is of increasing significance. Radcliffe (2008) sets out three leadership challenges that marketing leaders should embrace - first, having a clear sense of purpose and vision of the company's future; secondly, the ability to engage with employees and partners to create that future, and thirdly the capability to deliver the strategy in practice. This shapes the essence of the leadership marketing concept.

Leadership Marketing vs. Marketing Leadership

There are two terms "marketing leadership" and "leadership marketing" which sound very similar and can easily be confused, but have a completely different meaning. To ensure clarity between those two, a clear distinction needs to be made. While marketing leadership was a significant topic of the research back in 20th century, when automation and technological development were driving change in the business environment and the emphasis was only beginning to shift from production to marketing; back then, the idea of marketing leadership was gaining momentum, as it ascertained the importance of marketing for the success of any company, especially at the times of constant change. Marketing leadership emphasised the dynamism of marketing and evolved around a need "to see the enterprise as a whole and to understand how the various functions of the company depend on one another" (Felton, 1956). This formed a foundation for what is now known as a "holistic view of the organisation."

On the other hand, leadership marketing, which is the sole focus of this study, is a completely separate subject. Leadership marketing is a very novel concept, not previously researched, therefore there is no exact and acknowledged definition of the term. Therefore one of the aims of this study is to define the term of "marketing leadership." Based on the secondary research of the extant models and theories on leadership, marketing, culture and change, a comprehensive overview of leadership marketing concept is illustrated on Figure 3. Specifically, it proposes that marketing acts as an agent of change by being first to spot the changes in the external environment and understand trends in the industry e.g. changes in customer needs, economic climate, new technology. Then, together with other departments, e.g. production, IT and research and development, it creates solutions to address those external changes.

The process starts with changes in the business environment, where repositioning of the company's external brand is necessary often result in a need for realignment of the internal brand and culture amongst employees to reflect modified external image of the organisation. This consequently generates strategic change for the business. In particular, the theoretical model suggests that leadership marketing mediates the relationship between external positioning of the organisation and its internal culture and employee relations. These relationships and their underlying principles will be further explored as part of primary research, which follows.

Figure 3. Theoretical model of leadership marketing

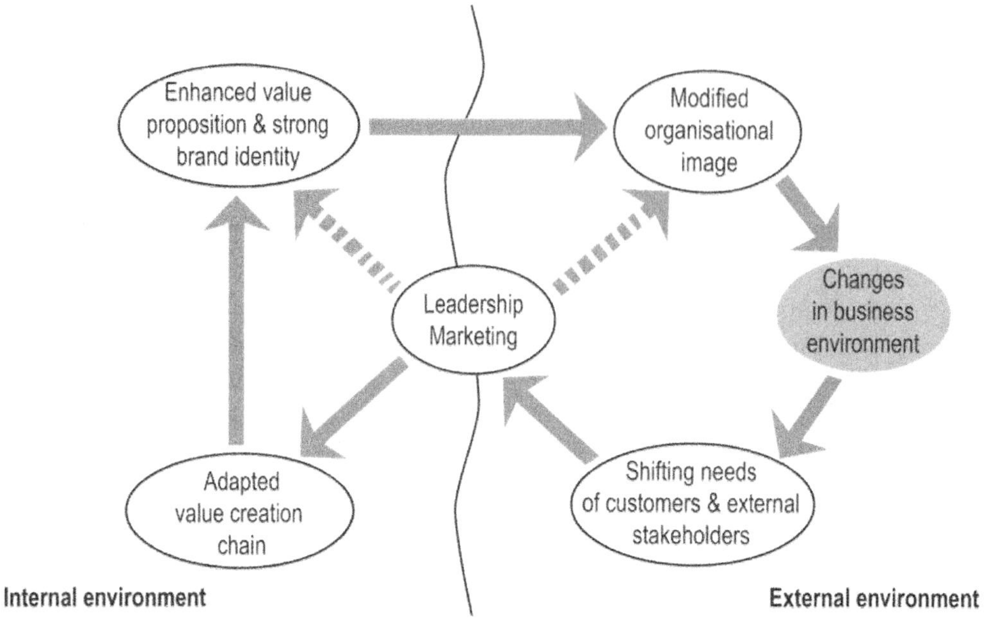

SOLUTIONS AND RECOMMENDATIONS

This chapter reveals that with the speed of change in the current business environment, marketing strategies quickly become out of date if not tuned in to market needs. While leadership develops employees to help organisation to adapt to external changes, marketing has external focus on the customer. The challenge that businesses need to address, as indicated in this study, is how to create alignment between organisational competencies and customer needs. Furthermore, it was discovered that internal and external perceptions of the brand need to be identical to ensure desired performance levels. As a result of the research, organisational alignment, agility and environmental awareness were established as key determinants of the new leadership marketing paradigm. It was also recognised that marketing drives change by anticipating future customer needs and communicating this information internally to adapt the organisation to the shifting business environment. Consequently, with the findings comes the challenge: conventional marketing lacks credibility and authenticity according to both - internal views of the leadership team and external views of customers – to lead the organisational change. Revolution of marketing itself is crucial for the discipline to regain its importance and respect within organisations. To achieve this, marketing needs to form a closer relationship with leadership by way of marketers become better leaders within their profession and business as well as marketing being represented on the top management board and having its own voice.

What follows is a framework for determining fundamental components of leadership marketing and essential interrelations of those elements with surrounding environment and stakeholders (see Figure 4). Based on existing academic marketing and leadership theories and primary research findings, the framework represents the DNA of the new leadership marketing paradigm. It allows organisations to adapt the concept of leadership marketing internally and enables the modification

Figure 4. New leadership marketing paradigm DNA

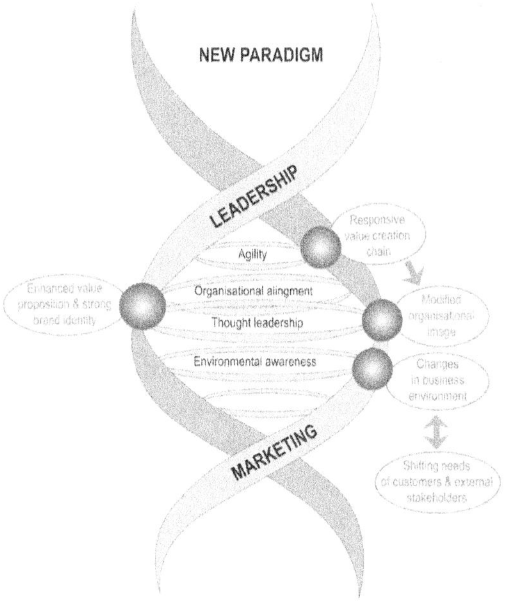

of its constituents and to tailor corporate strategy according to changes in external business conditions. Environmentally-aware adaptive organisations that deliver holistic consumer experiences and coherent messages to the market, have reached high levels of creativity, alignment, innovation and collaboration, which helps everyone make a leap in a way that wins for the business.

Throughout this chapter it was recognised that strong leadership and effective marketing are equally necessary for sustainable development of the organisation. Both of them are indispensable, but nonetheless insufficient in today's rapidly changing environment. For that reason, organisational ability to adapt to those changes was identified as another crucial capability. As the new leadership marketing paradigm offers a whole systems approach that strengthens the link between marketing and leadership and also enhances organisational agility, encouraging leadership marketing within the organisation will help the business to overcome its marketing challenges. Unified brand message, motivated employees and innovative ideas will be promoted to differentiate the company and create a holistic consumer experience and get customers believing in a brand and its reputation. The main recommendation from this research is that organisations challenge the conventional role of marketing within the business and look for innovative ways of adapting the new leadership marketing paradigm. From the marketing perspective, leadership is necessary for creating engagement and driving change. Thus, one of the recommendations to marketing professionals is to develop leadership skills in order to fulfil their roles in the organisation more successfully and help the organisation achieve its commercial goals. This in itself will become a catalyst for revolution of marketing and the role it plays in business, challenging the conventional view on marketing and raising awareness of the new paradigm.

From the leadership perspective, the importance of marketing needs to be formally and truthfully recognised by giving it a place on the board of management. In the last few years, marketing has lost its significance due to the perception of being content-driven and not having its own voice and, hence, credibility, while other business areas such as finance and operations have grown in importance. Leadership needs marketing as it focuses on understanding the market and being in tune with the customers' desires. Leadership relies on marketing to anticipate changes in consumer needs, identify opportunities for business success and deliver products or services in the most effective and profitable way for organisation and the customer. Organisations need to understand the dynamics of the organisation and how its various parts interconnect between themselves and external environment. The leadership marketing DNA model suggests the possible components and interaction between them as well as with the external environment. This allows for greater organisational agility to be developed as well as alignment of the internal and external view of the brand. By breaking silo barriers between the departments and increasing cross-functionality organisations will see the bigger picture, enhance collaboration, mutual sharing of accountabilities, transparency and teamwork. It will also allow businesses to use resources collectively and innovatively to differentiate themselves in communicating and meeting customer needs. Furthermore, change in remuneration and bonuses is needed, by way of performance review being based on aligned goals and elimination of silo budgeting.

Marketers need to spend more time working with teams and be interested in engaging with other departments, which may lead marketing to the higher echelons of the organisation, granting it more power and gaining more respect on the board of management. Leadership marketing creates a vision about the development of the marketing function within the organisation and chooses efficient ways to implement it by getting other departments aligned. Marketing needs to rebuild its credibility by communicating with authenticity, transparency and meaning. Vision of how marketing operates as a whole comes from greater understanding of consumer values and experiences. Marketing enables shared understanding across the leadership team about customer, strategy and markets and how they operate in a coherent way. Modern brands need to remember that nowadays customers appreciate collective experiences more than individual - everything that the company does takes place in networks. This study offers a contribution that marketers may consider for management of their function, and to a certain extent, the whole business. Throughout this study, a pressing need for change in business management as well as marketing was recognised. Numerous benefits of adopting the new leadership marketing paradigm were also named. Effective integration of various organisational and marketing components results in greater responsiveness of the business to the changes in the external environment, as well as successful alignment of employee perception to customer perception of the brand. The current study highlights the need for marketers to develop leadership skills, such as those mentioned above, to fulfil their role within the organisation. By being a leader in marketing and promoting marketing so as to achieve leadership in the marketplace, organisations embrace the new leadership marketing paradigm. Leadership needs to be more involved in marketing and marketing needs to make more leadership decisions. Organisations need to ensure alignment of vision and integrity of marketing with company's values and direction - marketing is required to have sound awareness of market needs and, through leadership, to align company's vision with the marketing message and demonstrate integrity in doing so. The leadership marketing paradigm ensures strong awareness of leadership and marketing alignment within the business. It is a mindset of the way organisations can operate, combining leadership and marketing at a senior level.

To successfully adopt leadership marketing to stay abreast of changes, the organisation's leadership needs to connect and empower marketing to have the power to transform and engage other functions and partners. Marketers should create a desire for change and also give the opportunity and resources for these departments to change, and this will shift employee behaviour. By addressing the point above regarding redefining marketing, it should be recognised that leadership marketing involves shifting mindsets in its definition. It sets the tone and drives change, gets people on board and inspires them to lead that challenge, facilitating change of organisational culture to enable delivery of brand promise internally and externally. Leaders should bring in new ideas and have awareness of what is happening outside, and marketing needs to be creative in proposing ways to reach the market. Marketing is a catalyst of organisational change and should get other departments to buy into the changes and incorporate them into strategy and activities. As previously mentioned, marketing should integrate more with other departments and adapt business internally by changing its offering externally. Ensuring that organisation has a united view on how it works with suppliers, partners and customers will assist in aligning value-creation chain with perceptions of stakeholders. It is necessary to connect organisational culture with the desired creative evolving strategy, which is based on listening and awareness of anticipation of clients' future needs. Organisations need a leadership marketing approach to ensure that a company brings to its markets a clearly defined product or service, which is aligned with the company's vision and values and meets the needs of customers, and where the message is clear for both employees and potential buyers alike. Thought the mindset of leadership marketing, organisations can deliver from the customer perspective by ensuring congruity between the way employees and customers perceive the brand. To strengthen the connection between internal employees' attitudes and external appearances of the brand to customers, organisations should analyse gaps in stakeholders' perceptions of the brand and use tailored marketing communication to translate brand values into customer experiences. Regular communication is necessary with an aim of aligning visions and building bonds between departments to ensure cohesive delivery of brand promise.

FUTURE RESEARCH DIRECTIONS

As this chapter introduced a novel concept of leadership marketing, information sources were limited and hence there was a higher reliance on extant conceptual theories. The research has covered vital aspects related to the role of marketing in leading organisational change within a number of UK-based enterprises operating in a range of industries. However, due to limited time and resources, the research was not able to explore and then analyse the opinions of a greater sample of marketing and leadership professionals.

The amount of data collected on investigating organisational change can be broadened to allow fuller exploration of some aspects, as well as the provision of practical examples and case studies to enhance the point. Additionally, quantitative research to justify the applicability of the findings to other organisations is necessary. Due to the exploratory nature of this research, further qualitative studies on the subject of the leadership marketing concept and quantitative studies on the impact of practical implementation of a new leadership marketing paradigm and implications for B2B and B2C organisations separately could be pursued as topics for independent research.

CONCLUSION

This chapter reveals that with the speed of change in the current business environment, marketing strategies quickly become out of date if not tuned in to market needs. While leadership develops employees to help organisation to adapt to external changes, marketing has external focus on the customer. The challenge that businesses need to address, as indicated in this study, is how to create alignment between organisational competencies and customer needs. Furthermore, it was discovered that internal and external perceptions of the brand need to be identical to ensure desired performance levels. As a result of the research, organisational alignment, agility and environmental awareness were established as key determinants of the new leadership marketing paradigm. It was also recognised that marketing drives change by anticipating future customer needs and communicating this information internally to adapt the organisation to the shifting business environment. Consequently, with the findings comes the challenge: conventional marketing lacks credibility and authenticity according to both - internal views of the leadership team and external views of customers – to lead the organisational change. Revolution of marketing itself is crucial for the discipline to regain its importance and respect within organisations. To achieve this, marketing needs to form a closer relationship with leadership by way of marketers become better leaders within their profession and business as well as marketing being represented on the top management board and having its own voice.

What follows is a framework for determining fundamental components of leadership marketing and essential interrelations of those elements with surrounding environment and stakeholders (see Figure 8). Based on existing academic marketing and leadership theories and primary research findings, the framework represents the DNA of the new leadership marketing paradigm. It allows organisations to adapt the concept of leadership marketing internally and enables the modification of its constituents and to tailor corporate strategy according to changes in external business conditions. Environmentally-aware adaptive organisations that deliver holistic consumer experiences and coherent messages to the market, have reached high levels of creativity, alignment, innovation and collaboration, which helps everyone make a leap in a way that wins for the business. Throughout this study it was recognised that strong leadership and effective marketing are equally necessary for sustainable development of the organisation. Both of them are indispensable, but nonetheless insufficient in today's rapidly changing environment. For that reason, organisational ability to adapt to those changes was identified as another crucial capability. As the new leadership marketing paradigm offers a whole systems approach that strengthens the link between marketing and leadership and also enhances organisational agility, encouraging leadership marketing within the organisation will help the business to overcome its marketing challenges. Unified brand message, motivated employees and innovative ideas will be promoted to differentiate the company and create a holistic consumer experience and get customers believing in a brand and its reputation. The main recommendation from this research is that organisations challenge the conventional role of marketing within the business and look for innovative ways of adapting the new leadership marketing paradigm. From the marketing perspective, leadership is necessary for creating engagement and driving change. Thus, one of the recommendations to marketing professionals is to develop leadership skills in order to fulfil their roles in the organisation more successfully and help the organisation achieve its commercial goals. This in itself will become a catalyst for revolution of marketing and the role it plays in business, challenging the conventional view on marketing and raising awareness of the new paradigm.

From the leadership perspective, the importance of marketing needs to be formally and truthfully recognised by giving it a place on the board of management. In the last few years, marketing has lost its significance due to the perception of being content-driven and not having its own voice and, hence, credibility, while other business areas such as finance and operations have grown in importance. Leadership needs marketing as it focuses on understanding the market and being in tune with the customers' desires. Leadership relies on marketing to anticipate changes in consumer needs, identify opportunities for business success and deliver products or services in the most effective and profitable way for organisation and the customer. Organisations need to understand the dynamics of the organisation and how its various parts interconnect between themselves and external environment. The leadership marketing DNA model suggests the possible components and interaction between them as well as with the external environment. This allows for greater organisational agility to be developed as well as alignment of the internal and external view of the brand. By breaking silo barriers between the departments and increasing cross-functionality organisations will see the bigger picture, enhance collaboration, mutual sharing of accountabilities, transparency and teamwork. It will also allow businesses to use resources collectively and innovatively to differentiate themselves in communicating and meeting customer needs. Furthermore, change in remuneration and bonuses is needed, by way of performance review being based on aligned goals and elimination of silo budgeting.

Marketers need to spend more time working with teams and be interested in engaging with other departments, which may lead marketing to the higher echelons of the organisation, granting it more power and gaining more respect on the board of management. Leadership marketing creates a vision about the development of the marketing function within the organisation and chooses efficient ways to implement it by getting other departments aligned. Marketing needs to rebuild its credibility by communicating with authenticity, transparency and meaning. Vision of how marketing operates as a whole comes from greater understanding of consumer values and experiences. Marketing enables shared understanding across the leadership team about customer, strategy and markets and how they operate in a coherent way. Modern brands need to remember that nowadays customers appreciate collective experiences more than individual - everything that the company does takes place in networks. This study offers a contribution that marketers may consider for management of their function, and to a certain extent, the whole business. Throughout this study, a pressing need for change in business management as well as marketing was recognised. Numerous benefits of adopting the new leadership marketing paradigm were also named. Effective integration of various organisational and marketing components results in greater responsiveness of the business to the changes in the external environment, as well as successful alignment of employee perception to customer perception of the brand. The current study highlights the need for marketers to develop leadership skills, such as those mentioned above, to fulfil their role within the organisation. By being a leader in marketing and promoting marketing so as to achieve leadership in the marketplace, organisations embrace the new leadership marketing paradigm. Leadership needs to be more involved in marketing and marketing needs to make more leadership decisions. Organisations need to ensure alignment of vision and integrity of marketing with company's values and direction - marketing is required to have sound awareness of market needs and, through leadership, to align company's vision with the marketing message and demonstrate integrity in doing so. The leadership marketing paradigm ensures strong awareness of leadership and marketing alignment within the business. It is a mindset of the way organisations can operate, combining leadership and marketing at a senior level. To successfully adopt leadership marketing to stay abreast of changes, the organisation's leadership needs to connect and empower marketing to have the power to transform and engage other functions and partners. Marketers should create a desire for change and also give the opportunity and resources for these departments to change, and this will shift employee behaviour. By addressing the point above regarding redefining marketing, it should be recognised that leadership marketing involves shifting mindsets in its definition. It sets the tone and drives change, gets people on board and inspires them to lead that challenge, facilitating change of organisational culture to enable delivery of brand promise internally and externally. Leaders should bring in new ideas and have awareness of what is happening outside, and marketing needs to be creative in proposing ways to reach the market. Marketing is a catalyst of organisational change and should get other departments to buy into the changes and incorporate them into strategy and activities. As previously mentioned, marketing should integrate more with other departments and adapt business internally by changing its offering externally. Ensuring that organisation has a united view on how it works with suppliers, partners and customers will assist in aligning value-creation chain with perceptions of stakeholders. It is necessary to connect organisational culture with the desired creative evolving strategy, which is based on listening and awareness of anticipation of clients' future needs. Organisations need a leadership marketing approach to ensure that a company brings to its markets a clearly defined product or service, which is aligned with the company's vision and values and meets the needs of customers, and where the message is clear for both employees and potential buyers alike. Thought the mindset of leadership marketing, organisations can deliver from the customer perspective by ensuring congruity between the way employees and customers perceive the brand. To strengthen the connection between internal employees' attitudes and external appearances of the brand to customers, organisations should analyse gaps in stakeholders' perceptions of the brand and use tailored marketing communication to translate brand values into customer experiences. Regular communication is necessary with an aim of aligning visions and building bonds between departments to ensure cohesive delivery of brand promise.

REFERENCES

Aaker, D. A., & Keller, K. L. (1990). Consumer Evaluations Of Brand Extensions. *Journal of Marketing, 54*(1), 27–41. doi:10.2307/1252171

Andersen, E. (2010). *Social Media Marketing: Game Theory and the Emergence of Collaboration*. Springer-Verlag. doi:10.1007/978-3-642-13299-5

Avlonitis, G. J., & Gounaris, S. P. (1999). Marketing orientation and its determinants: An empirical analysis. *European Journal of Marketing, 33*(11/12), 1003–1037. doi:10.1108/03090569910285896

Bass, B. M. (1995). Transformational Leadership. *Journal of Management Inquiry, 4*(3), 293–298. doi:10.1177/105649269543010

Berry, J., Hensel, S., & Burke, M. C. (1976). Improving Retailer Capability for Effective Consumerism Response. *Journal of Retailing, 52*(3), 3–14.

Berry, L. L., & Parasuraman, A. (1992). Services Marketing Starts from Within. *Marketing Management, 1*(1), 24–34.

Billire, P. (2009). *Leadership*. London: A&C Black Publishers Ltd.

Birkinshaw, J. (2010). *Reinventing Management: Smarter Choices For Getting The Work Done*. Chichester, UK: John Wiley & Sons, Ltd.

Boulding, K. E. (1956). *The Image*. Ann Arbor, MI: University of Michigan Press.

Bradshaw, P. (1998). *4x4 Leadership And The Purpose Of The Firm*. Binghampton, NY: The Haworth Press.

Brand Learning. (n.d.). *Conversation # 7 – Care about culture, 2011*. Retrieved from www.brandlearning.com/Whats-New/Brand-Learning-News/The-Conversations-for-2011-7.aspx

Brooke, J. (2002). *The Brand Inside*. Retrieved from www.cim.co.uk/filestore/resources/canons/brandinside.pdf

Carrig, K., & Wright, P. M. (2006). *Building profit through people: making your workforce the strongest link in the value-profit chain*. Society for Human Resource Management.

Charles, G. (2007, September). The CIM Definition: Fit for Purpose?. *Marketing*, 16.

Cohen, W. (2010). *Drucker on Leadership*. San Francisco, CA: Jossey-Bass.

Collins, J. C. (2001). *Good to Great: Why Some Companies Make The Leap..., & Others Don't*. London: Random House.

Conger, J. A., & Kanungo, R. N. (1998). *Charismatic Leadership in Organizations*. Thousand Oaks, CA: Sage.

Conger, J. A., Kanungo, R. N., & Menon, S. T. (2000). Charismatic leadership and follower effects. *Journal of Organizational Behavior*, *21*(7), 747–767. doi:10.1002/1099-1379(200011)21:7<747::AID-JOB46>3.0.CO;2-J

Courtney, H., Kirkland, J., & Viguerie, P. (1997, November/December). Strategy Under Uncertainty. *The McKinsey Quarterly*. PMID:10174798

Davies, E., Bannock, G., Uncles, M., & Trot, P. (n.d.). *The New Penguin Business Dictionary*. Penguin.

Day, D. V., & Lord, R. G. (1986). Executive leadership and organizational performance: Suggestions for a new theory and methodology. *Journal of Management*, *14*(3), 453–464. doi:10.1177/014920638801400308

Deshpande, R., & Webster, F. E. (1989). Organizational Culture and Marketing: Defining the Research. *Journal of Marketing*, *53*(1), 3–17. doi:10.2307/1251521

Drucker, P. F. (1973). *Management: Tasks, Responsibilities, Practices*. New York: Harper Collins.

Dunne, P. A., & Barnes, J.G. (2000). Internal Marketing: A relationships and value-creation view. *Internal Marketing: Directions for Management*, 192-220.

Elias, M. S. (2009). Employee Commitment in times of change: Assessing the importance of attitudes toward organisational change. *Journal of Management*, *35*(1), 37–55. doi:10.1177/0149206307308910

Evans, S. (1991). Strategic flexibility for high technology maneuvers. *Journal of Management Studies*, *28*, 69–89. doi:10.1111/j.1467-6486.1991.tb00271.x

Felton, A. P. (1956). Conditions Of Marketing Leadership. *Harvard Business Review*, *34*(2), 117–127.

Fomburn, C., & Van, R. C. (1997). The Reputational Landscape. *Corporate Reputation Review*, *1*(1/2), 5–13. doi:10.1057/palgrave.crr.1540024

Gardner, B., & Levy, S. (1955, March/April). The product and the brand. *Harvard Business Review*, 33–39.

Gavetti, G. (2011, July/August). The New Psychology Of Strategic Leadership. *Harvard Business Review*, 118–125. PMID:21800475

Goodyear, M. (1996). Divided by a Common Language: Diversity and Deception in the World of Global Marketing. *Journal of the Market Research Society. Market Research Society*, *38*(2), 105–122.

Grönroos, C. (1990). Relationship Approach to Marketing in Service Contexts: The Marketing and Organizational Behaviour Interface. *Journal of Business Research*, *20*(1), 3–11. doi:10.1016/0148-2963(90)90037-E

Gundlach, G., & Wilkie, W. (2009). The American Marketing Accusation's New Definition of Marketing: Perspective and Commentary on the 2007 Revision. *American Marketing Association*, *28*(2), 259-264.

Hatch, M., & Schultz, M. (1997). Relations between organizational culture, identity, and image. *European Journal of Marketing*, *31*(5-6), 356–365. doi:10.1108/eb060636

Heskett, J. L. (1994). Putting the service-profit chain to work. *Harvard Business Review*, *72*(2), 164.

Hofstede, G. (1980). *Cultures Consequences*. Beverly Hills, CA: Sage.

Hogg, G., & Carter, S. (2000). Employee attitudes and responses to internal marketing. In *Internal marketing: Directions for managers* (pp. 109–124). Academic Press. doi:10.4324/9780203207352.ch7

Ind, N. (2007). *Living the Brand: How to Transform Every Member of Your Organization into a Brand Champion* (3rd ed.). London: Kogan Page.

Jacobs, R. (2003). Turn employees into brand ambassadors. *ABA Bank Marketing, 35*(3), 22–26.

Jacobs, S. (n.d.). Flexible Working? It's About Culture, Not Rules. *People Management*. Retrieved from www.peoplemanagement.co.uk/articles/2011/flexible-working-its-about-culture-not-rules.htm

Jung, D. I. (2001). Transformational and Transactional Leadership and Their Effects on Creativity in Groups. *Creativity Research Journal, 13*(2), 185–195. doi:10.1207/S15326934CRJ1302_6

Kapferer, J. (1997). *Strategic Brand Management*. London: Kogan Page.

Kim, H. B., Kim, W. G., & An, J. (2003). The effect of consumer-based brand equity on firms' financial performance. *Journal of Consumer Marketing, 20*(4-5), 35–351.

Kohli, A. K., & Jaworski, B. J. (1990). Market orientation: The construct, research propositions, and managerial Implications. *Journal of Marketing, 54*(2), 1–18. doi:10.2307/1251866

Konopa, L. J., & Calabro, P. J. (1971). Adoption of the Marketing Concept by Large Northeastern Ohio Manufacturers. *Akron Business and Economic Review, 2*, 9–13.

Kotter, J. P. (1995). Leading Change: Why Transformation Efforts Fail. *Harvard Business Review, 73*(2), 59–67.

Low, G., & Fullerton, R. (1994). Brands, brand management and the brand manager system: A critical-historical evaluation. *JMR, Journal of Marketing Research, 31*(2), 173–190. doi:10.2307/3152192

Mark, M., & Pearson, C. S. (2001). *The Hero and The Outlaw: Building Extraordinary Brands Through the Power of Archetypes*. New York: McGraw-Hill.

Martin, A. (2007). The Changing Nature of Leadership, Research White Papers. *Centre for Creative Leadership*. Retrieved from www.ccl.org/leadership/pdf/research/NatureLeadership.pdf

McGrath, M. (2009). Why Marketing Leadership Matters. *Brand Learning*. Retrieved from http://www.brandlearning.com/Why-Marketing-Leadership-Matters.pdf

McGuire, J. P., Pasmore, W. C., & Rhodes, G. (2009). *Transforming Your Organisation*. San Francisco: Jossey-Bass.

Misiag, F. (2001). Metodyczne problemy badania orientacji marketingowej. *Marketing i Rynek, 10*.

Murphy, J. (1992). Assessing the Value of Brands. *Branding a Key Marketing Tool*, 184-197.

Narver, J. C., & Slater, S. F. (1990). The Effect of a Market Orientation On Business Profitability. *Journal of Marketing, 54*(4), 20–33. doi:10.2307/1251757

Nonaka, I., & Takeuchi, H. (2011, May). The Wise Leader. *Harvard Business Review*, 59–67. PMID:21548419

Olins, W. (1995). *The New Guide To Identity*. Aldershot, UK: Gower.

Pass, C., Lowes, B., Pendleton, A., Chadwick, L., & O'Reilly, D. (2006). *Collins Dictionary of Business*. Glasgow, UK: Harper-Collins.

Pfeffer, J. (1997). *New directions for organisation theory*. New York, NY: Oxford University Press.

Radcliffe, S. (2008). *Future - Engage - Deliver: The Essential Guide to Your Leadership*. Leicester, UK: Troubadour Publishing Ltd.

Rajagopalan, N., & Spreitzer, G. M. (1997). Toward a theory of strategic change: A multi-lens perspective and integrative framework. *Academy of Management Review*, *2*, 48–71.

Ries, A., & Trout, J. (1981). *Positioning: The Battle for your Mind*. Maidenhead, UK: McGraw-Hill.

Schein, E. (1992). *Organisational Culture and Leadership* (2nd ed.). San Francisco, CA: Jossey-Bass.

Shapiro, B. P. (2005). *Sustainable Marketing Leadership Model, Workshop I: Strategic Visioning and Integrated Planning*. Harvard Business Press Cases.

Sisodia, R., Sheth, J., & Wolfe, D. B. (2007). *Firms of Endearment: How World-class Companies Profit from Passion and Purpose*. Wharton School Publishing.

Smith, X. N., & Nunes, P. F. (2010). Will Marketing Get The Message. *Accenture Outlook*. Retrieved from www.accenture.com/Accenture_Outlook_Will_Marketing_Get_Message.pdf

Speak, K. D., & Hanson, G. (2008). Brand Inside Meets Brand Outside. *Design Management Review, 19*(2).

Stevens, M. (2011). UK Lacks Top Quality Leadership, Finds CIPD Survey. *People Management*. Retrieved from www.peoplemanagement.co.uk/pm/articles/2011/09/uk-lacks-top-quality-leadership

Ulrich, D., & Smallwood, N. (2007). *Leadership Brand: Developing Customer-Focused Leaders to Drive Performance and Build Lasting Value*. Boston: Harvard Business School Press.

Vrontis, D., Thrassou, A., & Razali, M. Z. (2010). Internal Marketing as an Agent of Change – Implementing a New Human Resource Information System for Malaysian Airlines. *Journal of General Management*, *36*(1), 21–41.

Werbach, A. (2009). *Leadership At All Levels: Inspiration As A Leadership Technique – A Strategy For Sustainability Starts With You*. Boston: Harvard Business Press.

Wu, C., Neubert, M. J., & Yi, X. (2007). Transformational leadership, cohesion perceptions and employee cynicism about organisational change: The mediating role of justice perceptions. *The Journal of Applied Behavioral Science*, *43*(3), 327–351. doi:10.1177/0021886307302097

KEY TERMS AND DEFINITIONS

Internal Marketing: Marketing that shapes organisational culture to transform the orientation of the organisation to focus upon employees, who are paramount in delivering the brand to external stakeholders.

Leadership: a collective activity of guiding, influencing and motivating others to achieve certain goals by interdependent decision-making, building shared direction, compelling vision and effective culture for employee alignment.

Leadership Marketing: A mindset of the way organisations operate, ensuring alignment of leadership and marketing within the business, whereby marketing acts as an agent attuned to customer needs and through leadership aligns company's vision to address those changes.

Marketing: the strategic business function responsible for creating, communicating and delivering offerings that have value for customers, clients, partners, and society at large.

Marketing Orientation: A shared set of beliefs and values that puts the consumer into the centre of the firm's thinking.

Organisational Change: A process of continuous evolvement, growth and development of the organization that is caused by the shifts in the external environment.

Organisational Culture: A mix of behaviours and attitudes of employees, often unsaid, intangible but deeply ingrained and embedded in every individual within the company.

Organisation's Identity: A commonly shared understanding of the values of the firm held by employees.

Chapter 8
The Impact of Marketing Strategy in Small Family Businesses

Anastasios Ntanos
A.T.E.I. of Piraeus, Greece

Stamatios Ntanos
A.T.E.I. of Piraeus, Greece

ABSTRACT

This chapter refers to small family businesses in Greece and examines the impact of their marketing strategy during an economic crisis period. The research took place in the broad area of Athens between December 2011 and March 2012. Data were collected to form a database of Greek independent private family companies (n=380) using personal interviews (structured questionnaire) with owners/managers of first- and second-generation family businesses. The chapter shows how small family businesses indicate marketing strategy using Carson's model. Limitations of expertise outline the marketing background, which can be described as "self-assisted." The research offers a verification of a previous model so that problems that arise from companies not putting into practice any marketing concepts can be examined. The significance of the chapter is that there have not formerly been any reviews made about Carson's model in Greece during the economic crisis period emphasizing family businesses.

INTRODUCTION

Family businesses constitute a dynamic segment of the economy that contributes to wealth creation, job generation and national competitiveness (Ward and Aronoff, 1990; Westhead and Cowling, 1995; Wang, 2002) and is a vital part of industrial change and innovation. In Greece, according to a research conducted by Grand Thornton (2003), family firms represent the 80% of all businesses. In addition, the last three years out of the 105.000 new businesses that started their operations in Greece a percentage of 70, 3 belonged to family businesses (Avramidis, 2007). Similar to all organizations, family firms have to make use of a number of organizational activities, structures and strategies in order to satisfy customers while overcoming competition. However, due to the fact that in this category of

DOI: 10.4018/978-1-4666-6232-2.ch008

business the social and economic system coexists and interacts, these companies, while choosing the appropriate courses of action, have to face all the pros and cons of family businesses as well as all positive and negative characteristics of economic firms in general. Consequently the need for these firms to use marketing strategies is considered to be a necessity and not a peripheral to their requirements; as their owners have to plan for the future while dealing with the essential daily matters from customer enquiries, production matters and financial control to employee recruitment and other operational details within severe resource constraints (Stanworth & Gray, 1991; Hogarth Scott et al., 1996).

However, the establishment of family business research as an academic field of study is relatively recent and even though a plethora of family businesses issues and marketing tactics exists there is a scarcity of both theory and practical implication in the use and impacts of marketing concept. In Greece it has not been explored in the extent it should have nor has it been given the importance it ought to have. As a result it is very important to investigate the marketing tactics in the most vital sectors.

According to (Getz & Carlsen, 2005) family business has not been explored as an independent sector, especially in Greece. The aim of the research is to identify the impact that the marketing mix has on family businesses in Greece. Furthermore, the current paper examines if these companies gives importance in understanding the market and competing at the same time.

BACKGROUND

Marketing Orientation and Family Business Limitations

Family firms could be defined as enterprises in which two different social systems, the business system and the family system intersect (Getz & Carlsen, 2005) (Kyriazopoulos & Terzidis, 2000).

However, a commonly accepted definition for family businesses does not exist (Sharma and al, 1996 in Getz & Carlsen, 2005). According to Yilmazer and Schrank (2006) a definition of a family business is: "businesses, in which at least two family members work and the business is owned and managed by one of the family members." Barry (1975, in Getz et al, 2005) on the other hand simply defines them as enterprises controlled by members of a single family. Getz and Carlsen (2005) state that by simply searching for the term family business the many relevant references are not revealed as a great part of the literature is subsumed under another heading such as entrepreneurship and small business.

The main characteristic of a family business is the succession ownership (Rosenblat et al, 1985) to the next generation. According to Chung et al (2003) "succession in family businesses is important as it does not require only the transfer of ownership and control but also a number of changes in the business model" and that the next generation's members who are usually more educated and innovating must make so as to compete in the market place (Sharma et al., 1996). However, in the companies that display distinctive patterns of power and authority (Poutziouris et al., 2003), first generation owners seem to be reluctant as they believe that despite the fact that the decision making within the business is affected by the entire family system (Poutziouris et al, 2003) next generation's members will not succeed in growing the company's size.

Getz et al., (2005) identify that the preparation level of owners and successors influence the transition and the future direction of businesses and have a significant impact on the firm's marketing concept.

It is well documented that small family businesses have unique characteristics that differentiate them from conventional marketing in large corporations (Getz et al., 2005). These characteristics may be determined by the inherent characteristics and behavior of the family members or owners;

and may be determined by the inherent size and stage of development of the enterprise.

Therefore it should be mentioned that Greek family businesses can be divided into two categories by ownership. The first one, which constitutes the majority of the family businesses, presents significant lacking in the ability of managing marketing techniques, technological advances and human resources. If the business size is not large enough to depend upon a large number of customers, the owners are not willing to take any risks.

These limitations can be summarized as: limited resources (such as finance, time, and marketing knowledge); lack of specialist expertise (owner-managers tend to be generalists rather than specialists); and limited impact in the marketplace.

In addition, family business owners do not conform to the conventional marketing rules since their implementation of marketing rules is haphazard and informal; they make most decisions on their own, respond to current opportunities and circumstances and therefore any decision making occurs in a loose, unstructured, spontaneous, way, according to personal and business priorities at any given point in time. Clearly such limitations will influence, indeed determine, the marketing concept of such businesses.

Thus, these characteristics restrain the dynamism of this segment as well as its survival and entrepreneurial development across generations (Poutziouris et al., 2003). In addition, these constraints prevent family firms from maintaining business planning while conditions of uncertainty turn them away from strategic planning activities, (Bhide, 1994; Hill, 2001); making marketing a relevant issue, a peripheral to their requirements.

Nevertheless, despite the fact that family businesses see marketing as an "unnecessary luxury" as businesses move along the growth-life cycle the pressure for planning and implementing marketing strategies increases (Kenny & Dyson, 1989) (Scott and Bruce, 1987; Watts et al., 1998). Family business owners have to develop strategies in order to allow the company to adapt to environmental changes, segmenting the market where it belongs, focusing on satisfying their customers as it is a major aim of the marketing concept (Dibb et al., 1994).

Therefore, the firm's main task is to determine the needs, wants, and interests of market's targets and to deliver the desired satisfaction more effectively and efficiently than competitors in a way that preserves or enhances the consumer's (Kotler, 2002) through the creation, distribution, promotion and pricing of goods, services and ideas (Kyriazopoulos & Terzidis, 2000).

The adopting of the marketing concept "tries to provide products that satisfy customer needs through co-ordinated sets of activities that allow the family firm to achieve its goals. Customer satisfaction is the major aim of the marketing concept" (Watts et al., 1998). The marketing concept is a management philosophy which guides the way in which an organization does business. Watts et al, (1998) emphasize that the marketing concept "is a way of thinking - a management philosophy guiding an organisation's overall activities." It is therefore important that family management is fully committed to the marketing concept and that it forms the basis for all goals and decisions within the company. The adoption of the marketing concept is the central theme of this article.

Environmental Scanning

Family businesses first priority is to get a full understanding of the market and the factors that influence it. Understanding the market by identifying opportunities that they can take advantage of, as well as threats that they must face is crucial for this kind of businesses. Nevertheless, family business owners especially those who founded the firm find it difficult and believe it to be a waist of time, money and resources to be occupied in a procedure like this. Unlike their successors that are, in their majority, more educated and make greater use of technology, founders believe that the best way to get market understanding is to stay in touch and keep a close personal contact with the clients. This is why they give great importance in keeping the selling procedure among the family members. Understanding the characteristics of rival competitors and each one's experience, market position, staying power, strength and predictability aids the company to find the most prosperous way in addressing the competitive market by leaning on its strengths and on characteristics that competitors lack. Especially in today's competitive marketplace identifying the size and features of competitors affects marketing decisions. Offering the product or service in a way that will outsell the competition is critical and so is the strategy that the company will choose to use in order to address the desired segments of the market (Watts et al., 1998).

In Greece, according to Macridakis et al., (1997) any kind of planning is difficult since managers tend to concentrate on the short term due to factors of frequent changes and unexpected events. They intent with their little or no formal marketing education and work experience to practice a simplified marketing strategy that is customer oriented due to the fact that part of their philosophy is to "please everyone" (Mc Tavish, 1996). However, in broad markets, a company cannot serve everyone as customers are numerous and diverse in their buying requirements. As a result, it researches its market to know how many potential customers it has, what their needs are and how to reach them (Mc Tavish, 1996). Afterwards it divides large, heterogeneous markets into smaller segments that can be reached and served more effectively (Kotler,1999; 2002).

However, while for the majority of large businesses the data of these segmentation variables are fairly readily available and it is easy for them to identify the segment or those segments for which they want to provide a product based on their objectives and their resources (Mc Tavish, 1996, Kotler, 2002), for the majority of family firms this rarely occurs. Financial restraints, lack of resources and technological innovation, low educational level of first generation owners and lack of managerial skills makes segmentation for this type of companies impossible. What the family business owner really wants, is to sell its products. In order to do so at the first stages of the business life cycle, especially when entering the market, he targets a single segment and uses a simple strategy.

Nevertheless, as the company moves on and seeks potential to increase aggregate sales what the business owner should do is use differing marketing mixes to target a multi-segment (Mc Tavish, 1996). Instead of doing that while at the same time examining the interrelation of cost - performance - and technology, as well as deciding whether they will follow an undifferentiated, a differentiated or a concentrated marketing, based on their resources, product variability, lifecycle stage and competitive marketing strategies (Kotler, 1999; 2002) what family business owners do is targeting multiple segments the same way they did with a single segment. Yet, the way the firm chooses to address the targeted markets constitutes its core strategy and it is supported by many practitioners that differentiation helps develop the strengths of the business so that they meet the needs of the target markets while market positioning develops and manages the way consumers view the company and its products (Kotler, 2002).

The Carson Model

The Carson Model addresses a number of issues relating to small firm marketing. These include the constraints affecting this type of marketing, the extent to which the general principles of marketing can be applied to each particular situation, the role of planning in marketing and the evolution of firms through different phases of development. Carson (1990) emphasized the importance of marketing planning and how it must be adapted to the circumstances of the business.

The first model describes three types of constraint affecting the way in which small firms undertake marketing. Limitations are classified as minimal, limited and substantial; they relate to resources and are described in terms of time and money devoted to marketing.

The second model identified three levels of general marketing principles adaptation to the situation in which a firm is operating.

The third model focuses on two categories of marketing decision and the extent to which there is a balance between the two in a firm's marketing. The fourth model focuses on the adaptation of family firms to the marketing planning concepts and the application of marketing techniques in suiting its opportunities.

The fifth model identified four stages from the date of its establishment to reactive, tinkering marketing, entrepreneurial marketing and proactive marketing.

The sixth model differentiates three levels of marketing activity and examines the techniques and operations of marketing in the context of marketing planning. It also includes: little or no marketing, implicit and simple marketing, explicit and sophisticated marketing.

MAIN FOCUS OF THE CHAPTER

Research Methodology

The sample that was used for the current research related to small family businesses that operate in Greece. We define a small family business as that which employs less than fifty employees and meets the independence criterion. As a very small business is the one that employs less than 10 employees. Eurostat's 2006 statistics show the dominance of small family businesses in Greece and the European Union. According to the table, self-employed that are rated as a business occupy 50.4% of all businesses and 10% of the employment.

Every effort to accurately defining small family businesses is not guaranteed neither in determining quantitative limits nor or annual sales and number of employees.

A questionnaire was developed specifically to collect the information among the first and second-generation owners about the impact of marketing concepts in the family business. The questionnaire was based on a review by Simpson et al., (2006). Drawing on the study of literatures above, the survey was devised with the five following questions in mind:

- Which factors in particular enforce the use of marketing practice in family business?
- Which limitations reduce the application of marketing techniques?
- Which is the implementation means that the family offers?
- Where should the business focus in order to gain a competitive advantage?

Therefore, the questionnaire designed was divided into four sections (Section A, B and C and D), each with its own subsections. Section A, asked the respondents questions to state their opinion for the product, price, channels of distribution and promotion. Section B included general and external environmental questions. The questions in each section were posed using the Likert scale. For instrument consistency, each scale included five items – 5=strongly agree, 4=agree, 3=neutral, 2=disagree; 1=strongly disagree.

To get answers to these questions, an interview based on a pilot questionnaire was conducted with five retailing companies in Greece. The respondents were the first-generation owners. The research was conducted from January to April 2007. The sample size was 550 family businesses, from a list provided by the Industrial and Commercial Chamber in Piraeus.

The database created specifically for this survey included owner-members of family businesses. The questionnaire was distributed by personal interviews. The survey team researched family businesses establishment 30 years ago and employed two officers or directors with the same last name. There were 380 companies, which participated in the survey. The overall response rate was 47,5%.

Family Business Demographic Characteristics

The sample companies' main characteristics can be summarized as follows:

Age distribution: the majority of family firms (41, 67%) have been established after 1980, while the rest of the firms (26, 67%) before 1980.

Turnover distribution: about 43,2% of family companies have annual turnover up to 100,000 euro, whilst 32,4% have up to 500,000 euro and a percentage of 8,2 surpass 1,000,000 euro.

Sector: it appears that family companies are more prolific in retail trade (41, 6%) and services (26, 3%) and construction activities (9, 7%) and less prolific in wholesale trade (8, 2%).

Business type: The main type of businesses is private enterprise (45%) with 38% being propriety unlimited and 17% propriety limited.

Business transfers: only 32, 4% of family companies have a second generation perspective and have been through ownership change.

Average percentage of sales from each market: 85% operate in the Greek market (50,6% local and 34,3% national) while the rest operate on a global scale (15, 69% of the respondents).

Financial resources: Financial recourses used by family business reflect a conservative borrowing profile.

Data Analysis

The external environment takes a lead role in planning the family business' strategy (Table 1). The economy situation, where there is a recession and is developed through reducing demand, lowering prices, profits and revenues is a matter that concerns the majority of the businesses. Family businesses suffer through a lack of knowledge of the customer base, the market and the understanding of marketing practices (74, 9%). Practices are often not suitable when adopted by family businesses. The result is often inadequate marketing and business mistakes. Moreover, marketing planning from family firms has limited adapta-

Table 1. General and external environment

	Yes %	No %
Does the instability of economies affect businesses?	90,5	9,5
Do the employees make any marketing mistakes in your industry?	74,9	25,1
Do changes in technology affect the way you do business?	64,9	35,1
Do government regulations affect family firm's marketing decisions?	63,5	36,5
Is the company's managers familiar with strategic planning?	62,7	37,3
Do your staff-members participate in marketing decisions?	50,9	49,1
Does the firm have any strategic plan in written?	19,0	81,0

tion as the firm only uses marketing techniques unsuitable to its needs.

MARKETING MIX OF SMALL FAMILY FIRMS

Product

The table below describes the lack of renewal and the need of family firms updating its portfolio by adding new products (Table 2).

The above fact, according to the findings, is due to the pressure that is put on by the external environment, in which the firm operates and the restricted resources that a family business disposes.

Sales Forecasting

Businesses create a sales budget, which in their majority is later used as a marketing tool. Those who took part in the questionnaire (Table 3) believe that quality combined with the creation of a long-term relationship with the customer and proper pricing policy are the main factors behind a business' survival in a competitive environment.

The firms of our sample present a lack of marketing strategy and this is reported by reducing the price in order to move customers, a technique that is continuously used by firms that lack in marketing, segmentation and positioning.

In the approval of the above, management sectors such as differentiation, management, innovation and technology are considered to be of

Table 2. Renewal (update) ratio of the product portfolio

		Recent product disconnection	New products adding to family business
		Valid percent	Valid percent
Valid	Yes	45,5	86,5
	No	54,5	13,5

Table 3. Sales forecasting

		Frequency	Percent	Valid Percent	Cumulative Percent
Valid	At all	4	1,1	1,1	1,1
	Very little	20	5,3	5,3	6,3
	Neutral	61	16,1	16,1	22,4
	Much	241	63,4	63,4	85,8
	Very much	54	14,2	14,2	100,0

secondary importance. The technological advance is verified to be one of the most important problems of small family businesses due to the lack of expenditure and specialization.

Limitations of expertise outlines the marketing background which can be described as self-assisted, where owners have taught themselves marketing through private study; in addition those firms which involve thinking about forecasting and developing low cost strategies and relationship as marketing is clearly orientated towards planning decisions. There is a balance between planning and operations decisions. Therefore, the policy that its competitors apply is vital to the firm, while the majority declares there is a seasoning in sales (Table 4).

Place

The management appears to be satisfied from the business' current location (Table 5). The management declares that there is flexibility in finding suppliers. This means that either not any significance is given in Logistics or many problems are solved due to a special relationship between them and the suppliers. According to Carson's model the evolution of marketing practices in the firm from the date of its establishment is the stage of entrepreneurial marketing that carried out instinctively as the owner learns about marketing and recognizes its value in general. Owners often have a craft or production background, which can lead to an approach incompatible with the marketing concept.

As far as the international expansion of the firm, globalization has not affected in creating aggressive policy with exports, since only 29.5% has examined this option (Table 6).

Family businesses are not interested in international activity except from opportunities that will arise in creating low cost products. This is perhaps due to the first generation's business founders, who cannot adapt to an ever changing and global economic environment in order to take the international market as a united one and segment the market it into various parts, where they will develop their activities.

The international activity of the businesses that responded positively is developing towards achieving a competitive cost (in order to face competition in a global economy) and Logistics economies.

Table 4. Competitors' policy

	Mean	Std. Deviation
Competitors policy affected the family business	3,50	0,87
Are there seasonal variations in your sales?	3,43	1,18

Table 5. Place

	Mean	Std. Deviation
Do you easily find new sources of suppliers?	3,90	0,83
Are you satisfied from your business' current location?	3,67	0,89

Table 6. Exporting/ importing opportunities

		Frequency	Percent	Valid Percent	Cumulative Percent
Valid	Yes	112	29,5	29,6	29,6
	No	267	70,3	70,4	100,0
	Total	379	99,7	100,0	
Missing	System	1	,3		
Total		380	100,0		

The portfolio creation of products (new products enhancement) could create conditions of profitability enrichment.

The activation (after a SWOT analysis) so that "product shortage" can be traced is an internationalization technique of a business unit.

On the contrary, modernization conditions of the management of a family business do not "move" these businesses for them to take advantage of the new economy.

Price

The competitive environment creates mimic motives as far as pricing of products is concerned (Table 7).

The increase of prices in raw material does not necessarily follow the supply chain. As far as pricing policy is concerned, half of the firms pursue the liberation of mark up, while the rest of them deem it should remain as in a closed economy (Table 8).

Question: Are there any standard mark-ups in your industry?

Promotion

Advertising campaigns through mass media is avoided (Table 9). Promotional activities are reduced, even though they have formerly proved beneficial. The trained staff can prove beneficial and many invest on them. Many focus on the means

Table 7. The influence of pricing policy in small family businesses

		Frequency	Percent	Valid Percent	Cumulative Percent
Valid	At all	47	12,4	12,6	12,6
	Very little	44	11,6	11,8	24,4
	Neutral	82	21,6	22,0	46,4
	Much	152	40,0	40,8	87,1
	Very much	48	12,6	12,9	100,0
	Total	373	98,2	100,0	
Missing	System	7	1,8		
Total		380	100,0		

Table 8. The race of the mark up

		Frequency	Percent	Valid Percent	Cumulative Percent
Valid	Yes	179	47,1	48,4	48,4
	No	191	50,3	51,6	100,0
	Total	370	97,4	100,0	
Missing	System	10	2,6		
Total		380	100,0		

Table 9. Promotion

	Mean	Std. Deviation
Do you give your staff regarding personal selling?	3,31	1,15
Have promotional efforts worked?	3,17	1,05
Do you use different selling techniques or promotional methods for: Older versus younger customers?	3,07	1,20
Do you use promotional efforts?	2,72	1,23
Do you use advertising?	2,56	1,26

of promoting sales and the employees that work on them. New and old customers are equally treated.

Limitations here arise from the minimal impact on expenditure and expertise. From the point where one firm spends the minimum amount of money necessary to communicate with its customers to the point where a firm and its products are known in the marketplace. Respondents determined that customers and the word of mouth are the advertising that works best. This describes reactive marketing a situation where all customers are personally known to the owner and business tends to develop through word-of-mouth recommendation based on product, price and delivery.

Maintaining customers in a business is easier than attracting new ones. This explains the focus on a more customer-orientated system

Generally, it should be noted that family businesses are thought of rather conservative in their majority and this should be due to first generation's culture, which can hardly absorb new economy conditions.

Table 10. Carson's model evaluation

Model	Classification categories		
(1) Marketing limitations			
Expenditure	Minimal	Limited	Substantial
Expertise	Self-help	Appreciation level	In-depth
Impact	Minimal	Limited	Substantial
(2) Levels of generalization	General consepts	Industry –specific	Situation-specific
(3) Planning versus operations	Minimal	Balanced	
(4) Marketing planning adapted	Limited adaptation	Substantial adaptation	
(5) Stages in marketing development	Reaction	Entrepreneurial tinkering	Expertly proactive
(6) Levels of activity	Little or no marketing	Implicit –Simple	Explicit Sophisticated

SOLUTIONS AND RECOMMENDATIONS

Carson's Model Evaluation

Taking into account the models that are presented below the following can be assumed: Classification categories in bold present the findings of the present research which verifies Carson's models (Table 10).

According to the findings, the limitations of expenditure relate to resources in terms of time and money devoted to marketing are described as minimal – where the firm spends the minimum amount of money necessary to communicate with its customers; The limitations of expertise outline the marketing background of the firm's management are described as self-assisted – where managers have taught themselves marketing terms through private study; and finally the limitations of impact arise from the limitations of expenditure and expertise.

The levels of generalization show how the general principles of marketing are adapted to the situation in which a firm is operating. It is identified as industry-specific and describes the situation where the firm follows the norms and practices of its industry.

The marketing plan versus operations the family business firms can be described as self-assisted – where owners have taught themselves marketing terms through private study; moreover firms are involved in thinking about the forecasting and developing strategies of low cost and relationship marketing, which are regarded as decision planning . There is a balance between planning and operations decisions therefore Carson planning versus operations model is verified

Marketing planning adapted for small firms', is found that family firms use marketing techniques unsuitable to its needs therefore the adaptation can be characterized as limited.

The evolution of marketing practices in the family firm from the date of its establishment identified as instinctive marketing went through as the owner-manager learns about marketing and recognizes its value in generating extra sales. Owner-managers often have a craft or production background, which can lead to an approach incompatible with any marketing concept.

The level of marketing activity in Model 6 is little since marketing occurs where a firm generally reacts to customer requirements, has little or no knowledge of the customer base or the market and has no clear purpose.

CONCLUSION

Family businesses face a number of challenges in order to survive to the next generations:

- The transition speed of the buying habits of their customers that is in many sectors rather big.
- The competition techniques of the large businesses, which are in position to shape market rules.
- The ever changing market policy of the suppliers in cost and condition issues and cooperation preconditions.
- The different growth perspectives that each family –member might have.
- The commercial consequences of technology advances.

The confrontation of competitive components means that a family business should:

- Be informed of market and customers trends.
- Obtain a broad view the changes that will occur in the business environment for the following five years as well as the business characteristics that started operating and had a success.
- Focus on the services or products it offers in order to create a competitive advantage in its sector. Family business should be very good and reputable in what it does.
- Gain advantages in the areas, where large businesses face problems, i.e. customer service, special relationships with the customers and suppliers and suppleness in providing services.

On the other hand, a businessman should:

- Develop banking system tools, which allow the improvement of financial data of a small business.
- Pursue business consulting help.

REFERENCES

(1991). 20 Years On: The Small Firm. InStanworth, J., & Gray, C. (Eds.), *The 1990s*. London: Paul Chapman.

Alba Economic Post. (2003, April 12). Grand Thorton Reserch In Staurou Kostea, E. *Alba Economic Post.*

Avramidis, N. (2007). Issues and necessities of small and medium size businesses. *Aluminium Profile Magazine, 7.*

Bhide, A. (1994, March-April). How Entrepreneurs Craft Strategies That Work. *Harvard Business Review*, 150–161.

Carson, D. (1990). Some Exploratory Models for Assessing Small Firms' Marketing Performance: A Qualitative Approach. *European Journal of Marketing*, *24*(11), 8–51. doi:10.1108/03090569010006056

Getz, D., & Petersen, T. (2005). Growth And Profit-Oriented Entrepreneurship Among Family Business Owners In The Tourism And Hospitality Industry. *Hospital Management*, *24*(2), 219–242. doi:10.1016/j.ijhm.2004.06.007

Hill, J. (2001). A Multidimensional Study Of The Key Determinants Of Effective SME Marketing Activity: Part 1. *International Journal Of Entrepreneurial Behaviour & Research*, *7*(5), 171–204. doi:10.1108/EUM0000000006006

Hogarth Scott, S., Watson, K., & Wilson, N. (1996). Do Small Businesses Have To Practice Marketing To Survive And Grow? *Marketing Intelligence & Planning*, *14*(1), 6–18. doi:10.1108/02634509610106197

Kenny, B., & Dyson, K. (1989). Marketing. In *Small Business*. London: Routledge.

Kotler, P. (2002). *Marketing Management*. Prentice-Hall, Inc.

Kotler, P., Armstrong, G., Saunders, J., & Wong, V. (1999). *Principles Of Marketing* (2nd ed.). Prentice Hall Europe.

Kyriazopoulos, P., & Terzidis, K. (2000). *Management SME in the 3rd Industrial Revolution*. Athens: Publisher Sychroni Ekdotiki.

Makridakis, S., Caloghirou, Y., Papagiannakis, L., & Trivellas, P. (1997). The Dualism Of Greek Firms And Management: Present State And Future Implications. *European Management Journal*, *15*(4), 381–402. doi:10.1016/S0263-2373(97)00018-2

Mctavish, A. R., Gunasekaran, S. G., & Yli-Olli, P. (1996). Establishing A Strategic Framework For Improving Productivity. *Integrated Manufacturing Systems*, *7*(4), 12–21. doi:10.1108/09576069610125067

Poutziouris, P. (2003). The Strategic Orientation Of Owner-Managers Of Small Ventures Evidence From The UK Small Business Economy. *International Journal Of Entrepreneurial Behaviour & Research*, *9*(5), 185–214. doi:10.1108/13552550310488929

Rosenblatt, P. C., De Milk, L., Anderson, R. M., & Jhonson, P. A. (1985). The Family. In *Business: Understanding The Dealing With The Challenges Entrepreneurial Families Face*. San Francisco: Jossey Bass.

Scott, M., & Bruce, R. (1987). Five Stages Of Growth In Small Businesses. *Long Range Planning*, *20*(3), 45–52. doi:10.1016/0024-6301(87)90071-9

Sharma, P., Chrisman, J., & Chua, J. (1996). *A Review And Annotated Bibliography Of Family Business Studies*. Boston: Kluwer. doi:10.1007/978-1-4419-8768-6

Wang, Y. (2002). *Succession Issues And Business Performance: Evidence From UK Small And Medium-Sized Family Businesses*. (Unpublished Doctoral Dissertation). Southampton Institute, Southampton, UK.

Ward, J. L., & Aronoff, C. E. (1990). To Sell Or Not To Sell? *Nation's Business*, *78*(1), 63–64.

Watts, G., Cope, J., & Hulme, M. (1998). Anshoff's Matrix, Pain And Gain Growth Strategies And Adaptive Learning Among Small Food Producers. *International Journal Of Entrepreneurial Behaviour & Research*, *4*(2), 101–111. doi:10.1108/13552559810224567

Westhead, P., & Cowling, M. (1995). Employment Change In Independent Owner-Managed High-Technology Firms In Great Britain. *Small Business Economics*, *7*(2), 111–140. doi:10.1007/BF01108686

Yilmazer, T., & Schrank, H. (2006). Financial Intermingling In Small Family Businesses. *Journal of Business Venturing*, *21*(5), 726–751. doi:10.1016/j.jbusvent.2005.04.011

KEY TERMS AND DEFINITIONS

Competitive Advantage: An advantage that allows the company to outperform its competitors, gained by offering consumers greater value, either by means of lower prices or by providing greater benefits and service that justifies higher prices.

Family Firm: An enterprise where the directors, the shareholders and sometimes many of the employees are members of the same family.

Mark Up: The amount that a seller of goods or services charges over and above the total cost of delivering its product or service in order to make a desired profit. For entrepreneurs in the process of starting a business, establishing markup is one of the most important parts of pricing strategy.

Marketing Plan: Marketing planning process is a logical sequence and series of activities leading to the setting of strategic planning objectives for an enterprise, and the formulation of strategic plans for achieving them. The marketing strategy provides the goals for the marketing plan.

Marketing Strategy: Product specific, market specific, or company-wide plan that describes activities involved in achieving specific marketing objectives within a set timeframe.

Strategic Planning: A systematic process that helps an organization to focus its resources and energy, in order to ensure that members of the organization are working toward the same goals or objectives.

SWOT Analysis: specifying the objective of a business venture and identifying the internal and external factors that are favorable and unfavorable to achieve that objective. It is used to evaluate the strengths, weaknesses, opportunities, and threats involved in a project.

Chapter 9
The Role of Brand Management in Emerging Markets

Kijpokin Kasemsap
Suan Sunandha Rajabhat University, Thailand

ABSTRACT

This chapter introduces the role of brand management in emerging markets, thus explaining the concepts of brand management system, corporate branding, brand performance, brand equity, brand awareness, perceived brand quality, brand association, and brand loyalty; the importance of brand strategy in emerging markets; and brand relationships toward effective brand management. Firms in emerging markets should take consideration of their brand management system, corporate branding, brand performance, brand equity, brand awareness, perceived brand quality, brand association, and brand loyalty in order to effectively achieve business success in emerging markets based on the conditions of their organizational structure, environment, and marketing contexts. Developing a good brand relationship is essential for brand management in emerging markets. Firms in emerging markets should recognize the importance of brand constructs (i.e., brand management system, corporate branding, brand performance, brand equity, brand awareness, perceived brand quality, brand association, and brand loyalty) and need to put more marketing efforts in building brand management system in order to enhance the marketing performance and achieve business goals in the global marketing environment.

INTRODUCTION

Knowledge of brand management actions is a central concern for practitioners and top managers (Dunes & Pras, 2013). Branding enables firms to achieve competitive advantage through building higher value perception of customers to get a higher price premium (Hsiao & Chen, 2013). Emerging markets are characterized by industrialization and rapid economic growth (Rugman & Collinson, 2009). Emerging markets are assuming an important position in the international strategy research (Cavusgil, Ghauri, & Agarwal, 2002). The adoption of developed nation-based theories or approaches to emerging markets and firms is the challenge in this stream of marketing research (Wright, Filatotchev, Hoskisson, & Peng 2005). The developed nations are characterized as mature, saturated, and highly competitive whereas emerging markets have unique characteristics such

DOI: 10.4018/978-1-4666-6232-2.ch009

as weak and shallow home country advantage, weak institutional structures, political instabilities, and lack of market-based management skills (Brouthers, O'Donnell, & Hadjimarsu, 2005). Emerging markets have experienced and are experiencing tremendous economic growth (Martin & Inchovichina, 2008). One of the challenges for brand managers in the twenty-first century is to comprehend the relations between brand loyalty and its antecedents (Taylor, Celuch, & Goodwin, 2004). Established brands (i.e., BMW, Ford, and Toyota) have established loyal customer bases over time, whereas the latecomer brands, i.e. brands from emerging countries now entering the global market, have yet to establish trust with consumers (Hamin, Baumann, & Tung, 2014). With a high level of customers' loyalty and perceived satisfaction, the long-term benefits of building up a strong brand can outweigh immediate costs (Hsiao & Chen, 2013). This chapter introduces the role of brand management in emerging markets, thus explaining the concepts of brand management system, corporate branding, brand performance, brand equity, brand awareness, perceived brand quality, brand association, and brand loyalty; the importance of brand strategy in emerging markets; and brand relationships toward effective brand management.

BACKGROUND

Branding is a powerful method of distinction (Pappu, Quester, & Cooksey, 2005). Brands play a central role in marketing and have attracted the attention of academics and practitioners over many years (Brodie, Glynn, & Little, 2006; Erdem, Swait, & Valenzuela, 2006). Strong brand names lead competitive advantages (Lee & Back, 2010), increase organizational cash flow, and accelerate liquidity in business (Miller & Muir, 2004), provide premium price, profitability and more loyalty for customers (Madden, Fehle, & Fournier, 2006). Branding supports the opportunity of brand extension (Yasin, Nasser Noor, & Mohamad, 2007). Building brand equity is considered as an important part of brand building (Pappu et al., 2005). Brand equity refers to the incremental utility or added value which brand adds to the product (Chen & Chang, 2008). In addition, brand equity is an appropriate metric for evaluating the long-run impact of marketing decision (Atilgan, Aksoy, & Akinci, 2005). Appropriate management of brand equity enhances: the increase in loyalty, flexible response to price fluctuations, more business support and cooperation, high effectiveness of marketing communications, licensing opportunities, additional opportunities for brand extension, more attraction and support from investors; and the decrease in risk of marketing activity and marketing crisis (VanAuken, 2005), and greater profit margins (Kim & Kim, 2005), thus increasing the ability to attract good employees (DelVecchio, Jarvis, Klink, & Dineen, 2007), and protecting the potential competitors which enter during outsourcing (Lim & Tan, 2009). Furthermore, brand equity is the result of consumers' perception (Yasin et al., 2007). The concept of brand can be traced back to product marketing where the role of brand and brand management has been primarily to create differentiation and preference for a product or service in the mind of the customer (Knox & Bickerton, 2003). The strong brand actually influences consumer perception; and brand loyalty primarily focuses on marketing mix variables. Brands can be successful when they are closely associated with consumers and are preferred by consumers over unbranded products (Rajagopal, 2009).

THE ROLE OF BRAND MANAGEMENT IN EMERGING MARKETS

This section introduces the concepts of brand management system, corporate branding, brand performance, brand equity, brand awareness, perceived brand quality, brand association, and brand loyalty; the importance of brand strategy in emerging markets; and brand relationships toward effective brand management.

Brand Management System

Branding activities are demonstrated that a portfolio of strong brands creates value for the shareholders (Madden et al., 2006); and the status of the marketing department within the firm depends on its ability to show its contribution in terms of return on investment (Verhoef & Leeflang, 2009). Lee et al., (2008) defined a brand management system (BMS) as a set of any systems, organizational structure, or culture of a firm supporting brand-building activities. Lee et al., (2008) conceptualized BMS as the degree of infrastructure-building activities (i.e., organization and culture; knowledge and education; and implementation and performance evaluation systems). Santos-Vijande et al., (2013) developed a BMS scale, with the Spanish sample of knowledge-intensive service firms, comprising three dimensions: brand orientation, internal branding, and strategic brand management. Brand orientation has been described as a component of the BMS (Santos-Vijande et al., 2013). Brand orientation is an organizational culture that drives the firm's marketing strategy (Wong & Merrilees, 2007; Baumgarth, 2010; Urde et al., 2013) in order to achieve a sustainable competitive advantage (Beverland et al., 2007; Wong & Merrilees, 2008; Baumgarth & Schmidt, 2010). Brand orientation is not only cultural but also behavioral (Bridson & Evans, 2004), with the development of management tools such as brand communication, brand charters, and controlling instruments. Brand orientation is also related to brand performance and profitability (Ind & Bjerke, 2007; Hirvonen et al., 2013).

In the area of strategic brand management, there is a tendency to over-concentrate on the important issue of brand building (John, 2006). John (2006) noted that four components of strategic brand management include: building brands, leveraging brands, identifying brands, and protecting brands. Brand values must be accepted by all organizational members, who must fully collaborate to achieve the goal of building strong brands (Punjaisri et al., 2009). All organizational members have to be educated and trained to understand and support the brand identity (De Chernatony & Cottam, 2006) and embrace the brand values in order to become the brand ambassadors (Vallaster & De Chernatony, 2006) and contribute to building the brand's image and reputation through their contacts with customers and stakeholders. A top-down, bottom-up approach to brand communication is a key ingredient of effective internal branding (Mzungu et al., 2010). To achieve effective internal branding, organizations also need to select candidates whose values are congruent with brand values and corporate culture (Hatch & Schultz, 2008) and reward employees who maintain and enhance the brand standards. Brand orientation and internal branding will be fully effective for corporate branding if a perfect alignment occurs between strategic vision, organizational culture, and corporate image (Rubin et al., 2008).

Corporate Branding

The concept of corporate branding has gained popularity in the marketing literature as corporate brands are said to add value to the products and services offered by the firms. A strong brand can lead to several marketing advantages and increase companies' competitive strength (Hoeffler & Keller, 2003). Abratt and Kleyn (2011) suggested four aspects of corporate branding that are crucial to the development of a strong brand identity. Four aspects of corporate branding are visual identity, brand promise, brand personality, and brand communication (Abratt & Kleyn, 2011). According to Souiden, Kassim, and Hong (2006), corporate branding encompasses the four dimensions of corporate name, image, reputation, and loyalty. The core concept of corporate branding is to adopt a monolithic brand name representing all products of the firms when communicating with stakeholders such as customers, employees, and shareholders (Xie & Boggs, 2006); and a successful corporate brand is underpinned by clear corporate missions and values defined by the senior management to guide the operations of all organizational departments (Abratt & Kleyn, 2011). With the specified strategic perspective, members of the organization act in conformity to achieve the desired brand identity (Pillai, 2012). Kowalczyk and Pawlish (2002) stated that in the current competitive environment, a firm's corporate brand is becoming increasingly important as a resource to be exploited in attaining sustainable competitive advantage. A corporate brand is considered as the sum of the corporation's marketing efforts to present a controlled representation of the corporation's value system and identity. A strongly cultivated corporate brand provides the firm with a sustainable competitive advantage that drives brand loyalty (Hatch & Schultz, 2003).

Corporate brand is considered as monetary assets (Olins, 2005). Kay (2006) stated that corporate brand is the way of creating trust, stability, and differentiation. In addition, corporate branding is a holistic brand management approach adopted by firms to provide a unique corporate identity (Abratt & Kleyn, 2011). Existing marketing studies have dealt with the issues of organizational performance (Chaudhuri, 2002; O'Cass & Ngo, 2007; Morgan & Rego, 2009) and how to build a successful brand (Matear, Gray, & Garrett, 2004; Yeniyurt, Townsend, & Talay, 2007). Although the complexities of corporate branding have been underlined (Gyrd-Jones et al., 2013), successful corporate branding is acknowledged as adding value for all stakeholders (Hawabhay et al., 2009). Branding is acknowledged as a potent tool for companies to use to their advantage in achieving competitive strength in the market, as branding generates marketing value for the producer and consumers (Keller, 2003). The implementation of a successful corporate branding strategy allows luxury firms to create distinguishable brands in return for customers' preferences and loyalty (Okonkwo, 2007; Chevalier & Mazzalovo, 2008). Branding strategy is less effective with luxury customers because customers are placing more emphasis on the emotional value, such as closeness and involvement with brands, when making their purchase decisions (Choo, Moon, Kim, & Yoon, 2012).

Brand Performance

Brand performance is a brand's strength in the market, and is defined as the relative measurement of the brand's success in the marketplace (O'Cass & Weerawardena, 2010). Brand performance is reflected in its attainment of organizational strategy and goals. A number of researchers such as Chaudhuri (2002), Reid (2002), and Wong and Merrilees (2007) considered brand reputation, brand awareness, and brand loyalty as a brand's crucial performance. The performance of the brand and the physical composition of the brand are some instances of product-related attributes; and product appearance, price of the product, user and usage imagery are some instances of non-product-related attributes (Tuan, 2014). Rajagopal (2008) stated that numerous firms engage in a variety of integrated marketing activities in order to monitor brand performance indicators (i.e., brand awareness, brand acquaintance, brand association, brand allegiance, and brand appraisal) over perceptional and financial factors in firms. Brand acquaintance refers to customers' familiarity with the brands of a firm; and brand association refers to customers' buying behavior toward the acquainted brands (Tuan, 2014).

Brand Equity

Pioneered by Aaker (1991), the managerial perspective considers brand equity as consisting of five brand assets (i.e., brand loyalty, brand awareness, perceived brand quality, brand associations, and other proprietary assets). Brand equity creates value for both the customer and the firm; and the value for the customer enhances the value for the firm (Aaker, 1991). Aaker (1991) considered that brand equity is a set of brand assets and liabilities linked to a brand, its name and symbol that add to or subtract from the value provided by a product or service to a firm/or to that firm's customers. Keller (2001) considered brand equity from a customer based view as being the differential effect of brand knowledge on consumer response to the marketing of the brand. According to the Customer-Based Brand Equity (CBBE) model (Keller, 2001), building a strong brand involves four steps: (1) establishing the suitable brand identity, that is, establishing breadth and depth of brand awareness related to brand salience; (2) creating the appropriate brand meaning through strong and unique brand associations related to brand performance and brand imagery; eliciting accessible brand responses related to brand judgment and brand feelings; and forging brand relations with customers related to brand resonance. In addition, Moisescu (2005) stated that CBBE involves customers' reactions to an element of the marketing mix for the brand in comparison with their reactions to the same marketing mix element attributed to a fictitiously named or unnamed version of the product or service.

Brand equity is the key and central concept in brand management and has been considered in different marketing perspectives (Boo, Busser, & Baloglu, 2009). Acquiring general awareness of the brand equity from the consumer perspective is essential for successful brand management (Tong & Hawley, 2009). Brand equity refers to the value inherent in a well-known brand name (Keller, 2008). Maintaining the determinants of brand equity will aid marketers in positioning their service in the market (Kumar, Dash, & Purwar, 2013). Practitioners must appreciate that brand equity is a major influencer on the customers' selection process, especially for a service as brand equity acts as a risk reliever (Mourad, Ennew, & Kortam, 2011). Brand equity has been measured with multiple constructs such as brand awareness (Pappu et al., 2005; Buil, De Chernatony, & Martinez, 2008), perceived quality (Pappu et al., 2005; Buil et al., 2008; Tong & Hawley, 2009), brand loyalty (Pappu et al., 2005; Buil et al., 2008; Tong & Hawley, 2009), brand image (Kim & Kim, 2004), brand association and brand personality (Pappu et al., 2005; Buil et al., 2008), and organizational association (Buil et al., 2008; Keller, 2008). Brand equity is the fundamental concept for the organizations in the recent 20 years (Leone, Rao, Keller, Luo, McAlister, & Srivastava, 2006). Ambler stated that brand equity is a key marketing asset. The emergence of brand equity increases the importance of marketing strategies and provides a focal point for researchers and managers (Chen, 2009). The idea of brand equity is related to the company's success, because when brand equity is created, it has more profits and less expense for the company (Keller, 2003; Myers, 2003). Brand equity, value equity, and communication equity are all parts of customer value (Severt & Palakurthi, 2008).

Brand Awareness

Aaker (1996) defined brand awareness as the strength of a brand's presence in the consumer's mind. Brand name is the most fundamental element of brand awareness (Davis, Golicic, & Marquardt, 2008). The creation of brand awareness is a key element of branding strategy (Munoz & Kumar, 2004; Homburg, Klarmann, & Schmitt, 2010). Only high-quality firms can afford high-level investments in brand awareness (Erdem et al., 2006). The maximum benefit of brand awareness is brand dominance, which takes place when in a brand recall most consumers recall a single brand. Brand awareness acts as a component, which plays an important role in consumer brand choice (Jiang, 2004; Desai, Kalra, & Murthi, 2008). Brand awareness arises from advertising awareness and is actually the same as advertising awareness (Romaniuk et al., 2004). In addition, brand advertising can increase both the scope and the frequency of brand appearance, thus empowering brand awareness (Chiaravalle & Schenck, 2007).

Perceived Brand Quality

As mentioned in session "brand equity," Aaker (1991) stated that brand equity involves five elements (i.e., brand loyalty, brand awareness, perceived brand quality, brand associations, and other proprietary assets). Aaker (1991) defined perceived brand quality as the customer's perception or subjective evaluation of the overall quality or superiority of a brand related to its intended purpose in brand alternatives. Perceived brand quality is considered as the overall preference or superiority, quite the same as approach assessment (Netemeyer, Krishnan, Pullig, Wang, Yagci, Dean, Ricks, & Wirth, 2004). In addition, perceived brand quality is the main dimension of consumer-based brand equity because it is related to brand choice and purchasing intention (Aaker, 1996; Kumar, Kim, & Pelton, 2009). Gottlieb et al., (1994) stated that perceived brand quality is a consumer's appraisal of a product's overall excellence or superiority. Service quality, personal contact, support services, and product's physical quality form the basis for competitive advantage in the firms (Morgan, Deeter-Schmelz, & Moberg, 2007; Spreng, Shi, & Page, 2009), and are critical to purchasing decisions and branding (Rauyruen & Miller, 2007; Beverland, 2009). Both perceived value and the distribution performance of industrial products have been identified as the main drivers of perceived product quality (Cater & Cater, 2009; Shi, Zhang, & Qu, 2010). Perceived brand quality is the main requirement of the perceived value (Boo et al., 2009).

Brand Association

Aaker (1991) defined brand association as any link in memory to a brand. Brand association is whatever that consumer relates to a brand (Aaker & Joachimsthaler, 2000). Brand association can include consumers' image-making, profile of the product, consumer's conditions, corporate awareness, brand characteristics, and symbols (Aaker & Joachimsthaler, 2000). Brand association is the heart of brand equity, as well as a key component of competitive advantage (Aaker & Joachimsthaler, 2000). Chen (2001) stated a number of reasons toward confirmation of this statement. Firstly, the brand awareness is a necessary condition to build brand equity but it is still not enough. Secondly, the other dimensions of brand equity can increase consumer's loyalty to the brand (Chen, 2001). Thirdly, the perceived brand quality is a kind of brand awareness (Chen, 2001). The corporate brand association and the equity sources emerging from partners associations offer a potential agenda for research and further theory development about the nature and design of corporate brand alliances (Uggla, 2006).

Brand Loyalty

Brand loyalty is defined as a deeply held commitment in order to consistently re-buy a preferred product or service in the future, thus causing repetitive same brand and purchasing, despite situational influences and marketing efforts, having the potential to cause switching behavior (Aaker, 1991). Rundle-Thiele (2005) stated that the concept of brand loyalty emerged in the marketing literature in the 1940s and it was first considered as one-dimensional. The definition of behavioral brand loyalty is considered to be synonymous with the repetitive purchasing behavior (Quester & Lim, 2003) while attitudinal brand loyalty is referred to the stated preferences, commitment or purchase intentions of the customers. Brand loyalty goes beyond repetitive purchasing behavior and implies a true commitment to a specific brand (Back & Parks, 2003; Quester & Lim, 2003). Brand loyalty is a result of the interplay between the consumer's attitude and repetitive purchasing behavior (Ogba & Tan, 2009). Brand loyalty is built on consumers' consistent satisfaction with the functions and performance of the brand (Reast, 2005). Customer loyalty is the consequence of perceived service quality (i.e., the quality of network coverage, quality value-added services, accurate data information, consistently courteous service staff, and good operating hours), brand image, brand trust and acceptable price (Syed Alwi & Melewar, 2013). In addition, brand loyalty reflects the desirability of product functionality and services. Advertisements enhance consumers' knowledge and perception pertaining to the brand and ultimately strengthen the brand loyalty (Ha, John, Janda, & Muthaly, 2011). Brand loyalty is directly linked with the customer satisfaction and brand image. There is a positive link between the retail brand and loyalty of the customers (Binninger, 2008).

The Importance of Brand Strategy in Emerging Markets

An emerging market has experienced a relatively rapid pace of economic development, and has initiated economic liberalization and a market economy. For emerging markets, building strong nation equity is important both for sustaining domestic consumption and for boosting overseas demand. With economic development and income growth, more consumers in emerging markets start to value product quality. Consumers in emerging markets often perceive products from developed economies to be of higher quality than domestic brands (Chu, 2013). Emerging markets not only provide a natural laboratory for testing theories and developing new ones, but they also offer practical relevance because success in emerging markets is crucial to the future of many companies (Burgess & Steenkamp, 2006). Compared with developed markets, emerging markets are characterized by rapid changes in their economic, political and social institutions (Hoskisson, Eden, Lau, & Wright, 2000; Peng, 2003). A feature of emerging markets is the rapid changes in their economic, political, and social institutions (Hoskisson et al., 2000; Burgess & Steenkamp, 2006). A fundamental challenge for firms operating in such environments is to predict the changes and respond to them, which would appear to make the adaption perspective particularly relevant in emerging markets (Wu, 2013). Companies from mature markets strive to win hearts and sales in emerging markets, which will account for most of the economic growth in the coming decades (Pauwels, K., Erguncu, S., & Yildirim, 2013). Brands from emerging markets, such as Lenovo and Haier, struggle to succeed in mature markets (Pukthuanthong & Roll, 2009) at least in part because they lack a strong emotional connection with their customers (Wang, 2008). Cayla and Arnould (2008) and Burgess and Steenkamp (2011) highlighted cultural differences in the importance of individual versus group decision making as a key reason for different branding strategies in emerging versus mature markets.

As market-supporting institutions develop in emerging economies, firms can rely less on network-based, personal relations-oriented strategies and more on arm's-length contracts and capability-based strategies (Peng, 2003). The relationship between perceived brand quality and brand loyalty, and the relationship between brand awareness and perceived brand quality are found to be significant in Thailand (Nguyen, Barrett, & Miller, 2011). The smaller, fast-growing emerging markets, such as Thailand, are the important destinations for foreign investors because of their location, market size and minimal interference from government. Thailand is widely accepted as a strategic location serving as a gateway for businesses and investors to the large growing markets of China, India and ASEAN countries. Mainland Chinese enterprises' poor performance in brand-building within China has hampered their pace of overseas expansion, even though they have been vying for global markets and global business leadership (Chu, 2013). Therefore, firms in emerging markets need to focus more on product quality and brand-building to increase their competitive advantage (Chu, 2013). Much of the extant research has been focused on market entry modes and foreign investment strategies of multinational enterprises in larger emerging markets such as China and India (Johnson & Tellis, 2008).

Emerging markets are attractive for at least three reasons (Nakata & Sivakumar, 1997). Firstly, many aspects are ready for an immediate extra sales effort in the developed countries, which can establish a presence and gain new customers quickly if they have a strong existing reputation (Nakata & Sivakumar, 1997). Secondly, saturation of the developed markets leads to the exploitation of new markets in emerging economies in order to shield firms from economic recessions (Nakata & Sivakumar, 1997). Thirdly, market size and market growth offer enormous potential for marketing success (Nakata & Sivakumar, 1997). Within emerging economies, market opportunities vary across industries and are not isolated from local environmental conditions (Luo, 2002). Research on emerging markets is a stream, thus attracting increased attention over years due to the dynamic environment found at the emerging markets (Ni & Wan, 2008). Firms in the emerging nations are taking active roles in the international arena, and many people believe that firms originating from emerging markets will act as the key factors in the future growth of world trade. Consistent with the strategic propositions in the extant literature (Brouthers & Xu, 2002; Brouthers et al., 2005), firms in emerging markets are pursuing aggressive and proactive strategies such as developing their own brands in international markets. In addition, there are numerous success stories of the companies and brands in the emerging markets challenging big multinational corporations (MNCs) in international markets (Anholt, 2003; Bilgin, Sriram, & Wuhrer, 2004; Chao, Samiee, & Yip, 2004). Most of the successful firms originate from China and Southeast Asia, followed by Latin America, Russia, Turkey, and Egypt (Luo, 2007). Firms in the emerging markets aspiring to compete in international markets face different conditions from those described in the literature (Cavusgil et al., 2002). In addition, firms in the emerging markets are at the growth stage of their internationalization; and standardization of brand strategies is generally considered a viable strategic option for international success in the emerging markets (Zou & Cavusgil, 2002).

Brand Relationships toward Effective Brand Management

This session explains the relationships among brand constructs toward effective brand management in emerging markets. Brand awareness is considered as an antecedent of brand loyalty (Aaker, 1991). Brand awareness plays a special role in driving brand equity in business markets (Davis et al., 2008). In addition, brand name and brand awareness show a significant amount of the variation in brand equity in industrial firms (Low & Blois, 2002; Davis et al., 2008). Consumer's satisfaction has positively influenced the brand loyalty (Chiou, Droge, & Hanvanich, 2002; Yang & Peterson, 2004; Da Silva & Syed Alwi, 2006; Ismail, Hasnah, Ibrahim, & Mohd Isa, 2006). When consumers are satisfied with the product/brand, they are more likely to recommend the product to others, are less likely to switch to other alternative brand, and are likely to repeat purchase (Bennett & Rundle-Thiele, 2004). However, researchers have found brand loyalty to be a desired outcome of publishing a brand, or brand equity (Van Riel, De Mortanges, & Streukens, 2005; Cater & Cater, 2009). In addition, Van Riel et al., (2005) found a direct positive relationship between industrial brand equity and brand loyalty. A product's value is enhanced when it is associated with a brand name (Keller, 2003).

Marketing literature shows empirical research in the field of relationship between brand equity dimensions (i.e., brand awareness, brand association, perceived brand quality, and brand loyalty) and overall brand equity (Yasin et al., 2007). High brand awareness, resulting from brand associations, is a signal of quality that assists consumers in making purchase decisions. Brand equity sources include consumers' brand awareness and strong, favorable and unique brand associations. The first step in creating brand equity is to develop a brand identity (Aaker, 1996; Keller, 2003) that is achieved through a unique set of brand associations that a firm aspires to create or maintain (Aaker, 1996). The perceived brand quality has a positive relationship with a brand that is distributed with a good brand image. Perceived brand quality has significant impact on customer satisfaction and brand loyalty (Nguyen et al., 2011). Hong-Youl and Kang-Hee (2012) stated that perceived brand quality have direct impact on brand loyalty and customers' satisfaction. Brand equity has been shown to be another significant antecedent of brand loyalty (Keller, 2003; Taylor et al., 2004). A brand that receives high attention from customers will have a competitive advantage in emerging markets (Nguyen et al., 2011). Keller (2003) stated that a positive brand equity can lead to more revenue, lower costs and higher profits, thus tending customer to seek new distribution channels, marketing communications effectiveness, and success in developing brand and selling licensing opportunities (Atilgan et al., 2005).

FUTURE RESEARCH DIRECTIONS

As the world continues to globalize, it is vital that the marketing research inquiry is focused on how to combine both brand management strategy and international marketing literature in order to establish a marketing research agenda for future international researchers to focus on international branding developments. Future marketing research should examine and broaden the case studies of brand strategies and how branding strategies have utilized in emerging markets. In addition, longitudinal studies of the marketing innovation process in brand strategy will further help to utilize the academic and practical applications of starting and maintaining a brand management-related international marketing venture in emerging markets.

CONCLUSION

This chapter introduced the role of brand management in emerging markets, thus explaining the concepts of brand management system, corporate branding, brand performance, brand equity, brand awareness, perceived brand quality, brand association, and brand loyalty; the importance of brand strategy in emerging markets; and brand relationships toward effective brand management. According to the marketing literature of brand management and brand constructs explained above, firms in emerging markets should take consideration of their brand management system, corporate branding, brand performance, brand equity, brand awareness, perceived brand quality, brand association, and brand loyalty in order to effectively achieve business success in emerging markets based on the conditions of their organizational structure, environment, and marketing contexts. Brand management should be strategic and holistic, as this is conducive to marketing longevity. The management of brands should be a higher level function than currently exists in many companies in emerging markets. Managers of brands are essentially involved in the creation of brand management and therefore the degree of brand strength or brand loyalty achieved. In addition, the higher the degree of brand strength achieved, the greater the competitive advantage in emerging markets. Developing a good brand relationship is essential for brand management in emerging markets. Firms in emerging markets should recognize the importance of brand constructs (i.e., brand management system, corporate branding, brand performance, brand equity, brand awareness, perceived brand quality, brand association, and brand loyalty) and need to put more marketing efforts in building brand management system in order to enhance the marketing performance and achieve business goals in the global marketing environment.

REFERENCES

Aaker, D. A. (1991). *Managing brand equity: Capitalizing on the value of a brand name*. New York, NY: Free Press.

Aaker, D. A. (1996). Measuring brand equity across products and markets. *California Management Review*, *38*(3), 102–120. doi:10.2307/41165845

Aaker, D. A., & Joachimsthaler, E. (2000). *Brand leadership*. London, UK: Free Press.

Abratt, R., & Kleyn, N. (2011). Corporate identity, corporate branding and corporate reputations: Reconciliation and integration. *European Journal of Marketing*, *46*(7-8), 1048–1063.

Ambler, T. (2003). *Marketing and the bottom line: Creating the measures of success*. London, UK: Prentice-Hall.

Anholt, S. (2003). *Brand new justice: The upside of global branding*. Stoneham, MA: Butterworth-Heinemann.

Atilgan, E., Aksoy, S., & Akinci, S. (2005). Determinants of the brand equity: A verification approach in the beverage industry in Turkey. *Marketing Intelligence & Planning*, *23*(3), 237–248. doi:10.1108/02634500510597283

Back, K. J., & Parks, S. (2003). A brand loyalty model involving cognitive, affective and conative brand loyalty and customer satisfaction. *Journal of Hospitality & Tourism Research (Washington, D.C.)*, *27*(4), 419–435. doi:10.1177/1096348003027403

Baumgarth, C. (2010). Living the brand: Brand orientation in the business-to-business sector. *European Journal of Marketing*, *44*(5), 653–671. doi:10.1108/03090561011032315

Baumgarth, C., & Schmidt, M. (2010). How strong is the business-to-business brand in the workforce? *Industrial Marketing Management*, *39*(8), 1250–1260. doi:10.1016/j.indmarman.2010.02.022

Bennett, R., & Rundle-Thiele, S. (2004). Customer satisfaction should not be the only goal. *Journal of Services Marketing*, *18*(7), 514–523. doi:10.1108/08876040410561848

Beverland, M. (2009). Boundary conditions to business relationships in China: The case of selling wine in China. *Journal of Business and Industrial Marketing*, *24*(1), 27–34. doi:10.1108/08858620910923676

Beverland, M., Napoli, J., & Lindgreen, A. (2007). Industrial global brand leadership: A capabilities view. *Industrial Marketing Management*, *36*(8), 1082–1093. doi:10.1016/j.indmarman.2006.08.007

Bilgin, F. Z., Sriram, V., & Wuhrer, G. (2004). *Drivers of global business success*. London, UK: Palgrave Macmillan.

Binninger, A. S. (2008). Exploring the relationships between retail brands and consumer store loyalty. *International Journal of Retail & Distribution Management*, *36*(2), 94–110. doi:10.1108/09590550810853057

Boo, S., Busser, J., & Baloglu, S. (2009). A model of customer-based brand equity and its application to multiple destinations. *Tourism Management*, *30*(2), 219–231. doi:10.1016/j.tourman.2008.06.003

Bridson, K., & Evans, J. (2004). The secret to a fashion advantage is brand orientation. *International Journal of Retail & Distribution Management*, *32*(8), 403–411. doi:10.1108/09590550410546223

Brodie, R. J., Glynn, M. S., & Little, V. (2006). The service brand and the service-dominant logic: Missing fundamental premise or the need for stronger theory. *Marketing Theory*, *6*(3), 363–379. doi:10.1177/1470593106066797

Brouthers, L. E., O'Donnell, E., & Hadjimarsu, J. (2005). Generic product strategies for emerging market exports into triad nation markets: A mimetic isomorphism approach. *Journal of Management Studies*, *42*(1), 225–245. doi:10.1111/j.1467-6486.2005.00495.x

Brouthers, L. E., & Xu, K. (2002). Product stereotypes, strategy, and performance satisfaction: The case of Chinese exporters. *Journal of International Business Studies*, *33*(4), 657–677. doi:10.1057/palgrave.jibs.8491038

Buil, I., De Chernatony, L., & Martinez, E. (2008). A cross-cultural validation of the consumer-based brand equity scale. *Journal of Product and Brand Management*, *17*(6), 384–392. doi:10.1108/10610420810904121

Burgess, S. M., & Steenkamp, J. B. E. M. (2006). Marketing renaissance: How research in emerging markets advances marketing science and practice. *International Journal of Research in Marketing*, *23*(4), 337–356. doi:10.1016/j.ijresmar.2006.08.001

Burgess, S. M., & Steenkamp, J. B. E. M. (2011). Call for papers: Special issue on marketing in emerging markets. *International Journal of Research in Marketing*, *28*(1), vi–vii. doi:10.1016/S0167-8116(11)00014-0

Cater, B., & Cater, T. (2009). Relationship-value-based antecedents of customer satisfaction and loyalty in manufacturing. *Journal of Business and Industrial Marketing*, *24*(7-8), 585–597. doi:10.1108/08858620910999457

Cavusgil, S. T., Ghauri, P. N., & Agarwal, M. R. (2002). *Doing business in emerging markets*. Thousand Oaks, CA: Sage.

Cayla, J., & Arnould, E. J. (2008). A cultural approach to branding in the global marketplace. *Journal of International Marketing*, *16*(4), 88–114. doi:10.1509/jimk.16.4.86

Chao, P., Samiee, S., & Yip, L. S. (2004). Guest editorial: International marketing in the Asia Pacific region. *International Marketing Review*, *21*(3), 243–246. doi:10.1108/02651330410539594

Chaudhuri, A. (2002). How brand reputation affects the advertising-brand equity link. *Journal of Advertising Research*, *42*(3), 33–43.

Chen, A. C. H. (2001). Using free association to examine the relationship between the characteristics of brand associations and brand equity. *Journal of Product and Brand Management*, *10*(7), 439–451. doi:10.1108/10610420110410559

Chen, C. F., & Chang, Y. (2008). Airline brand equity, brand preference, and purchase intentions – The moderating effects of switching costs. *Journal of Air Transport Management*, *14*(1), 40–42. doi:10.1016/j.jairtraman.2007.11.003

Chen, Y. S. (2009). The drivers of green brand equity: Green brand image, green satisfaction and green trust. *Journal of Business Ethics*, *92*(3), 307–319.

Chevalier, M., & Mazzalovo, G. (2008). *Luxury brand management: A world of privilege*. Singapore: John Wiley & Sons.

Chiaravalle, B., & Schenck, B. F. (2007). *Branding for dummies*. Indianapolis, In John Wiley & Sons.

Chiou, J. S., Droge, C., & Hanvanich, S. (2002). Does customer knowledge affect how loyalty is formed? *Journal of Service Research*, *5*(2), 113–124. doi:10.1177/109467002237494

Choo, H. J., Moon, H., Kim, H., & Yoon, N. (2012). Luxury customer value. *Journal of Fashion Marketing and Management*, *16*(1), 81–101. doi:10.1108/13612021211203041

Chu, J. (2013). Quantifying nation equity with sales data: A structural approach. *International Journal of Research in Marketing*, *30*(1), 19–35. doi:10.1016/j.ijresmar.2012.06.005

Da Silva, R. V., & Syed Alwi, S. F. (2006). Cognitive, affective and conative behavioural responses in retail corporate branding. *Journal of Product and Brand Management*, *15*(5), 293–305. doi:10.1108/10610420610685703

Davis, D. F., Golicic, S. L., & Marquardt, A. J. (2008). Branding a B2B service: Does a brand differentiate a logistics service provider? *Industrial Marketing Management*, *37*(2), 218–227. doi:10.1016/j.indmarman.2007.02.003

De Chernatony, L., & Cottam, S. (2006). Internal brand factors driving successful financial services brand. *European Journal of Marketing*, *40*(5-6), 611–633. doi:10.1108/03090560610657868

DelVecchio, D., Jarvis, C. B., Klink, R. R., & Dineen, B. B. (2007). Leveraging brand equity to attract human capital. *Marketing Letters*, *18*(3), 149–164. doi:10.1007/s11002-007-9012-3

Desai, P. S., Kalra, A., & Murthi, B. P. S. (2008). When old is gold: The role of business longevity in risky situations. *Journal of Marketing*, *72*(1), 95–107. doi:10.1509/jmkg.72.1.95

Dunes, M., & Pras, B. (2013). Practices in the brand management system: Identification and considerations for five business sectors. *Journal of Product and Brand Management*, *22*(7), 444–461. doi:10.1108/JPBM-09-2013-0396

Erdem, T., Swait, J., & Valenzuela, A. (2006). Brands as signals: A cross country validation study. *Journal of Marketing*, *70*(1), 34–49. doi:10.1509/jmkg.2006.70.1.34

Gottlieb, B. H., Grewal, D., & Brown, S. W. (1994). Consumer satisfaction and perceived quality: Complementary or divergent construct? *The Journal of Applied Psychology*, *79*(6), 875–885. doi:10.1037/0021-9010.79.6.875

Gyrd-Jones, R., Merriles, B., & Miller, D. (2013). Revisiting the complexities of corporate branding: Issues, paradoxes, solutions. *Journal of Brand Management*, *20*(7), 571–589. doi:10.1057/bm.2013.1

Ha, H. Y., John, J., Janda, S., & Muthaly, S. (2011). The effect of advertising spending on brand loyalty in services. *European Journal of Marketing*, *45*(4), 673–691. doi:10.1108/03090561111111389

Hamin, H., Baumann, C., & Tung, R. L. (2014). Attenuating double jeopardy of negative country of origin effects and latecomer brand - An application study of ethnocentrism in emerging markets. *Asia Pacific Journal of Marketing and Logistics*, *26*(1), 54–77. doi:10.1108/APJML-07-2013-0090

Hatch, M. J., & Schultz, M. (2003). Bringing the corporation into corporate branding. *European Journal of Marketing*, *37*(7-8), 1041–1064. doi:10.1108/03090560310477654

Hatch, M. J., & Schultz, M. (2008). *Taking brand initiative: How companies can align strategy, culture, and identity through corporate branding*. New York, NY: Jossey-Bass.

Hawabhay, B., Abratt, R., & Peter, M. (2009). The role of corporate communications in developing a corporate brand image and reputation in Mauritius. *Corporate Reputation Review*, *12*(1), 3–20. doi:10.1057/crr.2009.4

Hirvonen, S., Laukkanen, T., & Reijonen, H. (2013). The brand orientation-performance relationship: An examination of moderation effects. *Journal of Brand Management*, *20*(8), 623–641. doi:10.1057/bm.2013.4

Hoeffler, S., & Keller, K. (2003). The marketing advantages of strong brands. *Journal of Brand Management*, *10*(1), 421–445. doi:10.1057/palgrave.bm.2540139

Homburg, C., Klarmann, M., & Schmitt, J. (2010). Brand awareness in business markets: When is it related to firm performance? *International Journal of Research in Marketing*, *27*(3), 201–212. doi:10.1016/j.ijresmar.2010.03.004

Hong-Youl, H., & Kang-Hee, P. (2012). Effects of perceived quality and satisfaction on brand loyalty in China: The moderating effect of customer orientation. *African Journal of Business Management*, *6*(22), 6745–6753.

Hoskisson, R. E., Eden, L., Lau, C. M., & Wright, M. (2000). Strategy in emerging economies. *Academy of Management Journal*, *43*(3), 249–267. doi:10.2307/1556394

Hsiao, Y. C., & Chen, C. J. (2013). Branding vs. contract manufacturing: Capability, strategy, and performance. *Journal of Business and Industrial Marketing*, *28*(4), 317–334. doi:10.1108/08858621311313910

Ind, N., & Bjerke, R. (2007). The concept of participatory market orientation: An organization-wide approach to enhancing brand equity. *Journal of Brand Management*, *15*(2), 135–145. doi:10.1057/palgrave.bm.2550122

Ismail, I., Hasnah, H., Ibrahim, D. N., & Mohd Isa, S. (2006). Service quality, client satisfaction, and loyalty towards audit firms. Perceptions of Malaysian public listed companies. *Managerial Auditing Journal*, *22*(7), 738–756. doi:10.1108/02686900610680521

Jiang, P. (2004). The role of brand name in customization decision: A search vs. experience perspective. *Journal of Product and Brand Management*, *13*(2), 73–83. doi:10.1108/10610420410529708

John, D. R. (2006). *Strategic brand management on the cutting edge: Building, leveraging, identifying, and protecting brands*. Paper presented at the Institute for Research in Marketing's Carlson on Branding. Retrieved February 8, 2014, from http://www.carlsonschool.umn.edu/Assets/75903.pdf

Johnson, J., & Tellis, G. J. (2008). Drivers of success for market entry into China and India. *Journal of Marketing*, *72*(3), 1–13. doi:10.1509/jmkg.72.3.1

Kay, M. J. (2006). Strong brands and corporate brands. *European Journal of Marketing*, *40*(7-8), 742–760. doi:10.1108/03090560610669973

Keller, K. L. (2001). Building Customer-Based Brand Equity: A blueprint for creating strong brands. *Report Summary # 01-107*. Cambridge, MA: Marketing Science Institute. Retrieved February 8, 2014, from http://202.120.148.199/files/Custome%2BrBased%2Bbrand%2BEquity%2BModel.pdf

Keller, K. L. (2003). *Strategic brand management: Building, measuring, and managing brand equity*. Upper Saddle River, NJ: Pearson Education.

Keller, K. L. (2008). *Strategic brand management: Building, measuring, and managing brand equity*. Upper Saddle River, NJ: Prentice Hall.

Kim, H. B., & Kim, W. G. (2005). The relationship between brand equity and firms' performance in luxury hotels and chain restaurants. *Tourism Management*, *26*(4), 549–560. doi:10.1016/j.tourman.2004.03.010

Kim, W. G., & Kim, H. B. (2004). Measuring customer-based restaurant brand equity: Investigating the relationship between brand equity and firms' performance. *The Cornell Hotel and Restaurant Administration Quarterly*, *45*(2), 115–131. doi:10.1177/0010880404264507

Knox, S., & Bickerton, D. (2003). The six conventions of corporate branding. *European Journal of Marketing*, *37*(7-8), 998–1016. doi:10.1108/03090560310477636

Kowalczyk, S. J., & Pawlish, M. J. (2002). Corporate branding through external perception of organizational culture. *Corporate Reputation Review*, *5*(2-3), 159–174. doi:10.1057/palgrave.crr.1540172

Kumar, A., Kim, Y. K., & Pelton, L. (2009). Indian consumers' purchase behavior toward US versus local brands. *International Journal of Retail & Distribution Management*, *37*(6), 510–526. doi:10.1108/09590550910956241

Kumar, R. S., Dash, S., & Purwar, P. C. (2013). The nature and antecedents of brand equity and its dimensions. *Marketing Intelligence & Planning*, *31*(2), 141–159. doi:10.1108/02634501311312044

Lee, C., Baek, I., Park, S., & Lee, J. (2008). The impact of the brand management system on brand performance in B-B and B-C environments. *Industrial Marketing Management*, *37*(7), 848–855. doi:10.1016/j.indmarman.2008.04.005

Lee, J. S., & Back, K. J. (2010). Reexamination of attendee-based brand equity. *Tourism Management*, *31*(3), 395–401. doi:10.1016/j.tourman.2009.04.006

Leone, R. P., Rao, V. R., Keller, K. L., Luo, A. M., McAlister, L., & Srivastava, R. (2006). Linking brand equity to customer equity. *Journal of Service Research*, *9*(2), 125–138. doi:10.1177/1094670506293563

Lim, W. S., & Tan, S. J. (2009). Using brand equity to counter outsourcing opportunism: A game theoretic approach. *Marketing Letters*, *20*(4), 369–383. doi:10.1007/s11002-009-9071-8

Low, J., & Blois, K. (2002). The evolution of generic brands in industrial markets: The challenges to owners of brand equity. *Industrial Marketing Management*, *31*(5), 385–392. doi:10.1016/S0019-8501(00)00131-0

Luo, Y. (2002). Capability exploitation and building in a foreign market: Implications for multinational enterprises. *Organization Science*, *13*(1), 48–63. doi:10.1287/orsc.13.1.48.538

Luo, Y. (2007). From foreign investors to strategic insiders: Shifting parameters, prescriptions and paradigms for MNCs in China. *Journal of World Business*, *42*(1), 14–34. doi:10.1016/j.jwb.2006.08.009

Madden, T. J., Fehle, F., & Fournier, S. (2006). Brands matter: An empirical demonstration of the creation of shareholder value through branding. *Journal of the Academy of Marketing Science*, *34*(2), 224–235. doi:10.1177/0092070305283356

Martin, W., & Inchovichina, E. (2008). Economic development in emerging Asian markets: Implications for Europe. *European Review of Agriculture Economics*, *35*(3), 303–330. doi:10.1093/erae/jbn017

Matear, S., Gray, B. J., & Garrett, T. (2004). Market orientation, brand investment, new service development, market position and performance for service organizations. *International Journal of Service Industry Management*, *15*(3-4), 284–301. doi:10.1108/09564230410540944

Miller, J., & Muir, D. (2004). *The business of brands*. Chichester, UK: John Wiley & Sons.

Moisescu, O. I. (2005). *The concept of brand equity – A comparative approach*. Munich Personal RePEc Archive (MPRA) paper # 32013. Retrieved February 8, 2014, from http://mpra.ub.uni-muenchen.de/32013/1/MPRA_paper_32013.pdf

Morgan, F., Deeter-Schmelz, D., & Moberg, C. R. (2007). Branding implications of partner firm-focal firm relationships in business-to-business service networks. *Journal of Business and Industrial Marketing*, *22*(6), 372–382. doi:10.1108/08858620710780136

Morgan, N. A., & Rego, L. L. (2009). Brand portfolio strategy and firm performance. *Journal of Marketing*, *73*(1), 59–74. doi:10.1509/jmkg.73.1.59

Mourad, M., Ennew, C., & Kortam, W. (2011). Brand equity in higher education. *Marketing Intelligence & Planning*, *29*(4), 403–420. doi:10.1108/02634501111138563

Munoz, T., & Kumar, S. (2004). Brand metrics: Gauging and linking brands with business performance. *Journal of Brand Management*, *11*(5), 381–387. doi:10.1057/palgrave.bm.2540183

Myers, C. (2003). Managing brand equity: A look at the impact of attributes. *Journal of Product and Brand Management*, *12*(1), 39–51. doi:10.1108/10610420310463126

Mzungu, S., Merrilees, B., & Miller, D. (2010). Brand management to protect brand equity: A conceptual model. *Brand Management*, *17*(8), 605–617. doi:10.1057/bm.2010.15

Nakata, C., & Sivakumar, K. (1997). Emerging market conditions and their impact on first mover advantages: An integrative review. *International Marketing Review*, *14*(96), 461–472. doi:10.1108/02651339710192993

Netemeyer, R. G., Krishnan, B., Pullig, C., Wang, G., Yagci, M., & Dean, D. et al. (2004). Developing and validating measures of facets of customer based brand equity. *Journal of Business Research*, *57*(2), 209–224. doi:10.1016/S0148-2963(01)00303-4

Nguyen, T. D., Barrett, N. J., & Miller, K. E. (2011). Brand loyalty in emerging markets. *Marketing Intelligence & Planning*, *29*(3), 222–232. doi:10.1108/02634501111129211

Ni, N., & Wan, F. (2008). A configurational perspective of branding capabilities development in emerging economies: The case of the Chinese cellular phone industry. *Brand Management*, *15*(6), 433–451.

O'Cass, A., & Ngo, L. V. (2007). Balancing external adaptation and internal effectiveness: Achieving better brand performance. *Journal of Business Research*, *60*(1), 11–20. doi:10.1016/j.jbusres.2006.08.003

O'Cass, A., & Weerawardena, J. (2010). The effect of perceived industry competitive intensity and marketing-related capabilities: Drivers of superior brand performance. *Industrial Marketing Management*, *39*(4), 571–581. doi:10.1016/j.indmarman.2009.04.002

Ogba, I. E., & Tan, Z. (2009). Exploring the impact of brand image on customer loyalty and commitment in China. *Journal of Technology Management in China*, *4*(2), 132–144. doi:10.1108/17468770910964993

Okonkwo, U. (2007). *Luxury fashion branding: Trends, tactics, techniques*. New York, NY: Palgrave Macmillan. doi:10.1057/9780230590885

Olins, W. (2005). *On brands*. London, UK: Thames & Hudson.

Pappu, R., Quester, P. G., & Cooksey, R. W. (2005). Consumer-based brand equity: Improving the measurement – Empirical evidence. *Journal of Product and Brand Management*, *14*(3), 143–154. doi:10.1108/10610420510601012

Pauwels, K., Erguncu, S., & Yildirim, G. (2013). Winning hearts, minds and sales: How marketing communication enters the purchase process in emerging and mature markets. *International Journal of Research in Marketing*, *30*(1), 57–68. doi:10.1016/j.ijresmar.2012.09.006

Peng, M. W. (2003). Institutional transitions and strategic choices. *Academy of Management Review*, *28*(2), 275–296.

Pillai, A. (2012). Corporate branding literature: A research paradigm review. *Journal of Brand Management*, *19*(4), 331–343. doi:10.1057/bm.2011.43

Pukthuanthong, K., & Roll, R. (2009). Global market integration: An alternative measure and its application. *Journal of Financial Economics*, *94*(2), 214–232. doi:10.1016/j.jfineco.2008.12.004

Punjaisri, K., Evanschitzky, H., & Wilson, A. (2009). Internal branding: An enabler of employees' brand supporting behaviours. *Journal of Service Management*, *20*(2), 209–226. doi:10.1108/09564230910952780

Quester, P., & Lim, A. (2003). Product involvement/brand loyalty: Is there a link? *Journal of Product and Brand Management*, *12*(1), 22–38. doi:10.1108/10610420310463117

Rajagopal. (2008). Measuring brand performance through metrics application. *Measuring Business Excellence, 12*(1), 29-38.

Rajagopal. (2009). Branding paradigm for the bottom of the pyramid markets. *Measuring Business Excellence, 13*(4), 58-68.

Rauyruen, P., & Miller, K. E. (2007). Relationship quality as a predictor of B2B customer loyalty. *Journal of Business Research*, *60*(1), 21–31. doi:10.1016/j.jbusres.2005.11.006

Reast, J. (2005). Brand trust and brand extension acceptance: The relationship. *Journal of Product and Brand Management*, *14*(1), 4–13. doi:10.1108/10610420510583707

Reid, M. (2002). Building strong brands through the management of integrated marketing communications. *International Journal of Wine Marketing*, *14*(3), 37–52. doi:10.1108/eb008745

Romaniuk, J., Sharp, B., Paech, S., & Dreisener, C. (2004). Brand and advertising awareness: A replication and extension of a known empirical generalization. *Australasian Marketing Journal*, *12*(3), 70–80. doi:10.1016/S1441-3582(04)70107-X

Rubin, J., Schultz, M., & Hatch, M. (2008). Coming to America: Can Nordic brand values engage American stakeholders? *Brand Management*, *16*(1-2), 30–39. doi:10.1057/bm.2008.17

Rugman, A. M., & Collinson, S. C. (2009). *International business*. Harlow, UK: Prentice-Hall.

Rundle-Thiele, S. (2005). Exploring loyal qualities: Assessing survey-based loyalty measures. *Journal of Services Marketing*, *19*(7), 492–500. doi:10.1108/08876040510625990

Santos-Vijande, M., Del Rio-Lanza, A., Suarez-Alvarez, L., & Diaz-Martin, A. (2013). The brand management system and service firm competitiveness. *Journal of Business Research*, *66*(2), 148–157. doi:10.1016/j.jbusres.2012.07.007

Severt, K. S., & Palakurthi, R. (2008). Applying customer equity to the convention industry. *International Journal of Contemporary Hospitality Management*, *20*(6), 631–646. doi:10.1108/09596110810892209

Shi, J., Zhang, J., & Qu, X. (2010). Optimizing distribution strategy for perishable foods using RFID and sensor technologies. *Journal of Business and Industrial Marketing*, *25*(8), 596–606. doi:10.1108/08858621011088338

Souiden, N., Kassim, N. M., & Hong, H. J. (2006). The effect of corporate branding dimensions on consumers' product evaluation: A cross-cultural analysis. *European Journal of Marketing*, *40*(7-8), 309–566.

Spreng, R. A., Shi, H., & Page, T. F. (2009). Service quality and satisfaction in business-to-business services. *Journal of Business and Industrial Marketing*, *24*(7-8), 537–548. doi:10.1108/08858620910999411

Syed Alwi, S. F., & Melewar, T. C. (2013). Theme articles: Branding in Asia - Branding in the Asian context: A Malaysian perspective. *Asia Pacific Journal of Marketing and Logistics*, *25*(2), 287–297. doi:10.1108/13555851311314068

Taylor, S., Celuch, K., & Goodwin, S. (2004). The importance of brand equity to customer loyalty. *Journal of Product and Brand Management*, *13*(4), 217–227. doi:10.1108/10610420410546934

Tong, X., & Hawley, J. M. (2009). Measuring customer-based brand equity: Empirical evidence from the sport wear market in China. *Journal of Product and Brand Management*, *18*(4), 262–271. doi:10.1108/10610420910972783

Tuan, L. T. (2014). Corporate governance and brand performance. *Management Research Review*, *37*(1), 45–68.

Uggla, H. (2006). The corporate brand association base: A conceptual model for the creation of inclusive brand architecture. *European Journal of Marketing*, *40*(7-8), 785–802. doi:10.1108/03090560610669991

Urde, M., Baumgarth, C., & Merrilees, B. (2013). Brand orientation and market orientation – From alternatives to synergy. *Journal of Business Research*, *66*(1), 13–20. doi:10.1016/j.jbusres.2011.07.018

Vallaster, C., & De Chernatony, L. (2006). Internal brand building and structuration: The role of leadership. *European Journal of Marketing*, *40*(7-8), 761–784. doi:10.1108/03090560610669982

Van Riel, A. C. R., De Mortanges, C. P., & Streukens, S. (2005). Marketing antecedents of industrial brand equity: An empirical investigation in specialty chemicals. *Industrial Marketing Management*, *34*(8), 841–847. doi:10.1016/j.indmarman.2005.01.006

VanAuken, B. (2005). *The brand management checklist: Proven tools and techniques for creating winning brands*. London, UK: Kogan Page.

Verhoef, P., & Leeflang, P. (2009). Understanding the marketing department's influence within the firm. *Journal of Marketing*, *73*(2), 14–37. doi:10.1509/jmkg.73.2.14

Wang, J. (2008). *Brand new China: Advertising, media and commercial culture*. Cambridge, MA: Harvard University Press.

Wong, H., & Merrilees, B. (2007). Closing the marketing strategy to performance gap: The role of brand orientation. *Journal of Strategic Marketing*, *15*(5), 387–402. doi:10.1080/09652540701726942

Wong, H., & Merrilees, B. (2008). The performance benefits of being brand-orientated. *Journal of Product and Brand Management*, *17*(6), 372–383. doi:10.1108/10610420810904112

Wright, M., Filatotchev, I., Hoskisson, R. E., & Peng, M. W. (2005). Strategy research in emerging economies: Challenging the collective wisdom. *Journal of Management Studies*, *42*(1), 1–33. doi:10.1111/j.1467-6486.2005.00487.x

Wu, J. (2013). Marketing capabilities, institutional development, and the performance of emerging market firms: A multinational study. *International Journal of Research in Marketing*, *30*(1), 36–45. doi:10.1016/j.ijresmar.2012.07.001

Xie, H. Y., & Boggs, D. J. (2006). Corporate branding versus product branding in emerging markets: A conceptual framework. *Marketing Intelligence & Planning*, *24*(4), 347–364. doi:10.1108/02634500610672099

Yang, Z., & Peterson, R. (2004). Customer perceived value, satisfaction, and loyalty: The role of switching costs. *Psychology and Marketing*, *21*(10), 799–822. doi:10.1002/mar.20030

Yasin, N., Nasser Noor, M., & Mohamad, O. (2007). Does image of country-of-origin matter to brand equity? *Journal of Product and Brand Management*, *16*(1), 38–48. doi:10.1108/10610420710731142

Yeniyurt, S., Townsend, J. D., & Talay, M. B. (2007). Factors influencing brand launch in a global marketplace. *Journal of Product Innovation Management*, *24*(5), 471–485. doi:10.1111/j.1540-5885.2007.00264.x

Zou, S., & Cavusgil, S. T. (2002). The GMS: A broad conceptualization of global marketing strategy and its effect on firm performance. *Journal of Marketing*, *66*(4), 40–56. doi:10.1509/jmkg.66.4.40.18519

KEY TERMS AND DEFINITIONS

Brand: Unique design, sign, symbol, or a combination of these, employed in creating an image that identifies a product and differentiates it from its competitors.

Brand Association: Extent to which a particular brand calls to mind the attributes of a general product category.

Brand Awareness: Extent to which a brand is recognized by potential customers, and is associated with a particular product.

Brand Equity: A brand's power which translates into higher sales volume and higher profit margins against competing brands.

Brand Loyalty: The extent of the faithfulness of consumers to a particular brand, expressed through their repeat purchases.

Brand Management: The process of maintaining, improving, and upholding a brand so that the name is associated with positive results.

Brand Strategy: Long-term marketing support for a brand, based on the definition of the characteristics of the target consumers.

Emerging Markets: New market structures arising from digitalization, deregulation, globalization, and open-standards that are shifting the balance of economic power from the sellers to the buyers.

Marketing Strategy: An organizational strategy that combines all of its marketing goals into one comprehensive plan.

Chapter 10
The Antecedents of Word-of-Mouth Behaviour: The Service Quality Perspective

Ho Yin Wong
Deakin University, Australia

Anthony Perrone
La Trobe University, Australia

ABSTRACT

The aim of this study is to undertake empirical research investigating the nature and magnitude of the determinants of word-of-mouth behaviour from the point of view of service performance and post-purchase perceptions. A quantitative study was undertaken. A theoretical model linking service quality issues and word-of-mouth behaviour was developed and tested using structural equation modelling of 280 surveyed participants at various day spa locations. All major fit indices from structural equation modelling methods show satisfactory results for the measurement and structural models. The results confirm significant relationships between the constructs in the model. While the quality of the product, customer service, and servicescape atmosphere lead to customer satisfaction, it is servicescape atmosphere and customer satisfaction that drive word-of-mouth behaviour. The results of this study provide insights to aid service providers and marketing professionals in the service industry in fully understanding that the enhancement of the delivery of high quality service, an accommodating environment, and instilling feelings of satisfaction with their customers will more likely lead to positive word-of-mouth referrals. One major limitation is that the survey was conducted within one industry in one country. The major value of this chapter is the establishment of the role of service quality on word-of-mouth behaviour. This research provides empirical results of the impacts of service performance and post-purchase perceptions on word-of-mouth behaviour.

DOI: 10.4018/978-1-4666-6232-2.ch010

INTRODUCTION

Marketers have no control over the state of the economy. When times get tough, some firms choose to reduce their marketing budgets with an aim to protecting the bottom line. Customers know that there are a lot of products and services competing for their attention and businesses. If the customers do not get the level of service they expect, they know that plenty of firms in the market are prepared to offer those services. Service quality is found to have a positive impact on customers' re-purchase behaviour (Kordupleski, Rust, & Zahorik, 1993; Perrone & Wong, 2013). When managed properly, service quality can be treated as an investment rather than cost that is more likely to attract attention of those cost-cutting executives (Rust, Zahorik, & Keiningham, 1995a). It is further suggested that "if sales are declining, the last thing to do is take the problem out on customers by reducing quality while raising prices" (Quelch & Jocz, 2009, p. 60). Service quality can become a strategic tool that marketers can use to achieve competitive advantage over their competitors in fragile economic conditions. Marketing is not just about finding new customers, but also enhancing relationships with existing customers. Word of mouth (WOM) is an important marketing tool that can be used by marketers to look for existing customers and strengthen relationship with the existing ones.

There have been studies that have shown WOM is often a strong indicator of influencing consumer judgement of the services provided by an organisation. Service quality has become an increasingly indispensable aspect for service providers in managing a successful business operation in today's competitive service market (Blose, Tankersley, & Flynn, 2005; Schneider, Holcombe, & Whiete, 1997). The delivery of service performance results are exhibited by consumers demanding more from their relationships as well as a degree of rationalism, which are perceived to exist between those relationships (Bove & Johnson, 2001) with service providers as seen through WOM behaviour (Rust & Zahorik, 1993; Rust, Zahorik, & Keiningham, 1995b; V. Zeithaml, 2000). WOM is thereby a powerful mechanism as a form of promotion that is generally accepted in the transmittal of information communicated to others (Buttle, 1998; Dye, 2000). WOM communication plays a specifically essential role for service providers, as intangibility makes the pre-purchase assessment of services unfeasible (V. A. Zeithaml, 1981; V. A. Zeithaml, Parasuraman, & Berry, 1985), in particular those services provided by the day spa industry as indicated in this study. This is more so the case where people, who partake in intimate, relaxing and therapeutic experiences in a day spa setting, initiate communication processes in which they will share parts of their private experiences with various social partners (Dobele, Lindgreen, Beverland, Vanhamme, & van Wijk, 2007). While studies have examined WOM from the receiver perspective (Sweeney, Soutar, & Mazzarol, 2008), from the online experience perspective (Godes & Mayzlin, 2004), and from the customer satisfaction perspective (E. Anderson, 1998; Brown, Barry, Dacin, & Gunst, 2005); research gaps remain in the issues that affect WOM behaviour from the service quality perspective. This study is expected to provide empirical evidence to fill the research gaps. The research question of this proposed study is "what are the antecedents of word of mouth in service marketing?" This chapter will commerce with a literature review on WOM behaviour, followed by the developments of theoretical model, construct, and hypothesis. Research methodology and data analysis will then be discussed. Finally, the chapter will conclude with discussions on managerial implications and future studies.

LITERATURE REVIEW ON WOM BEHAVIOUR

Consumers prefer personal information sources when they are going to buy from or use a service provider due to the confidence they have in those sources (Murray, 1991). Many consumers are influenced more by WOM communications than they are by printed formats (Herr, Kardes, & Kim, 1991). Research, however in the WOM context has been generally regarded as opinion leadership research, or the process that an 'opinion leader' informally influences the actions or attitudes of others (Dobele, et al., 2007; Walker, 1995). Opinion leaders could spread information concerning a service provider and their products quickly over a populous starting within their own circles. Information may then continue to spread to other circles and so on, as effective opinion leaders can easily create instant positive WOM for an organisation in this way (Walker, 1995).

As WOM marketing by researcher's increases, the resulting effect has been the attention service providers are placing on its validity within the community and their decreasing reliability in more traditional marketing techniques (Hendricks, 1998; Rust, et al., 1995b; Silverman, 1997, 2001a, 2001b; A. Wilson, 1994; J. R. Wilson, 1994). Word-of-mouth marketing may therefore affect the implementation of new product categories as a result of consumer beliefs, preferences and the choice of products, which may decide the success or failure of those service providers' products (East, Hammond, & Lomax, 2008). In addition, organisations using viral marketing messages may tap into consumer's emotions thereby linking the service provider and or its products to their recipient base as a way of spreading their viral message (Dobele, et al., 2007; Keller & Fay, 2012). Studies have found that WOM communication has often exerted strong influence on consumer behavioural judgements on an organisation (Herr, et al., 1991). Researchers have identified that the quality of the experience, staff friendliness, expertise, source credibility, and the frequency of social sharing have been found positively related to WOM (Dobele & Lindgreen, 2010). Therefore service providers are placing more and more importance on WOM strategies.

Some studies suggest that service quality positively impacts those future customer behaviours, such as WOM, (Aydin & Ozer, 2005; Harrison-Walker, 2001; V. Zeithaml, Berry, & Parasuraman, 1996). While others report that customer service quality improves service provider efficiency, which is measured by an increase in overall WOM behavioural outcomes (Ferguson, Paulin, Pigeassou, & Gauduchon, 1999). It can then be understood from a service quality perspective, WOM is of great consequence to a service provider's service performance outcome as they relate to the behavioural factors in building relationships with current and prospective customers (Freiden & Goldsmith, 1988; Hennig-Thurau, Gwinner, & Gremler, 2002; Ng, David, & Dagger, 2001). Table 1 provides a sample of those researchers who have focused on the effects of WOM communication representations.

The review of the literature shows that WOM can have a big impact on a firm's sales due to the nature of WOM that involves the interpersonal relationships with acquaintances, friends and relatives. While there is argument that WOM is an important form of communication regarding customer service quality, few researchers offer insightful perspective for service providers. In addition, there has been little research looking at WOM communication from an organisations perspective (Wangenheim & Bayon, 2004). Research, in part, has focused on developing an understanding of the underlying phenomenon itself (Godes & Mayzlin, 2004) with previous studies having looked at WOM communication as a narrative process and the ability for consumers to recall 'stories' from memory as those stories relate to an organisations branding and the subsequent success/failure of those organisations who in turn try to understand consumers' perceptions of their respective products, services, and/or brands (Delgadillo & Escalas, 2004). Thus, there is a need to examine the antecedents of WOM to fill this research gap. The service setting is a complex array of environmental cues, which can potentially influence and affect the behavioural processes of the consumer. In the marketing literature, a num-

Table 1. Some key research on WOM communication

Researcher(s)	Research Focus
Dobele & Lingreen (2010)	Study conducted to understand consumer value in healthcare, focusing on one context – word-of-mouth referrals by new mothers.
De Bruyn & Lilien (2008)	Developed a model to study the influence of unsolicited electronic referrals within a multi-stage decision making framework.
Dobele (2007)	Studied what are the different types of positively referring clients of professional services firms and how do these types relate to the believability of the referral.
Garber, Goldenberg, Lbai, & Muller (2003); Foster & Rosenzweig (1995)	Studied the effects of WOM from the geographical evolution of sales data.
Godes & Mayzlin (2004)	Demonstrated a positive relationship between online WOM and its dispersion across communities and ratings mouth (WOM).
Derbaix & Vanhamme (2003)	Conducted research using the critical incident technique on the emotion of surprise and its influence on word-of-mouth (WOM).
Van den Bulte & Lilien (2001)	WOM played a significant role in the diffusion of tetracycline, and determined that a more-sophisticated decomposition of the physicians' adoption decision did, in fact, yield evidence for the role of interpersonal influence.
Biyalogorsky, Gerstner & Libai (2001)	The authors investigated the optimality of customer referral programs and show that the firm should offer rewards to customers only if they are somewhat demanding but not too demanding.
Feick & Price (1987)	Suggested that there exist 'market mavens' whose influence extends across categories.
Bloch & Richins (1983); Jacoby & Hoyer (1981)	Studied the important role played by category-level opinion leaders in the diffusion of information.
Trusov, Bucklin & Paulwels (2009)	Found that WOM referrals have substantially longer carryover effects than traditional marketing actions and produce substantially higher response elasticities.
Keller & Fay (2012)	Suggested the need for a new advertising model, one in which a key goal of the ad is to foster conversation; the conversation then persuades the prospect, which leads to purchase.
Libai, Muller & Peres (2013)	Investigated how acceleration and expansion combine to generate value in a wordof-mouth seeding program for a new product.
Meuter, McCabe & Curran (2013)	WOM is found to have more influence on behavioural intentions, trust in WOM, and attitude toward the firm compared to all eWOM channels explored.

ber of theoretical focuses have been proposed in an attempt to assimilate environmental attributes and consumer responses into the overall WOM framework. It is argued that consumers demanding more from their relationships with service providers as seen through WOM behaviour (Rust & Zahorik, 1993; Rust, et al., 1995b; V. Zeithaml, 2000). This research examines the relationships between various service aspects and their impacts on WOM.

CONCEPTUAL MODEL

A three tier theoretical model; which includes service performance, post purchase perception, and future customer behaviour, is established to examine the service environment and the subsequent customer perceptions and behaviours. The theoretical model suggests that service performance in terms of service quality leads to post purchase perception, which in turn affects future customers' behaviour. That is the outcome of how customers behave in a certain way following their engagement with the service provider. Service performance consists of product delivery, customer service, and servicescape atmosphere; while post purchase perception incorporates customer satisfaction; and future customer behaviour comprises WOM. The foundation of this service quality model framework was in part based on the seminal conceptualisation of service quality advanced by (Gronroos, 1982) whose theory postulated service quality was the result of customer perceptions based on the interaction that took place during customer service delivery (functional service quality) and product delivery (technical service quality). The addition of other constructs such as the servicescapes atmosphere (Baker, 1987; Bitner, 1992; Wagner, 2000), which refers to the physical surroundings in a service environment and how these surroundings affect and influence customers Bitner (1992), provides an informed measure in the development of service quality perceptions.

CONSTRUCTS DEVELOPMENT

WOM is the process in which clients tell others, external to the transaction, of their (dis)pleasure with a product or service provider. It indicates a customer's future referral intention. WOM is measured by five items adapted from (Arnold & Reynolds, 2003; Maxham & Netemeyer, 2002; V. Zeithaml, et al., 1996).

Product Delivery (PROD) is the delivery of those service products in which the product is to be delivered such as the quality of treatments, and the quality and selection of those products. It directly evaluates the quality of a product delivered by an organisation. In a day spa setting, it is the finished product or outcome dimension such as massages, treatments, towels and bathing areas. 12 items were used in this study adapted from (Braady & Cronin, 2001; Gronroos, 1984; V. Zeithaml, Parasuraman, & Berry, 1990).

Customer service (CSER) is defined as the manner in which the customer receives the service product. That is the manner in which the treatments and other products are provided, which is commonly called 'customer service' (adapted from Grönroos (Gronroos, 1982, 1984). Customer service quality reflects how well the organisation provides for consumers through the buyer-seller interaction. Customer service is measured by ten items adapted from (Braady & Cronin, 2001; Gronroos, 1984; V. Zeithaml, et al., 1990).

Servicescape atmosphere (ATOM) refers to the ambient atmospheric conditions of the physical surroundings of the service setting, in which the delivery of a product takes place. This includes background characteristics of the environment such as: lights, temperature, and noise (Baker, 1987; Bitner, 1992). It measures the overall amenities of a service provider. From a performance perspective, the servicescape includes those physical evidences organisations efficiently utilise to represent facets of their product delivery where customers experience the entire atmospheric physical environment. Eight items were adapted from (Baker, 1987; Bitner, 1992; Wagner, 2000; V. Zeithaml, et al., 1990).

Customer Satisfaction (CUSAT)—Customer satisfaction are feelings and judgements of customers towards a product after it has been used or consumed (Jamal & Naser, 2003). It relates to the overall satisfaction a consumer has with a service provider. Customer satisfaction was perceived as being evaluative and an emotion based response to a service encounter. Customer satisfaction reflects the degree to which a consumer believes the possession and/or use of a product evoked positive feelings. Six items from (Arnold & Reynolds, 2003; Babin, Darden, & Griffin, 1994; Garbarino & Johnson, 1999; Giese & Cote, 2000; Maxham & Netemeyer, 2002; Mittal, Ross, & Baldasare, 1998) were adapted and used to measure the construct.

HYPOTHESES DEVELOPMENT

Effect of Customer Perception of the Quality of the Product on Customer Satisfaction

Customers' positive perceptions can positively affect customer satisfaction. Customers often change suppliers due to the outcome of the finished product not satisfying or meeting their required needs (Schneider, et al., 1997). Customers assess what it is they need to obtain from an organisation, such as customer service, in choosing the product they desire or assortment options. When these service products are perceived as matching or exceeding customers' expectation, a positive customer satisfaction can be established. Therefore, we hypothesise that:

H1: Customer perception of the quality of the product is positively related to customer satisfaction.

Effect of Customer Perception of Customer Service on Customer Satisfaction

Customer service can affect the perceptions of service provider's quality (Gronroos, 1984; Parasuraman, Zeithaml, & Berry, 1985; Shavitt, 1989), which directly affects the level of satisfaction customers have towards that provider. The influence service providers can have on satisfying their customers by how they receive and experience the services or products delivered is thereby regarded as the functional service quality of an organisation (Gronroos, 1984). Customers look for social interaction from staff that can result in their needs being satisfied through this functional process (Noble, Girffith, & Adjei, 2006). Consumers who patronise a service provider, at times making a purchase, are actually forging a satisfied relationship with that organisation (McCracken, 1986; Thompson & Arsel, 2004). It shows the importance of the service staff in the customer service encounter. Service providers can further enhance and improve relationships by hiring staff that have previous skills, training in customer service, product knowledge, multi-functional and an ability to retain what they have learned (Friesen, 1989; Ng, et al., 2001). Staff performing their duties professionally can expect to enhance the customer satisfaction. Thus, a positive influence on customer perceptions and a significant relationship between a customer's perceptions of that customer service element can result in more satisfied customers. Quality customer service will have a positive effect on consumer perceptions with increased satisfaction levels (Gronroos, 2001). Therefore, we hypothesise that:

H2: Customer perception of customer service is positively related to customer satisfaction.

Effect of Customer Perception of Servicescape Atmosphere on Customer Satisfaction

Physical settings, the servicescape, are considered 'physical evidences' that service providers can effectively use to portray the specific elements of their product delivery in which they are conveying to the consumer, and consequently satisfying those consumers experiences as they relate to the physical setting in its entirety. Kotler (1973) suggests the importance of atmospherics and the influencing effect it has on consumer behaviour. The term atmospherics can influence consumer behaviour, and will evoke a satisfying effect on those consumers. The physical surroundings are significantly important in service settings because customers are affected by their surroundings (Bitner, 1992) resulting in a satisfied or dissatisfied experience. Atmospherics shows that it is not only the people dimension that can impact the level of customer satisfaction but also the physical environment which can be controlled by marketers. Proper management of the servicescape atmosphere such as music (Areni, 2003; North, Shilock, & hargreaves, 2003; Sweeney & Wyber, 2002), layout and design (Ang, Leong, & Lim, 1997; Smith & Burns, 1996) and aromas (Mattila & Wirtz, 2001; Michon, Chebat, & Turley, 2005; Spangenberg, Crowley, & Henderson, 1996), customer satisfaction levels can be enhanced. Therefore, we hypothesise that:

H3: Customer perception of the servicescape atmosphere is positively related to customer satisfaction.

Effect of Customer Perception of Customer Satisfaction on Word-Of-Mouth

Overall customer satisfaction has an influencing effect on future customer behaviour through WOM communication and the retention of those consumers (Nguyen & LeBlanc, 1998). Customer satisfaction reflects the degree in which a consumer believes the possession and/or use of a service evokes positive feelings and a willingness to communicate those feelings to others (E. Anderson, 1998; E. Anderson, Fornell, & Lehman, 1994; E. Anderson & Sullivan, 1993; Bitner & Hubbert, 1994; Bolton & Drew, 1991; Cronin & Taylor, 1992; Fornell, 1992; Rust & Oliver, 1994; Wangenheim & Bayon, 2004). Various studies have that examined the relationship between customer satisfaction and referral behaviours in several different industries such as; financial services and telecommunications. Thus, the link between the two has been acknowledged in the literature (Ranaweera & Prabhu, 2003). Perceived service quality, as cognitive judgement behaviour, allows the consumer to gain knowledge regarding an organisation through other means such as WOM communication, in addition to the usual experienced interaction a customer would have with that organisation (Liljander & Strandvik, 1994). In doing so consumers react and behave in a certain way such as referring a service provider to their friends based upon the positive service setting created by providers. Therefore, we hypothesise that:

H4: Customer perception of customer satisfaction is positively related to word-of-mouth behaviour.

Effect of Customer Perception of the Servicescape Atmosphere on Word-Of-Mouth Behaviour

The ability of the physical environment of a service setting to influence behaviour and to create an image has been particularly apparent for service providers in attracting new customers through WOM referrals such as hotels, restaurants, professional offices, banks and retail stores (Wall & Berry, 2007). The environment of a retail store can serve as an important differential or competitive advantage in attracting particular segments of shoppers through future behavioural response producing stimulus (Turley & Chebat, 2002). The physical environment can offer alternative cues, which consumers may share in a social setting to recommend a service provider and to further evaluate the quality of service provided (Bitner, 1990, 1992). Servicescape settings are considered as 'physical evidences' that service providers can effectively use to portray the specific elements of their product delivery they are conveying to the consumer. The consumers who experience the physical setting communicate their experience in its entirety to others. The physical environment can provide a basis for customers to express their approval or disapproval. Therefore, we hypothesise that:

H5: Customer perception of the servicescape atmosphere is positively related to word-of-mouth behaviour.

RESEARCH METHODOLOGY AND DATA ANALYSIS

With an aim at increasing the sample size and representativeness, various members of the day spa industry association were contacted to help facilitate this study with several day spas agreeing to participate. Surveys were conducted at various day spa locations in a period of one and a half months. A total of 280 usable questionnaires were received and consequently analysed. Reliability of the items was tested by Cronbach Alpha assessment. Items with low item-total correlation were taken out of the analysis. All Alphas are above 0.7, which indicates satisfactory internal consistency reliability (Francis, 2007; Hair, Anderson, Tatham, & Black, 1998). Table 2 shows the reliability results of all the constructs.

Convergent validity was tested using the criterion that the loadings of all items hypothesised to measure a latent variable must be statistically significant (J. C. Anderson & Gerbing, 1988; Dunn, Seaker, & Waller, 1994; Hair, et al., 1998). The critical ratios (c.r.) of all the items were found to be significant at the 0.05 level (c.r. > 1.96 = $p < 0.05$), showing strong convergent validity of the measurement model. Discriminant validity was tested using two methods. The first method was to measure the average variance extracted (AVE) in confirmatory factor analysis (CFA). If the average variance extracted (AVE) is greater than the squared correlation between pairs of factors, discriminant validity exists (Fornell & Larcker, 1981). Results of the tests were found to be satisfactory. All AVEs showed higher values than the squared correlations. The upper diagonal of Table 3 shows the results of the squared correlations among the constructs. The results suggested discriminant validity was supported.

The second method used to test discriminant validity was the examination of all constructs in pair in exploratory factor analysis (EFA). Discriminant validity exists if there are only two components extracted from each analysis (J. C. Anderson & Gerbing, 1988). EFA using principal components with varimax rotation was conducted. For all of the ten *pairs* of constructs in this study, there were always two components extracted for each pair of concepts. Thus, the results indicate discriminant validity.

Table 2. Results of Cronbach's alpha reliability test

Dimension	Initial # of Items	Initial Alpha	Items Deleted	Revised # of Items	Revised Alpha
Product Delivery (PROD)	11	0.72	8 (after reliability test and CFA)	3	0.84
Customer Service (CSER)	10	0.93	5 (after CFA)	5	0.92
Servicescape Atmosphere (ATOM)	8	0.78	5 (after CFA)	3	0.71
Customer Satisfaction (CUSAT)	6	0.88	3 (after CFA)	3	0.83
Word-of-Mouth (WOM)	5	0.83	3 (after CFA)	2	0.94

Note: Refer to Apendix A for revised test instrument items.

Table 3. Discriminant validity test using AVE and correlation methods

Constructs	AVE	PROD	CSER	ATOM	CUSAT	WOM
PROD	.64	---	.17	.12	.44	.09
CSER	.70		---	.16	.44	.24
ATOM	.50			---	.41	.32
CUSAT	.61				---	.41
WOM	.84					---

MEASUREMENT AND STRUCTURAL MODEL ANALYSIS

This study adopted a two-step approach in analysing the theoretical model as suggested by Anderson and Gerbing (1988), a measurement model analysis was conducted before a full structural model. Hair et al., (1998) propose a guideline for establishing acceptable fit using five typical fit indices to evaluate the theoretical model; namely χ^2, AGFI, CFI, RMSEA, and SRMR. In consideration of the limitation of the χ^2 value with a big sample size, normed χ^2 with a cut-off less than three instead of χ^2 should be used (E.G. Carmines & J.P. McIver, 1981; E.G. Carmines & J. P. McIver, 1981; R.B. Kline, 1998; R. B. Kline, 2005). All fit indices measures performed very well for the measurement models: χ^2 / DF = 1.54, AGFI = .92, CFI = .98, RMSEA = .04, and SRMR = .04. Thus, the items were found to measure their proposed latent constructs.

EVALUATION OF THE FULL STRUCTURE MODEL

Based on the protocol suggested by Cheng (2001) and Anderson and Gerbing (1988), evaluation of the full model starts with assessment of the model fit. The full conceptual model was analysed using the structural equation modelling method based on the indices of AGFI, RMSEA, CFI, Normed chi-square and SRMR. The results of all indices were satisfactory, indicating an acceptance of the full model. The results of all the fit indices for the structural model are also satisfactory: χ^2 / DF = 1.60, AGFI = .91, CFI = .98, RMSEA = .05 and SRMR = .04. The fit indices suggest an acceptance of the full model. Table 4 below summarises the values for all fit indices.

A graphical illustration of the fitted WOM model with correlations, the standardised regression coefficients, and the R-squared values are illustrated in Figure 1.

All five hypotheses in the structural model achieved statistical significant results; all with p-values less than 0.05. The paths demonstrate positive relationships *between* the constructs. The standardised coefficients of the five paths range from 0.14 to 0.55. The results of hypothesis testing in terms of the standardised coefficients, critical ratio (C.R.) and significant level (p-value) for the relationships between the three tiers of variables are summarised in Table 5.

DISCUSSION

The present study confirms that there is a statistically significant relationship between service quality and WOM. Various satisfactory fit indices demonstrate that the overall structural model of WOM presented in this paper works very well statistically. Each of the five paths has the hypothesised direction and is statistically significant. Of the significance of the findings in this study are the large and positive impacts of service quality on WOM. The three-tier model tested in this study es-

Table 4. Fit measures for the full structural model

Fit Indices	Statistics	Benchmark	Acceptable of Not
Chi-square	153.15 (96 df. P<0.01	p>0.05	N/A
AGFI	0.91	>0.90	Yes
RMSEA	0.05	<0.08	Yes
CFI	0.98	>0.90	Yes
Normed chi-square	1.60	<3	Yes
Standardised root mean square residual (SRMR)	0.06	<0.08	Yes

Figure 1. WOM structural model

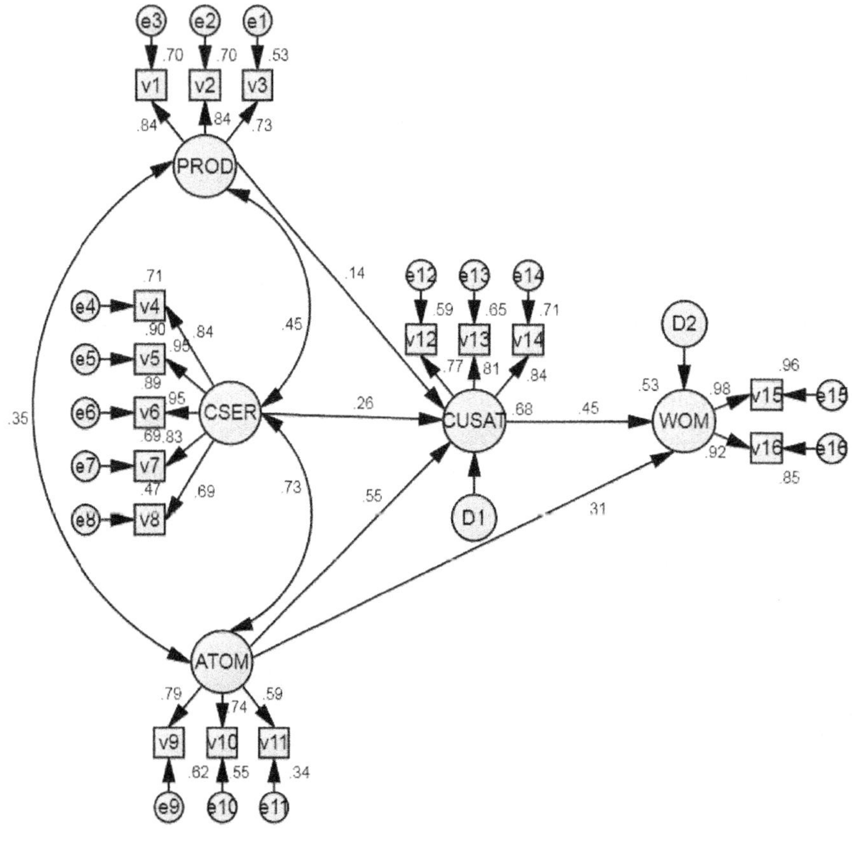

tablishes two critical aspects. First, perceived service performance positively affects post purchase perception, which is customer satisfaction. The biggest effect in perceived service performance is servicescape atmosphere (standardised beta coefficient of 0.55), followed by customer service (0.26) and product delivery (0.14). Servicescape atmosphere is about four times as important as product delivery in terms of influencing customer satisfaction. It may be partly due to the fact that the environmental effects play a more important role in the spa industry. Second, both servicescape

Table 5. Results of hypotheses testing

Model Hypotheses		Results
H1: Customer perceptions of the quality of the product are positively related to customer satisfaction.	Coefficient C.R. Significant?	0.14 2.40 (p 0.017) Significant
H2: Customer perceptions of customer service are positively related to customer satisfaction.	Coefficient C.R. Significant?	0.26 2.93 (p-0.003) Significant
H3: Customer perceptions of the servicescape atmosphere are positively related to customer satisfaction.	Coefficient C.R. Significant?	0.55 5.21 (p 0.001) Significant
H4: Customer perceptions of customer satisfaction are positively related to word-of-mouth behaviour.	Coefficient C.R. Significant?	0.45 2.40 (p 0.001) Significant
H5: Customer perceptions of the servicescape atmosphere are positively related to word-of-mouth behaviour.	Coefficient C.R. Significant?	0.31 2.40 (p 0.004) Significant

atmosphere (standardised beta coefficient of 0.31) and customer satisfaction (0.45) have positive significant impacts on future customer behaviour, which is WOM. WOM referral is comparatively more likely to occur with higher customer satisfaction than servicescape atmosphere. However, considering that servicescape atmosphere has a big influence on customer satisfaction, and relatively high impact of WOM, it is important to recognise the role of servciescape atmosphere plays in the model. All in all, adding together the direct and indirect effects, the results advocate that both perceived service performance and post purchase perception can positively affect WOM behaviour.

MANAGERIAL IMPLICATIONS

Overall results of this study have provided beneficial insights of service quality in the day spa industry as it relates to service performance and the subsequent WOM behavioural intentions of consumers. In order to enhance the chance of positive WOM, marketing managers need to deal with the basic service quality issues such as services products, personal customer service, and servicescape atmosphere. These three basic service quality issues have effects on the perceived customer service. When the perceived customer service is positive, the chance of spreading positive WOM has also increased. Marketers can strengthen their product delivery with better service quality and wider selection; and professional personalised customer service for customers. Customer satisfaction is expected to increase with the better management of the three service quality issues. Among all three service quality issues, servicescape is especially important because it has the highest statistically significant effects on customer satisfaction. Moreover, it has a direct effect on WOM, meaning that if servicescape is managed properly, both the customer satisfaction level and the likelihood of spreading positive WOM will increase.

CONCLUSION

WOM plays an important role in marketing. When facing a fragile economy, marketers need to go much further to defend their position in the market and to attack their competitors. Positive WOM can be a useful strategic tool for marketers in such an economic situation. The impacts of WOM have been well researched, but the antecedents of WOM have been somewhat overlooked. The current study has developed a theoretical model that places service quality performance as the pivot of a model of WOM. The theoretical model has been tested using structural equation modelling on a sample of 280 respondents from various day spas. The results reveal the theoretical model has overall validity with all five key paths in the model being statistically significant. Therefore the model offers a good explanation of WOM behaviour with special significance in the findings confirming WOM is affected by customer satisfaction and servicescape atmosphere. In addition, service performance can drive customer satisfaction. Organisations in the service industry are encouraged to pay extra attention on managing service performance as service performance can directly and indirectly influence consumers WOM behavioural intentions. Future research could apply this model to other service industries and countries to test the validity of the model. It would also be useful to compare the model from other theoretical perspectives that could explain WOM behaviour. Additional research could also examine the moderation effect of the macro marketing environment such as economic situation.

REFERENCES

Anderson, E. (1998). Customer satisfaction and word of mouth. *Journal of Service Research*, *1*(1), 5–17. doi:10.1177/109467059800100102

Anderson, E., Fornell, C., & Lehman, D. (1994). Customer satisfaction, marketing share and profitability: Findings from Sweden. *Journal of Marketing*, *58*(3), 53–66. doi:10.2307/1252310

Anderson, E., & Sullivan, M. (1993). The antecedents and consequences of customer satisfaction for firms. *Marketing Science*, *12*(2), 125–143. doi:10.1287/mksc.12.2.125

Anderson, J. C., & Gerbing, D. W. (1988). Structural equation modeling in practice: A review and recommended two-step approach. *Psychological Bulletin*, *103*(3), 411–423. doi:10.1037/0033-2909.103.3.411

Ang, S., Leong, S. M., & Lim, J. (1997). The mediating influence of pleasure and arousal on layout and signage effects. *Journal of Retailing and Consumer Services*, *4*(1), 13–24. doi:10.1016/0969-6989(95)00091-7

Areni, C. (2003). Exploring managers' implicit theories of atmospheric music: Comparing academic analysis to industry insight. *Journal of Services Marketing*, *17*(2), 161–184. doi:10.1108/08876040310467925

Arnold, M., & Reynolds, K. (2003). Hedonic shopping motivations. *Journal of Retailing and Consumer Services*, *79*(2), 77–95.

Aydin, S., & Ozer, G. (2005). The analysis of antecedents of customer loyalty in the Turkishmobile telecommunication makret. *European Journal of Marketing*, *39*(7/8), 910–925. doi:10.1108/03090560510601833

Babin, B., Darden, W., & Griffin, M. (1994). Work and/or fun: Measuring hedonic and utilitarian shopping value. *The Journal of Consumer Research*, *20*(4), 644–556. doi:10.1086/209376

Baker, J. (1987). The role of the environment in marketing services: The consumer perspective. In J. Czepiel, C. Congram, & J. Shanahan (Eds.), *The Services challenge: Integrating for competitive Advantage* (pp. 77–84). Chicago: American Marketing Association.

Bitner, M. (1990). Evaluating service encounters: The effects of physical surroundings and employee responses. *Journal of Marketing*, *54*(4), 69–82. doi:10.2307/1251871

Bitner, M. (1992). Servicescapes: The impact of they physical surroundings on customers and employees. *Journal of Marketing*, *56*(2), 57–71. doi:10.2307/1252042

Bitner, M., & Hubbert, A. (1994). Encounter satisfaction versus overall satisfaction versus quality. In R. Rust, & R. Oliver (Eds.), *Service quality: New directions in theory and practice* (pp. 72–84). New York: Sage Publications.

Blose, J., Tankersley, W., & Flynn, L. (2005). Managing service quality using data envelopment analysis. *The Quality Management Journal*, *12*(2), 7–24.

Bolton, R., & Drew, J. (1991). A multistage model of customers' assessments of service quality and value. *The Journal of Consumer Research*, *17*(4), 375–384. doi:10.1086/208564

Bove, L., & Johnson, W. (2001). Customer relationships with service personnel: Do we measure closeness, quality or strength? *Journal of Business Research*, *54*(3), 189–197. doi:10.1016/S0148-2963(00)00122-3

Braady, M., & Cronin, J. (2001). Some new thoughts on conceptualizing perceived service quality: A hierarchical approach. *Journal of Marketing*, *65*(3), 34–49. doi:10.1509/jmkg.65.3.34.18334

Brown, T., Barry, T., Dacin, P., & Gunst, R. (2005). Spreading the word: Investigating antecedents of consumers' positive word-of-mouth intentions and behaviors in a retailing context. *Journal of the Academy of Marketing Science*, *33*(2), 123–138. doi:10.1177/0092070304268417

Buttle, F. A. (1998). Word of mouth: Understanding and managing referral marketing. *Journal of Strategic Marketing*, *6*(3), 241–254. doi:10.1080/096525498346658

Carmines, E. G., & McIver, J. P. (1981). analyzing models with unobserved variables: Analysis of covariance structure. In G. Bohrnstedt & E. Borgatta (Eds.), Social measurement: Current Issues. Beverly Hills, CA: Sage Publications.

Carmines, E. G., & McIver, J. P. (1981). Analyzing models with unobserved variables: Analysis of covariance structures. In G. Bohrnstedt, & E. Borgatta (Eds.), *Social Measurement: Current Issues*. Beverly Hills, CA: Sage.

Cheng, E. W. L. (2001). SEM being more effective than multiple regression in parsimonious model testing for management development research. *Journal of Management Development*, *20*(7), 650–667. doi:10.1108/02621710110400564

Cronin, J., & Taylor, S. (1992). Measuring service quality: A re-examination and etension. *Journal of Marketing*, *56*(3), 55–68. doi:10.2307/1252296

Delgadillo, Y., & Escalas, J. E. (2004). Narrative word-of-mouth communication: Exploring memory and attitude effects of consumer storytelling. *Advances in Consumer Research. Association for Consumer Research (U. S.)*, *31*(1), 186–192.

Dobele, A., & Lindgreen, A. (2010). Exploring the nature of value in the word-of-mouth referral equation for health care. *Journal of Marketign Management*, *27*(3/4), 269–290.

Dobele, A., Lindgreen, A., Beverland, M., Vanhamme, J., & van Wijk, R. (2007). Why pass on viral message? Because they connect emotionally. *Business Horizons*, *50*(4), 291–304. doi:10.1016/j.bushor.2007.01.004

Dunn, S. C., Seaker, R. F., & Waller, M. A. (1994). Latent variables in business logistics research: Scale development and validation. *Journal of Business Logistics*, *15*(2), 145–172.

Dye, R. (2000). The buzz on buzz. *Harvard Business Review*, *78*(6), 139–146. PMID:11184968

East, R., Hammond, K., & Lomax, W. (2008). Measuring the impact of positive and negative word-of-mouth on brand purchase probability. *International Journal of Research in Marketing*, *25*(3), 215–224. doi:10.1016/j.ijresmar.2008.04.001

Ferguson, R., Paulin, M., Pigeassou, C., & Gauduchon, R. (1999). Assessing service management effectiveness in a health resort: Implications of technical and functional quality. *Managing Service Quality*, *9*(1), 58–65. doi:10.1108/09604529910248821

Fornell, C. (1992). A national customer satisfaction barometer: The Swedish experience. *Journal of Marketing*, *56*(1), 6–21. doi:10.2307/1252129

Fornell, C., & Larcker, D. F. (1981). Evaluating structural equation models with unobservable variables and measurement error. *JMR, Journal of Marketing Research*, *18*(1), 39–50. doi:10.2307/3151312

Francis, G. (2007). Introduction to SPSS for Windows (5th ed.). Frenchs Forest: Pearson.

Freiden, J., & Goldsmith, R. (1988). Correlates of consumer information search for professional services. *Journal of Professional Services Marketing*, *4*(1), 15 29. doi:10.1080/15332969.1988.9984906

Friesen, J. (1989). Product knowledge shoot out fires' em up in the heartland. *Bank Marketing*, *21*(7), 30–33.

Garbarino, E., & Johnson, M. (1999). The different roles of satisfaction, trust, and commitment in customer relationships. *Journal of Marketing*, *63*(2), 70–87. doi:10.2307/1251946

Giese, J., & Cote, J. (2000). Defining consumer satisfaction. *Academy of Marketing Science Reivew*. Retrieved from http://www.amsreview.org/articles/giese01-2000.pdf

Godes, D., & Mayzlin, D. (2004). Using online conversation t ostudy word of mouth communication. *Marketing Science*, *23*(4), 545–560. doi:10.1287/mksc.1040.0071

Gronroos, C. (1982). An applied service marketing theory. *European Journal of Marketing*, *16*(7), 30–41. doi:10.1108/EUM0000000004859

Gronroos, C. (1984). A service quality model and its marketing implications. *European Journal of Marketing*, *18*(4), 36–44. doi:10.1108/EUM0000000004784

Gronroos, C. (2001). The perceived service quality concept - A mistake? *Managing Service Quality*, *11*(3), 150–152. doi:10.1108/09604520110393386

Hair, J. F. J., Anderson, R. E., Tatham, R. L., & Black, W. C. (1998). *Multavariate Data Analysis* (5th ed.). Upper Saddle River, NJ: Prentice Hall.

Harrison-Walker, L. J. (2001). The measurement of word-of-mouth communication and investigation of service quality and customer commitment as potential antecedents. *Journal of Service Research*, *4*(1), 60–75. doi:10.1177/109467050141006

Hendricks, M. (1998). Spread teh word: Advertising by word-of-mouth. *Entrepreneur*, *26*(2), 120–126.

Hennig-Thurau, T., Gwinner, K., & Gremler, D. (2002). Understanding relationship marketing outcomes: An integration of relationship benefits and relationship quality. *Journal of Service Research*, *4*(3), 230–247. doi:10.1177/1094670502004003006

Herr, P., Kardes, F., & Kim, J. (1991). Effects of word-of-mouth and product-attibute information on persuasion: An accessibility-diagnosticity perspective. *The Journal of Consumer Research*, *17*(4), 454–462. doi:10.1086/208570

Jamal, A., & Naser, K. (2003). Factors influencing customer satisfaction in the retail banking sector in Pakistan. *International Journal of Commerce & Management*, *13*(2), 29–53. doi:10.1108/eb047465

Keller, E., & Fay, B. (2012). Word-of-mouth advocacy: A new key to advertising effectiveness. *Journal of Advertising Research*, *52*(4), 459–464. doi:10.2501/JAR-52-4-459-464

Kline, R. B. (1998). *Principles and Practice of Structural Equation Modeling*. New York: The Guilford Press.

Kline, R. B. (2005). *Principles and Practices of Structural Equation Modeling* (2nd ed.). New York: The Guildford Press.

Kordupleski, R., Rust, R. T., & Zahorik, A. (1993). Why improving quality doesn't improve quality. *California Management Review*, *35*(3), 82–95. doi:10.2307/41166745

Kotler, P. (1973). Anmospherics as a marketing tool. *Journal of Retailing*, *49*(4), 48–64.

Liljander, V., & Strandvik, T. (1994). The relation between service quality, satisfaction and intentions. In P. PKunst & J. Lemmink (Eds.), Quality Management in Service II. Van Gorcum: Assen/Maastricht.

Mattila, A., & Wirtz, J. (2001). Congruency of scent and music as a driver of in-store evaluations and behaviour. *Journal of Retailing*, *77*(2), 273–289. doi:10.1016/S0022-4359(01)00042-2

Maxham, J. III, & Netemeyer, R. (2002). A longitudinal study of complaining customers' evvaluations of multiple service failures and recovery efforts. *Journal of Marketing*, *66*(4), 57–71. doi:10.1509/jmkg.66.4.57.18512

McCracken, G. (1986). Culture and consumption: A theoretical account of the structure and movement of the cultural menaing of consumer goods. *The Journal of Consumer Research*, *13*(1), 71–84. doi:10.1086/209048

Michon, R., Chebat, J., & Turley, L. (2005). Mall atmospherics: The interaction effects of the mall environment on shopping behaviour. *Journal of Business Research*, *58*(5), 576–583. doi:10.1016/j.jbusres.2003.07.004

Mittal, V., Ross, W., & Baldasare, P. (1998). The asymmetric impact of negative and positive attribute-level performance on overall satisfaction and repurchase intentions. *Journal of Marketing*, *61*(1), 33–47. doi:10.2307/1251801

Murray, K. (1991). A test of servcies marketing theory: Consumer information acquisition activities. *Journal of Marketing*, *55*(1), 10–25. doi:10.2307/1252200

Ng, S., David, M., & Dagger, T. (2001). Generating positive word-of-mouth in the servcie experience. *Managing Service Quality*, *21*(2), 133–151. doi:10.1108/09604521111113438

Nguyen, N., & LeBlanc, G. (1998). The mediating role of corporate image on customers retention decisions: An investigation in financial servccie. *International Journal of Bank Marketing*, *16*(2), 52–65. doi:10.1108/02652329810206707

Noble, S., Girffith, D., & Adjei, M. (2006). Drivers of local merchant loyalty: Understanding the influence of gender and shopping motives. *Journal of Retailing*, *83*(3), 177–189. doi:10.1016/j.jretai.2006.05.002

North, A., & Shilock, A. (2003). The effect of musical style on restaurant customers spending. *Environment and Behavior*, *35*(5), 712–718. doi:10.1177/0013916503254749

Parasuraman, A., Zeithaml, V., & Berry, L. (1985). A conceptual model of service quality and its implications for future research. *Journal of Marketing*, *49*(4), 41–50. doi:10.2307/1251430

Perrone, A., & Wong, H. Y. (2013). The antecedents of re-purchase intentions: The service quality perspective. *International Journal of Services. Economics and Management*, *5*(3), 203–221.

Quelch, J. A., & Jocz, K. E. (2009). How to market in a downturn. *Harvard Business Review*, *87*(4), 52–62.

Ranaweera, C., & Prabhu, J. (2003). The influence of satisfaction, trust and switching barriers on customer retention in a continuous purchasing setting. *International Journal of Service Industry Management*, *14*(4), 374–395. doi:10.1108/09564230310489231

Rust, R., & Oliver, R. (1994). Service quality: Insights and managerial implications from the frontier. In R. Rust, & R. Oliver (Eds.), *Service Quality: New Directions in Theory and Practice* (pp. 1–19). London: Sage Publications. doi:10.4135/9781452229102.n1

Rust, R., & Zahorik, A. (1993). Customer satisfaction, customer retention and market share. *Journal of Retailing*, *69*(2), 193–215. doi:10.1016/0022-4359(93)90003-2

Rust, R., Zahorik, A., & Keiningham, T. (1995a). Return on quality (ROQ), Making service quality financially accountable. *Journal of Marketing*, *59*(April), 58–70. doi:10.2307/1252073

Rust, R., Zahorik, A., & Keiningham, T. (1995b). Return on quality: Making service quality financially accountable. *Journal of Marketing*, *59*(2), 58–70. doi:10.2307/1252073

Schneider, B., Holcombe, K., & Whiete, S. (1997). Lessons learned about servcie quality: What it is, how to manage it and how to become a service quality organization. *Consulting Psychology Journal*, *49*(1), 35–50. doi:10.1037/1061-4087.49.1.35

Shavitt, S. (1989). Products, personality and situations in attitude functions: Implications for consumer behaviour. In T. Srull (Ed.), Advances in Consumer Research (pp. 300-305). Provo, UT: Association for consumer Research.

Silverman, G. (1997). How to harness the awesome power of word of mouth: Generating desired customer response through word of mouth. *Direct Marketing*, *60*(7), 32–36.

Silverman, G. (2001a). The power of word of mouth. *Direct Marketing*, *64*(5), 47–52.

Silverman, G. (2001b). *The Secrets of Word-of-Mouth Marketing: How to Trigger Exponential Sales thourgh Runsway Word of Mouth*. New York: American Management Association.

Smith, P., & Burns, D. (1996). Atmospherics and retail enviornments: The case of the power aisle. *International Journal of Retail & Distribution Management*, *31*(2), 80–94.

Spangenberg, E., Crowley, A., & Henderson, P. (1996). Improving the store environment: Do Olfactory cues affect evaluations and behaviours? *Journal of Marketing*, *60*(2), 67–80. doi:10.2307/1251931

Sweeney, J., Soutar, G., & Mazzarol, T. (2008). Factors influencing word of mout heffectiveness: Receiver perspectives. *European Journal of Marketing*, *42*(3/4), 344–364. doi:10.1108/03090560810852977

Sweeney, J., & Wyber, F. (2002). The role of cognitions and emotions in the music apporach avoidance behaviour relationship. *Journal of Services Marketing*, *16*(1), 51–59. doi:10.1108/08876040210419415

Thompson, C., & Arsel, Z. (2004). The Starbucks brandscape and consumers' (anticorporate) experiences of globalization. *The Journal of Consumer Research*, *31*(3), 631–642. doi:10.1086/425098

Turley, L., & Chebat, J. (2002). Linking retail strategy, atmospheric design and shopping behaviour. *Journal of Marketing Management*, *18*(1/2), 125–144. doi:10.1362/0267257022775891

Wagner, J. (2000). A model of aesthetic alue in the servciescape. In T. A. Swartz, & D. Iacobucci (Eds.), *Handbook of Servccies Marketing and Management*. Thousand Oaks, CA: Sage Publications.

Walker, C. (1995). Word of mouth. *American Demographics*, *17*(7), 38–44.

Wall, E., & Berry, L. (2007). The combined effects of the physical environment and employee behavior on customer perception of restaurant service quality. *The Cornell Hotel and Restaurant Administration Quarterly*, *48*(1), 59–70. doi:10.1177/0010880406297246

Wangenheim, F., & Bayon, T. (2004). The effect of word of mouth on services switching. *European Journal of Marketing*, *38*(9/10), 1173–1185. doi:10.1108/03090560410548924

Wilson, A. (1994). Stimulating referrals'. *Management Decision*, *32*(7), 13–15. doi:10.1108/00251749410068102

Wilson, J. R. (1994). *Word-of-Mouth Marketing* (2nd ed.). New York: John Wiley.

Zeithaml, V. (2000). Service quality, profitability, and the economic worth of customers: What we know and waht we need to learn. *Journal of the Academy of Marketing Science*, *28*(1), 67–85. doi:10.1177/0092070300281007

Zeithaml, V., Berry, L., & Parasuraman, A. (1996). The behavioural consequences of service quality. *Journal of Marketing*, *60*(2), 31–46. doi:10.2307/1251929

Zeithaml, V., Parasuraman, A., & Berry, L. (1990). *Delivering quality servcie: Balancing customer perceptions and expectations*. New York: Free Press.

Zeithaml, V. A. (1981). How consumer evaluation processes differ between goods and servcies. In J. H. Donnelly, & W. R. George (Eds.), *Marketing of Services* (pp. 186–190). Chicago: American Marketing Association.

Zeithaml, V. A., Parasuraman, A., & Berry, L. (1985). Problems and strategies in services marketing. *Journal of Marketing*, *49*(2), 33–46. doi:10.2307/1251563

KEY TERMS AND DEFINITIONS

Customer Satisfaction: Feelings and judgements of customers towards a product after it has been used or consumed.

Customer Service: The manner in which the customer receives the service product.

Product Delivery: The delivery of those service products in which the product is to be delivered such as the quality of treatments, and the quality and selection of those products.

Service Quality: Is an evaluation of how well a delivered service conforms to the client's expectations.

Servicescape Atmosphere: The ambient atmospheric conditions of the physical surroundings of the service setting, in which the delivery of a product takes place.

Strategic Marketing: A process that can allow an organization to concentrate its resources on the optimal opportunities with the goals of increasing sales and achieving a sustainable competitive advantage.

Word-of-Mouth: The process in which clients tell others, external to the transaction, of their (dis)pleasure with a product or service provider.

APPENDIX

Table 6. Items used to measure the five constucts

Product Delivery (PROD)
1. The quality of massages were excellent (v1) 2. The selection of other treatments were excellent (v2) 3. The quality of other treatments were excellent (v3)
Customer Service (CSER)
1. I received a welcome when I arrived (v4) 2. Staff appeared neat and tidy (v5) 3. Staff were polite (v6) 4. Staff performed their duties professionally (v7) 5. I was served in an acceptable time (v8)
Servicescape Atmosphere (ATOM)
1. I like the decor (v9) 2. The Day Spa has a nice atmosphere (v10) 3. The Day Spa had a pleasant smell (v11)
Customer Satisfaction (CUSAT)
1. Services I received were adequate (v12) 2. I felt comfortable with the physical surroundings of the facility (v13) 3. Overall, I was satisfied with the product(s) and services(s) (v14)
Word-of-Mouth Behaviour (WOM)
1. I will refer this Day Spa to other people (v15) 2. If asked to recommend a day Spa facility to other people, I would tell them about this Day Spa (v16)

Chapter 11
How is Internal Marketing Understood?
An Examination of Stakeholder Perspective

Wilson Ozuem
University of Gloucestershire, UK & Regents University, UK

Natalie Limb
University of Wales, UK

ABSTRACT

The service industry and business-to-business companies have remained at the forefront of studies into internal marketing due to the close contact between employees and customers in such companies. Marketers and industry experts have shown particular interest to the supermarket sector over the past years due to the varied fluctuations in performance that have been reported. Consumers have negligible switching costs and the threat of substitute products is high, with little product differentiation. Therefore, there is the opportunity to create sustainable competitive advantage through intangible offerings. As of yet, there is little evidence supporting benefits of internal market orientation in the food retail industry. One reason for this may be the difficulty of measuring its benefits in such a context. Although the UK food retail industry has been extensively researched, researchers are yet to address it properly in regard to internal market orientation. This chapter examines it from a stakeholder perspective.

INTRODUCTION

Internal marketing, although widely practiced by corporations, is not properly understood, either by firms or academics, leading to problems implementing such strategies in the workplace (Papasolomou-Doukakis, 2003; Ahmed & Rafiq, 2003; Gounaris, 2006). This study aims to provide insight into how companies in the food retail industry can use internal marketing to create a competitive advantage, drawing on a stakeholder perspective. Marketers are constantly faced with the challenge of implementing effective marketing strategies in such difficult environments. In recent years, as the business environment in which firms operate has become increasingly turbulent, organisations have been seeking new ways to create competitive advantage. For many

DOI: 10.4018/978-1-4666-6232-2.ch011

years, adopting a strong customer-orientation was seen as one method of achieving this, but it appears that this approach to marketing is no longer relevant in the current environment. According to Bhattacharya and Korschun (2008), there is urgent need for new research to examine the impact of marketing on groups other than the customer, who is normally the dominant target of marketing activities. They outline potential areas for fruitful research discussed at a conference of the Stakeholder Marketing Consortium. [1]Traditionally, stakeholders are seen as mutually exclusive, however they instigate that all stakeholders may be embroiled in a network of relationships and that actions of a firm can have a reverberating effect on them all, whether directly or indirectly. Harrison and Freeman (1999) believe that the stakeholder models in the literature are not very sophisticated and assert that examining large stakeholder groups can lead to a lack of understanding about differences that exist within them. Therefore, they call for further, fine-grained research on individual stakeholder groups. This study puts the internal customer stakeholder group as the focus of the discussion and aims to provide further insight into the importance of internal marketing. Much of the existing literature and theory on the subject of internal marketing approaches this topic from the Human Resources perspective (e.g. Collins & Payne, 1991; Harris & Ogbonna, 2001). Wieseke et al., (2009) take a different perspective and discuss the role of internal marketing through adopting a social identity theory perspective. However, these critical streams of research have not looked at internal marketing from a stakeholder perspective. This is unfortunate as it has impeded researchers and practitioners from understanding how and why management fails to formulate effective product offerings that address the needs of internal marketers. To partially bridge this research gap, the current study aims to examine internal marketers from a stakeholder's perspective.

THEORETICAL FRAMEWORKS AND CONTEXT

While in the past, firms tended to adopt a transactional approach, whereby the stockholders were seen as the primary stakeholder of an organisation, stakeholder theory attempts to correct this narrow definition of the corporation. Stakeholder theory argues that the purpose of a company is not solely to maximise shareholder wealth, and that a firm must change along with the context in which it functions (Buchholz & Rosenthal, 2005). Stakeholder orientation is a modern concept to the academic and corporate literature and is a business philosophy that recognises the importance of the needs of multiple stakeholders. This stakeholder perspective has stemmed from the traditional customer perspective of the firm. Following a significant work by Levitt (1960), emphasising the importance of acknowledging the needs of customers, many companies have shifted towards adopting a customer-orientation approach to their strategies. Customer-orientation has been the subject of many influential papers in the last half century and is now considered to be a very well-researched area of marketing. However, it is becoming evident that this approach to marketing is seen as myopic by some authors and companies risk distorting their strategic vision by adopting such a narrow approach (Bhattacharya & Korschun, 2008; Smith, Drumwright & Gentile, 2010). This market-oriented approach entails visualising the customer as the primary focus of marketing activities whereas stakeholder orientation recognises the importance of valuing all stakeholders. A stakeholder can be defined as "all of those groups and individuals that can affect, or are affected by, the accomplishment of organisational purpose" (Freeman, 2010, p46)[2] and this definition has come to be generally the most well accepted among academics (Fassin, 2009), although Mitchell, Agle & Wood (1997) argue that, while it is widely used, it is not universally accepted among scholars. Stakeholder groups can include suppliers, manufacturers, families, government, local communities and trade unions in addition to customers, employees and shareholders. Hung (2011) even proposes that the organisation itself can be viewed as a stakeholder in the society. Freeman's (2010) original stakeholder model is shown in Figure 1.

Freeman (2010) initially raised the question of whether all stakeholders have an equally legitimate claim on the resources of the corporation but left this question open to discussion. Perhaps in such an early stage in research on stakeholder theory, it would not have been possible to explore all aspects of the theory in just one book. While Donaldson and Preston (1995) agree that the subject of stakeholder legitimacy is important, Phillips (2003) believes that this subject is realised by authors but often ignored with no clear definition leading to ambiguity within stakeholder theory. Phillips (2003) believes that giving such a broad definition to stakeholder theory could mean that everyone is a stakeholder of everyone else. He believes that this threatens its meaning and detracts from the value that the theory can provide. Therefore, Phillips (2003) theorises that stakeholders can be classified under different types: normative, derivative, and non-stakeholders, as a way of including them all and being able to distinguish between them. Following this line of thoughts, he identified three dimensions of stakeholders:

- Normative stakeholders can be described as "those stakeholders to whom the organisation has a moral obligation, an obligation of stakeholder fairness, over and above that due other social actors simply by virtue of their being human" (Phillips, 2003: p30).
- Derivative stakeholders are "those groups whose actions and claims must be accounted for by managers due to their potential effects upon the organisation and its normative stakeholders" (Phillips, 2003: p31).

Figure 1. Freeman's (2010) stakeholder model

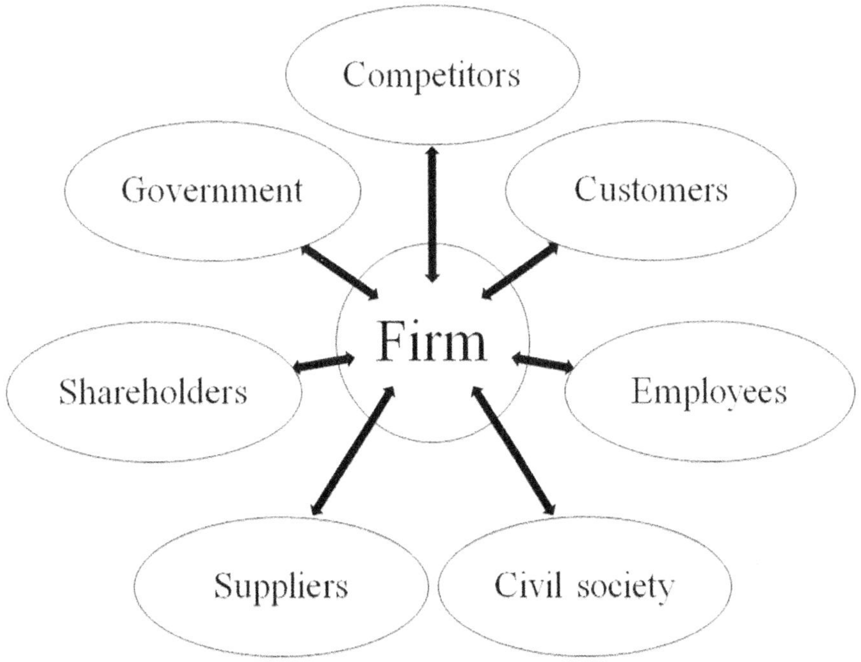

- Non-stakeholders are "the set of groups and individuals that are not stakeholders at all" (Phillips, 2003: p33). The organisation has no moral obligations towards these groups and the likelihood of these groups affecting a firm is extremely small but nonetheless this group of stakeholders is named for such instances.

Phillips, Freeman and Wicks (2003) claim that the breadth, ambiguities and complexity of stakeholder theory leads to various flaws in the theory and is subject to critique. Although Freeman's (2010) definition seen above remains the most widely accepted, the subject of stakeholder theory is open to much interpretation and many authors have taken different viewpoints on it. Fissan (2009) believes that two viewpoints- the managerial and legal interpretations of stakeholder concept- have led to some different understandings. Fissan (2009) argues that these two perspectives are opposing visions and Kaler (2002) agrees that the use of two such contrasting definitions has increased the lack of clarity of its meaning.

An organisation has many stakeholders but a debate has arisen into which is the most important to the firm. For a long while, customers have been seen as the most important since they directly influence sales and hence profitability. Sasser and Arbeit (1976) believed that, in service industries, a company's personnel, namely the employees, are the most important market, and demote the customer to second place. It is generally understood that a fundamental axiom of contemporary marketing is that the external customer has primacy (Rafiq and Ahmed, 2000), and most marketing activities are undertaken in order to satisfy these external customers, with Rafiq and Ahmed (1993) claiming that the external customers are the *'raison d'être'* of any company. Gounaris, Vassilikopoulou and Chatzipanagiotou (2010) agree that customer value is the primary objective since the ability to create value for the customer directly influences revenues. However, under modern marketing philosophy, they propose that "it appears more appropriate to consider customers as *primus inter pares*: first among equally significant stakeholders" (p. 1683). Some authors are now debating the role of the external customer as the most important stakeholder of an organisation (Bhattacharya & Korschun, 2007; Smith, Drumwright & Gentile, 2010). This notion that questions the external customer as the most important, and considers the needs of others serves as the foundation of the stakeholder orientation business philosophy.

Some organisations undertaking a shift towards stakeholder orientation focus on individual stakeholder groups whereas others adopt a multiple stakeholder orientation profile (MSOP) whereby orientations exist to satisfy multiple stakeholder groups simultaneously. According to Greenley et al., (2004), due to the complexity of satisfying multiple stakeholder groups simultaneously, adopting a MSOP can create sustainable competitive advantage as it is not easy to imitate. Recent years have seen an ongoing debate on stakeholder theory amongst academics in the literature as its importance and relevance in the marketplace is becoming more apparent, however its roots can be traced back to the early sixties. Freeman and Reed (1983, p89) found the first notion of a stakeholder mentioned in a document of the Stanford Research Institute in 1963 and believed the term refers to "those groups without whose support the organisation would cease to exist."

Many authors (e.g. Donaldson & Preston, 1995; Clarkson, 1995; Mitchell, Agle & Wood, 1997; Matten & Crane, 2005; Steurer et al., 2005) cite Freeman's (2010) work as a landmark book which has largely influenced much of the work on stakeholder theory. Until this publication, stakeholder theory was relatively unknown in the literature which may have been due to the confusion and lack of clarity of its definition and application within an organisation. Despite the apparent importance of stakeholders in marketing, the word "stakeholder" was not used in the

American Marketing Association's definition of marketing until 2004. Tortosa, Moliner and Sánchez (2009) noted that this highlights the need for organisations to consider all stakeholders in the process of creating value for customers. However it was subsequently removed from the 2007 version in order to broaden the term and provide a basis for moving forward in the future (Gundlach & Wilkie, 2010). It is clear that stakeholder theory is increasing its presence in the literature and that stakeholders are becoming increasingly important in marketing. In fact, stakeholder theory has been in the literature for a while but it was rarely used in the marketing literature until recently. Polonsky (1995) believed that stakeholder theory has not had any significant input to conventional marketing practices and theories, however it appears that this is beginning to change. Stakeholder marketing can be defined as "activities and processes within a system of social institutions that facilitate and maintain value through exchange relationships with multiple stakeholders" (Hult *et al.*, 2011, p44). In essence it is the way in which the marketing strategy is designed to satisfy multiple stakeholders rather than only the customer. Stakeholder theory is also becoming an increasingly important topic in the subject of business ethics. While there is a debate centred around viewing profit maximisation as the core function of a business, as indicated in the introduction, stakeholder theory can be viewed as a powerful heuristic device, intended to broaden management's vision of its roles and responsibilities beyond the profit maximisation function to include interests and claims from non-stockholding groups (Mitchell, Agle & Wood, 1997).

Transition from Market Orientation to Stakeholder Orientation

Traditionally, firms were very product-oriented and business operations consisted solely of transactional processes. Levitt (1960) argued that being product-oriented was the reason many businesses failed to continue growing and Freeman (2010) also agreed that organisations adopting this so-called "production view of the firm" would surely fail. He added that the business environment has changed drastically in recent years and that in order to succeed in this new environment, a conceptual shift was required towards the "managerial view of the firm" whereby owners, customers, employees and suppliers are all taken into account. Many agree that there has been a shift towards a modern turbulent business environment, which has prompted the need for firms to reconsider their approach to marketing (Freeman & Reed, 1983; Doyle, 1995; Morgan & Hunt, 1994). Following Levitt's (1960) influential paper, the past half century has seen a surge in research into customer relationship management and key account management added to the literature in a bid for companies to be more customer-focused.

For a long time, marketers were under the impression that the customer was required to be the primary focus of marketing activities. In particular, many firms have invested large amounts of money into customer relationship management (CRM) schemes in a bid to build strong relationships with customers and become more profitable. However, many CRM projects fail, leading to the belief that adopting the customer perspective alone may not be sufficient to create a competitive advantage in the marketplace. According to Gartner Group (Rigby, Reichheld & Schefter, 2002), 55% of all CRM projects do not produce results and can even drive customers away. The 1970s and 1980s saw a drastic shift from a product-orientation to a customer-orientation and it appears that mainstream marketing is currently undergoing a paradigm shift towards a stakeholder-orientation. According to Malhotra and Agarwal (2002, p4), "There is a fundamental paradigm shift in the way marketing is being redefined." Whilst firms were traditionally accustomed to the transactional approach, relationship marketing requires a fundamentally different approach. Malhotra and Agarwal (2002) examine the relationship marketing paradigm from the stakeholder perspective and note the importance of strategic alliances and building close relationships with multiple stakeholder groups.

In the past, relationship marketing has been fairly limited to the idea of building close working relationships with customers, however, some marketers are of the belief that relationship marketing involved more than just developing close relationships with customers. Morgan and Hunt (1994) identify that most definitions of relationship marketing fail to recognise that often there is not a customer as an exchange participant. They define relationship marketing as "all marketing activities directed toward establishing, developing, and maintaining successful relational exchanges" (Morgan & Hunt, 1994: p22). According to Payne, Ballantyne and Christopher (2005), the conventional marketing literature has shown little regard to the value of building relationships with the customer in addition to other stakeholders. However, in contrast, the relationship marketing literature focuses strongly on the importance of stakeholder relationships.

The advantages of adopting an internal market orientation have been seen in the literature for many years, however implementing such a strategy can be difficult. Recently, it has been seen that internal marketing can be effective in developing a successful market orientation (eg Conduit & Mavondo, 2001; Harris & Ogbonna, 2000). In particular, this approach to marketing can lead an organisation to fulfil its end goal of customer satisfaction. Since the employees play a large part in communicating value to the customer whether directly or indirectly, satisfying the employees can lead to an enhanced service to the customer. According to Gounaris, Vassilikopoulou and Chatzipanagiotou (2010), competitors can easily replicate services and operations that exist within an organisation, however personnel-specific capabilities are not easily copied and therefore can produce competitive advantage. Such employee training requires substantial time and requires the adoption of internal market orientation. Lings and Brooks (1998) found that implementing an internal marketing model in an organisation led to increased service quality both internally and externally, but call for further empirical evidence to assess the effect of internal marketing on service quality. They also add that when all employees can see how they can affect the customer's service quality, this may provide an incentive to adopt a more customer focused approach to their work since they are able to really see how they are important to the company.

Furthermore, there is evidence that indicates that adopting a stakeholder orientation can have a positive effect on a company's financial performance. García de los Salmones, Herrero Crespo and Rodriguez del Bosque (2005) deduced that companies who have well-defined ethical codes, who truly understand their social commitment, and that have honest relationships with all stakeholders are in a position to achieve better economic results. Rais and Goedegebuure (2009) also found a positive correlation between stakeholder marketing and financial success. They deduced that, in the case of manufacturing companies, firms adopt a stakeholder orientation with the view of maximising economic return and stakeholder orientation is used to achieve shareholder return. Other empirical evidence suggests that adopting such an approach to marketing can have significant financial rewards. Jones (1995) concludes that firms who operate on behaviour that is trustworthy and cooperative will have a competitive advantage. When repeated transactions with stakeholders are based on trust, it can motivate honest and trustworthy behaviour, since these companies understand that returns to this type of ethical behaviour are high.

Internal Marketers as Stakeholders

While there has been much discussion on stakeholder theory in the literature, little has been said about its implications for management. Donaldson and Preston (1995) believe that it acts as a justification for the internal marketing literature, whereby of all the stakeholders that contribute to the business, the workforce is one that needs extra consideration. According to Varey and Lewis (1999), while external marketing focuses on economic transactions, internal marketing has a larger focus on social values. In adopting a stakeholder perspective, many firms tend to focus on the external stakeholders as the primary target however many seem to fail to realise the importance of satisfying internal stakeholders also. Drucker (2002, p77) says that "employees may be our greatest liability, but people are our greatest opportunity." He believes that employees need to be viewed as people as well, and that developing talent is a business's most important task. While the market-orientation perspective proposes that companies should build long-term, lasting relationships with their customers, the internal stakeholder perspective proposes that companies should build relationships with its employees. This concept is reinforced by Balmer (2011), who found that organisations that value the importance of corporate marketing and corporate identity understand that powerful corporate brands can be a large source of competitive advantage. In particular, Balmer (2011) believes that organisations need to have multiple relationships, not just with their customers but with other stakeholders and society as a whole. Lings and Greenley (2009) speculate that in addition to developing relationships with employees, managers should also develop a better understanding of the wants and needs of them, and how to balance them with the objectives of the firm. According to Schlosser and McNaughton (2007), external stakeholders are often the target of marketing efforts. In particular, when adopting a market orientation strategy, they are put at the forefront and internal stakeholders are ignored, despite the internal stakeholders providing the link between the strategy-makers and the targets. Upon attempting to implement some strategy within an organisation, they believe that all employees should be involved in the strategy, however doing this can cause some problems because there may be issues of role conflict and some employees believing that the strategy is not of value to them. Welch and Jackson (2007) examine internal communication from a stakeholder perspective. In particular, this new approach broadened many previous approaches to the topic. They define internal corporate communication as "communication between an organisation's strategic managers and its internal stakeholders, designed to promote commitment to the organisation, a sense of belonging to it, awareness of its changing environment and understanding of its evolving aims" (Welch & Jackson, 2007: p193). They argue that doing so can help them create a sense of belonging and engage the employees.

METHODS AND ANALYSIS

The current study adopted an embedded multiple case study strategies, utilising inductive data generation (Yin, 2004; Denzin & Lincoln, 2000). As the case with qualitative research, the study aims to examine the multiple frames of meaning to understand complex reality. Internal marketing involves the management of multiple relationships within, or/and between organisations, seeking to identify their challenges, and understanding how to leverage the differences to organisational success. Adams and Van Manen (2008 p.608) argued that the focus of qualitative interview is to elicit the 'direct description of a particular situation or event as it is lived through without offering causal explanations or interpretive generalisations'. Drawing on the work of Adams and Van Manen (2011), Roulston (2011) identified two inter-related dimensions of qualitative interviews – the 'phenomenological interview' that explores and gathers descriptions of lived experience, and 'hermeneutic interview' that seeks to examine the interpretive meaning aspects of lived experience material. Whilst the current study seeks to examine participants' experience on how they perceived the effects internal marketing in facilitating organisation success, we are more concerned on exploring the study participants lived experience material through their personal interpretations. The selection of participants was based on mutual exclusivity – that is, participants were 'purposively sampled' to enhance and facilitate the data collection process (Creswell, 2009). Thirty-two participants were recruited and interviewed for approximately 45 minutes each. The interviews were recorded verbatim and manually transcribed by the researchers. The emerged data was analysed, using thematic analytic approach. The underlying reason is to find out what was, and generally is, in the minds of the interviewees (Gomm, 2008; Ozuem, Howell, & Lancaster 2008). Based on the interviewees' perspectives, we identified several patterns and statements, which were later categorised into themes (see Figure 2).

MOTIVATION

One of the major issues identified by the study participants was the issue of motivation. When asked about what motivates employees as individuals, what particularly stood out was the variation in the type of motivation seen across the respondents. When there is such a wide range of levels in such large companies such as those under investigation, and when the variety of positions is so large, there are inevitably going to be a wide range of people who will be motivated by varying factors. For instance, one checkout assistant said:

It's worth noting that, when the pay is as low as it was, pay isn't a factor. I'm getting a basic wage for

Figure 2. Themes

doing a basic job, so there's no financial incentive for performing well or going above and beyond.

For some people, perhaps a low salary is little motivation to put more effort into their work. In addition, a number of employees recalled a mystery shopper programme that the company implemented to staff working in stores. While they all agreed that this was an incentive to keep alert and on their toes, they said that a £50 reward for performing well to a mystery shopper was not an overwhelming incentive to do an outstanding job. However, when it comes to managers at board level, some respondents agreed that perhaps when executives are rewarded and given a bonus based on their performance, then it may be more motivation for them. In addition, it was noted that many employees were middle-aged ladies with families and children to support. These employees enjoyed their jobs, chatting to the customers, and were motivated by the shift work available and keen to take on more in order to support families. The work enabled them to be able to pick up children from school, and so on, but earn money at the same time. This theme recurred in addition in an interview with a head office employee. This respondent believed that an employee with young children may perhaps benefit from the shift work associated with the stores, as it may allow them to work around their children. The respondent said:

At the end of the day, not everyone wants to be a manager, it's not everyone's goal. Motivation is completely different for different people, and it's also different with the level you're at.

One respondent recalled a time, a few years previously, when the organisation had funded a postgraduate qualification. This respondent was extremely passionate about the type of work he was doing, and expressed gratitude that the organisation had provided this particular opportunity. The respondent noted:

I couldn't have done it without that money, certainly in the first few years, there was a sense of 'I owed them'...

An interesting issue that emerged was that of the benefits provided to employees, and their effects on motivation.

From my perspective, I don't think knowing I'm going to get those things makes me work harder- even if they didn't do it, that's not why I go to work. My experience in my last company was a lot more generous, and it never motivated me to work- I still feel the same way.

However, despite these feelings, the majority of respondents did agree that staff enjoyed the benefits that were available to them, even if they weren't motivators to work harder. The consensus among head office employees was that happiness of the job was vital. One employee in quite a specialist role declared his main motivation as passion and interest for the job, and the principal reason for liking his job was that he was interested in the work. This respondent said:

I found the work I was involved with very interesting. It is generally the case that the various company specialists tend to be very interested in their field. It was noticeable that the same interest in the role didn't extend elsewhere.

As one respondent concurred with these sentiments and stated:

If you enjoy what you do, you're going to perform better, whereas I think if you hate what you do and you resent doing it every day, you're not going to perform to the best of your ability, and you're not going to get the same level of achievement, because it's always going to be obvious I think. That's how I felt when I did a job for a year that I hated.

Another head office employee noted the importance of selecting the right people for a job. This respondent recalled times he had interviewed potential employees and could immediately sense passion or disinterest in the job at hand. The respondent felt the most crucial element of motivation was to select the right staff in order that they are interested in their work, else they lack passion and motivation. This sentiment was shared among other respondents, with one respondent noting the issue of fairness in selecting people for jobs. This respondent said:

I don't think every person who goes up to management is going to be favoured or liked by everyone understandably, but unfortunately its often a case of who you know rather than what you know as well. In an ideal world, it should be done fairly and treated by who does the best job rather than who gets on best with each other. I think there are some people in the business who shouldn't be where they are, but they've been put there because of someone who's pushed them to be there who was in the right position at the right time, and they've been able to do that.

It is common knowledge that this practice happens in many workplaces, and perhaps may be something that is difficult to control. The same respondent went on to describe the way in which this impacts on other employees:

It's going to have a big impact on them, and probably a negative impact on them, because, if someone's going into a position that the people below, and people that work with them, don't think they're suited for, then they're not going to have that respect there. They might try and do the best they can, but other people aren't going to respect them.

This theme occurred throughout the data, with another agreeing saying,

If you get the people bit right, all the task will happen. You've got a Venn diagram of things being done. It's team, it's task and individual. And if you get all those three things right, then the outcome is always going to be positive.

This emphasises the importance of valuing the people within an organisation. If workers do not feel surrounded by people who are supportive of them there will be a lack of respect and motivation.

Engaged Workforce

Another key theme that emerged from the study participants was the issue of engaging with the company and its other personnel. Respondents generally agreed that it was important for employees not only to be engaged with their own work and the workforce, but also the organisation. One respondent recalled a time after a period of falling profits, when the company reconfigured its visions and goal in an attempt to redirect the company. They were communicated to all employees through various channels but this respondent claimed:

Beyond the bullet points of the aims and objectives of the company, there was a lot of effort put into trying to develop a sense of belonging.

In addition, the importance of knowing the company's visions was noted by some respondents. This was interesting as it relates to the issue of organisational identity seen in chapter two. By training the staff in the core values of the company, they become more engaged with it and perhaps identify with it more, sharing in the values. In particular, it was found that by understanding the company's values can help to engage the staff more in day to day activities. For example one respondent said:

We're told what the values of the company are, so it's those sorts of values that are instilled into us, and we're supposed to live by them, and if we're not doing, then we can have action taken against us.

Furthermore, other respondents all repeated that the company's goals and values are emphasised in the staff training and that is forms an important part of the induction process. One respondent noted:

We had an induction day about the company's history, vision, goals, policies- and given loads of booklets about them. Then we were tested on them. The inside of the store was FULL of posters and company buzzwords about their vision and goals- it was everywhere, but the reality didn't live up to them.

If the company is unable to demonstrate the company's visions and goals among the workforce, then it may be more difficult for them to be put into practice. Many respondents acknowledged that it the company goals and visions on paper were not replicated in the majority of the workforce, and were ignored by many. There was general agreement that it was vital to engage all staff across all levels of the company, however simply informing employees about what is expected does mean things live up to the expectations. In addition it was noted by some respondents that perhaps the store divisions and head office were not fully integrated with each other. Many respondents acknowledged a rift but a problem in how to solve it. One respondent recalled one way in which the company tried to redirect its focus:

The company regarded itself previously as three companies: distribution, head office, and the stores, hence the push to foster the image of being one team with common goal and to break down those barriers... Over the years, along with the ditching of the term 'staff', which we weren't to use anymore, it was to be 'colleagues' and an inverting of the traditional pyramid hierarchy with head office at the top commanding success of levels downwards to the shop floor, that we should do away with that and that basically the central office, the store support centre, is there to support the stores. They wanted it viewed as an upside down pyramid.

Another respondent noted a rift between stores and head office, acknowledging that it is quite common in this industry where, at either end, people are doing very different jobs and do not understand the other. For instance, as one respondent explained the situation for their company:

Like most head offices, they install all these ideas of grandeur, but they're all these visionary plans that have been brought in by someone who has probably never walked into a store in the first place. We get a visit every so often, and people from head office do come down to see how we're getting on.

This was an issue that occurred repeatedly in the data. Head office employees insisted that the store staff didn't understand their roles and vice versa. It is something that occurs in many organisations but is a difficult obstacle to overcome. One respondent noted how their organisation, head office employees must do compulsory store placements. This respondent said:

When you join, you do a store placement, it's before you get into your head office role...partly I think that is a really great way of breaking down barriers...they're grateful to have people there.

One respondent recalled the issues with Walmart in the USA and the major strikes before Black Friday whereby some employees protested against pay and working conditions, noting the importance of considering needs and wants of employees at all levels of the company. Stores generally have targets which the managers are responsible for, and fulfilling these targets may have become the ultimate aim of the managers and perhaps they could become too narrowly focused on this. One respondent added that:

I think big companies need to realise that there is no one-size fits all approach to running a store, that the targets for one store might be impossible to achieve in another, that that staff in one might have different concerns than staff elsewhere.

The issue here demonstrate the need for large organisations to ensure communication across all levels of the organisation. It is vital for employees within an organisation to understand the roles of others, above and below them in order to gain a deeper understanding of the core functions of the business.

Feeling of Importance

This theme- the feeling of importance occurred throughout the data. In particular, perhaps due to the nature of the work, some respondents noted that they believe that many shop floor workers feel like their job isn't very important, and do not understand their role within the company. This was mentioned by one respondent when they said:

I think it's important to be able to understand what they're doing, what impacts what you're doing, and how it impacts other things and other people. Just a little thing, for example if one person on checkouts calls in sick, its understanding- well we need to get someone else from another department to cover, but then they've lost somebody, so they can't get all their jobs done, then that's impacting on the next day. Understanding makes them feel a bit more responsibility for it as well.

At the end of the day, all employees are working for the same company, and all have an important role to play be it large or small. Everything that everybody does contributes in some way and it is important for employees to feel important and understand the importance of the role they play in the company. Work done by an individual will always have an effect on others and their work, across all levels of a company. Even if the role is deemed to be unimportant, it is still important for the business. One respondent agreed and noted how even workers at the lowest level of the organisation can feel important:

When I joined as weekend staff, I was made to feel part of the team, and I've stayed here ever since. Even as a weekend assistant, I had specific responsibilities in certain areas, and was made to feel part of the team, valued and appreciated, but also motivated to achieve more.

In particular, one respondent recalled in their organisation how this was noticed, and steps were taken to improve employees' understandings of their roles:

Since the manager has changed, he's pushed for development and wants to see more people being progressed and developed and now people have more of an understanding, rather than just turning up, doing their job and going home. I think now people have got a bit more pride of the place, and they want to progress and learn more about it.

Another interesting aspect that emerged was the issue of staff feeling like they are not thanked enough for their job. One respondent said:

A lot of the team that I work with, or work for me- I make sure that I go to them and say thank you, and well done, to try and inspire them. Many of them do say that they don't get thanked for a job well done- it's one of the things we're working towards. In the survey done every year to get colleagues' views on things- one of the things that comes out of it all the time is they feel like they don't get thanked for a job well done.

Many respondents agreed that staff can encounter angry, rude and aggressive customers in day to day life. For example one person noted its occurrence in this sector:

With retail, you're always going to get, for example, unhappy customers and unfortunately that is the way of retail- we're not going to be able to please everyone all the time, and you do get customers that scream and shout because we haven't got something. It's about trying to understand that, for the colleagues, they're doing the best job they can, and it's a case of saying to them- I know you've had to put up with a lot today, thank you for that, we'll have a better day tomorrow.

Perhaps by ensuring that staff are all courteous towards each other, it can spark some positivity that is not felt from these sorts of customers. One respondent noted the importance of implementing such practices in a workplace:

I think the majority of people do get on well- even if its someone they don't particularly know, they'll still walk past each other and say hello etc- general pleasantry towards each other which is nice to see. I try and make sure that if I walk past people I say hello to everybody, but 9 times out of 10 there's always going to be one person that you miss, but you should try and say it as much as you can.

An issue identified by one store employee was the size of the companies. When asked whether the fact that many food retailers have now grown so large was important, the respondent replied:

Yes, it's too impersonal now…because it's so big, it's become very target driven, plus there's a feeling that you are detached from anybody of importance.

Another respondent also agreed that the size of the companies has become and issue, and that it can affect the employees and how they feel valued. For instance, this respondent noted:

Because the company has got bigger, I think that you do become more of a number than you have a colleague. Nowadays, because of the recession going on, people are watching what they spend, but then obviously that impacts on our wages- so you've got the same amount of work being expected, with two thirds of the people to do it because you can't afford more people. It is hard, and the business itself has become a lot harder to work in, but it's just about making sure that the people do feel valued and they're not going to try and go elsewhere.

It has become apparent in this study, that in such large companies when one store alone can have 600 employees working there, it is important that all staff members feel like part of the same team. An employee in such a large organisation can begin to feel more of a cog in a machine and less like an individual. Even small things such as kindness among workers and gratitude from others can boost morale. In addition, when workers understand how their own role contributes to the organisation, they may be inclined to feel like a more important part of the firm.

Shopping Experience

Another theme that emerged from the interviews was the shopping experience that customers have in store. Many respondents concurred that the shopping experience was not hugely important to them and convenience was more important to them. For instance, one respondent claimed the following:

I think the choice of supermarket mostly relies on practical issues, like affordable prices, location, the range and quality of items you can buy there. Of course, the service the employees provide is important too but in my mind are not predominant in the case of the supermarket. Shopping in the supermarket, in most cases, is a matter of habit.

This sentiment was shared by another who said:

I won't walk 10minutes in the wrong direction if the one with bad service was the most convenient.

This feeling recurred among many respondents, who all agreed that going to the supermarket was simply just another chore, and they wouldn't be phased by a rude or unhelpful member of staff. However, as one respondent pointed out:

Even the people that say it's like a chore- I think they would still be unhappy if people didn't give them a good service, it's going to deter them. It might not be something they look out for, but they will notice it.

It was evident from the responses that some customers particularly valued the service they experienced in store. As one respondent said:

I once arrived at a store as it was nearing its closing time, and was therefore unable to complete my shopping. Unfortunately the Website had not updated its new opening hours and so I expressed to the manager how this had inconvenienced me. Although I was a bit annoyed, I just planned to return the next day. Then, however, the store manager presented me with a bouquet of flowers as a way of apologising. I was very surprised, and I don't think I would receive the same treatment elsewhere. I now am very loyal to this branch, and have told several people about my experience!

A head office employee noted the important role that the store staff play in enhancing a customer's shopping experience. For instance this respondent said:

Head office have an impact on the company and lead big changes, but the store staff, they're the face of the company really...one of our new goals/ values is making moments matter, that's where we're working at the moment. As much as they (store staff)get lower pay, they are the people that drive business performance. Having engaged staff in store is hugely important, they are much closer to the customers.

The same respondent emphasised how a simple pleasant experience in store can hugely impact a customer's day. Respondents agreed that a particularly good experience can be a pleasant surprise, and that it can enhance their shopping experience. One respondent mentioned:

I feel that the extent of friendliness goes along way to improving the shopping experience. Staff are present to provide assistance, so in treating them with respect I would expect and hope to receive the same.

Organisations in this industry are beginning to realise the importance of enhancing the customer's shopping experience. When there is little differentiation between products sold across stores, superior service is a way of improving the shopping experience that will make customers want to return.

Customer Loyalty

One interesting theme that emerged from the study participants was the issue of customer loyalty and switching behaviour. One issue that significantly stood out was the fact that consumers were well aware of their purchasing power. Furthermore, when asked whether they would be inclined to stop using a particular store after a bad service, the majority of respondents replied that it would bother them and if it was repeated bad experience then if possible they would take their custom elsewhere. For instance one respondent replied:

With so many supermarkets to choose from, it would not inconvenience me to go elsewhere.

Although some respondents appeared they would remain undeterred by such an incident- prices and proximity were more important in some cases- some respondents were more passionate about this issue. Another replied:

Any organisation (including supermarkets) which offers a poor quality service should not benefit from repeat business. I wouldn't be permanently driven away, on the first occasion, but if the service was bad on multiple occasions I would.

This sentiment is reinforced by another who replied:

Definitely it would prevent me from using the company again - my power is to take my custom elsewhere.

It was also shared with another who insisted:

Unhelpfulness or rudeness are unnecessary. I would much rather a pay a bit more/travel a little further to not get annoyed at useless staff.

However a number of respondents insisted that if they could, they would go elsewhere however a lack of choice in their area meant they could not do this. Those perhaps living in less populated areas have fewer choices in where to shop. The feeling among some, was that groceries are commodities, and although superior service may be a bonus, it is not something they look for when going to a supermarket, and all they seek is the products themselves. On the other hand, when asked about whether or not they were likely to share a good experience, most respondents replied that it is not the type of thing they tell people about, although if the topic came up on conversation they may mention it. One young respondent, a student mentioned that this would be something he would be particularly interested in sharing on social media sites, and this sentiment was shared among others in the same age group. Many respondents who said they were loyal to one particular supermarket stated their main reason for this as the good service they always receive there. It appears to be down to individual preference, and personality types. One respondent said:

Loyalty stems from the quality of service and the quality of the food; when you are happy with the food that you buy, and the quality of service, over and above that received in other supermarkets, then it is sensible to continue to use the supermarket.

Despite the many of the respondents saying they would not be inclined to talk about particularly good shopping experiences, others said if the service they received was particularly exceptional or outstanding, they are more likely to spread good word of mouth. An outstanding service could act as a way of deterring switching behaviour and encouraging loyalty, and even good word of mouth recommendations. Overall, there are many substitute products and services and among all respondents, the general consensus was that in the majority of cases there are many to choose from. Although one bad experience may not deter some people, others would feel strongly about it and would not hesitate to take their custom elsewhere. There is little differentiation in this industry, and perhaps delivering exceptional service could provide a firm with a strong intangible asset that may drive customer loyalty.

Company Ethos

While for many, convenience will always be the deciding factor in choosing a supermarket, other respondents mentioned how other things can sway their decision. In addition to service levels and shopping experiences outlined previously, some respondents noted the importance of other factors. For instance, one respondent said:

Having always just shopped for food where ever in the past, about a year ago we made a conscious effort to THINK about where we shopped and how we shopped. We are more environmentally friendly in insisting in NO bag for every shop! Only recently I watched a C4 programme called the peoples supermarket and for me this raised many questions and made me think even more so about shopping and a better way forward - more thought & planning .....less waste!

Another respondent agreed that ethical considerations were taken into account when shopping, and noted:

Ethics plays a big part in supermarket choice for me - is the brand making an effort to be a better citizen & have a positive impact on society & the environment.

It appears that some consumers are increasingly paying more attention to how they shop and where they spend their money. Although only a small proportion of the respondents mentioned these types of issues in their answers, it is important to consider that there others who feel the same way. In addition, these sentiments may be felt not only in the case of supermarkets, but across the entire retail industry. In particular, as an increasing number of unethical work practices are being uncovered, perhaps more people are becoming more concerned about where their money is going.

RECOMMENDATIONS AND FUTURE RESEARCH DIRECTIONS

It seems sensible that perhaps companies should invest more time and money into improving training and the working environment of store employees. It was generally agreed that those who progressed with training from the basic level generally had a deeper understanding of, not only their own value to the company, but of all the functions that make up the organisation. As was found in this study, when employees feel that their work is of little importance, they feel less valued and important to the organisation. Providing a supportive working environment would not only ensure that they feel more important and valued, but at the same time it would lead to them feeling more positive and therefore deliver a better service.

Whilst in some organisations, employees were kept up to date with the company strategy and values through newsletters or emails, this may not suffice to keep them engaged with the organisation. While respondents reported that all new employees were given an induction about the company upon joining the organisation, less is done to maintain corporate training. Since the business environment is constantly changing, it may be worthwhile for all employees to participate in regular training. While it would not be required to be compulsory, updating employees about the organisation, and teaching them about the role they play in a more formal manner may prove beneficial in the long term. This may help to enhance corporate identification, which as shown by Maxham, Netemeyer and Lichtenstein (2008), can lead to superior performance. In addition, feeling more engaged with the company may lead to changing employees' attitudes towards their work, which in turn will reflect well on the customer.

It also became apparent throughout the study that respondents strongly felt that it is important to have the right people in the right jobs, both in head office and the stores. On one hand, respondents noted the importance of selecting somebody who is interested in that role. This means that they will enjoy their job more, which in turn will increase their motivation to perform well. Some customers reported encounters with rude and uncaring staff. If service is something that the companies aim to pride themselves on, then people who behave badly to customers should not be employed by the company. Perhaps one way of ensuring that the right people are chosen as employees is to tighten the recruitment process to ensure enthusiastic staff in all levels of the company. It perhaps may be something that is overlooked in the case of the shop floor staff, but securing the right staff for individual or specific roles is essential. This study attempted to analyse the employee stakeholder group, however further fine-grained research is required on other stakeholder groups. Within the food retail industry, there is the opportunity to investigate other stakeholder groups such as suppliers and manufacturers. Naturally, employees' and customers' views will vary according to geographical area, and so further research should be carried out across the United Kingdom. Outside the industry investigated in this study, there is also the opportunity to apply the internal marketing and stakeholder concepts to other businesses and industries.

REFERENCES

Adams, J. S. (1963). Toward an understanding of inequity. *Journal of Abnormal and Social Psychology*, *67*(5), 422–436. doi:10.1037/h0040968 PMID:14081885

Ahmed, P. K., & Rafiq, M. (2003). Internal marketing issues and challenges. *European Journal of Marketing*, *37*(9), 1177–1186. doi:10.1108/03090560310498813

Ashforth, B. E., & Mael, F. (1989). Social Identity Theory and the Organization. *Academy of Management Review*, *14*(1), 20–39.

Balmer, J. M. T. (2011). Corporate marketing myopia and the inexorable rise of a corporate marketing logic: Perspectives from identity-based views of the firm. *European Journal of Marketing*, *45*(9/10), 1329–1352. doi:10.1108/03090561111151781

Berry, L. L. (1981). The Employee as a Customer. *Journal of Retail Banking*, *3*, 25–28.

Berry, L. L., Hensel, J. S., & Burke, M. C. (1976). Improving retailer capability for effective consumerism response. *Journal of Retailing*, *52*(3), 3–14.

Berry, L. L., & Parasuraman, A. (1992). Services Marketing Starts from Within. *Marketing Management*, *1*(1), 24–34.

Bhattacharya, C. B., & Korschun, D. (2008). Stakeholder Marketing: Beyond the Four Ps and the Customer. *Journal of Public Policy & Marketing*, *27*(1), 113–116. doi:10.1509/jppm.27.1.113

Blumberg, B., Cooper, D. R., & Schindler, P. S. (2005). *Business Research Methods*. London: McGraw-Hill.

Boyatzis, R. E. (1998). *Transforming Qualitative Information*. Thousand Oaks, CA: Sage.

Braun, V., & Clarke, V. (2006). Using thematic analysis in psychology. *Qualitative Research in Psychology*, *3*(2), 77–101. doi:10.1191/1478088706qp063oa

Bryman, A., & Bell, E. (2007). Business Research Methods (2nd ed.). New York: Oxford.

Buchanan, D. A. (2012). Case Studies in Organizational Research. In *Qualitative Organizational Research: Core Methods and Current Challenges*. London: Sage.

Buchholz, R. A., & Rosenthal, S. B. (2005). Toward a Contemporary Conceptual Framework for Stakeholder Theory. *Journal of Business Ethics*, *58*(1-3), 137–148. doi:10.1007/s10551-005-1393-8

Clarkson, M. E. (1995). A Stakeholder Framework for Analysing and evaluating corporate social performance. *Academy of Management Review*, *20*(1), 92–117.

Collins, B., & Payne, A. (1991). Internal Marketing: A new perspective for HRM. *European Management Journal*, *9*(3), 261–270. doi:10.1016/0263-2373(91)90006-C

Collins, J., & Hussey, R. (2003). *Business Research: A Practical Guide for Undergraduate and Postgraduate Students* (2nd ed.). Basingstoke, UK: Macmillan.

Collins, J., & Hussey, R. (2009). *Business Research: A Practical Guide for Undergraduate and Postgraduate Students* (3rd ed.). Basingstoke, UK: Macmillan.

Conduit, J., & Mavondo, F. T. (2001). How Critical Is Internal Customer Orientation to Market Orientation? *Journal of Business Research*, *51*(1), 11–24. doi:10.1016/S0148-2963(99)00044-2

Corbin, J., & Strauss, A. (2008). *Basics of Qualitative Research: Techniques and Procedures for Developing Grounded Theory* (3rd ed.). Thousand Oaks, CA: Sage.

Dabholkar, P. A., & Abston, K. A. (2008). The role of customer contact employees as external customers: A conceptual framework for marketing strategy and future research. *Journal of Business Research*, *61*(9), 885–1026. doi:10.1016/j.jbusres.2007.10.004

Davies, F. M., Goode, M. M. H., Moutinho, L. A., & Ogbonna, E. (2001). Critical factors in consumer supermarket shopping behaviour: A neural network approach. *Journal of Consumer Behaviour*, *1*(1), 35–49. doi:10.1002/cb.52

Donaldson, T., & Preston, L. E. (1995). The stakeholder theory of the corporation: Concepts, evidence and implications. *Academy of Management Review*, *20*, 65–91.

Doyle, P. (1995). Marketing in the new millennium. *European Journal of Marketing*, *29*(13), 23–41. doi:10.1108/03090569510147712

Drucker, P. F. (2002). They're not employees, they're people. *Harvard Business Review*, *80*(2), 70–77. PMID:11894680

Easterby-Smith, M., Thorpe, R., & Jackson, P. R. (2008). *Management Research* (3rd ed.). London: Sage.

Eisenhardt, K. M. (1989). Building theories from case study research. *Academy of Management Review*, *14*(4), 532–550.

Eriksson, P., & Kovalainen, A. (2008). *Qualitative Methods in Business Research*. London: Sage. doi:10.4135/9780857028044

Esbjerg, L., Jensen, B. B., Bech-Larsen, T., Dutra de Barcellos, M., Boztug, Y., & Grunert, K. G. (2012). An integrative conceptual framework for analyzing customer satisfaction with shopping trip experiences in grocery retailing. *Journal of Retailing and Consumer Services*, *19*(4), 445–456. doi:10.1016/j.jretconser.2012.04.006

Euromonitor International. (2012). *Grocery Retailers in the United Kingdom*. Retrieved from www.euromonitor.com

Fassin, Y. (2009). The Stakeholder Model Refined. *Journal of Business Ethics*, *84*(1), 113–135. doi:10.1007/s10551-008-9677-4

Ferrell, O., Gonzalez-Padron, T., Hult, G., & Maignan, I. (2010). From Market Orientation to Stakeholder Orientation. *Journal of Public Policy & Marketing*, *29*(1), 93–96. doi:10.1509/jppm.29.1.93

Freeman, R. E. (2010). *Strategic Management: A Stakeholder Approach*. Boston: Pitman.

Freeman, R. E., & Reed, D. (1983). Stockholders and Stakeholders: A New Perspective on Corporate Governance. *California Management Review*, *25*(3), 88–106. doi:10.2307/41165018

Friedman, M. (2002). Capitalism and Freedom (40th anniversary Ed.). Chicago: The University of Chigago Press.

Galbreath, J. (2009). Building corporate social responsibility into strategy. *European Business Review*, *21*(2), 109–127. doi:10.1108/09555340910940123

Garcia de los Salmones, M., Herrero Crespo, A., & Rodriguez del Bosque, I. (2005). Influence of Corporate Social Responsibility on Loyalty and Valuation of Services. *Journal of Business Ethics*, *61*(4), 369–385. doi:10.1007/s10551-005-5841-2

Garriga, E., & Melé, D. (2004). Corporate Social Responsibility Theories: Mapping the Theory. *Journal of Business Ethics*, *53*(1/2), 51–71. doi:10.1023/B:BUSI.0000039399.90587.34

George, W. R. (1990). Internal marketing and organisational behaviour: A partnership in developing customer-conscious employees at every level. *Journal of Business Research*, *20*(1), 63–70. doi:10.1016/0148-2963(90)90043-D

Gill, J., & Johnson, P. (2010). *Research Methods for Managers* (4th ed.). Thousand Oaks, CA: Sage.

Gilmore, A., & Carson, D. (1995). Managing and marketing to internal customers. In *Understanding Services Management*. Chichester, UK: Wiley and Sons.

Goodpaster, K. E. (1991). Business Ethics and Stakeholder Analysis. *Business Ethics Quarterly*, *1*(1), 53–73.

Gounaris, S. (2006). Internal-market orientation and its measurement. *Journal of Business Research*, *59*(4), 432–448. doi:10.1016/j.jbusres.2005.10.003

Gounaris, S., Vassilikopoulou, A., & Chatzipanagiotou, K. C. (2010). Internal-market orientation: A misconceived aspect of marketing theory. *European Journal of Marketing*, *44*(11/12), 1667–1699. doi:10.1108/03090561011079837

Greene, W. E., Walls, G. D., & Schrest, L. J. (1994). Internal Marketing: The Key to External Marketing Success. *Journal of Services Marketing*, *8*(4), 5–13. doi:10.1108/08876049410070682

Greenley, G. E., & Foxall, G. R. (1998). External moderation of associations among stakeholder orientations and company performance. *International Journal of Research in Marketing*, *15*(1), 51–69. doi:10.1016/S0167-8116(97)00018-9

Greenley, G. E., Hooley, G. J., Broderick, A. J., & Rudd, J. M. (2004). Strategic planning differences among different multiple stakeholder orientation profiles. *Journal of Strategic Marketing*, *12*(3), 163–182. doi:10.1080/0965254042000262887

Gremler, D. D., Gwinner, K. P., & Brown, S. W. (2001). Generating positive word-of-mouth communication through customer-employee relationships. *International Journal of Service Industry Management*, *12*(1), 44–59. doi:10.1108/09564230110382763

Grönroos, C. (1990). Relationship Approach to Marketing in Service Contexts: The Marketing and Organizational Behavior Interface. *Journal of Business Research*, *20*(1), 3–11. doi:10.1016/0148-2963(90)90037-E

Grönros, C. (1994). From Marketing Mix to Relationship Marketing: Towards a Paradigm Shift in Marketing. *Management Decision*, *32*(2), 4–20. doi:10.1108/00251749410054774

Guest, G., MacQueen, K. M., & Namey, E. E. (2012). *Applied Thematic Analysis*. Thousand Oaks, CA: Sage.

Gummesson, E. (1991). Marketing-orientation revisited: The crucial role of the part-time marketer. *European Journal of Marketing*, *25*(2), 60–75. doi:10.1108/03090569110139166

Gummesson, E. (2000). *Qualitative Methods in Management Research* (2nd ed.). Thousand Oaks, CA: Sage.

Gundlach, G. T., & Wilkie, W. L. (2010). Stakeholder Marketing: Why Stakeholder Was Omitted from the American Marketing Association's Official 2007 Definition of Marketing and Why the Future Is Bright for Stakeholder Marketing. *Journal of Public Policy & Marketing*, *29*(1), 89–82. doi:10.1509/jppm.29.1.89

Harris, L. C., & Ogbonna, E. (2000). The Responses of Front-line Employees to Market-oriented Culture Change. *European Journal of Marketing*, *34*(3/4), 318–340. doi:10.1108/03090560010311885

Harris, L. C., & Ogbonna, E. (2001). Strategic human resource management, marketorientation, and organizational performance. *Journal of Business Research*, *51*(2), 157–166. doi:10.1016/S0148-2963(99)00057-0

Harrison, J. S., & Freeman, R. E. (1999). Stakeholders, Social Responsibility, and Performance: Empirical Evidence and Theoretical Perspectives. *Academy of Management Journal*, *42*(5), 479–485. doi:10.2307/256971

Hult, G., Mena, J., Ferrell, O., & Ferrell, L. (2011). Stakeholder marketing: A definition and conceptual framework. *Academy of Marketing Science*, *1*(1), 44–65.

Hung, H. (2011). Directors' Roles in Corporate Social Responsibility: A Stakeholder Perspective. *Journal of Business Ethics*, *103*(3), 385–402. doi:10.1007/s10551-011-0870-5

James, K., & Vinnicombe, S. (2002). Acknowledging the Individual in the Researcher. In *Essential Skills for Management Research*. London: Sage. doi:10.4135/9781848605305.n5

Jones, T. (1995). Instrumental stakeholder theory: A synthesis of ethics and economics. *Academy of Management Review*, *20*(2), 404–437.

Kaler, J. (2002). Morality and Strategy in Stakeholder Identification. *Journal of Business Ethics*, *39*(1/2), 91–99. doi:10.1023/A:1016336118528

Kohn, A. (1993). Why incentive plans cannot work. *Harvard Business Review*, *71*(5), 54–60.

Levinson, H. (1965). Reciprocation: The relationship between man and organization. *Administrative Science Quarterly*, *9*(4), 370–390. doi:10.2307/2391032

Levitt, T. (1958). The dangers of social responsibility. *Harvard Business Review*, *36*(5), 41–50.

Levitt, T. (1960). Marketing Myopia. *Harvard Business Review*, *38*(4), 45–56. PMID:15252891

Levitt, T. (2004). Marketing Myopia. *Harvard Business Review*, *82*(7/8), 138–149. PMID:15252891

Lings, I., & Brooks, R. F. (1998). Implementing and measuring the effectiveness of internal marketing. *Journal of Marketing Management*, *14*(4/5), 325–351. doi:10.1362/026725798784959426

Lings, I., & Greenley, G. (2005). Measuring internal market orientation. *Journal of Service Research*, *7*(3), 290–305. doi:10.1177/1094670504271154

Lings, I. N., & Greenley, G. E. (2009). The impact of internal and external market orientations on firm performance. *Journal of Strategic Marketing*, *17*(1), 41–53. doi:10.1080/09652540802619251

Maignan, I., Ferrell, O. C., & Ferrell, L. (2005). A stakeholder model for implementing social responsibility in marketing. *European Journal of Marketing*, *39*(9/10), 956–977. doi:10.1108/03090560510610662

Malhotra, N. K., & Agarwal, J. (2002). A Stakeholder Perspective on Relationship Marketing: Framework and Propositions. *Journal of Relationship Marketing*, *1*(2), 3–37. doi:10.1300/J366v01n02_02

Markwick, N., & Fill, C. (1995). Towards a framework for managing corporate identity. *European Journal of Marketing*, *31*(5), 396–409. doi:10.1108/03090569710167619

Matten, D., & Crane, A. (2005). What is stakeholder democracy? Perspectives and issues. *Business Ethics (Oxford, England)*, *14*(1), 6–13. doi:10.1111/j.1467-8608.2005.00382.x

Maxham, J. G. III, Netemeyer, R. G., & Lichtenstein, D. R. (2008). The Retail Value Chain: Linking Employee Perceptions to Employee Performance, Customer Evaluations, and Store Performance. *Marketing Science*, *27*(2), 147–167. doi:10.1287/mksc.1070.0282

McWilliams, A., Siegel, D. S., & Wright, P. M. (2006). Corporate Social Responsibility: Strategic Implications. *Journal of Management Studies*, *43*(1), 1–18. doi:10.1111/j.1467-6486.2006.00580.x

Mitchell, R. K., Agle, B. R., & Wood, D. J. (1997). Toward a Theory of Stakeholder Identification and Salience: Defining the Principle of Who and What Really Counts. *Academy of Management Review*, *22*(4), 853–886.

Morgan, R. M., & Hunt, S. D. (1994). The Commitment-trust theory of relationship marketing. *Journal of Marketing*, *58*(3), 20–38. doi:10.2307/1252308

Niglas, K. (2010). The Multidimensional Model of Research Methodology: An Integrated Set of Continua. In *The Sage Handbook of Mixed Methods in Social and Behavioural Research*. Thousand Oaks, CA: Sage.

Nohria, N., Groysberg, B., & Lee, L. E. (2008). Employee Motivation: A Powerful New Model. *Harvard Business Review*, *86*(7/8), 78–84. PMID:18681299

Panigyrakis, G. G., & Theodoridis, P. K. (2009). Internal marketing impact on business performance in a retail context. *International Journal of Retail & Distribution Management*, *37*(7), 600–628. doi:10.1108/09590550910964620

Papasolomou-Doukakis, I. (2003). Internal Marketing in the UK Retail Banking Sector: Rhetoric or Reality? *Journal of Marketing Management*, *19*(1/2), 197–224.

Payne, A., Ballantyne, D., & Christopher, M. (2005). A stakeholder approach to relationship marketing strategy: The development and use of the six markets model. *European Journal of Marketing*, *39*(7), 855–871. doi:10.1108/03090560510601806

Phillips, R. (2003). Stakeholder Legitimacy. *Business Ethics Quarterly*, *13*(1), 25–41. doi:10.5840/beq20031312

Phillips, R., Freeman, E., & Wicks, A. (2003). What Stakeholder Theory is not. *Business Ethics Quarterly*, *13*(4), 479–502. doi:10.5840/beq200313434

Polonsky, M. J. (1995). A stakeholder theory approach to designing environmental marketing strategy. *Journal of Business and Industrial Marketing*, *10*(3), 29–46. doi:10.1108/08858629510096201

Rafiq, M., & Ahmed, P. K. (1993). The scope of internal marketing: Defining the boundary between marketing and human resource management. *Journal of Marketing Management*, *9*(3), 219–232. doi:10.1080/0267257X.1993.9964234

Rafiq, M., & Ahmed, P. K. (2000). Advances in the internal marketing concept: Definition, synthesis and extension. *Journal of Services Marketing*, *14*(6), 449–462. doi:10.1108/08876040010347589

Rais, S., & Goedegebuure, R. V. (2009). Stakeholder Orientation and financial performance: Evidence from Indonesia. *Problems and Perspectives in Management*, *7*(3), 62–75.

Reed, D. (1999). Stakeholder Management Theory: A Critical Theory Perspective. *Business Ethics Quarterly*, *9*(3), 453–483. doi:10.2307/3857512

Rigby, D. K., Reichheld, F. F., & Schefter, P. (2002). Avoid the four perils of CRM. *Harvard Business Review*, *80*(2), 101–109. PMID:11894676

Sasser, W. E., & Arbeit, S. F. (1976). Selling jobs in the service sector. *Business Horizons*, *19*(3), 61–65. doi:10.1016/0007-6813(76)90053-7

Saunders, M., Lewis, P., & Thornhill, A. (2012). *Research Methods for Business Students* (6th ed.). Harlow, UK: Pearson.

Schlosser, F. K., & McNaughton, R. B. (2007). Internal stakeholder views of a market orientation strategy: Implications for implementation. *Journal of Strategic Marketing*, *15*(4), 307–325. doi:10.1080/09652540701320944

Sekaran, U., & Bougie, R. (2009). *Research Methods for Business: A Skill Building Approach* (5th ed.). Chichester, UK: Wiley & Sons Ltd.

Sergeant, A., & Frenkel, S. (2000). When do customer contact employees satisfy customers? *Journal of Service Research*, *3*(1), 18–34. doi:10.1177/109467050031002

Smith, N., Drumwright, M., & Gentile, M. (2010). The New Marketing Myopia. *Journal of Public Policy & Marketing*, *29*(1), 4–11. doi:10.1509/jppm.29.1.4

Steurer, R., Langer, M. E., Konrad, A., & Martinuzzi, A. (2005). Corporations, Stakeholders and Sustainable Development I: A Theoretical Exploration of Business–Society Relations. *Journal of Business Ethics*, *61*(3), 263–281. doi:10.1007/s10551-005-7054-0

Thomas, J. L., Vitell, S. J., Gilbert, F. W., & Rose, G. M. (2002). The Impact of Ethical Cues on Customer Satisfaction with Service. *Journal of Retailing*, *78*(3), 167–173. doi:10.1016/S0022-4359(02)00062-3

Tortosa, V., Moliner, M. A., & Sánchez, J. (2009). Internal market orientation and its influence on organisational performance. *European Journal of Marketing*, *43*(11), 1435–1456. doi:10.1108/03090560910989975

van Riel, C. B. M. (1995). *Principles of Corporate Communication*. Hemel Hempstead, UK: Prentice Hall.

Varey, R. J., & Lewis, B. R. (1999). A broadened conception of internal marketing. *European Journal of Marketing*, *33*(9), 926–944. doi:10.1108/03090569910285869

Welch, M., & Jackson, P. R. (2007). Rethinking internal communication: A stakeholder approach. *Corporate Communications: An International Journal*, *12*(2), 177–198. doi:10.1108/13563280710744847

Wieseke, J., Ahearne, M., Lam, S. K., & van Dick, R. (2009). The Role of Leaders in Internal Marketing. *Journal of Marketing*, *73*(2), 123–145. doi:10.1509/jmkg.73.2.123

Wilcox, M., & O'Callaghan, E. (2001). The strategic response of Dublin's traditional department stores to intensifying competition. *Journal of Retailing and Consumer Services*, *8*(4), 213–225. doi:10.1016/S0969-6989(00)00027-8

Wilson, J. (2010). *Essentials of Business Research: A Guide to Doing Your Research Project*. London: Sage.

Yin, R. K. (1993). *Applications of Case Study Research*. Newbury Park, CA: Sage.

Yin, R. K. (2004). *The Case Study Anthology*. Thousand Oaks, CA: Sage.

Yin, R. K. (2009). *Case Study Research: Design and Methods* (4th ed.). Thousand Oaks, CA: Sage.

KEY TERMS AND DEFINITIONS

Case Study: A qualitative research strategy that investigate contemporary research problem in its real-life context.

Internal Marketing: To describe various management initiatives used to improve the effectiveness and efficiency of organisational resources that could enhance customers and employees relationships.

Marketing Concept: The fulfilment of corporate marketing goals through meeting customer's needs and wants better than competitors.

Qualitative Research: Aims at understanding meaning that involves human action in a given context.

Service Offer: The intangible component of any product that cannot be dropped on customer's foot.

Stakeholders: Individuals directly or indirectly affected by the activities of a particular organisation.

Thematic Analysis: A qualitative data analytic approach that identifies the relationships between respondents' comments, and comparing and contrasting the emerged themes to formulate theory.

ENDNOTES

1. The Stakeholder Marketing Consortium is a forum which enables marketing scholars and practitioners to collaborate with innovative research on stakeholder marketing. It is a joint project between Boston University and the Aspen Institute.
2. It is important to note that, for the purposes of this dissertation, the author used the reprinted edition of Freeman's book. The book was originally published in 1984 but was reprinted in 2010 to celebrate the 25th anniversary of the original publication. Therefore the concepts cited in this dissertation are from 1984.

Section 3
E-Marketing

Chapter 12
Growing E-Marketing Trends in India

Laxhminarayan Das
Ravenshaw University, India

ABSTRACT

Internet growth in India is increasing at an alarming rate, which is indicating a fast growth future for the many e-marketing companies in India. The young population of the country prefers the new technology. The phenomenon is not only confined to urban India but has also spread to rural India. Due to the popularity of Internet usage, there will be a big boom of e-commerce market in India. Young buyers of India prefer to buy online due to easy mode of transaction, preferred mode of payment, safe delivery, and effective after sales service, in terms of return and refund policy. These changing shopping habits of the consumer open the door of opportunity for many e-marketing companies in India. The consumer in India buys many products online, from food to non-food categories. This is explored in this chapter.

INTRODUCTION

As e-marketing is basically an internet enabled transaction process, hence it has a global reach. Today internet user across the globe is increasing spontaneously including India. Sitting across at any place of globe, consumer can order their choice of product and received the same during a stipulated time period.

This kind of transaction cost is too less for the consumer and also he/she saves time (Berryman et al, 1998). Consumer also saves money from transportation cost to go to a market place, parking cost, entry fees where applicable in the big shopping complex etc. On the other hand internet is now a convenient tool to handle easily according to the consumer's wish and cost towards using the high speed internet in India is extremely cheap.

As e-marketing is just click based model, hence rate of conversion from offline mode of shopping to online mode of shopping in India is increasing periodically. Once a consumer finalizes the product in the company's web page then only a click matters the future and growth of the company (Berryman et al, 1998).

Latest information about the products is highly personal in nature as the information are supposed to send to the consumer in his/her e-mail addresses. Hence based on their need they will order for the product. As online transactions is one-to- one

DOI: 10.4018/978-1-4666-6232-2.ch012

marketing, hence it suited to the buyers and all the transactions are held in a tight privacy. Consumer enjoys the privacy of shopping and continues to a part of the shopping for a long time.

THEORETICAL APROACH

Benefits to Customers through E-Marketing

Many new buyers are adding themselves to the online mode of shopping due to easy, protected, and lesser cost of internet usage. Online companies are respecting the consumer's privacy. Online transaction symbolizes the scope of shopping with freedom. Hence online companies first try to persuade the consumer about the availability of the product near to their hand and then tempt them to buy through various sales plans where they succeed. Consumer enjoys his/her free time to spend behind the online shopping (Chaffey et al, 2006) . There is no pressure from the seller's end. All the transactions are highly secured and can be taken place at any point of time according to the consumers wish. Choice of a particular brand also goes to consumer as he/she will select the same according to the search he/she had made in due course of time. Companies can further strengthened the scope by uploading more and more latest category of the product the consumer is looking for. Door step delivery of the consignment is another strong benefit of the company, where he/she has been assured about the delivery of the item by any means. Under no circumstances online companies can lost the consumer's items. Many new features in the company's webpage enhances the knowledge of the consumer and according to the modify version of the technology consumers also updated themselves. Taking care of the consumer queries through 24x7 ways in also improves the value of online shopping (Chaffey et al, 2006).

Merits: De-Merits of E-Marketing

Low startup cost i.e. initial investment to start the venture attracts low funds. It encourages immediate action i.e. the decision making process is highly authentic and quick. Easy mode of maintaining the relationship with customer. Provides great opportunity to target consumers with many kinds of personalization services. Sometime it creates difficulty to contact the consumers due to server problem or wrong e-mail id provided by the consumers. Initial link with consumers bring a smile in the face of e-marketing companies, but subsequently it is very difficult to retain the consumers as they are always not prepared to shop through online due to low internet presence and non-habitual nature of many Indian consumers.

It is very difficult to segment the consumers according to their product preference, brand they like, preferred price, level of after- sales service they are looking for in an e-commerce platform. Due to this every registered consumer in the internet database may not be a prospect consumer.

Bringing additional resources like merchandising and man power in to the board is a herculean task for the e-marketing company (Quelch and Klein, 1996).

Reasons Behind the Growing Popularity of E-Marketing Companies in India: Internet Evaluation in India

Today India is third largest internet user country after China and USA. According to TRAI (Telecom Regulatory Authority of India) the total number of internet subscribers in India was 165 million by the end of 31st March, 2013. Out of the above users, three fourth of India's online community is below the age of 35. In terms of gender basis, male under the age 35 and female in between the age of 35 to 44 are the heavy users of internet. Today most popular search engine among Indians

Table 1. User status

URBAN		RURAL	
Year	In Million	Year	In Million
December 2013	130	December 2013	27
June 2014	185	June 2014	32

is Google; best social platforms are Face book and twitter. Orkut is in a decline stage in India. There is more bigger world is waiting for India as the no is increasing rapidly day by day. Today the users' ratio in between India and China is 1:5, which may narrow further in the near future. According to IAMAI (Internet and Mobile Association of India), the no of internet users in India is expected to grow 185 million by the end of June, 2014. The users rate in an increasing trend both in urban as well as rural India.

By June 2014, India will have 243 million internet users, at which point of time, it is expected to overtake the US as the second largest Internet base in the world. China currently leads with more than 300 million internet users while the US currently has estimated 207 million internet users.

Currently more than 50% of the urban internet users access Internet daily. Remarkably however, this high frequency usage is not restricted to only the youth and the working men. This habit of accessing the Internet daily is seen among other demographic segments as well, including Older Men and Non-Working Women.

In Rural India, 70% of the active internet users also access internet using mobile phones, while 32% use internet only through mobile. The Community Service Centres and Cyber Cafes are the main point of access for 40% of them.

Recent past has shown about the growth of internet community in India. Due to this reason many e-commerce and e-marketing companies are coming up in the recent time in Indian market.

The companies are highly consumer friendly in nature and the rising growth of the e-marketing in India is due the below few factors:

- Many starts up ventures are receiving funds from venture capital funds/private equity funds.
- Aggressive marketing plan by the online companies, where they try to push their products into the gadget platform of the consumers like mobile phone, laptop, PC, tablet, Smartphone. Strong online presence and unique brand appealing are few causes for the popularity of e-marketing companies in India.

Figure 1. Overall internet users

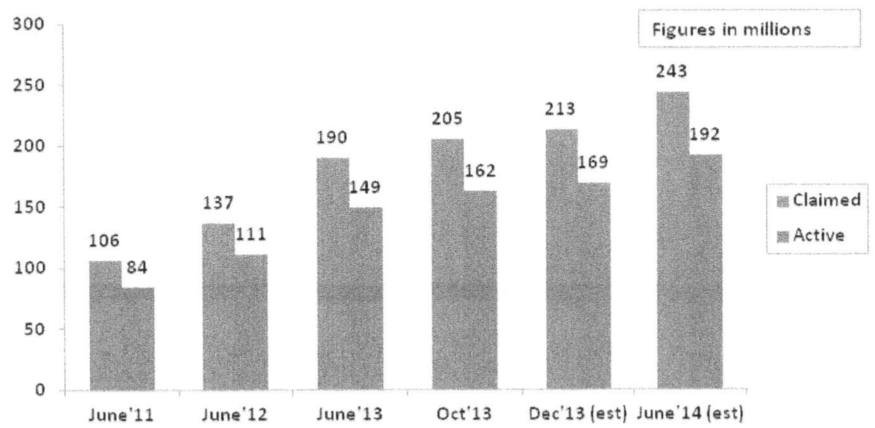

Figure 2. Rural internet users

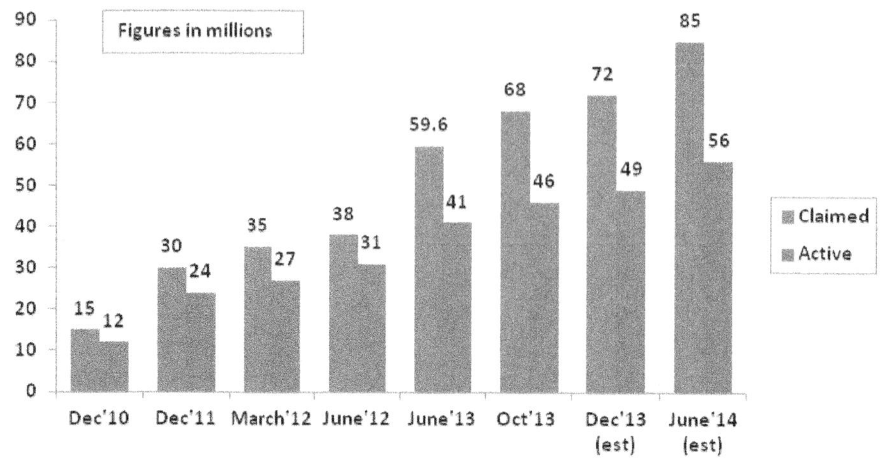

- Extremely user friendly web page with many lucidly written information about the products the company is offering with price comparison meter, flexible mode of receiving the consignment, help line no to contact the customer care executive in case of any difficulty during placing of the order, wish list link to create a data base of the consumer's about the various category of the product what currently he/she doesn't want to buy, rather buy during another occasion or any time he/she feels fit to the buying situation.

E-Marketing Success Basically Rest on Four Pillars of Online Science

- **Technology:** Many e-marketing companies are using latest technologies like enterprise java, Microsoft technologies to keep their websites user friendly and free from any kind of technical shutdown.

Figure 3. Mobile internet users

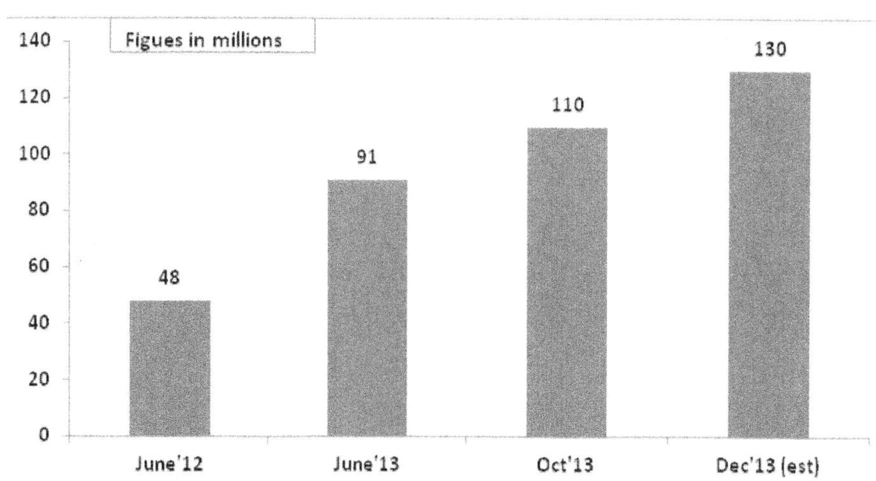

Figure 4. Frequency of access in urban India

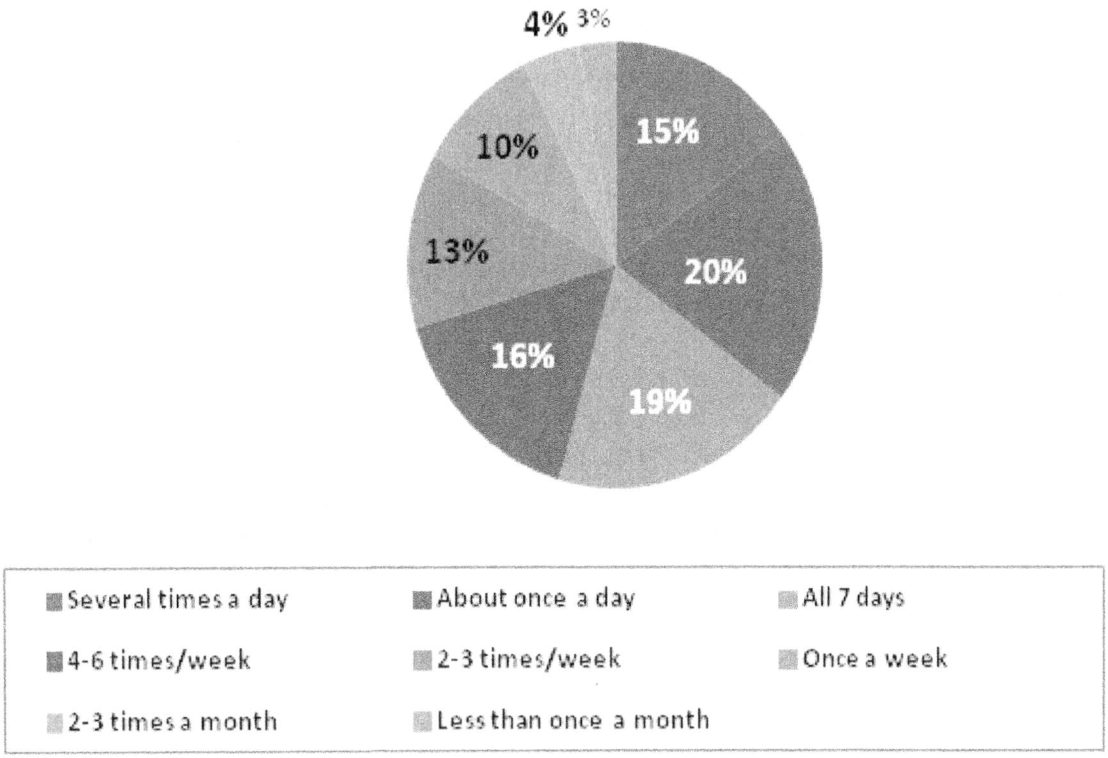

Figure 5. Points of access in rural India

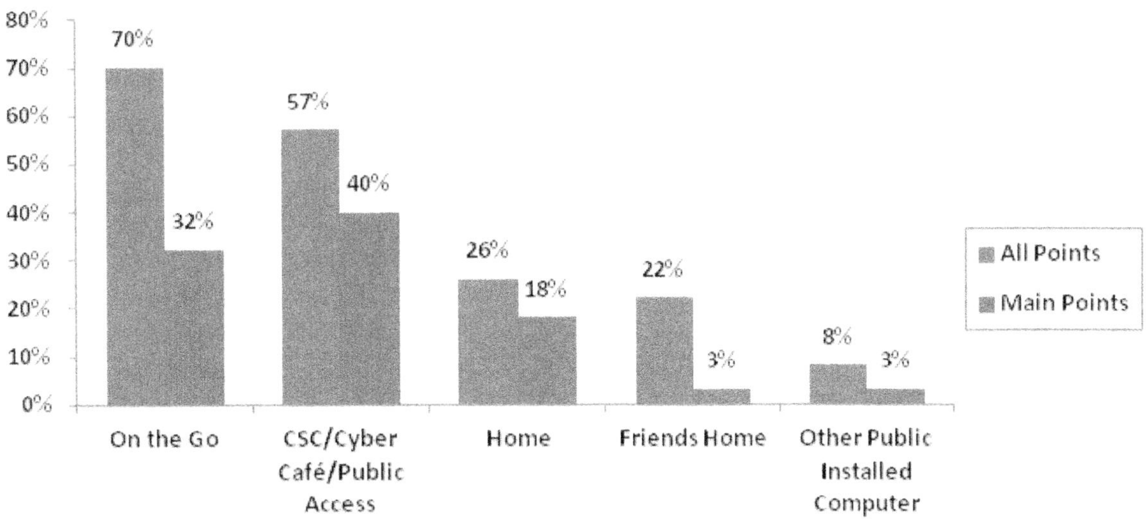

- **Payment:** Indian consumers are highly price sensitive in nature. The rising rate of cyber crimes prevents them to use their plastic cards like debit cards/credit cards. To encourage consumers to shop more on online mode many e-marketing companies in India are offering one of the most popular and convenient option of payment i.e. COD(CASH ON DELIVERY), where consumer have to pay the amount against the consignment after the delivery of the product at their door step.
- **Logistics:** Logistics solution in recent years have gone to that level where consumer is the ultimate decision maker to advice the company about the date and time of the consignment he/she wish to take. Such kind of arrangement of delivery can only be possible with a committed vendor who understands the speed of logistics in the modern market.
- **Marketing:** Today in the competitive world where majority of the buyers still prefer to shop traditionally, online companies have left no stone unturned to make their venture a successful one by adopting many consumer friendly marketing plan like continuous bombardment of information, latest sales promotional schemes of the products, easy search of their websites, hassle free transaction, developing an excellent relationship with the consumers by sending the latest information about any new launch. Besides that tie up with Google, social platforms like twitter, Face book are also few marketing tools that e-marketing companies are adopting looking at to the new generation buyers' presence in those social networks. Today Face book has been used as more a marketing platform than a social chatting platform.

Several Norms of Internet Marketing

Online shopping is one of the new modes of shopping for Indian buyers. Still many consumers prefer to buy through offline mode; hence promoting business through online is a gigantic task in India. To make the online shopping more popular, friendly and effective, few norms should be practiced by the e-marketing companies (Ohmae, 1999):

- Design a user friendly web page with lucidly described products and services which may create an impact in the consumer's mind and tempt to buy the same.
- Clarity in expression and visual aids combination will create more favorable situation of buying for the consumer. Technically embedded products should narrate properly to avoid any kind of misunderstanding and confusion in the consumer's mind.
- Continuous flow of consultancy services through the shopping guide and feedback from the existing consumers may help the company to increase their data base.
- Easy and convenient mode of payment like Cash on delivery should be adopted to win the consumer's faith and confidence. This kind of arrangement motivates the consumer to repeat the purchase in the other categories also.
- Company should adopt the hassle free mode of return and refund policy in case of any defective products and dislike of the product by the consumers.
- Product transit should be made through a effective SCM. Committed vendors and courier service companies should be empanelled for the same and allow customer to receive the product according to their own convenience. An Indian e-marketing company www.exictinglives.com is of-

fering a consumer based delivery service, where consumers are free to take their consignments according to the date and time they have mentioned in the ordered section of the company's web page.

- Finest quality of after sales service, where consumer can get information starting from product availability to product description, discount if any, refund policy, any feedback etc.

Consumer's Norms While Considering an E-Marketing Company

Consumer's need and want differs due to demographical differences such as age, income, education, gender, race etc. Hence e- marketing company should design their web page in such a manner that it will fulfill the need of individual consumer. Consumer should understand the interpretation of internet use in the country and the changing life style of the consumer in terms of richer, easier and faster. As online transaction is a technology based operation, hence all the functions of the operation should be easier and consumer friendly in nature. Young Indian consumers with high income base should be focused by the e-marketing companies to popularize the trend of online shopping (Siegel, 2000). Online mode of shopping vested the power to consumer of making final decision about the transaction. More no of the consumers who still buy their products through off line mode should make aware about the growing trends and its benefits by the e-marketing companies. India still lives in village. Hence e-marketing companies should not forget about the highly untapped and unexplored rural market in India. After the successful creation of the consumer's database by the e-marketing companies, it should be managed properly in terms of individual consumer's need and want. Understanding the expectation of the young consumers: Today young consumers in India buy books to jewellery from the e-marketing companies. Hence e-marketing companies should try to bridge the gap of consumer's expectation and the category of the merchandise. Quality is another parameter to justify the expectation of the consumer. Effective communication of the product/service: Any product/service offered by the e-marketing company should passed through the stringent norms of quality parameters, guaranteed promise of result, refund and replacement in case of any defect, zero defect delivery and a consumer friendly after sales service. These norms should communicate to the potential buyers through a proper medium of channel. Delivering the stated promise fulfilling the promise and commitment increase the credibility of the company in the society. Promise is a social yardstick and company should maintain the same to create the confidence in the consumer's mind (Siegel, 2000).

Barriers in Online Marketing

Few barriers are also observed in the recent past which should be addressed by the company time to time. Getting difficult in a business is not a new preposition, but company should learn every time from any kind of loop holes which occurred in the business (Quelch and Klein, 1996). Technology is not a suitable title for every customer to engage in shopping. PCs usage are not too high in India, Consumers buying more laptop, tablets and Smart phones for their official and social purposes, not for e-commerce transaction. Due to virtual mode of transaction, sometime company unable to handle the query of the consumers about the product they ask. Mismatch in between the delivery schedule of the consignment and consumer's availability in their home. Due to this reason many consignments have been return back to the e-marketing companies' leads to loss of the company in terms of revenue generation (Press releases, 2013). Difficulty in returning back the defective products by the consumers to the companies as many does not have a provision of reverse courier. Few categories such as white

Table 2. Indian companies offering services

Categories	List of the companies
Ticket, Holiday and Hotel Booking	MakeMy Trip, IRCTC, Cleartrip, Yatra, redBus, TravelGuru
Online financial services	ICICI direct, Bank Baazar, Policy Bazaar, Sharekhan
Online Classified	Quikr, 99 acrea, OLX, MagicBricks, Simply Merry, Bharatmatrimony, Timesjobs, Naukari
Food, Entertainment	FoodPanda, Zomato, Bookmyshow

goods, furniture, jewellery items have been limited to transaction due to their expensive nature and practice to examine and verify those product's quality and authenticity before buying. Word of mouth spread is extremely low in India about the success of e-commerce transaction. Consumers are avoiding all the promotional materials provided by the e-marketing companies. Today Indian law protected the consumer by bringing a law where the consumer is fully free to select which promotional messages he/she wants to receive and which he/she does not want to see or receive (ComScore report, 2013). There are few successful journeys of Indian e-marketing companies.

Table 3. E-marketing companies in India (2013)

Name of the e-marketing company	Rank in 2013
Mobile Phones	1st
Clothing	2nd
PCs and Tablets	3rd
Home and Kitchen	4th
Books	5th
Shoes	6th
Sporting goods	7th
Watches	8th
Beauty care products	9th
Jewellery	10th

Changing Shopping Trends in India

E-marketing trend changes gradually both in product as well as service industries. Many service institutions today focus more on online transaction of their services for better and easy mode of transfer of their services to the consumers. Few service institutions in India are pushing their service brands more aggressively due to consumer's preference and growing popularity of their services and have been designed uniquely to offer the same in a suitable way, according to the consumer's convenient approach.

Benefits from the E-Marketing Model of Business

Many benefits are currently reflecting in the Indian market due to e-marketing ventures and its rapid growth in Indian market. E-marketing is a cheaper mode of transaction for the consumer other than the traditional mode of transaction. It also helps to the companies to get a wider audience who can be their prospect buyers in the near future. Revenue pools of many e-marketing companies are increasing steadily due to the increase of online community as well as the online shoppers in the country.

There will be no geographical barrier to do a business through online. Indian buyers do not prefer a particular type of seller in the market place. Hence any global marketer can be added in to the database of the consumer's prefer destination to buy a product of their choice. Easy mode of payment option creates the whole online story successful in the Indian market. The mode can be fastest one or wait for arrival model according to the consumer's wish. Many kinds of tips, advice and other general content in the web page add value and satisfaction to the consumer's purchase. This kind of support from the company helps the consumer to retain the name of the concerned web page and tempt to purchase the products repeatedly. Providing right kind of the product according to the consumer's wish improve the credibility of the e-marketing companies in the society. Research before buying the products, taking the help of the reference groups before taking a final decision about the purchase of the product may considered by a consumer and final short listing of the company can possible due to the worth of the company in the market.

CONCLUSION

E-marketing may be a fresh concept to the traditional buyers in India, but the concept is gaining ground among the new generation buyers from Indian market. The actual flavor of online marketing rests on think and decide model, transaction can be done immediately or can be postponed to further period as per the need of the consumer, easy mode of payment, less interaction from the sales force and more genuine and confidence of the company's web site and reorder process of the same product, if the consumer unable to receive the same due to his/her tight schedule. Around 1,000 plus online companies are offering their products/services to Indian consumers' ranges from vegetables to gold products. In near future India will be a hub for the e-marketing companies.

Managerial Implications

Future of e-marketing companies in India is bringing a digital revolution in Indian market. Due to the growing popularity of much verse of gadgets in India, the future of the online marketing is highly net worth. Search engine optimization is a key future and will remain dominant in the e-marketing transaction. Pay per click (PPC) method is also a popular tool which supports the future of the e-marketing companies. Within a time span of one decade many Indian e-marketing companies have attained the level of e-bay or Amazon range of success from the Indian market.

REFERENCES

Berryman, K., Harrington, L., Layton-Rodin, D., & Rerolle, V. (1998). Electronic commerce: Three emerging strategies. *The McKinsey Quarterly*, *1*, 152–159.

Chaffey, D., Mayer, R., Johnston, K., & Ellis-Chadwick, F. (2006). *Internet marketing: Strategy, implementation and practice* (3rd ed.). Harlow, UK: Financial Times/Prentice Hall.

ComScore Report. (2013). *India is now world's third largest internet used after US, China*. Retrieved from www.digitsmith.com

Ohmae, K. (1999). *The borderless world: Power and strategy in the interlinked economy*. New York: Harper Business.

Press Releases. (2013). *Internet users in India crosses 200 million mark*. Retrieved from www.iamai.in

Quelch, J., & Klein, L. (1996, Spring). The internet and international marketing. *Sloan Management Review*, 61–75.

Siegel, D. (2000). Futurize Your Enterprise. In *Business strategy in the age of the e-customer*. New York: John Wiley.

KEY TERMS AND DEFINITIONS

Anticipation: What consumer really wants to buy through online may be an absolute anticipation. Hence companies should spend maximum quality time behind the consumers to know their exact need and the bifurcation of purchase in between online and off line. For example, consumers across the globe avoid white goods purchase, gold product purchase, furniture purchase through online.

Definition of E-Marketing: In general speaking, the marketing of products or services over the internet is called as E-marketing. It can also be defined as an act of achieving all the well designed marketing objectives through the mode of any kind of electronics devices.

Features of E-Marketing: According to Smith and Chaffey (2001), e-marketing can be achieved through the following objectives.

Identify: Consumers must know the universal application of the internet and its need in the current business context.

Satisfy: Customer satisfaction is the path way to success. Hence seam less flow of services from every quarter of the company should provide to the consumers before as well as after purchase of the product.

Chapter 13
Tourism Promotion through Web

Nilanjan Ray
Royal Thimphu College, Bhutan

Dillip Kumar Das
Sikkim Central University, India

Somnath Chaudhuri
Royal Thimphu College, Bhutan

ABSTRACT

This chapter studies the application of information technology in tourism promotion, particularly through Internet. In the context of tourism management, this chapter penetrates different usage of Web technology to disseminate maximum level of information for tourism promotion. This chapter is designed to determine the conditions of Websites as well as application of different application of Web technology like Virtual Reality (VR), CRS, etc. used in tourism promotion to identify the obstacles faced in this type of promotion via Web. The chapter adopts a survey from 200 respondents. Collected data is analyzed through different statistical tools like correlation analysis, simple average method, and Cronbach Alfa for reliability of the data. The results show that tourism promotion through the Web helps to increase competition as well as tourism demand if Web design helps to disseminate information about the tourism offers to the tourists' desire. Both sexes consider the Website design as a means helps to ensure the information veracity of tourism offers. The chapter recommends continuing development of the role of tourism promotion through the Internet in spreading information about tourism offers, so as to achieve the greatest possible benefits. This study also indicates how to develop and upgrade Web for promotion of tourism information and offer better tourism service excellence, while promoting less popular tourist spots.

DOI: 10.4018/978-1-4666-6232-2.ch013

INTRODUCTION

Tourism is one of the fastest growing industries. Tourism has emerged as a new mantra for alternative economic development. Tourism concept has been tested and already applied for alternative development of a nation and proved to give positive result. As per World Tourism Council tourism is contributing around 10% to the world wide GDP projected to rise nearly 11% by 2014. Increase in supply of information to the tourists is the biggest advantage of information technology in the tourism industry. Information Technology breaks the geographical boundaries so it is shared to the global audiences. Information Technology integrates between tourism product and requirement of the tourists. Due to changes in tourists or visitors behavior, the tourism market is becoming more segmented with each potential tourist belonging to a number of market segments. Tourist operators need to be aware of these changes and be equipped to respond or better still, take a proactive approach .Technological revolution during1990s brought with it new opportunities and challenges for the tourism industries. Technology has become fundamental to the ability of the global tourism industry to operate effectively and competitively. Information technology is being rapidly diffused throughout the tourism industry and that no player will escape from information technologies impacts. These technological innovations started in the 1970s when the main airlines set up CRSs (Computerized Reservation Systems), with the strategic aim of building a global distribution network for their products. Connecting travel agencies to the CRSs set off a process of distribution automation involving an ever-increasing number of tour operators, carriers, and car hire firms, individual hotels, hotel chains, and other hospitality firms.

SURVEY OF EXISTING LITERATURE

Tourism is now one of the fastest growing smokeless industries. It is also an interdisciplinary sector. A more technical definition of tourism was provided by Prof. Hunziker and Kraf (1942), tourism is the totality of the relationship and phenomena arising from the travel and the stay of strangers, provided that the stay does not imply the establishment of the permanent residence and is not connected with a remunerated activity. Tourism is a hybrid industry since even though it is dominated by the provision of information; essentially it is about a physical product Driver J. (1999). Technology behind the modern information society, particularly by the way of the Internet, has bought about four key changes for the way in which business is conducted Cheng C. and Piccoli G.(2002). These changes which apply equally to the tourism sector. The ability to turn ideas into marketable innovation for a wide range of customer, with reduced buyer search costs and costs of access to market, Increased speed to market and access to new product offerings via. Internet, Changed processes and sharing of information within and between organizations, a shift in the balance of power between suppliers and customers due to the increased availability of information.

In the area of tourism, tourist information search has mainly focused on the uses of various information sources Gitelson, R.J., and Perdue (1987), Chervenak, L (1993). The tourism industry can be seen as one of the first business sectors where business functions are almost exclusively using information and communication technology Galloway, L, et al. (2004). Information mechanism leads to the establishment of specific product distribution. Online technologies within the tourism industry have significantly impacted on communications, transactions and relationships between the various industry operators and with the customer, as well as between regulators and operators .The Internet provides many advantages in the tourism industry,. Technology behind the modern information society, particularly by way of the Internet, has bought about four key changes for the way in which business is conducted Cheng C. and Piccoli G. (2002).

THEORETICAL FRAMEWORK

Impact of IT in tourism is very vital. For instance, a guide requires historical and cultural information about the destinations, tour agency requires information on transformation, reservations, accommodation in Hotel, and for marketing, a tourist requires information from Cell Phone Application (SMS), Internet, Wireless (Wi-Fi), VOIP, GPS, GIS, Digital Radio, On demand application and so on. Role of Information Technology in tourism industry cannot be underestimated because it has vital contributions. Once the tourism information or data is in the system (computer) this may be transmitted to the proposed tourists through different channels viz. FAX, GPS, Website etc. For instance, The Orissa Tourism Website was refurbished to highlight the Tourism products of the State which attracted considerable cyber- visitors. First time Orissa Tourism in association with NIC has Web cast the programmes of the Mukteswar Dance Festival. The objective of this Web cast was to market Orissa in general and the cultural heritage of Orissa in particular through the use of Internet amongst the Cyber Savvy visitors. According to Ray et al. (2011) Geospatial Information Technology (GIT) helps to identify the boundaries of the proposed tourism attraction and destination location around the surrounding communities. It also helps to identify the auxiliary utilities available in the destination .it also helps in Promoting utilization, development, and preservation of the land. GIS is an information system that provides functions including visual presentation about the tourism destination, advanced analyses, etc., of digital geospatial information by processing it in an integrated manner on electronic maps of the tourist site. Electronic tourism distribution channels dictate the choice of product as the difference between products becomes secondary to the easiness of getting an entire transaction completed. CRM plays a vital role in tourism sector which turns prospects into repeat customers. It also helps regarding flexibility of information rendering about travel, lodging, fooding and trip management. Apart from CRM, public relation cell communicates with travel agents, corporate houses, national and international airlines. Tourism technology especially that related to Web 2.0 plays a vital role in marketing and promoting tourist destinations. Web 2.0 has resulted in an explosive increase of not only travel-related content, but also applications and technology for effective destination marketing. It also usefulness in customer relationship management (CRM) through virtual communities where social ties between customer and DMOs can be enhanced. PR cell may be entrusted with advertisements and develop informative Web sites about the destination. Operation includes reservation and guest management, financial management (e-banking, budget vs. actual), sales and catering, cleaning, property management, maintenance, procurement. Technological innovation and the growth of the Internet as an electronic medium have led to the emergence of online travel distribution channels. The study verifies the practices that frequently appear in relationship marketing process within online operations or whether their Internet presence mainly depends on the basic actions of ‘supplying information’ and ‘reservations’. Also, it investigates the effects of e-CRM system on customer loyalty and satisfaction as well as the impact of relationship marketing practices to customer retention and acquisition. They have understood the importance of using electronic channels instead of traditional ones to implement their marketing strategies. Thus, e-CRM system has assisted hotel business to manage more effectively their reservations and serve their customers as fast and as effective as possible. They did not seem to apply many of the relationship marketing strategies to emphasize customer retention and continual satisfaction because of difficulties in staff training (Samanta 2011).

RESEARCH HYPOTHESIS

H_0 = The tourism promotion through Web does not help to disseminate the tourism information.

H_0= The tourism promotion through Web does not increase prices of tourism offers.

H_0 = The tourism market remains fixed with the application of Web technology

ANALYSIS AND DISCUSSIONS

$$\chi 2 = \sum_{i=1}^{k} \frac{(Oi - Ei)^2}{Ei},$$

Calculated value of $\chi 2$ is 19.Using the $\chi 2$ -Test goodness of fit ascertains whether there is an existence of relation between Web and dissemination of the tourism information. The critical value of the $\chi 2$ at 0.01 level of significance with 3(k-1) the table value of d.f. is $\chi 2$=11.345. Therefore, the estimated value of $\chi 2$ is greater than the critical value (tabulated); therefore, null hypothesis is rejected. Virtual Learning Environments (VLEs) helps to support their class teaching, distribute notes and link to resources, and stimulate discussion and facilitating marking and course administration. E-Learning is also utilized as an essential feature of training delivery of guide, but the application of such system and adoption differ one company to another. It has been accepted as a means of increasing skills and knowledge, and is being integrated into their training strategy along with other methods of delivering training. Reservation is a core function of tourism. Now days today, the user has direct access to essential travel information and can find further information in all CRSs about trade shows, visa regulations, particular events etc. Passenger Name Record (PNR) or Guest Name Record (GNR) is created for each passenger or each group of passengers at the time of reservation. These records contain all services-related customer information. Multimedia plays a vital role in tourism offline information, which is unilaterally exposed to travelers, the Web allows people from around the world to virtually interact with a destination through three-dimensional (3D) virtual tours (2007, 2001) [23, 5]. Mobile and Wi-Fi technology are most interesting tools. Travelers can retrieve tour related data from GSM, WAP, and GPRS. In addition, mobile services now enable travelers to book hotel rooms and air-tickets, car rentals, retrieve information about transportation schedules, travel guides for destinations, and dining guides.

Table 1. $H_{0=}$ The tourism promotion through Web does not help to disseminate the tourism information

Parameters	Expected Frequency	Observed Frequency
Strongly Agree	50	70
Disagree	50	35
Strongly disagree	50	60
Neither agree nor disagree	50	35

$$\chi 2 = \sum_{i=1}^{k} \frac{(Oi - Ei)^2}{Ei},$$

Calculated value of $\chi 2$ is 33 Using the $\chi 2$ -Test goodness of fit proves that Web has a positive impact to increase the price of the tourism prod-

Table 2. $H_{0=}$ The tourism promotion through Web does not increase prices of tourism offers

Parameters	Expected Frequency	Observed Frequency
Strongly Agree	50	75
Disagree	50	60
Strongly disagree	50	45
Neither agree nor disagree	50	20

ucts. The critical value of the $\chi2$ at 0.01 level of significance with 3(k-1) the table value of d.f. is x^2=11.345.Therefore, the estimated value of $\chi2$ is greater than the critical value (tabulated), therefore, null hypothesis is rejected. Web is the use of information and communications technologies in all activities of a firm both internally and in relation to its outside partners. The tourism industry consists of many companies dabbling in various activities, ranging from tour operators to cafes and restaurants. The companies include SMEs and the types of enterprises that comprise the tourism industry are: (1) tour operators (2) travel agents (3) tourist guide services (4) airlines (5) transportation (6) restaurants and cafes (7) hotels and guesthouses (8) museums and historical sites and buildings (9) nature reserve services (10) tourism education and training institutions; (11) local tourist offices. Within the discourse on the information society and the e-economy, ICTs are seen as major tools with the potential to fundamentally change business behavior and company strategies. The Internet has provided a new business environment in which virtual business can be conducted. The adoption of ICT in the tourism industry can provide detailed up-to-date information on the availability and prices (Islam S, 2012).

Table 3. $H_{0=}$ The tourism market remains fixed with the application of Web technology

Parameters	Expected Frequency	Observed Frequency
Strongly Agree	50	49
Disagree	50	35
Strongly disagree	50	68
Neither agree nor disagree	50	48

$$\chi2 = \sum_{i=1}^{k} \frac{(Oi - Ei)^2}{Ei},$$

Calculated value of $\chi2$ is 11.08

Using the $\chi2$ -Test goodness of fit it has proved that the statement of null hypothesis is incorrect.

The critical value of the $\chi2$ at 0.01 level of significance with 3(k-1) the table value of d.f. is x^2=11.345.Therefore, the estimated value of $\chi2$ is greater than the critical value (tabulated); therefore, null hypothesis is rejected. E-business in the tourism sector is important because it has the potential of improving the productivity of firms operations. The significance of the responses to marketing communications is that tourism firms seem to understand that the Internet is a useful marketing communication tool, integral to getting them to establish a global presence.

POLICY IMPLICATIONS

Transportation is a vital key factor of tourism sector. Now a day's different mode of transportation vouches are well equipped with good communication equipment. Aviation takes help of modern technology information about weather, altitude, air traffic control. In-flight entertainment like videos, movies, video games. Other than these services CSR helps fare quote and ticketing, internal administration, agent commission, invoicing, accounting, customer and quota management increasingly depend on this particular system. The core functions which a PMS can handle are reservations, front office operations, some back office operations and some managerial functions. A PMS is commonly used for handling the accounting functions of the various departments in a Hotel. With the ever increasing need to use the net, Tourism has entered a new era. Virtual travel has gained popularity and a tourist if he wishes can use the various tools and Internet and sit at the comfort of his office or home and do a virtual travel. Earlier there used to armchair travelogue creators who used to design the show from articles and hearsays. But now travel writing has been simplified just because there is a plethora of information in CD's, brochures and on the net. There are even virtual travel agencies on the net which offers a tour through its gallery and offers a great deal of information. Gone are the days when a guide used to take travelers for ride narrating several cock and bull stories and feeding the customers with false information. Virtual travelers are more informed and many of them do not even need an introduction to a destination which they plan to visit. For the last 5-6 years with the massive popularity of the social networking sites like, google+, twitter, LinkedIn etc. and none other than face book, most of the travel agencies are trying to promote themselves through these popular Websites. Though, all most all the travel agencies have their personal Websites, then also they are using these social networking sites as a tool for promotion; as it's easy to reach more number of people just by creating a single profile and that too free of cost. Promotion of less popular tourist spots can be done through these sites. On the other hand, when we are discussing about virtual tour that too is possible in these Websites. People who are not physically fit to hike or trek in hilly remote regions, they can enjoy and feel the charm of those places by going through the snapshots or videos taken and uploaded by their virtual friends in these popular social networking sites.

So, information technology can be used not only for operational purposes, but also for tactical and strategic management. As a result tourism sector is empowered to communicate directly and more efficiently with prospective travelers and suppliers as well as to achieve competitive advantage. Information Technology is a combination of hard ware and software. Hardware and software include keyboard, mouse, touch screen, optical bar code, etc. Software application includes both system and application of software. Operating systems are DOS, Windows98, Novell Netware and UNIX becoming more user-friendly and less proprietary allowing different software packages to be used on different traveling operating system. Application software used in tourism includes both generic business software such as spreadsheet, database, desktop publishing etc. Airline Sector is a part of Tourism sector. This sector (airline) is a heavy user of information technology. CRS (Computerized Reservation System) is one of them. Computer reservations system (CRS) is a computerized system used to store and retrieve information and conduct transactions related to air travel. Originally designed and operated by airlines, CRSs were later extended for the use of travel agents; major CRS operations that book and sell tickets for multiple airlines are known as global distribution systems (GDS). CRS helps to store information of schedule, travel routes, fares, fare rules, ticketing, passenger's seat plan etc. Most vital application of information technology used by travel agencies. Amadeus is one of the Computerized Reservation software which provides customer management solutions in aviation sector like Solutions Get rid of paper tickets and quickly interline with more than 100 airlines, Fares and Availability Management, fast, flexible and competitive travel solutions, Revenue, Secures revenue with Amadeus' portfolio of automated integrity tools, Feed Up-to-date PNR information direct link to data warehouse. They may be used to run other varieties updated software applications like TPS (Travel Policy Software) which helps Agent Details, Agent Pad, Renewals, Agent Returns - Manual from pads and electronic transfer, Agent Invoicing, Premium Calculation, Annual Renewals - Direct Sales or by Agent, tour Operators Returns, Import/Export Data E-mail and Fax Facilities, FAS (Fare Auditing Software). They often use back office software for their accounting process, tracking their commission, customer information for marketing purpose. These special Web application tools and software packages are gaining popularity in the tourism industry to maintain data in a secured but fast accessible database. Now it's much easier for the travel agencies to maintain an organized database, generating reports, creating balance sheets and taking proper strategic plans just on a click. At the same time, it becomes easy for the policy makers to take some strategic decisions very fast, as all the reports and analysis are produced by these software tools. New Policies and limitations including the privacy and security issues by the Government have significant effect on the Internet and its potential development. This enforces the Internet providers to consider on the ethical matters and the usage of personal data stored within the networks. For the fullest utilization of the commercial potential of e-commerce and Internet to be exploited by the tourism industry and its consumers, several issues have to be taken into consideration which includes an increase of security of transmissions, copyright issues, reduction of confusion and dissatisfaction among users, establishment of pricing structures for information distribution and reservations, enhancement of the standardization of information and reservation procedures. Credibility and accountability of the information needs to be secured and equal access for smaller and larger partners should be developed. In the case of Web marketing .It is anticipated that eventually GDS's will take advantage of the openness of the World Wide Web (WWW) and develop suitable interfaces for consumers and the industry. Sabre has already launched Travelocity, an electronic travel agency, while other GDS's have announced similar actions or cooperation's with travel providers on the Internet. These include World span with Expedia and Amadeus with the Internet Travel Network. IT and the Internet have transformed distribution of the tourism product to form an electronic marketplace where access to information is instantly achievable. Principals and consumers continue to experience unprecedented interactivity. The dramatic ongoing development of the Internet has resulted in the re-engineering of the entire production and distribution process for tourism products. As a consequence of this technological explosion, the packaging of tourism is becoming much more individualistic, leading inevitably to a certain degree of channel disintermediation, a process that will offer new opportunities and threats to all tourism partners.

CONCLUSION

The discussed study showed that the tourism promotion through the Web helps to increase competition as well as tourism demand if Web design helps to disseminate information about the tourism offers to the tourists' desire. Less popular tourist spots can be promoted to limelight through the Web information services. Both sexes consider that the Website design as a means helps to ensure the information veracity of tourism offers. Recommendation on continuing development of the role of tourism promotion through the Internet in spreading information about the tourism offers, so as to achieve the greatest possible benefits. So, in a nutshell we can conclude that the Web service can be used as one of the most of important tool for promoting tourism as a whole by minimizing the manual work of the tourism companies involved as well as the tourists, sharing information among the tourists, promoting less popular tourist spots and maintaining relevant data in a much secured but easy accessible way. At the same time quenching the thirst of travelling for some tourists by providing the virtual tour service, though the social networking sites are playing a vital role in this field but more involvement of virtual tour companies are required.

REFERENCES

Bernstein, J., & Awe, S. (1999). "Wired travelers": Travel and tourism Web sites. *RSR. Reference Services Review*, *27*(Iss: 4), 364–375. doi:10.1108/00907329910303536

Buhalis, D. (1998). Strategic use of information technologies in the tourism industry. *Tourism Management*, *19*(5), 409–421. doi:10.1016/S0261-5177(98)00038-7

Cederle A., (2005): The process began in the 1970s with Sabre and Apollo, two CRSs run by American Airlines and United Airlines, respectively.

Cheng, C., & Piccoli, G. (2002). Web-Based Training in the Hospitality Industry: A Conceptual Definition, Taxonomy and Preliminary Investigation. *International Journal of Hospitality Information Technology*, *2*(2), 19–33. doi:10.3727/153373402803617737

Chervenak, L. (1993). Hotel Technology at the start of the New Millennium. *Hospitality Research Journal.*, *17*(1), 113–120. doi:10.1177/109634809301700110

Cho, Y., & Fesenmaier, D. R. (2001). A new paradigm for tourism and electronic commerce: Experience marketing using the virtual tour. In E. Laws, & D. Buhalis (Eds.), *tourism distribution channels: practices, issues and transformation* (pp. 351–370). Thomson.

Clayton, T., & Criscuolo, C. 2002, *Electronic commerce and business change*, National Statistics, viewed 16 April 2005, http://www.statistics.gov.uk/cci/article.asp?ID=139>

Collins, C., Buhalis, D., & Peters, M. (2003). Enhancing SMTEs' Business Performance Through the Internet and U-learning Platforms. *Education + Training*, *45*(8/9), 483–494. doi:10.1108/00400910310508874

Daniele, R., & Frew, A. (2005). Using Concept Maps to Examine Business Models and Drivers of Competitive Advantage for Travel eMediaries. In A. Frew (Ed.), *Information and Communication Technologies in Tourism 2005* (pp. 497–507). Vienna: Springer. doi:10.1007/3-211-27283-6_45

Davin, K. (1997). Effects of Computer Support on Group Decisions. *Journal of Hospitality & Tourism Research (Washington, D.C.)*, *21*(2), 44–57. doi:10.1177/109634809702100204

Dogac, A., Kabak, Y., Laleci, G., Sinir, S., Yildiz, A., Kirbas, S., & Gurcan, Y. (2004). Semantically enriched web services for the travel industry. *SIGMOD Record*, *33*(3), 21–27. doi:10.1145/1031570.1031575

Driver, J. (1999). Developments in Airline Marketing Practice [enhancing the participatory role of travelers and exploiting their collective intelligence.]. *Journal of Marketing Practice: Applied Marketing Science*, *5*(5), 134–150. doi:10.1108/EUM0000000004571

Fesenmaier, D. R., Vogt, C. A., & Stewart, W. P. (1993). Investigating the influence of welcome center information on travel behavior. *Journal of Travel Research*, *31*(3), 47–52. doi:10.1177/004728759303100308

Fodor, O., & Werthner, H. (2005). Harmonise: A step toward an interoperable tourism Marketplace. *International Journal of Electronic Commerce*, *9*(2), 11–39.

Galloway, L., Mochrie, R., & Deakins, D. (2004). ICT-enabled collectivity as a positive Rural business strategy. *International Journal of Entrepreneurial Behaviour And Research*, *10*(4), 247–259. doi:10.1108/13552550410544213

Garzotto, F., Paolini, P., Speroni, M., & Pröll, B. Retschitzegger, Schwinger, W 2004, *'Ubiquitous access to cultural tourism portals', paper presented to Database and Expert Systems Applications*, 15th International Workshop on (DEXA'04), Zaragoza, Spain, August 30 - September 03, 2004.

Gascó-Hernández & T. Torres-Coronas (Ed.), *Information communication technologies and city.*

Gitelson, R. J., & Perdue, R. R. (1987). Evaluating the role of state welcome centers in disseminating travel related information in North Carolina. *Journal of Travel Research*, *25*(4), 15–19. doi:10.1177/004728758702500403

ICT & Tourism USAID from the American People,, Arusha, Tanzania Information Science Reference. *International Journal of Knowledge and Learning, 3*(6), 628-648. doi:10.1504/IJKL.2007.016837

In, M., & Fesenmaier, D. R. (1994). Traveler use of visitor information centers: Implications for development in Illinois. *Journal of Travel Research, 33*(1), 44–50. doi:10.1177/004728759403300106

Islam, S. (2012), E-Business- A Tool to Enhance Tourism Industry: A Study from Bangladesh, ASA University Review, Vol.6, No.1 Jan-Jun 2012

IT and Internet's Impact on Tourism and Hospitality Industry. Implementations of technologies for Hilton Hotels <http://www.ivoryresearch.com/sample24.php> online document [Accessed 2nd November 2010]

Jafar Jafari. (2003). *Encyclopedia of Tourism* (p. 308).

Jakkilinki, R., Georgievski, M., & Sharda, N. (2007). Connecting Destinations with an Ontology-Based e-Tourism Planner. In M. Sigala, L. Mich, & J. Murphy (Eds). Information and Communication Technologies in Tourism 2007, (pp. 21-32), Springer-Verlag Wien.

John A. Quelch and Lisa R. Klein. April 15, 1996. Is the internet just another marketing channel like direct mail or home shopping?

Kim, E., Nam, D., & Stimpert, J. L. (2004). The Applicability of Porter's Generic Strategies in the Digital Age: Assumptions, Conjectures and Suggestions. *Journal of Management, 30*(5), 569–589. doi:10.1016/j.jm.2003.12.001

Klein, S. (2002). Web impact on the distribution structure for flight tickets. In K. W. Wöber, A. J. Frew, & M. Hitz (Eds.), *Information and Communication Technologies in Tourism 2002* (pp. 219–228). New York: Springer-Verlag Wien. doi:10.1007/978-3-7091-6132-6_22

Lashley, *C. and* Rowson, *B (*2005*)* Getting IT Right: Exploring information technology in the hospitality curriculum, *International Journal of Contemporary* vol 17, no 1, pp 94-105. *marketing: Digital opportunities for cities around the world* (pp. 220 – 244). Hershey, PA:

Poon, A. (1993). *Tourism, Technology and Competitive Strategies, CAB International: Wallingford; relationship, Springer Computer Science.* Vienna, Austria: Springer.

Ray, N., et al. (2011). A Study on Application of Information Technology on Tourism Development. In *Management and Service Science (MASS), International Conference on* (pp. 1-7). IEEE. doi:10.1109/ICMSS.2011.5998707

Ray, N., et al. (2011): Information Technology and Its Impact on Tourism: An Overview. In Khurana, R., Agrawal, R., Debnath, C (Eds) Computing Business Application and Legal Issues ISBN 978-81-7446-936-6 Excel Book Publication Edition 1st. 2011 from IMT Gaziabad, India

Ray N; Das D K (2011): Marketing Practices for Promotion of Rural Tourism: A Study On Kamarpukur, India, *Journal of Business and Economics* ISSN 2155- 7950 Academic Star Publishing Co. May 2011, *2*(5), New York, USA

Samanta, I. (2009). The impact of e-customer relationship marketing in hotel industry. *International Journal of Knowledge and Learning*, *5*(3/4), 333–346. doi:10.1504/IJKL.2009.031228

Samanta, I. (2011). *Digital Culture and è-Tourism: Technologies Applications and Management Approaches IGI Global* (pp. 90–104). Hershey, PA: Information Science Reference.

Sharma, P, Carson, D & DeLacy, T 2000, 'National online tourism policy initiatives

Sheldon, P. J. (1998). *Tourism information technology*. New York: CABI Publishing.

Sigala, M. (2007). Integrating Web 2.0 in e-learning environments: A socio-technical approach.

Sigala, M. (2008). WEB 2.0, social marketing strategies and distribution channels for city destinations:

Stabb, S., & Werthner, H. (2002). Intelligent Systems for Tourism. IEEE Intelligent Systems, November/December, 53-55.Statistics, viewed 16 April 2005

Werthner, H., & Klein, S. (1999). ICT and the changing landscape of global tourism Distribution. *Electronic Markets*, *9*(4), 256–262. doi:10.1080/101967899358941

Wolff, C. (1998a). Microsoft Sees Integration Chaning Face of PMS. *Lodging Hospitality.*, *54*(3), 41.

World Travel and Tourism Council 2004, *Progress and priorities 2004/2005*, World Travel and Tourism Council, viewed 7 March 2005,

KEY TERMS AND DEFINITIONS

ICT: Information and Communication Technologies, it refers to technologies that provide information through telecommunications. ICT and Information Technology (IT) are more or less similar, but ICT focuses primarily on communication technologies. This includes the Internet, wireless networks, cell phones, satellite systems and other communication mediums.

Tourism: Tourism is a social, cultural and economic phenomenon related to the movement of people to places outside their usual place of residence. Tourism comprises the activities of persons travelling to and staying in places outside their usual environment for not more than one consecutive year for leisure, business and other purposes not related to the exercise of an activity remunerated from within the place visited.

Tourist: Someone who travels for pleasure and recreation and exchange of culture.

APPENDIX

Websites Accessed

www.orissatourism.com
www.EzineArticles.com/?expert=Venugopal_C_K
http://www.acrwebsite.org/volumes/display.asp?id=11652

Chapter 14
The Effect of E-Business in B2B Relationships

Irene Samanta
Graduate Technological Education Institute of Piraeus, Greece

Nondas Pitticas
University of the West of Scotland, Greece

ABSTRACT

This chapter examines whether the changes that take place in the global business environment have modulated the way firms do business or whether it is simply transient details that have caused such excitement. Should firms be wary of any proclamations of "new" ways of doing business? Or should they ignore changes of the business environment? Semi-structured in-depth interviews were conducted in 3 focus groups of managers from 3 major firms operating in Greece. In addition, a quantitative research in 29 B2B firms was conducted. The influence of globalization, the intense competition, and new technologies in B2B e-commerce are external factors that raise problems and complexities in the future direction of firms. There is also a gap caused by the lack of an innovation culture between top and lesser management. Businesses are required to modernise their practices to move from their present situation at the level of the second industrial revolution of "old economy" to the third industrial revolution of "new era economy."

INTRODUCTION

According to (Shapiro & Varian,1999) the business environment for most organizations is rarely a stable state. There is no certainty that the future will follow the pattern of the recent past. For B2B companies operating in a low-tech, low-scale environment, adaptation to change may be quite easy, but for a large organization which has to invest heavily for the future, the risks can be enormous (Kanter et al, 1992). The Internet is more than just another sales channel or marketing medium, it is also an entirely new business model. In order for B2B firms to be successful it is therefore essential for them appreciate the sea change the Internet is bringing about in marketing strategy. It soon becomes apparent that B2B e-commerce itself represents an entirely new game plan for the e-marketer to consider (Day & Schoemaker, 2000). The structure and politics of an organiza-

DOI: 10.4018/978-1-4666-6232-2.ch014

tion affect the manner in which it responds to environmental change.

The internal culture of an organization, as (Jones, 1996) states, can greatly affect the way it responds to organizational change. Organizational culture can be shared in a number of ways that include: the way the work is organized and experienced; how authority is exercised and delegated; how people are rewarded, organized and controlled; and the roles and expectations of staff and managers. Employees are the biggest cause of delay in responding to change; it therefore becomes apparent that having the right staff in the right place at the right time is more likely to enable the firm to share in the threats and opportunities which environmental change presents through the Internet. Consequently, every organization can be considered to comprise an internal marketplace where employees engage in exchanges between each other making it possible for the organization to respond to environmental change in a rapid and coordinated manner (Lei, 1991). Business-to-business firms have received widespread attention by adopting an Internet marketing strategy, as it consists of one of the key drivers to face the changes of the business environment, and in building and sustaining an organization's competitive advantage (Barbian, 2000).

Technology provides obvious benefits for organizations, such as the ability to carry out transactions around the clock, and also increase confidence of business partners due to their online transaction ability and enhance relationships (Malhotra, 2001). It can also have a detrimental effect if the appropriate strategy is not applied. B2B Internet usage is growing in popularity for many reasons, ranging from cost savings to gaining benefits in the value within a supply chain. This allows businesses to extend their relationships with customers, suppliers, retailers, brokers, co-producers, employees and shareholders, and achieve a more personalized relationship with them. The development of such personalized relationships is a key goal of marketing, because they tend to be more sustainable (Kalakota & Robinson, 1999).

Recently, the European Information Technology Observatory (EITO) estimated that the value of B2B e-commerce activities for the year 2007 would reach approximately $6.4 trillion US dollars, indicating that a third of all B2B purchases will have been carried out online and B2B markets are expected to dominate the world of online trading. As a result, EITO estimated that transactions would reach $3.4 trillion US dollars by the end of 2007. There is a growing trend for some companies to refuse to transact with companies that do not use Web facilities in their operations, which shows the importance of using Internet facilities in B2B relationships (European Commission, 2000). According to (Narayanan, 2001) there are five marketing strategies that can lead to a sustainable competitive advantage in relation to e-commerce:

- Actively collaborating with supply chain partners
- Extending the company's reach up and down the supply chain
- Changing the supply chain flow path
- Growing revenue
- Transforming capabilities into new business.

Most of these elements involve benefits filtering to the supply chain and are therefore relevant when assessing B2B relationships. The way in which a business adapts to the changes of the business environment and addresses each of these marketing strategies has an impact on its B2B relationships and it is therefore important that this is sufficiently assessed by the organization (Waddell, 2000). These various changes have fundamentally reshaped marketing strategies due to globalization via thc Internet. The present research attempts to verify whether the structure of the business environment has changed because of the new economy. This study also analyses how external and internal factors evolve in Greek markets and, especially, in the areas of B2B relationships.

BACKGROUND

Threats and Opportunities of Globalization

According to (Whipple & Frankel, 2000), globalization can be considered as a process of transformations in the organization of transactions and social relations around the globe, bringing inter-regional flows, activity networks, interactive environment and power. The following types of change describe it adequately: it extends the economic, political and also the social activities across regions, nations or even continents; it supports the substantial connection between different nations and the growing magnitude of flows of trade, culture, investment and movement of population; it quickens the transactions and the processes between nations, since the new technology of communication and transportation makes any transmission of information, goods or people easier and faster every day; it creates an environment where every incident (no matter how significant it may be) may affect other communities elsewhere. The consequences of a local event can be spread to the whole globe, making it clear that the frontiers of every country cannot seclude it from this system of globalization (Parkhe, 1991). According to (Lado et al., 1997) the global business firm operates in more that one country and ensures advantages of research and development, production, distribution, marketing and finances in respect to its expenses and status that the purely domestic competitors do not have. Globalization has affected firms around the world, which have managed impressive reductions in the barriers of trade and have established important agreements to promote the trade of products, services and investment globally. Therefore, a major characteristic of globalization is that it forms an international industrial and financial business structure (Lei, 1991, Lado et al., 1997; Pearce, 1997).

A very interesting statement issued by (UNCTAD 2003) shows the effects of globalization on small- and medium-sized firms. The study estimated that a great number of firms are in jeopardy and will face difficulties of orientation. It reported that in 2005 about 40% of firms will not survive in their present form without making significant changes in their operation costs, in the quality of their products and their management practices. Only one-third of the business firms are capable of becoming competitive internationally and of making proper use of the increasing globalization phenomenon.

Global competition has reached a point where the competition policies in most advanced countries and regions have assumed an international and cooperative character. The harmonization came about precisely because national competition policy was unable to keep up with globalization. The competitive environment that globalization has created complicates the survival and the self-adjustment of medium-sized companies

Shift from 'Old' to 'New' World of Business

E-business has been at the forefront of change during the past decades, bringing new products, transforming the way of life and changing the rules of the marketplace. The trends shaping e-business will have a significant impact on the way technology is used to conduct business in the future, and the nature of business itself. There are essentially two arguments. The first holds that although e-business will have a significant impact on organizations and the conduct of business in the future, the fundamental imperatives and underlying business principles will remain the same. (Shapiro & Varian, 1999) attest to the durability of economic principles, despite the fact that some of these principles are relatively new. The second is the counterclaim that the old imperatives of business will become obsolete, creating a fundamental paradigm shift in the nature and operation of organizations in the future, and a fundamentally new business environment. The latter is the more realistic in light of the current trends that are shaping and altering the conduct of e-business. In this light, organizations must constantly monitor, respond and adapt to the environment to ensure that they are not left behind in the face of intense competition.

Market and technical expertise are intertwined and will be equally important in those organizations that achieve success. The new business paradigm emerging in the domain of e-business has resulted in the significant restructuring of organizations (Blumenthal & Haspeslagh, 1994). This raises complex economic, strategic, legal, and social and conflict management issues, as well as major changes in both organizational and technological practices. The new business paradigm emerging is one that requires a rethinking and redesign of core business processes and new organizational forms. The new business models emerging are relationship focused and, hence, involve a more collaborative process that focuses on customer needs and wants and the building of business relationships. The move to relationship-focused business models therefore involves a return to basics. This includes identifying the significance of existing business relationships and real customer service, so advantages can be enhanced through collaboration. Generally, companies are now centring on procedural effectiveness and the need to utilize resources in deploying and raising business relationships. The implication is that there are many key areas that organizations will have to manage in the future (Burn & Robins, 2003). (Malhotra, 2001) suggests there are three phases of technology that enable change from the 'old' to the 'new' world of business:

- **Automation:** For increased operational efficiency
- **Rationalization of Procedures:** Streamlining of procedures and elimination of bottlenecks
- **Re-Engineering:** Thorough redevelopment of procedures and work flows with the use of technology.

Knowledge management is the closest approach that can facilitate all the procedures of an organization. Using the knowledge along with the technology and the potentiality of the employees, an organization can arrive at much better outcomes. In order to overcome the barriers and enhance e-business implications a firm is required to manage the changes. These changes in pattern have a consequence on the following:

- **Role of Senior Management:** The character of management will be changed from 'command and control' to 'sense and respond', emphasizing the building commitment to the organizational vision while at the same time the organization, treated as a 'human community', could vary substantially according to the information produced from technological systems. This demands additional skills of managers to anticipate the consequences of the introduction of such technology. The three trends – globalization, time compression and technology integration – require managers to adopt a global perspective, enhance organizational speed of response, and work with other organizations to adapt to technological changes as well as fully to exploit the potential of new technology. Nevertheless, it is crucial that managers are fully cognisant with the management of technology, particularly in such a changing environment (Pearlson, 2001).

- **Job Content and Tasks:** The development of e-business requires changes in work processes and automated routine tasks. This will allow organizations to reduce staff levels and re-engineer job descriptions and the business structure. Through the maintenance of e-business employees learn new work processes and skills to fulfil their expanded roles. It is the responsibility of the human resource departments to acknowledge the impact of technology and e-business on employee satisfaction, morale, status, productivity and training.
- **Use of Technology:** Current information systems tend to be inflexible, especially where there are static assumptions supporting transaction processing; there will be an inclination towards communication building and people networks as well as on-the-job learning.
- **Organizational Knowledge Processes:** In the past it was assumed that problems were a given and that a solution was based on understanding of the business environment; the shift will be towards a characterization of the given difficulty from the current knowledge of each occasion, while any divergence of meanings will converge around the organizational mission.
- **Organizational Design:** There will be a shift from where 'best practices' are institutionalized with a high level of structure and control to a relative lack of structure, external control, plenty of freedom and only some determinate information; assumptions will be constantly under review with a continuous pursuit of 'better practices'. This will result in the world of 'e-everything'. Organizations will constantly question and adapt operating assumptions and logic. There will be less focus on predefined rules and more on adapting to changes in the rules, and the game itself. It would be true to say that yesterday's best practices become today's core rigidities. Therefore, organizations should have the skill to produce and afterwards easily adopt new knowledge. This will be achieved in part with ongoing renewal of existing archived knowledge (May, 2000).
- **Role Ambiguity:** Technology has changed the role and tasks employees perform in organizations, creating new positions while making others redundant. Individuals may experience role confusion, with organizational departments unsure who will be responsible for the implementation, use and maintenance of e-business (Zinkhan, 2002).
- **Breakdown of Relationships:** Also e-business influences the way organizations, customers and employees communicate. Before the creation of e-business, sales staff built a relationship with customers in an effort to produce a sale. These relationships were built with the salesperson taking responsibility for servicing the customer's business requirements.
- **Process Technology:** Pertains to the techniques of producing and marketing goods and services. It also includes work methods, equipment, distribution and logistics, process technology changes that are much less visible in the marketplace. Such changes are much more difficult to detect by either a firm's customers or its competitors. Changes in process technology may bring about changes in the organization, including its human resource practices, logistics and marketing functions.

The development of technology and e-business in organizations requires a change in management thinking and practice. It means a change in job content and task, role ambiguity, changes in technology and communication requirements, changes in management and supervision style, availability of information and breakdown of relationships (Naude & Holland, 1996).

Management E-Business

With such a chaotic and unpredictable business environment, there are many implications for the management of change that distinguish it from other stable and predictable situations. The technological environment is dynamic and needs to be tracked on an ongoing basis. From an open-systems perspective, management of organizations, including technology, should be predicated based on the environment facing organizations. The domino effect on the strategies for change is particularly evident with such change (Bensaou & Earl, 1998). Tracking technological changes whether it is in the external or internal environment, requires managers to penetrate the organizations and networks that conduct and facilitate technology development. There are significant implications for this change management strategy. Successful management of technology requires that the problem solving within the organization should take into account both technical and market considerations. Also, learning through environmental intelligence, innovation and imitation are central to effective problem solving (Day & Schoemaker,. 2000).

Therefore, change interventions which consider globalization, time compression and technology integration as vital are positioned to heighten the need for faster and more effective problem solving. Managing technology in a changing environment is not a daunting experience – it is a fact of life. For change agents, the development of problem solutions can be accomplished either within the organization in collaboration with others, or simply by adopting innovations from outside. However, the method of organizational development should be a deliberate and informed managerial choice (Lawrence, 2000). In order to change management, one should bear in mind the factors of failure or success, the application of the knowledge of the executive staff and also the methodologies needed for those applications. Thus the strategies have to be developed for all the stages before, during and after that implementation. The company can make some procedures easier at the corporate level (Kuruppuarachchi et al., 2002) by creating a project organization plan, supporting the team work, building an information system or even providing employees with adequate training for the project.

In facilitating the successful implementation of e-business into an organization, leaders must develop effective methods for managing employee resistance. Individuals resist change for three main reasons: a lack of information, a lack of understanding or mistrust of the changes occurring. Resistance can be demonstrated by stop-work action, protests, lockouts, go-slows, high turnover rates, absenteeism and theft. The development of technology and e-business in an organization can be the cause of resistance if leaders do not address employee concerns. Employees resist change because they feel inadequately consulted, their job may be threatened, their job description and task may change or, simply, they fear the unknown. Organization leaders must implement training programmes and communication, which will allow employees to be kept well informed and address their concerns (Coltman et al., 2001).

Business-To-Business Relationships in E-Business Network

Having considered the factors that relate to the e-business implementation as key components to successful marketing implementation in order to meet the needs of the present research, the importance of B2B relationships are researched in an e-marketing context. On this point, B2B firms are defined as markets where a firm sells goods and services to another business firm for internal use, or for resale to other customers (Wright, 2004). According to (Wilkinson & Young, 2002), there are five groups of factors that require consideration in relation to business networks. These characteristics refer to the relationships and interactions in which a firm is involved, the characteristics of the firm's relationship partners, the characteristics of connected relations and their interactions, the characteristics of a firm's network positions and the characteristics of the network as a whole (Wright, 2004). These factors influence the potential success and longevity of a relationship. In general, B2B relationships tend to be relatively long term and stable. Overall, it is the interaction of the stakeholders that influences exchanges in such relationships.

Ultimately, the understanding of the changes in the business environment is becoming imperative, and has been defined as the subjective probability by which an organization believes that the underlying technology infrastructure and control mechanisms are capable of facilitating inter-organizational transactions (Turban et al, 2002). Therefore, the development of e-marketing strategies in B2B transactions has affected relationships quite drastically, allowing more competition and more control over processes and employees. According to (Wright, 2004), the value trust networks (VNTs) will develop into collaborative networks in which related companies will be motivated to work together based upon the mutual creation of value. Consequently, the rapid alterations of the business environment mainly influence B2B relationships and this qualitative research is an attempt to identify the firms' intentions to deal with these changes. Based on strategic issues focused on marketing, proportionately to the positive or negative response of B2B firms, we can then identify how firms move from the traditional to the new era in order to develop successful relationships.

The Greek Business Environment

In this contemporary business environment, therefore, the question is whether Greece is ready to seize the opportunities and reinforce its competitiveness and productivity. Greece is still far-removed from the northern countries that monopolize the research and technology industry, spending large sums of money in this area. More specifically, according to recent Eurostat data, Greece has the lowest access to the new economy and the information society of all the countries in the European Union, given that it has the lowest expenditure on research and technology. Furthermore, the lack of specialized executives in positions concerning new technologies and electronic business constitutes a very important issue for all countries and especially for countries with a high development rate, such as Greece. Last but not least, incorporating new technologies into the activities of Greek companies is viewed, at least at present, as unsatisfactory.

According to the annual Report of Competitiveness from the International Institute for Management Development (IMD), the application of electronic commerce is not adequately developed in creating business opportunities (Greece is rated 44th out of 49 countries), the incorporation of new technologies in informatics is not part of companies' demands (Greece is rated 41st out of 49 countries) and the lack of cooperation in technologies between companies is also noted (Greece is rated 39th out of 49) (McDonald, 2005).

To settle these problems, more extended cooperation between the state and the business world is required. Greek companies must keep up with the new business requirements in matters that concern new technologies, towards reinforcing their technological infrastructure and offering wider training of their executives. In order to meet the expectations and changes of the business environment, contemporary companies have to react positively to competition by accepting and undertaking the risks of entrepreneurship, which means continuously undertaking new initiatives and adopting innovations, organizing access in business or departmental networks and adjusting production to the international models, by putting into action the techniques of benchmarking (Burn et al., 2002). Also, by changing their structure, the companies will succeed in becoming cross-national while also addressing the continuous improvement of the cost by taking measures for increasing productivity and full visibility of the supply chain while orientating on the world market. When companies focus on the above efforts, they should take into account the constant broadening of the knowledge of their personnel and invest in it, by understanding that knowledge constitutes today the strongest advantage for competitiveness, in order to move to broad applications of informatics and new technologies.

On the other hand, the state has constantly to reinforce companies' efforts in establishing adequate corporate and extra-corporate infrastructures, in order to accomplish the much desired progress and international awards. Actions and measures that will be concerned with the reassessment of the framework that today still creates boundaries (deregulation of the markets, cutback of the civil services, motivation for mergers, creation of venture capital, etc.) are required, with the development of the capital markets for making the financing of these adjustments easier. The improvement of information networks for on-time information concerning the international changes and the importance of adjustments as well as radical restructures in education and training, stressing new systems of informatics and the positive connection of education and production, are also two additional actions that are required.

In conclusion, the new economy seems to be changing the world dramatically. It creates new possibilities for development in countries such as Greece. It creates a global economy obliging everyone to be properly prepared to confront the pressures of international competition. The responsibilities of both the state and the business world are immense and any delays will have a negative effect on both industry and government. In this significant part of the 'brave new world', businesses in Greece are asked to answer the call for further development and modernization of their practices. From this standpoint, a qualitative research has been conducted to provide a better understanding of the issues at stake.

RESEARCH METHODOLOGY

Qualitative Research

In the present research the qualitative method was used through focus groups to create a base for a deeper and more complete understanding of the studied phenomenon. The method used for the qualitative research based on a snowball sampling technique. Semi-structured in-depth interviews were conducted in three focus groups of managers from three major firms operating in Greece. A case-study methodology was considered to be the most appropriate because of the qualitative nature of the data collected. Relationships are complex and dynamic by nature, and their study necessitates in-depth knowledge of the organizational context. Yin (1994) defines a case study as an empirical inquiry that investigates a contemporary phenomenon within its real-life context, especially when the boundaries between phenomenon and context are not clearly evident.

To achieve that goal it was important to have the largest possible variation among the samples. It was also crucial to use respondents who were expected to have a profound knowledge of the studied phenomenon. Therefore, the sample used consists of representatives from three firms: The first was from firm Alpha, a leading multinational firm producing a wide range of consumer goods which was chosen as one of the target companies for this purpose. Their biggest sellers and customers are equally large corporations from a multitude of industries. Firm Beta is a multinational company in the consumer goods sector. The third firm, Gamma, is a leading Greek domestic firm producing a wide range of consumer goods, whose biggest sellers and customers are equally large corporations from a multitude of industries.

The steps directing every focus group were first the preparation for each group, second the selection of a focus group facility, third the recruitment of participants and, finally, the creation of a discussion guide. In total three focus groups were carried out over a six-month period. The interviews that were conducted were semi-structured, and encompassed a discussion of buyer–seller relationship dimensions. The participants were staff from high and middle management. Selection was based on their position and duties within the organizations. The participants had responsibilities for external relations with regard to purchasing and supply, and their position varied in the hierarchical structure. These provided multiple sources of evidence bearing in mind that the complex interactions that take place between organizations cover a wide range of functions and activities in the firm. The researcher was aided by an interview framework. This warranted internal validity (Yin, 1994) and ensured the comparability of data collected. In order to ensure internal validity and avoid subjective and personally held views by the interviewees, the researcher ensured that the documented perceptions were supported with evidence. Reliability was enhanced through the taping of discussions. This ensured the traceability of data (McCutcheon & Meredith, 1993). These were later transcribed, documented and coded.

The questions were direct and to the point. The response from one person stimulated other responses. The time allowed for each focus group was one hour. The goal was to learn and understand what executives have to say and to allow questions formulated in the focus groups to be accurately recorded to use in interviews where appropriate. The emphasis was also upon encouraging the executives to talk in detail. The survey took place in the area of Attica where firms are established. The research took place in September 2005 and February 2006.

The questionnaire was developed for the accomplishment of the research objectives, taking into account external factors of Greece's economic environment. Participants were asked to respond to questions that included issues which influence their main relationships with their partners and to reflect on the interactions they have with them. More analytically, the questions raised were relative to the internal as well as to the external environment of the firm, which allowed managers to express their views as summarized below:

Does the globalization influence firms' strategy and culture?

Which variables affecting the organizational structure that the B2B firm could adjust or change to suit its changing environment (innovation diffusion)?

Which changes in the business environment that create threats and opportunities are usually beyond the control of management?

Can the existing planning of the organization hold relationships of seller–buyer together?

Do the managers recognize the potential benefits of e-commerce applications?

What organizational change factors are necessary for successfully deploying B2B relationships? Has the firm a strategic vision for utilizing Internet technologies?

Quantitative Research

For the accomplishment of the research objectives, the questionnaire developed by Andrew Cox, Lorna Chicksand, Paul Ireland (2002) was used. Modifications made to the instruments included semantic changes to suit the needs of this study. For the purpose of the research, taking into account the economic environment of Greece, questions were including regarding the globalization and the free market economy, the pressure from the competitors, the reduction of physical distance between the business workers and the use of modern technology.

The questionnaire consists of 38 questions of ordinal type. The items of the questionnaire was in the form statements on the 5-point Likert –type scale anchored on 1=not important, through 5=critically important. The applied questionnaire refereed to issues, which are essential for the recording of the opinions of respondents. The topics were included on:

- Strategic factors of a B2B e-marketing strategy
- The adoption of the business strategy in the new era
- Business process of organization structure
- The impact of business process in a customer-centric system
- The impact of new strategy to revenue generation

Sample Frame

The survey took place in Greece where according to ICAP (2003) 1525 Medium sized firms operated in this area. From this population, 920 firms operate in e-commerce activities. We addressed 46 firms (5%) of the total population and 29 responded.

The research took place in April 2008 to and 15th of June 2008. The usable questionnaires which were returned constitute the 63% of the total sample operating in e-commerce.

The factor analysis used in order to uncover the correlation patterns between variables. Orthogonal Factor Model, with the Principal Component Method was used. Furthermore the ordinal symmetric measures, Kendall's tau-b were used to indicate the significance, strength and direction of the relationship between the row and column variables of a cross tabulation. Finally the whole procedure was worked out with the statistical program SPSS V.15.

Qualitative Research Findings: Firms' Profiles

The three firms studied in this research are briefly introduced. Owing to limitations of space only a concise description of their background is presented. For reasons of confidentiality, the identity of case-organizations remains anonymous.

Alpha is a leading multinational firm producing a wide range of chemical consumer goods and has a history that goes back 50 years. In its Greek subsidiary it has around 300 employees and trades well-known brands. Clients can choose from a large array of categories of products. The firm is very effective in its delivery and always manages to keep delivery dates as promised to its clients. Alpha is organized along a rigid hierarchical structure. The firm purchases materials and products used in the production process on a JIT basis exclusively from local suppliers. Every purchase is registered through a purchase order with the supplier who then delivers as per specific instructions.

Beta is a leading Greek domestic firm that produces a wide range of agriculture consumer goods, whose biggest sellers and customers are equally large corporations from a multitude of industries employing around 200 employees. The majority of their staff are technical and well-educated personnel. Beta produces its own quality brand and has a strong R and D department. It has been established for 60 years. Beta's purchases from the local suppliers consist mainly of laboratory equipment, consumables, spare parts and packaging material. It also buys technical expertise in the form of maintenance and calibration for all its equipment. Beta is 'ready to build a supplier/customer relation' because time is an important factor, especially when technical expertise is required.

Gamma is a fully owned subsidiary of a multinational organization involved in the consumer chemical goods. Gamma has been established for 25 years and employs around 300 highly skilled employees. The firm's main purchases from Greek suppliers consist of packaging material, machine tools and printed matter. They consider it easier to make these purchases from local firms both from an operational point of view (JIT) and because they can solve occurring problems more rapidly and with less bother because suppliers can visit in a relatively short time. They believe that their key suppliers are their partners in their continual effort to deliver quality products to their clients worldwide. They work 'hand in- hand' with their suppliers and expect them to be involved in the R and D of their product and in the re-engineering of their processes.

Results and Discussions

Guided by the literature, analysis yielded some main themes as identified in this research that are reproduced below. First we examined the factors from the business environment that have been recognized by B2B firms as crucial in order to develop 'new' ways of doing business and adopt an e-marketing strategy. It was discovered that in those questioned a very significant motive is globalization and the free market economy, as the global economy requires an understanding of the foreign marketing environment. With the availability of international delivery, it is important for the firms to design a logistical system that allows them to deliver their products/services across nations efficiently.

Firm Beta represents a very significant motive of the B2B collaboration for successful relationships. The marketing manager said: '*The enlargement of business relations in the new economy will reinforce the development of interactive e-relationships involving real customer relationships, as it contributes to forming the exchange of the required information among B2B firms.*' Customer acceptance is another significant motive relevant to externally related factors and includes all the special efforts to motivate their partners to make the move to an online environment. The use of new technologies appears to be of crucial importance, while globalization and the reduction of natural distances due to e-commerce is the second reason. Also, competition is extremely important. .Summarizing the aspects of the three focus groups relevant to the motives that lead industries to their activation of the digital environment the findings amount to statements which are generated from:

- The pressure in order to lessen the working costs,
- The pressure from collaborators, who have proceeded in electronic operational solutions,
- The pressure from competitive threats, as they are formed at the digital environment,
- The pressure for the exact monitoring and satisfaction of the request,
- The pressure for the reinforcement of the relationships with the customers, and
- The pressure for better financial circles between offer and demand.

Apart from several external factors that may urge a firm to adopt a B2B e-marketing strategy, there are, as well, the most crucial internal motives that seemed to play a large role. According to firm Beta, the most important were contribution to the process cost, along with the impact on the speed of activities and business internal coordination that such a strategy might produce. Also rather crucial, seemed to be the contribution to customer relationships management and to the development of competitive advantage and added-value.

Obvious benefits that firm Alpha delivered due to new economy principles are cost savings and benefits in the value chain. E-commerce provides the ability to carry out transactions around the clock, in addition to increasing confidence of business partners due to their online transaction ability. Firms' expectations with regard to the benefits that are achievable by using e-marketing applications appear to be high. The organizations surveyed agreed that e-business will provide opportunities to reduce the cost base. The respondents believed that e-business will enable the enlargement of business relations and of the clientele.

The adaptation of an e-marketing strategy contributes to the regulation of prices. It also contributes to a better control of the supply chain and influences the speed of processes in the internal environment of the organization as well as increasing the growth rate between departments.

It helps to organize production and to collaborate successfully with supply, marketing and sales departments.

The respondents consider that e-marketing does not contribute absolutely to relationship management and their retention. There is not plenary trust among B2B firms. They are cautious about the dispersion of information which is more personal than professional.

The implementation of an e-marketing strategy offers time reduction and saving money but it cannot be achieved in the short run. There is a doubt that the use of technology through e-marketing is unable to acquire buyers but can operate better in acquiring customers of raw materials. However, e-marketing assists in products being upgraded because it contributes to discovering any weaknesses. Consequently, the major advantage is the cost reduction, as well as the supply management, and time reduction in the distribution of goods. In addition, they consider the personalization and customization that the firm implements to respond to their customers' needs do not succeed through e-marketing as most customers have many individual features. The organization is responsive to the customer's needs as most of the partners in Greece operate in a traditional way keeping their own individual structure.

Based on strategic issues with a focus on marketing, proportionately to the positive or negative response of B2B firms, we can then identify how firms move from the traditional to the new era in order to develop successful relationships.

The participants agree that an adequate information technology infrastructure is considered a vital factor in successful B2B e-marketing implementation; hence, the availability of equipment for access and services is required. Therefore, the implementation of e-marketing practices creates a shared vision for an operational Website. The results of the research show that firm Beta uses Intranet technologies and the ERP system.

Firm Alpha's department of information technology is in a reformation stage and regarding the use of EDI is at an embryonic stage. Firm Gamma had specified the launch of the EDI system but the parent company decided itself to establish, finance and organize the EDI system.

Currently, firm Gamma has established the 'VELUM' system through the Internet which is funded by the subsidiary in Greece. The main characteristic of the system is to communicate on a national level with agents who are responsible for the firm's customers. This system's operating cost is low while it gives an added value to the organization by reducing the costs.

Two years ago the new manager at firm Alpha introduced a new vision to the organization in order to become e-business oriented. The decision of higher management was to put in place the necessary procedures to change from the 'old' to the 'new' world of business but they faced resistance from lower management. This situation created a gap between high and low management and as a result several employees transferred from the marketing department while other employees left their jobs because they could not adapt to the new regulations.

Beta, which is a domestic firm, higher management's future plan is to adopt an e-marketing strategy because it has experience from the firm's participation in an e-marketplace. The benefits for the firm are the promotion of the company, information on partner activities and exchange of standardized information such as orders, price lists and bills of sales, research for possible suppliers or buyers and participation in online auctioning.

In order to deal with these changes in the operational environment that has affected B2B relationships, companies have to take into account the employees' resistance to e-business changes. In fact, the participants in the study totally agreed that the most difficult task they face is to encourage an innovative culture of sharing and networking in the employees, while at the same time maintaining a high level of individual expertise and excellence.

They are in agreement that they have to lead and encourage employees towards the development of an innovation culture in the firm's internal processes by motivating them. Organizations that participated in this research stated that many modifications have to take place and they have to change their structure in order to adopt and implement e-business standards. Therefore, investments in IT infrastructure are required in order to facilitate networking.

Together, they emphasized that the transition of the firm to e-business changes the way that B2B relationships occurred. The participants classified some important criteria to accomplish effective e-relationships between B2B firms and their partners: the distribution and communication of relevant private and secure information; and the need to re-align their marketing strategy with new perspectives to increase the 'lifetime value' of relationships.

Quantitative Research Findings

At first we examined the factors that motivate firms to develop a new strategy. It was identified in Table 1 that a very significant motive of those questioned consist the globalization and the free market economy as the global economy requires an understanding of the foreign marketing environment as long as vary from one country to another. As well the international delivery availability which has been reduced by physical distance, it is important for the firms to design a logistical system that allow them to deliver its products/services across nations efficiently.

Table 1.Foreign marketing environment

	Variables	Mean	Standard Deviation
1	The use of technology	4.57	0.728
2	Globalization	4.17	0.913
3	The reduce of the physical distance	4.07	1.015
4	Competition	3.90	0.759

Also the internal factors that motivate firms to develop a new strategy was examined. As well the international delivery availability which has been reduced by physical distance, it is important for the firms to design a logistical system that allow them to deliver its products/services across nations efficiently. Thus external related factors consist also a very significant motive of the B2B collaboration this of the successful relationships. The enlargement of business relations reinforces the development of an interactive Web site involving real customer relationships, as it contributes being formed the exchange of the required information among of B2B firms. Customer acceptance is another significant motive interesting in external related factor and including all the special efforts to motivate customers to make the move to an online environment.

The combination of technology and e-marketing creates shared vision for an operational Web site. Considered an adequate information technology infrastructure as a vital factor in successful B2B e-marketing implementation the availability of equipment for access and services is required. Table 2.

In order to uncover the correlation patterns between variables used factor analysis. The questionnaire consists of 38 questions of ordinal type. Nevertheless, not all of them are adequate for participating in factor analysis due to resulting in non positive definite sample correlation matrix Table 3.

The development of the new strategy according to first factor in B2B Internet usage has involved transformations particularly in the area of organization expectations of creating value within a supply chain..In the second factor the internal culture is based on old beliefs and corporate values that often are no longer appropriate or useful in the new environment of doing business. Therefore an organization must conform to the new values, management processes and communication styles

Table 2. Technology and e-marketing

	Variables	Mean	Standard Deviation
1	Contributes significantly to the creation of competitive advantage and added value	3.87	0.860
2	Significantly influences the speed of activities and the internal coordination of the enterprise	3.73	0.868
3	Significantly contributes to the configuration of the cost of processes	3.73	0.868
4	Achieves the best coordination of the supply chain	3.57	0.774
5	Contributes significantly to the better management of relationships with the customers	3.53	0.900
6	Creates significant interdependence between the collaborating enterprises	3.53	1.196

Table 3. Factor analysis

Factors	Variables
1. The new strategy influence the supply chain».	New strategy effect on Logistics (Logistics practices' improvement) **(0.852).** New strategy effect on cost (Deterioration of improvement of products' or services' sales conditions) **(0.793).** New strategy strategy adoption (achieve the coordination of the supply chain) **(0.769).** new strategy effects on Logistics (Reduction of time in stock taking) **(0.709).** New strategy effect on the Reduction of time for goods delivery(0.597).
2. **The new strategy** influence **firm's internal culture**	New strategy adoption (influence the speed of activities and the internal coordination of the firm) **(0.786).** New strategy adoption (Contributes to the configuration to the cost of processes) **(0.692).**
3. The new strategy effect on the relationships of the enterprise with internal and external customers.	new strategy adoption (Better management of relationships with the customers) **(0.834).** effect on cost (effective use of Personnel) **(0.786).**
4. The new strategy effect on a B2B collaboration	Benefits from a B2B collaboration(Enlargement of clientele) **(0.806)** Benefits from a B2B collaboration (Business' relationships broadening) **(0.709)** Benefits from a B2B collaboration (Creation of competitive advantage) **(0.644)** New strategy adoption (create interdependence between the collaborating enterprises) **(-0.725).**
5. The new strategy effect the B2B co-operation	Benefits from a B2B cooperation(Money saving) **(0.749)** Benefits from a B2B cooperation(Time saving) **(0.738)**

that are being created by new methods. Worldwide companies are finding success by investing in a combination of innovative implementations of technology business process enhancements and organizational changes that are part of the overall new strategy. Factor 3 was called an "*effect on the relationships of the enterprise* with internal and external customers. The inter-organizational relationships are critical in B2B e-transactions. The statement in fourth factor explains that top management didn't develop dynamic and just-in-time collaborations attitude and responsiveness. Defining who the external and internal audience to be targeted is one of the primary task of the firm. The opportunities offered by the Internet have concluded that in business to business the technology offers customers the benefit of a convenient, very rapid mechanism through which to obtain goods at the lowest available price.

SOLUTIONS AND RECOMMENDATIONS

Globalization creates huge new opportunities for firms. National boundaries, due to globalization, have become meaningless in the business world, and the managerial process in global companies has changed to reap the rewards of this new climate. Firms in the industrial sector taking advantage of the new environment pursue the increasingly universal objective of the generation of wealth through globalization. Companies who want to use the Internet to do business internationally have to revise their operations, strategies and business models in order to exploit to their full potential the opportunities offered by the Internet.

Since companies have identified the external factors that force them to be global, it is necessary to consider the factors that relate to the internal environment that include technological infrastructure, internal/innovation culture and the importance of training programmes. This means how marketing activities through the Internet can be coordinated by the general strategic perspective of the industry for the successful implementation and strengthening of the new era.

The completion of those activities with the marketing activities which take place in traditional markets is the best way to encompass the efficient exploitation of those chances that are provided by the electronic environment. According to Porter (1986), the weakness of reconciliation of the electronic with the ordinary activities to the strategic frame of operational development comprises one of the main reasons for failure of the electronic markets. Moreover, many industries have not succeeded in understanding the strategic environment of the Internet and have tried to operate their electronic expressions with mechanisms of the ordinary market, a fact that quickly led to operational failures.

The B2B organizations must understand and conform to the new values, management processes and communication styles, and strategies applied aim to associate innovation with business targets, and the application of the innovation values into the firm's internal environment. The fieldwork sought to define the firm's innovative core and create frameworks to integrate innovation throughout the range of enterprise leaders and teams in order to sustain the level of innovation by generating and implementing ideas, strategies and plans that cultivate a thinking organization.

The findings introduce the concepts of globalization, the Internet and the technological changes that have impacted the business environment, forcing B2B firms to develop an e-commerce strategy. This research has gone some way in the exploration of how B2B e-commerce can fundamentally change the inter-organizational processes at the buyer–seller interface. More specifically, it emphasizes the importance of developing a B2B e-marketing strategy. It has been shown that electronic B2B marketing can provide support for e-relationships. At one end of the continuum, electronic marketing can create joint, inter-organizational processes, while at the other end creating increased efficiency and reduced transaction costs with partners. The development of close business partnerships to optimize inter-organizational processes remains one of the most difficult aspects, as well as problems that are met, related to business culture.

REFERENCES

Barbian, J. (2000). IT in 2000 and beyond. *Computer User, 19*(1).

Bensaou, M., & Earl, M. (1998). The right mind-set for managing information technology. *Harvard Business Review*, *76*(5). PMID:10185427

Blumenthal, B., & Haspeslagh, P. (1994). Toward a definition of corporate transformation. *Sloan Management Review*.

Burn, J., Marshall, P., & Barnett, M. (2002). *E-business Strategies for Virtual Organisations*. Oxford, UK: Butterworth-Heinemann.

Burn, J., & Robins, G. (2003). Moving towards e-government: A case study of organizational change processes. *Logistics Information Management*, *16*(1), 25–35. doi:10.1108/09576050310453714

Burnes, B. (2000). *Managing Change: A Strategic Approach to Organizational Dynamics*. London: Pearson Education.

Cao, L. (2002). Corporate and product identity in the post national economy: Rethinking US trade laws. *California Law Review*, *90*(2), 401–484. doi:10.2307/3481283

Coltman, T., Devinney, T., Latukefu, A., & Midgley, D. (2001). E-business: Revolution, evolution or hype? *California Management Review*, *44*(61).

Day, G., & Schoemaker, P. (2000). Avoiding the pitfalls of emerging technologies. *California Management Review*, *42*(52).

European Commission. (2000). *SMEs Access to the Digital Economy*. Brussels: Directorate C of DG Information Society.

Evans, P., & Warster, T. S. (1999). *Blown to Bits: How the New Economic of Information Transforms Strategy*. Boston, MA: Harvard Business School Press.

Jones, R. (1996). Digital equipment corporation: creating new business. In *The Internet Strategy Handbook: Lessons from the New Frontier of Business*. Boston, MA: Harvard Business School Press.

Kalakota, R., & Robinson, M. (1999). *E-business, Roadmap for Success*. Reading, MA: Addison-Wesley.

Kanter, R., Stein, B., & Jick, T. (1992). *The Challenge of Organizational Change: How CompaniesExperience It and Leaders Guide It*. New York: Maxwell Macmillan Int.

Kotter, J. (1996). *Leading Change*. Boston, MA: Harvard Business School Press.

Kuruppuarachchi, P., Mandal, P., & Smith, R. (2002). IT project implementation strategies for effective changes: A critical review. *Logistics Information Management*, *15*(2), 126–137. doi:10.1108/09576050210414006

Lado, A. A., Boyd, N. G., & Hanlon, S. C. (1997). Competition, cooperation, and the search for economic rents: A syncretic model. *Academy of Management Review*, *22*(1), 110–141.

Lawrence, E., Corbitt, B., Fisher, J., Lawrence, J., & Tidwell, A. (2000). *Internet Commerce: Digital Models for Business* (2nd ed.). Milton, Australia: John Wiley & Sons, Inc.

Lei, D., & Slocum, J. W. Jr. (1991). Global strategic alliances: Payoffs and pitfalls. *Organizational Dynamics*, *19*(3), 44–62. doi:10.1016/0090-2616(91)90093-O

Lei, D., & Slocum, J. W. Sr. (1992). Global strategy, competence-building and strategic alliances. *California Management Review*, *35*(1), 81–97. doi:10.2307/41166714

Malhotra, Y. (Ed.). (2001). *Knowledge Management and Business Model Innovation*. Hershey, PA: Idea Group.

May, P. (2000). *The Business of E-commerce: From Corporate Strategy to Technology*. New York: Cambridge University Press.

McCutcheon, D. M., & Meredith, J. R. (1993). Conducting case study research in operations management. *Journal of Operations Management*, *11*(3), 239–256. doi:10.1016/0272-6963(93)90002-7

Narayanan, V. (2001). *Managing Technology and Innovation for Competitive Advantage*. Upper Saddle River, NJ: Prentice Hall.

Naude, P., & Holland, C. (1996). Business-to-business relationships. In *Relationship Marketing, Theory and Practice*. London: Paul Chapman Publishing. doi:10.4135/9781446252062.n4

Parkhe, A. (1991). Interfirm diversity, organizational learning, and longevity in global strategic alliances. *Journal of International Business Studies*, *22*(4), 579–601. doi:10.1057/palgrave.jibs.8490315

Parkhe, A. (1993). Strategic alliances structuring: A game theoretic and transaction cost examination of interfirm cooperation. *Academy of Management Journal*, *38*(4), 794–829. doi:10.2307/256759

Pearce, R. J. (1997). Toward understanding joint venture performance and survival: A bargaining and influence approach to transaction cost theory. *Academy of Management Review*, *22*(1), 203–225.

Pearlson, K. (2001). *Managing and Using Information Systems: A Strategic Approach*. New York: John Wiley & Sons.

Porter, M. (1986). *Competition in Global Industries*. Cambridge, MA: Harvard Business School.

Shapiro, C., & Varian, H. (1999). *Information Rules: A Strategic Guide to the Network Economy*. Boston, MA: Harvard Business School Press.

Turban, E., King, D., Warkentin, M., & Chung, H. (2002). *E-commerce: A Managerial Perspective*. Upper Saddle River, NJ: Prentice Hall.

Turban, E., Lee, J., King, D., & Chung, H. (2000). Electronic Commerce: A Managerial Perspective (Int. Ed.). Upper Saddle River, NJ: Prentice-Hall International.

Turban, E., McLean, E., & Wetherbe, J. (2000). *Information Technology for Management: Making Connection for Strategic Advantage* (2nd ed.). New York: John Wiley & Sons Inc.

Waddell, D., Cummings, T., & Worley, C. (2000). *Organisation Development and Change*. Melbourne: Nelson Thomson Learning.

Whipple, J.M., & Frankel, R. (2000). Strategic alliance success factors. *Journal of Supply Chain Management*, 21-26.

Wilkinson, I., & Young, L. (2002). On cooperating: Firms, relations and networks. *Journal of Business Research*, *55*(2), 123–132. doi:10.1016/S0148-2963(00)00147-8

Wright, R. (2004). *Business to Business Marketing: A step by step guide*. Harlow, UK: Prentice Hall.

Yin, R. K. (1994). *Case Study Research - Design and Methods*. Thousand Oaks, CA: Sage Publications.

Zinkhan, M. G. (2002). Promoting services via the internet: New opportunities and challenges. *Journal of Services Marketing*, *16*(5), 412–423. doi:10.1108/08876040210436885

KEY TERMS AND DEFINITIONS

B2B Firms: Are defined as markets where a firm sells goods and services to another business firm for internal use, or for resale to other customers (Wright, 2004).

B2B Relationships: Involves a more collaborative process that focuses on customer needs and wants and the building of business relationships.

E-Commerce Benefits: Actively collaborating with supply chain partners, Extending the company's reach up and down the supply chain, Changing the supply chain flow path, Growing revenue, Transforming capabilities into new business.

Globalization: It can be considered as a process of transformations in the organization of transactions and social relations around the globe, bringing inter-regional flows, activity networks, interactive environment and power.

New Business Paradigm: Requires a rethinking and redesign of core business processes and new organizational forms. New business models emerging are relationship focused.

Organizational Culture Sharing: The way the work is organized and experienced; how authority is exercised and delegated; how people are rewarded, organized and controlled; and the roles and expectations of staff and managers.

Technology: Benefits for organizations, such as the ability to carry out transactions around the clock and also increase confidence of business partners due to their online transaction ability and enhance relationships.

Chapter 15
Electrotextiles:
A Novel Product for the Textile Industry

Georgios Priniotakis
TEI of Piraeus, Greece

ABSTRACT

During the last decade, the textile Industry in Europe collapsed due to the competition with the low labor countries. The textile industry in Europe refused to adapt to the new market conditions. The competitive advantage of the design and the quality were not enough to keep it in the leading position. Nevertheless, in the last few years, the textile industry has completely changed. New products have been launched in the market. Electrotextiles is one of them: a new category of textile products that has conducting properties contrary to the traditional textile products but keeps the "textile" properties like softness, lightness, and "washableness." Fabric is the best intermediary between the human being and a computer. Fabrics and cloths are almost all the time in contact with our body. Therefore, they can "feel" us and "cure" us. A fabric can also cover a large space, having low weight and cost, so it could be perfect if it can have electrical properties and work as photovoltaic. This chapter explores electrotextiles.

1. INTRODUCTION

Electrotextiles are a novel category of textiles. Textiles offer a unique way to fabricate novel large area, flexible clothing for use in military, medical and commercial systems. There is a unique research and development in basic yarn components, textile circuits, device manufacturing CAD and device simulation, fabric based system simulation, design and modelling for that reason. This includes a very important condition to talk about "Electro" textiles, which is the possibility to conduct an electrical current. In this section different methods will be discussed to produce such fibres, yarns and garments (Seyam, 2003).

However, electro-textiles are not expected to compete with high-density, high-performance electronic systems typified by current computer of telecommunications products because of higher resistance, thus slower charge transport (data transport). Electro-textiles can have other unique applications that are determined by the need of flexible and conformable systems or systems that require large surface areas. Distribution of elementary sensors, actuators, logic, and power sources combined with reconfigurable network

DOI: 10.4018/978-1-4666-6232-2.ch015

architecture with fault tolerance and operational long-term stability is needed. It is expected that lower production cost for these types of applications will be achieved through the use of textile manufacturing processes that are appropriately modified and optimized to incorporate electronic components (conventional or yarn based).

Textiles structures are characterized by their high strength, flexibility, and conformability to almost any desired shape. They can be manufactured continuously at high speed with extremely low production cost. Textiles structures are produced and used in forms such as fibres, yarns, twisted structures, braided, woven, knitted, non-woven, or a combination thereof. They can be modified and structured with piles, spaces and multi-layers to accommodate inserts and devices. They exist everywhere around us in many forms. There are numerous end uses of textile structures for small surface areas (such as apparel, seat covers, and seat belts) large surface area (such as rugs, parachutes, weather balloons, and parafoils) and exceptional large surface areas (such as carpets, wall covers, houst wraps, geo-textiles, scientific balloon, air structures and tensioned structures). It is the aim to develop electro-textiles that keep the advantages of conventional textiles but allow charge transport through its structure.

2. ELECTRO-TEXTILE STRUCTURE AND PRODUCTION METHODS

There is a wide variety of structures in electro-textiles, which are mainly based on the technology used to produce such fibers.

- Production of pure metallic fibres. The structure is the one of the metal and charge conduction is obtained through the entire fiber.
- Metallization is a process in which a metal ion is absorbed by a conventional fibre, followed by chemical reduction of the absorbed metal ions to its metallic phase. In this case also conduction is obtained through the entire fibre but with a limited rate, dependent of the density of metal ion absorbed in the fibre and adsorbed at the surface of the fiber.
- Chemical deposition, is the method that conductive materials are deposited through chemical methods, thus the conductivity properties are obtained exclusively at the surface of the fibre.
- Inclusion of conductive material, such as carbon particles, during melt spinning production of the fibres.

Fibres obtained by these methods are then further manufactured in yarns, clothing and garments. The production methods are described more in detail in the sections below.

2.1. Melt Spinning Process

One of the cost and process effective methods is blending common plastics with conductive fillers, such as carbon black, metal powders, during the melt spinning production of fibres. The method is not still optimised. There are several efforts to develop conductive fibres with melt spinning process. (Ikkala et al., 1995) described the development of conductive polymer blends by blending thermoplastic bulk polymers such as polyolefins, polystyrene or a polyaniline salt complex. In their report 1-20 S/cm of conductivity has been achieved in the range of 1-30 wt% of the polyaniline complex. (Kim et al., 2004). have prepared conductive composite fibres by mixing polyaniline emeraline salt, polypyrrole and graphite with polypropylene or low-density polyethylene using a co-rotating twin-crew extruder. Low polyaniline concentrations (6-10 wt.%) were used for polyaniline particles dispersion in Polypropylene via melt blending.

Dall'Acqua reported the development of conductive fibres made by cellulose-based fibres embedded with polypyrrole (Dall'Acqua et al, 2004). Several efforts with cotton, viscose, cupro and lyonell have been followed. The conductivity is directly related to polypyrrole amount, oxidant ratio and fibre structure with significant differences between viscose and lyonell. Polymerisation occurs uniformly inside the fibre bulk, by producing a coherent composite polypyrrole/cellulose. The mechanical and physical properties of cellulose fibres were not significantly modified.

A serious remark should be given here about the difference of electroconductivity and ion conductivity. Electroconductivity means that charge is conducted by electrons that move freely through the conductive fibre. This mechanism is present in metal fibres, fibres obtained through metallization if enough metal is dispersed in the fibre and through modification of fibre surfaces with metallic coatings. Ion conductivity also allows to conduct charge but in this case it is not an electron that moves freely but electrons that jump from one place to another leaving a positive gap behind and it is the movement of that positive gap that allows conduction. This is the mechanism present in conductive polymers, such as polypyrrole and polyaniline. This type of conduction is inferior to electroconductive mechanism because of much smaller rate of charge transfer and limited capacity to conduct charge (Priniotakis, 2005).

2.2. Conductive Fibres Obtained Through Chemical Deposition of Coatings

Chemical deposition of different polymers, such as polyaniline, polypyrrole and polythiophene that possess conductive properties is obtained through deposition of the monomer followed by polymerization in presence of an initiator (e.g. FeCl3). In this method the surface to be coated is enriched either with a monomer, or an oxidizing agent (through spontaneous deposition, using auxiliary reagents that promote the adsorption), followed by treatment with a solution of either oxidizing agent or monomer, respectively. A major advantage of this process is that the polymerization occurs almost exclusively at the surface, and there is no bulk polymerization in the solution. The enrichment of the surface by an oxidizer can occur either by ion-exchange mechanism, or by the deposition of an insoluble layer of oxidizer. The process is limited by materials that can be covered or enriched with a layer of either monomer or oxidizer in a separate stage, preceding the surface polymerization (Cospodinova et al, 1998; Tan & Ge 1998).

An alternative of chemical polymerization is electro-polymerization of monomers at electrodes performed either in aqueous, or in organic solutions is another method for coating. However, Electro-polymerization is strongly restricted by the use of conducting materials because an activation potential needs to be applied and an electrical current should be able to flow in the electrodes. This implies that the initial fibre to be coated should already have conductive properties which limits the use of this method (Huang 1995). Frequently, electro-polymerization is used as a finishing touch after that fibres were treated with a chemical deposition, the latter providing the conductive properties to the fibre necessary to perform electro-polymerization.

Alternative methods like spraying a solution containing the polymer at the surface of a textile, followed by solvent evaporation is not discussed here because of its poor reproducibility, poor adhesion of the polymer to the substrate, inhomogeneous distribution of the polymer of the fibre surface, large fluctuations in layer thickness and co-deposition of impurities present in the solution (De Jesus et al, 1997).

Another method is by depositing a thin layer of soft metal like gold onto polypyrrole- and copper-coated para-aramid yarns in an electroless way. The coating method result to a gold deposition and the deposition solution was used contained a gold salt, sulfite and thiosulfate. Performance tests showed that the coated yarns offered an excellent electrical conductivity combined with good mechanical properties and satisfying resistance to washing. In addition, electrochemical impedance measurements revealed that the gold coated yarns are promising electrode materials to measure biomedical signals (Schwarz et al, 2010).

3. THE ELECTRO-TEXTILE CHALLENGES

Textiles offer a unique combination of attributes to facilitate the fabrication of electrotextile systems. They are lightweight, flexible and conformable. Two and three dimensional fabrication techniques are available to provide a preformed network to incorporate and connect a large number of nodes. Also available are a large number of crossover points that can be exploited for fault-tolerance in signal routing and low level computing. Multilayered textile systems can be made to mimic film transistor and printed wiring board structures. Textile market economics drives manufacturing toward large-area, high-throughput, and cost-effectiveness.

There is a broad spectrum of functions that may be incorporated into textiles:

- **Sensing:** Large areas, simple modification methods, large number of sensors, platform modular sensors (acoustic, chem/bio, thermal, optical, etc.)
- **Actuation-multiple nano/micro actuation:** To achieve macro effect, shaping, conforming, variable porosity, affecting surrounding environment/fluid.
- **Power sources/ generation:** Fibre batteries/ fuel cells/solar cells.
- **Communication/connectivity:** Fibre optics.

4. MAKE ELECTRO-TEXTILES FABRIC

Despite that in each fabric production methodology the potential is present to form innovative electro-textile products, weaving is the most promising technology to produce electro-textiles. This is due to the combined advantages of weaving and woven structures that cannot be found with any other methodology. Woven fabrics are characterised by their lightweight, conformability, flexibility, durability, high tensile and tear strength, possibility to obtain multilayers, high thread density, dimensionally stable, easy recovery from high stresses and high fabric width of up to 12 metres. The weaving technology is good for short nuns as well as long run, highly automated, versatile and can handle a wide range of yarn types including ribbon yarns, broad range of yarn size, highly twisted yarns, rigid rods. Additional advantages that are relevant to the formation of electro-textiles by the weaving process are:

Weaving zone is spacious and can accommodate additional devices to automate the formation of interconnects/disconnects while weaving.

Different yarns of different physical and mechanical properties can be woven in the same fabric by adding creel behind the weaving machine or by adjusting filling yarn feeders.

Woven fabrics have ordered structure in which warp and filling yarns are precisely addressed and controlled.

4.1 Electro-Textile Applications

For the last twenty years, the textile industry had provided very simple electro-textile products. Several novel uses of Electro-textiles have been developed for lab testing, while others have been utilised in products on the commercial market, as well as items used in space science (Langenhove et al, 2005).

The ability to integrate electrical functionality into textile garments is becoming increasingly desired for consumer devices, military applications and for the companies with large distributed workforces. This technology has the potential to facilitate the transfer of information and increase efficiency in many areas. Nevertheless these products should be electrically conductive, but must also exhibit superior flexibility, enhanced wearability, and the ability to withstand multiple washing environments. The electrotextiles should be tested and evaluated accordingly (Slade et al, 2003).

Clothes are worn for long periods and worn next to our skin and are therefore convenient hosts for physiological monitoring of a person. Integration of sensors onto clothes would enable comfortable monitoring.

Conductive and pressure sensitive textiles have been incorporated in the advanced development of space suits (I-Suit) as switch controls for lights and as signal transmission cables.

Conductive fibres have been used in several stitched applications for electrostatic charge dissipation, including large pharmaceutical containment enclosures where fine powders are being captured for transfer between manufacturing facilities, as well as impact attenuation airbags used in landing spacecraft on the surface of Mars. In both cases, conductive threads are uniquely located in seams and panel locations (Catogan et al,1998).

Electrically conductive and semi conductive fabrics have been used in applications such as electromagnetic interference, and microwave attenuation.

Electromagnetic interface shielding is the most common application. Conductive fibres braided into a shield or sock offer superior performance against electromagnetic interference and they present the following advantages:

- **More Uniform Coverage:** The large number of very fine fibres, together with the tendency of yarn bundles to flatten and spread, makes it easy to obtain high coverage.
- **Better High-Frequency Shielding:** The fine fibres provide a very high surface-to-volume ratio. Together with the excellent coverage, the extra surface yields improved high-frequency electromagnetic interface shielding performance.
- **Reduced Weight:** Weight savings can be especially important in aerospace and similar applications where every milligram saved is important.
- **Flexibility:** Braid made from these fibres has successfully replaced copper braid in military applications where freedom of movement and durability are critical.
- **Compatibility:** Yarns of conductive fibres are fully compatible with standard braiding equipment.

Battlefield acoustic sensors are required to detect, localize, track, and classify or identify targets of interest, which typically includes vehicles aircraft and personnel.

More advanced electro-textile products such as thermal blankets for human and animal use, computer keyboard, smart shirt to monitor physiological conditions, etc. are appeared in the market over the last years. Researchers are conducting research and development in electro-textiles to come up with new generation of multi-functional and active "smart textiles" that are able to harvest energy for self-powering, sense, response, and adjustment to stimuli such as pressure, temperature and/or electrical charge.

Examples of large deployable structures featuring very thin, large flexible circuits for use in space include synthetic aperture radar (SAR) antennas, communications antenna reflectarrays, and active variable reflectance solar sails (Hertleer et al, 2007).

In order to improve volume efficiency and reduce payload weight for arbital earth remote sensing applications, low-mass membrane-based

Synthetic Apenture Radar array concepts are being developed. One such system is an inflatable deployable SAR consisting of thin fabrics or membranes that are deployed for L-band operation with dual polarization. The entire assembly is flexible before employment and is rolled up onto the spacecraft bus. The antenna is comprised of three membranes positioned vertically over one another: the ground plane, the radiation patch, and the microstrip transmission line membranes.

The increasing desire for localisation of soldiers on the battlefield requires a new approach for the garments of the soldier. This includes the implementation of communications systems through electro-textiles. Conductive fibres are used in a conformal sensate liner garment for the detection of wound locations and medical sensor signal transmission for soldier health monitoring while on the battlefield.

Textile based antennas have already introduced in similar products giving some key features including small size while highly efficient, consuming 15 times less power than conventional antenna technology and synthesizes its own radiation requiring no power amplifier (Hertleer et al, 2009).

In some other cases they are mentioned electro-textiles with properties as fibres whose stiffness or colour can be controlled by applying an electrical load (Cough, 2004).

4.2 Electro-Textile Research For The Future

4.2.1 Basic Yarn Component Development

Functional Fibres, filaments, and yarns are the basic building blocks of electro-textiles. The textile industry has demonstrated a remarkable capability to incorporate both natural and manmade filaments into yarns and fabrics to satisfy a wide range of physical parameters that survive the manufacturing process and are tailored to specific application environments. Electronic components can be fabricated within and/or on the surface of filaments and subsequently be processes into functional yarns and woven into fabrics. Passive components such as resistors, capacitors, and inductors can be fabricated in several different manners. Diodes and transistors can be made on long, thin, flat strands of silicon or formed in a coaxial way. Progress had been made in the development of fibre batteries and fibre-based solar cells. In addition, a variety of actuated materials (piezoelectric, etc.) can be made into multiple long strands (filaments) and subsequently be woven into fabric.

4.2.2 Textile Circuits

Basic Yarn components along with conventional filament/yarns, constitute the feedstock of the weaving process. Selectively fed into a loom and manipulated through advanced textile manufacturing process, this feedstock can be woven into a complex variety of designs that result in a structurally sound, environmentally compatible fabric that provides electrical and mechanical functionality. Electronic circuits can be formed from the selective interconnection of fibre components during the weaving process.

4.2.3 Device Manufacturing CAD

The electronics industry has demonstrated a remarkable ability to develop computer-aided design (CAD) tools for developing complex integrated circuits and printed wiring board products. The textile industry has demonstrated a similar computer-aided design capability for the design and development of advanced fabrics. Tailoring of existing electronic CAD and the textile CAD tools are required for new electronic textiles manufacturing processes. Device and circuit characterization (both electrical and mechanical parameters) can be used to develop macros and design libraries and be incorporated into the tailored electronic textiles design tools.

CONCLUSION

Electrotextiles can be a great chance for the west countries textile industry. These products usually are high tech products based in novel technology. In most cases are high customized products with high selling price. There is no doubt that the competition is less than the traditional textile product, and day every day they got bigger market share.

REFERENCES

Anand, J., Palaniappan, S., & Sathyanarayana, D. N. (1998). Conducting polyaniline blends and composites. *Progress in Polymer Science*, *23*(6), 993–1018. doi:10.1016/S0079-6700(97)00040-3

Cough, P. (2004). *Electronic and Clothes: Watt to wear?* Leeds, UK: Wearable Electronic and Smart Textiles.

Dall'Acqua, L., Tonin, C., Peila, R., Ferrero, F., & Catellani, M. (2004). Performances and properties of intrinsic conductive cellulose-polypyrrole textiles. *Synthetic Metals*, *146*(2), 213–221. doi:10.1016/j.synthmet.2004.07.005

De Jesus, M. C., Fu, Y., & Weiss, R. A. (1997). Conductive polymer blends prepared by in situ polymerization of pyrrole: A review. *Polymer Engineering and Science*, *37*(12), 1936–1943. doi:10.1002/pen.11844

Gospodinova, A., & Terlemezyan, L. (1998). Conducting polymers prepared by oxidative polymerization: Polyaniline. *Progress in Polymer Science*, *23*(8), 1443–1481. doi:10.1016/S0079-6700(98)00008-2

Hertleer, C., Rogier, H., Vallozzi, L., & Van Langenhove, L. (2009). Textile Antenna for Off-Body Communication Integrated into Protective Clothing for Firefighter. *IEEE Transactions on Antennas and Propagation*, *57*(4), 919–925. doi:10.1109/TAP.2009.2014574

Hertleer, C., Tronquo, A., Rogier, H., Vallozzi, L., & Van Langenhove, L. (2007). Aperture-Coupled Patch Antenna for Integration Into Wearable Textile Systems. *IEEE Antennas and Wireless Propagation Letters*, *6*(11), 392–395. doi:10.1109/LAWP.2007.903498

Huang, J. C. (1995). EMI shielding plastics: A review. *Advances in Polymer Technology*, *14*(2), 137–150. doi:10.1002/adv.1995.060140205

Ikkala, O. T., Laakso, J., Vakiparta, K., Virtanen, E., Ruohonen, H., & Järvinen, H. et al. (1995). Counter-ion induced processibility of polyaniline: Conducting melt processible polymer blends. *Synthetic Metals*, *69*(1-3), 97–100. doi:10.1016/0379-6779(94)02376-A

Kaswell, E. (1953). *Textile Fibers, Yarns, and Fabrics*. New York: Reihold Publishing.

Kim, B., Koncar, V., Devaux, E., Dufour, C., & Viallier, P. (2004). Electrical and morphological properties of PP. and PET conductive polymer fibers. *Synthetic Metals*, *146*(2), 167–174. doi:10.1016/j.synthmet.2004.06.023

Langenhove, L., Hertleer, C., Priniotakis, G., & Lanfer, B. (2005). *Smart textiles: Dream or fact?* Paper presented at the 5th World Textile Conference AUTEX. Portoroz, Slovenia.

McAdams, E. T., McLaughlin, J., & Anderson, J. (2004). *Wearable and Implantable Monitoring Systems: 10 Years Experience*. Paper presented at the Wearable Electronic and Smart Textiles. Leeds, UK.

Orth, M. (2003). Defining Flexibility and Sewability in Conductive Yarns. In *Proceedings of Materials Research Society Symposium Proceedings* (Vol. 736, p. 47). Academic Press.

Priniotakis, G. (2005). *Study of Conductive Textile Electrodes as Analytical Tool for Detection of Parameters related to human body by (EIS) Electrochemical Impedance Spectroscopy*. (PhD Thesis). University of Ghent, Ghent, Belgium.

Schwarz, A., Hakuzimana, J., Kaczynska, A., Banaszczyk, J., Westbroek, P., & McAdams, E. et al. (2010). Gold coated para-aramid yarns through electroless deposition. *Surface and Coatings Technology*, *204*(9-10), 1412–1418. doi:10.1016/j.surfcoat.2009.09.038

Seyam, A. M. (2003). Formation of Textiles Structures for Giant-Area Applications, Electronics on Unconventional Substrates. *Electrotextiles and Giant Area Flexible Circuits*, *736*, 25–36.

Slade, J., Catogan, D., Sandy, C., & Grahne, M. (1998). *Development and Evaluation of the Mars Pathfinder Inflatable Airbag Landing System*. Paper presented at the 49th International Astronautical Congress. Washington, DC.

Tan, S. N., & Ge, H. L. (1998). Analysis of some cytokinins in cocnut water by micellar electrokinetic capillary chromatography after solid extraction. *New Polymer Materials*, *5*, 169–176.

KEY TERMS AND DEFINITIONS

Conducting Yarn: Yarn that conducts electricity. There are several methods known to manufacture electrically conductive textiles. The simplest way is to incorporate metal wires or wire meshes into fabrics. another approach is to use metalized yarns.

Conductive Fabrics: Fabrics that conducts electricity. They are used for several uses nd later for smart textiles.

Electrotextiles: Textiles with electrical properties. They're mostly used for electromagnetic shielding, anti-static and heating purposes, and also for soft circuits: electric circuits or sensors made out of a combination of special fabrics, threads, yarns and electronic components.

Flexible Photovoltaic: Solar cells that are manufactured by depositing photovoltaic material on flexible substrates, such as ordinary fabric, using chemical vapor deposition technology.

Light Membrane: A selective light barrier that allows the passage of certain constituents and retains other constituents found in the liquid. The degree of selectivity of a membrane depends on the membrane pore size. Depending on the pore size, they can be classified as microfiltration (MF), ultrafiltration (UF), nanofiltration (NF) and reverse osmosis (RO) membranes.

New Product Development: Process of developing a new product or service for the market. This type of development is considered the preliminary step in product or service development and involves a number of steps that must be completed before the product can be introduced to the market. New product development is essential to any business that must keep up with market trends and changes.

Smart Textiles: Fabrics that enable digital and electronics to be embedded in them. The intelligent clothing, smart clothing, wearable technology, and wearable computing are characterized as smart textiles.

Compilation of References

(1991). 20 Years On: The Small Firm. InStanworth, J., & Gray, C. (Eds.), *The 1990s*. London: Paul Chapman.

Aacker, D. A. (1989). Managing assets and skills: The key to a sustainable competitive advantage. *California Management Review*.

Aaker, D. A. (1991). *Managing brand equity: Capitalizing on the value of a brand name*. New York, NY: Free Press.

Aaker, D. A. (1996). Measuring brand equity across products and markets. *California Management Review*, *38*(3), 102–120. doi:10.2307/41165845

Aaker, D. A., & Joachimsthaler, E. (2000). *Brand leadership*. London, UK: Free Press.

Aaker, D. A., & Keller, K. L. (1990). Consumer Evaluations Of Brand Extensions. *Journal of Marketing*, *54*(1), 27–41. doi:10.2307/1252171

Abratt, R., & Kleyn, N. (2011). Corporate identity, corporate branding and corporate reputations: Reconciliation and integration. *European Journal of Marketing*, *46*(7-8), 1048–1063.

Adams, J. S. (1963). Toward an understanding of inequity. *Journal of Abnormal and Social Psychology*, *67*(5), 422–436. doi:10.1037/h0040968 PMID:14081885

Adams, J. S., & Freedman, S. (1976). Equity theory revisited: Comments and an annotated bibliography. In L. Berkowitz, & E. Walster (Eds.), *Equity theory: Toward a general theory of social interaction* (pp. 43–90). New York: Academic Press. doi:10.1016/S0065-2601(08)60058-1

Afsar, B., Rehman, Z. U., Qureshi, J. A., & Shahjehan, A. (2010). Determinants of customer loyalty in the banking sector: The case of Pakistan. *African Journal of Business Management*, *4*(6), 1040–1047.

Agatz, N. A. H., Fleischmann, M., & van Nunen, J. A. E. E. (2008). E-fulfillment and multi-channel distribution – A review. *European Journal of Operational Research*, *187*(2), 339–356. doi:10.1016/j.ejor.2007.04.024

Ahluwalia, R., Burnkrant, R. E., & Unnava, H. R. (2000). Consumer response to negative publicity: The moderating role of commitment. *JMR, Journal of Marketing Research*, *37*(2), 203–214. doi:10.1509/jmkr.37.2.203.18734

Ahmed, P. K., & Rafiq, M. (2003). Internal marketing issues and challenges. *European Journal of Marketing*, *37*(9), 1177–1186. doi:10.1108/03090560310498813

Akhtar, M. N., Hunjra, A. I., Akbar, S. W., Rehman, K. U., & Niazi, C. S. K. (2011). Relationship between customer satisfaction and service quality of Islamic banks. *World Applied Sciences Journal*, *13*(3), 453–459.

Alba Economic Post. (2003, April 12). Grand Thorton Reserch In Staurou Kostea, E. *Alba Economic Post*.

Aliouat, B. (2004). Un regard nouveau et global sur l'organisation en réseau: Compétences relationnelles et métamorphoses des organisations. *Revue Management International*, *8*(2), 51–56.

Ambler, T. (2003). *Marketing and the bottom line: Creating the measures of success*. London, UK: Prentice-Hall.

Amit, R., & Schoemaker, P. G. H. (1993). Strategic assets and organizational rent. *Strategic Management Journal*, 14.

Amit, R., & Zott, C. (2001). Value creation in e-business. *Strategic Management Journal*, *22*(6/7), 493–520. doi:10.1002/smj.187

Anand, J., Palaniappan, S., & Sathyanarayana, D. N. (1998). Conducting polyaniline blends and composites. *Progress in Polymer Science*, *23*(6), 993–1018. doi:10.1016/S0079-6700(97)00040-3

Andersen, E. (2010). *Social Media Marketing: Game Theory and the Emergence of Collaboration*. Springer-Verlag. doi:10.1007/978-3-642-13299-5

Anderson, E. (1998). Customer satisfaction and word of mouth. *Journal of Service Research*, *1*(1), 5–17. doi:10.1177/109467059800100102

Anderson, E. W., Fornell, C., & Lehmann, D. R. (1994). Customer satisfaction, market share and profitability: Findings from Sweden. *Journal of Marketing*, *58*(3), 53–66. doi:10.2307/1252310

Anderson, E., & Sullivan, M. (1993). The antecedents and consequences of customer satisfaction for firms. *Marketing Science*, *12*(2), 125–143. doi:10.1287/mksc.12.2.125

Anderson, J. C., & Gerbing, D. W. (1988). Structural equation modeling in practice: A review and recommended two-step approach. *Psychological Bulletin*, *103*(3), 411–423. doi:10.1037/0033-2909.103.3.411

Ang, S., Leong, S. M., & Lim, J. (1997). The mediating influence of pleasure and arousal on layout and signage effects. *Journal of Retailing and Consumer Services*, *4*(1), 13–24. doi:10.1016/0969-6989(95)00091-7

Anholt, S. (2003). *Brand new justice: The upside of global branding*. Stoneham, MA: Butterworth-Heinemann.

Aoki, K., & Lennerfors, T. (2013a). The new improved Keiretsu. *Harvard Business Review*, 109–113.

Aoki, K., & Lennerfors, T. (2013b). Whither Japanese keiretsu? The transformation of vertical keiretsu in Toyota, Nissan and Honda 1991-2011. *Asia Pacific Business Review*, *19*(1), 70–84. doi:10.1080/13602381.2011.652832

Aoki, M. (1988). *Information, incentives, and bargaining in the Japanese economy*. Cambridge, UK: Cambridge University Press. doi:10.1017/CBO9780511571701

Aoki, M. (1995). Towards a Comparative Institutional Analysis. *The Japanese Economic Review*, *47*(1), 1–19. doi:10.1111/j.1468-5876.1996.tb00031.x

Aoki, M., & Okuno-Fujiwara, M. (Eds.). (1996). *Comparative Institutional Analysis: A New Approach to Economic Systems*. Tokyo: University of Tokyo Press.

Arbore, A., & Busacca, B. (2009). Customer satisfaction and dissatisfaction in retail banking: Exploring the asymmetric impact of attribute performances. *Journal of Retailing and Consumer Services*, *16*(4), 271–280. doi:10.1016/j.jretconser.2009.02.002

Areni, C. (2003). Exploring managers' implicit theories of atmospheric music: Comparing academic analysis to industry insight. *Journal of Services Marketing*, *17*(2), 161–184. doi:10.1108/08876040310467925

Arli, V., Dylke, S., Burgess, R., & Soldo, E. (2013). Woolworths Australia and Walmart US: Best practices in supply chain collaboration. *Journal of Economics, Business, and Accountancy Ventura*, *16*(1), 27–46.

Armstrong, J. S., & Overton, T. S. (1977). Estimating nonresponse bias in mail surveys. *JMR, Journal of Marketing Research*, *14*(3), 396–402. doi:10.2307/3150783

Arnold, M., & Reynolds, K. (2003). Hedonic shopping motivations. *Journal of Retailing and Consumer Services*, *79*(2), 77–95.

Arrow, K.J. (1973). *Information and economic behavior*. Stockholm: Federation of Swedish Industries.

Arrow, K. J. (1974). *The limits of organization. New-York*. W. W. Norton & Company.

Arrow, K. J. (1975). Gifts and Exchanges. In *Altruism, Morality, and Economic Theory* (pp. 13–28). New York: Academic Press.

Asanuma, B. (1989). Manufacturer-Supplier Relationships in Japan and the Concept of Relation-Specific Skill. *Journal of the Japanese and International Economies*, *3*(1), 1–30. doi:10.1016/0889-1583(89)90029-4

Ashforth, B. E., & Mael, F. (1989). Social Identity Theory and the Organization. *Academy of Management Review*, *14*(1), 20–39.

Assens, C. (2003). Le réseau d'entreprises: Vers une synthèse des connaissances. *Management international*, *24*(1), 120-136.

Athanasopoulos, A., & Gounaris, S. (2001). Behavioural responses to customer satisfaction: An empirical study. *European Journal of Marketing*, *35*(5/6), 687–707. doi:10.1108/03090560110388169

Atilgan, E., Aksoy, S., & Akinci, S. (2005). Determinants of the brand equity: A verification approach in the beverage industry in Turkey. *Marketing Intelligence & Planning*, *23*(3), 237–248. doi:10.1108/02634500510597283

Avlonitis, G. J., & Gounaris, S. P. (1999). Marketing orientation and its determinants: An empirical analysis. *European Journal of Marketing*, *33*(11/12), 1003–1037. doi:10.1108/03090569910285896

Avramidis, N. (2007). Issues and necessities of small and medium size businesses. *Aluminium Profile Magazine, 7*.

Axelrod, R. (1984). *The Evolution of Cooperation*. New York: Basic Books.

Aydin, S., & Ozer, G. (2005). The analysis of antecedents of customer loyalty in the Turkishmobile telecommunication makret. *European Journal of Marketing*, *39*(7/8), 910–925. doi:10.1108/03090560510601833

Babin, B., Darden, W., & Griffin, M. (1994). Work and/or fun: Measuring hedonic and utilitarian shopping value. *The Journal of Consumer Research*, *20*(4), 644–556. doi:10.1086/209376

Back, K. J., & Parks, S. (2003). A brand loyalty model involving cognitive, affective and conative brand loyalty and customer satisfaction. *Journal of Hospitality & Tourism Research (Washington, D.C.)*, *27*(4), 419–435. doi:10.1177/10963480030274003

Baier, A. (1986). Trust and Antitrust. *Ethics*, *96*(2), 231–260. doi:10.1086/292745

Bain, J. S. (1956). *Barriers to new competition*. Cambridge, MA: Harvard University Press. doi:10.4159/harvard.9780674188037

Baker, J. (1987). The role of the environment in marketing services: The consumer perspective. In J. Czepiel, C. Congram, & J. Shanahan (Eds.), *The Services challenge: Integrating for competitive Advantage* (pp. 77–84). Chicago: American Marketing Association.

Ballantyne, D. (2003). A relationship mediated theory of internal marketing. *European Journal of Marketing*, *37*(9), 1242–1260. doi:10.1108/03090560310486979

Ball, D., Coelho, P. S., & Machás, A. (2004). The role of communication and trust in explaining customer loyalty: An extension to the ECSI case. *European Journal of Marketing*, *38*(9–10), 1272–1293. doi:10.1108/03090560410548979

Balmer, J. M. T. (2011). Corporate marketing myopia and the inexorable rise of a corporate marketing logic: Perspectives from identity-based views of the firm. *European Journal of Marketing*, *45*(9/10), 1329–1352. doi:10.1108/03090561111151781

Bamberg, S., & Moser, G. (2007). Twenty years after Hines, Hungerford, and Tomera: A new meta-analysis of psycho-social determinants of pro-environmental behaviour. *Journal of Environmental Psychology*, *27*(1), 14–25. doi:10.1016/j.jenvp.2006.12.002

Barber, B. (1983). *The Logic and Limits of Trust*. New Brunswick, NJ: Rutgers University Press.

Barbian, J. (2000). IT in 2000 and beyond. *Computer User, 19*(1).

Barney, J. B. (1991). Firm resources and sustained competitive advantage. *Journal of Management*, *17*(1), 99–120. doi:10.1177/014920639101700108

Barney, J. B., & Clark, D. N. (2007). *Resource-Based Theory: Creating and Sustaining Competitive Advantage*. New York: Oxford University Press.

Barney, J. B., & Hansen, M. H. (1994). Trust-worthiness as a source of competitive advantage. *Strategic Management Journal*, *15*(S1), 175–190. doi:10.1002/smj.4250150912

Barringer, B. R., & Greening, D. W. (1998). Small business growth through geographic expansion: A comparative case study. *Journal of Business Venturing*, *13*(5), 467–492. doi:10.1016/S0883-9026(97)00038-4

Bass, B. M. (1995). Transformational Leadership. *Journal of Management Inquiry*, *4*(3), 293–298. doi:10.1177/105649269543010

Baumgarth, C. (2010). Living the brand: Brand orientation in the business-to-business sector. *European Journal of Marketing*, *44*(5), 653–671. doi:10.1108/03090561011032315

Baumgarth, C., & Schmidt, M. (2010). How strong is the business-to-business brand in the workforce? *Industrial Marketing Management*, *39*(8), 1250–1260. doi:10.1016/j.indmarman.2010.02.022

Bendapudi, N., & Berry, L. L. (1997). Customers' motivations for maintaining relationships with service providers. *Journal of Retailing*, *73*(1), 15–37. doi:10.1016/S0022-4359(97)90013-0

Bennett, R., & Rundle-Thiele, S. (2004). Customer satisfaction should not be the only goal. *Journal of Services Marketing*, *18*(7), 514–523. doi:10.1108/08876040410561848

Bensaou, M., & Earl, M. (1998). The right mind-set for managing information technology. *Harvard Business Review*, *76*(5). PMID:10185427

Berglof, E., & Perotti, E. (1994). The Governance Structure of the Japanese Financial Keiretsu. *Journal of Financial Economics*, *36*(2), 259–284. doi:10.1016/0304-405X(94)90026-4

Bernhardt, K. L., Donthu, N., & Kennett, P. A. (2000). A longitudinal analysis of satisfaction and profitability. *Journal of Business Research*, *47*(2), 161–171. doi:10.1016/S0148-2963(98)00042-3

Bernstein, J., & Awe, S. (1999). "Wired travelers": Travel and tourism Web sites. *RSR. Reference Services Review*, *27*(Iss: 4), 364–375. doi:10.1108/00907329910303536

Berry, J., Hensel, S., & Burke, M. C. (1976). Improving Retailer Capability for Effective Consumerism Response. *Journal of Retailing*, *52*(3), 3–14.

Berry, L. L. (1981). The Employee as a Customer. *Journal of Retail Banking*, *3*, 25–28.

Berry, L. L., Hensel, J. S., & Burke, M. C. (1976). Improving retailer capability for effective consumerism response. *Journal of Retailing*, *52*(3), 3–14.

Berry, L. L., & Parasuraman, A. (1992). Services Marketing Starts from Within. *Marketing Management*, *1*(1), 24–34.

Berryman, K., Harrington, L., Layton-Rodin, D., & Rerolle, V. (1998). Electronic commerce: Three emerging strategies. *The McKinsey Quarterly*, *1*, 152–159.

Beverland, M. (2009). Boundary conditions to business relationships in China: The case of selling wine in China. *Journal of Business and Industrial Marketing*, *24*(1), 27–34. doi:10.1108/08858620910923676

Beverland, M., Napoli, J., & Lindgreen, A. (2007). Industrial global brand leadership: A capabilities view. *Industrial Marketing Management*, *36*(8), 1082–1093. doi:10.1016/j.indmarman.2006.08.007

Bhattacharya, S. (2011). Consumer Attitude towards Green Marketing in India. *The IUP Journal of Marketing Management*, 62-70.

Bhattacharya, C. B., & Korschun, D. (2008). Stakeholder Marketing: Beyond the Four Ps and the Customer. *Journal of Public Policy & Marketing*, *27*(1), 113–116. doi:10.1509/jppm.27.1.113

Bhide, A. (1994, March-April). How Entrepreneurs Craft Strategies That Work. *Harvard Business Review*, 150–161.

Bies, R. J., & Tripp, T. M. (1996). Beyond Distrust: Getting Even and the Need for Revenge. In *Trust in Organizations: Frontiers of Theory and Research* (pp. 246–260). Thousand Oaks, CA: Sage. doi:10.4135/9781452243610.n12

Bigley, G. A., & Pearce. (1998). Straining for Shared Meaning in Organization Science: Problems of Trust and Distrust. *Academy of Management Review*, *23*, 405–421.

Bilgin, F. Z., Sriram, V., & Wuhrer, G. (2004). *Drivers of global business success*. London, UK: Palgrave Macmillan.

Billire, P. (2009). *Leadership*. London: A&C Black Publishers Ltd.

Binninger, A. S. (2008). Exploring the relationships between retail brands and consumer store loyalty. *International Journal of Retail & Distribution Management*, *36*(2), 94–110. doi:10.1108/09590550810853057

Birkinshaw, J. (2010). *Reinventing Management: Smarter Choices For Getting The Work Done*. Chichester, UK: John Wiley & Sons, Ltd.

Bitner, M. (1992). Servicescapes: The impact of they physical surroundings on customers and employees. *Journal of Marketing*, *56*(2), 57–71. doi:10.2307/1252042

Bitner, M. J. (1990). Evaluating service encounters: The effects of physical surroundings and employee responses. *Journal of Marketing*, *54*(2), 69–82. doi:10.2307/1251871

Bitner, M. J., & Hubbert, A. R. (1994). Encounter satisfaction versus overall satisfaction versus quality. In *Service Quality: New Directions in Theory and Practice*. London: Sage.

Bitner, M., & Hubbert, A. (1994). Encounter satisfaction versus overall satisfaction versus quality. In R. Rust, & R. Oliver (Eds.), *Service quality: New directions in theory and practice* (pp. 72–84). New York: Sage Publications.

Blanchot, F., & Kalika, M. (2002). The Renault-Nissan Alliance, Case study. (Y. Meyer, Trans.). Paris: Centrale de Cas et de Médias Pédagogiques (CCMP).

Bloemer, J., Ruyter, K., & Peeters, P. (1998). Investigating drivers of bank loyalty: The complex relationship between image, service quality and satisfaction. *International Journal of Bank Marketing*, *16*(7), 279–286. doi:10.1108/02652329810245984

Blose, J., Tankersley, W., & Flynn, L. (2005). Managing service quality using data envelopment analysis. *The Quality Management Journal*, *12*(2), 7–24.

Blumberg, B., Cooper, D. R., & Schindler, P. S. (2005). *Business Research Methods*. London: McGraw-Hill.

Blumenthal, B., & Haspeslagh, P. (1994). Toward a definition of corporate transformation. *Sloan Management Review*.

Bodgett, J. G., & Anderson, R. D. (2000). A Bayesian network case of the consumer complaint process. *Journal of Service Research*, *2*(4), 321–338. doi:10.1177/109467050024002

Bolton, R., & Drew, J. (1991). A multistage model of customers' assessments of service quality and value. *The Journal of Consumer Research*, *17*(4), 375–384. doi:10.1086/208564

Boo, S., Busser, J., & Baloglu, S. (2009). A model of customer-based brand equity and its application to multiple destinations. *Tourism Management*, *30*(2), 219–231. doi:10.1016/j.tourman.2008.06.003

Bouder, F., Bertok, F., & Beschel, R. (2001). Fostering Public Ethics and Preventing Corruption. In Schiavo-Campo & Sundaram (Eds.), To Serve and Preserve: Improving Public Administration in a Competitive World. Manila: Asian Development Bank.

Boulding, K. E. (1956). *The Image*. Ann Arbor, MI: University of Michigan Press.

Bove, L., & Johnson, W. (2001). Customer relationships with service personnel: Do we measure closeness, quality or strength? *Journal of Business Research*, *54*(3), 189–197. doi:10.1016/S0148-2963(00)00122-3

Bowen, J. T., & Shoemaker, S. (1998). Loyalty: A strategic commitment. *The Cornell Hotel and Restaurant Administration Quarterly*, *39*(1), 12–25. doi:10.1177/001088049803900104

Bowen, T. J., & Chen, S. (2001). The relationship between customer loyalty and customer satisfaction. *International Journal of Contemporary Hospitality Management*, *13*(5), 213–217. doi:10.1108/09596110110395893

Boyatzis, R. E. (1998). *Transforming Qualitative Information*. Thousand Oaks, CA: Sage.

Braady, M., & Cronin, J. (2001). Some new thoughts on conceptualizing perceived service quality: A hierarchical approach. *Journal of Marketing*, *65*(3), 34–49. doi:10.1509/jmkg.65.3.34.18334

Bradshaw, P. (1998). *4x4 Leadership And The Purpose Of The Firm*. Binghampton, NY: The Haworth Press.

Brady, M. K., Cronin, J. J. Jr, & Brand, R. R. (2002). Performance-only measurement of service quality: A replication and extension. *Journal of Business Research*, *55*(1), 17–31. doi:10.1016/S0148-2963(00)00171-5

Brand Learning. (n.d.). *Conversation # 7 – Care about culture,2011*. Retrieved from www.brandlearning.com/Whats-New/Brand-Learning-News/The-Conversations-for-2011-7.aspx

Bratt, C., Hallstedt, S., Robèrt, K.-H., Broman, G., & Oldmark, J. (2011). Assessment of eco-labelling criteria development from a strategic sustainability perspective. *Journal of Cleaner Production*, *19*(14), 1631–1638. doi:10.1016/j.jclepro.2011.05.012

Braun, V., & Clarke, V. (2006). Using thematic analysis in psychology. *Qualitative Research in Psychology*, *3*(2), 77–101. doi:10.1191/1478088706qp063oa

Breton, A., & Wintrobe, R. (1982). *The logic of bureaucratic conduct: An economic analysis of competition, exchange and efficiency in private and public organizations*. Cambridge, UK: Cambridge University Press. doi:10.1017/CBO9780511896033

Bridson, K., & Evans, J. (2004). The secret to a fashion advantage is brand orientation. *International Journal of Retail & Distribution Management*, *32*(8), 403–411. doi:10.1108/09590550410546223

Brodie, R. J., Glynn, M. S., & Little, V. (2006). The service brand and the service-dominant logic: Missing fundamental premise or the need for stronger theory. *Marketing Theory*, *6*(3), 363–379. doi:10.1177/1470593106066797

Bromiley, P., & Harris, J. (2006). Trust, transaction cost economics, and mechanisms. In R. Bachmann, & A. Zaheer (Eds.), *Handbook of Trust Research* (pp. 124–143). Northampton, MA: Edward Elgar. doi:10.4337/9781847202819.00014

Brooke, J. (2002). *The Brand Inside*. Retrieved from www.cim.co.uk/filestore/resources/canons/brandinside.pdf

Brouthers, L. E., O'Donnell, E., & Hadjimarsu, J. (2005). Generic product strategies for emerging market exports into triad nation markets: A mimetic isomorphism approach. *Journal of Management Studies*, *42*(1), 225–245. doi:10.1111/j.1467-6486.2005.00495.x

Brouthers, L. E., & Xu, K. (2002). Product stereotypes, strategy, and performance satisfaction: The case of Chinese exporters. *Journal of International Business Studies*, *33*(4), 657–677. doi:10.1057/palgrave.jibs.8491038

Brown, T., Barry, T., Dacin, P., & Gunst, R. (2005). Spreading the word: Investigating antecedents of consumers' positive word-of-mouth intentions and behaviors in a retailing context. *Journal of the Academy of Marketing Science*, *33*(2), 123–138. doi:10.1177/0092070304268417

Brucks, M. (1985). The effects of product class knowledge on information search behavior. *The Journal of Consumer Research*, *12*(1), 1–16. doi:10.1086/209031

Bryman, A., & Bell, E. (2007). Business Research Methods (2nd ed.). New York: Oxford.

Buchanan, D. A. (2012). Case Studies in Organizational Research. In *Qualitative Organizational Research: Core Methods and Current Challenges*. London: Sage.

Buchholz, R. A., & Rosenthal, S. B. (2005). Toward a Contemporary Conceptual Framework for Stakeholder Theory. *Journal of Business Ethics*, *58*(1-3), 137–148. doi:10.1007/s10551-005-1393-8

Buhalis, D. (1998). Strategic use of information technologies in the tourism industry. *Tourism Management*, *19*(5), 409–421. doi:10.1016/S0261-5177(98)00038-7

Buil, I., De Chernatony, L., & Martinez, E. (2008). A cross-cultural validation of the consumer-based brand equity scale. *Journal of Product and Brand Management*, *17*(6), 384–392. doi:10.1108/10610420810904121

Bunse, S., & Fritz, V. (2012). *Making Public Sector Reforms Work Political and Economic Contexts, Incentives and Strategies* (working paper 6174). The World Bank.

Burgess, S. M., & Steenkamp, J. B. E. M. (2006). Marketing renaissance: How research in emerging markets advances marketing science and practice. *International Journal of Research in Marketing*, *23*(4), 337–356. doi:10.1016/j.ijresmar.2006.08.001

Burgess, S. M., & Steenkamp, J. B. E. M. (2011). Call for papers: Special issue on marketing in emerging markets. *International Journal of Research in Marketing*, *28*(1), vi–vii. doi:10.1016/S0167-8116(11)00014-0

Burnes, B. (2000). *Managing Change: A Strategic Approach to Organizational Dynamics*. London: Pearson Education.

Burn, J., Marshall, P., & Barnett, M. (2002). *E-business Strategies for Virtual Organisations*. Oxford, UK: Butterworth-Heinemann.

Burn, J., & Robins, G. (2003). Moving towards e-government: A case study of organizational change processes. *Logistics Information Management*, *16*(1), 25–35. doi:10.1108/09576050310453714

Butler, J. K. Jr, & Cantrell, R. S. (1984). A behavioral decision theory approach to modeling dyadic trust in superiors and subordinates. *Psychological Reports*, *55*(1), 19–28. doi:10.2466/pr0.1984.55.1.19

Buttle, F. A. (1998). Word of mouth: Understanding and managing referral marketing. *Journal of Strategic Marketing*, *6*(3), 241–254. doi:10.1080/096525498346658

Buzzell, R., & Gale, B. (1987). *The PIMS principles*. New York: Free Press.

Cahill, D. (2007). *Customer loyalty in third party logistics relationships: Findings from studies in Germany and the USA*. New York: Springer.

Cao, L. (2002). Corporate and product identity in the post national economy: Rethinking US trade laws. *California Law Review*, *90*(2), 401–484. doi:10.2307/3481283

Carmines, E. G., & McIver, J. P. (1981). Analyzing models with unobserved variables: Analysis of covariance structures. In G. Bohrnstedt, & E. Borgatta (Eds.), *Social Measurement: Current Issues*. Beverly Hills, CA: Sage.

Carr, A. S., & Pearson, J. N. (2002). The impact of purchasing and supplier involvement on strategic purchasing and its impact on firm's performance. *International Journal of Operations & Production Management*, *22*(9/10), 1032–1055. doi:10.1108/01443570210440528

Carrig, K., & Wright, P. M. (2006). *Building profit through people: making your workforce the strongest link in the value-profit chain*. Society for Human Resource Management.

Carson, D. (1990). Some Exploratory Models for Assessing Small Firms' Marketing Performance: A Qualitative Approach. *European Journal of Marketing*, *24*(11), 8–51. doi:10.1108/03090569010006056

Cater, B., & Cater, T. (2009). Relationship-value-based antecedents of customer satisfaction and loyalty in manufacturing. *Journal of Business and Industrial Marketing*, *24*(7-8), 585–597. doi:10.1108/08858620910999457

Cavusgil, S. T., Ghauri, P. N., & Agarwal, M. R. (2002). *Doing business in emerging markets*. Thousand Oaks, CA: Sage.

Cayla, J., & Arnould, E. J. (2008). A cultural approach to branding in the global marketplace. *Journal of International Marketing*, *16*(4), 88–114. doi:10.1509/jimk.16.4.86

Cederle A., (2005): The process began in the 1970s with Sabre and Apollo, two CRSs run by American Airlines and United Airlines, respectively.

Chaffey, D., Mayer, R., Johnston, K., & Ellis-Chadwick, F. (2006). *Internet marketing: Strategy, implementation and practice* (3rd ed.). Harlow, UK: Financial Times/Prentice Hall.

Chanley, V. A. (2002). Trust in Government in the Aftermath of 9/11: Determinants and Consequences. *Political Psychology*, *23*(3), 469–483. doi:10.1111/0162-895X.00294

Chanley, V. A., Rudolph, T. J., & Rahn, W. M. (2000). The origins and consequences of public trust in government: A time series analysis. *Public Opinion Quarterly*, *64*(3), 239–256. doi:10.1086/317987 PMID:11114267

Chanley, V. A., Rudolph, T. J., & Rahn, W. M. (2001). Public trust in government in the Reagan years and beyond. In J. R. Hibbing, & E. Theiss-Morse (Eds.), *What is it about government that Americans dislike?* (pp. 59–78). Cambridge, UK: Cambridge University Press.

Chan, R. Y. K. (2004). Consumer responses to environmental advertising in China. *Marketing Intelligence & Planning*, *22*(4), 427–437. doi:10.1108/02634500410542789

Chao, P., Samiee, S., & Yip, L. S. (2004). Guest editorial: International marketing in the Asia Pacific region. *International Marketing Review*, *21*(3), 243–246. doi:10.1108/02651330410539594

Charles, G. (2007, September). The CIM Definition: Fit for Purpose?. *Marketing*, 16.

Charley, B. (1997). Organisational Infidelity: How Violations of Trust Affect the Employee-Employer Relationship. *The Academy of Management Executive*, *11*(4), 94–99.

Chaudhuri, A. (2002). How brand reputation affects the advertising-brand equity link. *Journal of Advertising Research*, *42*(3), 33–43.

Chen, A. C. H. (2001). Using free association to examine the relationship between the characteristics of brand associations and brand equity. *Journal of Product and Brand Management*, *10*(7), 439–451. doi:10.1108/10610420110410559

Chen, C. F., & Chang, Y. (2008). Airline brand equity, brand preference, and purchase intentions – The moderating effects of switching costs. *Journal of Air Transport Management*, *14*(1), 40–42. doi:10.1016/j.jairtraman.2007.11.003

Cheng, C., & Piccoli, G. (2002). Web-Based Training in the Hospitality Industry: A Conceptual Definition, Taxonomy and Preliminary Investigation. *International Journal of Hospitality Information Technology*, *2*(2), 19–33. doi:10.3727/153373402803617737

Cheng, E. W. L. (2001). SEM being more effective than multiple regression in parsimonious model testing for management development research. *Journal of Management Development*, *20*(7), 650–667. doi:10.1108/02621710110400564

Chen, Y. S. (2009). The drivers of green brand equity: Green brand image, green satisfaction and green trust. *Journal of Business Ethics*, *92*(3), 307–319.

Cherian, J., & Jacob, J. (2012). Green Marketing: A Study of Consumers' Attitude towards Environment Friendly Products. *Asian Social Science*, *8*(12).

Chervenak, L. (1993). Hotel Technology at the start of the New Millennium. *Hospitality Research Journal.*, *17*(1), 113–120. doi:10.1177/109634809301700110

Chevalier, M., & Mazzalovo, G. (2008). *Luxury brand management: A world of privilege*. Singapore: John Wiley & Sons.

Chiaravalle, B., & Schenck, B. F. (2007). *Branding for dummies*. Indianapolis, In John Wiley & Sons.

Chi, C. G., & Gursoy, D. (2009). Employee satisfaction, customer satisfaction and financial performance: An empirical examination. *International Journal of Hospitality Management*, *28*(2), 245–253. doi:10.1016/j.ijhm.2008.08.003

Child, J. (2001). Trust–the fundamental bond in global collaboration. *Organizational Dynamics*, *29*(4), 274–288. doi:10.1016/S0090-2616(01)00033-X

Chiou, J. S., Droge, C., & Hanvanich, S. (2002). Does customer knowledge affect how loyalty is formed? *Journal of Service Research*, *5*(2), 113–124. doi:10.1177/109467002237494

Cho, J. J.-K., Ozment, J., & Sink, H. (2008). Logistics capability, logistics outsourcing and firm performance in an e-commerce market. *International Journal of Physical Distribution & Logistics Management*, *38*(5), 336–359. doi:10.1108/09600030810882825

Choo, H. J., Moon, H., Kim, H., & Yoon, N. (2012). Luxury customer value. *Journal of Fashion Marketing and Management*, *16*(1), 81–101. doi:10.1108/13612021211203041

Cho, Y., & Fesenmaier, D. R. (2001). A new paradigm for tourism and electronic commerce: Experience marketing using the virtual tour. In E. Laws, & D. Buhalis (Eds.), *tourism distribution channels: practices, issues and transformation* (pp. 351–370). Thomson.

Chu, J. (2013). Quantifying nation equity with sales data: A structural approach. *International Journal of Research in Marketing*, *30*(1), 19–35. doi:10.1016/j.ijresmar.2012.06.005

Clarkson, M. E. (1995). A Stakeholder Framework for Analysing and evaluating corporate social performance. *Academy of Management Review*, *20*(1), 92–117.

Clayton, T., & Criscuolo, C. 2002, *Electronic commerce and business change*, National Statistics, viewed 16 April 2005, http://www.statistics.gov.uk/cci/article.asp?ID=139>

Coase, R. (1937). The Nature of the Firm. *Economica*, *4*(16), 386–405. doi:10.1111/j.1468-0335.1937.tb00002.x

Cohen, D., & Prusak, L. (2001). *In Good Company: How Social Capital Makes Organizations Work*. Boston, MA: Harvard Business School Press.

Cohen, W. (2010). *Drucker on Leadership*. San Francisco, CA: Jossey-Bass.

Coleman, J. S. (1988). Social capital in the creation of human capital. *American Journal of Sociology*, *94*(s1 Supplement), S95–S120. doi:10.1086/228943

Collier, J.E., & Bienstock, C.C. (2006, Fall). How do customers judge quality in an e-tailor?. *MIT Sloan Management Review,* 35–40.

Collins, B., & Payne, A. (1991). Internal Marketing: A new perspective for HRM. *European Management Journal, 9*(3), 261–270. doi:10.1016/0263-2373(91)90006-C

Collins, C., Buhalis, D., & Peters, M. (2003). Enhancing SMTEs' Business Performance Through the Internet and U-learning Platforms. *Education + Training, 45*(8/9), 483–494. doi:10.1108/00400910310508874

Collins, J. C. (2001). *Good to Great: Why Some Companies Make The Leap..., & Others Don't.* London: Random House.

Collins, J., & Hussey, R. (2003). *Business Research: A Practical Guide for Undergraduate and Postgraduate Students* (2nd ed.). Basingstoke, UK: Macmillan.

Colquitt, J. A., Scott, B. A., & LePine, J. A. (2007). Trust, Trustworthiness, and Trust Propensity: A Meta-Analytic Test of Their Unique Relationships With Risk Taking and Job Performance. *The Journal of Applied Psychology, 92*(4), 909–927. doi:10.1037/0021-9010.92.4.909 PMID:17638454

Coltman, T., Devinney, T., Latukefu, A., & Midgley, D. (2001). E-business: Revolution, evolution or hype? *California Management Review, 44*(61).

ComScore Report. (2013). *India is now world's third largest internet used after US, China.* Retrieved from www.digitsmith.com

Conduit, J., & Mavondo, F. T. (2001). How Critical Is Internal Customer Orientation to Market Orientation? *Journal of Business Research, 51*(1), 11–24. doi:10.1016/S0148-2963(99)00044-2

Conger, J. A., & Kanungo, R. N. (1998). *Charismatic Leadership in Organizations.* Thousand Oaks, CA: Sage.

Conger, J. A., Kanungo, R. N., & Menon, S. T. (2000). Charismatic leadership and follower effects. *Journal of Organizational Behavior, 21*(7), 747–767. doi:10.1002/1099-1379(200011)21:7<747::AID-JOB46>3.0.CO;2-J

Conner, K. R. (1991). A historical comparison of resource-based theory and five schools of thought within IO economics: Do we have a new theory of the firm? *Journal of Management, 17*(1). doi:10.1177/014920639101700109

Cook, J., & Wall, T. (1980). New work attitude measures of trust, organizational commitment, and personal need nonfulfillment. *Journal of Occupational Psychology, 53*(1), 39–52. doi:10.1111/j.2044-8325.1980.tb00005.x

Corbin, J., & Strauss, A. (2008). *Basics of Qualitative Research: Techniques and Procedures for Developing Grounded Theory* (3rd ed.). Thousand Oaks, CA: Sage.

Cough, P. (2004). *Electronic and Clothes: Watt to wear?* Leeds, UK: Wearable Electronic and Smart Textiles.

Courtney, H., Kirkland, J., & Viguerie, P. (1997, November/December). Strategy Under Uncertainty. *The McKinsey Quarterly.* PMID:10174798

Cox, D., La Caze, M., & Levine, M. P. (1999). Should We Strive for Integrity? *The Journal of Value Inquiry, 33*(4), 519–530. doi:10.1023/A:1004614232579

Cramton, C. D. (2001). The mutual knowledge problem and its consequences for dispersed collaboration. *Organization Science, 12*(3), 346–371. doi:10.1287/orsc.12.3.346.10098

Cronin, J., & Taylor, S. (1992). Measuring service quality: A re-examination and etension. *Journal of Marketing, 56*(3), 55–68. doi:10.2307/1252296

Crutchfield, T. N. (2001). The Effect of Trust and Commitment on Retention of High-Risk Professional Service Customers. *Services Marketing Quarterly, 22*(2), 17–27. doi:10.1300/J396v22n02_02

Cullen, J. B., Johnson, J. L., & Sakano, T. (1995). Japanese and local partner commitment to IJVs: Psychological consequences of outcomes and investments in the IJV relationship. *Journal of International Business Studies, 26*(1), 91–115. doi:10.1057/palgrave.jibs.8490167

Cullen, J. B., Johnson, J. L., & Sakano, T. (2000). Success through commitment and trust: The soft side of strategic alliance management. *Journal of World Business, 35*(3), 223–240. doi:10.1016/S1090-9516(00)00036-5

Currall, S. C., & Inkpen, A. (2002). A Multilevel Approach to Trust in Joint Ventures. *Journal of International Business Studies*, *33*(3), 479–495. doi:10.1057/palgrave.jibs.8491027

Currall, S. C., & Inkpen, A. C. (2006). On the Complexity of Organizational Trust: A Multi-level Co-Evolutionary Perspective and Guidelines for Future Research. In R. Bachmann, & A. Zaheer (Eds.), *Handbook of Trust Research* (pp. 235–246). Edward Elgar. doi:10.4337/9781847202819.00021

D'Aveni, R., & MacMillan, I. C. (1994). *Hypercompetition*. New York: Free Press.

D'Souza, C., Taghian, M., & Lamb, P. (2006). An empirical study on the influence of environmental labels on consumers. *Corporate Communications: An International Journal*, *11*(2), 162–173. doi:10.1108/13563280610661697

D'Souza, C., Taghian, M., Lamb, P., & Peretiatko, R. (2007). Green decisions: Demographics and consumer understanding of environmental labels. *International Journal of Consumer Studies*, *31*, 371–376. doi:10.1111/j.1470-6431.2006.00567.x

Da Silva, R. V., & Syed Alwi, S. F. (2006). Cognitive, affective and conative behavioural responses in retail corporate branding. *Journal of Product and Brand Management*, *15*(5), 293–305. doi:10.1108/10610420610685703

Dabholkar, P. A., & Abston, K. A. (2008). The role of customer contact employees as external customers: A conceptual framework for marketing strategy and future research. *Journal of Business Research*, *61*(9), 885–1026. doi:10.1016/j.jbusres.2007.10.004

Daft, R. (1983). *Organization Theory and Design*. New York: West Publishing.

Daidj, N. (2009). The evolution of corporate governance in Japan: The case of vertical keiretsu groups. In G. Aras & D. Crowther D. (Eds.), Global perspectives on Corporate Governance and Corporate Social Responsibility (pp. 73-106). Aldershot, UK: Gower Publishing Limited.

Daidj, N. (2011). The evolution of KM practices: The case of the Renault-Nissan International strategic alliance. In *Knowledge Management 2.0: Organizational Models and Enterprise Strategies*. IGI Global. doi:10.4018/978-1-61350-195-5.ch010

Daidj, N. (2013a). Different perspectives on KM 2.0 new practices and Web 2.0 tools at Renault-Nissan alliance since 2000. *International Journal of Strategic Information Technology and Applications*, *4*(2), 1–20. doi:10.4018/jsita.2013040101

Daidj, N. (2013b). The evolution of new entrants' strategies in the media sector in a context of convergence: The case of Apple, Google and Microsoft. In S. Ben Letaifa, A. Gratacap, & T. Isckia (Eds.), *Understanding business ecosystems: How firms succeed in the new world of convergence* (pp. 165–192). De Boeck.

Daidj, N., Gardet, E., & Mothe, C. (2008). The manufacturing keiretsu: A changing inter-company network? The case of the car industry. In S. Dzever, J. Jaussaud, & B. O'Callaghan (Eds.), *Evolving corporate structures and cultures in Asia* (pp. 97–117). London: ISTE/Wiley Ltd.

Daley, D. M., & Vasu, M. L. (1998). Fosternig Organizational Trust in North Carolina, The Pivotal Role Of Administrators And Political Leaders. *Administration & Society*, *30*(1), 62–84. doi:10.1177/009539979803000105

Dall'Acqua, L., Tonin, C., Peila, R., Ferrero, F., & Catellani, M. (2004). Performances and properties of intrinsic conductive cellulose-polypyrrole textiles. *Synthetic Metals*, *146*(2), 213–221. doi:10.1016/j.synthmet.2004.07.005

Dalton, D. (2000). Understanding High Performance Organizations. *Security*, *37*, 69.

Daniele, R., & Frew, A. (2005). Using Concept Maps to Examine Business Models and Drivers of Competitive Advantage for Travel eMediaries. In A. Frew (Ed.), *Information and Communication Technologies in Tourism 2005* (pp. 497–507). Vienna: Springer. doi:10.1007/3-211-27283-6_45

Das, A., Kumar, V., & Saha, G. C. (2010). Retail service quality in the context of transition economies. *International Journal of Quality & Reliability Management*, *27*(6), 658–683. doi:10.1108/02656711011054542

David, F. R. (2005). *Strategic Management*. New York: Prentice-Hall.

Davies, E., Bannock, G., Uncles, M., & Trot, P. (n.d.). *The New Penguin Business Dictionary*. Penguin.

Davies, F. M., Goode, M. M. H., Moutinho, L. A., & Ogbonna, E. (2001). Critical factors in consumer supermarket shopping behaviour: A neural network approach. *Journal of Consumer Behaviour*, *1*(1), 35–49. doi:10.1002/cb.52

Davin, K. (1997). Effects of Computer Support on Group Decisions. *Journal of Hospitality & Tourism Research (Washington, D.C.)*, *21*(2), 44–57. doi:10.1177/109634809702100204

Davis, D. F., Golicic, S. L., & Marquardt, A. J. (2008). Branding a B2B service: Does a brand differentiate a logistics service provider? *Industrial Marketing Management*, *37*(2), 218–227. doi:10.1016/j.indmarman.2007.02.003

Day, D. V., & Lord, R. G. (1986). Executive leadership and organizational performance: Suggestions for a new theory and methodology. *Journal of Management*, *14*(3), 453–464. doi:10.1177/014920638801400308

Day, G., & Schoemaker, P. (2000). Avoiding the pitfalls of emerging technologies. *California Management Review*, *42*(52).

De Chernatony, L., & Cottam, S. (2006). Internal brand factors driving successful financial services brand. *European Journal of Marketing*, *40*(5-6), 611–633. doi:10.1108/03090560610657868

De Furia, G. L. (1997). *Facilitators Guide to the Interpersonal Trust Surveys*. Pfeiffer & Co.

De Jesus, M. C., Fu, Y., & Weiss, R. A. (1997). Conductive polymer blends prepared by ın sıtu polymerization of pyrrole: A review. *Polymer Engineering and Science*, *37*(12), 1936–1943. doi:10.1002/pen.11844

Delgadillo, Y., & Escalas, J. E. (2004). Narrative word-of-mouth communication: Exploring memory and attitude effects of consumer storytelling. *Advances in Consumer Research. Association for Consumer Research (U. S.)*, *31*(1), 186–192.

DelVecchio, D., Jarvis, C. B., Klink, R. R., & Dineen, B. B. (2007). Leveraging brand equity to attract human capital. *Marketing Letters*, *18*(3), 149–164. doi:10.1007/s11002-007-9012-3

Desai, P. S., Kalra, A., & Murthi, B. P. S. (2008). When old is gold: The role of business longevity in risky situations. *Journal of Marketing*, *72*(1), 95–107. doi:10.1509/jmkg.72.1.95

Deshpande, R., & Webster, F. E. (1989). Organizational Culture and Marketing: Defining the Research. *Journal of Marketing*, *53*(1), 3–17. doi:10.2307/1251521

Deutsch, M. (1958). Trust and suspicion. *The Journal of Conflict Resolution*, *2*(4), 265–279. doi:10.1177/002200275800200401

Deutsch, M. (1973). *The Resolution of Conflict: Constructive and Destructive Processes*. New Haven, CT: Yale University Press.

Dick, A., & Basu, K. (1994). Customer loyalty: Toward an integrated conceptual framework. *Journal of Marine Science*, *22*(2), 99–113.

Dietz, & Hartog. (2006). Measuring trust inside organisations. *Personnel Review*, *35*(5), 557 – 588.

Dirks, K. T. (2000). Trust in leadership and team performance: Evidence from NCAA basketball. *The Journal of Applied Psychology*, *85*(6), 1004–1012. doi:10.1037/0021-9010.85.6.1004 PMID:11125648

Dobele, A., & Lindgreen, A. (2010). Exploring the nature of value in the word-of-mouth referral equation for health care. *Journal of Marketign Management*, *27*(3/4), 269–290.

Dobele, A., Lindgreen, A., Beverland, M., Vanhamme, J., & van Wijk, R. (2007). Why pass on viral message? Because they connect emotionally. *Business Horizons*, *50*(4), 291–304. doi:10.1016/j.bushor.2007.01.004

Dogac, A., Kabak, Y., Laleci, G., Sinir, S., Yildiz, A., Kirbas, S., & Gurcan, Y. (2004). Semantically enriched web services for the travel industry. *SIGMOD Record*, *33*(3), 21–27. doi:10.1145/1031570.1031575

Donaldson, T., & Preston, L. E. (1995). The stakeholder theory of the corporation: Concepts, evidence and implications. *Academy of Management Review*, *20*, 65–91.

Dono, J., Janine, W., & Ben, R. (2010). The relationship between environmental activism, pro-environmental behaviour and social identity. *Journal of Environmental Psychology*, *30*(2), 178–186. doi:10.1016/j.jenvp.2009.11.006

Doyle, B. (2008). Customer Advocacy: How US Consumers Rate Their Banks, Brokerages, And Insurers. *Forrester Research Inc*. Retrieved September 2, 2013, from http://www.forrester.com/rb/Research/customer_advocacy_2008_how_us_consumers _rate/q/id/46083/t/2

Doyle, P. (1995). Marketing in the new millennium. *European Journal of Marketing*, *29*(13), 23–41. doi:10.1108/03090569510147712

Doz, Y., & Hamel, G. (1998). *Alliance Advantage*. Boston: Harvard Business School Press.

Driver, J. (1999). Developments in Airline Marketing Practice[enhancing the participatory role of travelers and exploiting their collective intelligence.]. *Journal of Marketing Practice: Applied Marketing Science*, *5*(5), 134–150. doi:10.1108/EUM0000000004571

Drucker, P. F. (1954). *The Practice of Management*. New York: Harper and Row.

Drucker, P. F. (1973). *Management: Tasks, Responsibilities, Practices*. New York: Harper Collins.

Drucker, P. F. (2002). They're not employees, they're people. *Harvard Business Review*, *80*(2), 70–77. PMID:11894680

Duffy, D. (2003). Internal and external factors which affect customer loyalty. *Journal of Consumer Marketing*, *20*(5), 480–485. doi:10.1108/07363760310489715

Dunes, M., & Pras, B. (2013). Practices in the brand management system: Identification and considerations for five business sectors. *Journal of Product and Brand Management*, *22*(7), 444–461. doi:10.1108/JPBM-09-2013-0396

Dunne, P. A., & Barnes, J.G. (2000). Internal Marketing: A relationships and value-creation view. *Internal Marketing: Directions for Management*, 192-220.

Dunn, S. C., Seaker, R. F., & Waller, M. A. (1994). Latent variables in business logistics research: Scale development and validation. *Journal of Business Logistics*, *15*(2), 145–172.

Dye, R. (2000). The buzz on buzz. *Harvard Business Review*, *78*(6), 139–146. PMID:11184968

Easterby-Smith, M., Thorpe, R., & Jackson, P. R. (2008). *Management Research* (3rd ed.). London: Sage.

East, R. (1997). *Consumer Behaviour: Advances and Applications in Marketing*. London: Prentice Hall.

East, R., Hammond, K., & Lomax, W. (2008). Measuring the impact of positive and negative word-of-mouth on brand purchase probability. *International Journal of Research in Marketing*, *25*(3), 215–224. doi:10.1016/j.ijresmar.2008.04.001

Edelenbos, J., & Klijn, E. (2007). Trust in complex decision-making networks: A theoretical and empirical exploration. *Administration & Society*, *39*(1), 25–50. doi:10.1177/0095399706294460

Edvardsson, B., Kristensson, P., Magnusson, P., & Sundström, E. (2012). Customer integration within service development. *Technovation*, *32*(7-8), 419–429. doi:10.1016/j.technovation.2011.04.006

Ehigie, B. (2006). Correlates of customer loyalty to their bank: A case study in Nigeria. *International Journal of Bank Marketing*, *24*(7), 494–508. doi:10.1108/02652320610712102

Eisenhardt, K. (1989). Building theories from case study research. *Academy of Management Review*, *14*, 532–550.

Elias, M. S. (2009). Employee Commitment in times of change: Assessing the importance of attitudes toward organisational change. *Journal of Management*, *35*(1), 37–55. doi:10.1177/0149206307308910

Ellis, K. & Shockley-Zalabak. (1999). Communicating with management: Relating trust to job satisfaction and organizational effectiveness. Paper presented at the National Communication Association Convention. Chicago, IL.

Eltantawy, R. A., Giunipero, L., & Fox, G. L. (2009). A strategic skill based model of supplier integration and its effect on supply management performance. *Industrial Marketing Management*, *38*(8), 925–936. doi:10.1016/j.indmarman.2008.12.022

Erdem, T., Swait, J., & Valenzuela, A. (2006). Brands as signals: A cross country validation study. *Journal of Marketing*, *70*(1), 34–49. doi:10.1509/jmkg.2006.70.1.34

Eriksson, P., & Kovalainen, A. (2008). *Qualitative Methods in Business Research*. London: Sage. doi:10.4135/9780857028044

Esbjerg, L., Jensen, B. B., Bech-Larsen, T., Dutra de Barcellos, M., Boztug, Y., & Grunert, K. G. (2012). An integrative conceptual framework for analyzing customer satisfaction with shopping trip experiences in grocery retailing. *Journal of Retailing and Consumer Services*, *19*(4), 445–456. doi:10.1016/j.jretconser.2012.04.006

Esper, T. L., Jensen, T. D., Turnipseed, F. L., & Burton, S. (2003). The last mile: An examination of effects of online retail delivery strategies on consumers. *Journal of Business Logistics*, *24*(2), 177–203. doi:10.1002/j.2158-1592.2003.tb00051.x

Euromonitor International. (2012). *Grocery Retailers in the United Kingdom*. Retrieved from www.euromonitor.com

European Commission. (2000). *SMEs Access to the Digital Economy*. Brussels: Directorate C of DG Information Society.

Eurostat. (2013). *Government statistics*. Retrieved September the 1st from http://epp.eurostat.ec.europa.eu/portal/page/portal/government_finance_statistics/data/database

Evans, W. (2012). *Trust in Japanese Culture and Management*. (Unpublished doctoral dissertation). Telecom Ecole de Management, Evry, France.

Evans, P., & Warster, T. S. (1999). *Blown to Bits: How the New Economic of Information Transforms Strategy*. Boston, MA: Harvard Business School Press.

Evans, S. (1991). Strategic flexibility for high technology maneuvers. *Journal of Management Studies*, *28*, 69–89. doi:10.1111/j.1467-6486.1991.tb00271.x

Ewing, M. T. (2000). Brand and retailer loyalty: Past behaviour and future intensions. *Journal of Product and Brand Management*, *9*(2), 120–127. doi:10.1108/10610420010322161

Ezezika, O. C., Deadman, J., Murray, J., Mabeya, J., & Daar, A. S. (2013). To trust or not to trust: A model for effectively governing public-private partnerships. *AgBioForum*, *16*(1), 27–36.

Fairholm, G. W. (1994). *Leadership and the Culture of Trust*. Westport, CT: Praeger.

Farris, G., Senner, E., & Butterfield, D. (1973). Trust, culture, and organizational behavior. *Industrial Relations*, *12*(2), 144–157. doi:10.1111/j.1468-232X.1973.tb00544.x

Fassin, Y. (2009). The Stakeholder Model Refined. *Journal of Business Ethics*, *84*(1), 113–135. doi:10.1007/s10551-008-9677-4

Fathollahzadeh, M., Hashemi, A., & Kahreh, M. S. (2011). Designing a new model for determining customer value satisfaction and loyalty towards banking sector of Iran. *European Journal of Economics. Finance and Administrative Sciences*, *28*(1), 126–138.

Felton, A. P. (1956). Conditions Of Marketing Leadership. *Harvard Business Review*, *34*(2), 117–127.

Ferguson, R., Paulin, M., Pigeassou, C., & Gauduchon, R. (1999). Assessing service management effectiveness in a health resort: Implications of technical and functional quality. *Managing Service Quality*, *9*(1), 58–65. doi:10.1108/09604529910248821

Ferrell, O., Gonzalez-Padron, T., Hult, G., & Maignan, I. (2010). From Market Orientation to Stakeholder Orientation. *Journal of Public Policy & Marketing*, *29*(1), 93–96. doi:10.1509/jppm.29.1.93

Ferrin, D. L. (2001). The role of trust in organizational settings. *Organization Science*, *12*(4), 450–467. doi:10.1287/orsc.12.4.450.10640

Fesenmaier, D. R., Vogt, C. A., & Stewart, W. P. (1993). Investigating the influence of welcome center information on travel behavior. *Journal of Travel Research*, *31*(3), 47–52. doi:10.1177/004728759303100308

File, K. M., & Prince, R. A. (1992). Positive word of mouth: Customer satisfaction and buyer behaviour. *International Journal of Bank Marketing*, *10*(1), 25–29. doi:10.1108/02652329210007867

Financial Times. (1990). Mobile Communications: How Motorola Plans to Cut Off its Competitors. *Financial Times*, *6*, 12.

Fodor, O., & Werthner, H. (2005). Harmonise: A step toward an interoperable tourism Marketplace. *International Journal of Electronic Commerce*, *9*(2), 11–39.

Fomburn, C. J. (1996). *Reputation*. Boston: Harvard Business School Press.

Fomburn, C., & Van, R. C. (1997). The Reputational Landscape. *Corporate Reputation Review*, *1*(1/2), 5–13. doi:10.1057/palgrave.crr.1540024

Fornell, C. (1992). National satisfaction barometer: The Swedish experience. *Journal of Marketing*, *56*(1), 6–21. doi:10.2307/1252129

Fornell, C., & Larcker, D. F. (1981). Evaluating structural equation models with unobservable variables and measurement error. *JMR, Journal of Marketing Research*, *18*(1), 39–50. doi:10.2307/3151312

Fornell, C., & Wernerfelt, B. (1987). Defensive marketing strategy by customer complaint management: A theoretical analysis. *JMR, Journal of Marketing Research*, *24*(4), 337–346. doi:10.2307/3151381

Fox, A. (1974). *Beyond Contract: Work, Power and Trust Relations*. Faber.

Francis, G. (2007). Introduction to SPSS for Windows (5th ed.). Frenchs Forest: Pearson.

Frederique, S., & Sorge, A. (2008). Creating a High-Trust Organisation: An Exploration into Organisational Policies that Stimulate Interpersonal Trust Building. *Journal of Management Studies*, *45*(5), 857–884. doi:10.1111/j.1467-6486.2007.00763.x

Freeman, R. E. (2010). *Strategic Management: A Stakeholder Approach*. Boston: Pitman.

Freeman, R. E., & Reed, D. (1983). Stockholders and Stakeholders: A New Perspective on Corporate Governance. *California Management Review*, *25*(3), 88–106. doi:10.2307/41165018

Freiden, J., & Goldsmith, R. (1988). Correlates of consumer information search for professional services. *Journal of Professional Services Marketing*, *4*(1), 15–29. doi:10.1080/15332969.1988.9984906

Freyssenet, M. (2003). Renault: Globalization, But For What Purpose? In M. Freyssenet, K. Shimizu, & G. Volpato (Eds.), *Globalization or Regionalization of European Car Industry?* (pp. 103–131). London: Palgrave Macmillan. doi:10.1057/9780230554818

Friedman, M. (2002). Capitalism and Freedom (40th anniversary Ed.). Chicago: The University of Chigago Press.

Friesen, J. (1989). Product knowledge shoot out fires' em up in the heartland. *Bank Marketing*, *21*(7), 30–33.

Fujiki, K. (2002). Keiretsu Kaitai – Kawaru Jiodousha Buhin Torihiki. In *The Breakdown of Keiretsu – The Changing Automobile Parts Transactions*. Tokyo: Ekonomisto Sha.

Fujimoto, T., & Arturo Heller, D. (2001). Recent Trends in Alliance-Enabled Capability Building: Implications for Firm Performance in the Global Auto Industry: A Dynamic View of the Ford-Mazda, Renault-Nissan & DaimlerChryslerMitsubishi. Paper presented at the Ninth GERPISA International Colloquium: Reconfiguring the Auto Industry: Merger & Acquisition, Alliances and Exit. Paris, France.

Fukuyama, F. (1995). *Trust: The Social Virtues and the Creation of Prosperity*. The Free Press.

Fukuyama, F. (2001). Social capital, civil society, and development. *Third World Quarterly*, *22*(1), 7–20. doi:10.1080/713701144

Gabarro, J. J. (1978). The Development of Trust, Influence, and Expectations. In *Interpersonal Behavior: Communication and Understanding in Relationships* (pp. 290–303). Englewood Cliffs, NJ: Prentice-Hall.

Galbreath, J. (2009). Building corporate social responsibility into strategy. *European Business Review*, *21*(2), 109–127. doi:10.1108/09555340910940123

Galford, R., & Drapeau, A. S. (2002). *The Trusted Leader: Bringing Out the Best in Your People and Your Company*. The Free Press.

Galford, R., & Drapeau, A. S. (2003). Enemies of Trust. *Harvard Business Review*, *81*(2), 1–8. PMID:12577656

Galford, R., & Drapeau, A. S. (2003). Trusted Leadership. *Executive Excellence*, *20*(1), 12.

Galloway, L., Mochrie, R., & Deakins, D. (2004). ICT-enabled collectivity as a positive Rural business strategy. *International Journal of Entrepreneurial Behaviour And Research*, *10*(4), 247–259. doi:10.1108/13552550410544213

Gambetta, D. (1988). *Trust: Making and Breaking Cooperative Relations*. Oxford, UK: Blackwell.

Gambetta, D. G. (1988). Can we trust trust? In D. G. Gambetta (Ed.), *Trust* (pp. 213–237). New York: Basil Blackwell.

Garbarino, E., & Johnson, M. (1999). The different roles of satisfaction, trust, and commitment in customer relationships. *Journal of Marketing*, *63*(2), 70–87. doi:10.2307/1251946

Garcia de los Salmones, M., Herrero Crespo, A., & Rodriguez del Bosque, I. (2005). Influence of Corporate Social Responsibility on Loyalty and Valuation of Services. *Journal of Business Ethics*, *61*(4), 369–385. doi:10.1007/s10551-005-5841-2

Gardner, B., & Levy, S. (1955, March/April). The product and the brand. *Harvard Business Review*, 33–39.

Garriga, E., & Melé, D. (2004). Corporate Social Responsibility Theories: Mapping the Theory. *Journal of Business Ethics*, *53*(1/2), 51–71. doi:10.1023/B:BUSI.0000039399.90587.34

Garzotto, F., Paolini, P., Speroni, M., & Pröll, B. Retschitzegger, Schwinger, W 2004, 'Ubiquitous access to cultural tourism portals', paper presented to Database and Expert Systems Applications, 15th International Workshop on (DEXA'04), Zaragoza, Spain, August 30 - September 03, 2004.

Gascó-Hernández & T. Torres-Coronas (Ed.), *Information communication technologies and city*.

Gavetti, G. (2011, July/August). The New Psychology Of Strategic Leadership. *Harvard Business Review* 118–125. PMID:21800475

George, W. R. (1990). Internal marketing and organisational behaviour: A partnership in developing customer-conscious employees at every level. *Journal of Business Research*, *20*(1), 63–70. doi:10.1016/0148-2963(90)90043-D

Gerald, A. E. (2010). Ethics of Innovation for Public Service Professionals. *The Innovation Journal: The Public Sector Innovation Journal, Volume, 15*(3), Article 2.2.

Gerlach, M. (1992). *Alliance Capitalism: The Social Organization of Japanese Business*. Berkeley, CA: University of California Press.

Getz, D., & Petersen, T. (2005). Growth And Profit-Oriented Entrepreneurship Among Family Business Owners In The Tourism And Hospitality Industry. *Hospital Management*, *24*(2), 219–242. doi:10.1016/j.ijhm.2004.06.007

GfK Global Trust. (n.d.). Germans place more trust in government again. *GfK Global Trust Report2013*. Retrieved August 26, 2013, from http://www.gfk-verein.org/index.php?article_id=301&clang=1

Giese, J., & Cote, J. (2000). Defining consumer satisfaction. *Academy of Marketing Science Reivew*. Retrieved from http://www.amsreview.org/articles/giese01-2000.pdf

Giffin, K. (1967). The contribution of studies of source credibility to a theory of interpersonal trust in the communication process. *Psychological Bulletin*, *68*(2), 104–120. doi:10.1037/h0024833 PMID:6065581

Gill, J., & Johnson, P. (2010). *Research Methods for Managers* (4th ed.). Thousand Oaks, CA: Sage.

Gilmore, A., & Carson, D. (1995). Managing and marketing to internal customers. In *Understanding Services Management*. Chichester, UK: Wiley and Sons.

Gitelson, R. J., & Perdue, R. R. (1987). Evaluating the role of state welcome centers in disseminating travel related information in North Carolina. *Journal of Travel Research*, *25*(4), 15–19. doi:10.1177/004728758702500403

Gittell, J. H., & Douglass, A. (2012). Relational Bureaucratic Form: Embedding Reciprocal Relationships into Roles. *Academy of Management Review*, *37*(4), 709–733. doi:10.5465/amr.2010.0438

Glueck, W. F. (1980). *Business Policy & Strategic Management*. New York: McGraw-Hill.

Godes, D., & Mayzlin, D. (2004). Using online conversation t ostudy word of mouth communication. *Marketing Science*, *23*(4), 545–560. doi:10.1287/mksc.1040.0071

Goodpaster, K. E. (1991). Business Ethics and Stakeholder Analysis. *Business Ethics Quarterly*, *1*(1), 53–73.

Goodyear, M. (1996). Divided by a Common Language: Diversity and Deception in the World of Global Marketing. *Journal of the Market Research Society. Market Research Society*, *38*(2), 105–122.

Gorbatenko, A. (2011). *Customer loyalty as the factor of a company's competitiveness in the time of depression*. Retrieved September the 15th from http://www.changing-europe.org/download/CESS2011/gorbatenko.pdf

Gospodinova, A., & Terlemezyan, L. (1998). Conducting polymers prepared by oxidative polymerization: Polyaniline. *Progress in Polymer Science*, *23*(8), 1443–1481. doi:10.1016/S0079-6700(98)00008-2

Gottlieb, B. H., Grewal, D., & Brown, S. W. (1994). Consumer satisfaction and perceived quality: Complementary or divergent construct? *The Journal of Applied Psychology*, *79*(6), 875–885. doi:10.1037/0021-9010.79.6.875

Gounaris, S. (2006). Internal-market orientation and its measurement. *Journal of Business Research*, *59*(4), 432–448. doi:10.1016/j.jbusres.2005.10.003

Gounaris, S., & Stathakopoulos, V. (2004). Antecedents and consequences of brand loyalty: An empirical study. *Journal of Brand Management*, *11*(4), 283–306. doi:10.1057/palgrave.bm.2540174

Gounaris, S., Vassilikopoulou, A., & Chatzipanagiotou, K. C. (2010). Internal-market orientation: A misconceived aspect of marketing theory. *European Journal of Marketing*, *44*(11/12), 1667–1699. doi:10.1108/03090561011079837

Governance and Public Sector Management. (n.d.). Retrieved September 5, 2013, from http://siteresources.worldbank.org/PUBLICSECTORANDGOVERNANCE/Resources/285741-1348676611027/PSGDataSheet.pdf

Granger, C. H. (1964). The Hierarchy of Objectives. *Harvard Business Review*.

Granovetter, M. (1985). Economic Action and Social Structure: The Problem of Embeddedness. *American Journal of Sociology*, *91*(3), 481–510. doi:10.1086/228311

Grant, J. H., & King, W. R. (1982). *The Logic of Strategic Planning*. New York: Little Brown and Co.

Grant, R. M. (1991). The resource-based theory of competitive advantage: Implications for strategy formulation. *California Management Review*, *33*(3), 114–135. doi:10.2307/41166664

Grant, R. M. (1996). Prospering in dynamically-competitive environments: Organizational capability as knowledge integration. *Organization Science*, *7*(4), 375–387. doi:10.1287/orsc.7.4.375

Greene, W. E., Walls, G. D., & Schrest, L. J. (1994). Internal Marketing: The Key to External Marketing Success. *Journal of Services Marketing*, *8*(4), 5–13. doi:10.1108/08876049410070682

Green, K. W. Jr, Whitten, D., & Inman, R. A. (2008). The impact of logistics performance on organizational performance in a supply chain context. *Supply Chain Management: An International Journal*, *13*(4), 317–327. doi:10.1108/13598540810882206

Greenley, G. E., & Foxall, G. R. (1998). External moderation of associations among stakeholder orientations and company performance. *International Journal of Research in Marketing*, *15*(1), 51–69. doi:10.1016/S0167-8116(97)00018-9

Greenley, G. E., Hooley, G. J., Broderick, A. J., & Rudd, J. M. (2004). Strategic planning differences among different multiple stakeholder orientation profiles. *Journal of Strategic Marketing*, *12*(3), 163–182. doi:10.1080/0965254042000262887

Gremler, D. D., Gwinner, K. P., & Brown, S. W. (2001). Generating positive word-of-mouth communication through customer-employee relationships. *International Journal of Service Industry Management*, *12*(1), 44–59. doi:10.1108/09564230110382763

Gronroos, C. (1982). An applied service marketing theory. *European Journal of Marketing*, *16*(7), 30–41. doi:10.1108/EUM0000000004859

Gronroos, C. (1984). A service quality model and its marketing implications. *European Journal of Marketing*, *18*(4), 36–44. doi:10.1108/EUM0000000004784

Grönroos, C. (1990). Relationship Approach to Marketing in Service Contexts: The Marketing and Organizational Behaviour Interface. *Journal of Business Research*, *20*(1), 3–11. doi:10.1016/0148-2963(90)90037-E

Gronroos, C. (2001). The perceived service quality concept - A mistake? *Managing Service Quality*, *11*(3), 150–152. doi:10.1108/09604520110393386

Grönros, C. (1994). From Marketing Mix to Relationship Marketing: Towards a Paradigm Shift in Marketing. *Management Decision*, *32*(2), 4–20. doi:10.1108/00251749410054774

Guest, G., MacQueen, K. M., & Namey, E. E. (2012). *Applied Thematic Analysis*. Thousand Oaks, CA: Sage.

Gummesson, E. (1991). Marketing-orientation revisited: The crucial role of the part-time marketer. *European Journal of Marketing*, *25*(2), 60–75. doi:10.1108/03090569110139166

Gummesson, E. (2000). *Qualitative Methods in Management Research* (2nd ed.). Thousand Oaks, CA: Sage.

Gundlach, G., & Wilkie, W. (2009). The American Marketing Accusation's New Definition of Marketing: Perspective and Commentary on the 2007 Revision. *American Marketing Association, 28*(2), 259-264.

Gundlach, G. T., & Wilkie, W. L. (2010). Stakeholder Marketing: Why Stakeholder Was Omitted from the American Marketing Association's Official 2007 Definition of Marketing and Why the Future Is Bright for Stakeholder Marketing. *Journal of Public Policy & Marketing*, *29*(1), 89–82. doi:10.1509/jppm.29.1.89

Gupta, S., Lehmann, D. R., & Stuart, J. A. (2004). Valuing Customers. *JMR, Journal of Marketing Research*, *41*(1), 7–18. doi:10.1509/jmkr.41.1.7.25084

Gupta, Y., & Torkzadeh, G. (1988). Re-designing bank service: Systems for effective marketing. *Long Range Planning*, *21*(6), 38–43. doi:10.1016/0024-6301(88)90157-4

Gyrd-Jones, R., Merriles, B., & Miller, D. (2013). Revisiting the complexities of corporate branding: Issues, paradoxes, solutions. *Journal of Brand Management*, *20*(7), 571–589. doi:10.1057/bm.2013.1

Haakansson, H., & Johanson, J. (1992). A model of industrial networks. In *Industrial networks: A new view of reality* (pp. 28–34). London, UK: Routledge.

Haakansson, H., & Johanson, J. (1993). The Network as a Governance Structure: Interfirm Cooperation Beyond Markets and Hierarchies. In G. Grabher (Ed.), *The Embedded Firm On the Socioeconomics of Industrial Networks* (pp. 35–51). London: Routledge.

Hagedoorn, J. (1996). Trends and Patterns in Strategic Technology Partnering since the Early Seventies. *Review of Industrial Organization*, *11*(5), 601–616. doi:10.1007/BF00214825

Ha, H. Y., John, J., Janda, S., & Muthaly, S. (2011). The effect of advertising spending on brand loyalty in services. *European Journal of Marketing*, *45*(4), 673–691. doi:10.1108/03090561111111389

Hair, J. F. J., Anderson, R. E., Tatham, R. L., & Black, W. C. (1998). *Multavariate Data Analysis* (5th ed.). Upper Saddle River, NJ: Prentice Hall.

Hallowel, R. (1996). The relationships of customer satisfaction, customer loyalty and profitability: An empirical study. *International Journal of Service Industry Management*, *7*(4), 27–42. doi:10.1108/09564239610129931

Hamel, G., & Prahalad, C. K. (1989). Strategic Intent. *Harvard Business Review*. PMID:10303477

Hamin, H., Baumann, C., & Tung, R. L. (2014). Attenuating double jeopardy of negative country of origin effects and latecomer brand - An application study of ethnocentrism in emerging markets. *Asia Pacific Journal of Marketing and Logistics*, *26*(1), 54–77. doi:10.1108/APJML-07-2013-0090

Hansen, G., & Wernerfelt, B. (1989). Determinants of Firm Performance: The relative importance of economic and organizational factors. *Strategic Management Journal*, 10.

Harris, L. C., & Ogbonna, E. (2000). The Responses of Front-line Employees to Market-oriented Culture Change. *European Journal of Marketing*, *34*(3/4), 318–340. doi:10.1108/03090560010311885

Harris, L. C., & Ogbonna, E. (2001). Strategic human resource management, marketorientation, and organizational performance. *Journal of Business Research*, *51*(2), 157–166. doi:10.1016/S0148-2963(99)00057-0

Harrison, J. S., & Freeman, R. E. (1999). Stakeholders, Social Responsibility, and Performance: Empirical Evidence and Theoretical Perspectives. *Academy of Management Journal*, *42*(5), 479–485. doi:10.2307/256971

Harrison-Walker, L. J. (2001). The measurement of word-of-mouth communication and investigation of service quality and customer commitment as potential antecedents. *Journal of Service Research*, *4*(1), 60–75. doi:10.1177/109467050141006

Hatch, M. J., & Schultz, M. (2003). Bringing the corporation into corporate branding. *European Journal of Marketing*, *37*(7-8), 1041–1064. doi:10.1108/03090560310477654

Hatch, M. J., & Schultz, M. (2008). *Taking brand initiative: How companies can align strategy, culture, and identity through corporate branding*. New York, NY: Jossey-Bass.

Hatch, M., & Schultz, M. (1997). Relations between organizational culture, identity, and image. *European Journal of Marketing*, *31*(5-6), 356–365. doi:10.1108/eb060636

Hawabhay, B., Abratt, R., & Peter, M. (2009). The role of corporate communications in developing a corporate brand image and reputation in Mauritius. *Corporate Reputation Review*, *12*(1), 3–20. doi:10.1057/crr.2009.4

Hax, A., & Majluf, N. (1991). *The strategy concept and process: A pragmatic approach*. New York: Prentice-Hall.

Hayes, R. H. (1985). Strategic Planning--Forward in Reverse? *Harvard Business Review*.

Heikkila, J. (2002). From supply to demand chain management: Efficiency and customer satisfaction. *Journal of Operations Management*, *20*(6), 747–767. doi:10.1016/S0272-6963(02)00038-4

Hendricks, M. (1998). Spread teh word: Advertising by word-of-mouth. *Entrepreneur*, *26*(2), 120–126.

Hennig-Thurau, T., Gwinner, K., & Gremler, D. (2002). Understanding relationship marketing outcomes: An integration of relationship benefits and relationship quality. *Journal of Service Research*, *4*(3), 230–247. doi:10.1177/1094670502004003006

Herr, P., Kardes, F., & Kim, J. (1991). Effects of word-of-mouth and product-attibute information on persuasion: An accessibility-diagnosticity perspective. *The Journal of Consumer Research*, *17*(4), 454–462. doi:10.1086/208570

Hertleer, C., Rogier, H., Vallozzi, L., & Van Langenhove, L. (2009). Textile Antenna for Off-Body Communication Integrated into Protective Clothing for Firefighter. *IEEE Transactions on Antennas and Propagation*, *57*(4), 919–925. doi:10.1109/TAP.2009.2014574

Hertleer, C., Tronquo, A., Rogier, H., Vallozzi, L., & Van Langenhove, L. (2007). Aperture-Coupled Patch Antenna for Integration Into Wearable Textile Systems. *IEEE Antennas and Wireless Propagation Letters*, *6*(11), 392–395. doi:10.1109/LAWP.2007.903498

Heskett, J. L. (1994). Putting the service-profit chain to work. *Harvard Business Review*, *72*(2), 164.

Hetherington, J. M. (2005). *Why Trust Matters: Declining political Trust and the demise of American Liberalism*. Princeton, NJ: Princeton University Press.

Hill, C. (1995). National institutional structures, transaction cost economizing, and competitive advantage: The case of Japan. *Organization Science*, *6*(1), 119–131. doi:10.1287/orsc.6.1.119

Hill, J. (2001). A Multidimensional Study Of The Key Determinants Of Effective SME Marketing Activity: Part 1. *International Journal Of Entrepreneurial Behaviour & Research*, *7*(5), 171–204. doi:10.1108/EUM0000000006006

Hirvonen, S., Laukkanen, T., & Reijonen, H. (2013). The brand orientation-performance relationship: An examination of moderation effects. *Journal of Brand Management*, *20*(8), 623–641. doi:10.1057/bm.2013.4

Hitt, M. A., Ireland, R. D., & Hoskisson, R. E. (1995). *Strategic Management: Competitiveness & Globalization*. New York: West Publishing.

Hoeffler, S., & Keller, K. (2003). The marketing advantages of strong brands. *Journal of Brand Management*, *10*(1), 421–445. doi:10.1057/palgrave.bm.2540139

Hofer, C., & Schendel, D. (1978). *Strategy Formulation: Analytical Concepts*. New York: West Publishing.

Hofstede, G. (1980). *Cultures Consequences*. Beverly Hills, CA: Sage.

Hofstede, G. (1991). *Cultures and Organizations: Software of the Mind*. London: McGraw-Hill Book Company.

Hogarth Scott, S., Watson, K., & Wilson, N. (1996). Do Small Businesses Have To Practice Marketing To Survive And Grow? *Marketing Intelligence & Planning*, *14*(1), 6–18. doi:10.1108/02634509610106197

Hogg, G., & Carter, S. (2000). Employee attitudes and responses to internal marketing. In *Internal marketing: Directions for managers* (pp. 109–124). Academic Press. doi:10.4324/9780203207352.ch7

Homburg, C., Giering, A., & Menon, A. (2003). Relationship Characteristics as Moderators of the Satisfaction-Loyalty Link: Findings in a Business-to-Business Context. *Journal of Business-To-Business Marketing*, *10*(3), 35–62. doi:10.1300/J033v10n03_02

Homburg, C., Klarmann, M., & Schmitt, J. (2010). Brand awareness in business markets: When is it related to firm performance? *International Journal of Research in Marketing*, *27*(3), 201–212. doi:10.1016/j.ijresmar.2010.03.004

Hong-Youl, H., & Kang-Hee, P. (2012). Effects of perceived quality and satisfaction on brand loyalty in China: The moderating effect of customer orientation. *African Journal of Business Management*, *6*(22), 6745–6753.

Hoopes, D. G., Madsen, T. L., & Walker, G. (2003). Guest Editors' Introduction to the Special Issue: Why is There a Resource-Based View? Toward a Theory of Competitive Heterogeneity. *Strategic Management Journal*, *24*(10), 889–902. doi:10.1002/smj.356

Hoq, H. Z., & Amin, M. (2010). The role of customer satisfaction to enhance customer loyalty. *African Journal of Business Management*, *4*(12), 2385–2392.

Horne, R. E. (2009). Limits to labels: The role of eco-labels in the assessment of product sustainability and routes to sustainable consumption. *International Journal of Consumer Studies*, *33*(2), 175–182. doi:10.1111/j.1470-6431.2009.00752.x

Hoskisson, R. E., Eden, L., Lau, C. M., & Wright, M. (2000). Strategy in emerging economies. *Academy of Management Journal*, *43*(3), 249–267. doi:10.2307/1556394

Hoy, W. K., & Tschannen-Moran, M. (1999). Five faces of Trust: An Empirical Confirmation in Urban Elementary Schools. *Journal of School Leadership*, *9*(3), 184–208.

Hrebiniak, L. G., & Joyce, W. (1984). *Implementing Strategy*. New York: Macmillan.

Hrebiniak, L. G., & Snow, C. (1982). Top management agreement and organizational performance. *Human Relations*, *3*(12).

Hsiao, M.-H. (2009). Shopping mode choice: Physical store shopping versus e-shopping. *Logistics and Transportation Review*, *45*(1), 86–95. doi:10.1016/j.tre.2008.06.002

Hsiao, Y. C., & Chen, C. J. (2013). Branding vs. contract manufacturing: Capability, strategy, and performance. *Journal of Business and Industrial Marketing*, *28*(4), 317–334. doi:10.1108/08858621311313910

Huang, J. C. (1995). EMI shielding plastics: A review. *Advances in Polymer Technology*, *14*(2), 137–150. doi:10.1002/adv.1995.060140205

Hult, G., Mena, J., Ferrell, O., & Ferrell, L. (2011). Stakeholder marketing: A definition and conceptual framework. *Academy of Marketing Science*, *1*(1), 44–65.

Hung, H. (2011). Directors' Roles in Corporate Social Responsibility: A Stakeholder Perspective. *Journal of Business Ethics*, *103*(3), 385–402. doi:10.1007/s10551-011-0870-5

ICT & Tourism USAID from the American People,, Arusha, Tanzania Information Science Reference. *International Journal of Knowledge and Learning*, *3*(6), 628-648. doi:10.1504/IJKL.2007.016837

Ikkala, O. T., Laakso, J., Vakiparta, K., Virtanen, E., Ruohonen, H., & Järvinen, H. et al. (1995). Counter-ion induced processibility of polyaniline: Conducting melt processible polymer blends. *Synthetic Metals*, *69*(1-3), 97–100. doi:10.1016/0379-6779(94)02376-A

Imai, K., & Itami, H. (1984). Interpenetration of Organization and Market. *International Journal of Industrial Organization*, *2*(4), 285–310. doi:10.1016/0167-7187(84)90001-8

Ind, N. (2007). *Living the Brand: How to Transform Every Member of Your Organization into a Brand Champion* (3rd ed.). London: Kogan Page.

Ind, N., & Bjerke, R. (2007). The concept of participatory market orientation: An organization-wide approach to enhancing brand equity. *Journal of Brand Management*, *15*(2), 135–145. doi:10.1057/palgrave.bm.2550122

Ingham, M., & Mothe, C. (2003). Apprentissages et confiance au sein d'une alliance technologique. *Revue Française de Gestion*, *29*, 111–128. doi:10.3166/rfg.143.111-128

In, M., & Fesenmaier, D. R. (1994). Traveler use of visitor information centers: Implications for development in Illinois. *Journal of Travel Research*, *33*(1), 44–50. doi:10.1177/004728759403300106

Islam, S. (2012), E-Business- A Tool to Enhance Tourism Industry: A Study from Bangladesh, ASA University Review, Vol.6, No.1 Jan-Jun 2012

Ismail, I., Hasnah, H., Ibrahim, D. N., & Mohd Isa, S. (2006). Service quality, client satisfaction, and loyalty towards audit firms. Perceptions of Malaysian public listed companies. *Managerial Auditing Journal*, *22*(7), 738–756. doi:10.1108/02686900610680521

IT and Internet's Impact on Tourism and Hospitality Industry. Implementations of technologies for Hilton Hotels <http://www.ivoryresearch.com/sample24.php> online document [Accessed 2nd November 2010]

Itami, H. (1987). *Mobilizing Invisible Assets*. Harvard University Press.

Jackson, G., & Moerke, A. (2005). Continuity and Change in Corporate Governance: Comparing Germany and Japan. *Corporate Governance: An International Review*, *13*(3), 351–361. doi:10.1111/j.1467-8683.2005.00429.x

Jacobs, S. (n.d.). Flexible Working? It's About Culture, Not Rules. *People Management*. Retrieved from www.peoplemanagement.co.uk/articles/2011/flexible-working-its-about-culture-not-rules.htm

Jacobs. (2013). What can HR do to change the banking culture and rebuild trust? *JD Power and Associates*. Retrieved August 24, 2013, from http://www.jdpower.com/autos/ratings/auto-insurance-provider-ratings/

Jacobs, R. (2003). Turn employees into brand ambassadors. *ABA Bank Marketing*, *35*(3), 22–26.

Jacoby, J., & Chestnut, R. W. (1978). *Brand Loyalty: Measurement and Management*. New York: Wiley.

Jacoby, J., & Kyner, D. B. (1973). Brand loyalty vs repeat purchasing behaviour. *JMR, Journal of Marketing Research*, *10*(1), 1–9. doi:10.2307/3149402

Jafar Jafari. (2003). *Encyclopedia of Tourism* (p. 308).

Jakkilinki, R., Georgievski, M., & Sharda, N. (2007). Connecting Destinations with an Ontology-Based e-Tourism Planner. In M. Sigala, L. Mich, & J. Murphy (Eds). Information and Communication Technologies in Tourism 2007, (pp. 21-32), Springer-Verlag Wien.

Jamal, A., & Naser, K. (2002). Customer satisfaction and retail banking: An assessment of some of the key antecedents of customer satisfaction in retail banking. *International Journal of Bank Marketing*, *20*(4), 146–160. doi:10.1108/02652320210432936

Jamal, A., & Naser, K. (2003). Factors influencing customer satisfaction in the retail banking sector in Pakistan. *International Journal of Commerce & Management*, *13*(2), 29–53. doi:10.1108/eb047465

James, K., & Vinnicombe, S. (2002). Acknowledging the Individual in the Researcher. In *Essential Skills for Management Research*. London: Sage. doi:10.4135/9781848605305.n5

Jarillo, J. C. (1988). On strategic networks. *Strategic Management Journal*, *9*(1), 31–41. doi:10.1002/smj.4250090104

Jarvenpaa, S. L., Tractinsky, N., & Vitale, M. (1998). *Consumer trust in an internet store* (Working Paper). Department of MSIS, University of Texas, Austin, TX.

Jiang, P. (2004). The role of brand name in customization decision: A search vs. experience perspective. *Journal of Product and Brand Management*, *13*(2), 73–83. doi:10.1108/10610420410529708

Jimenez, G., Ongena, Peydro, & Saurina. (2008). *Hazardous times for monetary policy: What do twenty-three million bank loans say about the effects of monetary policy on credit risk-taking?*. Banco de España documento de Trabajo 0833.

John A. Quelch and Lisa R. Klein. April 15, 1996. Is the internet just another marketing channel like direct mail or home shopping?

John, D. R. (2006). *Strategic brand management on the cutting edge: Building, leveraging, identifying, and protecting brands*. Paper presented at the Institute for Research in Marketing's Carlson on Branding. Retrieved February 8, 2014, from http://www.carlsonschool.umn.edu/Assets/75903.pdf

Johnson, G., Scholes, K., & Whittington, R. (2005). Exploring Corporate Strategy. *Financial Times*, pp. 150-157.

Johnson-George, C., & Swap, W. (1982). Measurement of specific interpersonal trust: Construction and validation of a scale to assess trust in a specific other. *Journal of Personality and Social Psychology*, *43*(6), 1306–1317. doi:10.1037/0022-3514.43.6.1306

Johnson, J., & Tellis, G. J. (2008). Drivers of success for market entry into China and India. *Journal of Marketing*, *72*(3), 1–13. doi:10.1509/jmkg.72.3.1

Johnston, D. A., McCutcheon, D. M., Stuart, F. I., & Kerwood, H. (2004). Effects of supplier trust on performance of cooperative supplier relationships. *Journal of Operations Management*, *22*(1), 23–38. doi:10.1016/j.jom.2003.12.001

Jones, R. (1996). Digital equipment corporation: creating new business. In *The Internet Strategy Handbook: Lessons from the New Frontier of Business*. Boston, MA: Harvard Business School Press.

Jones, T. (1995). Instrumental stakeholder theory: A synthesis of ethics and economics. *Academy of Management Review*, *20*(2), 404–437.

Jones, T. O., & Sasser, W. E. Jr. (1995, November-December). Why satisfied customers defect. *Harvard Business Review*, 88–99.

Jordan, S. A. (1999). Innovative Cultures + Empowered Employees = High Perfomanse Organizations. *Public Productivity and management. RE:view*, *23*, 109–115. doi: doi:10.2307/3380798

Julia, J. (2006). Organisation-Stakeholder-relationships: Exploring Trust and Transparency. *Journal of Management Development*, *25*(10), 942–945. doi:10.1108/02621710610708577

Jung, D. I. (2001). Transformational and Transactional Leadership and Their Effects on Creativity in Groups. *Creativity Research Journal*, *13*(2), 185–195. doi:10.1207/S15326934CRJ1302_6

Kalakota, R., & Robinson, M. (1999). *E-business, Roadmap for Success*. Reading, MA: Addison-Wesley.

Kaler, J. (2002). Morality and Strategy in Stakeholder Identification. *Journal of Business Ethics*, *39*(1/2), 91–99. doi:10.1023/A:1016336118528

Kalwani, M. U., & Narayandas, N. (1995). Long-term manufacturer supplier relationships: Do they pay off for supplier firms? *Journal of Marketing*, *59*(1), 1–16. doi:10.2307/1252010

Kang, N.-H., & Sakai, K. (2000). International Strategic Alliances: Their Role in Industrial Globalisation. *STI Working Paper, 5*.

Kanning, U. P., & Bergmann, N. (2009). Predictors of customer satisfaction: Testing the classical paradigms. *Managing Service Quality*, *19*(4), 377–390. doi:10.1108/09604520910971511

Kanter, R., Stein, B., & Jick, T. (1992). *The Challenge of Organizational Change: How CompaniesExperience It and Leaders Guide It*. New York: Maxwell Macmillan Int.

Kapferer, J. (1997). *Strategic Brand Management*. London: Kogan Page.

Karatepe, O. M., & Ekiz, E. H. (2004). The effects of organisational responses to complaints on satisfaction and loyalty: A study of hotel guests in Northern Cyprus. *Managing Service Quality*, *14*(6), 476–486. doi:10.1108/09604520410569810

Karpinski. (1999). The logistics of e-business—Web commerce demands new approach to inventory, shipping. *Internet Week, 767*, 1096.

Kaswell, E. (1953). *Textile Fibers, Yarns, and Fabrics*. New York: Reihold Publishing.

Kay, M. J. (2006). Strong brands and corporate brands. *European Journal of Marketing*, *40*(7-8), 742–760. doi:10.1108/03090560610669973

Keisidou, E., Sarigiannidis, L., Maditinos, D. I., & Thalassinos, E. I. (2013). Customer satisfaction, loyalty and financial performance: A holistic approach of the Greek banking sector. *International Journal of Bank Marketing*, *31*(4), 259–288. doi:10.1108/IJBM-11-2012-0114

Keller, K. L. (2001). Building Customer-Based Brand Equity: A blueprint for creating strong brands. *Report Summary # 01-107*. Cambridge, MA: Marketing Science Institute. Retrieved February 8, 2014, from http://202.120.148.199/files/Custome%2BrBased%2Bbrand%2BEquity%2BModel.pdf

Keller, E., & Fay, B. (2012). Word-of-mouth advocacy: A new key to advertising effectiveness. *Journal of Advertising Research*, *52*(4), 459–464. doi:10.2501/JAR-52-4-459-464

Keller, K. L. (2003). *Strategic brand management: Building, measuring, and managing brand equity*. Upper Saddle River, NJ: Pearson Education.

Kenny, B., & Dyson, K. (1989). Marketing. In *Small Business*. London: Routledge.

Kester, C. (1990). *Japanese Takeovers: The Global Contest for Corporate Control*. Cambridge, MA: Harvard Business School Press.

Kim, B., Koncar, V., Devaux, E., Dufour, C., & Viallier, P. (2004). Electrical and morphological properties of PP. and PET conductive polymer fibers. *Synthetic Metals*, *146*(2), 167–174. doi:10.1016/j.synthmet.2004.06.023

Kim, E., Nam, D., & Stimpert, J. L. (2004). The Applicability of Porter's Generic Strategies in the Digital Age: Assumptions, Conjectures and Suggestions. *Journal of Management*, *30*(5), 569–589. doi:10.1016/j.jm.2003.12.001

Kim, H. B., & Kim, W. G. (2005). The relationship between brand equity and firms' performance in luxury hotels and chain restaurants. *Tourism Management*, *26*(4), 549–560. doi:10.1016/j.tourman.2004.03.010

Kim, H. B., Kim, W. G., & An, J. (2003). The effect of consumer-based brand equity on firms' financial performance. *Journal of Consumer Marketing*, *20*(4-5), 35–351.

Kim, W. G., & Kim, H. B. (2004). Measuring customer-based restaurant brand equity: Investigating the relationship between brand equity and firms' performance. *The Cornell Hotel and Restaurant Administration Quarterly*, *45*(2), 115–131. doi:10.1177/0010880404264507

Kim, Y., & Choi. (2005). Antecedents of green considerations purchase behaviour: An examination of collectivism, environmental concern and PCE. *Advances in Consumer Research. Association for Consumer Research (U. S.)*, *32*(1), 592–599.

Klein, S. (2002). Web impact on the distribution structure for flight tickets. In K. W. Wöber, A. J. Frew, & M. Hitz (Eds.), *Information and Communication Technologies in Tourism 2002* (pp. 219–228). New York: Springer-Verlag Wien. doi:10.1007/978-3-7091-6132-6_22

Kline, R. B. (1998). *Principles and Practice of Structural Equation Modeling*. New York: The Guilford Press.

Kline, R. B. (2005). *Principles and Practices of Structural Equation Modeling* (2nd ed.). New York: The Guildford Press.

Knemeyer, A. M., Corsi, T. M., & Murphy, P. R. (2003). Logistics Outsourcing Relationships: Customer Perspectives. *Journal of Business Logistics*, *24*(1), 77–109. doi:10.1002/j.2158-1592.2003.tb00033.x

Knott, A. M. (2003). The organizational routines factor market paradox. *Strategic Management Journal*, 24.

Knox, S., & Bickerton, D. (2003). The six conventions of corporate branding. *European Journal of Marketing*, *37*(7-8), 998–1016. doi:10.1108/03090560310477636

Kohli, A. K., & Jaworski, B. J. (1990). Market orientation: The construct, research propositions, and managerial Implications. *Journal of Marketing*, *54*(2), 1–18. doi:10.2307/1251866

Kohn, A. (1993). Why incentive plans cannot work. *Harvard Business Review*, *71*(5), 54–60.

Konopa, L. J., & Calabro, P. J. (1971). Adoption of the Marketing Concept by Large Northeastern Ohio Manufacturers. *Akron Business and Economic Review*, *2*, 9–13.

Kordupleski, R., Rust, R. T., & Zahorik, A. (1993). Why improving quality doesn't improve quality. *California Management Review*, *35*(3), 82–95. doi:10.2307/41166745

Kotler, P. (1973). Anmospherics as a marketing tool. *Journal of Retailing*, *49*(4), 48–64.

Kotler, P., Armstrong, G., Saunders, J., & Wong, V. (1999). *Principles Of Marketing* (2nd ed.). Prentice Hall Europe.

Kotler, P., & Keller, K. (2009). *Marketing Management* (13th ed.). Pearson.

Kotter, J. (1996). *Leading Change*. Boston, MA: Harvard Business School Press.

Kotter, J. P. (1995). Leading Change: Why Transformation Efforts Fail. *Harvard Business Review*, *73*(2), 59–67.

Kowalczyk, S. J., & Pawlish, M. J. (2002). Corporate branding through external perception of organizational culture. *Corporate Reputation Review*, *5*(2-3), 159–174. doi:10.1057/palgrave.crr.1540172

Kraaijenbrink, J., Spender, J.C., & Groen. (2009). The resource-based view: A review and assessment of its critiques. *MPRA Paper No. 21442*. Retrieved from http://mpra.ub.uni-muenchen.de/21442/

Kumar, A., Kim, Y. K., & Pelton, L. (2009). Indian consumers' purchase behavior toward US versus local brands. *International Journal of Retail & Distribution Management*, *37*(6), 510–526. doi:10.1108/09590550910956241

Kumar, R. S., Dash, S., & Purwar, P. C. (2013). The nature and antecedents of brand equity and its dimensions. *Marketing Intelligence & Planning*, *31*(2), 141–159. doi:10.1108/02634501311312044

Kuruppuarachchi, P., Mandal, P., & Smith, R. (2002). IT project implementation strategies for effective changes: A critical review. *Logistics Information Management*, *15*(2), 126–137. doi:10.1108/09576050210414006

Kyriazopoulos, P., & Terzidis, K. (2000). *Management SME in the 3rd Industrial Revolution*. Athens: Publisher Sychroni Ekdotiki.

Ladhari, R., Ladhari, I., & Morales, M. (2011). Bank service quality: Comparing Canadian and Tunisian customer perceptions. *International Journal of Bank Marketing*, *29*(3), 224–246. doi:10.1108/02652321111117502

Lado, A. A., Boyd, N. G., & Hanlon, S. C. (1997). Competition, cooperation, and the search for economic rents: A syncretic model. *Academy of Management Review*, *22*(1), 110–141.

Lado, A. A., Boyd, N. G., & Wright, P. (1992). A competency-based model of sustainable competitive advantage: Toward a conceptual integration. *Journal of Management*, *18*(1), 77–91. doi:10.1177/014920639201800106

Lane, P. J., Salk, J. E., & Lyles, M. A. (2001). Absorptive capacity, learning, and performance in international joint ventures. *Strategic Management Journal*, *22*(12), 1139–1161. doi:10.1002/smj.206

Langenhove, L., Hertleer, C., Priniotakis, G., & Lanfer, B. (2005). Smart textiles: Dream or fact? Paper presented at the 5th World Textile Conference AUTEX. Portoroz, Slovenia.

Laroche, M., Rosenblatt, J., & Manning, T. (1986). Services used and factors considered important in selecting a bank: An investigation across diverse demographic segments. *International Journal of Bank Marketing*, *4*(1), 35–55. doi:10.1108/eb010771

Lashley, C.and Rowson, B *(*2005*)* Getting IT Right: Exploring information technology in the hospitality curriculum, *International Journal of Contemporary* vol 17, no 1, pp 94-105. *marketing: Digital opportunities for cities around the world* (pp. 220 – 244). Hershey, PA:

Lau, A. K. W., Yam, R. C. M., & Tang, E. P. Y. (2010). Supply chain integration and product modularity: An empirical study of product performance for selected Hong Kong manufacturing industries. *International Journal of Operations & Production Management*, *30*(1), 20–56. doi:10.1108/01443571011012361

Lawrence, E., Corbitt, B., Fisher, J., Lawrence, J., & Tidwell, A. (2000). *Internet Commerce: Digital Models for Business* (2nd ed.). Milton, Australia: John Wiley & Sons, Inc.

Lee, C., Baek, I., Park, S., & Lee, J. (2008). The impact of the brand management system on brand performance in B-B and B-C environments. *Industrial Marketing Management*, *37*(7), 848–855. doi:10.1016/j.indmarman.2008.04.005

Lee, J. S., & Back, K. J. (2010). Reexamination of attendee-based brand equity. *Tourism Management*, *31*(3), 395–401. doi:10.1016/j.tourman.2009.04.006

Lee, T., Chung, W., & Taylor, R. (2011). A strategic response to the financial crisis: An empirical analysis of financial services advertising before and during the financial crisis. *Journal of Services Marketing*, *25*(3), 150–164. doi:10.1108/08876041111129146

Lei, D., & Slocum, J. W. Jr. (1991). Global strategic alliances: Payoffs and pitfalls. *Organizational Dynamics*, *19*(3), 44–62. doi:10.1016/0090-2616(91)90093-O

Lei, D., & Slocum, J. W. Sr. (1992). Global strategy, competence-building and strategic alliances. *California Management Review*, *35*(1), 81–97. doi:10.2307/41166714

Leidecker, J., & Bruno, A. (1984). Identifying and Using Critical Success Factors. *Long Range Planning*, *17*(1), 23–32. doi:10.1016/0024-6301(84)90163-8

Leinwand, P., Moeller, L. H., & Shriram, K. (2008). *Consumer Spending in the Economic Downturn: The wide ranging Impact on consumer behaviour*. Booz & Company. Retrieved from www.interbrand.com/.../33_IP_Consumer_Spending_in_a_Recession.pdf

Leone, R. P., Rao, V. R., Keller, K. L., Luo, A. M., McAlister, L., & Srivastava, R. (2006). Linking brand equity to customer equity. *Journal of Service Research*, *9*(2), 125–138. doi:10.1177/1094670506293563

Levesque, T., & McDougall, G. H. C. (1996). Determinants of customer satisfaction in retail banking. *International Journal of Bank Marketing*, *14*(7), 12–20. doi:10.1108/02652329610151340

Levinson, H. (1965). Reciprocation: The relationship between man and organization. *Administrative Science Quarterly*, *9*(4), 370–390. doi:10.2307/2391032

Levitt, T. (1958). The dangers of social responsibility. *Harvard Business Review*, *36*(5), 41–50.

Levitt, T. (1960). Marketing Myopia. *Harvard Business Review*, *38*(4), 45–56. PMID:15252891

Lewicki & Wiethoff. (2000). Trust, Trust Development, and Trust Repair. In *The Handbook of Conflict Resolution: Theory and Practice* (pp. 86–107). San Francisco: Jossey-Bass Publishers.

Lewicki, R. J., & Bunker, B. B. (1996). Developing and Maintaining trust in work relationships. In *Trust in Organisations* (pp. 119–124). Thousand Oaks, CA: Sage Publications. doi:10.4135/9781452243610.n7

Lewicki, R. J., McAllister, D. J., & Bies, R. J. (1998). Trust and distrust: New relationships and realities. *Academy of Management Review*, *23*, 438–458.

Lewicki, R. J., & Wiethoff, C. (2000). Trust, Trust development and Trust Repair. In *The Handbook of Conflict Resolution*. San Francisco: Jossey-Bass.

Lewiski, R., Tomlinson, E., & Gillespie, N. (2006). Models of interpersonal trust development: Theoretical approaches, empirical evidence and future directions. *Journal of Management*, *32*(6), 991–1022. doi:10.1177/0149206306294405

Liljander, V., & Strandvik, T. (1994). The relation between service quality, satisfaction and intentions. In P. PKunst & J. Lemmink (Eds.), Quality Management in Service II. Van Gorcum: Assen/Maastricht.

Lim, W. M. (2012). The Voyage of the Renault-Nissan Alliance: A Successful Venture. *Advances in Management*, *5*(9), 25–29.

Lim, W. S., & Tan, S. J. (2009). Using brand equity to counter outsourcing opportunism: A game theoretic approach. *Marketing Letters*, *20*(4), 369–383. doi:10.1007/s11002-009-9071-8

Lincoln, J. R., Gerlach, M. L., & Ahmadjian, C. L. (1996). Keiretsu Networks and Corporate Performance in Japan. *American Sociological Review*, *61*(1), 67–88. doi:10.2307/2096407

Lings, I. N., & Greenley, G. E. (2009). The impact of internal and external market orientations on firm performance. *Journal of Strategic Marketing*, *17*(1), 41–53. doi:10.1080/09652540802619251

Lings, I., & Brooks, R. F. (1998). Implementing and measuring the effectiveness of internal marketing. *Journal of Marketing Management*, *14*(4/5), 325–351. doi:10.1362/026725798784959426

Lings, I., & Greenley, G. (2005). Measuring internal market orientation. *Journal of Service Research*, *7*(3), 290–305. doi:10.1177/1094670504271154

Lin, H.-F. (2007d). Knowledge sharing and firm innovation capability: An empirical study. *International Journal of Manpower*, *28*(3/4), 315–332. doi:10.1108/01437720710755272

Lippman, S., & Rumelt, R. (1982). Uncertain Imitability: An Analysis of Interfirm Differences in Efficiency under Competition. *The Bell Journal of Economics*, 13.

Liu, Y. (2013). Sustainable Competitive advantage in turbulent business environments. *International Journal of Production Research*, *51*(10), 2821–2841. doi:10.1080/00207543.2012.720392

Lovelock, C. (2007). *Services Marketing*. Prentice Hall.

Low, G., & Fullerton, R. (1994). Brands, brand management and the brand manager system: A critical-historical evaluation. *JMR, Journal of Marketing Research*, *31*(2), 173–190. doi:10.2307/3152192

Low, J., & Blois, K. (2002). The evolution of generic brands in industrial markets: The challenges to owners of brand equity. *Industrial Marketing Management*, *31*(5), 385–392. doi:10.1016/S0019-8501(00)00131-0

Luhmann, N. (1988). Familiarity, confidence, trust: Problems and alternatives. In D. G. Gambetta (Ed.), *Trust* (pp. 94–107). New York: Basil Blackwell.

Luhmann, N. (n.d.). Familiarity, Confidence, Trust: Problems and Alternatives. In *Trust: Making and Breaking Cooperative Relations* (pp. 94–107). New York: Blackwell.

Luo, Y. (2002). Capability exploitation and building in a foreign market: Implications for multinational enterprises. *Organization Science*, *13*(1), 48–63. doi:10.1287/orsc.13.1.48.538

Luo, Y. (2007). From foreign investors to strategic insiders: Shifting parameters, prescriptions and paradigms for MNCs in China. *Journal of World Business*, *42*(1), 14–34. doi:10.1016/j.jwb.2006.08.009

Madden, T. J., Fehle, F., & Fournier, S. (2006). Brands matter: An empirical demonstration of the creation of shareholder value through branding. *Journal of the Academy of Marketing Science*, *34*(2), 224–235. doi:10.1177/0092070305283356

Magnusson, P. R., Matthing, J., & Kristensson, P. (2003). Managing user involvement in service innovation. *Journal of Service Research*, *6*(2), 111–124. doi:10.1177/1094670503257028

Maignan, I., Ferrell, O. C., & Ferrell, L. (2005). A stakeholder model for implementing social responsibility in marketing. *European Journal of Marketing*, *39*(9/10), 956–977. doi:10.1108/03090560510610662

Makridakis, S., Caloghirou, Y., Papagiannakis, L., & Trivellas, P. (1997). The Dualism Of Greek Firms And Management: Present State And Future Implications. *European Management Journal*, *15*(4), 381–402. doi:10.1016/S0263-2373(97)00018-2

Malhotra, N. K., & Agarwal, J. (2002). A Stakeholder Perspective on Relationship Marketing: Framework and Propositions. *Journal of Relationship Marketing*, *1*(2), 3–37. doi:10.1300/J366v01n02_02

Malhotra, Y. (Ed.). (2001). *Knowledge Management and Business Model Innovation*. Hershey, PA: Idea Group.

Manrai, A. K., & Manrai, A. L. (1993). Consumer switching behaviour of banking services: A conceptual case. In Proceedings of the Sixth Bi-Annual International Conference of the Academy of Marketing Science, (vol. 6, pp. 100-104). Istanbul: World Marketing Congress.

Mansoor, D. (2011). The Global Business Crisis and Consumer Behavior: Kingdom of Bahrain as a Case Study. *International Journal of Business and Management*, *6*(1), 104–115.

March & Simon. (1958). *Organizations*. New York: John Wiley and Sons.

Mark, M., & Pearson, C. S. (2001). *The Hero and The Outlaw: Building Extraordinary Brands Through the Power of Archetypes*. New York: McGraw-Hill.

Markwick, N., & Fill, C. (1995). Towards a framework for managing corporate identity. *European Journal of Marketing*, *31*(5), 396–409. doi:10.1108/03090569710167619

Martin, A. (2007). The Changing Nature of Leadership, Research White Papers. *Centre for Creative Leadership*. Retrieved from www.ccl.org/leadership/pdf/research/NatureLeadership.pdf

Martin, W., & Inchovichina, E. (2008). Economic development in emerging Asian markets: Implications for Europe. *European Review of Agriculture Economics*, *35*(3), 303–330. doi:10.1093/erae/jbn017

Maslow, A. H. (1943). A Theory of Human Motivation. *Psychological Review*, *50*(4), 374. doi:10.1037/h0054346

Matear, S., Gray, B. J., & Garrett, T. (2004). Market orientation, brand investment, new service development, market position and performance for service organizations. *International Journal of Service Industry Management*, *15*(3-4), 284–301. doi:10.1108/09564230410540944

Matten, D., & Crane, A. (2005). What is stakeholder democracy? Perspectives and issues. *Business Ethics (Oxford, England)*, *14*(1), 6–13. doi:10.1111/j.1467-8608.2005.00382.x

Mattila, A., & Wirtz, J. (2001). Congruency of scent and music as a driver of in-store evaluations and behaviour. *Journal of Retailing*, *77*(2), 273–289. doi:10.1016/S0022-4359(01)00042-2

Mavondo, F. T., Chimhanzi, J., & Stewart, J. (2005). Learning orientation and market orientation: Relationship with innovation, human resource practices and performance. *European Journal of Marketing*, *39*(11-12), 1235–1263. doi:10.1108/03090560510623244

Maxham, J. G. III, & Netemeyer, R. G. (2002). Caseling customer perceptions of complaint handling over time: The effects of perceived justice on satisfaction and intent. *Journal of Retailing*, *78*(4), 252–259. doi:10.1016/S0022-4359(02)00100-8

Maxham, J. G. III, Netemeyer, R. G., & Lichtenstein, D. R. (2008). The Retail Value Chain: Linking Employee Perceptions to Employee Performance, Customer Evaluations, and Store Performance. *Marketing Science*, *27*(2), 147–167. doi:10.1287/mksc.1070.0282

Maxham, J. III, & Netemeyer, R. (2002). A longitudinal study of complaining customers' evvaluations of multiple service failures and recovery efforts. *Journal of Marketing*, *66*(4), 57–71. doi:10.1509/jmkg.66.4.57.18512

Mayer, R. C., Davis, & Schoormann. (1995). An Integrative Model of Organisational Trust. *Academy of Management Review*, *20*(3), 709–734.

Mayer, R. C., Davis, J. H., & Schoorman, F. D. (1995). An integrative model of organizational trust. *Academy of Management Review*, *20*, 709–734.

May, P. (2000). *The Business of E-commerce: From Corporate Strategy to Technology*. New York: Cambridge University Press.

McAdams, E. T., McLaughlin, J., & Anderson, J. (2004). Wearable and Implantable Monitoring Systems: 10 Years Experience. Paper presented at the Wearable Electronic and Smart Textiles. Leeds, UK.

McCauley, D. P., & Kuhnert, K. W. (1992). A Theoretical Review and Empirical Investigation of Employee Trust in Management. *Public Administration Quarterly*, *16*, 265–285.

McCracken, G. (1986). Culture and consumption: A theoretical account of the structure and movement of the cultural menaing of consumer goods. *The Journal of Consumer Research*, *13*(1), 71–84. doi:10.1086/209048

McCutcheon, D. M., & Meredith, J. R. (1993). Conducting case study research in operations management. *Journal of Operations Management*, *11*(3), 239–256. doi:10.1016/0272-6963(93)90002-7

McEvily, B., Perrone, V., & Zaheer, A. (2003). Trust as an Organizing Principle. *Organization Science*, *14*(1), 91–103. doi:10.1287/orsc.14.1.91.12814

McGrath, M. (2009). Why Marketing Leadership Matters. *Brand Learning*. Retrieved from http://www.brandlearning.com/Why-Marketing-Leadership-Matters.pdf

McGuire, J. P., Pasmore, W. C., & Rhodes, G. (2009). *Transforming Your Organisation*. San Francisco: Jossey-Bass.

McKnight, D. H., & Chervany, N. L. (n.d.). While trust is cool and collected, distrust is fiery and frenzied: A model of distrust concepts. In D. Strong, D. Straub, & J.I. DeGross (Eds.), Proceedings of the Seventh Americas Conference on Information Systems (pp. 883–888). Boston: Omnipress.

Mctavish, A. R., Gunasekaran, S. G., & Yli-Olli, P. (1996). Establishing A Strategic Framework For Improving Productivity. *Integrated Manufacturing Systems*, *7*(4), 12–21. doi:10.1108/09576069610125067

McWilliams, A., Siegel, D. S., & Wright, P. M. (2006). Corporate Social Responsibility: Strategic Implications. *Journal of Management Studies*, *43*(1), 1–18. doi:10.1111/j.1467-6486.2006.00580.x

Michon, R., Chebat, J., & Turley, L. (2005). Mall atmospherics: The interaction effects of the mall environment on shopping behaviour. *Journal of Business Research*, *58*(5), 576–583. doi:10.1016/j.jbusres.2003.07.004

Mihelis, G., Grigoroudis, E., Siskos, Y., Politis, Y., & Malandrakis, Y. (1998). *Customer Satisfaction Measurement in the Private Bank Sector*. Decision Support Systems Laboratory, University of Chania.

Milgrom, P., & Roberts, J. (1992). *Economics, Organization and Management*. Englewood Cliffs, NJ: Prentice Hall.

Miller, J., & Muir, D. (2004). *The business of brands*. Chichester, UK: John Wiley & Sons.

Mishra, A. K. (1996). Organizational responses to crisis: The centrality of trust. In R. M. Kramer, & T. R. Tyler (Eds.), *Trust in Organizations: Frontiers of Theory and Research* (pp. 261–287). Thousand Oaks, CA: Sage. doi:10.4135/9781452243610.n13

Mishra, A. K., & Mishra, K. E. (1994). The role of mutual trust in effective downsizing strategies. *Human Resource Management*, *33*(2), 261–279. doi:10.1002/hrm.3930330207

Mishra, A. K., & Spreitzer, G. M. (1998). Explaining How Survivors Respond to Downsizing: The Roles of Trust, Empowerment, Justice, and Work Redesign. *Academy of Management Review*, *23*(3), 567–588.

Misiag, F. (2001). Metodyczne problemy badania orientacji marketingowej. *Marketing i Rynek*, *10*.

Mitchell, C. (2011). *Achieving Customer-led Growth in Insurance-Three steps to improve retention and return to growth* (IBM Global Business Services, White Paper). IBM Corporation.

Mitchell, R. K., Agle, B. R., & Wood, D. J. (1997). Toward a Theory of Stakeholder Identification and Salience: Defining the Principle of Who and What Really Counts. *Academy of Management Review*, *22*(4), 853–886.

Mittal, V., Ross, W., & Baldasare, P. (1998). The asymmetric impact of negative and positive attribute-level performance on overall satisfaction and repurchase intentions. *Journal of Marketing*, *61*(1), 33–47. doi:10.2307/1251801

Miyashita, K., & Russel, D. W. (1994). *Keiretsu: Inside the hidden Japanese conglomerates*. New York: McGraw Hill.

Mohr, J., & Spekman, R. (1994). Characteristics of partnership success: Partnership attributes, communication behavior, and conflict resolution techniques. *Strategic Management Journal*, *15*(2), 135–152. doi:10.1002/smj.4250150205

Moisescu, O. I. (2005). *The concept of brand equity – A comparative approach*. Munich Personal RePEc Archive (MPRA) paper # 32013. Retrieved February 8, 2014, from http://mpra.ub.uni-muenchen.de/32013/1/MPRA_paper_32013.pdf

Moon. (2003). Can IT Help Government to Restore Public Trust? Declining Public Trust and Potential Prospects of IT in the Public Sector. In *Proceedings of the 36th Hawaii International Conference on System Sciences*. Retrieved September 9, 2013, from http://citeseerx.ist.psu.edu/viewdoc/download?doi=10.1.1.4.2836&rep=rep1&type=pdf

Morgan, F., Deeter-Schmelz, D., & Moberg, C. R. (2007). Branding implications of partner firm-focal firm relationships in business-to-business service networks. *Journal of Business and Industrial Marketing*, *22*(6), 372–382. doi:10.1108/08858620710780136

Morgan, N. A., & Rego, L. L. (2009). Brand portfolio strategy and firm performance. *Journal of Marketing*, *73*(1), 59–74. doi:10.1509/jmkg.73.1.59

Morgan, R. M., & Hunt, S. D. (1994). The Commitment-Trust Theory of Relationship Marketing. *Journal of Marketing*, *58*(3), 20–38. doi:10.2307/1252308

Morris, M., & Koçak, A., & Özer. (2007). Coopetition as a Small Business Strategy: Implications for Performance. *Journal of Small Business Strategy*, *18*(1), 35–55.

Mourad, M., Ennew, C., & Kortam, W. (2011). Brand equity in higher education. *Marketing Intelligence & Planning*, *29*(4), 403–420. doi:10.1108/02634501111138563

Moutinho, L., & Smith, A. (2000). Caseling bank customer satisfaction through mediation of attitudes towards human and automated banking. *International Journal of Bank Marketing*, *18*(3), 124–134. doi:10.1108/02652320010339699

Mowery, D. C. (Ed.). (1988). *International Collaborative Ventures in U.S. Manufacturing*. Cambridge, MA: Ballinger.

Munoz, T., & Kumar, S. (2004). Brand metrics: Gauging and linking brands with business performance. *Journal of Brand Management*, *11*(5), 381–387. doi:10.1057/palgrave.bm.2540183

Muraskin, W. (2002). The last years of the CVI and the birth of GAVI. In M. R. Reich (Ed.), *Public-private partnerships for public health* (pp. 115–168). Cambridge, MA: Harvard University Press.

Murphy, J. (1992). Assessing the Value of Brands. *Branding a Key Marketing Tool*, 184-197.

Murray, K. (1991). A test of servcies marketing theory: Consumer information acquisition activities. *Journal of Marketing*, *55*(1), 10–25. doi:10.2307/1252200

Myers, C. (2003). Managing brand equity: A look at the impact of attributes. *Journal of Product and Brand Management*, *12*(1), 39–51. doi:10.1108/10610420310463126

Mytelka, L. K. (1991). *Strategic Partnerships and the World Economy*. London.

Mzungu, S., Merrilees, B., & Miller, D. (2010). Brand management to protect brand equity: A conceptual model. *Brand Management*, *17*(8), 605–617. doi:10.1057/bm.2010.15

Nakamura, M. (2003). Corporate Governance and Management Practices in Japan: Current issues. Paper presented at the EAMSA 20th Annual Conference. Stockholm, Sweden.

Nakata, C., & Sivakumar, K. (1997). Emerging market conditions and their impact on first mover advantages: An integrative review. *International Marketing Review*, *14*(96), 461–472. doi:10.1108/02651339710192993

Narayanan, V. (2001). *Managing Technology and Innovation for Competitive Advantage*. Upper Saddle River, NJ: Prentice Hall.

Narver, J. C., & Slater, S. F. (1990). The Effect of a Market Orientation On Business Profitability. *Journal of Marketing*, *54*(4), 20–33. doi:10.2307/1251757

Naude, P., & Holland, C. (1996). Business-to-business relationships. In *Relationship Marketing, Theory and Practice*. London: Paul Chapman Publishing. doi:10.4135/9781446252062.n4

Neal, W. D. (1999). Satisfaction is Nice, But Value Drives Loyalty. *Marketing Research*, *11*(1), 20–23.

Netemeyer, R. G., Krishnan, B., Pullig, C., Wang, G., Yagci, M., & Dean, D. et al. (2004). Developing and validating measures of facets of customer based brand equity. *Journal of Business Research*, *57*(2), 209–224. doi:10.1016/S0148-2963(01)00303-4

Neustadt, R. (1990). *Presidential Power and the Modern Presidents: The Politics of Leadership from Roosevelt to Reagan*. New York: Free Press.

Newman, K., & Cowling, A. (1996). Service quality in retail banking: The experience of two British clearing banks. *International Journal of Bank Marketing*, *14*(6), 3–11. doi:10.1108/02652329610130127

Ng, S., David, M., & Dagger, T. (2001). Generating positive word-of-mouth in the servcie experience. *Managing Service Quality*, *21*(2), 133–151. doi:10.1108/09604521111113438

Nguyen, N., & LeBlanc, G. (1998). The mediating role of corporate image on customers retention decisions: An investigation in financial servccie. *International Journal of Bank Marketing*, *16*(2), 52–65. doi:10.1108/02652329810206707

Nguyen, T. D., Barrett, N. J., & Miller, K. E. (2011). Brand loyalty in emerging markets. *Marketing Intelligence & Planning*, *29*(3), 222–232. doi:10.1108/02634501111129211

Niglas, K. (2010). The Multidimensional Model of Research Methodology: An Integrated Set of Continua. In *The Sage Handbook of Mixed Methods in Social and Behavioural Research*. Thousand Oaks, CA: Sage.

Nikolopoulou, R. (2006, March 15). The importance of the right customer service in franchise networks. *Express*, p. 40.

Ni, N., & Wan, F. (2008). A configurational perspective of branding capabilities development in emerging economies: The case of the Chinese cellular phone industry. *Brand Management*, *15*(6), 433–451.

Noble, S., Girffith, D., & Adjei, M. (2006). Drivers of local merchant loyalty: Understanding the influence of gender and shopping motives. *Journal of Retailing*, *83*(3), 177–189. doi:10.1016/j.jretai.2006.05.002

Nohria, N., Groysberg, B., & Lee, L. E. (2008). Employee Motivation: A Powerful New Model. *Harvard Business Review*, *86*(7/8), 78–84. PMID:18681299

Nonaka, I., & Takeuchi, H. (2011, May). The Wise Leader. *Harvard Business Review*, 59–67. PMID:21548419

North, A., & Shilock, A. (2003). The effect of musical style on restaurant customers spending. *Environment and Behavior*, *35*(5), 712–718. doi:10.1177/0013916503254749

O'Cass, A., & Ngo, L. V. (2007). Balancing external adaptation and internal effectiveness: Achieving better brand performance. *Journal of Business Research*, *60*(1), 11–20. doi:10.1016/j.jbusres.2006.08.003

O'Cass, A., & Weerawardena, J. (2010). The effect of perceived industry competitive intensity and marketing-related capabilities: Drivers of superior brand performance. *Industrial Marketing Management*, *39*(4), 571–581. doi:10.1016/j.indmarman.2009.04.002

Ogba, I. E., & Tan, Z. (2009). Exploring the impact of brand image on customer loyalty and commitment in China. *Journal of Technology Management in China*, *4*(2), 132–144. doi:10.1108/17468770910964993

Ohmae, K. (1988). Getting Back to Strategy. *Harvard Business Review*.

Ohmae, K. (1999). *The borderless world: Power and strategy in the interlinked economy*. New York: Harper Business.

Okabe, M. (2001). Are cross-holdings of Japanese corporations dissolving? Evolution and implications. *Nissan Occasional Paper Series, 33*.

Okonkwo, U. (2007). *Luxury fashion branding: Trends, tactics, techniques*. New York, NY: Palgrave Macmillan. doi:10.1057/9780230590885

Olins, W. (1995). *The New Guide To Identity*. Aldershot, UK: Gower.

Olins, W. (2005). *On brands*. London, UK: Thames & Hudson.

Oliver, R. L. (1980). A cognitive model of the antecedents and consequences of satisfaction decisions. *JMR, Journal of Marketing Research*, *17*(4), 460–469. doi:10.2307/3150499

Oliver, R. L. (1997). *Satisfaction: A Behavioural Perspective on the Consume*. New York: McGraw-Hill Companies, Inc.

Oliver, R. L. (1999). Whence consumer loyalty? *Journal of Marketing*, *63*, 33–44. doi:10.2307/1252099

Orth, M. (2003). Defining Flexibility and Sewability in Conductive Yarns. In Proceedings of Materials Research Society Symposium Proceedings (Vol. 736, p. 47). Academic Press.

Osborn, C. (Ed.). (2000). *Public-private partnerships: Theory and practice in international perspective*. London: Routledge.

Panigyrakis, G. G., & Theodoridis, P. K. (2009). Internal marketing impact on business performance in a retail context. *International Journal of Retail & Distribution Management*, *37*(7), 600–628. doi:10.1108/09590550910964620

Paolo. (2003). Banks Can Reduce Running Cost by 20%. *Kathimerini*, 24.

Papasolomou-Doukakis, I. (2003). Internal Marketing in the UK Retail Banking Sector: Rhetoric or Reality? *Journal of Marketing Management*, *19*(1/2), 197–224.

Pappu, R., Quester, P. G., & Cooksey, R. W. (2005). Consumer-based brand equity: Improving the measurement – Empirical evidence. *Journal of Product and Brand Management*, *14*(3), 143–154. doi:10.1108/10610420510601012

Parasuraman, A., Zeithaml, V., & Berry, L. (1985). A conceptual model of service quality and its implications for future research. *Journal of Marketing*, *49*(4), 41–50. doi:10.2307/1251430

Parasuraman, B., & Radhakrishnan, B. (2011). Employee participation in the Public sector in Malayasia: A General Overview. *Journal of Arts. Science and Commerce*, *2*(1), 55–69.

Parkhe, A. (1991). Interfirm diversity, organizational learning, and longevity in global strategic alliances. *Journal of International Business Studies*, *22*(4), 579–601. doi:10.1057/palgrave.jibs.8490315

Parkhe, A. (1993). Strategic Allaince Structure, A Game theoretic and transaction cost examination of inter-firm cooperation. *Academy of Management Journal*, *24*(4), 794–829. doi:10.2307/256759

Parkhe, A. (1998). Understanding Trust in International Alliances. *Journal of World Business*, *33*(3), 219–240. doi:10.1016/S1090-9516(99)80072-8

Pascale, R. T. (1984). Perspectives on Strategy: The Real Story Behind Honda's Success. *California Management Review*, *26*(3), 47–72. doi:10.2307/41165080

Pass, C., Lowes, B., Pendleton, A., Chadwick, L., & O'Reilly, D. (2006). *Collins Dictionary of Business*. Glasgow, UK: Harper-Collins.

Pauwels, K., Erguncu, S., & Yildirim, G. (2013). Winning hearts, minds and sales: How marketing communication enters the purchase process in emerging and mature markets. *International Journal of Research in Marketing*, *30*(1), 57–68. doi:10.1016/j.ijresmar.2012.09.006

Payne, A., Ballantyne, D., & Christopher, M. (2005). A stakeholder approach to relationship marketing strategy: The development and use of the six markets model. *European Journal of Marketing*, *39*(7), 855–871. doi:10.1108/03090560510601806

Pearce, R. J. (1997). Toward understanding joint venture performance and survival: A bargaining and influence approach to transaction cost theory. *Academy of Management Review*, *22*(1), 203–225.

Pearlson, K. (2001). *Managing and Using Information Systems: A Strategic Approach*. New York: John Wiley & Sons.

Penga, M. W., & Leea, S.-H. (2001). The keiretsu in Asia: Implications for multilevel theories of competitive advantage. *Journal of International Management*, *7*(4), 253–276. doi:10.1016/S1075-4253(01)00047-3

Peng, M. W. (2003). Institutional transitions and strategic choices. *Academy of Management Review*, *28*(2), 275–296.

Peppers, D., & Rogers, M. (2004). *Managing customer relationships: A strategic framework*. New York: John Wiley and Sons.

Perrone, A., & Wong, H. Y. (2013). The antecedents of re-purchase intentions: The service quality perspective. *International Journal of Services. Economics and Management*, *5*(3), 203–221.

Peteraf, M. A. (1993). The Cornerstones of Competitive Advantage: A Resource-Based View. *Strategic Management Journal*, *14*(3), 179–191. doi:10.1002/smj.4250140303

Peter, P. J., & Olson, J. C. (1996). *Consumer behaviour and Marketing Strategy* (4th ed.). Irwin.

Peters, T., & Waterman, R. (1982). *In Search of Excellence*. New York: Warner Books.

Pew Research Center. (2013). Majority Says the Federal Government Threatens Their Personal Rights. *Pew Research Center for the People and & the Press*. Retrieved September 4, 2013, from http://www.people-press.org/2013/01/31/majority-says-the-federal-government-threatens-their-personal-rights/2/

Pfeffer, J. (1997). *New directions for organisation theory*. New York, NY: Oxford University Press.

Pfeffer, J. (1998). *The Human Equation*. Boston, MA: Harvard Business School Press.

Phillips, C. J. (1997). Do you Trust me? *Executive Excellence*, *14*, 7–10.

Phillips, R. (2003). Stakeholder Legitimacy. *Business Ethics Quarterly*, *13*(1), 25–41. doi:10.5840/beq20031312

Phillips, R., Freeman, E., & Wicks, A. (2003). What Stakeholder Theory is not. *Business Ethics Quarterly*, *13*(4), 479–502. doi:10.5840/beq200313434

Pillai, A. (2012). Corporate branding literature: A research paradigm review. *Journal of Brand Management*, *19*(4), 331–343. doi:10.1057/bm.2011.43

Piricz, N., & Mandják, T. (2012). The relationship among trust conflicts and perceived satisfaction in B2B context. Paper presented at the 28th Annual IMP Conference. Rome, Italy.

Pollalis, Y. A., & Grant, J. H. (1994). Information Resources & Corporate Strategy Development. *Information Strategy*, *11*(1), 12–28.

Polonsky, M. J. (1995). A stakeholder theory approach to designing environmental marketing strategy. *Journal of Business and Industrial Marketing*, *10*(3), 29–46. doi:10.1108/08858629510096201

Poon, A. (1993). *Tourism, Technology and Competitive Strategies, CAB International: Wallingford; relationship, Springer Computer Science*. Vienna, Austria: Springer.

Porter, M. (1986). *Competition in Global Industries*. Cambridge, MA: Harvard Business School.

Porter, M. E. (1980). *Competitive Strategy*. New York: Free Press.

Porter, M. E. (1981). The contributions of industrial organization to strategic management. *Academy of Management Review*, *15*(1).

Porter, M. E. (1985). *Competitive Advantage*. New York: Free Press.

Porter, M., & Fuller, M. B. (1986). Coalitions and Global Strategy. In M. Porter (Ed.), *Competition in Global Industries* (pp. 315–343). Boston, MA: Harvard Business.

Poutziouris, P. (2003). The Strategic Orientation Of Owner-Managers Of Small Ventures Evidence From The UK Small Business Economy. *International Journal Of Entrepreneurial Behaviour & Research*, *9*(5), 185–214. doi:10.1108/13552550310488929

Praest Knudsen, M. (2007). The relative importance of inter firm relationships and knowledge transfer for new product development success. *Journal of Product Innovation Management*, *24*(2), 117–138. doi:10.1111/j.1540-5885.2007.00238.x

Prahalad, C. K., & Hamel, G. (1990). The core competence of the corporation. *Harvard Business Review*, *68*(3), 79–91.

Press Association. (n.d.). Financial crisis, five years on: trust in banking hits new low. *Press Association*. Retrieved September 15, 2013, from http://www.theguardian.com/business/2012/aug/09/financial-crisis-anniversary-trust-in-banks

Press Releases. (2013). *Internet users in India crosses 200 million mark*. Retrieved from www.iamai.in

Priem, P., & Butler, J. E. (2001). Is the resource-based view a useful perspective for strategic management research? *Academy of Management Review*, *26*(1), 22–40. doi:10.5465/AMR.2001.4011928

Priniotakis, G. (2005). *Study of Conductive Textile Electrodes as Analytical Tool for Detection of Parameters related to human body by (EIS) Electrochemical Impedance Spectroscopy*. (PhD Thesis). University of Ghent, Ghent, Belgium.

Public Sector Integrity Reviews. (n.d.). Fighting corruption in the public sector - Why integrity matters for governments? *Public Sector Integrity Reviews*. Retrieved August 24, 2013, from http://www.oecd.org/governance/ethics/publicsectorintegrityreviews.htm

Pukthuanthong, K., & Roll, R. (2009). Global market integration: An alternative measure and its application. *Journal of Financial Economics*, *94*(2), 214–232. doi:10.1016/j.jfineco.2008.12.004

Punjaisri, K., Evanschitzky, H., & Wilson, A. (2009). Internal branding: An enabler of employees' brand supporting behaviours. *Journal of Service Management*, *20*(2), 209–226. doi:10.1108/09564230910952780

Quelch, J. A., & Jocz, K. E. (2009). How to market in a downturn. *Harvard Business Review*, *87*(4), 52–62.

Quelch, J., & Klein, L. (1996, Spring). The internet and international marketing. *Sloan Management Review*, 61–75.

Quester, P., & Lim, A. (2003). Product involvement/brand loyalty: Is there a link? *Journal of Product and Brand Management*, *12*(1), 22–38. doi:10.1108/10610420310463117

Quinn, J. B. (1992). *The Intelligence Enterprise*. New York: Free Press.

Radcliffe, S. (2008). *Future - Engage - Deliver: The Essential Guide to Your Leadership*. Leicester, UK: Troubadour Publishing Ltd.

Rafiq, M., & Ahmed, P. K. (1993). The scope of internal marketing: Defining the boundary between marketing and human resource management. *Journal of Marketing Management*, *9*(3), 219–232. doi:10.1080/0267257X.1993.9964234

Rafiq, M., & Ahmed, P. K. (2000). Advances in the internal marketing concept: Definition, synthesis and extension. *Journal of Services Marketing*, *14*(6), 449–462. doi:10.1108/08876040010347589

Rais, S., & Goedegebuure, R. V. (2009). Stakeholder Orientation and financial performance: Evidence from Indonesia. *Problems and Perspectives in Management*, *7*(3), 62–75.

Rajagopal. (2008). Measuring brand performance through metrics application. *Measuring Business Excellence*, *12*(1), 29-38.

Rajagopal. (2009). Branding paradigm for the bottom of the pyramid markets. *Measuring Business Excellence*, *13*(4), 58-68.

Rajagopalan, N., & Spreitzer, G. M. (1997). Toward a theory of strategic change: A multi-lens perspective and integrative framework. *Academy of Management Review*, *2*, 48–71.

Ramanathan, R. (2010). The moderating roles of risk and efficiency on the relationship between logistics performance and customer loyalty in e-commerce. *Transportation Research Part E, Logistics and Transportation Review*, *46*(6), 950–962. doi:10.1016/j.tre.2010.02.002

Ranaweera, C., & Prabhu, J. (2003). The influence of satisfaction, trust and switching barriers on customer retention in a continuous purchasing setting. *International Journal of Service Industry Management*, *14*(4), 374–395. doi:10.1108/09564230310489231

Rauyruen, P., & Miller, K. E. (2007). Relationship quality as a predictor of B2B customer loyalty. *Journal of Business Research*, *60*(1), 21–31. doi:10.1016/j.jbusres.2005.11.006

Ray N; Das D K (2011): Marketing Practices for Promotion of Rural Tourism: A Study On Kamarpukur, India, *Journal of Business and Economics* ISSN 2155- 7950 Academic Star Publishing Co. May 2011, *2*(5), New York, USA

Ray, N., et al. (2011). A Study on Application of Information Technology on Tourism Development. In Management and Service Science (MASS), International Conference on (pp. 1-7). IEEE. doi:10.1109/ICMSS.2011.599870710.1109/ICMSS.2011.5998707

Ray, N., et al. (2011): Information Technology and Its Impact on Tourism: An Overview. In Khurana, R., Agrawal, R., Debnath, C (Eds) Computing Business Application and Legal Issues ISBN 978-81-7446-936-6 Excel Book Publication Edition 1st. 2011 from IMT Gaziabad, India

Reast, J. (2005). Brand trust and brand extension acceptance: The relationship. *Journal of Product and Brand Management*, *14*(1), 4–13. doi:10.1108/10610420510583707

Reed, D. (1999). Stakeholder Management Theory: A Critical Theory Perspective. *Business Ethics Quarterly*, *9*(3), 453–483. doi:10.2307/3857512

Reichheld, F. (2003). The one number you need to grow. *Harvard Business Review*, *81*(12), 46–54. PMID:14712543

Reichheld, F. (2009). Closing the customer feedback loop. *Harvard Business Review*, *87*(12), 43–47.

Reichheld, F. F., Markey, R. G. J., & Hopton, C. (2000). The loyalty effect - The relationship between loyalty and profits. *European Business Journal*, *12*(3), 134–139.

Reichheld, F. F., & Sasser, W. C. J. (1990). Zero defections: Quality comes to services. *Harvard Business Review*, *68*(5), 105–111. PMID:10107082

Reid, M. (2002). Building strong brands through the management of integrated marketing communications. *International Journal of Wine Marketing*, *14*(3), 37–52. doi:10.1108/eb008745

Reinartz, W., & Kumar, V. (2002, July). The mismanagement of customer loyalty. *Harvard Business Review*, 86–94. PMID:12140857

Reis, D., Pena, L., & Lopes, P. A. (2003). Customer satisfaction: The historical perspective. *Management Decision*, *41*(2), 195–198. doi:10.1108/00251740310457641

Reitchheld, F. F. (1996). *The Loyalty Effect*. Cambridge, MA: Harvard Business School Press.

Rex, E., & Baumann, H. (2007). Beyond ecolabels: What green marketing can learn from conventional marketing. *Journal of Cleaner Production*, *15*(6), 567–576. doi:10.1016/j.jclepro.2006.05.013

Ries, A., & Trout, J. (1981). *Positioning: The Battle for your Mind*. Maidenhead, UK: McGraw-Hill.

Rigby, D. K., Reichheld, F. F., & Schefter, P. (2002). Avoid the four perils of CRM. *Harvard Business Review*, *80*(2), 101–109. PMID:11894676

Rocco, M. A., & Andrew, N. V. (2011). *Hospitality Today: An Introduction* (7th ed.). Educational Institute of the American Hotel Motel Association.

Rockart, J. (1979). Chief Executives Define their Own Data Needs. *Harvard Business Review*, *57*(2). PMID:10297607

Romaniuk, J., Sharp, B., Paech, S., & Dreisener, C. (2004). Brand and advertising awareness: A replication and extension of a known empirical generalization. *Australasian Marketing Journal*, *12*(3), 70–80. doi:10.1016/S1441-3582(04)70107-X

Rosenblatt, P. C., De Milk, L., Anderson, R. M., & Jhonson, P. A. (1985). The Family. In *Business: Understanding The Dealing With The Challenges Entrepreneurial Families Face*. San Francisco: Jossey Bass.

Rotter, J. (1980). Interpersonal trust, trustworthiness and gullibility. *The American Psychologist*, *35*(1), 1–7. doi:10.1037/0003-066X.35.1.1

Rotter, J. B. (1967). A new scale for the measurement of interpersonal trust. *Journal of Personality*, *35*(4), 651–665. doi:10.1111/j.1467-6494.1967.tb01454.x PMID:4865583

Rousseau, D. M., Sitkin, S. B., Burt, R. S., & Camerer, C. (1998). Not so Different After All: A Cross-Discipline View of Trust. *Academy of Management Review*, *23*(3), 393–404. doi:10.5465/AMR.1998.926617

Rowe, & Calnan. (2006). Trust relations in health care: Developing a theoretical framework for the new NHS. *Journal of Health Organization and Management, 20* (5), 376 – 396.

Rowen, H. S., & Toyoda, A. M. (2002). *From Keiretsu to Startups: Japan's Push for High Tech Entrepreneurship* (Working Paper). Asia/Pacific Research Center, Stanford University. Retrieved from http://iis-db.stanford.edu/pubs/20027/rowen_toyoda.pdf

Rowley, J. (2005). The four Cs of customer loyalty. *Marketing Intelligence & Planning*, *23*(6), 574–581. doi:10.1108/02634500510624138

Rubin, J., Schultz, M., & Hatch, M. (2008). Coming to America: Can Nordic brand values engage American stakeholders? *Brand Management*, *16*(1-2), 30–39. doi:10.1057/bm.2008.17

Rugman, A. M., & Collinson, S. C. (2009). *International business*. Harlow, UK: Prentice-Hall.

Rundle-Thiele, S. (2005). Exploring loyal qualities: Assessing survey-based loyalty measures. *Journal of Services Marketing*, *19*(7), 492–500. doi:10.1108/08876040510625990

Rust, R., & Oliver, R. (1994). Service quality: Insights and managerial implications from the frontier. In R. Rust, & R. Oliver (Eds.), *Service Quality: New Directions in Theory and Practice* (pp. 1–19). London: Sage Publications. doi:10.4135/9781452229102.n1

Rust, R., & Zahorik, A. (1993). Customer satisfaction, customer retention and market share. *Journal of Retailing*, *69*(2), 193–215. doi:10.1016/0022-4359(93)90003-2

Rust, R., Zahorik, A., & Keiningham, T. (1995a). Return on quality (ROQ), Making service quality financially accountable. *Journal of Marketing*, *59*(April), 58–70. doi:10.2307/1252073

Sabel, C. F. (1993). Studied trust: Building new forms of cooperation in a volatile economy. *Human Relations*, *46*(9), 1133–1170. doi:10.1177/001872679304600907

Sako, M. (1992). *Price, Quality and Trust*. Cambridge, UK: Cambridge University Press. doi:10.1017/CBO9780511520723

Salzman, M., & O'Reilly, A. (2010). *10 trends in mindful consumption*. Retrieved 25/09/2013 from http://www.thenewconsumer.com/2010/10/29/10-trends-in-mindful-consumption/

Samanta, I. (2006). The reinforcement of competitiveness of medium sized firms. *Applied Research Review Periodical Scientific, 11*(2).

Samanta, I. (2008). Innovation Culture Assists Knowledge Management in new era. In *Web 2.0: The business model*. Springer.

Samanta, I. (2009). The impact of e-customer relationship marketing in hotel industry. *International Journal of Knowledge and Learning*, *5*(3/4), 333–346. doi:10.1504/IJKL.2009.031228

Samanta, I. (2011). *Digital Culture and è-Tourism: Technologies Applications and Management Approaches IGI Global* (pp. 90–104). Hershey, PA: Information Science Reference.

Santos-Vijande, M., Del Rio-Lanza, A., Suarez-Alvarez, L., & Diaz-Martin, A. (2013). The brand management system and service firm competitiveness. *Journal of Business Research*, *66*(2), 148–157. doi:10.1016/j.jbusres.2012.07.007

Sarker, A. E. (2006). New Public Management in Developing Countries – An analysis of success and failure with particular reference to Singapore and Bangladesh. *International Journal of Public Sector Management*, *19*(2), 180–203. doi:10.1108/09513550610650437

Sasser, W. E., & Arbeit, S. F. (1976). Selling jobs in the service sector. *Business Horizons*, *19*(3), 61–65. doi:10.1016/0007-6813(76)90053-7

Saunders, M., Lewis, P., & Thornhill, A. (2003). Research Methods for Business Studies. *Financial Times*, pp. 81–105.

Saunders, M., Lewis, P., & Thornhill, A. (2012). *Research Methods for Business Students* (6th ed.). Harlow, UK: Pearson.

Savage, D. (1982). Trust as a Productivity Management Tool. *Training and Development Journal*, *36*, 54–57.

Schein, E. (1992). *Organisational Culture and Leadership* (2nd ed.). San Francisco, CA: Jossey-Bass.

Schein, E. H. (1992). *Organizational Culture and Leadership*. San Francisco: Jossey-Bass Publishers.

Schelling, T. C. (1956). An essay on bargaining. *The American Economic Review*, *46*, 281–306.

Schlosser, F. K., & McNaughton, R. B. (2007). Internal stakeholder views of a market orientation strategy: Implications for implementation. *Journal of Strategic Marketing*, *15*(4), 307–325. doi:10.1080/09652540701320944

Schneider, B., Holcombe, K., & Whiete, S. (1997). Lessons learned about servcie quality: What it is, how to manage it and how to become a service quality organization. *Consulting Psychology Journal*, *49*(1), 35–50. doi:10.1037/1061-4087.49.1.35

Schon, D. (1983). *The Reflective Practitioner*. New York, NY: Basic Books.

Schultz, R. L., & Slevin, D. P. (1975). *Implementing Operations Research/Management Science*. New York: Elsevier.

Schumpeter, J. A. (1950). *Capitalism, Socialism, and Democracy*. New York: Harper & Row.

Schwarz, A., Hakuzimana, J., Kaczynska, A., Banaszczyk, J., Westbroek, P., & McAdams, E. et al. (2010). Gold coated para-aramid yarns through electroless deposition. *Surface and Coatings Technology*, *204*(9-10), 1412–1418. doi:10.1016/j.surfcoat.2009.09.038

Schweizer, B. (2008). *An Examination of Factors Leading to Abating Customer Loyalty Towards Magazine Subscriptions*. Berlin: GRIN Verlag.

Scott, M., & Bruce, R. (1987). Five Stages Of Growth In Small Businesses. *Long Range Planning*, *20*(3), 45–52. doi:10.1016/0024-6301(87)90071-9

Sekaran, U., & Bougie, R. (2009). *Research Methods for Business: A Skill Building Approach* (5th ed.). Chichester, UK: Wiley & Sons Ltd.

Sergeant, A., & Frenkel, S. (2000). When do customer contact employees satisfy customers? *Journal of Service Research*, *3*(1), 18–34. doi:10.1177/109467050031002

Severt, K. S., & Palakurthi, R. (2008). Applying customer equity to the convention industry. *International Journal of Contemporary Hospitality Management*, *20*(6), 631–646. doi:10.1108/09596110810892209

Seyam, A. M. (2003). Formation of Textiles Structures for Giant-Area Applications, Electronics on Unconventional Substrates. *Electrotextiles and Giant Area Flexible Circuits*, *736*, 25–36.

Shapiro, B. P. (2005). *Sustainable Marketing Leadership Model, Workshop I: Strategic Visioning and Integrated Planning*. Harvard Business Press Cases.

Shapiro, C., & Varian, H. (1999). *Information Rules: A Strategic Guide to the Network Economy*. Boston, MA: Harvard Business School Press.

Sharland, A., Eltantawy, R. A., & Giunipero, L. C. (2003). The impact of cycle time on supplier selection and subsequent performance outcomes. *Journal of Supply Chain Management*, *39*(3), 4–12. doi:10.1111/j.1745-493X.2003.tb00155.x

Sharma, P, Carson, D & DeLacy, T 2000, 'National online tourism policy initiatives

Sharma, P., Chrisman, J., & Chua, J. (1996). *A Review And Annotated Bibliography Of Family Business Studies*. Boston: Kluwer. doi:10.1007/978-1-4419-8768-6

Shavitt, S. (1989). Products, personality and situations in attitude functions: Implications for consumer behaviour. In T. Srull (Ed.), Advances in Consumer Research (pp. 300-305). Provo, UT: Association for consumer Research.

Sheard, P. (1994). The Main Bank System and Corporate Monitoring and Control in Japan. *Journal of Economic Behavior & Organization*, *11*(3), 399–422. doi:10.1016/0167-2681(89)90037-1

Sheldon, P. J. (1998). *Tourism information technology*. New York: CABI Publishing.

Shi, J., Zhang, J., & Qu, X. (2010). Optimizing distribution strategy for perishable foods using RFID and sensor technologies. *Journal of Business and Industrial Marketing*, *25*(8), 596–606. doi:10.1108/08858621011088338

Shin, H., Collier, D. A., & Wilson, D. D. (2000). Supply management orientation and supplier/buyer performance. *Journal of Operations Management*, *18*(3), 317–333. doi:10.1016/S0272-6963(99)00031-5

Shockley-Zalabak, P., Ellis, K., & Winograd, G. (2000). Organizational Trust: What it Mean and Why it Matters. *Organization Development Journal*, *18*, 35–48.

Siegel, D. (2000). Futurize Your Enterprise. In *Business strategy in the age of the e-customer*. New York: John Wiley.

Sigala, M. (2007). Integrating Web 2.0 in e-learning environments: A socio-technical approach.

Sigala, M. (2008). WEB 2.0, social marketing strategies and distribution channels for city destinations:

Silverman, G. (1997). How to harness the awesome power of word of mouth: Generating desired customer response through word of mouth. *Direct Marketing*, *60*(7), 32–36.

Silverman, G. (2001a). The power of word of mouth. *Direct Marketing*, *64*(5), 47–52.

Silverman, G. (2001b). *The Secrets of Word-of-Mouth Marketing: How to Trigger Exponential Sales thourgh Runsway Word of Mouth*. New York: American Management Association.

Sisodia, R., Sheth, J., & Wolfe, D. B. (2007). *Firms of Endearment: How World-class Companies Profit from Passion and Purpose*. Wharton School Publishing.

Sitkin, S. B., & Roth, N. L. (1993). Explaining the Limited Effectiveness of Legalistic Remedies for Trust / Distrust. *Organization Science*, *4*(3), 367–392. doi:10.1287/orsc.4.3.367

Skowron, L., & Kristensen, K. (2012). The impact of the recent banking crisis on customer loyalty in the banking sector. Developing versus developed countries. *The TQM Journal*, *24*(6), 480–497. doi:10.1108/17542731211270052

Slade, J., Catogan, D., Sandy, C., & Grahne, M. (1998). Development and Evaluation of the Mars Pathfinder Inflatable Airbag Landing System. Paper presented at the 49th International Astronautical Congress. Washington, DC.

Smith, X. N., & Nunes, P. F. (2010). Will Marketing Get The Message. *Accenture Outlook*. Retrieved from www.accenture.com/Accenture_Outlook_Will_Marketing_Get_Message.pdf

Smith, A. M.Characteristics on the Dimensionality of the Service Quality Construct. (2000). The impact of scale characteristics on the dimensionality of the service quality construct. *Service Industries Journal*, *20*(3), 167–190. doi:10.1080/02642060000000037

Smith, N., Drumwright, M., & Gentile, M. (2010). The New Marketing Myopia. *Journal of Public Policy & Marketing*, *29*(1), 4–11. doi:10.1509/jppm.29.1.4

Smith, P., & Burns, D. (1996). Atmospherics and retail enviornments: The case of the power aisle. *International Journal of Retail & Distribution Management*, *31*(2), 80–94.

Souiden, N., Kassim, N. M., & Hong, H. J. (2006). The effect of corporate branding dimensions on consumers' product evaluation: A cross-cultural analysis. *European Journal of Marketing*, *40*(7-8), 309–566.

Soulaki, A. (2010). *Can a financial crisis shaken Greek consumers' brand loyalty?* Retrieved September the 20th from http://www.ihu.edu.gr/gateway/files/document/dissertations/Soulaki_Antonia.pdf

Spangenberg, E., Crowley, A., & Henderson, P. (1996). Improving the store environment: Do Olfactory cues affect evaluations and behaviours? *Journal of Marketing*, *60*(2), 67–80. doi:10.2307/1251931

Speak, K. D., & Hanson, G. (2008). Brand Inside Meets Brand Outside. *Design Management Review*, *19*(2).

Spreng, R. A., MacKenzie, S. B., & Olshavsky, R. W. (1996). A Reexamination of the Determinants of Consumer Satisfaction. *Journal of Marketing*, *60*(3), 15–32. doi:10.2307/1251839

Spreng, R. A., Shi, H., & Page, T. F. (2009). Service quality and satisfaction in business-to-business services. *Journal of Business and Industrial Marketing*, *24*(7-8), 537–548. doi:10.1108/08858620910999411

Stabb, S., & Werthner, H. (2002). Intelligent Systems for Tourism. IEEE Intelligent Systems, November/December, 53-55.Statistics, viewed 16 April 2005

Stank, T. P., Goldsby, T. J., & Vickery, S. K. (1999). Effect of service supplier performance on satisfaction and loyalty of store managers in the fast food industry. *Journal of Operations Management*, *17*(4), 429–447. doi:10.1016/S0272-6963(98)00052-7

Stern, S., Manning, H., & Connor, C. O. (2013). *Sharpen Customer Experience Focus With Employee Engagement*. Retrieved September 3, 2013, from http://www.forrester.com/Sharpen+Customer+Experience+Focus+With+Employee+Engagement /fulltext/-/E-res101141

Steurer, R., Langer, M. E., Konrad, A., & Martinuzzi, A. (2005). Corporations, Stakeholders and Sustainable Development I: A Theoretical Exploration of Business–Society Relations. *Journal of Business Ethics*, *61*(3), 263–281. doi:10.1007/s10551-005-7054-0

Stevens, M. (2011). UK Lacks Top Quality Leadership, Finds CIPD Survey. *People Management*. Retrieved from www.peoplemanagement.co.uk/pm/articles/2011/09/uk-lacks-top-quality-leadership

Stewart, D., & Kamins, M. (1993). *Secondary Research: Information, Sources, and Methods*. Thousand Oaks, CA: Sage Publications.

Sweeney, J., Soutar, G., & Mazzarol, T. (2008). Factors influencing word of mout heffectiveness: Receiver perspectives. *European Journal of Marketing*, *42*(3/4), 344–364. doi:10.1108/03090560810852977

Sweeney, J., & Swait, J. (2008). The effects of brand credibility on customer loyalty. *Journal of Retailing and Consumer Services*, *15*(3), 179–193. doi:10.1016/j.jretconser.2007.04.001

Sweeney, J., & Wyber, F. (2002). The role of cognitions and emotions in the music apporach avoidance behaviour relationship. *Journal of Services Marketing*, *16*(1), 51–59. doi:10.1108/08876040210419415

Syed Alwi, S. F., & Melewar, T. C. (2013). Theme articles: Branding in Asia - Branding in the Asian context: A Malaysian perspective. *Asia Pacific Journal of Marketing and Logistics*, *25*(2), 287–297. doi:10.1108/13555851311314068

Sztompka, P. (1999). *Trust: A sociological theory*. Cambridge, UK: Cambridge University Press.

Tabeta, N. (1998). The Kigyo keiretsu organization and opportunism in the Japanese automobile manufacturing industry. *Asia Pacific Journal of Management*, *15*(1), 1–18. doi:10.1023/A:1015428707475

Tan, S. N., & Ge, H. L. (1998). Analysis of some cytokinins in cocnut water by micellar electrokinetic capillary chromatography after solid extraction. *New Polymer Materials*, *5*, 169–176.

Taylor, S. A., & Baker, T. L. (1994). An assessment of the relationship between service quality and customer satisfaction in the formation of consumer's purchase intentions. *Journal of Retailing*, *70*(2), 163–178. doi:10.1016/0022-4359(94)90013-2

Taylor, S., Celuch, K., & Goodwin, S. (2004). The importance of brand equity to customer loyalty. *Journal of Product and Brand Management*, *13*(4), 217–227. doi:10.1108/10610420410546934

Teece, D. (1984). Economic Analysis and Strategic Management. *California Management Review*, *25*(3).

Temkin. (n.d.). Customer Experience Boosts Revenue. *Forrester Research, Inc.* Retrieved September 5, 2013, from http://www.forrester.com/rb/Research/customer_experience_boosts_revenue/q/id/54750/t/2

Tepper, B. J. (1995). Upward maintenance tactics in supervisory mentoring and nonmentoring relation-ships. *Academy of Management Journal*, *38*(4), 1191–1205. doi:10.2307/256626

Tepper, B. J. (2000). Consequences of abusive supervision. *Academy of Management Journal*, *43*(2), 178–190. doi:10.2307/1556375

Thomas, J. L., Vitell, S. J., Gilbert, F. W., & Rose, G. M. (2002). The Impact of Ethical Cues on Customer Satisfaction with Service. *Journal of Retailing*, *78*(3), 167–173. doi:10.1016/S0022-4359(02)00062-3

Thompson, C., & Arsel, Z. (2004). The Starbucks brandscape and consumers' (anticorporate) experiences of globalization. *The Journal of Consumer Research*, *31*(3), 631–642. doi:10.1086/425098

Thwaites, D., & Vere, L. (1995). Bank selection criteria – A student perspective. *Journal of Marketing Management*, *11*(1–3), 133–149. doi:10.1080/0267257X.1995.9964334

Tong, X., & Hawley, J. M. (2009). Measuring customer-based brand equity: Empirical evidence from the sport wear market in China. *Journal of Product and Brand Management*, *18*(4), 262–271. doi:10.1108/10610420910972783

Tortosa, V., Moliner, M. A., & Sánchez, J. (2009). Internal market orientation and its influence on organisational performance. *European Journal of Marketing*, *43*(11), 1435–1456. doi:10.1108/03090560910989975

Tracey, M., & Tan, C. L. (2001). Empirical analysis of supplier selection and involvement, customer satisfaction, and firm performance. *Supply Chain Management: An International Journal*, *6*(4), 174–188. doi:10.1108/EUM0000000005709

Tracy, A. P., & Oskamp, S. (1984). Relationships among ecologically responsible behaviors. *Journal of Environmental Systems*, *13*(2), 115–126. doi:10.2190/6TN8-48WT-63XT-CHEN

Tuan, L. T. (2014). Corporate governance and brand performance. *Management Research Review*, *37*(1), 45–68.

Tucker, T. (1998). A Critical Analysis of the Procurement Procedures of the World Bank. In S. Arrowsmith, & A. Davies (Eds.), *Public Procurement: Global Revolution* (pp. 139–157). London: Kluwer Law International.

Tullock, G. (1965). *The Politics of Bureaucracy*. Washington, DC: Public Affairs Press.

Turban, E., Lee, J., King, D., & Chung, H. (2000). Electronic Commerce: A Managerial Perspective (Int. Ed.). Upper Saddle River, NJ: Prentice-Hall International.

Turban, E., King, D., Warkentin, M., & Chung, H. (2002). *E-commerce: A Managerial Perspective*. Upper Saddle River, NJ: Prentice Hall.

Turban, E., McLean, E., & Wetherbe, J. (2000). *Information Technology for Management: Making Connection for Strategic Advantage* (2nd ed.). New York: John Wiley & Sons Inc.

Turley, L., & Chebat, J. (2002). Linking retail strategy, atmospheric design and shopping behaviour. *Journal of Marketing Management*, *18*(1/2), 125–144. doi:10.1362/0267257022775891

Turnbull, S. (1997). Corporate governance: Its scope, concerns & theories, *Corporate Governance. International Review (Steubenville, Ohio)*, *5*(4), 180–205.

Uggla, H. (2006). The corporate brand association base: A conceptual model for the creation of inclusive brand architecture. *European Journal of Marketing*, *40*(7-8), 785–802. doi:10.1108/03090560610669991

Ulrich, D., & Smallwood, N. (2007). *Leadership Brand: Developing Customer-Focused Leaders to Drive Performance and Build Lasting Value*. Boston: Harvard Business School Press.

University of Michigan Business School. (2001). *American Customer Satisfaction Index*. Retrieved from www.bus.umich.edu/research/nqrc/asci.html

Urde, M., Baumgarth, C., & Merrilees, B. (2013). Brand orientation and market orientation – From alternatives to synergy. *Journal of Business Research*, *66*(1), 13–20. doi:10.1016/j.jbusres.2011.07.018

Vallaster, C., & De Chernatony, L. (2006). Internal brand building and structuration: The role of leadership. *European Journal of Marketing*, *40*(7-8), 761–784. doi:10.1108/03090560610669982

Van Riel, A. C. R., De Mortanges, C. P., & Streukens, S. (2005). Marketing antecedents of industrial brand equity: An empirical investigation in specialty chemicals. *Industrial Marketing Management*, *34*(8), 841–847. doi:10.1016/j.indmarman.2005.01.006

van Riel, C. B. M. (1995). *Principles of Corporate Communication*. Hemel Hempstead, UK: Prentice Hall.

VanAuken, B. (2005). *The brand management checklist: Proven tools and techniques for creating winning brands*. London, UK: Kogan Page.

Varey, R. J., & Lewis, B. R. (1999). A broadened conception of internal marketing. *European Journal of Marketing*, *33*(9), 926–944. doi:10.1108/03090569910285869

Verhoef, P., & Leeflang, P. (2009). Understanding the marketing department's influence within the firm. *Journal of Marketing*, *73*(2), 14–37. doi:10.1509/jmkg.73.2.14

Vesel, P., & Zabkar, V. (2009). Managing customer loyalty through the mediating role of satisfaction in the DIY retail loyalty program. *Journal of Retailing and Consumer Services*, *16*(5), 396–406. doi:10.1016/j.jretconser.2009.05.002

Voinea, L., & Filip, A. (2011). Analyzing the Main Changes in New Consumer Buying Behavior during Economic Crisis. *International Journal of Economic Practices and Theories*, *1*(1), 14–19.

Vonderembse, M. A., & Tracey, M. (1999). The impact of supplier selection criteria and supplier involvement on manufacturing performance. *Journal of Supply Chain Management*, *35*(3), 33–39. doi:10.1111/j.1745-493X.1999.tb00060.x

Vrontis, D., Thrassou, A., & Razali, M. Z. (2010). Internal Marketing as an Agent of Change – Implementing a New Human Resource Information System for Malaysian Airlines. *Journal of General Management*, *36*(1), 21–41.

Waddell, D., Cummings, T., & Worley, C. (2000). *Organisation Development and Change*. Melbourne: Nelson Thomson Learning.

Wagner, J. (2000). A model of aesthetic alue in the servciescape. In T. A. Swartz, & D. Iacobucci (Eds.), *Handbook of Servccies Marketing and Management*. Thousand Oaks, CA: Sage Publications.

Walker, C. (1995). Word of mouth. *American Demographics*, *17*(7), 38–44.

Wall, E., & Berry, L. (2007). The combined effects of the physical environment and employee behavior on customer perception of restaurant service quality. *The Cornell Hotel and Restaurant Administration Quarterly*, *48*(1), 59–70. doi:10.1177/0010880406297246

Wallenburg, C. M. (2004). *Kundenbindung in der Logistik: Eine empirische Untersuchung zu ihren Einflussfaktoren*. Bern: Academic Press.

Wang, Y. (2002). *Succession Issues And Business Performance: Evidence From UK Small And Medium-Sized Family Businesses*. (Unpublished Doctoral Dissertation). Southampton Institute, Southampton, UK.

Wangenheim, F., & Bayon, T. (2004). The effect of word of mouth on services switching. *European Journal of Marketing*, *38*(9/10), 1173–1185. doi:10.1108/03090560410548924

Wang, J. (2008). *Brand new China: Advertising, media and commercial culture*. Cambridge, MA: Harvard University Press.

Ward, J. L., & Aronoff, C. E. (1990). To Sell Or Not To Sell? *Nation's Business*, *78*(1), 63–64.

Watts, G., Cope, J., & Hulme, M. (1998). Anshoff's Matrix, Pain And Gain Growth Strategies And Adaptive Learning Among Small Food Producers. *International Journal Of Entrepreneurial Behaviour & Research*, *4*(2), 101–111. doi:10.1108/13552559810224567

Webb, E. J. (1996). Trust and Crisis. In *Trust in Organizations: Frontiers of Theory and Research* (pp. 288–301). Thousand Oaks, CA: Sage.

Week, B. (1989, November 13). The Rival Japan Respects, Motorola's Secrets. *Business Week*, pp. 108-114.

Welch, M., & Jackson, P. R. (2007). Rethinking internal communication: A stakeholder approach. *Corporate Communications: An International Journal*, *12*(2), 177–198. doi:10.1108/13563280710744847

Werbach, A. (2009). *Leadership At All Levels: Inspiration As A Leadership Technique – A Strategy For Sustainability Starts With You*. Boston: Harvard Business Press.

Wernerfelt, B. (1984). A Resource-Based View of the Firm. *Strategic Management Journal*, *5*(2), 171–180. doi:10.1002/smj.4250050207

Wernerfelt, B. (1989). From Critical Resources to Corporate Strategy. *Journal of General Management*, *14*(3).

Werthner, H., & Klein, S. (1999). ICT and the changing landscape of global tourism Distribution. *Electronic Markets*, *9*(4), 256–262. doi:10.1080/101967899358941

Westhead, P., & Cowling, M. (1995). Employment Change In Independent Owner-Managed High-Technology Firms In Great Britain. *Small Business Economics*, *7*(2), 111–140. doi:10.1007/BF01108686

Whipple, J.M., & Frankel, R. (2000). Strategic alliance success factors. *Journal of Supply Chain Management*, 21-26.

Whitener, E. M., Brodt, Korsgaard, & Werner. (1998). Managers as Initiators of Trust: An Exchange Relationship Framework for Understanding Managerial Trustworthy Behavior. *Academy of Management Review*, *23*(3), 513–530.

Wicks, A. C., Berman, S. L., & Jones, T. M. (1999). The Structure of Optimal Trust: Moral and strategic Implications. *Academy of Management Review*, *24*(1), 99–116.

Wieseke, J., Ahearne, M., Lam, S. K., & van Dick, R. (2009). The Role of Leaders in Internal Marketing. *Journal of Marketing*, *73*(2), 123–145. doi:10.1509/jmkg.73.2.123

Wiggenhorn, W. (1990). Motorola University: When Training Becomes an Education. *Harvard Business Review*.

Wilcox, M., & O'Callaghan, E. (2001). The strategic response of Dublin's traditional department stores to intensifying competition. *Journal of Retailing and Consumer Services*, *8*(4), 213–225. doi:10.1016/S0969-6989(00)00027-8

Wilkinson, I., & Young, L. (2002). On cooperating: Firms, relations and networks. *Journal of Business Research*, *55*(2), 123–132. doi:10.1016/S0148-2963(00)00147-8

Williamson, O. E. (1975). *Markets and Hierarchies*. New York: Free Press.

Williamson, O. E. (1981). The Economics of Organization: The Transaction Cost Approach. *American Journal of Sociology*, *87*(3), 548–577. doi:10.1086/227496

Williamson, O. E. (1985). *The Economic Institutions of Capitalism*. New York: Free Press.

Williamson, O. E. (1993). Opportunism and its critics. *Managerial and Decision Economics*, *14*(2), 97–107. doi:10.1002/mde.4090140203

Williams, P., & Naumann, E. (2011). Customer satisfaction and business performance: A firm-level analysis. *Journal of Services Marketing*, *25*(1), 20–32. doi:10.1108/08876041111107032

Wilson, A. (1994). Stimulating referrals'. *Management Decision*, *32*(7), 13–15. doi:10.1108/00251749410068102

Wilson, E. J., Bunn, M. D., & Savage, G. T. (2010). Anatomy of a social partnership: A stakeholder perspective. *Industrial Marketing Management*, *39*(1), 76–90. doi:10.1016/j.indmarman.2008.06.005

Wilson, J. (2010). *Essentials of Business Research: A Guide to Doing Your Research Project*. London: Sage.

Wilson, J. R. (1994). *Word-of-Mouth Marketing* (2nd ed.). New York: John Wiley.

Wisner, J. D. (2003). A structural equation model of supply chain management strategies and firm performance. *Journal of Business Logistics*, *24*(1), 1–26. doi:10.1002/j.2158-1592.2003.tb00030.x

Wolff, C. (1998a). Microsoft Sees Integration Chaning Face of PMS. *Lodging Hospitality.*, *54*(3), 41.

Wong, C. Y., Boonitt, S., & Wong, C. W. Y. (2011). The contingency effects of environmental uncertainty on the relationship between supply chain integration and operational performance. *Journal of Operations Management*, *29*(6), 604–615. doi:10.1016/j.jom.2011.01.003

Wong, H., & Merrilees, B. (2007). Closing the marketing strategy to performance gap: The role of brand orientation. *Journal of Strategic Marketing*, *15*(5), 387–402. doi:10.1080/09652540701726942

Wong, H., & Merrilees, B. (2008). The performance benefits of being brand-orientated. *Journal of Product and Brand Management*, *17*(6), 372–383. doi:10.1108/10610420810904112

Worcester, R. M. (1997). Managing the image of your bank: The glue that binds. *International Journal of Bank Marketing*, *15*(5), 146–152. doi:10.1108/02652329710175244

Worchel, P. (1979). Trust and Distrust. In *The Social Psychology of Intergroup Relations* (pp. 174–187). Wadsworth.

World Bank. (2009). *Governance and Anticorruption in Lending Operations: A Benchmarking and Learning Review*. Retrieved from http://siteresources.worldbank.org/EXTLAWJUSTINST/Resources/GAC_review_2009.pdf

World Travel and Tourism Council 2004, *Progress and priorities 2004/2005*, World Travel and Tourism Council, viewed 7 March 2005,

Wright, B. E., & Pandey, S. K. (2010). Transformational Leadership in the Public Sector: Does Structure Matter? *Journal of Public Administration: Research and Theory*, *20*(1), 75–89. doi:10.1093/jopart/mup003

Wright, M., Filatotchev, I., Hoskisson, R. E., & Peng, M. W. (2005). Strategy research in emerging economies: Challenging the collective wisdom. *Journal of Management Studies*, *42*(1), 1–33. doi:10.1111/j.1467-6486.2005.00487.x

Wright, R. (2004). *Business to Business Marketing: A step by step guide*. Harlow, UK: Prentice Hall.

Wu, C., Neubert, M. J., & Yi, X. (2007). Transformational leadership, cohesion perceptions and employee cynicism about organisational change: The mediating role of justice perceptions. *The Journal of Applied Behavioral Science*, *43*(3), 327–351. doi:10.1177/0021886307302097

Wu, J. (2013). Marketing capabilities, institutional development, and the performance of emerging market firms: A multinational study. *International Journal of Research in Marketing*, *30*(1), 36–45. doi:10.1016/j.ijresmar.2012.07.001

Wu, L. W. (2011). Beyond satisfaction: The relative importance of locational convenience, interpersonal relationships, and commitment across service types. *Managing Service Quality*, *21*(3), 240–263. doi:10.1108/09604521111127956

Wulf, K. D., & Schröder, G. O. (2003). Assessing the impact of a retailer's relationship efforts on consumers' attitudes and behavior. *Journal of Retailing and Consumer Services*, *10*(2), 95–108. doi:10.1016/S0969-6989(02)00013-9

Xie, H. Y., & Boggs, D. J. (2006). Corporate branding versus product branding in emerging markets: A conceptual framework. *Marketing Intelligence & Planning*, *24*(4), 347–364. doi:10.1108/02634500610672099

Yang, C.-C., Marlow, P. B., & Lu, C.-S. (2009). Assessing resources, logistics service capabilities, innovation capabilities and the performance of container shipping services in Taiwan. *International Journal of Production Economics*, *122*(1), 4–20. doi:10.1016/j.ijpe.2009.03.016

Yang, Z., & Peterson, R. (2004). Customer perceived value, satisfaction, and loyalty: The role of switching costs. *Psychology and Marketing*, *21*(10), 799–822. doi:10.1002/mar.20030

Yasin, N., Nasser Noor, M., & Mohamad, O. (2007). Does image of country-of-origin matter to brand equity? *Journal of Product and Brand Management*, *16*(1), 38–48. doi:10.1108/10610420710731142

Yeniyurt, S., Townsend, J. D., & Talay, M. B. (2007). Factors influencing brand launch in a global marketplace. *Journal of Product Innovation Management*, *24*(5), 471–485. doi:10.1111/j.1540-5885.2007.00264.x

Yilmazer, T., & Schrank, H. (2006). Financial Intermingling In Small Family Businesses. *Journal of Business Venturing*, *21*(5), 726–751. doi:10.1016/j.jbusvent.2005.04.011

Yin, R. (1989). *Case study research: Design and methods*. Newbury Park, CA: Sage Publishing.

Yin, R. K. (1993). *Applications of Case Study Research*. Newbury Park, CA: Sage.

Yin, R. K. (1994). *Case Study Research - Design and Methods*. Thousand Oaks, CA: Sage Publications.

Yin, R. K. (2004). *The Case Study Anthology*. Thousand Oaks, CA: Sage.

Yin, R. K. (2009). *Case Study Research: Design and Methods* (4th ed.). Thousand Oaks, CA: Sage.

You, J. (2005). A Study of Social Trust in South Korea, with Comparative Perspectives. Paper presented at the Annual Conference of the American Sociological Association. Philadelphia, PA.

Yu, Y., & Dean, A. (2001). The contribution of emotional satisfaction to consumer loyalty. *International Journal of Service Industry Management*, *12*(3), 234–250. doi:10.1108/09564230110393239

Zaheer, A., McEvily, B., & Perrone, V. (1998). Does trust matter? Exploring the effects of inter-organizational and interpersonal trust on performance. *Organization Science*, *9*(2), 141–159. doi:10.1287/orsc.9.2.141

Zairi, M. (2000). Managing customer dissatisfaction through effective complaints management systems. *The TQM Magazine*, *12*(5), 331–337. doi:10.1108/09544780010341932

Zalabak, P. S., & Winograd, G. (2000). Organizational Trust: What It Means, Why It Matters. *Organization Development Journal*, *18*(4), 35–49.

Zand, D. E. (1972). Trust and Managerial Problem Solving. *Administrative Science Quarterly*, *17*(2), 229–239. doi:10.2307/2393957

Zand, D. E. (1997). *The Leadership Triad – Knowledge, Trust and Power*. Oxford University Press.

Zeithaml, V. (2000). Service quality, profitability, and the economic worth of customers: What we know and waht we need to learn. *Journal of the Academy of Marketing Science*, *28*(1), 67–85. doi:10.1177/0092070300281007

Zeithaml, V. A. (1981). How consumer evaluation processes differ between goods and servcies. In J. H. Donnelly, & W. R. George (Eds.), *Marketing of Services* (pp. 186–190). Chicago: American Marketing Association.

Zeithaml, V. A., Berry, L. L., & Parasuraman, A. (1996). The behavioural consequences of service quality. *Journal of Marketing*, *60*(2), 31–46. doi:10.2307/1251929

Zeithaml, V. A., Parasuraman, A., & Berry, L. (1985). Problems and strategies in services marketing. *Journal of Marketing*, *49*(2), 33–46. doi:10.2307/1251563

Zeithaml, V., Parasuraman, A., & Berry, I. (1990). *Developing Quality Service-Balancing Customer Perceptions and expectations*. New York: The Free Press.

Zineldin, M. (1992). *Bank-Corporate Client Interactions and Relationships-A New Marketing Approach (Research Report Series, No. 4)*. Stockholm University.

Zineldin, M. (1996, March). Bank strategic positioning and some determinants of bank selection. *International Journal of Bank Marketing*, *14*(6), 12–22. doi:10.1108/02652329610130136

Zinkhan, M. G. (2002). Promoting services via the internet: New opportunities and challenges. *Journal of Services Marketing*, *16*(5), 412–423. doi:10.1108/08876040210436885

Zou, S., & Cavusgil, S. T. (2002). The GMS: A broad conceptualization of global marketing strategy and its effect on firm performance. *Journal of Marketing*, *66*(4), 40–56. doi:10.1509/jmkg.66.4.40.18519

Zucker, L. G. (1986). Production of Trust: Institutional Sources of Economic Structure. *Research in Organizational Behavior*, *8*, 53–111.

About the Contributors

Irene Samanta obtained a degree (BA) in Business Administration, MSc in International Marketing from University of Paisley (UK), and PhD from the University of the West of Scotland (UK). Her PhD research was on modelling the relationships in B2B firms under e-marketing practices. Her main research interests are in the areas of e-relationships, e-marketing, international marketing, and research methods. She is works as an Assistant Professor in the above fields in the Department of Business Administration of Graduate Technological Educational Institute of Piraeus (TEI). She is moderator in two modules in the MSc in International Business Management, and she has taught for six years in MSc in International Marketing of the University of the West of Scotland and in MSc program International MBA in Graduate Education Technological Institute of Piraeus. She has supervised a large number of MSc dissertations concentrated in the area of electronic relationships and social media. She is author or co-author of several papers in various scientific journals, books, conference proceedings, and several articles in economic journals. She is the co-author of three textbooks. She participates as an active member in academic associations, including the European Association of Operations Management, European Academy of Management, and the Hellenic Institution of Operational Research. In addition, she participates in professional associations, including the Industrial and Commercial Chamber of Piraeus and Commercial Association of Piraeus. She is a member of the editorial board of several journals and chapter books.

* * *

Somanth Chaudhuri is a Lecturer in Faculty of IT and Maths at Royal Thimphu College Affiliated to Royal University of Bhutan Royal Thimphu College. His responsibilities include: teaching and supervising final year students' projects for different government and private organisations. He is a member of the RTC Conference Committee, Examination Committee, and the RTC Database Management team. He has published several scientific papers in scientific journals. His research interests are VLSI, Nano Technology, Cloud Computing, Automated System, and Application of Information Technology in Business and Industry Sectors.

Nabyla Daidj is Associate Professor in Strategy at Telecom Business School (known as Telecom Ecole de Management). Her teaching and research interests are corporate strategy, inter-organizational relationships (business ecosystems, clusters, strategic alliances, networks, *keiretsu*), and conglomerates' performance and corporate governance in a context of hypercompetition and coopetition. Currently, she is studying the sources of value creation for ICT groups in a context of convergence. She has published on these issues in academic journals such as *Communications & Strategies, Critical Perspectives on Ac-*

counting, Journal of Media Business Studies, Journal of Media Business Studies, International Journal of Strategic Information Technology and Applications (IJSITA). She has published in 2008 a book about cooperation, games theory, and strategic management.

Dillip Kumar Das is Assistant Professor in Tourism in Department of Tourism Management in The University of Burdwan, GolapBag, Burdwan. He has attended many training programs. He has attended many conferences, and he has published in many scientific journals. He is a project co-coordinator of different research projects, has organized two research methodology workshops and other academic activities.

Laxhminarayan Das has around 15 years of experience in teaching to the undergraduates as well as postgraduate level students in Management Science. Currently, he is working as Faculty in Marketing Area at Ravenshaw Business School, an affiliated school of Ravenshaw University, CUTTACK, a state university. He also works as a corporate consultant, who devises plans and executions of many upcoming educational ventures in his locality. He is a student mentor for placement cell of his parent university. He has around 20 research papers published in various research journals and conference proceedings to his credit. He is also a reviewer for several journals across the globe in his area of expertise. He is also the question paper setter as well as evaluator to several prestigious institutes across India. He also writes self-learning materials for MBA programs for a few universities across the country.

Kijpokin Kasemsap received his BEng degree in Mechanical Engineering from King Mongkut's University of Technology Thonburi, his MBA degree from Ramkhamhaeng University, and his DBA degree in Human Resource Management from Suan Sunandha Rajabhat University. He is a Special Lecturer at Faculty of Management Sciences, Suan Sunandha Rajabhat University based in Bangkok, Thailand. He is a Member of International Association of Engineers (IAENG), International Association of Engineers and Scientists (IAEST), International Economics Development and Research Center (IEDRC), International Association of Computer Science and Information Technology (IACSIT), International Foundation for Research and Development (IFRD), and International Innovative Scientific and Research Organization (IISRO). He also serves on the International Advisory Committee (IAC) for International Association of Academicians and Researchers (INAAR). He has numerous original research articles in top international journals, conference proceedings, and book chapters on business management, human resource management, and knowledge management published internationally.

Vedantam Leela is Assistant Professor, Faculty of Management Studies, National Law University, Jodhpur, and is the Executive Director of the Centre for Human Resource Management Initiatives and Industrial Relations Studies. She specialises in areas like Organisational Behaviour, Human Resource Management, Compensation Management, and Cross-Cultural and Global HRM. She has actively participated in various national and international conferences. She has published her works in various journals of national and international repute.

Natalie Limb holds a Master of Science in Marketing from University of Wales (UK) and Bachelor of Science in Mathematics from the University of Durham. Her research interests lie primarily in the field of stakeholder theory and internal marketing, especially how these thoughts can be applied to increase efficiency of large corporations. She is also interested in other aspects of branding and communications. Following her passion for marketing communications, Natalie now works at Blue Hive, a full service communications agency based in London.

Ray Nilanjan obtained MBA (Mktg), MCom (Mktg), BCom (Hons), and PhD at Burdwan University, Department of Business Administration. He has a Certificate Course on Financial Modeling and Risk Management from Humanities and Social Science Department and Vinod Gupta School of Management, Indian Institute of Technology Kharagpur, India. He is a Lecturer at Faculty of Business Studies Royal Thimpu College, and his responsibilities are teaching, mentoring, and tutoring service marketing, tourism principles and practices, and corporate law. He has a lot of publications in scientific journals, book chapters, and conference proceedings. He is editor of three chapter books.

Anastasios S. Ntanos was born at Orion, Evia. He is Professor at the Department of Business Administration, Technological Educational Institute of Piraeus. He has a law degree and a degree at the Department of Public Law and Political Sciences of the National and Kapodistrian University of Athens. He is also a graduate of the Theological Faculty at Theology School of the National and Kapodistrian University of Athens. He has a postgraduate in Administrative Law and Pedagogy as well. He holds a PhD from the National and Kapodistrian University of Athens. His PhD thesis is related to the Organization and Management of Organizations and Education. He teaches, at the Technological Educational Institute of Piraeus, courses related to Law, Management, and Humanities since the Academic Year 1988. He has participated as a speaker in scientific meetings and international conferences and as a scientific researcher in European programs. Moreover, he teaches in postgraduate studies "International Business Administration," "Health Management," and "Educational Technology and Human Resource Development." His scientific articles have been published in leading Greek and international scientific journals and honorary and massive scientific volumes. He has authored scientific books and textbooks for students. His total work and overall contribution to science has been recognized by the Greek Academic Community and well-known international researchers.

Stamatios Ntanos (MSc), Economist-Accountant, holds degrees in both areas of Business Administration and Accounting from the University of Piraeus and the Technological Educational Institute of Piraeus, with postgraduate studies in Industrial Management Systems (University of Piraeus and The National Technical University – NTUA). He is currently a PhD Candidate in the University of Piraeus. Mr. Stamatis Ntanos has over 13 years of teaching experience as a Laboratory Associate in the Technological Educational Institute of Piraeus, Department of Business Administration. His teaching areas include Statistics, Operational Research, Management, Computing, and Marketing, and he has also taught for several years as a professor in Public Institutes of Vocational Training (IEK). He has published nine academic papers in scientific journals, and he has participated in several international conferences. His professional experience includes consulting for EU projects and manpower for the Municipality of Athens (2005-2010) and as an official in the Agricultural Bank of Greece (2008-2010). He is a Member of the Economic Chamber of Greece and holder of an accountant license.

Alina O'Keeffe is a marketing professional. She holds a Master's degree in marketing from the University of Wales, and an undergraduate degree from the Chartered Institute of Marketing. Alina's research interests are marketing, leadership, business and change management. Her work examines the novel concept of "leadership marketing," which challenges the conventional view of marketing and leadership as two separate fields and offers a holistic approach to business management and brand alignment. Alina presented a paper on leadership marketing at the 2012 Global Business and Technology Association (GBATA) international conference in New York. Her article "Leadership Marketing: The Role of Marketing in Leading Organisational Change" was published in the *GBATA Journal*.

Wilson Ozuem is Associate Professor of Digital Marketing at Regents University, London (UK). His research interests include the implications of information technology for decision making by marketers and consumers. The results of his research have been published in scholarly journals and international conference papers, including *European Journal of Marketing, Social Responsibility Journal,* and *World Business Congress*. Dr. Ozuem teaches in a number of UK universities, including the University of Gloucestershire, the University of Hertfordshire, and GSM (London). He currently teaches MSc and MBA courses in marketing communications, Internet marketing, research methodology, and marketing management. He is a Fellow of the Chartered Institute of Marketing (FCIM) and has worked as a marketing consultant for several companies and organizations. He received his BA in Business from the University of Portsmouth, MA Marketing from University of West London, MBA from London Metropolitan University, MEd (Educational Leadership and Management) from Open University (UK), Doctorate from Anglia Ruskin University, and Postgraduate Degree in Educational Research from University of Cambridge.

Anthony Perrone has overlapping backgrounds in education and psychology with specific expertise in marketing, management, consumer behavior and service quality. Anthony has inclusions in several international marketing texts, published journal articles as well as presenting at related conferences. Anthony has been a course coordinator and lecturer, has taught subjects on the principles of marketing, international economics, marketing research, consumer behavior, organizational behavior and managing organizational change. Anthony has done curriculum design as well as developing on-line written learning materials and assessments for Marketing/Management units. In addition Anthony has held numerous industry executive management positions including Vice President for Fred Hayman Beverly Hills (the creator of Giorgio Beverly Hills) and senior positions for Neiman Marcus, Ethan Allen and David Jones as well as owning two successful companies.

Nondas Pitticas is a Senior Lecturer at the University of the West of Scotland, based in the town of Paisley in Scotland. He specialises in the use of geo-informatics for decision-making, marketing analysis with particular application in the real estate sector. Until 2010 and for a period of 25 years, in addition to his teaching duties, he was also the Director of the University's Land Value Information Unit. After the Unit's closure in 2010, his teaching and research interests have focused on strategic management and global citizenship issues.

Yannis A. Pollalis is a Professor of Strategic Management and Policy in the Department of Economic Sciences since 1999 at the University of Piraeus in Greece. He has consulted, researched, and published numerous articles on strategic management of information systems, e-business development, IS planning, and strategic management and marketing. He has also published 13 books in the areas of information management, e-business, marketing management, organizational behavior, and business strategy. His research has been funded by the Onassis Public Benefit Foundation, NATO's Science & Research Program, the European Network for SMEs Research, and others. He is on the editorial board for the *International Journal for Information Management* (IJIM) and Associate Editor for the *Journal of Applied Systems Studies* (JASS) and the *International Journal of Economics & Business* (SPOUDAI). He has served as a faculty member for iSchool during 1993-1998, and since 2002, he has been a visiting professor for the Summer Leadership Institute at Syracuse University, New York.

Georgios Priniotakis, PhD in Textiles Sensors ("Simulation of Human Body Behavior during Sweat Production Measured at Textile Electrodes"), is an Assistant Professor, TEI of Piraeus, School of Applied Technology, Dept. of Textile Engineering (Piraeus, Greece). He is a National Representative of Greece to boards and committees in the activities of the European Research Area and its cooperation with intergovernmental organizations in embedded systems. He is a co-writer of the popular book *Analytical Electrochemistry in Textiles* (P. Westbroek, G. Priniotakis, P. Kiekens, Woodhead Publishing Ltd., UK, ISBN 1 85573 919 4, August 2005), and number other books. He has published 14 A1 papers and 38 publications in international conferences over the last 10 years. He is a referee in scientific journals, *Transactions of the Institute of Measurement and Control*, *Applied Polymer Science*, *Textile Research Journal*, and *Journal of Applied Electrochemistry*. He is a member of scientific committee of various international conferences and has participated in numerous research and education projects. He has international educational experience from nine countries.

Ritu Sinha, (NET - Qualified) PGDBM in Marketing from Birla-Institute of Management and Technology, New Delhi, is presently working as Faculty Member with IES Management College and Research Centre, Mumbai. She holds an extensive professional experience in pharmaceutical sector with multinational corporations. Her interest areas include environment, research methodology, marketing research, and retailing. She has been actively participating in various forums related to her areas of interests. She has published numerous articles and papers on diverse topics and worked on many edited books.

Dimitra Skoumpopoulou is a Senior Lecturer in Information Management and joined Newcastle Business School in 2008. She worked as a business consultant both in the UK and abroad. Her research interests include information systems and approaches to information systems implementation. Her most recent work is in the area of integrated systems and in particular the implementation of SITS in the UK Higher Education sector.

Ilias P. Vlachos is a Reader in Logistics and Supply Chain Management with Northumbria University. He holds a PhD from Cranfield University, UK. From 2002-2012, Ilias was assistant professor in the University of Athens as well as adjunct professor at Hellenic Open University, Greece. His current research interests revolve around supply chain management, sustainable food logistics, and adoption of technological innovation. Ilias has been actively involved in competitive Greek and European research projects. He has published articles in a number of refereed journals. He co-edited the book titled *Intelligent Agrifood Chains and Networks*, which was published by Wiley-Blackwell in 2011.

Ho Yin Wong is a senior lecturer at Deakin Graduate School of Business, Faculty of Business and Law, Deakin University, Burwood Campus, Australia. He has published in *International Marketing Review, Journal of Strategic Marketing, Journal of Product and Brand Management, Journal of Global Marketing*, and *Asia Pacific Journal of Marketing and Logistics*, among others. He co-authored an article for the *Journal of Asia Pacific Journal of Marketing and Logistics*, which was chosen as an Outstanding Paper Award Winner at the Emerald Literati Network Awards for Excellence 2013. He is also a co-author of a book, *Building a Marketing Plan: A Complete Guide*. His main research interests are international marketing, branding, and marketing strategy.

Index

CPSIA information can be obtained at www.ICGtesting.com
Printed in the USA
BVOW08*1348050914

364562BV00007BB/34/P